Lecture Notes in Computer Science 12190

More information about this series at http://www.springer.com/series/7409

Jessie Y. C. Chen · Gino Fragomeni (Eds.)

Virtual, Augmented and Mixed Reality

Design and Interaction

12th International Conference, VAMR 2020
Held as Part of the 22nd HCI International Conference, HCII 2020
Copenhagen, Denmark, July 19–24, 2020
Proceedings, Part I

 Springer

Editors
Jessie Y. C. Chen
U.S. Army Research Laboratory
Aberdeen Proving Ground, MD, USA

Gino Fragomeni
U.S. Army Combat Capabilities
Development Command
Orlando, FL, USA

ISSN 0302-9743   ISSN 1611-3349 (electronic)
Lecture Notes in Computer Science
ISBN 978-3-030-49694-4   ISBN 978-3-030-49695-1 (eBook)
https://doi.org/10.1007/978-3-030-49695-1

LNCS Sublibrary: SL3 – Information Systems and Applications, incl. Internet/Web, and HCI

This Springer imprint is published by the registered company Springer Nature Switzerland AG
The registered company address is: Gewerbestrasse 11, 6330 Cham, Switzerland

Foreword

The 22nd International Conference on Human-Computer Interaction, HCI International 2020 (HCII 2020), was planned to be held at the AC Bella Sky Hotel and Bella Center, Copenhagen, Denmark, during July 19–24, 2020. Due to the COVID-19 coronavirus pandemic and the resolution of the Danish government not to allow events larger than 500 people to be hosted until September 1, 2020, HCII 2020 had to be held virtually. It incorporated the 21 thematic areas and affiliated conferences listed on the following page.

A total of 6,326 individuals from academia, research institutes, industry, and governmental agencies from 97 countries submitted contributions, and 1,439 papers and 238 posters were included in the conference proceedings. These contributions address the latest research and development efforts and highlight the human aspects of design and use of computing systems. The contributions thoroughly cover the entire field of human-computer interaction, addressing major advances in knowledge and effective use of computers in a variety of application areas. The volumes constituting the full set of the conference proceedings are listed in the following pages.

The HCI International (HCII) conference also offers the option of "late-breaking work" which applies both for papers and posters and the corresponding volume(s) of the proceedings will be published just after the conference. Full papers will be included in the "HCII 2020 - Late Breaking Papers" volume of the proceedings to be published in the Springer LNCS series, while poster extended abstracts will be included as short papers in the "HCII 2020 - Late Breaking Posters" volume to be published in the Springer CCIS series.

I would like to thank the program board chairs and the members of the program boards of all thematic areas and affiliated conferences for their contribution to the highest scientific quality and the overall success of the HCI International 2020 conference.

This conference would not have been possible without the continuous and unwavering support and advice of the founder, Conference General Chair Emeritus and Conference Scientific Advisor Prof. Gavriel Salvendy. For his outstanding efforts, I would like to express my appreciation to the communications chair and editor of HCI International News, Dr. Abbas Moallem.

July 2020   Constantine Stephanidis

HCI International 2020 Thematic Areas and Affiliated Conferences

Thematic areas:

- HCI 2020: Human-Computer Interaction
- HIMI 2020: Human Interface and the Management of Information

Affiliated conferences:

- EPCE: 17th International Conference on Engineering Psychology and Cognitive Ergonomics
- UAHCI: 14th International Conference on Universal Access in Human-Computer Interaction
- VAMR: 12th International Conference on Virtual, Augmented and Mixed Reality
- CCD: 12th International Conference on Cross-Cultural Design
- SCSM: 12th International Conference on Social Computing and Social Media
- AC: 14th International Conference on Augmented Cognition
- DHM: 11th International Conference on Digital Human Modeling and Applications in Health, Safety, Ergonomics and Risk Management
- DUXU: 9th International Conference on Design, User Experience and Usability
- DAPI: 8th International Conference on Distributed, Ambient and Pervasive Interactions
- HCIBGO: 7th International Conference on HCI in Business, Government and Organizations
- LCT: 7th International Conference on Learning and Collaboration Technologies
- ITAP: 6th International Conference on Human Aspects of IT for the Aged Population
- HCI-CPT: Second International Conference on HCI for Cybersecurity, Privacy and Trust
- HCI-Games: Second International Conference on HCI in Games
- MobiTAS: Second International Conference on HCI in Mobility, Transport and Automotive Systems
- AIS: Second International Conference on Adaptive Instructional Systems
- C&C: 8th International Conference on Culture and Computing
- MOBILE: First International Conference on Design, Operation and Evaluation of Mobile Communications
- AI-HCI: First International Conference on Artificial Intelligence in HCI

HCI International 2020 Thematic Areas and Affiliated Conferences

Thematic areas:

- HCI 2020: Human-Computer Interaction
- HIMI 2020: Human Interface and the Management of Information

Affiliated conferences:

- EPCE: 17th International Conference on Engineering Psychology and Cognitive Ergonomics
- UAHCI: 14th International Conference on Universal Access in Human-Computer Interaction
- VAMR: 12th International Conference on Virtual, Augmented and Mixed Reality
- CCD: 12th International Conference on Cross-Cultural Design
- SCSM: 12th International Conference on Social Computing and Social Media
- AC: 14th International Conference on Augmented Cognition
- DHM: 11th International Conference on Digital Human Modeling and Applications in Health, Safety, Ergonomics and Risk Management
- DUXU: 9th International Conference on Design, User Experience and Usability
- DAPI: 8th International Conference on Distributed, Ambient and Pervasive Interactions
- HCIBGO: 7th International Conference on HCI in Business, Government and Organizations
- LCT: 7th International Conference on Learning and Collaboration Technologies
- ITAP: 6th International Conference on Human Aspects of IT for the Aged Population
- HCI-CPT: Second International Conference on HCI for Cybersecurity, Privacy and Trust
- HCI-Games: Second International Conference on HCI in Games
- MobiTAS: Second International Conference on HCI in Mobility, Transport and Automotive Systems
- AIS: Second International Conference on Adaptive Instructional Systems
- C&C: 8th International Conference on Culture and Computing
- MOBILE: First International Conference on Design, Operation and Evaluation of Mobile Communications
- AI-HCI: First International Conference on Artificial Intelligence in HCI

Conference Proceedings Volumes Full List

1. LNCS 12181, Human-Computer Interaction: Design and User Experience (Part I), edited by Masaaki Kurosu
2. LNCS 12182, Human-Computer Interaction: Multimodal and Natural Interaction (Part II), edited by Masaaki Kurosu
3. LNCS 12183, Human-Computer Interaction: Human Values and Quality of Life (Part III), edited by Masaaki Kurosu
4. LNCS 12184, Human Interface and the Management of Information: Designing Information (Part I), edited by Sakae Yamamoto and Hirohiko Mori
5. LNCS 12185, Human Interface and the Management of Information: Interacting with Information (Part II), edited by Sakae Yamamoto and Hirohiko Mori
6. LNAI 12186, Engineering Psychology and Cognitive Ergonomics: Mental Workload, Human Physiology, and Human Energy (Part I), edited by Don Harris and Wen-Chin Li
7. LNAI 12187, Engineering Psychology and Cognitive Ergonomics: Cognition and Design (Part II), edited by Don Harris and Wen-Chin Li
8. LNCS 12188, Universal Access in Human-Computer Interaction: Design Approaches and Supporting Technologies (Part I), edited by Margherita Antona and Constantine Stephanidis
9. LNCS 12189, Universal Access in Human-Computer Interaction: Applications and Practice (Part II), edited by Margherita Antona and Constantine Stephanidis
10. LNCS 12190, Virtual, Augmented and Mixed Reality: Design and Interaction (Part I), edited by Jessie Y. C. Chen and Gino Fragomeni
11. LNCS 12191, Virtual, Augmented and Mixed Reality: Industrial and Everyday Life Applications (Part II), edited by Jessie Y. C. Chen and Gino Fragomeni
12. LNCS 12192, Cross-Cultural Design: User Experience of Products, Services, and Intelligent Environments (Part I), edited by P. L. Patrick Rau
13. LNCS 12193, Cross-Cultural Design: Applications in Health, Learning, Communication, and Creativity (Part II), edited by P. L. Patrick Rau
14. LNCS 12194, Social Computing and Social Media: Design, Ethics, User Behavior, and Social Network Analysis (Part I), edited by Gabriele Meiselwitz
15. LNCS 12195, Social Computing and Social Media: Participation, User Experience, Consumer Experience, and Applications of Social Computing (Part II), edited by Gabriele Meiselwitz
16. LNAI 12196, Augmented Cognition: Theoretical and Technological Approaches (Part I), edited by Dylan D. Schmorrow and Cali M. Fidopiastis
17. LNAI 12197, Augmented Cognition: Human Cognition and Behaviour (Part II), edited by Dylan D. Schmorrow and Cali M. Fidopiastis

http://2020.hci.international/proceedings

12th International Conference on Virtual, Augmented and Mixed Reality (VAMR 2020)

Program Board Chairs: **Jessie Y. C. Chen, U.S. Army Research Laboratory, USA, and Gino Fragomeni, U.S. Army Combat Capabilities Development Command Soldier Center, USA**

- Daniel W. Carruth, USA
- Shih-Yi Chien, Taiwan
- Jeff Hansberger, USA
- Fotis Liarokapis, Czech Republic
- Joseph B. Lyons, USA
- Phillip Mangos, USA
- Crystal Maraj, USA
- Rafael Radkowski, USA
- Maria Olinda Rodas, USA
- Jose San Martin, Spain
- Andreas Schreiber, Germany
- Peter Smith, USA
- Simon Su, USA
- Tom Williams, USA
- Kevin Wynne, USA
- Denny Yu, USA

The full list with the Program Board Chairs and the members of the Program Boards of all thematic areas and affiliated conferences is available online at:

http://www.hci.international/board-members-2020.php

HCI International 2021

The 23rd International Conference on Human-Computer Interaction, HCI International 2021 (HCII 2021), will be held jointly with the affiliated conferences in Washington DC, USA, at the Washington Hilton Hotel, July 24–29, 2021. It will cover a broad spectrum of themes related to Human-Computer Interaction (HCI), including theoretical issues, methods, tools, processes, and case studies in HCI design, as well as novel interaction techniques, interfaces, and applications. The proceedings will be published by Springer. More information will be available on the conference website: http://2021.hci.international/.

General Chair
Prof. Constantine Stephanidis
University of Crete and ICS-FORTH
Heraklion, Crete, Greece
Email: general_chair@hcii2021.org

http://2021.hci.international/

Contents – Part I

Gestures and Haptic Interaction in VAMR

Cognitive, Psychological and Health Aspects in VAMR

Robots in VAMR

Contents – Part II

Learning, Narrative, Storytelling and Cultural Applications of VAMR

VAMR for Health, Well-being and Medicine

Design and User Experience in VAMR

Guerilla Evaluation of Truck HMI with VR

Frederik Diederichs[1]([✉]), Friedrich Niehaus[2], and Lena Hees[3]

[1] Fraunhofer IAO, 70569 Stuttgart, Germany
`frederik.diederichs@iao.fraunhofer.de`
[2] Daimler Trucks and Busses, Inselstr. 140, 12345 Stuttgart, Germany
[3] University of Stuttgart IAT, 70569 Stuttgart, Germany

Abstract. HMI development requires user centered testing of HMI prototypes in realistic scenarios. Typical problems are the acquisition of a representative user group and the setup of realistic scenarios. The paper describes the method of Guerilla interviews on truck stops along highways in order to approach truck drivers as participants in a user centered HMI development process. A truck steering wheel with cluster display mockup from earlier on-site interviews was compared to a new virtual reality (VR) truck cockpit simulator. The Guerilla method proofed its value to involve truck drivers in HMI evaluation as a fast and efficient approach, as long as mobile HMI prototypes are available. As a limitation of the Guerilla method we found the time limits given by the strict truck drivers' break time and little control of the participant sample. Regarding the HMI prototype comparison, we conclude that the steering wheel mockup still requires less efforts and costs for testing, however the VR simulator shows a better context representation for the function and hence better external validity of the results. Slightly longer test duration of the VR simulator is mainly attributed to the time for introducing the new technology to participants. The outlook describes how the mobile VR simulator is further developed to overcome its limitations.

Keywords: VR simulator · Truck HMI · Guerilla interviews

1 Introduction

HMI development requires user centered testing and hence the involvement of potential users with HMI prototypes in a realistic context. Typical problems are the acquisition of a representative user group and the setup of a realistic context, e.g. driving scenarios that degrade the HMI function to a secondary task (Alfes et al. 2014).

In our case, it is difficult to get a truck driver to a certain residential test laboratory for testing an HMI. Those who are willing to come are a highly selective sub-group of truck drivers, causing a clear bias to the study. In order to overcome these problems, we adapted the Guerilla Interview technique (Jacobsen and Meyer 2018) and took our HMI prototype to the users.

© Springer Nature Switzerland AG 2020
J. Y. C. Chen and G. Fragomeni (Eds.): HCII 2020, LNCS 12190, pp. 3–17, 2020.
https://doi.org/10.1007/978-3-030-49695-1_1

The original Guerilla technique was proposed for website testing by Martin Belam (2010). The characteristics of the Guerilla approach are to find the users where they are and to get a few minutes in between their regular daily routine in order to test the HMI prototype rather quick and dirty. In order to meet our users, we selected truck stops along German highways and approached truck drivers in their normal work and break routine.

On site Guerilla testing requires portable HMI prototypes that can be used in the given environment where the users are found. In the past we used a portable HMI mockup, consisting of a truck steering wheel and a tablet behind the wheel representing the instrument cluster content. This solution allowed for HMI function tests, but did not provide any context or scenario.

To overcome this limitation VR with head mounted displays (HMD) have been used recently in different studies to assess vehicle HMI (Krupenia et al. 2017; Lottermoser et al. 2018; van der Veer et al. 2019; Bopp-Bertenbreiter et al., in press). In our approach we combined the VR simulation with the Guerilla method, hence a portable VR simulator was set up in the back of a Mercedes-Benz V-Class (Fig. 1). This allowed us to simulate automated driving and integrate the HMI prototype in a mixed-mock-up environment of a full truck cabin (see also Figs. 3 and 4).

Fig. 1. Mercedes-Benz V-Class with integrated VR simulator in the rear seat compartment (Daimler AG 2018)

2 Method

The Guerilla method allows to find a representative user group in the field and in their regular work environment. It requires a mobile HMI prototype of which we compared two different versions, a truck steering wheel mockup and a VR simulator.

2.1 Guerilla Interviews

In user centred HMI development a large variety of methods to involve potential users and to gain their feedback on early prototypes have been reported (e.g. Jacobsen und Meyer 2018; Pollmann 2018). Apart from standardized usability tests, these methods also include the remote or Guerrilla testing. According to Lämmler (2017), the advantages of this method are to obtain data fast and efficiently without having to invest lots of time or money (Lämmler 2017).

Especially in the case of truck drivers, the Guerilla interview allows to approach truck drivers efficiently in their break time on truck stops. Driving time regulations mean drivers have 45 min break time a day and hence the total length of the interview in relation to the remaining break time determines whether drivers take part.

By this approach, also truck drivers are included in the test sample who would not come to a test laboratory. The time requirements for the test participants are minimized with this approach and hence it can increase the efficiency of the participant acquisition and the positive response rate when asking for participation.

In addition, Guerilla interviews approach end-users to test the product directly in its usual environment and context and hence the feedback quality provides higher external validity.

For an objective, reliable and valid data analysis back in the office, a structured interview guide helps to retrieve all relevant information (Mayring 2010; Niehaus 2014; Lämmler 2017). The qualitative results are analyzed according to the content analysis process introduced by Mayring and Frenzl (2014). The content analysis is the standard method for analyzing large quantities of qualitative data (Mayring 2010). It assures the classic test quality criteria: objectivity, reliability and validity (Mayring and Brunner 2009).

2.2 Mobile Truck Steering Wheel Mockup and Click Dummy

The first developed UX simulator is a dummy steering wheel with functional keypads from the simulated vehicle (Fig. 2). The rapid-prototyping casing has the geometry of a generic truck steering wheel with integrated series production steering wheel keypads. The HMI prototype is implemented on a Tablet PC positioned behind the steering wheel mockup equivalent to the Instrument Cluster (IC) position in the real truck.

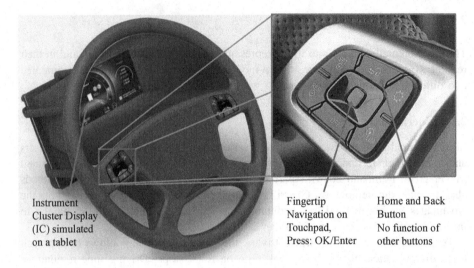

Instrument
Cluster Display
(IC) simulated
on a tablet

Fingertip   Home and Back
Navigation on   Button
Touchpad,   No function of
Press: OK/Enter   other buttons

Fig. 2. Click dummy buttons in the steering wheel controls (Daimler AG 2018)

The simulator with the setup allows test participants to carry out interactive activities in the represented context. The test participants can look at individual screens as part of the evaluation and interact with the HMI via the steering wheel buttons. Like in the real vehicle, the left keypad is used to control the IC. As the function of the IC is limited, only a few of the interface elements actually create events in the software prototype. To navigate through the individual menus and screens, a user can press the home/back button and the multifunctional touch control button. The home/back button enables the user to navigate in the menu structure and by pressing the touch control button an action is selected. The touch control button also works like a touchpad. It can be used to toggle between elements on the display. Unlike the left keypad, the right keypad does not have any saved functions. The driver uses this keypad in the vehicle to operate the centre console display (IVI), which was not installed in this setup.

2.3 Mobile VR Truck Cockpit Simulator and Click Dummy

The second UX simulator uses VR technology. Apart from the head mounted display (HMD), the simulator requires an avatar tracking device, a steering wheel with optical tracker as well as functional keypads, comparable to the steering wheel mockup described above. A processing unit with the simulation and the SW prototype allow the VR representation of the complete truck cockpit.

During a test run with the simulator, the test participant must put on the HMD. When looking through the lenses of the HMD, the test participant perceives the image shown in Fig. 3. The driver sits in a virtual truck cab and recognizes the changing surroundings. The avatar tracking device tracks the test participant's hands and provides a model for the simulation to create virtual hands in the relevant position in relation to reality. The visualization of the whole cab and the exterieur, as well as the sounds perceived through the speakers in the HMDs integrated headphones, provide a rich contextual environment for the simulation. The driver has the sensation of actually sitting and driving in the cab.

Fig. 3. View through the HMD - detail from the VR simulation (Daimler AG 2018)

The simulator also includes a series production steering wheel as a hardware component and at the same time as a digital representation in the VR (Fig. 4). This allows the test participant to intervene interactively in the simulation and to receive tactile feedback. As a result, the test participant can put themselves into their everyday driving situation, test the available interface and experience the surroundings in a lifelike way. The driver can also turn the real steering wheel during the interview. To display this turning motion reflected in the VR, an optical tracker is installed in the center of the steering wheel.

Fig. 4. Mixed mockup of hardware seat and steering wheel (Daimler AG 2018)

In the VR simulator both keypads on the steering wheel include functions. With the left keypad, the buttons can be used to operate the IC, with the right keypad participants control the centre console display (IVI).

To carry out tests flexibly and quickly with the Guerilla method, the simulator is built into a Mercedes-Benz V-Class (Fig. 1). This provides a mobile UX lab. As Fig. 5 shows, the test participant is located during the interview on the rotated simulator seat and wears the HMD with built-in headphones. The HMD require two sensors for positioning in the space, which are shown in Fig. 5 as red boxes.

The original truck steering wheel with the function keypads and optical tracker in the center are placed straight in front of the test participant. The steering wheel is placed at the same height as in the truck.

During the test phase, the interviewer sits on the rear bench of the V-Class, controls the simulation via the laptop and asks questions associated with the selected scenarios.

The test team also includes an observer and a note taker. The observer takes up the position on the co-driver's seat and observes the interview scene closely. The observer documents how the test participant interacts with the simulator and the interviewer. An additional note-taker in the driver's seat documents what the test participant says.

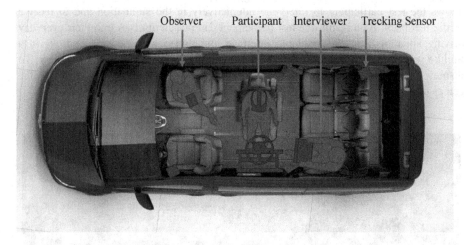

Fig. 5. Installation of the VR simulator in a Mercedes-Benz V-Class (Daimler AG 2018)

3   Experimental Evaluation

Both HMI mockups, the steering wheel and the VR environment, include the same HMI concept of the new Daimler Trucks Actros Cluster Display. This concept was exemplarily evaluated during the test phase. Additionally, it is important to mention that in this paper we only report on the differences encountered for the two different simulators and not the results of the HMI-evaluation. Both evaluations where carried out with identical procedure and material.

The evaluations took place at truck parking lots. Once there, truck drivers are approached impromptu and recruited for an interview, without offering any payment. The interviewer introduced the team, stated the reason for the study and mentioned that the interview will take around 20 min.

In total 78 participants were approached on truck stops in Germany, resulting in 10 test participants for each HMI mockup. Once a participant has agreed to take part, the driver's demographic data are collected and their consent to record the interview.

After an introduction of the technology, the structured interview on usability and UX of the HMI prototype started. The interviewer asks the questions from the structured interview guide. The test participant answers, normally resulting in a fluid conversation and interacts parallel with the simulator and the HMI. The note-taker documents the statements. In our particular setup, the observer monitored the interaction between participant and interviewer as well as the interaction with the simulator during the whole interview in order to collect data about the use of the particular mockup.

4   Results

The results compare both HMI testing prototypes in order to identify benefits and disadvantages of each concept.

4.1   Test Participants Data

Among all drivers approached to take part in the study, one quarter accepted to participate. Main hindering were limited time due to soon departure or missing German language skills.

Table 1 shows that our test participant sample mainly consists of male drivers. Just one female truck driver was encountered at the truck stops and she agreed to participate to the test with the steering wheel mockup. Female truck drivers represent only 1.8% of the truck drivers in Germany (Statista 2020) and some apparently prefer to stay in their truck cabin while the male often stand outside of their trucks during break time.

The test participants with the steering wheel mockup have an average age of 54, with the VR simulator an average age of 49. The age is also reflected in the professional experience. On average, the older test participants of the steering wheel mockup have seven years more experience driving a truck. Two test participants already actively used VR. The others had no practical experience with this technology. Furthermore, mainly drivers with German license plates took part in the two evaluations. Given that the interviews require good German skills, this is a consequence of this selection criteria. All participants haul freight nationally and, in some cases in adjacent EU countries. The test participants of both interview phases constitute typical representatives of their vocational group (Statista 2020).

Table 1. Test participants statistics

Interview participants	Steering wheel mockup	VR simulator
Number of test participants	10	10
Gender	90% male	100% male
Average age [year]	Ø 54	Ø 48,8
Professional experience as a truck driver [year]	Ø 27,84	Ø 20,4
VR experience	–	20% yes, 80% no
Truck brand	60% Mercedes-Benz 30% other brands	50% Mercedes-Benz 50% other brands
Country license plate	100% GER	90% GER 10% NL
Dispatching range	100% DE 70% EU 30% INT (in the past)	100% DE 50% EU 0% INT

4.2   Interview Duration

Due to the time constraints of the test participants it is important to gain as much information as possible in little time. Table 2 shows that the VR simulator tests require 3.5 min more than the test sessions in the steering wheel mockup.

Table 2. Interview duration

Test trial	Interview duration steering wheel	Interview duration VR simulator
1	0:17:12	0:24:52
2	0:23:58	–
3	0:23:28	0:22:51
4	0:17:58	0:19:03
5	0:18:36	0:29:40
6	0:21:40	0:22:50
7	–	0:16:30
8	0:22:48	0:25:20
9	0:19:16	0:27:20
10	0:15:55	0:22:53
Ø Interview duration	00:20:05	00:23:29

4.3   Answer Quality and Variance

The longer test duration with VR is partly a consequence of more relatedness of the test situation to truck drivers' daily routines. The VR achieved a far higher immersion into the situation, due to the representation of the avatar hands and the steering wheel position and buttons in VR. This could be achieved even though the VR prototype still suffered from some technical insufficiency that resulted in problems in the interaction.

Due to this wider scope of imagination and relating the test situation more to their daily life, the participants address a wider scope of their problems and personal solutions. Not all of them are relevant for the specific HMI test, but some represent situations that are relevant and were not mentioned with the steering wheel mockup. On the other hand, the variance of answers directly related to the HMI was higher with the steering wheel mockup, as the post hoc cluster analysis of qualitative answers indicates. A reason might be, that the HMI can be less intuitive without context. A relevant context often explains HMI functions that are misleading without the context. Based on observation we would say that the rich VR context did not distract the participants' attention from the relevant HMI function. Hence, their answers may provide a higher external validity and decisions taken based on VR testing may better fit to the real use cases.

4.4   Utility Analysis of Both Simulators

The method utility analysis provides a tool for the specific, detailed assessment of the different demonstrator alternatives (Windolph 2015). This shows the clear, transparent representation of decisions (Müller 2008) and enables a detailed documentation, which allows anyone interested to trace the individual steps (Windolph 2015). As a result, it documents which simulator offers the greater utility.

The first step in the utility analysis includes the determination of comparable criteria. Therefore a cluster analyses is important. The result of the analysis is presented in the column "criteria". Moreover, a valuation of the criteria is necessary. Windolph (2015) recommends an expert workshop to define the weightings. In such a workshop, an expert team from Daimler Trucks first defined the importance of the different criteria and second evaluated the forms in both simulators.

Next the implementation-rating per simulator of the shown criteria is represented in the column (c) and reaches from 0 to 10, while 10 being the best value.

In Table 3 the weighting factors of the respective subcriteria are multiplied by the target values ($d = b * c$) and then the sum formed of all part utility values for each superordinate criterion ($e = \sum d$). This value is then multiplied by the weighting factor of the superordinate criterion ($e * a$), giving its utility value per superordinate criterion (Haedrich und Tomczak 1996).

The results are presented in Table 3.

Table 3. Utility analyses comparing steering wheel mockup and VR simulator

Category	Mass factor		Steering wheel			VR simulator			Winning prototype
	a	b	c	b * c	a * ∑d	c	b * c	a * ∑d	
Technical components	0,21				0,64			1,43	VR
Vehicle		0,23	5	1,15		8	1,84		
Scenario		0,23	2	0,46		10	2,30		
Environment (-simulation)		0,15	3	0,45		8	1,20		
Driving task		0,08	1	0,08		3	0,24		
Control		0,31	3	0,93		4	1,24		
∑		1,00		3,07			6,82		
Mobility of the test environment	0,29				1,45			2,03	VR
Mobility of the test environment		1,00	5	5,00		7	7,00		
∑		1,00		5,00			7,00		
Human perception	0,29				1,84			2,25	VR
Driving immersion		0,12	2	0,24		9	1,08		
Body immersion		0,06	3	0,18		7	0,42		
Simulator sickness		0,23	10	2,30		8	1,84		
(real) interaction		0,23	5	1,15		8	1,84		
Visual feedback		0,18	9	1,62		8	1,44		
Haptic feedback		0,12	6	0,72		6	0,72		
Auditive feedback		0,06	2	0,12		7	0,42		
∑		1,00		6,33			7,76		
Main quality criteria	0,07				0,40			0,49	VR
Objectivity		0,33	5	1,65		5	1,65		
Reliability		0,22	2	0,44		10	2,20		
Validity		0,45	8	3,60		7	3,15		
∑		1,00		5,69			7,00		
Secondary quality criteria	0,14				1,18			0,93	S. wheel
Economy		0,31	8	2,48		5	1,55		
Reasonableness		0,23	10	2,30		8	1,84		
Safety		0,23	10	2,30		8	1,84		
Data Protection		0,23	6	1,38		6	1,38		
∑		1,00		8,46			6,61		
Sum ∑	1,00				5,51			7,13	VR

The first criterion in Table 3 is representation of technical components. The VR simulator is the winner by comparison, because it allows the test participants to locate themselves in the future cab design in the relevant driver position and in the context of driving. Thereby the 360° video and the rotatable steering wheel enables an interaction with the simulation.

The second criterion in the technology area is the mobility of the test environment. As it turned out the steering wheel mockup is much more unwieldy than expected. It is difficult to find a suitable place during the test. Either there is no interaction between the test participant and simulator, or the test participant must hold it all the time. This is solved much better by the V-Class with the VR simulator.

The third criterion is human perception, whereby the VR simulator dominated again with its high degree of interaction. It enables the driver to be fully immersed in the fictitious world and perceive themselves and their hands in the VR and point actively to virtual objects. In addition the VR setup provided ambient noises which increase the immersion. However, the ambient noise combined with the questions sometimes lead to sensory overload. None of the test participants reported any discomfort.

When analyzing the main quality criteria it turns out that the objectivity is a distinct shortcoming of the Guerrilla testing method. The objectivity of the result depends substantially on the structured interview guide, and the number and selection of participants. This was kept constant for both simulators. The VR Simulator dominated in the other both subcategories, especially in the validity of the answers.

The last comparable category are the secondary quality criteria, where the steering wheel mockup shows better results. It is much cheaper than the VR setup, requires little effort to create and transport and requires a little less time to conduct quick user tests.

4.5   Technical Readiness of the VR Simulator

The VR simulator prototype was used for the first time in regular HMI testing and already unveiled its benefits regarding representation of the technical components, mobility of the test setup, human perception and immersion as well as the main quality criteria. However several technical limitations were noticed.

During the interaction of the participants with the HMI, they comment on what they see and sometimes point at it. For the interviewer this context was not visible.

The HMD got too warm after prolonged use, which explicitly constitutes a comfort problem when carrying out studies in the summer. The HMD is difficult to clean due to their foam pads and adjustment straps.

The viewing angle of the HMD is modestly restricted and the resolution requires bending forward in order to read text on the cluster display.

Depending on the individual's stature, a bigger or smaller distance to the steering wheel mockup is required, and hence an adjustable steering wheel is needed. In addition, many test participants noted that the virtual representation of the buttons on the steering wheel do not meet their requirements. A great deal of practice is needed to use these in VR due to imperfect matching for the use of such small buttons.

Also the realization of a real driving task or at least a moving steering wheel with force feedback would be an important improvement, since we found that many participants missed the actual driving as primary task while evaluating the HMI as secondary task. They note the desire for a test in reality, underscoring the limits of the fictitious world.

5 Discussion

The comparison of the steering wheel and the VR simulator show the respective benefits and disadvantages of both approaches. The Guerilla interview method is applicable with both prototypes.

With the VR simulator, interviews take approx. 3 min longer which is a relevant time when quick tests are necessary. These 3 min can be attributed to the time needed to equip the participants and for the tracking calibration. This procedure may become a bit faster in future when more participants have experience with VR and the tracking procedure. Also some technical issues of the VR prototype added some minutes to the test duration in some trials. In the further development, the robustness should be addressed in order to reduce testing time. The VR simulator also provides much more impressions, especially the whole truck cockpit and a driving scenario. For this reason test participants also tell more anecdotes about their work life when they are remembered by the complex driving scenario. This also adds some extra time to the test duration, however improves the external validity of the statements and contributes to higher answer quality.

The higher external validity of the answers lead to a better transfer of the HMI results into the later product. On the other hand the steering wheel mockup created more answers directly related to the specific HMI under investigation. It might be, that the context provided in the VR simulator reduced some doubts resulting from the HMI when it is presented without the context. It may also be, that the richer context in the VR distracted the participants focus on the specific HMI under investigation. Both hypothesis need more attention and data in following studies.

The utility analysis replicated these findings and shows the main benefits of VR simulation over traditional mockups. It also shows the disadvantage of slightly higher effort. This might be the main decision criteria when selecting the best testing environment. The traditional steering wheel is cheaper to produce and to maintain and a bit quicker in application, while the VR simulator provides higher external validity.

There is still a lot of improvement possible in the VR simulator. The technical readiness is already now acceptable and provides relevant results in HMI testing. However it is obvious that technical development is fast and can eliminate many disadvantages encountered in this study. Given the higher benefit of the VR solution it is recommendable to keep on improving this approach.

6 Conclusion

By way of conclusion, the initial question regarding the improvement of the contextual integration can be answered. The VR simulator constitutes a sound tool as part of UX studies. With its aid, test participants can immerse themselves in fictitious worlds and so experience an immersive user experience. Thanks to the realistic context integration, high-quality, verified UX statements are generated.

The VR simulator in comparison with the click-dummy convinces in two categories: utility and generating enthusiasm. The fully-fledged immersion and presence within the VR also leads to a higher degree of acceptance and taking the interviews seriously among the test participants.

This may result in more verified decisions regarding the utility of the presented display functions. To conclude the relevance of this aspect shall be investigated in further studies.

The extent to which the recorded statements can be transferred to reality can also be validated based on the gained insights. The analysis of the feedback shows that the test participants set the HMI prototype in the context of their personal everyday working lives. They not only answer the questions in the interview guide, but also recount related anecdotes from their professional lives.

The integration requires, however, for the method and the presentation tool to have a certain degree of flexibility, efficiency, agility and mobility. The use of the VR simulator in combination with the evaluation methodology implements all the required aspects.

Solely with regard to controlling the displays, the HMI exhibits a shortcoming due to the discrepancy between the real and fictitious steering wheel in relation to the generated hand representations.

Given the lack of implementation of driving tasks in the simulation, no conclusions could be drawn about the control of the displays while driving during this study.

At the same time, high-quality HMI statements are generated with a minimum outlay of time, human resources and money. To this end, the interviews are conducted at truck stops and so in the familiar working environment of the drivers. This additional effort compared with stationary test environments, however, proves worthwhile. The experienced respect by having the field researchers approach the test participants and the specialist interest in their working environment leads to a successful test sequence most of the time.

The qualitative analysis of huge amounts of data is the only shortcoming with the evaluation methodology. It takes a long time to complete and is as of now the most costly element of the process. Development of an alternative method for the time-consuming qualitative analysis should be developed and is in fact the next step in a following study.

The analysis shows many technical shortcoming of the first technical implementation of the VR system. Apart from optimizing the precision of hand & actuator positions, also risk of simulator sickness must be further reduced to allow longer test times. Readability of HMI text should be further enhanced to remove this distraction from the perceived user experience. System resources have to increase drastically to cover up need for higher frame-rates and resolution.

7 Outlook

In the meantime, many conclusions of this study have found its way into implementation:

- Hand tracking has been improved by hardware & software updates & changes of the tracking strategy
- Resolution has been elevated by using a new generation of HMD
- Tracking loss has been reduced using redundant sensors
- Interview and protocol interfaces are now wireless and separated to the different roles
- Active driving and steering in an 3D environment is implemented
- Seating and packaging of the Mercedes-Benz V-Class has been adjusted for the interview situation
- Computing power has been increased using a fixed tower PC unit in the V-Class separated from the interfaces.
- Eye tracking & real time tracking of driving behavior and HMI usage indicators has been implemented

Apart from fixing technical difficulties & quality enhancements, the biggest additions to the setup will be an active driving task & adding real time tracking of driving & other behavioral data.

Future evaluations of the simulator will tell us in which extent we can draw conclusions about real driving behavior in respect to HMI usage out of those additions to our VR driving simulation.

Through the further development of optical systems, we are getting closer and closer to actual human perception. With each hardware generation new applications open up that were previously not suitable to be displayed in VR due to their quality requirements. Especially now it is very important to look at applications that we previously excluded from our research, since the possibilities are developing very rapidly. Therefore, simulations will definitely gain importance for user experience and usability testing in the future.

But aside from our "Deep UX" development project, VR has a lot more useful applications in automotive research and development. For example, the technology allows designers to view our vehicles in their original size at a very early stage in the design process. We can implement changes to the virtual vehicle live and assess their design impact directly. Therefore, using virtual reality in simulations is a powerful tool in many use cases—no matter if it is about looking at complex driving scenarios, facing geometric challenges or working on three-dimensional models of future products.

The long-term aim must be to fully implement virtual reality. This should be no different from the real world, allow for any interaction and be deployable worldwide. Implementing all these ascertained aspects will promote even better statements, greater utility and a better fusion between evaluation methodology and simulator.

References

Alfes, S., Von Querfurth, A., Raiser, H., Niehaus, F.: Interactive flexible remote-diagnosis. ATZelektronik Worldwide **9**(4), 46–49 (2014)

Belam, M.: 10 tips for ambush Guerilla user testing (2010). http://www.currybet.net/cbet_blog/2010/06/10-tips-for-ambush-Guerilla-us.php

Bopp-Bertenbreiter, A.V., Diederichs, F., Mathis, L.-A., Widlroither, H.: Accessibility and inclusion: what automated vehicles mean to users limited by age and physical disabilities. In: 7th International Humanist Conference, Greece, September 2020 (2020, in press)

Haedrich, G., Tomczak, T.: Produktpolitik (Kohlhammer-Edition Marketing). Kohlhammer, Stuttgart (1996)

Krupenia, S., et al.: The process and challenges of introducing a VR simulator capability to the automotive industry: a Scania use case. In: DSC 2017 Europe VR, Stuttgart (2017)

Jacobsen, J., Meyer, L.: Praxisbuch Usability & UX. Was jeder wissen sollte, der Websites und Apps entwickelt, Rheinwerk Computing, 1. Auflage, 1, korrigierter Nachdruck. Rheinwerk Verlag GmbH, Bonn (2018)

Lämmler, R.: (Testing Time, Hrsg.) Guerrilla Testing: Mutig und rasch zu Resultaten (2017). https://www.testingtime.com/ux-testing/guerrilla-testing/

Lottermoser, L.-M., Dittrich, F., Langer, D.: Keine frage des alters. Virtual Reality als Evaluationsmethode für die nutzerzentrierte Entwicklung von AAL-Anwendungen. In: Hess, S., Fischer, H. (eds.) Mensch und Computer 2018 – Usability Professionals, Bonn, pp. 41–51 (2018). https://dl.gi.de/bitstream/handle/20.500.12116/16756/Beitrag_189_final_a.pdf

Mayring, P., Brunner, E.: Qualitative inhaltsanalyse. In: Buber, R., Holzmüller, H.H. (eds.) Qualitative Marktforschung. Konzepte - Methoden – Analysen, Lehrbuch, 2, überarbeitete Auflage, pp. 671–680. Gabler Verlag/GWV, Wiesbaden (2009)

Mayring, P.: Qualitative Inhaltsanalyse. Grundlagen und Techniken. Beltz, Weinheim (2010)

Mayring, P., Frenzl, T.: Qualitative inhaltsanalyse. In: Baur, N., Blasius, J. (eds.) Handbuch Methoden der empirischen Sozialforschung, pp. 543–548. Springer, Wiesbaden (2014). https://doi.org/10.1007/978-3-531-92052-8_42

Müller, P.D.W.: Methoden der Produktgestaltung (Reihe Forschungspapiere Band 18). Institut für Angewandtes Markt-Management der FH Dortmund, Dortmund (2008)

Niehaus, F., Kehrein, T.: Gestaltungsprinzipien für herstellerproprietäre, mobilfunkbasierte Arbeitsmittel Applikationen – Die Zielgruppenbefragung In: Krzywinski, J., Linke, M., Wölfel, C., Kranke, G. (eds.) Proceedings of the Conference on "Entwerfen – Entwickeln – Erleben", EEE 2014. Gemeinsames Kolloquium Konstruktionstechnik (KT 2014), 26–27 Juni 2014, Dresden, Germany, pp. 263–277 (2014)

Pollmann, K., Fronemann, N., Krüger, A.E., Peissner, M.: PosiTec – how to adopt a positive, need-based design approach. In: Marcus, A., Wang, W. (eds.) DUXU 2018. LNCS, vol. 10920, pp. 52–66. Springer, Cham (2018). https://doi.org/10.1007/978-3-319-91806-8_5

Statista (2020). https://de.statista.com/statistik/daten/studie/202938/umfrage/hoehe-des-frauenanteils-bei-den-kraftfahrzeugfuehrern-in-deutschland/

van der Veer, A., et al.: The influence of the viewpoint in a self-avatar on body part and self-localization. In: ACM Symposium on Applied Perception 2019, pp. 1–11, September 2019

Windolph, A.: Fundierte Entscheidungen treffen mit der Nutzwertanalyse (2015) http://projekte-leicht-gemacht.de. https://projekte-leicht-gemacht.de/blog/pm-methoden-erklaert/nutzwertanalyse/

A Mixed-Reality Shop System Using Spatial Recognition to Provide Responsive Store Layout

Hao Dou$^{(\boxtimes)}$ ⓘ and Jiro Tanaka$^{(\boxtimes)}$ ⓘ

Waseda University, Kitakyushu, Japan
douhao@fuji.waseda.jp, jiro@aoni.waseda.jp

Abstract. Environment is very important for consumers shopping. In-store characteristics such as store layout, decoration, music and store employee are the key of consumers shopping experience. However, the current online shop system lacks environment information and in-store characteristics, which are very important for consumers shopping experience. In this paper, we designed a new mixed-reality (MR) shop system by mixing virtual in-store characteristics and real environment, which might be the possible direction for the future online shop system. Technically, we developed a new spatial understanding algorithm and layout mechanism to support responsive spatial layout. In our system, store designers only need to design once, and our system can make any place to the mixed reality shop. We have invited some participants to test the usability and efficiency of our system. We have obtained a positive feedback through the preliminary user study.

Keywords: Mixed-reality · E-commerce · Spatial recognition · Responsive layout

1 Introduction

The current online shop system lacks environment information and in-store characteristics. It is difficult to imagine whether the product is suitable in the real environment. Because of the lack of in-store characteristics. It is also difficult to express the brand characteristics [1].

Recently, with the development of mixed reality (MR) technology, it has become possible to use only head-mounted devices to scan the environment and bring a mixed reality experience. Evolving MR technology has brought new opportunity to the shopping system.

In this study, we proposed the concept of the MR shop system, which might be the possible direction of the future shopping system. The MR shop system consists of three main parts. Spatial recognition, responsive store layout, and store interaction (see Fig. 1). First, we scan the space through depth cameras and use a spatial understanding algorithm to understand the surfaces. Next, we have designed a layout algorithm which is based on the understood surfaces and layout preference of shop items, to generate the responsive MR store layout. Last, after building the designed shop, the user can use

© Springer Nature Switzerland AG 2020
J. Y. C. Chen and G. Fragomeni (Eds.): HCII 2020, LNCS 12190, pp. 18–36, 2020.
https://doi.org/10.1007/978-3-030-49695-1_2

gestures to move or rotate virtual products or use voice commands to communicate with the virtual store employee.

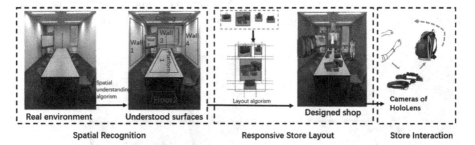

Fig. 1. The process of generating a mixed reality shop.

2 Goal and Approach

Our research tries to build a mixed-reality (MR) shop system which can recognize the space and mix virtual in-store characteristics and real environment, to provide: Immersive virtual preview and interaction in the real environment. It also provides in-store characteristics, such as store layout, decoration, music and virtual store employee.

As the Fig. 2 shows, after scanning the environment. The same room can be different MR shops. The Virtual products placed on the real table and chairs and the real walls and ceiling is decorated with virtual store characteristics. The user can use gestures to manipulate virtual products or use voice commands to communicate with the virtual store employee. This system can automatically make the real environment to be the MR shop and give users an immersive shop experience just like a physical shop.

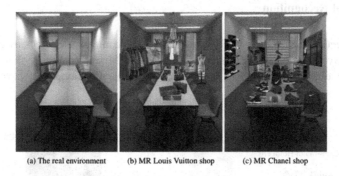

(a) The real environment   (b) MR Louis Vuitton shop   (c) MR Chanel shop

Fig. 2. Different MR shop in the same environment.

If the user is in a different room, this system would automatically build another MR shop by using the same elements (see Fig. 3). This system is very convenient for shop designers. Designers only need to design the elements once, this system will automatically adapt these elements to all spaces. Although the elements are the same, each user has their own unique MR shop because they are in a different environment.

(a) The seminar room   (b) Another real environment

Fig. 3. The same MR shop in the different environment.

3   Mixed-Reality Shop System

To generate a MR shop, there are three steps: spatial recognition, responsive store layout, and store interaction.

3.1   Spatial Recognition

Spatial Detection. As the Fig. 4 shows, we use depth cameras to detect surfaces of the real world. By using the spatial understanding API of Mixed Reality Toolkit (MRTK) [2]. We can obtain the metadata of detected surfaces: Position, size, horizontal or vertical.

Fig. 4. The process of spatial detection

Spatial Metadata Processing. In a real store layout, different store elements tend to have different layout characteristics. For example, chandeliers are often placed on the ceiling, and merchandise is often placed on a table for easy viewing. Some advertisements may be posted on the wall to attract the attention of the user. Based on these placement preferences, we need to understand the specific meaning of each plane in the space. As the Fig. 5 shows, we designed an algorithm to understand detected surfaces. First, we remove all surfaces that are smaller than the smallest item of the store. Then understand the specific surface by judging the metadata.

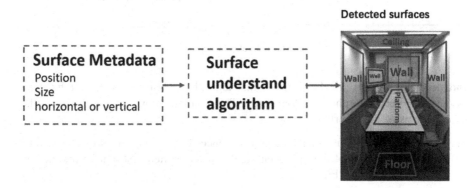

Fig. 5. The process of surface understanding

The specific spatial understanding mechanism is shown as Table 1.

Table 1. The specific spatial understanding mechanism.

Type	Spatial understanding mechanism
Ceiling	The highest horizontal surfaces in space
Wall	Vertical surfaces
Platform	Horizontal surface in the middle of the ceiling floor
Floor	The lowest horizontal surfaces in space

Through this spatial understanding algorithm, we simplify complex, non-specific spatial metadata into concrete surfaces that can be understood by store designers and can be used for design, which is the basis for generating responsive stores.

3.2 Responsive Store Layout

After understanding the surfaces, we can generate the layout of the store. In order to get a regular store layout, we developed several layout mechanisms to correspond to store elements and the detected surfaces. These layout mechanisms depend on the placement characteristics of the store elements.

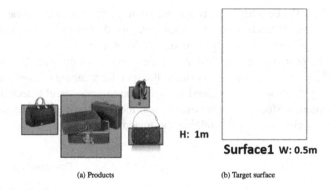

H: 1m

Surface1 W: 0.5m

(a) Products   (b) Target surface

Fig. 6 Products and target surface.

Independent Layout Mechanism. In this algorithm, shop items do not have an association. This algorithm has four steps. The example shown in Fig. 6 shows the specific steps of the algorithm:

1. Arrange the shop items into an ordered sequence. The order of this sequence will be used as the priority of the placement, and the item sorted first will be placed first when traversing (see Fig. 7).

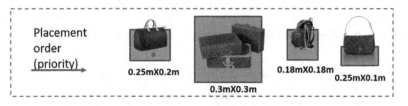

Fig. 7. Arrange the shop items into an ordered sequence.

2. Specify the direction of traversal for the target surface. In this example, Placement direction: row down. It means we'll traverse the surface along the row, and from top to bottom (see Fig. 8).

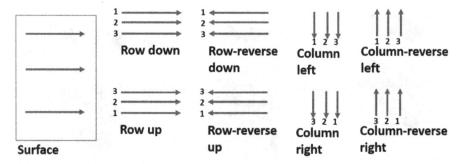

Fig. 8. The direction of traversal.

The first and second steps are all the attributes that the store designer needs to configure. Next, we will start the layout. The principle of layout: Try to ensure that high-priority products can be placed.

3. For each shop item, this algorism traverses the surface from the first line (alone the direction). If there is enough space for the placement, place it, if not, go to the next line (see Fig. 9).

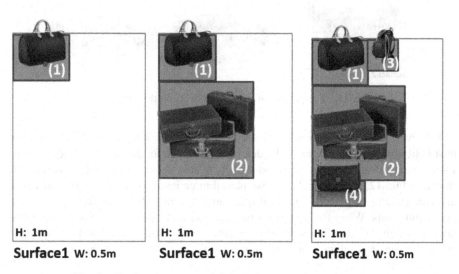

Fig. 9. The layout sequence of the independent layout algorithm

4. Let the items have the same spacing between rows and columns (see Fig. 10).

- Make the same spacings between each row. (H − Hrow1 − Hrow2 − Hrow3)/4.
- Make the same spacings in each row.

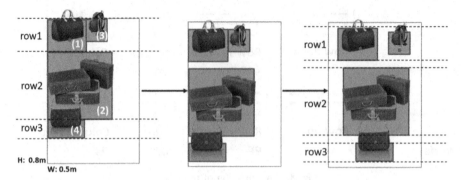

Fig. 10. Make the same spacing between rows and columns.

In some cases, if there is not enough space, lower priority items may not be placed. As shown in Fig. 11, if we say that the four items are placed on the smaller flat surface2, the fourth item will not be placed because there is not enough space after the first three items are placed.

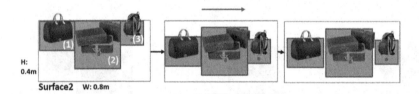

Fig. 11. The process of placing products on the surface2.

However, Users may also be interested in items that are not placed. We Designed a float indicator to indicate there are hidden items available for display. We Added a new voice command "show other items" to show available items that are not displayed. As shown in Fig. 12, in the initial case, we placed three items. Since there are four items that can actually be placed, we will display an indicator "3/4" to indicate the current placement status. When the user gazes the indicator and says, "show more", the items that are not displayed will be displayed, and the status of the indicate will also change. When the user says "show more" again, we will return to the state of the initial display of three items.

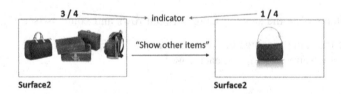

Fig. 12. Products indicator.

Independent layout has some limitation. The placement of shop items usually has an association. For example. Sometimes we may want to put some shop items to the platform on this structure. In this case, we cannot implement such layout just using the independent layout mechanism. So, it is very important to have a group layout mechanism to solve this problem.

Group Layout Mechanism. In the independent layout, the placement of the shop items is independent. However, in the real shop, items usually have associations (bags group, shoes group, belts group). These kinds of association are very important for shop layout.

Moreover, we may place multiple groups on one surface. The placement of different groups may also have a structure (see Fig. 13), but different surface in the different environment may have different size, we cannot define the fixed size of each group to describe the layout structure.

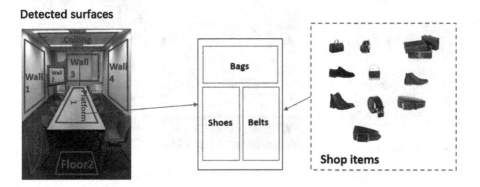

Fig. 13. Group layout example.

In order to describe the same structure on the different surfaces. We introduced a new concept of size: flex size. Flex size is described by a percentage that less than 100%. Its real size depends on the surface on which it is placed.

For example, there is a flex block which has flex size: 40% width and 50% height. When it is place on surface1, its real size will be 0.4 m width and 0.5 m height, while it is place on surface2, its real size is 0.4 m width and 0.35 m height (see Fig. 14). By defining flex size, we can describe the proportion structure between different surfaces, and calculate the real size of each group base on the real surfaces, in this way, we keep the same layout preference in different environment (see Fig. 15).

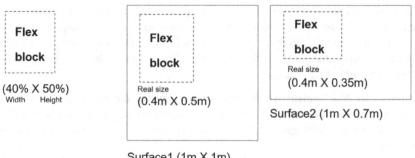

Fig. 14. The flex size and the real size

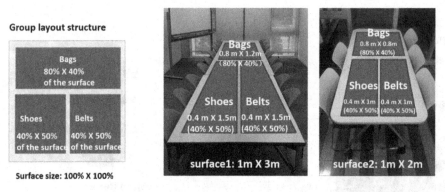

Fig. 15. Same layout structure in different surfaces.

It's not enough, A fixed structure may not be suitable for all surfaces. For example, as the Fig. 16 shows, because the width of surface3 is very small. If we use the same layout structure as surface1 and surface2, we may not have enough width to place any items.

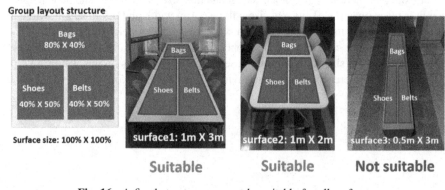

Fig. 16. A fixed structure may not be suitable for all surfaces.

In order to solve this problem. We allow store designers to give multiple sets of structures and specify their size range (see Fig. 17). In different surfaces, this system uses the related structure to generate the layout. For example. If we put these three groups on the surface 1, we'll use the structure1 while we put them to surface 3, use structure2.

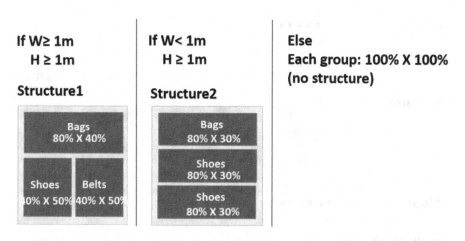

Fig. 17. Multiple sets of structures.

If there is no specified range, we'll give each group 100% × 100%. It means has no structure. And One group will take one whole surface. Like the Fig. 18 shows. In this way, we can get suitable group layout in any environment.

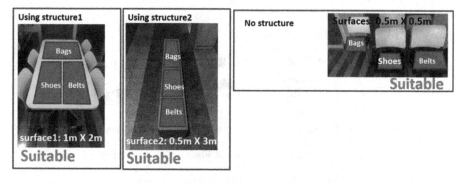

Fig. 18. Different layout structures in different surfaces.

Here is the summary of the layout mechanism.

1. Arrange shop items groups of each kind of surfaces (ceiling, wall, platform, floor) into an ordered sequence. We will traverse from ceiling to floor. In each kind of surface, from largest surface to smallest surface (see Fig. 19).

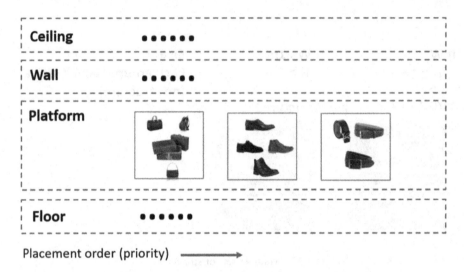

Placement order (priority) ⟶

Fig. 19. Arrange shop items groups into an ordered sequence.

2. Describe multiple sets of layout structures (set the percentage size of each group) and set a traversal direction of each group. When generating the layout within each group. We will use this traversal direction (see Fig. 20).

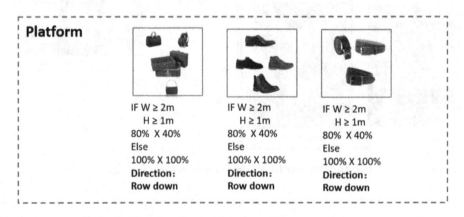

Fig. 20. Describe multiple sets of layout structures.

The first and second steps are all the attributes that the store designer needs to configure. Next, we will start the layout.

3. In the real environment, choose the related structure base on the real size of current surface.
4. Calculate the real size of each group using the structure. Then use independent layout algorism to generate the layout of each group.

After these four steps, we generated an MR shop. And the user can interact with it.

3.3 Spatial Sound

Many studies have shown that in the store system, sound feedback may affect the consumer's shopping experience [3]. Background music is an important symbol of brand culture, and different background music highlights different shopping environments [4]. We offer store designers two different modes of music interaction. One is the global mode, which allows users to hear the same sound anywhere in the virtual store. The other is space sound. Spatial sounds allow store designers to place a certain type of sound on a particular store element, which provides new interaction possibilities for the elements of the store item. For example, a store designer can place a dynamic show video near a particular item. Or specify a sound command that is sent when a particular item is in use. In this way, users can get a more immersive shopping experience.

3.4 Virtual Store Employee

In the physical store, interaction with the store employee is very important. When a user is interested in a product, it is often necessary to ask the store employee for details. The employee's description of the design source of products often enhances the user's trust and delivers a brand culture [5, 6]. In our system, after getting the designed shop. The user can use voice commands to communicate with the virtual store employee, and there are three kinds of voice commands:

1. I want to visit the Prada shop.
2. Introduce this product.
3. What's the price of the product? I'll take it.

After getting the voice commands, we use Microsoft speech to text and text analytics API to get the keywords of the voice command and get the related information from the store server.

3.5 Virtual Product Manipulation

The user can also use two-hand manipulation gesture to move or rotate virtual 3D objects (see Fig. 21). We use cameras of HoloLens to detect the user's gestures, then use the mixed-reality toolkit to achieve rotate and move operations [7].

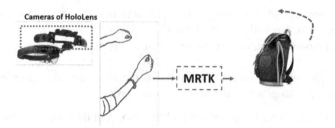

Fig. 21. Two-hand manipulation gesture.

In this chapter, we introduced the system design of our system:

1. We use spatial recognition technology to build a mixed-reality shop system which provides immersive virtual preview and interaction in the real environment.
2. We propose a layout mechanism to automatically mix virtual in-store characteristics with the real environment to provide a responsive mixed-reality store layout.

4   Implementation

4.1   Hardware

We divided this system into two parts: HMD client and server. To achieve the system, we need:

1. Depth sensors to detect the environment to recognize the space.
2. Microphones and speakers to capture the user's voice commands and provide feedback.
3. Head-mounted display to show the MR shop.
4. A computer as a server to store the shop elements.

We choose Microsoft HoloLens. It is a see-through type head-mounted display with built-in depth camera set and microphone. It blends cutting-edge optics and depth sensors to deliver 3D holograms pinned to the real world around the user. Built-in microphones and speakers are used to capture the user's voice and provide audio feedback. When the user makes a voice command, we use the HoloLens dictation system to convert the user's voice commands into text. Then proceed to the next operation based on the text instructions.

In order to store shop elements and store layout preferences, we use a laptop as a store server. Laptops and head-mounted displays are in the same network environment to increase access speed.

The other technical supports are:

1. Mixed-Reality Toolkit (MRTK), it Supports environment data analysis and gestures input functionality of my system.
2. Microsoft speech-to-text API, it converts the user's voice commands into text.

3. Microsoft text analytics API, it extracts keywords from user commands that have been converted to text. For example, when the user says, "I want to go to the Prada store" or "Take me to the Prada store", we will extract the keyword "Prada store" and perform the same operation (generating the Prada mixed reality store).

4.2   Graphical User Interface for Shop Designer

As the Fig. 22 shows, we provide the store designer with a user interface for the web server. The store designer only needs to upload the elements of the store, specifying the attributes of the store elements, such as size and placement preferences. We will store the store elements in the store server and generate a mixed reality store using the corresponding store elements and placement preferences when the user accesses with voice commands.

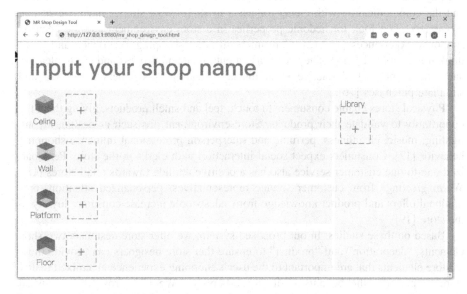

Fig. 22. Graphical user interface for shop designer.

4.3   Voice Command

In order to provide users with a more natural approach [8]. to interact with our assistant system, we designed our system to allow voice input. With the help of existing speech recognition techniques, the system can extract the user's command and keywords, and it can provide responses in real-time response [9, 10]. Users can say a sentence including the mixed reality shop that they desire, our system will generate the related mixed reality shop in the real time.

4.4   Two-Hands Manipulation

We built a shop server to store the 3D models of shop items and the layout preference designed by the shop designer. Each product in our system has its own 3D virtual object. So that when the products result is returned, the 3D virtual objects can also be shown. We pre-processed the virtual models to make sure that they can be operated successfully. Using MRTK, bounding box around the virtual objects is used to help users judge the size of the objects. By adding two-hand manipulation scripts in MRTK, users can use their hands to drag and rotate the virtual objects.

5   Related Works

5.1   Related Works on In-Store Shopping

For physical stores, many studies have shown the importance of in-store characteristics and the communication with clerks for users to shop. Most studies have shown that consumers often look for hedonic properties in a store environment and are keen on shopping experiences [11, 12]. Consumers like the shopping experience and don't think it's a chore [13, 14]. They see it as an entertainment process and enjoy pleasure and enjoyment [15]. Attractive retail displays motivate consumers to browse and stimulate purchases [16].

Physical stores enable consumers to touch, feel and smell products, giving them the opportunity to validate their products. Store environment tips such as design, layout, lighting, music, cleanliness, perfume and salesperson professional influence shopping behavior [17]. Consumers expect social interaction with clerks in the store. Personalized one-to-one customer service also has a positive attitude towards retail stores [18]. Warm greetings from customer service representatives, personalized attention, promotional offers and product knowledge from salespeople increase consumer loyalty to the store [19].

Based on these studies. In our proposed system, we offer store designers two shop elements, "decoration" and "product" to ensure that store designers can provide these in-store elements that are important to the user's shopping experience in a mixed reality store to preserve the benefits of in-store shopping. We also provide the "virtual employee" function to provide communication functions similar to physical stores, which not only meets the social needs of users in shopping, but also further strengthens the brand characteristics. By Comparing consumer's shopping channel choice motivations, we added the most important in-store factors that are lacking in the online shop to the mixed-reality shop system, and also provided speech input and voice feedback (virtual store employee interaction) to give users a natural shopping experience.

5.2   Related Works on Responsive Layout

Placer and Packer Algorithms. In the geometry management system of tcl/tk. The packer arranges widgets around the edges of an area. The placer provides simple fixed and "rubber sheet" placement of widgets [20].

In a real store system, we also have the need to separate objects from a single plane to a specific plane, so I introduced an independent layout method in the store layout algorithm which is similar with the "placer". But in fact, commodity groups with a certain pattern are more common in stores, so I also introduced a group layout method which is similar with the "packer" to allow individual items to be packaged into groups, thus providing a more realistic layout unit.

Responsive Web Layout. A web browser is a dynamic medium, it allows a user to re-size the browser window itself, and users can also change the size of the font as well. And when this happens, web pages created with pixel-perfect web design principles often break. If a web page was optimized for a 1024 × 768-pixel screen size, that web page will look quite wrong in a smaller or bigger screen. As the number of mobile devices that have a variety of screen sizes grows, pixel-perfect web design has become problematic. Responsive web design [21] is an attempt to solve this problem. Its core concept is "flexible layout".

Responsive web design makes a web page adjust itself in response to the screen size of a device. This means that there is no longer one fixed layout in which the elements of a web page are permanently placed. Instead, as the size of the screen changes, the layout of a web page adjusts itself and rearranges the elements of the page.

In my mixed reality store system, in order to create a corresponding virtual store with the same material in different environments, I designed a traversal-based responsive layout algorithm. It dynamically generates the corresponding layout on different planes based on the product placement priority. Unlike tcl/tk and web responsive layouts, real environments have fixed and non-expandable sizes. Therefore, I also designed a layout indicator to extend the size of the store, which in turn expands the capacity of the real environment.

6 Preliminary Evaluation

We asked participants to accomplish their shopping tasks in our mixed-reality shop system. The main purpose of this study was to test whether our system can provide brand characteristics in the mixed-reality shop to give users a good shopping experience and whether the interaction of our system is easy to use.

6.1 Participants

We invited 10 participants (2 females and 8 males), ranging from 22 to 25 years of age. All participants have basic computer skills. Two of them had experience with head-mounted displays.

6.2 Method

All participants are given a brief introduction of the system. Before each study, we introduced the basic operations of Microsoft HoloLens to the participants. After the participants became familiar with the device, we asked them to visit two mixed-reality shops (one is the Prada shop, another is a flower shop), and try to find the products that they are interested.

After that, the participants will be asked to fill in a questionnaire. The questionnaire has following 7 questions and these questions use the 5-point Likert scale.

1. The system is easy to use.
2. The interaction with virtual store employee is useful or interesting.
3. The gestures interaction is useful or interesting.
4. I can easily find products of interest in the mixed-reality shop.
5. I can easily understand the details of the products in the mixed-reality shop
6. I can feel the brand characteristics in the mixed-reality shop.
7. The system can provide a good shopping experience.

6.3 Results

Question 1, 2 and 3 are used to test the ease of use and usability of the system. The average score of question 1 is 4.5. The results prove that the system is easy to operate. Question 2 is used to test the usability of the store employee interaction, the average score of question 2 is 4.8, the results shows that participants agree that voice interaction with virtual clerk is useful. Question 3 is used to test the usability of the gesture's interaction, the average score is 4.2. All the results show that even though users are not familiar with the operation of the head-mounted display, our voice and gestures-based system is still easy to use.

Questions 4, 5, 6 and 7 are used to determine whether our system can give users a good shopping experience. The average score of question 4, 5, 6, 7 is 4, 4, 4.5 and 4.6. The results show that participants agree that using our system can easily find products of interest, feel the brand characteristics and get a good shopping experience. One participant thought that using our system can better understand products information than traditional mobile shopping systems. Traditional mobile shopping systems typically use limited 2D images and captions to describe the specifics of the product, and users may not be able to get more specific information from these descriptions. Our system allows users to understand the product more fully by visually displaying a rotatable virtual 3D product with descriptive information.

In general, all participants rated our system higher than the traditional system. This may signify that our system is designed to be reasonable and practical. It demonstrates that our system can build a new way of shopping, allowing users to intuitively get high-quality recommended products based on the current scene and make quick shopping decisions.

Overall, we got a positive feedback through the preliminary user study.

7 Conclusion and Future Work

7.1 Conclusion

Our research compared current shop systems' advantages and disadvantages, then proposed the concept of a new shop system, mixed reality shop, which may be the possible direction of the future shopping system.

Technically, we developed a spatial understanding algorithm that divides the complex environment metadata into detected surfaces. This algorithm simplifies the information in space then reduce the amount of calculations. we also designed several matching layout mechanisms to generate the store layout. Under these mechanisms, we can generate the responsive store layout just through simple calculations.

For shop designers, we provide a simple layout interface, and store designers can easily complete the design of a mixed-real store by simply uploading store elements, grouping them, and specifying their order. When consumers use a mixed reality store on the client side, we will use a comprehensive layout algorithm to automatically generate the corresponding store based on the current environment. We also designed a virtual voice employee system and a simple gesture interaction system to allow consumers to interact with the mixed reality store.

We received feedback from the users by conducting a user study. Overall, we received positive feedback.

7.2 Future Work

Although we have proposed a prototype of mixed reality shop system, there are still some limitations and future possibilities to improve its efficiency. In this system, for the designer's design interface, it is still a 2D web interface. However, for the final mixed reality store, it is displayed in a real 3D environment. Therefore, there is a process of conversion between design and real layout, and store designers may not be able to imagine the final 3D store just through the 2D layout page. We hope this can be solved by a 3D design interface (for example, a store designer designs a store directly in a real environment). Also, we are thinking of the possibility of involving machine learning ability In the store's layout algorithm, because the store layout is subjective and difficult to measure with data, it may be related to the store style, related to the characteristics of the real environment, and related to the commodity elements. Through machine learning methods, we can not only be limited to a layout algorithm, but also consider the most possible layout factors to provide a better store layout.

References

1. Haridasan, A.C., Fernando, A.G.: Online or in-store: unravelling consumer's channel choice motives (2018)
2. Microsoft: MixedRealityToolkit-Unity (2018). https://github.com/Microsoft/MixedReality Toolkit-Unity. Accessed 29 Mar 2018

3. Sikström, E., Høeg, E.R., Mangano, L., Nilsson, N.C., De Götzen, A., Serafin, S.: Shop'til you hear it drop: influence of interactive auditory feedback in a virtual reality supermarket. In: Proceedings of the 22nd ACM Conference on Virtual Reality Software and Technology, pp. 355–356. ACM (2016)
4. Yalch, R., Spangenberg, E.: Effects of store music on shopping behavior. J. Consum. Market. **7**(2), 55–63 (1990)
5. Kim, M., Lee, M.K., Dabbish, L.: Shop-i: Gaze based interaction in the physical world for in-store social shopping experience. In: Proceedings of the 33rd Annual ACM Conference Extended Abstracts on Human Factors in Computing Systems, pp. 1253–1258. ACM (2015)
6. Li, F.-L., et al.: AliMe assist: an intelligent assistant for creating an innovative e-commerce experience. In: Proceedings of the 2017 ACM on Conference on Information and Knowledge Management, pp. 2495–2498. ACM (2017)
7. Funk, M., Kritzler, M., Michahelles, F.: HoloLens is more than air tap: natural and intuitive interaction with holograms. In: Proceedings of the Seventh International Conference on the Internet of Things, p. 31. ACM (2017)
8. Amalberti, R., Carbonell, N., Falzon, P.: User representations of computer systems in human-computer speech interaction. Int. J. Man Mach. Stud. **38**(4), 547–566 (1993)
9. Microsoft.github.io: Getting Started with MRTK | Mixed Reality Toolkit Documentation (2019). https://microsoft.github.io/MixedRealityToolkit-Unity/Documentation/Getting StartedWithTheMRTK.html
10. Singh, P., Katiyar, N., Verma, G.: Retail shop ability: the impact of store atmospherics & store layout on consumer buying patterns. Int. J. Sci. Technol. Res. **3**(8), 15–23 (2014)
11. Sloot, L.M., Verhoef, P.C., Franses, P.H.: The impact of brand equity and the hedonic level of products on consumer stock-out reactions. J. Retail. **81**(1), 15–34 (2005)
12. Verhoef, P.C., Lemon, K.N., Parasuraman, A., Roggeveen, A., Tsiros, M., Schlesinger, L. A.: Customer experience creation: determinants, dynamics and management strategies. J. Retail. **85**(1), 31–41 (2009)
13. Van Rompay, T.J.L., Krooshoop, J., Verhoeven, J.W.M., Pruyn, A.T.H.: With or without you: interactive effects of retail density and need for affiliation on shopping pleasure and spending. J. Bus. Res. **65**(8), 1126–1131 (2012)
14. Terblanche, N.S.: Revisiting the supermarket in-store customer shopping experience. J. Retail. Consum. Serv. **40**, 48–59 (2018)
15. Mortimer, G.: Toward a shopping typology of primary male grocery shoppers. Int. J. Retail Distrib. Manag. **40**(10), 790–810 (2012)
16. Nsairi, Z.B.: Managing browsing experience in retail stores through perceived value: implications for retailers. Int. J. Retail Distrib. Manag. **40**(9), 676–698 (2012)
17. Helmefalk, M., Hultén, B.: Multi-sensory congruent cues in designing retail store atmosphere: effects on shoppers' emotions and purchase behavior. J. Retail. Consum. Serv. **38**, 1–11 (2017)
18. Pantano, E., Gandini, A.: Exploring the forms of sociality mediated by innovative technologies in retail settings. Comput. Hum. Behav. **77**, 367–373 (2017)
19. Seock, Y.-K., Lin, C.: Cultural influence on loyalty tendency and evaluation of retail store attributes: an analysis of taiwanese and american consumers. Int. J. Retail Distrib. Manag. **39** (2), 94–113 (2011)
20. Johnson, E.F., Foster-Johnson, E.: Graphical Applications with TCL and TK. Hungry Minds, Incorporated (1996)
21. Kim, B.: Responsive web design, discoverability, and mobile challenge. Libr. Technol. Rep. **49**(6), 29–39 (2013)

Mixed Mock-up – Development of an Interactive Augmented Reality System for Assembly Planning

Florian Dyck$^{(\boxtimes)}$, Jörg Stöcklein, Daniel Eckertz,
and Roman Dumitrescu

Fraunhofer Institute for Mechatronic Systems Design IEM, Paderborn, Germany
{florian.dyck,joerg.stoecklein,daniel.eckertz,
roman.dumitrescu}@iem.fraunhofer.de

Abstract. Virtual assembly simulations are used in the industry to save costs in early stages of product development. As previous work, the so called mixed mock-up was developed to support the assembly planning of an automotive supplier. The mixed mock-up extends cardboard engineering through Augmented Reality (AR) visualizations. Virtual components are assembled virtually at the physical assembly mock-up. The evaluation of the first mixed mock-up prototype revealed various deficits in the technical implementation and the user interaction. This paper describes the further development of the existing system with the aim of making the simulation more realistic and increasing the practical suitability of the application. Based on a generic system description, the system has been improved in its individual components. A new pair of AR glasses is used to extend the field of vision. In addition, innovative force feedback gloves are used to support the user interaction. The gloves enhance the handling and ensure a natural interaction with the system and the virtual components. The effort for the preparation of the simulation data and the configuration of the assembly scene is reduced by a semi-automatic data processing step. This makes it easy to exchange CAD data and enables a productive use of the system. An evaluation by experts of the industry partner resulted in a thoroughly positive feedback. The mixed mock-up application has become more realistic and intuitive overall.

Keywords: Virtual assembly · Augmented Reality · Interaction · Haptics · Force feedback

1 Introduction

In today's global market, manufacturing companies face major challenges. Products are becoming increasingly complex and varied, batch sizes are shrinking and product life cycles are shortening [1]. In order to keep up with the competition, companies have to save costs and time in the various stages of the product life cycle [2]. It is well known that about 70% of the final production costs are already determined during the design stage [3] and that product costs are strongly linked to the assembly processes [2]. Practices like planning and training assembly operations can ensure that a product is

© Springer Nature Switzerland AG 2020
J. Y. C. Chen and G. Fragomeni (Eds.): HCII 2020, LNCS 12190, pp. 37–49, 2020.
https://doi.org/10.1007/978-3-030-49695-1_3

manufactured as efficiently as possible [4]. Digital methods such as computer-aided assembly planning allow for an early planning based on digital product models. However, the important aspects of ergonomics and operator safety are not considered [2]. For this reason, many companies still rely on analog methods like cardboard engineering. Cardboard structures are designed for assembly stations in order to be able to realistically simulate the assembly processes with the involvement of the human operator. Since physical prototypes of the components and tools need to be created, this procedure is time-consuming and particularly cost-intensive.

These circumstances gave rise to the idea of mixed mock-ups, in which cardboard engineering is extended by digital product models with the help of AR [5]. The use of Virtual Reality (VR) or AR in this context has the potential to provide the system operator with a realistic and immersive assembly simulation and to experience the effects of his interaction in real-time [1]. This supports the aim of the mixed mock-up to focus on the human operator who plans the assembly systems. The need for physical product parts is eliminated in early stages, which ultimately saves costs.

A German automotive supplier provided an industrial use case for the mixed mock-up by facing the problems described when planning new assembly systems. In cooperation with the research institute Fraunhofer IEM, a prototype was developed with which new assembly systems could be playfully tested and analyzed [5]. The company expects cost and time savings through the replacement of physical prototypes as well as immediate validation results. Even though the realization of Stöcklein et al. [5] was promising and well received by the users, the work can only be regarded as proof-of-concept. Due to technical restrictions, productive usage in the company could not be ensured. The implementation did not enable the integration of further construction data and the technical devices were criticized with regard to field of view and haptics.

Based on the first implementation, an enhanced system was developed. The points of criticism were revised in consideration of the current state of research. The focus was on data processing for virtual assembly systems and realistic interaction techniques. Novel hardware components were used to provide the system operator with a realistic impression of the virtual assembly and allow an intuitive handling of virtual components. For the development of the new system a generic approach was followed in order to create a better understanding of the system and to facilitate future work in the context of mixed mock-ups. The developed system was evaluated by means of a user test.

The further course of the present paper is structured as follows. Section 2 deals with related work, which includes the preliminary work as well as the state of research with focus on interaction in AR environments. Section 3 outlines the development of the enhanced mixed mock-up application followed by an evaluation. Finally, a conclusion is drawn and the need for action for future research is identified.

2   Related Work

This chapter is intended to provide an overview of the preliminary work on the mixed mock-up and the respective evaluation results. Subsequently, the state of research is investigated addressing the identified deficits of the first mixed mock-up implementation and the respective fields of action.

2.1   First Realization of the Mixed Mock-up and Its Deficits

As preliminary work, a first virtual assembly simulation prototype was developed by Fraunhofer IEM in Paderborn for an automotive supplier [5]. Physical cardboard mock-ups are extended using AR. This so-called mixed mock-up allows the virtual assembly of components of a headlamp based on predefined assembly steps.

Such a virtual simulation could also be done completely virtually. But there are several reasons for choosing AR over VR. On the one hand, these mock-ups are carried out in interdisciplinary teams. Since the participants communicate and discuss a lot with each other, it is not desirable to isolate individuals with VR glasses. In addition, AR can be used to adapt already existing work stations. In the case of VR this would involve greater effort, since the assembly station would first have to be digitized. A further point is that the tangible cardboard structures should remain in place for all workshop participants, so that rapid changes to the structure can be made in reality for all to see.

Fig. 1. First mixed mock-up prototype (photo composition)

Hardware and Software Setup

Figure 1 shows the actual setup for the first prototype of the mixed mock-up as a photo composition. The user stands in front of a workstation consisting of a workbench and two racks built from cardboard and wood. Using a HoloLens, Microsoft's Mixed Reality (MR) glasses, the virtual components and assemblies on the real racks as well as a virtual case, a virtual screwdriver and a virtual screw container on the physical workbench are visualized. A so-called marker in form of a 2D image is used for a geometrically correct superposition of the virtual elements on the physical structure. It is located on the workbench surface and recognized as a reference point by the AR application during an initialization step. After the initialization step the marker can be removed from the workbench as indicated in Fig. 1. Based on this reference point, the virtual contents are correctly registered within the real environment. As the HoloLens does not provide sufficient interaction support for this use case, Oculus touch controllers are used to interact with the virtual objects. With the help of these controllers, the user is able to grab and release virtual objects, move them freely and operate the virtual screwdriver. An additional feature of the Oculus touch controllers is the ability to provide simple haptic feedback (vibration) when touching virtual objects. This eases the interaction to the extent that users can also grab virtual objects even if they are outside the HoloLens' field of view. The prototype was realized using the 3D render engine Unity, whereby one part of the application is executed natively on the HoloLens, the other part on a PC connected via WLAN. This was necessary because the Oculus touch controllers could not be connected natively to the HoloLens. The application on the PC is responsible for transmitting the transformation (position and rotation) and the states of the buttons of both controllers to the application running on the HoloLens. The application on the HoloLens was responsible for visualizing all virtual objects as well as the entire logic.

Evaluation

Once the prototype was completed, it was tested with the help of experts of the company and evaluated on the basis of a System Usability Scale (SUS) questionnaire. This showed that the first prototype had both technical and functional deficits [5]. For instance, users often complained about the HoloLens' field of view being too small. Since users stand very close to the workstation, the HoloLens' small field of view of $30° \times 17.5°$ is very restrictive, so that users often have to move their entire head to see the virtual content. Inexperienced users of the HoloLens are not always aware of this limitation, so they often state that they can't see the virtual content as they usually just move their eyes. Another point of concern is the handling of the controllers and the unrealistic haptic feedback. Inexperienced users of the Oculus touch controllers often had difficulties with the controllers and could only handle them properly after a short instruction. The hard-coded scenario is a further restriction for the productive use of the first prototype. This means that only a few predefined assembly steps can be simulated with it. A use for further design data, new workflows and other setups of the real working area were not planned. Exactly these aspects should be considered and improved in the development of an extended and optimized prototype. Therefore the following fields of action for improvement are captured:

- **Visualization**: A new visualization solution with a larger field of view is to be utilized in the enhanced mixed mock-up. The goal is to give the user a better overview of the virtual contents without restricting his freedom of movement.
- **Interaction:** A new interaction medium is to be used to make the system easier to handle. Hereby a realistic and natural interaction shall be essential in order to simulate the virtual assembly activities.
- **Data processing:** The processing of assembly data should run (semi) automatically. New design data should thus be easily enabled for virtual assembly.

2.2 Existing Virtual Assembly Systems

In research there are many approaches regarding virtual assembly, therefore the presented related work is limited to AR systems. A special focus will be on the previously captured fields of action.

A methodology for implementing virtual assembly using natural interfaces was presented by Valentini et al. [6]. This system uses an AR head-mounted display in combination with hand tracking for natural interaction. The hand tracking was realized using Leap Motion Control, which recognizes bone segments of the users hand to interpret the hands' pose und thereby the users' intent. The system can detect different hand poses for interacting with spherical and cylindrical objects as well as pinching. The interpretation of interactions can take place between a hand and a component or between two components. The management of assembly conditions between components is done with the help of algebraic equations that constrain the degrees of freedom of virtual objects.

Wang et al. [7] developed an AR based interactive manual assembly design system (ARIMAD). In this implementation users can simulate an assembly by manipulating the virtual objects through hand tracking. The management of assembly data is realized by algorithms which extract assembly constraints out of geometric features of the considered CAD models. Interaction was realized with two virtual spheres registered on the users' fingertips. A manipulation of a virtual object can only take place when both spheres are in contact with the object.

Zaldivar-Colado et al. [8] presented a MR system which integrated a virtual assembly environment. Users can perform assembly tasks either in a completely computer generated (VR) environment or in an AR environment where only the components are virtual. For both approaches data gloves were used to track the movements of fingers and wrists. An experiment proved that the AR approach showed a statistically significant improvement in the assembly task execution compared to the task realized in VR.

The approaches presented so far work with hand tracking, but haptic feedback was left out of consideration. Murakami et al. [9] combined a wearable haptic device with marker-less AR technology. The aim of this approach was to identify differences of the operability of virtual objects in an assembly task to evaluate effects of the haptic feedback provided by HapticGEAR. The results indicate that haptic feedback is subjectively and objectively effective in assembly task completion.

There are also approaches that can provide force feedback in addition to haptic feedback. This enables the palpation of form and density of virtual objects. However, existing approaches are only available for VR environments. Al-Ahmari et al. [4] proposed a system that can be used for evaluating assembly decisions and training assembly operations. This is realized with the help of an interactive workbench inside a virtual environment. The system provides visual, auditory, tactile, as well as force feedback. The force feedback is provided through the Phantom Desktop device, which is basically a freely movable stylus mounted on a fixed stand. This device is also used by others to provide force feedback in virtual assembly tasks [10, 11].

Up to this point of time, the authors are not aware of another use case in research that describes an AR system with the utilization of force feedback data gloves.

3 Enhanced Mixed Mock-up

The first prototype of the mixed mock-up by Stöcklein et al. [5] met with a positive response. It showed that the combination of cardboard engineering and AR made it possible to dispense with expensive component prototypes. This saves costs and time in the planning of assembly lines. Nevertheless, there are the fields of action described in Sect. 2.1 which are addressed in the further development described in this chapter. To ensure future adaptations for new versions of the mixed mock-up, the development of the presented realization follows a generic approach.

3.1 System Overview

To provide a better understanding of the current state of development, the mixed mock-up system was initially analyzed and all relevant elements identified. These elements and their interdependencies were modelled using the specification technique CON-SENS[1]. In addition to the elements of the actual system, the model includes environmental elements that are important for the system (see Fig. 2). The model describes the system on an abstract level without addressing the concrete technical solutions. Thus, it can be used independently of the specific solution and accordingly enables a systematic evolution of the system. The actual mixed mock-up, shown in blue in Fig. 2, is divided into two parts, the AR system and the physical mock-up. Then there are the user who is working with the system and the virtual data or content necessary for the assembly planning as environment elements.

The **physical mock-up** is basically the cardboard setup. The **AR system** consists of four elements that are closely linked together.

- The **processing unit** runs the software and does all the computations. It gets external data like 3D models and assembly information for the assembly simulation as input. The processing unit provides visual content for the visualization device.

---

[1] CONSENS is a specification technique for mechatronic systems developed at the Heinz Nixdorf Institute in Paderborn, Germany.

- The **visualization device** displays all the virtual content necessary for the assembly simulation additional to the physical mock-up to the user. This could be models of assembly components, storage boxes and tools as well as visual feedback and additional information.
- An **interaction solution** is needed as an interface between the user and the processing unit. Special devices like controllers or a functionality like gesture or speech control can be used to allow the user to interact with the virtual content, grab objects and go through the assembly process virtually. Depending on the interaction solution, the user can get feedback like vibrations or sound to make the interaction more realistic. By using the visualization device and the interaction solution, the user influences their movement and spatial transformation.
- In order to provide a correct visualization and simulation a **tracking system** is needed. The world anchor of the tracking system is based on the cardboard setup. The tracking system tracks the visualization device and the interaction solution relatively to the world anchor and sends the tracking information to the processing unit. In this way the virtual content is always visualized in the correct position relatively to the physical mock-up.

With such a system, the user is able to carry out the assembly activities for selected assemblies virtually.

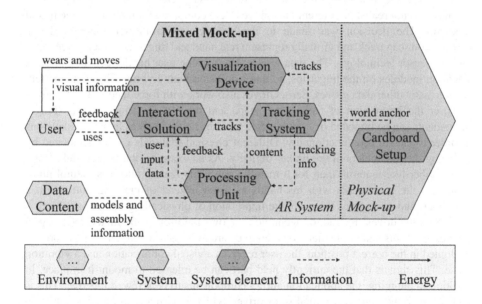

Fig. 2. System model of the mixed mock-up using CONSENS

3.2   Realization

This section describes the concrete implementation with the integration of the individual hardware components and the resulting advantages.

Visualization and Processing. Since a major criticism of the first prototype was the small field of view, new visualization technology is used for the enhanced mixed mock-up. After evaluating and comparing different AR glasses, the Meta 2 AR glasses from Metavision[2] were chosen. This selection was made due to the display resolution of 2560×1440 pixels and the field of view of 90° (diagonal). This means that about four times as much virtual content can be displayed on the Meta 2 as on the previously used HoloLens with a field of view of 35° (diagonal). This has the advantage that the user of the system gets a better overview of all virtual content around him, which increases the level of immersion. Because the Meta 2 is a wired AR device, all data is processed on an external computer. This has the disadvantage that the user is tied to a cable and thus slightly restricted in his movements. But much more complex AR visualizations can be realized with this system variant, because the computing power is no longer limited by the HoloLens processor.

Interaction. In terms of interaction, the preliminary work was criticized since many participants felt uncomfortable using the Oculus touch controllers. A main requirement for the new interaction solution is that the handling is more realistic and haptic feedback is provided. In a first approach, the gesture control of the Meta 2 AR glasses was tested and examined for its applicability in the mixed mock-up. This type of interaction did not work as desired and did not provide any haptic feedback to the user.

Therefore haptic interaction devices were necessary. Since game controllers were evaluated as not realistic, different data gloves were compared for their use in the mixed mock-up. The decision was made to use data gloves from SenseGlove[3]. These exoskeletons can track and virtually represent real hand and finger movements due to the built-in sensor technology. The data gloves can give the user haptic feedback through vibration modules on the fingertips, so that a collision with a virtual object can be felt. Unlike many other data gloves, SenseGloves also work with force feedback. This gives the user the impression of feeling the shape and density of virtual objects. Finger movements can be impeded or even blocked with the help of brakes in the exoskeletons in order to ensure this functionality. Different physical materials can be simulated by adjusting the parameters of the brakes digitally. As an example, the brakes yield faster for a rubber-like material than for a metallic one. This feature allows a natural inter-action, as the user works with his hands as usual instead of pressing buttons on a controller, and even gives the users the impression of physically grabbing an object.

The SenseGloves' interaction technology allows the user of the mixed mock-up to grab components and guide them to where they are to be assembled. Once a component is aligned in the correct position, the user receives a visual confirmation and a vibration pulse. This signals that the currently held part can be released to mount it in place. In addition to plugging, the application allows components to be screwed together. This is realized with the help of a virtual screwdriver, which is virtually attached to the table and enables the user to screw parts together vertically. To do this, a virtual screw must first be taken from a container and then placed on the bit of the screwdriver. Then the screwdriver can be grabbed and guided to the joint. Again, the user receives visual and

---

[2] https://www.metavision.com/.

[3] https://www.senseglove.com/.

haptic feedback as soon as the screw has been guided to a correct position. To start the screwing process, the handle of the virtual screwdriver can be pressed together. For this procedure, the ability of the SenseGloves to map elastic materials was applied. Compressing the virtual handle up to a defined threshold value is the trigger for the virtual screwing. This simulates the handling of real screwdrivers, which often have a trigger on the back of the handle.

A challenge in this realization was the handling of the screws. Since these geometries are usually very small, gripping them is difficult. To solve this problem, the colliders of these small standard parts had to be enlarged. As described in Sect. 3.3 later on, colliders are automatically added to the geometries in the data processing. This procedure had to be adapted for this special case. This reduced the realism of the application slightly, but increased the usability significantly.

Fig. 3. User mounting parts virtually with the enhanced mixed mock-up

Tracking. A tracking system is needed in order to display the virtual contents correctly positioned according to the physical mock-up. The Meta 2 AR glasses provide its own SLAM[4] tracking. However, the selected data gloves by SenseGlove need trackers of the HTC VIVE lighthouse[5] system. In order to bring the virtual contents visualized by the Meta 2 glasses and the gloves for the interaction into the same coordinate system, the two tracking systems need to be synchronized. Script based approaches did not achieve the intended results, so the tracking of the Meta 2 had to be switched off completely. Instead, a lighthouse tracker was attached on top of the glasses (see Fig. 3) and could thus be integrated into a uniform coordinate system with the other devices.

---

[4] Simultaneous localization and mapping.

[5] https://www.vive.com/.

3.3   Assembly Data Processing

The basis for a virtual assembly is the design data whose assembly process is to be investigated. This data must first be loaded into the AR environment in a suitable format. At this point, however, it is only the geometries of components without any knowledge about their assembly relationships. These relationships contain information about position and orientation in the finished state as well as the joining principle, such as plugging or screwing. By storing this information in the individual parts of an assembly, virtual work processes can be simulated. In order to enable any CAD data for a virtual assembly simulation, a methodology to enrich this data was developed. The steps involved in assembly data processing are pictured on Fig. 4 and explained below.

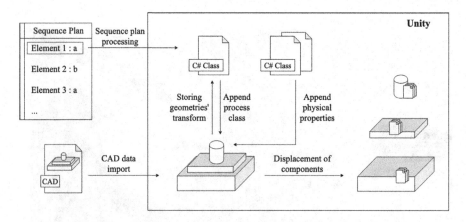

Fig. 4. Scheme of assembly data processing

CAD Data Import. The data processing takes the CAD data that is to be assembled as input. It is important that the CAD data is provided in its assembled state, as information about the position and rotation of the individual parts within the assembly is required. Besides the CAD data, a sequence plan is given as input. This plan is a text file which contains a list of all components to be assembled. Each list entry consists of a unique component designation as well as a corresponding joining process code. This code stands for the respective joining process of the component and is represented through a single alphabetical character. As an example the character "b" represents the process of screwing a component. Since in the present use case a large part of the work steps can be covered by placing and screwing components, the implementation is initially limited to these assembly processes. However, the system can easily be extended with new joining process codes.

Sequence Plan Processing. The individual parts in the sequence plan are processed iteratively. For each list entry a predefined process class gets instantiated with the information of the joining process. Since the parts have a unique designation in the sequence plan, an allocation to the corresponding geometries (loaded in the first step) can take place.

Storing Geometries' Transform. The geometries' information about position and rotation in the finished state gets stored in the instantiated process class. During virtual assembly later on, this information is used to place the components correctly.

Append Process Class. The instantiated process class gets applied to the corresponding geometry so that each component owns the required information such as final position, rotation and joining process.

Append Physical Properties. In order to be able to interact with these components, further classes such as rigid bodies and colliders are added to the objects. This supplies the components with physical properties so that gravity can be simulated and the parts can be grabbed with an interaction device. These classes are provided by the development environment Unity.

Displacement of Components. The individual parts are moved so that the work station is represented in a stage, where the components are not yet assembled.

In summary, the data processing serves to identify the parts that have to be assembled at the considered workstation and to enrich them with appropriate functionality. New assemblies can be loaded into the AR environment without great effort and prepared for assembly simulation. This procedure can ensure productive use in the company, since the simulation is no longer restricted to a specific product.

3.4 Evaluation

To evaluate the new prototype, it was tested at the automotive supplier. Test persons were invited who already knew the first prototype and were therefore able to evaluate the further development accordingly. After the demonstration phase, the 13 volunteers received a questionnaire to evaluate the application in its individual aspects. This questionnaire contained statements to which the subjects were asked to give their agreement on a 5-step evaluation scale. The statements concerned the field of view of the new AR glasses, the interaction with virtual components, the operation of the enhanced prototype and the general impression of closeness to reality. Figure 5 summarizes the results of the survey.

The results of the survey show that the field of view of the new AR glasses in particular was perceived by the test persons as a significant improvement. If one considers the agreement to the statements as a scale of points, an average value of 4.6 points results for the first statement, whereby 5 is the maximum number of points. The second and third statement concerns mainly the operation with the haptic gloves. With an average score of 3.8, a positive tendency can also be seen here. However, there was also a test person who only awarded one point in each case (disagree at all). This may be due to the fact that this test person was already able to handle the controller handling of the existing demonstrator very well and therefore rated the operation with the data gloves as negative. Another explanation could be that the test person did not feel comfortable wearing the gloves and already had a negative opinion due to the difficulty of putting on the gloves. The last statement should ask to what extent the new application has become more realistic overall. For this statement, all test persons gave a positive assessment and an average score of 4.5 points was obtained. For all statements, therefore, positive evaluations were given in comparison to the old prototype.

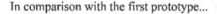

... the field of view of the AR glasses has improved significantly.

... the haptic gloves allow virtual parts to be grasped and joined more realistically.

... operation has become simpler and more intuitive overall.

... the enhanced application as a whole has become more realistic.

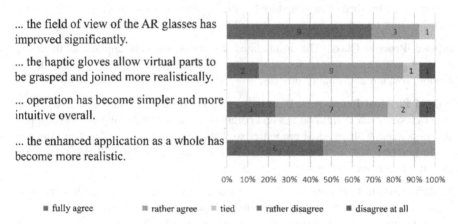

Fig. 5. Evaluation results of the enhanced mixed mock-up implementation

4 Conclusion and Future Work

The mixed mock-up system proposed in this paper combines cardboard engineering with AR in an industrial use case provided by an automotive supplier. The realization allows an interactive assembly simulation by virtually picking and placing components as well as screwing them together at a physical cardboard mock-up.

The paper is based on a previous implementation of a mixed mock-up system and its evaluation. This evaluation showed that several functional and technical aspects needed to be improved to enable a productive usage of the system. Thus as a first step a generic system model was developed to provide a better understanding and enable a systematic improvement of the system.

Based on this system model new hardware components were identified and used in the enhanced mixed mock-up system to address and improve the identified aspects such as field of view and haptics. Particularly noteworthy is the use of the force feedback data gloves by SenseGlove. The evaluation of the new system confirmed that the improvements enable a more realistic simulation of the assembly processes and a more intuitive operation of the system. In addition, a data processing procedure was developed in order to provide the basis for an easy exchangeability of CAD data. New models can now be easily integrated into the mixed mock-up system which makes it more suitable for productive use.

For future developments, the system should be expanded with further joining processes, so that a wider range of assembly activities can be represented. An automated abstraction of assembly dependencies and sequences could further automate data processing. Furthermore, the hardware devices are still connected to the computing unit by cables. For the future it is desirable to find a wireless alternative so that the user's freedom of movement is not restricted.

Acknowledgements. The results were developed within the project "IviPep - Work 4.0 in product development". The joint project is funded by the German Federal Ministry of Education and Research (BMBF) and the European Social Fund (ESF) as part of the "Future of Work" programme.

References

1. Wang, X., Ong, S., Nee, A.: Real-virtual interaction in AR assembly simulation based on component contact handling strategy. Assembly Autom. **35**(4), 376–394 (2015). https://doi.org/10.1108/AA-02-2015-012
2. Jayasekera, R.D.M.D., Xu, X.: Assembly validation in virtual reality—a demonstrative case. Int. J. Adv. Manuf. Tech. **105**(9), 3579–3592 (2019). https://doi.org/10.1007/s00170-019-03795-y
3. Boothroyd, G.: Product design for manufacture and assembly. Comput. Aided Des. **26**(7), 505–520 (1994). https://doi.org/10.1016/0010-4485(94)90082-5
4. Al-Ahmari, A.M., Abidi, M.H., Ahmad, A., Darmoul, S.: Development of a virtual manufacturing assembly simulation system. Adv. Mech. Eng. **8**(3) (2016). https://doi.org/10.1177/1687814016639824
5. Stöcklein, J., Bansmann, M., Berssenbrügge, J., Foullois, M.: AR-basierte Arbeitsplatzgestaltung für manuelle Montageabläufe. Virtuelle und Erweiterte Realität. In: 15. Workshop der GI-Fachgruppe VR/AR (2018). https://doi.org/10.2370/9783844062151
6. Valentini, P.P.: Natural interface for interactive virtual assembly in augmented reality using leap motion controller. Int. J. Interact. Des. Manuf. **12**(4), 1157–1165 (2018). https://doi.org/10.1007/s12008-018-0461-0
7. Wang, Z.B., Ong, S.K., Nee, A.Y.C.: Augmented reality aided interactive manual assembly design. Int. J. Adv. Manuf. Tech. **69**, 1311–1321 (2013). https://doi.org/10.1007/s00170-013-5091-x
8. Zaldívar-Colado, U., Garbaya, S., Tamayo-Serrano, P., Zaldívar-Colado, X., Blazevic, P.: A mixed reality for virtual assembly. In: International Symposium on Robot and Human Interactive Communication, vol. 26, pp. 739–744. IEEE, Lisbon (2017). https://doi.org/10.1109/ROMAN.2017.8172385
9. Murakami, K., Kiyama, R., Narumi, T., Tanikawa, T., Hirose, M.: Poster: a wearable augmented reality system with haptic feedback and its performance in virtual assembly tasks. In: Symposium on 3D User Interfaces (3DUI), pp. 161–162. IEEE (2013). https://doi.org/10.1109/3DUI.2013.6550228
10. Gonzalez-Badillo, G., Medellín-Castillo, H.I., Lim, T.: Development of a haptic virtual reality system for assembly planning and evaluation. Procedia Tech. **7**, 265–272 (2013). https://doi.org/10.1016/j.protcy.2013.04.033
11. Carlson, P., Vance, J.M., Berg, M.: An evaluation of asymmetric interfaces for bimanual virtual assembly with haptics. Virtual Reality **20**, 193–201 (2016). https://doi.org/10.1007/s10055-016-0290-z

Interactive AR Models in Participation Processes

Jonas Hansert, Mathias Trefzger[(⊠)], and Thomas Schlegel

Institute of Ubiquitous Mobility Systems, Karlsruhe University of Applied
Sciences, Moltkestr. 30, 76133 Karlsruhe, Germany
{iums,mathias.trefzger}@hs-karlsruhe.de

Abstract. It is getting more and more important to enable stakeholders from
different backgrounds to collaborate efficiently on joint projects. Physical
models provide a better understanding of spatial relationships while using video
mapping of suitable visualizations enables a meaningful enrichment of information. We therefore developed a demonstrator using a physical architectural
model as base and projected additional data via video mapping onto it. In this
paper, we describe the initial situation and the requirements for the development
of our demonstrator, its construction, the software developed for this purpose,
including the calibration process as well as the implementation of tangible
interaction as a means to control data and visualizations. In addition, we
describe the whole user interface and lessons learned. Ultimately, we present a
platform that encourages discussions and can enrich participation processes.

Keywords: Video mapping · Spatially augmented reality · Architectural model

1 Introduction

1.1 Initial Project and Background Information

The campus of Karlsruhe University of Applied Sciences is undergoing an architectural
rearrangement. To support the planning phase for these changes, we developed a
demonstrator that is able to show changes of the buildings as well as changes in the
mobility to, from and on the campus. The ambitious overarching goal of the project
was the establishment of a CO_2 neutral campus until 2030. An additional goal was
enhancing the quality of stay and several other requirements and constraints were also
in place. Due to the multitude of goals and responsibilities, many different participants
and stakeholders were involved in the planning process. Those were civil engineers,
architects, traffic engineers, computer scientists, students, employees, representatives of
the city of Karlsruhe, the local transport and transportation sharing companies and
many more.

Therefore, the field of participants was very heterogeneous. Because of that, we
searched for a suitable possibility to bring these different disciplines together and to
provide a basis for a joint discussion. Our approach was the construction of an interactive demonstrator using interactive spatially augmented reality. For the development
of the demonstrator, we pursued a prototyping approach.

© Springer Nature Switzerland AG 2020
J. Y. C. Chen and G. Fragomeni (Eds.): HCII 2020, LNCS 12190, pp. 50–62, 2020.
https://doi.org/10.1007/978-3-030-49695-1_4

The demonstrator was used for meetings with stakeholders, presentations, explorative surveys and participation workshops. During the planning process, new ideas were constantly being added, which influenced the planning. In the course of the project the concept was adapted and further developed in several steps. Thus, an important requirement for the demonstrator was to be able to visualize new ideas and measures quickly and easily. In addition, it should also be ensured that as much information as possible can be understood and memorized by those involved. The demonstrator should be able to display spatial data, architectural data, data concerning the mobility on campus and visualizations of key figures.

Looking for a suitable medium for this purpose, we decided to develop a construction with an architectural model as centerpiece onto which information is projected with video mapping. Already the old Egyptians used physical models to design and communicate [1]. Physical models make it easier to understand and evaluate forms and at the same time present spatial relationships and proportions. According to Stanford Hohauser, architectural models are the most easily understood presentational technique [2].

Especially for people that are not familiar with a project it can be difficult to perceive a planning clearly. Architectural models can directly communicate ideas to the stakeholders and public and therefore facilitates understanding. At the same time, the campus reconstruction project does not only focus on architectural changes. Due to the goal to achieve a CO_2 neutral campus, mobility and energy information is also relevant. These data are related to buildings and other architectural aspects of the campus, but cannot easily be displayed on an architectural model on its own. The video mapping can augment the architectural model and integrate additional data with architectural information.

1.2 Requirements

In the course of half a year, several events, meetings, explorative surveys and participation workshops on campus were held with different participants. The demonstrator should promote discussion and encourage participation. After each meeting there were new ideas that were to be incorporated into the planning. For this reason, the demonstrator had the requirement that it should be possible to incorporate changes of the visualizations at short notice.

In cooperation with the partners a number of requirements were identified. Some of them were already defined at the beginning of the project, but some were only determined during the course of the project. The requirements are briefly summarized below:

- Different groups of people should be able to understand and memorize the planned measures as easily as possible
- The demonstrator should be suitable to be independently operated by people for self-information. (Later, the requirement was added, that it should additionally be usable for presentations.)
- Interaction with the model should be self-explanatory
- Discussions should be encouraged to strengthen the participation process
- It should be possible to change visualizations on the model quickly

- The demonstrator should attract attention and arouse interest
- The demonstrator should be transportable and able to be installed in rooms with a height of at least three meters

2 Related Work

Generally, Augmented Reality on interactive architecture models is generated by projections from above [3]. Depth, thermal, or infrared cameras provide real-time interaction possibilities with physical models [4].

Video mapping is an established technology that is used for entertaining, cultural [5] and somewhat less frequently for educational and planning purposes [6, 7]. A series of projects with Tangible-User Interfaces (TUIs) and Video mapping were developed for collaboration at the beginning of the millennium [3, 8] and have since been refined and implemented for a multitude of purposes. Mainly, video mapping is used to map pictures and video files onto real architecture.

Interactive projection can be used in augmented workplaces in production. For example, Korn et al. [9] shows, that assembly workers can understand manuals faster if they are projected directly on the worktop. They use hand detection for interaction with their system. A time consuming calibration is necessary.

Huber et al. automated the calibration process in the project LightBeam. It can project images on any planar object. It can be controlled with tangibles detected by a camera. The calibration works fast and without markers. Unfortunately, the accuracy is not fine enough for our use case [10].

Narazani et al. use 3D printed architectural prototypes with a conductive wireframe and combined them with touch gestures [11]. They use augmented reality on a mobile phone to show additional buildings and floors on existing buildings and use some common gestures for interaction.

3 Construction of the Demonstrator

3.1 Hardware

Basic components of the demonstrator are an Optoma 4K550st Short Throw beamer, an Intel RealSense D435 depth camera, the architectural model plus the remaining tabletop around the model. The beamer provides 4500 lumens and the camera provides 30 frames per second (FPS) at a resolution of 3840 × 2160 Pixels.

In addition, a scaffold can be attached around the table to which the beamer and the depth image camera can be attached (see Fig. 1).

3.2 Dimensions

The total table size of the demonstrator is 2.49 m length and 1.40 m width. Center piece of the demonstrator is an architectural model with 1,40 m length an 1,00 m width. The model was built in scale 1:500. The relationship between the height and width as well as the orientation of the table ultimately depends on the architectural model. The horizontal alignment of the model, the beamer and limited room height influenced the entire design of the demonstrator. The dimensions of the table allow for up to 30 people to have a good view of the model.

The used beamer is able to cover the whole table with a distance of 200 cm from beamer lens to the table surface. The height of the table is 60 cm. This meets the requirement to fit into a room with a height of at least three meters. The height is chosen because both public buildings and apartments in old buildings usually have this minimum height.

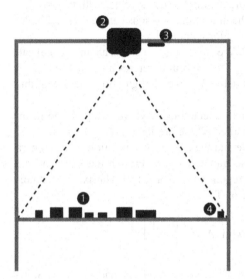 

Fig. 1. Construction of the demonstrator. Left: The beamer (2) projects onto the architectural model (1) and rest of the table. The depth camera (3) recognizes the four markers in every edge of the table to calibrate the picture onto the table. It also recognizes the marker on the tangible (4). Right: The Demonstrator in construction.

4 Software and Interaction Technique

We used python for our implementation. The pyrealsense2 library was used to read the images from the RealSense depth camera. All computer vision tasks are solved by using the open source computer vision library OpenCV. For the detection of markers, we used the ArUco library.

For an exact projection of content on our table and detection of the position of tangibles, a correlation between the coordinate systems of the camera, projector and table is necessary. One of the issues of computing this affine transformation, is finding some similar points in the camera image, projector image and the real world. This can be done manual with a large amount of time. Because a new calibration is necessary after moving the construction as well as after the effects of any other vibration, manual calibration is not useful in our use case.

We solved this by ArUco markers [12] painted on predefined positions on our table and ArUco markers projected on predefined positions in the projector image on the table and by detecting their position in the camera image.

In order to use only a minimum amount of space on the table for the markers, we decided to print them as small as possible even if the detection of them is more difficult.

For calibration of the system and transformation of the content we used OpenCV, a common open source computer vision framework. In the following part, we want to give an overview of the algorithm we implemented for calibration.

The registration procedure starts with reading the position of the markers on the table and the markers in the projected image from a JSON based configuration file. The ArUco dictionary, the size of the markers and the marker IDs together with the position of their center are defined in this file too. The unit of the positions can be selected in the configuration file but has to remain the same throughout the project.

In the next step, one color frame is read. We convert it to a grayscale image and call the detection algorithm of the ArUco library. This algorithm returns a list of all detected markers. We filter this list for the markers defined in the configuration and repeat this steps until the four markers are detected.

To avoid inaccuracy if one corner is not detected exactly, we compute the mean value of all x and y positions for every marker. These are the centers of the markers.

Now we have four positions on the table and their associated position in the camera image. With that we can compute an affine transformation between the table and the camera and the inverse direction. This is represented as a 4×4 Matrix as a combination of a Matrix R and a translation vector T.

$$A \begin{pmatrix} x \\ 1 \end{pmatrix} = \begin{pmatrix} x' \\ 1 \end{pmatrix} \text{ with } A = \begin{bmatrix} R & T \\ 0 & 1 \end{bmatrix}$$

Now we have to get the transformation between the projector and the camera. To compute it, we project four markers to positions defined in the configuration file. These positions are predefined so that they are on the table and do not cover any parts of the architectural model. Then we use the algorithm described before to compute the affine transformations between the projector and the camera.

Only the affine transformation between the table and the projector and the inverse direction is missing at this point. This can be computed by a multiplication of the transformation matrices between the camera and the projector and between the table and the camera:

$$A_{projector \rightarrow table} = A_{camera \rightarrow projector} \cdot A_{table \rightarrow camera}$$
$$A_{table \rightarrow projector} = A_{camera \rightarrow table} \cdot A_{projector \rightarrow camera}$$

With the transformation between the table and projector $A_{table \rightarrow projector}$ we transform all media in the startup process of our solution. Depending on the number of images, length of the videos and their resolution this may take several minutes. The results of the calibration process are saved and the calibration process can be skipped as long as the construction has not been moved.

```json
{
    "path": "/home/katze/",
    "start_image": "start.png",
    "table": {
        "width": 24900,
        "height": 14000,
        "marker": {
            "size": 500,
            "marker": [0,1,2,3],
            "position": [[200,200], [200,200], [200,200], [200,200]]
        }
    },
    "projector": {
        "width": 3840,
        "height": 2160,
        "marker": {
            "size": 120,
            "marker": [5,6,7,8],
            "position": [[200,250], [300,300], [300,200], [400,200]]
        }
    },
    "areas": [
        {
            "name": "area1",
            "positon_x": 1000,
            "position_y": 1000,
            "length": 20000,
            "width": 15000
        }
    ],
    "content": [
        {
            "name": "image1",
            "area": "area1",
            "url": ["image1.png", "image2.png"],
            "type": "slideshow",
            "duration": [5, 10],
            "conditions": [
                {
                    "type": "marker",
                    "id": 4,
                    "position_x": 0,
                    "position_y": 5000,
                    "width": 1500,
                    "height": 4000
                }
            ]
        }
    ]
}
```

Fig. 2. Listing 1: Example of a configuration file

On the top of our tangible we printed an ArUco marker. We use a separate thread for detection and all related computations for performance reasons. After marker detection we filter the list of detected markers for the used IDs. Then we use the transformation between the camera and the table $A_{camera \rightarrow table}$ for the computation of the position on the Table. The interaction that is triggered when the tangible is in a certain position is defined in the configuration file. As a next step, the interaction is therefore determined from this file.

We decided to use a configuration file in JSON format [Listing 1]. The path of all media is defined at first. It is still possible to use subfolders in this path. Then an image shown after startup and the position of the calibration markers are defined. We define multiple areas of the table in a sequence. They can be used to change the content on just a part of the table. In a sequence of content, every entry contains a name, an area, a type and a sequence of conditions. Depending on the type, additional properties can be necessary (Fig. 2).

The condition contains the type, in our example always marker, but it is possible to expand it and to add hand detection or object detection. Additionally, it contains an ID and a rectangular area on the table, where the object with the given ID has to be detected. If multiple conditions are defined, we combine them with an AND operation. An OR operation is possible by adding the same content with the second condition.

4.1 Integration of Visualizations

Visualizations that should be projected on the model and worktop around were created with common graphic programs. The image must have the same proportions as the real world model. A resolution of 10 pixel per mm can be chosen, for example. We created a template to simplify and speed up the creation process. This was done to meet the requirement that visualizations should be quickly realizable. The template contained a 2D plan of the architectural model and the dimensions of the table. In the template, the information could be visualized and finally be exported.

The images can then be used in the following steps to create animations. In the next step, the images and videos only have to be stored in the file folder of the program and the file names have to be written in the JSON file.

After each insertion of new images, the transformations of the images and videos must be recomputed. For this purpose, the variable "–calc-transformation" must be passed to the program. After the calibration run, the projection starts.

5 Information Presentation and Visualization

One major challenge concerning the demonstrator was the balancing act of not showing too much information at once to the spectators while giving them a good insight into relevant planning data. Also the visualizations should be designed in a way that the most important information draws the attention first. As shown in Fig. 3 the proposed and planned measures on the campus were visualized using icons on the architectural model itself. Because of the limited space directly on the model, which would have had a huge impact on readability, we included the frame around the model to display information. The space around the model was used to give additional information about measures located in the model. Furthermore, we halved the space below the model. On the left half, we showed pictures of the modifications of campus buildings. The right half was mainly used to show graphs with the impact of the planned measures on CO_2 developments, the modal split and the energy mix. The timeline below this space provided a clear structure of the planned measures in each phase. The following explains the structure and design of the user interface.

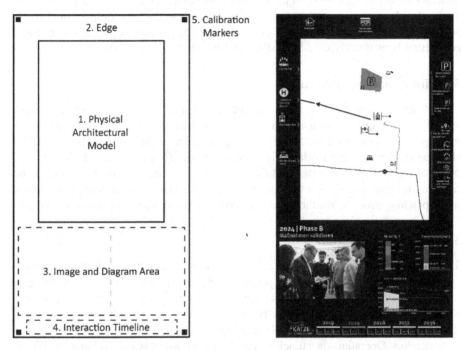

Fig. 3. Layout of the user interface. Left: Schematic representations of the divided areas. Right: Example of a displayed slide.

5.1 Architectural Model

The physical model is the centerpiece of the demonstrator. Some buildings can be exchanged to show the planned structural changes. A striking feature of the model is the characteristic forest around the campus, which is permanently implemented on the model. On the one hand, this ensured a high recognizability of the model. On the other hand, this limited the possibilities of visualizations. Icons were used to locate and represent the results of planned measures.

Areas (e.g. parking lots, solar plants) and paths (routes to the campus, bus route) were also used for visualization Icons with a size of 4 by 4 cm turned out to be easily recognizable. Due to the relatively close proximity of the buildings to each other, it was not possible to use a font with a clearly legible size directly on the model. For this reason, we used the frame around the model for any written information.

5.2 Frame

The frame was used to show additional information to the displayed information in the model. It serves as a summary of the measures for the viewers due to its bullet word based structure. The respective measures are displayed iteratively, triggered by interaction and highlighted in green to draw attention to the specific issues to be discussed in this step. In addition, the icons from the architecture model are also displayed on the margin in order to support the reception of information for the participants. An arrow indicates the connection between the measures displayed in the model and the labels on the border. A connection with a dash was omitted due to the large proportion of forest area around the campus, which is not a good projection surface. In addition, many connecting lines quickly create a restless and muddled presentation.

5.3 Image and Diagram Area

The left half area of the image and diagram area is used for the projection of images related to the respective measures. Pictures are used as eye catchers and support the message of the presented measures and diagrams. The right half is mainly used for showing diagrams of the modal split, energy mix and CO_2 emissions. In the starting phase of our project, the image and diagram area were strictly separated. During the first presentations we saw that the information provided overstrained many participants in the planning process. We therefore decided to show diagrams only on as a summary.

5.4 Interaction Timeline

The timeline enables interaction and allows a user to navigate through different years of campus development. Shown five phases, starting 2019 until 2036. Each phase is divided into three categories: green, social and mobility measures (see Fig. 4). By moving the tangible onto the respective measures, the respective images, figures and diagrams are shown. The selected field is always highlighted in order to give feedback to the spectators. Operation via a timeline was chosen because it is self-explanatory: people who have not yet been involved in the project can easily also discover the phases. Furthermore, the interaction using a tangible is also suitable for presentations in front of an audience. It can be used to move through the timeline and each category successively. The placement of the timeline determines the operating side and viewing direction.

Fig. 4. Interactive Timeline that can be controlled via a tangible.

5.5   Coloring

Initially the project partners set the requirement to only use grey tones, black and white for the complete design. This turned out not to be appropriate, as the visualizations and fonts were hardly visible on the physical model. So it was necessary to use bright colors in the model. We then tested two color schemes: one with dark font on a white background and an inverted color scheme. The inverted version turned out to be a much more popular variant and could offer further advantages. Of 18 people interviewed 16 preferred the inverted variant and two were undecided. The inverted version also has other advantages: The black border around the model highlights the architectural model. In addition, the black border ensures an invisible transition beyond the edge of the table.

5.6   Font Sizes

During the development process, different font sizes were tested and defined. In the model itself, the use of lettering did not make sense, because the existing areas on the model are too small, so that no sufficiently large lettering is possible. Only the margin is therefore used to provide textual information. The required font size was tested with ten people. The people stood at the bottom edge of the table and gave feedback which font size was legible for them. The tested writing was thus between 2.09 and 2.29 meters away from the test persons. We asked whether the persons could read a word with the font size. And afterwards we asked which font size they preferred. Eight people stated that they could read the font with 46 pt, but preferred 54 pt. Two people preferred a larger font size. Due to the limited edge and the possibility to walk around the table, a font size of 54 pt. was finally chosen.

6 Evaluation

We conducted a study with eight participants (3 female, 5 male) to evaluate the interface and to investigate, how much information could be memorized. For this purpose, we showed the participants the different visualizations of the mobility measures in phase 2024. This phase was chosen because it contained the most information of all phases. While the visualizations on the demonstrator were running, a previously recorded audio file was played, to simulate an oral presentation. After the five-minute presentation, the test persons had to fill out a questionnaire. We used six questions to check, how many facts were remembered by the participants. Those were:

- Which means of transport will be the most used to the campus?
- Which means of transport will be the least used to the campus?
- In which way will the university cover most of its energy needs?
- What is the main source of the university's CO_2 emissions?
- By what percentage is the CO_2 requirement of the university to be reduced from 2019 to 2024?
- Please tick which measures have been planned in this phase to reduce the CO_2 requirements of the university.

Of those six, the first four answers were not contained in the audio information and could only be perceived by looking at the diagrams (see Fig. 3).

The result was that the test persons could answer these questions very poorly or not at all. To evaluate if the participants were able to capture the information shown on the three diagrams. They were asked about the most and least used means of transport (3 out of eight correct answers and no correct answer). The question of how the university can cover the largest part of its energy requirements could not be answered either. Only the information that most of the university's emissions are produced by transport could be answered correctly by seven of the respondents.

Better results could be achieved when asked about the planned measures in this phase. Here the test persons were able to classify 67% of a list of 18 proposed measures as correct or incorrectly correct. At this point it was noticeable that six of the test persons had always left three of the measures presented in the presentation unchecked. These measures were sub-items of the measure "Mobility Centre". This leads to the conclusion that an enumeration of such sub-items was not observed. We are convinced that this information would have been memorized better without the use of sub-items.

Furthermore, participants were asked to rate the clarity of the interface. On a scale between clear (100%) and unclear (0%) the interface was rated as rather clear (59%). The test persons generally liked the demonstrator (85% - good (100%), bad (0%)). Four people would prefer a presentation with the demonstrator to a PowerPoint presentation, two were undecided and two would prefer a PowerPoint presentation.

The results show that there was a tendency to display too much information. The test persons were able to remember a large part of the information on the first visualizations, where no diagrams were displayed. In contrast, the last visualization that used three different diagrams contained too much information. For this reason, a maximum of one diagram should be displayed at a time.

The evaluated variant is therefore not ideally suited in this form for presentations where each visualization is only displayed for a certain period of time. In order to be able to capture all the information presented, it is necessary that users can go through the information at their own pace. This is also possible through interaction with the timeline and was the primary use case at the beginning of the project.

7   Conclusion and Discussion

In this paper, we presented a demonstrator utilizing interactive spatially augmented reality that can be used in planning processes. It was designed so that the visualizations are easily and quickly adaptable and to support an iterative planning process over several workshops. The developed user interface is appropriate for the use case that participants can navigate through the different project phases in their own pace. For presentations with a tight time frame, the interface has a novelty effect, but visualizations should be chosen carefully, if viewers are supposed to memorize information. The demonstrator as a medium of participation was well received by stakeholders and other participants. Future phases and scenarios could be prepared and presented in an understandable way with simple visualizations: The relationships of location and time information were clearly worked out by many spectators and project participants. The involvement of the demonstrator strengthened the interdisciplinary participation process and helped to develop new ideas. For this reason, the use of similar setups in comparable projects can be recommended.

Acknowledgements. This work was conducted within the scope of two research projects. The first is "KATZE" as part of the idea competition "Mobility concepts for the emission-free campus" and was funded by the German Federal Ministry of Education and Research. The second is "View-BW – Visualization of the energy transformation Baden-Württemberg" that was funded by the German Federal Ministry of Environment (Funding ID: BWED19004). We like to thank Prof. Robert Pawlowski, Prof. Jan Riel, Prof. Jochen Eckart, Prof. Susanne Dürr, Jonas Fehrenbach, Isabelle Ginter and Lena Christ for their contribution to this work. We would also like to thank our stakeholders, the students and all other participants for their good cooperation over the course of the project.

References

1. Smith, A.: Architectural Model as Machine – A New View of Models From Antiquity to the Present Day. Elsevier, Oxford (2004)
2. Hohauser, S.: Architectural and Interior Models, p. 6. Van Nostrand Reinhold, New York (1970)
3. Piper, B.; Ratti, C., Ishii, H.: Illuminating clay: a 3-D tangible interface for landscape analysis. In: Proceedings of the SIGCHI Conference on Human Factors in Computing Systems (2002)
4. Schubert, G.: Interaktionsformen für das digitale Entwerfen: Konzeption und Umsetzung einer rechnergestützten Entwurfsplattform für die städtebaulichen Phasen in der Architektur. Dissertation. Technical University of Munich (2014)

5. Catanese, R.: 3D architectural videomapping. In: International Archives of the Photogrammetry, Remote Sensing and Spatial Information Sciences, vol. XL-5/W2 (2013)
6. Alonso, L., et al.: CityScope: a data-driven interactive simulation tool for urban design. use case volpe. In: Morales, A.J., Gershenson, C., Braha, D., Minai, A.A., Bar-Yam, Y. (eds.) ICCS 2018. SPC, pp. 253–261. Springer, Cham (2018). https://doi.org/10.1007/978-3-319-96661-8_27
7. Grignard, A., et al.: Simulate the impact of the new mobility modes in a city using ABM. In: ICCS 2018 (2018)
8. Ishii, H., et al.: Augmented urban planning workbench: overlaying drawings, physical models and digital simulation. In: Proceedings of the 1st International Symposium on Mixed and Augmented Reality, p. 203. IEEE Computer Society (2002)
9. Korn, O., Schmidt, A., Hörz, T.: The potentials of in-situ-projection for augmented workplaces in production: a study with impaired persons. In CHI 2013 Extended Abstracts on Human Factors in Computing Systems (CHI EA 2013), pp. 979–984. Association for Computing Machinery, New York (2013). https://doi.org/10.1145/2468356.2468531
10. Huber, J., Steimle, J., Liao, C., Liu, Q., Mühlhäuser, M.: LightBeam: interacting with augmented real-world objects in pico projections. In: Proceedings of the 11th International Conference on Mobile and Ubiquitous Multimedia, MUM 2012, pp. 16:1–16:10 (2012). https://doi.org/10.1145/2406367.2406388
11. Narazani, M., Eghtebas, C., Jenney, S.L., Mühlhaus, M.: Tangible urban models: two-way interaction through 3D printed conductive tangibles and AR for urban planning. In: Adjunct Proceedings of the 2019 ACM International Joint Conference on Pervasive and Ubiquitous Computing and Proceedings of the 2019 ACM International Symposium on Wearable Computers (UbiComp/ISWC 2019 Adjunct), pp. 320–323. Association for Computing Machinery, New York (2019). https://doi.org/10.1145/3341162.3343810
12. Garrido-Jurado, S., Muñoz-Salinas, R., Madrid-Cuevas, F.J., Marín-Jiménez, M.J.: Automatic generation and detection of highly reliable fiducial markers under occlusion. Pattern Recogn. **47**(6), 2280–2292 (2014). https://doi.org/10.1016/j.patcog.2014.01.005

Calibration of Diverse Tracking Systems to Enable Local Collaborative Mixed Reality Applications

Adrian H. Hoppe[1][✉], Leon Kaucher[1], Florian van de Camp[2], and Rainer Stiefelhagen[1]

[1] Karlsruhe Institute of Technology (KIT), Karlsruhe, Germany
{adrian.hoppe,rainer.stiefelhagen}@kit.edu, leon.kaucher@student.kit.edu
[2] Fraunhofer IOSB, Karlsruhe, Germany
florian.vandecamp@iosb.fraunhofer.de

Abstract. Mixed reality (MR) devices offer advantages for a wide range of applications, e.g. simulation, communication or training purposes. Local multi user applications allow users to engage with virtual worlds collaboratively, while being in the same physical room. A shared coordinate system is necessary for this local collaboration. However, current mixed reality platforms do not offer a standardized way to calibrate multiple devices. Not all systems offer the required hardware that is used by available algorithms, either because the hardware is not available or not accessible by developers. We propose an algorithm that calibrates two devices using only their tracking data. More devices can be calibrated through repetition. Two MR devices are held together and moved around the room. Our trajectory-based algorithm provides reliable and precise results when compared to SfM or marker based algorithms. The accurate, but easy to use rotational calibration gesture can be executed effortlessly in a small space. The proposed method enables local multi user collaboration for all six degrees of freedom (DOF) MR devices.

Keywords: Calibration · Shared coordinate system · Trajectory · Rigid body · Virtual reality · Augmented reality · Local collaboration · Quantitative evaluation · Qualitative evaluation

1 Introduction

With mixed reality (MR) systems, the virtual and the real world merge together. MR devices range from small handheld tablets over virtual/augmented reality (VR/AR) headsets to large cave automatic virtual environment (CAVE) systems. Applications provide useful information or enable easy understanding of complex data by utilizing spatial rendering. Besides solo usage, users can engage in multi-user collaboration to support each other in a local (on-site) or remote (distant) context.

© Springer Nature Switzerland AG 2020
J. Y. C. Chen and G. Fragomeni (Eds.): HCII 2020, LNCS 12190, pp. 63–80, 2020.
https://doi.org/10.1007/978-3-030-49695-1_5

However, especially local collaboration needs the virtual worlds of the different users to align. Systems with 6-DOF employ tracking techniques using sensors such as inertial measurement units (IMU), RGB or infrared cameras and/or depth sensors. This allows each device to track its location and rotation in a self-defined coordinate system to enable accurate perspective changes, e.g. on the user's head movement.

The meta review of collaborative MR systems from 2013–2018 of de Belen et al. [4] shows that 103 of 259 systems use a local collaboration of multiple users in a shared physical environment. For example, multiple users can train work flows in safe and controlled virtual environments [23]. In order to achieve the local collaboration, a shared coordinate system is needed. This involves calibrating the different devices (see Fig. 1). However, there exists no standardized way to calibrate different MR systems as current services [7,21] are only available for specific devices and not extendable to other platforms.

We propose a new algorithm that calibrates two MR devices based on their interlinked movement on a trajectory. The algorithm is integrated in an open architecture that allows calibrating a shared coordinate system for any amount of local devices. We evaluate our algorithm and compare it to commonly used structure from motion (SfM) and fiducial marker based solutions.

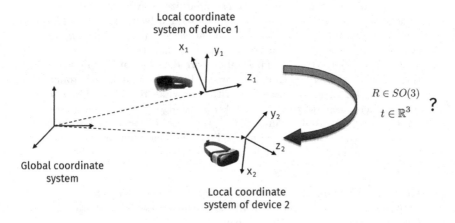

Fig. 1. Two MR devices with 6-DOF tracking have their own local coordinate system, but lack a shared global coordinate system.

2   Related Work

User can share an experience in a virtual environment (VE) by being in the same room (local) or by collaborating across the globe via the internet (remote). While collaborating remotely, users do not need to calibrate their MR systems towards a shared coordinate system, because their relative positions do not matter. However, while engaging in a local collaboration users need to know where the other user is to avoid collisions [12] or in order to be able to work together using tools [30]. There exists several systems that support the calibration of two local MR systems. SynchronizAR [13] uses a ultra-wideband (UWB) module, wifi and a Google Tango device. The system measures the position of each device and the distance between the different devices. An algorithm minimizes the an euclidean transformation and solves for the shared calibration of the devices. The system calibrates devices during usage. However, due to the high error of the distance measurement of the UWB module the resulting calibration has a RMSE of about 25 cm. Also, the algorithm is restricted to two dimensions (2D), which requires the users to hold the devices at approximately the same height. Futhermore, the UWB module is not included in any commercial off-the-shelf MR product. Krohn et al. [17] also calibrate different devices in a 2D plane using infrared light.

Billinghurst et al. [5] and Kalkusch et al. [15] use devices with cameras and fiducial markers placed around the room to calibrate the devices in a coordinate system relative to the room. Different patterns can be used for the marker detection [29]. Modern AR frameworks allow to track arbitrary images as well as 3D models [10,37]. Bai et al. [2] use this technique to integrate a HTC Vive controller interaction with a Microsoft HoloLens device. Hoppe et al. [11] use the internal cameras of a HTC Vive headset to track an acrylic glass surface for touch input. Zheng [40] implemented a similar system for an AR device.

Wahlstrom et al. [38] calibrate a smart phone to a car using an unscented Kalman filter and the device's IMUs. But, the precision allows only to determine the approximate location of the phone in the car and is not an accurate calibration. Visual simultaneous localization and mapping (SLAM) algorithms use a camera to reconstruct the environment of the device (e.g. [34]). SLAM algorithms provide tracking to popular MR systems such as HoloLens [19] or Oculus Quest and Rift S [20]. They create a map of the environment and track the device with respect to this map using a RGB camera [9]. Also depth information can be included [34]. By matching the generated environment maps of the different devices, a shared calibration can be found.

Most of the existing work either has high requirements for the sensors of the device or the environment, or is only usable by a specific operating system or type of device. Therefore, we propose an algorithm that calibrates two devices using only the tracking data of each device. Details about the algorithm and an evaluation of its precision are presented below.

3   Trajectory-Based Calibration Algorithm

We propose a new method that registers the trajectories of two interlinked devices with 6-DOF tracking. Through repetition, any number of devices can be calibrated towards a shared coordinate system. The algorithm has low requirements, as it only demands the position and angular velocity of each device. The position can be obtained through the 6-DOF tracking and the angular velocity can be measured by an IMU or calculated by differentiating with respect to the position. It does not require a camera, but is based on the bare minimum sensory output that any 6-DOF MR system offers.

In the beginning, two devices are interlinked (or held closely together) to form a rigid body and then moved around the room. During the movement, users should try to minimize any relative movement in between devices so that both devices form a rigid body system. Then, the rigid body system offers the following guarantees: (g_1) the distance of two arbitrary points is constant, and (g_2) the angular velocity ω at a certain point in time is identical for all points.

The algorithm uses the guarantees of the interlinked-bodies to calibrate two devices towards a shared coordinate system. It consists of a time synchronization and mapping step and then finds the rotation offset and the translation offset of the two coordinate systems.

First, data recordings on both devices are triggered by a server. The devices record data in the form of $(a_i) = ((p_{a_1}, \omega_{a_1}), (p_{a_2}, \omega_{a_2}), \ldots, (p_{a_N}, \omega_{a_N}))$ for data of *device A* and $(b_i) = ((p_{b_1}, \omega_{b_1}), (p_{b_2}, \omega_{b_2}), \ldots, (p_{b_M}, \omega_{b_M}))$ for data of *device B*, with p_{i_j} being the jth position of device i and ω_{i_j} the jth angular velocity of device i.

A resampling of the trajectory series allows the algorithm to calibrate two systems, even if they have different tracking rates. The position is resampled using linear interpolation $\hat{p}_j$ between consecutive points p_j and p_{j+1} and is calculated as follows:

$$\hat{p}_j = p_j + \frac{p_{j+1} - p_j}{t_{j+1} - t_j} \cdot (\delta t \cdot i - t_j) \tag{1}$$

The norm of the angular velocity is interpolated using spherical linear interpolation (slerp) because its axis is not constant:

$$\|\hat{\omega}_j\| = \|\omega_j\| + \frac{\|\omega_{j+1}\| - \|\omega_j\|}{t_{j+1} - t_j} \cdot (\delta t \cdot i - t_j) \tag{2}$$

We resample the tracking data with a frequency of $f_s = 90\,\text{Hz}$. This yields the series $(a_i') = ((p_{a_1}', \|\omega_{a_1}'\|), \ldots, (p_{a_{N'}}', \|\omega_{a_{N'}}'\|))$ as well as $(b_i') = ((p_{b_1}', \|\omega_{b_1}'\|), \ldots, (p_{b_{M'}}', \|\omega_{b_{M'}}'\|))$.

Yet, the resulting series are not guaranteed to be time-synchronous due to network delay. One way to solve this is to synchronize the clocks of the two devices using a network time protocol [8,22]. Our approach uses the cross-correlation function [28] to synchronize the two trajectories by finding the maximum of the cross-correlation function of the angular velocity magnitude time series. The method uses (g_2) and is based on the equation:

$$xCorr_{\omega_a' \omega_b'}(r) = \sum_{i=1}^{M'-r} \|\omega_{a_i}'\| \|\omega_{b_{i+r}}'\| \quad , \text{w.l.o.g. let M' < N'} \tag{3}$$

Explicitly, the discrete series $\|\omega_b'\|$ of the norms of angular velocities of *device B* is shifted over the series $\|\omega_a'\|$ with an offset of r and the resulting sum reflects the similarity of the series at time r. To ensure that (b_i') lies inside of (a_i'), we remove $t_r = 1$ second from the beginning and end of the data recording (b_i') by setting the respective values to $\mathbf{0}$ which yields (b_i''). Because (b_i'') lies inside (a_i')

the factor $\frac{1}{M'-r}$ of the cross correlation is not needed. By maximizing the rank correlation coefficient, the time offset Δt of (a_i') and (b_i'') can be found using:

$$\Delta t = \frac{1}{f_s} \cdot \underset{1 \leq r \leq M'}{arg\,max} \, xCorr_{\omega_a' \omega_b''}(r) - t_r \tag{4}$$

The time offset Δt is applied to the original series (b_i).

A dynamic time warping (DTW) algorithm is used to receive a pairwise mapping between the series (a_i) and (b_i). DTW reqires both series to start at the same time and end at the same time. We therefore adjusted the DTW algorithms finish condition to soften the requirement of the same ending time.

Based on the previous steps, we can define the algorithm for the calibration of the devices. Data points in the series (a_i) are excluded, if the distance between successive points p_{a_i} and $p_{a_{i+1}}$ is less than 1 cm. The respective mapped points in (b_i) are excluded as well.

Given the cleaned series (a_i) and (b_i), both of length M, with the same start time, we find the optimal rotation $\hat{R}$ between the coordinate systems of the two devices by minimizing the angle between the axis for the pairs of angular velocities using a rotation offset R:

$$\hat{R} = \underset{R \in SO(3)}{arg\,min} \sum_{i=1}^{M} \measuredangle \left(\omega_{a_i}, R \cdot \omega_{b_i} \right) \tag{5}$$

Using the solved optimal rotation $\hat{R}$ and the guarantee (g_1), the optimal translation $\hat{t}$ can be determined. Because the distance between the devices is fixed, $\hat{t}$ can be found by minimizing the variance of the differences for the distances between the tracked positions points:

$$\hat{t} = \underset{t \in \mathbb{E}^3}{arg\,min} \frac{1}{M} \sum_{i=1}^{M} \left(d_i - \tilde{d} \right)^2 \tag{6}$$

with $d_{t_i} = p_{a_i} - \left(\hat{R} \cdot p_{b_i} + t \right)$ defined as the distance between the tracking positions of *device A* and the rotated positions of *device B* including a translation offset t, and $\tilde{d}$ the median of all distances.

Our algorithm uses COBYLA (constrained optimization by linear approximation) [26], to optimize the functions $\hat{R}$ and $\hat{t}$. The implementation uses unit quaternions instead of the rotation matrix to calculate $\hat{R}$. This decreases the number of parameters to optimize from 9 to 4. The unit quaternion (x_q, y_q, z_q, w_q) is optimized under the constraint of $1 - x_q^2 + y_q^2 + z_q^2 + w_q^2 < 0.01$.

The equation $\hat{t}$ is adjusted to avoid that COBYLA optimizes towards an unwanted local minimum:

$$\hat{t}' = \underset{t \in \mathbb{E}^3}{arg\,min} \frac{1}{M} \sum_{i=1}^{M} \left(d_{t_i}' - \tilde{d}_t \right)^2 \cdot \frac{1}{M} \sum_{i=1}^{M} d_{t_i}' \tag{7}$$

The additional factor of the average point distance favors solutions where the distance between the two HMDs is smaller. The value t that needs to be optimized is initially estimated as $t\star$.

$$t\star = \frac{1}{M}\sum_{i=1}^{M} p_{a_i} - \frac{1}{M}\sum_{i=1}^{M} \hat{R}p_{b_i} \tag{8}$$

$t\star$ represents the distance between the centroid of both trajectories (analogous to [1]). The translation t is represented as $t = t \star +(x_t, y_t, z_t)$ and optimized under the constraint of $x_t^2 \leq 0.01 \Leftrightarrow ||x_t|| \leq 0.1$, $y_t^2 \leq 0.1$ and $z_t^2 \leq 0.1$, so that $\hat{t}'$ cannot be to far away from the estimated translation. Finally, the Eq. 7 is optimized with $d'_{t_i} = p_{a_i} - \left(\hat{R} \cdot p_{b_i} + t \star +(x_t, y_t, z_t)\right)$.

As a result, $\hat{R}$ and $\hat{t}$, or rather $\hat{t}'$, yield the calibration matrix from *device B* to *device A*. Figure 2 shows the movement of two devices that were calibrated using the trajectory-based calibration algorithm.

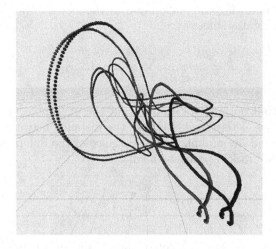

Fig. 2. Calibrated trajectory of two interlinked devices that were picked up from a table, moved around and then set back on the table again.

4   Evaluation

To evaluate the performance of the trajectory-based calibration algorithm, proposed in the previous chapter, we implemented two other algorithms commonly used for calibration and tracking for comparison.

One algorithm is based on the SfM technique. SfM [16,36] algorithms allow to generate a virtual map of the user's surroundings and track the positions of a device in this environment using camera and IMU input. The virtual maps of two devices can be aligned to get the calibration matrix. This approach is comparable to the shared anchor methods of [7,21]. We use COLMAP [31,32] to calibrate two devices by feeding the algorithm with a series of pictures from both cameras. COLMAP finds SIFT features in each image to obtain the relative camera poses for each image which in turn gives the calibration between the two devices.

The other algorithm uses marker detection to calibrate two devices. This approach requires each device to have a camera and one fiducial marker to be placed in the room. Systems such as Chilitags [6] or AprilTags [25, 39] can be used to detect the marker and calculate the position and orientation of the devices with respect to its location. This yields a shared calibration for both devices. Prior to the marker detection algorithm, the cameras were calibrated using Kalibr [27] (COLMAP finds the camera calibration matrix during the solving process).

4.1 Setup

The system is designed as a service and features an easy-to-use graphical user interface (GUI) to allow quick calibration. The GUI is implemented in Unity3D [35] as it allows to deploy the system do a diverse set of MR devices. Since all calculations are done on a server, the system is also appropriate for hardware with limited resources such as computing power or battery life and operating system independent. Our calibration suite currently offers the three calibration algorithms described above, but can be extended further.

We use two HTC Vive Pro VR head-mounted displays (HMDs) as their Lighthouse tracking system is very precise if tracking is not lost [24]. Therefore, the SteamVR calibration setup for each Vive Pro was executed before each test and in case the tracking was lost to avoid errors due to large offsets. The Lighthouse system tracks one or more VR devices using infrared light emitted from two base stations which is captured by several diodes on the devices. To evaluate the calibration accuracy of the three algorithms, we calculate a ground truth calibration. For this, we retrieve the positions of the Lighthouse base stations for both Vive Pro HMDs. By matching the position of both base stations, the calibration matrix from one Vive to the second Vive can be calculated.

We recorded 30 s of data for each of the following calibration setups:

I. Trajectory-based calibration algorithm:

I.1	Slow translation	I.2	Fast translation
I.3	Slow rotation	I.4	Fast rotation
I.5	Slow spherical movement	I.6	Fast spherical movement
I.7	Slow spontaneous movement (*)	I.8	Fast spontaneous movement (*)

II. SfM-based calibration algorithm:

II.9	Table scene (*)	II.10	Room corner scene (*)

III. Marker-based calibration algorithm:

III.11	Moving camera (*)	III.12	Static camera

Some movements are predefined and executed by the authors. All data recordings highlighted with (*) were executed by users, because their movement cannot be defined or is open to interpretation. For the recording of the user data sets, we invited 11 participants to perform the tasks. Each data set contains 44 records. In case of a user data set, each of the 11 users performed 4 calibration movements. The HMDs position was recorded with 60 Hz. *Device A's* camera recorded videos with 40 Hz and *device B* had a camera sampling rate of 30 Hz.

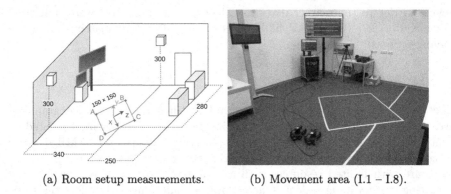

(a) Room setup measurements.   (b) Movement area (I.1 – I.8).

Fig. 3. Setup for the room and trajectory-based algorithm.

4.2   Data Recording

I. Trajectory-Based Calibration Algorithm. All trajectory based algorithms were executed in two ways, slow and fast movements in order to evaluate the calibration difference at different speeds. For I.1–I.6, the authors executed the movements with a factor of $f_m = 3$ in the slow condition and $f_m = 6$ in the fast condition. All movements were executed inside the calibration space defined by the square ABCD (see Fig. 3a and 3b)

Translation (I.1 and I.2). The two HMDs that form the rigid body system are oriented to face the negative x-direction and positioned in the center of the calibration space. The authors then executed translational movements along the different axis:

$$([-x \ \rightarrow][x \ \rightarrow][x \ \rightarrow][-x \ \rightarrow]) \times f_m$$
$$([-z \ \rightarrow][z \ \rightarrow][z \ \rightarrow][-z \ \rightarrow]) \times f_m$$
$$([-y \ \rightarrow][y \ \rightarrow][y \ \rightarrow][-y \ \rightarrow]) \times f_m$$

Rotation (I.3 and I.4). The two HMDs that form the rigid body system are oriented to face the negative x-direction and positioned in the center of the calibration space. The authors then executed rotational movements along the different axis:

$$([-y \ \circlearrowleft][y \ \circlearrowleft][y \ \circlearrowleft][-y \ \circlearrowleft]) \times f_m$$
$$([z \ \circlearrowleft][-z \ \circlearrowleft][-z \ \circlearrowleft][z \ \circlearrowleft]) \times f_m$$
$$([-x \ \circlearrowleft][x \ \circlearrowleft][x \ \circlearrowleft][-x \ \circlearrowleft]) \times f_m$$

Spherical Movement (I.5 and I.6). The two HMDs that form the rigid body system are oriented to face the negative x-direction. The system is moved 75 cm in negative x-direction in between the points A and B (see Fig. 3a). The authors then executed spherical movements along the different axis:

$$([-y \; \curvearrowright] [y \; \curvearrowright] [y \; \curvearrowright] [-y \; \curvearrowright]) \times 3$$
$$([z \; \curvearrowright] [-z \; \curvearrowright] [-z \; \curvearrowright] [z \; \curvearrowright]) \times 3$$
$$([-x \; \circlearrowleft] [x \; \circlearrowleft] [x \; \circlearrowleft] [-x \; \circlearrowleft]) \times 3$$

Spontaneous Movement (I.7 and I.8). The participants were informed about the goal of their movement. They were asked to perform any movement that comes to their mind while moving 'not too fast' in the slow condition and 'move fast' in the fast condition. Users were encouraged to find a suitable grip that fixes the relative position of the headsets. Also, users were asked not to leave the calibration space during the movements.

II. SfM-Based Calibration Algorithm. Two scenes were prepared for the SfM algorithm. The video stream was displayed on the large display so that users could judge the camera's viewing angle. Users first captured the scenes using *device A*. Then each user performed four calibrations using *device B*. Users were asked to 'not move too fast' to avoid camera blur. Users were encouraged to capture the scenes from different angles and with different distances.

Table Scene (II.9). A table with a prepared scene was placed so that the leading edge of the table was parallel to the line AB (see Fig. 3a). The scene was filled with objects that contained many color contrasts and brightness variations, to obtain as many SIFT features as possible (see Fig. 4a).

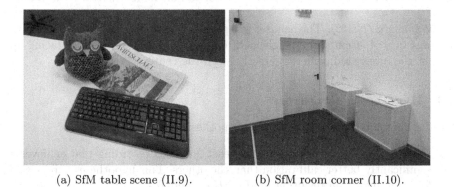

(a) SfM table scene (II.9).   (b) SfM room corner (II.10).

Fig. 4. Setup for SfM-based algorithm.

Room Corner Scene (II.10). The room corner scene contains mostly large and white surfaces (see Fig. 4b). Users were asked to not get closer as 2.5 m towards the target, which was indicated by a line on the ground (see Fig. 3a). This data recording therefore contains an environment with large monotonous surfaces but movements with large spatial extension.

Fig. 5. Setup for Marker-based algorithm (III.11 and III.12).

III. Marker-Based Calibration Algorithm. A table was placed in the room as described in the table scene (II.9) above. A 8 × 6 AprilTag board, printed on a A3 sheet, was placed on the table (see Fig. 5). The marker board was placed orthogonal to the table, with a 8° offset towards the ceiling of the room. Again, users first captured the scene using *device A* and then performed four calibrations using *device B*.

Moving Camera (III.11). Users were asked to 'not move too fast' to avoid camera blur, and to perform movements within a distance of 20–60 cm and to avoid flat angles in order to keep the perspective distortion of the markers at a minimum.

Static Camera (III.12). The headset was placed on a box facing the marker board at a distance of 30 cm and a height of 20 cm. The headset was slightly facing up so that the integrated cameras directly faced the center of the markers.

4.3 Hypotheses and Errors

For the outcome of the evaluation we hypothesized:

H_A For each algorithm, there exists at least one data recording that achieves a significantly better calibration than the others. This hypotheses is reviewed for each algorithm resulting in H_{A_I}, $H_{A_{II}}$ and $H_{A_{III}}$.

H_B One algorithm (I, II or III) reaches a significantly better calibration than the others.

The null hypothesis H_{A0} and H_{B0} are formulated as follows: The arithmetic mean of no data set or algorithm differs significantly from any other data set or algorithm.

The rotation $R_A = \Delta R \cdot R_{GT}$ calculated by an algorithm differs from the reference rotation R_{GT} by an error ΔR. ΔR can be represented as an angle and an axis. The angle describes the rotational error and can be calculated as $\theta_{\Delta R} = 2*arccos\left(\left|q_A * q_{GT}^{-1}\right|\right)$ with q_A and q_{GT} as the unit quaternions of R_A and R_{GT} [14]. The translational error is described as the euclidean distance between the position vectors contained in the calibration and ground truth matrices.

4.4 Quantitative Results

Table 1. Statistical values for the translational error (in m) of the cleaned data sets.

Data set	N	Ø	SD	SE	95% CI	RMSE
[I.1] Slow translation	44	0.1056	0.0154	0.0023	0.1010	0.1067
[I.2] Fast translation	44	0.1177	0.0094	0.0014	0.1149	0.1181
[I.3] Slow rotation	44	0.0196	0.0073	0.0011	0.0174	0.0209
[I.4] Fast rotation	44	0.0237	0.0039	0.0006	0.0225	0.0240
[I.5] Slow spherical movement	42	0.0290	0.0115	0.0018	0.0255	0.0312
[I.6] Fast spherical movement	44	0.0317	0.0042	0.0006	0.0304	0.0319
[I.7] Slow spontaneous movement	42	0.0595	0.0456	0.0070	0.0455	0.0746
[I.8] Fast spontaneous movement	43	0.0480	0.0287	0.0044	0.0393	0.0557
[II.9] Table scene	44	0.0904	0.0540	0.0081	0.0742	0.1050
[II.10] Room corner scene	44	0.0590	0.0379	0.0057	0.0477	0.0699
[III.11] Moving camera	44	0.5138	0.3034	0.0457	0.4231	0.5949
[III.12] Static camera	44	0.1505	0.0673	0.0101	0.1304	0.1646

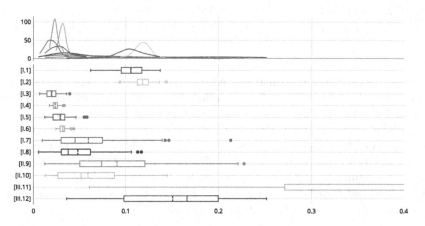

Fig. 6. Distribution of the translational error (in m) of the cleaned data sets. The x-axis is truncated to increase the resolution for the lower errors.

The results of the evaluation are reported as average value (Ø) with standard deviation (SD), standard error (SE), 95% confidence interval (CI) and root-mean-square error (RMSE). For a statistical analysis, ANOVA significances tests and Tukey HSD post-hox tests are used. The Tukey HSD post-hoc-test is adjusted with a familywise error rate (FWER) of 1% to avoid the inflation of a type-1 error. All data sets contain $N = 44$ data recordings. Points with a larger distance than 3 standard deviations from the average value were excluded from the results. The translational and rotational errors are described in the Tables 1 and 2. The distribution of the errors are displayed in Figs. 6 and 7. Both Figures show Box-Whisker-Plots [3] and probability density functions using a kernel density estimation (KDE) [18]. The bandwidth of the KDE is calculated using the Scott-rule [33].

Table 2. Statistical values for the rotational error (in °) of the cleaned data sets.

Data set	N	Ø	SD	SE	95% CI	RMSE
[I.1] Slow translation	43	1.2288	0.4389	0.0669	1.0961	1.3031
[I.2] Fast translation	44	1.9148	0.8080	0.1218	1.6733	2.0747
[I.3] Slow rotation	44	0.7474	0.2982	0.0450	0.6583	0.8035
[I.4] Fast rotation	43	0.9718	0.1603	0.0245	0.9233	0.9846
[I.5] Slow spherical movement	43	0.6000	0.2430	0.0371	0.5265	0.6462
[I.6] Fast spherical movement	44	1.0746	0.1747	0.0263	1.0224	1.0884
[I.7] Slow spontaneous movement	42	1.6462	1.3073	0.2017	1.2461	2.0925
[I.8] Fast spontaneous movement	43	1.4547	1.1148	0.1700	1.1175	1.8248
[II.9] Table scene	44	2.9294	2.3461	0.3537	2.2282	3.7364
[II.10] Room corner scene	44	1.4075	0.8107	0.1222	1.1651	1.6197
[III.11] Moving camera	44	20.0404	16.7612	2.5268	15.0306	26.0033
[III.12] Static camera	44	4.5872	2.0914	0.3153	3.9621	5.0316

I. Trajectory-Based Calibration Algorithm. The ANOVA for the translational error included $N = 347$ observations in $p = 8$ groups with $F(7, 339) = 148.6$ and $p < 0.001$. Therefore, we can reject the null hypothesis H_{A0_I} for the translational error. A Tukey HSD test yields the following: The data sets form three clusters where each data set is not significantly different to the other data sets in the cluster, but is significantly different to any data sets from the other cluster. All significant differences have a value of $p < 0.001$. The three clusters are slow and fast translation (I.1 and I.2), slow and fast spontaneous movement (I.7 and I.8) and slow and fast rotation and spherical movement (I.3–I.6).

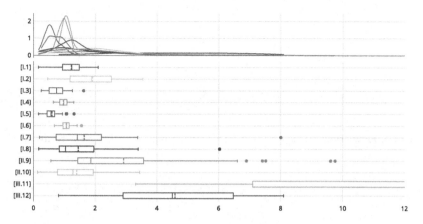

Fig. 7. Distribution of the rotational error (in °) of the cleaned data sets. The x-axis is truncated to increase the resolution for the lower errors.

The ANOVA for the rotational error included $N = 346$ observations in $p = 8$ groups with $F(7, 338) = 17.65$ and $p < 0.001$. Therefore, we can reject the null hypothesis H_{A0_I} for the rotational error. A Tukey HSD test shows that the data set with the lowest error, I.5, has no significant differences to the data sets I.3, I.4 and I.6. However, I.5 is significantly different to all other data sets with $p < 0.001$. I.2 is significantly different to I.1, I.3, I.4 and I.6 with $p < 0.001$. I.7 is significantly different to I.3 and I.4 with $p < 0.001$ and to I.6 with $p = 0.0047$. Also I.8 is significantly different to I.3 with $p < 0.001$.

II. SfM-Based Calibration Algorithm. The ANOVA for the translational error included $N = 88$ observations in $p = 2$ groups with $F(1, 86) = 9.97$ and $p = 0.0022$. Therefore, we can reject the null hypothesis $H_{A0_{II}}$ for the translational error. The difference between II.9 and II.10 is significant.

The ANOVA for the rotational error included $N = 88$ observations in $p = 2$ groups with $F(1, 86) = 16.54$ and $p < 0.001$. Therefore, we can reject the null hypothesis $H_{A0_{II}}$ for the rotational error. The difference between II.9 and II.10 is significant.

III. Marker-Based Calibration Algorithm. The ANOVA for the translational error included $N = 88$ observations in $p = 2$ groups with $F(1, 86) = 60.13$ and $p < 0.001$. Therefore, we can reject the null hypothesis $H_{A0_{III}}$ for the translational error. The difference between III.11 and III.12 is significant.

The ANOVA for the rotational error included $N = 88$ observations in $p = 2$ groups with $F(1, 86) = 36.83$ and $p < 0.001$. Therefore, we can reject the null hypothesis $H_{A0_{III}}$ for the rotational error. The difference between III.11 and III.12 is significant.

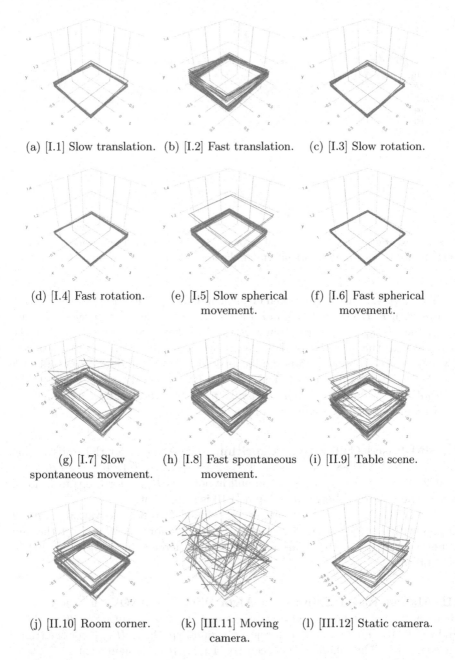

(a) [I.1] Slow translation.   (b) [I.2] Fast translation.   (c) [I.3] Slow rotation.

(d) [I.4] Fast rotation.   (e) [I.5] Slow spherical movement.   (f) [I.6] Fast spherical movement.

(g) [I.7] Slow spontaneous movement.   (h) [I.8] Fast spontaneous movement.   (i) [II.9] Table scene.

(j) [II.10] Room corner.   (k) [III.11] Moving camera.   (l) [III.12] Static camera.

Fig. 8. Simulated trajectories that show the error introduced during the calibration process for a device that was moved along the sides of a square.

Comparison of Algorithms I, II and III. The hypothesis H_B is checked based on the best data sets from the three algorithms. The test includes I.3 and I.5, as well as II.10 and III.12. The ANOVA for the translational error included $N = 174$ observations in $p = 4$ groups with $F(3, 170) = 100.40$ and $p < 0.001$. Therefore, we can reject the null hypothesis H_{B0} for the translational error. A Tukey HSD test yields the following: Again, I.3 and I.5 are not significantly different. However, all other differences are significant with $p < 0.001$, with the exception of I.5 and II.10 with $p = 0.0031$.

The ANOVA for the rotational error included $N = 175$ observations in $p = 4$ groups with $F(3, 171) = 117.50$ and $p < 0.001$. Therefore, we can reject the null hypothesis H_{B0} for the rotational error. A Tukey HSD test yields the following: As for the translation, I.3 and I.5 are not significantly different. Algorithm III with III.12 is significantly worse than all other algorithms with $p < 0.001$. Algorithm I (I.5) and II (II.10) have a significant difference with $p = 0.0064$.

4.5 Qualitative Results

To evaluate the quality of the different calibration results, we simulated how the translational and rotational errors would impact the user's experience during usage. For this we positioned *device B* at the center of the simulated space at a height of 1 m. *Device A* is moved around the XZ-plane in the shape of a square with the length of 1.5 m at a height of 1 m. For each algorithm and each data set we have the ground truth matrix T_{GT} and the calculated calibration matrix $T_C = \Delta T \cdot T_{GT}$ with some calibration error ΔT. The movement of *device A* is now projected into an uncalibrated space by transforming it using the inverse ground truth matrix and then reprojected into calibrated space by transforming it using the calibration matrix. The resulting point $p_i' = T \cdot T_{GT}^{-1} \cdot p_i = \Delta T \cdot T_{GT} \cdot T_{GT}^{-1} \cdot p_i = \Delta T \cdot p_i$ contains the error that is introduced by the calibration process. The series (p_i') of the simulated points for each algorithm and data set is shown in Fig. 8.

5 Discussion

As the results of the evaluation and the simulated trajectories show, algorithm I provides a reliable and accurate way to calibrate two devices towards a shared coordinate system. Slow rotational or spherical movements provide better results than fast movements or translational and spontaneous movements. Furthermore, slow rotations can be executed easily in a small space without much effort.

The SfM algorithm achieves a better calibration results in the room corner scene. This was not expected, as the table scene should provide more SIFT features. However, the larger movements and different viewing angles seem to result in a more precise calibration. The marker-based algorithm seems unsuitable for MR headsets with a wide field-of-view camera. This supports the work of Zhen et al. [40], who show that a Vive camera can yield errors of several cm at short distances.

6   Conclusion and Future Work

Local user collaboration requires different MR systems to move in a shared coordinate system. Currently, there exists no easy way to calibrate the different coordinate systems of a variety of devices. We propose an algorithm that captures tracking data from two devices that are moved around the room on an interlinked trajectory. The algorithm is integrated in a service that allows calibrating two or more local MR systems using a user-friendly guidance interface. Slow rotational or spherical movements yield the best results for the proposed algorithm. Especially the rotational movements require minimal effort and are easy to explain and perform. The trajectory-based calibration offers higher precision when compared to camera-based calibration methods such as SfM or marker tracking. Our solution enables cross-platform local MR applications and opens up an easy way to implement collaborative systems. For future work, we would like to extend the algorithm to allow calibrating devices during application usage.

References

1. Arun, K.S., Huang, T.S., Blostein, S.D.: Least-squares fitting of two 3-D point sets. IEEE Trans. Pattern Anal. Mach. Intell. **9**(5), 698–700 (1987). https://doi.org/10.1109/TPAMI.1987.4767965. ISSN: 0162–8828
2. Bai, H., Gao, L., Billinghurst, M.: 6DoF input for Hololens using vive controller. In: SIGGRAPH Asia 2017 Mobile Graphics & Interactive Applications on - SA 2017. SIGGRAPH Asia 2017 Mobile Graphics & Interactive Applications, Bangkok, Thailand, p. 1. ACM Press (2017). https://doi.org/10.1145/3132787.3132814. ISBN: 978-1-4503-5410-3
3. Becker, T., Herrmann, R., Sandor, V., Schäfer, D., Wellisch, U.: Stochastische Risikomodellierung und statistische Methoden. SA. Springer, Heidelberg (2016). https://doi.org/10.1007/978-3-662-49407-3
4. de Belen, R.A.J., et al.: A Systematic review of the current state of collaborative mixed reality technologies: 2013–2018. AIMS Electron. Electr. Eng. **3**(2), 181–223 (2019). https://doi.org/10.3934/ElectrEng.2019.2.181. ISSN: 2578–1588
5. Billinghurst, M., et al.: Mixing realities in shared space: an augmented reality interface for collaborative computing. In: 2000 IEEE International Conference on Multimedia and Expo. ICME 2000. Proceedings. Latest Advances in the Fast Changing World of Multimedia (Cat. No.00TH8532), July 2000, vol. 3, pp. 1641–1644. https://doi.org/10.1109/ICME.2000.871085
6. Bonnard, Q., et al.: Chilitags 2: Robust Fiducial Markers for Augmented Reality and Robotics (2013). http://chili.epfl.ch/software. Accessed 28 Feb 2020
7. Microsoft Corporation. Microsoft Spatial Anchors (2019). https://azure.microsoft.com/de-de/services/spatial-anchors/. Accessed 28 Feb 02 2020
8. Correll, K., Barendt, N., Branicky, M.: Design considerations for software only implementations of the IEEE 1588 precision time protocol. In: Conference on IEEE, vol. 1588, pp. 11–15 (2005)
9. Daoud, H.A., et al.: SLAMM: visual monocular SLAM with continuous mapping using multiple maps. PLoS ONE **13**(4), 1932–6203 (2018). https://doi.org/10.1371/journal.pone.0195878.pmid:29702697

10. Google Developers. Recognize and Augment Images – ARCore. https://developers. google.com/ar/develop/c/augmented-images. Accessed 28 Feb 2020
11. Hoppe, A.H., et al.: VirtualTablet: extending movable surfaces with touch interaction. In: 2019 IEEE Conference on Virtual Reality and 3D User Interfaces (VR), March 2019, pp. 980–981. https://doi.org/10.1109/VR.2019.8797993
12. Hoppe, A.H., Reeb, R., van de Camp, F., Stiefelhagen, R.: Capability for collision avoidance of different user avatars in virtual reality. In: Stephanidis, C. (ed.) HCI 2018. CCIS, vol. 851, pp. 273–279. Springer, Cham (2018). https://doi.org/10. 1007/978-3-319-92279-9_37
13. Huo, K., et al.: SynchronizAR: instant synchronization for spontaneous and spatial collaborations in augmented reality. In: Proceedings of the 31st Annual ACM Symposium on User Interface Software and Technology. UIST 2018, Berlin, Germany, pp. 19–30. ACM (2018). https://doi.org/10.1145/3242587.3242595. ISBN: 978-1-4503-5948- 1
14. Jain, A., Dellaert, F.: Fast 3D pose refinement with RGB images, 17 November 2019
15. Kalkusch, M., et al.: Structured visual markers for indoor pathfinding. In: The First IEEE International Workshop Agumented Reality Toolkit, First IEEE International Augmented Reality Toolkit Workshop, Darmstadt, Germany, p. 8. IEEE (2002). https://doi.org/10.1109/ART.2002.1107018. ISBN: 978-0-7803-7680-9
16. Koenderink, J.J., Van Doorn, A.J.: Affine structure from motion. JOSA A **8**(2), 377–385 (1991)
17. Krohn, A., et al.: Using fine-grained infrared positioning to support the surface-based activities of mobile users. In: 25th IEEE International Conference on Distributed Computing Systems Workshops, June 2005, pp. 463–468 (2005). https:// doi.org/10.1109/ICDCSW.2005.139
18. Lang, S.: Skript Zur Vorlesung Computerintensive Verfahren in Der Statistik (2004). https://www.uibk.ac.at/statistics/personal/lang/publications/compstat_ aktuell.pdf. Accessed 28 Feb 2020
19. Liu, Y., et al.: Technical evaluation of hololens for multimedia: a first look. IEEE Multimedia **25**(4), 8–18 (2018). https://doi.org/10.1109/MMUL.2018.2873473. ISSN: 1070–986X
20. Facebook LLC. Powered by AI: Oculus Insight. https://ai.facebook.com/blog/ powered-by-ai-oculus-insight/. Accessed 28 Feb 2020
21. Google LLC. ARCore Cloud Anchor (2019). https://developers.google.com/ar/ develop/java/cloud-anchors/overview-android. Accessed 28 Feb 2020
22. Mills, D.L.: Internet time synchronization: the network time protocol. IEEE Trans. Commun. **39**(10), 1482–1493 (1991)
23. Mujber, T.S., Szecsi, T., Hashmi, M.S.J.: Virtual reality applications in manufacturing process simulation. J. Mater. Process. Technol. **155–156**, 1834–1838 (2004). https://doi.org/10.1016/j.jmatprotec.2004.04.401. ISSN: 09240136
24. Niehorster, D.C., Li, L., Lappe, M.: The accuracy and precision of position and orientation tracking in the HTC vive virtual reality system for scientific research. i-Perception **8**(3), 204166951770820 (2017). https://doi.org/10.1177/ 2041669517708205
25. Olson, E.: AprilTag: a robust and exible visual fiducial system. In: Proceedings of the IEEE International Conference on Robotics and Automation (ICRA), May 2011, pp. 3400–3407. IEEE (2011)
26. Powell, M.J.D.: Direct search algorithms for optimization calculations. Acta Numerica **7**, 287–336 (1998). https://doi.org/10.1017/S0962492900002841. ISSN: 0962–4929, 1474–0508

27. Rehder, J., et al.: Extending Kalibr: calibrating the extrinsics of multiple IMUs and of individual axes. In: 2016 IEEE International Conference on Robotics and Automation (ICRA), May 2016, pp. 4304–4311 (2016). https://doi.org/10.1109/ICRA.2016.7487628

28. Rhudy, M.: Time alignment techniques for experimental sensor data. Int. J. Comput. Sci. Eng. Surv. **5** (2014). https://doi.org/10.5121/ijcses.2014.5201

29. Saito, S., et al.: Indoor marker-based localization using coded seamless pattern for interior decoration. In: 2007 IEEE Virtual Reality Conference, March 2007, pp. 67–74 (2007). https://doi.org/10.1109/VR.2007.352465

30. Salzmann, H., Jacobs, J., Froehlich, B.: Collaborative interaction in co-located two-user scenarios. In: Proceedings of the 15th Joint virtual reality Eurographics conference on Virtual Environments. Eurographics Association, pp. 85–92 (2009)

31. Schönberger, J.L., Frahm, J.-M.: Structure-from-motion revisited. In: Conference on Computer Vision and Pattern Recognition (CVPR) (2016)

32. Schönberger, J.L., et al.: Pixelwise view selection for unstructured multi-view stereo. In: European Conference on Computer Vision (ECCV) (2016)

33. Scott, D.W.: Multivariate density estimation and visualization. In: Gentle, J.E., Härdle, W.K., Mori, Y. (eds.) Handbook of Computational Statistics, pp. 549–569. Springer, Heidelberg (2012). https://doi.org/10.1007/978-3-642-21551-3_19. ISBN: 978-3-642-21550-6 978-3-642-21551-3

34. Taketomi, T., Uchiyama, H., Ikeda, S.: Visual SLAM algorithms: a survey from 2010 to 2016. IPSJ Trans. Comput. Vis. Appl. **9**(1), 1–11 (2017). https://doi.org/10.1186/s41074-017-0027-2

35. Unity Technologies. Unity3D. https://unity.com/. Accessed 28 Feb 2020

36. Ullman, S.: The interpretation of structure from motion. Proc. Royal Soc. London. Series B. Biol. Sci. **203**(1153), 405–426 (1979)

37. Vuforia. Image Targets. https://library.vuforia.com/articles/Training/Image-Target-Guide. Accessed 28 Feb 2020

38. Wahlström, J., et al.: IMU-based smartphone-to-vehicle positioning. IEEE Trans. Intell. Veh. **1**(2), 139–147 (2016). https://doi.org/10.1109/TIV.2016.2588978. ISSN: 2379–8904

39. Wang, J., Olson, E.: AprilTag 2: efficient and robust fiducial detection. In: Proceedings of the IEEE/RSJ International Conference on Intelligent Robots and Systems (IROS), October 2016

40. Zheng, Z., et al.: Aristo: an augmented reality platform for immersion and interactivity. In: Proceedings of the 2017 ACM on Multimedia Conference - MM 2017. The 2017 ACM. Mountain View, California, USA, pp. 690–698. ACM Press (2017). https://doi.org/10.1145/3123266.3123308. ISBN: 978-1-4503-4906-2

Contrast and Parameter Research of Augmented Reality Indoor Navigation Scheme

Wen-jun Hou[1,2] and Lixing Tang[1,2(✉)]

[1] Beijing University of Posts and Telecommunications,
No. 10 Xitucheng Road Haidian District, Beijing, China
182377718@qq.com
[2] Beijing Key Laboratory of Network Systems and Network Culture,
Beijing, China

Abstract. We are committed to using various indoor and outdoor images, 3D objects and static scenes as recognition objects to build an augmented reality world. This paper focuses on the research and application of indoor augmented reality navigation. Indoor navigation has a variety of technical solutions, such as Wi-Fi Based and indoor sensor based. As one of them, augmented reality has the advantages of no need to deploy additional hardware devices in advance, six degrees of freedom and high precision. By analyzing the development of augmented reality indoor navigation and the underlying technology, we summarize and implement three solutions: map based (MB), point-cloud based (PCB), image based (IB). We first conducted a control experiment, and compared these schemes with the flow theory and the experimental data. At the same time, we collected the feedback and suggestions during the experiment, and carried out a second experiment on some components of augmented reality navigation (such as path, point of interest), and obtained the corresponding quantitative data.

Keywords: Augmented reality · Indoor navigation · User experience

1 Introduction

With the birth of applications such as pokémon go, augmented reality (AR) has received great attention. People began to explore the application of augmented reality in medical, education, entertainment, navigation and other scenarios. However, in order to provide a better experience in each scenario, a large number of technical problems and interaction problems still need to be solved.

Navigation, especially based on smart phones, has always been the focus of attention. Different from outdoor navigation based on GPS, there is no uniform technical solution for indoor navigation, which is generally recognized and used by the public. However, in the complex environment of places such as museums, airports and shopping malls, the navigation scheme based on smart phones is urgently needed. Despite unremitting efforts, progress has been slow.

© Springer Nature Switzerland AG 2020
J. Y. C. Chen and G. Fragomeni (Eds.): HCII 2020, LNCS 12190, pp. 81–96, 2020.
https://doi.org/10.1007/978-3-030-49695-1_6

Indoor navigation needs to know where the user is first, and the corresponding camera information is usually the result of location and direction. The camera's attitude relative to the whole indoor environment can be expressed by at least six parameters, three of which represent translation and the other three represent rotation. These parameters are called degrees of freedom (DOF).

Some technical solutions are based on infrared ray, ultrasonic wave or RFID technology [1–3], which can only be used in a short distance, and need to have advanced hardware system deployment. Some technical solutions are located through Wi Fi, which requires a high coverage and stable network system, and the accuracy is only 1–3 m, and only three degrees of freedom [4]. There are also some technical schemes to estimate the position and direction information of the device based on the inertial sensors of mobile phones such as gyroscopes and accelerometers. There is a serious drift problem in inertial tracking, which cannot provide accurate tracking in continuous operation [5, 6].

Different from the above scheme, augmented reality indoor navigation is based on the visual elements that can be seen everywhere in the indoor environment as the basis of recognition features and continuous tracking. It does not need to arrange other hardware systems in advance, and has high accuracy and six degrees of freedom. In order to know where the user is in the room, such applications usually need to turn on the camera for image acquisition, and use the collected image to determine the location and orientation. At the beginning of the development of augmented reality, the collected image features are some specific images, which are widely used by various AR platforms [7, 8]. However, this kind of pre-determined mark needs to be installed and maintained. For this reason, people propose markless AR, which extracts the natural visual features of the environment to work with good accuracy. However, this scheme usually brings users extra burden of navigation between information points [9]. With the gradual improvement of the underlying technology and supporting equipment of augmented reality, at present, the feature is no longer just a static picture, but also a 3D object or the corresponding point cloud information of the whole indoor space.

The three solutions we analyze and implement are based on one or more of the above technologies. We collect data through experiments to analyze the advantages and disadvantages of these technical schemes in many aspects. At the same time, we pay attention to the components during navigation that few people pay attention to in the past, and explore the appropriate parameters of these components (such as path, point of interest) through secondary experiments.

2   Related Work

So far, there are many solutions with the development of augmented reality indoor navigation. The first one is based on static pictures. For example, Reitmayr [10], Höllerer [11], Wagner [12], etc. all use arrows to describe where users need to go next. Based on this, Mulloni et al. [13] proposed the indoor navigation of hand-held augmented reality based on the activity instruction. By setting multiple identification pictures in the room, the user's location can be accurately obtained and informed, and the user's next walking direction can be informed at the same time. For the navigation from one map to another, the user's steps and turns are calculated by devices such as gyroscopes and accelerometers. On the interface display, it uses the activity instruction, which means how many steps you need to take next and whether you should turn left or right, etc. Kasprzak et al. [14] proposed a feature-based augmented reality indoor navigation, which uses the trademark extracted in the space environment as the recognition image, and provides enough abundant marks to enable users to scan anytime, anywhere. This scheme demonstrates the practicability and advantages of augmented reality indoor navigation scheme in complex environment.

The above schemes usually need users to look for specific recognition images in the navigation, and the navigation is discontinuous, so there are errors in the navigation between points. With the continuous development of technology, AR indoor navigation began to have some new solutions. For example, Huang et al. [15] use panoramic images to estimate the location and direction information of users in indoor environment. Jiang et al. [16] proposed an iMoon solution based on SfM technology for large-scale 3D reconstruction of unordered images, which enables users to scan everywhere and then locate and navigate. Noreikis et al. [17] put forward SeeNav based on iMoon. The attitude estimation based on SfM is combined with inertial tracking rather than SLAM, so as to achieve high-precision tracking in the environment without features, and the scheme is more energy-saving.

The above schemes usually need to be built on the basis of special equipment or using a large number of static pictures to build 3D scenes. There are also programs that offer different directions of technology and experience exploration. For example, Gerstweiler et al. [18] proposed a new method named HyMoTrack, which combines two visual feature tracking algorithms. In the first phase, the location and direction information is detected by static pictures, and in the second phase, continuous tracking is realized in almost all indoor environments by SLAM algorithm. At the same time, the data of inertial sensor is used to compensate for the short-term tracking loss to provide a more continuous and accurate navigation experience. Rustagi et al. [19] proposed a scheme building augmented reality indoor navigation map based on MapBox. This scheme provided small map and navigation and rendering of POI, and implemented a user-defined user interface to get a better user experience.

There are also some researches on the space division and user experience in the navigation process. For example, Becker et al. [20] proposed a framework of semantic space division, which allows the integration of conceptually separated interior space models in multi-level representation. Goetz et al. [21] developed a navigation network to provide users with adaptive and optimal length paths, and defined images containing semantic information such as room tags or the accessibility constraints of the door. Krūminaitė et al. [22] proposed a spatial division of navigation network based on the principle of human behavior and perception of environment. In this scheme, for example, the queuing area waiting at the information desk is included in the unnavigable area, so that the navigation is more accurate.

3 System Overview

3.1 Image Based Navigation Scheme

The first scheme IB returns to the most basic function of augmented reality based on recognition image. This scheme is based on the scheme proposed by Mulloni et al. [13]. When users navigate, they first need to scan a picture in the environment. After scanning successfully, a virtual two-dimensional or three-dimensional map will be superimposed on the picture to inform location. When the user selects the destination, the map will display the next path information, and the required steps will be displayed in the upper area of the screen, and a series of activity lists (such as go straight, turn left, etc.) will be displayed in the lower part of the screen. When the user leaves the picture, the upper area will become larger, and a virtual arrow will be added in the real environment to inform the user of the next direction. The upper area will display the number of steps that have been walked in real time. When the user completes an action (such as straight walking 26 steps), it is necessary to manually click the button in the lower part of the screen for the next action. In the long-distance navigation, this scheme may produce some deviation, so the user can search for and scan a new picture during the navigation to refresh the real-time position. When the user completes the last action, the navigation ends.

We have made some improvements to the above scheme. We display all the original instruction information on the lower area of the interface, so that there will be more visible areas on the screen during navigation. When the user completes an action, the instruction automatically switches to the next one. At the same time, we add more activity instructions to enrich the action set, as go upstairs or go downstairs. Due to the different step size of each person, we record the difference between the actual steps and the predicted steps when the user completes a navigation task, which is used for more accurate navigation in the future. The scheme interface is as follows (Fig. 1):

Fig. 1. Scheme IB: static recognition image and inertial tracking.

In order to realize the above scheme, developers need to select enough locations in the navigation environment, and each location corresponds to a recognition image. Developers also need to prepare maps corresponding to the environment and routes between each location. After the user scans the recognition image and selects the destination, the path is generated according to Dijkstra algorithm and rendered on the virtual map in real time. When the user moves, the system uses the pedometer and gyroscope to obtain the number of steps and the rotation information of the mobile phone.

3.2   Point-Cloud Based Navigation Scheme

The second scheme is mainly based on iMoon [16] and SeeNav [17], creating 3D model of indoor environment (point cloud form), and using Structure-from-Motion (SfM) to realize image-based positioning. At first, the user opens the camera, takes one static picture around him and uploads it to the server. After a few seconds of calculation, the screen displays the map, real-time location and orientation. At this time, the user can directly select the destination preset by the system, or upload another photo to find the corresponding location. Next, similar to scheme I, the user starts according to the instruction information above. When the user completes the last instruction, the navigation ends. The scheme interface is as follows (Fig. 2):

Fig. 2. Scheme PCB: SfM and inertial tracking.

One of the highlights of the scheme is the generation of map, which uses SfM technology to build an initial 3D model from crowdsourced photos or videos. The 3D model becomes more complete by constantly updating photos. The system uses the map generated by this 3D model to provide navigation. When the user uploads one image around him, the system queries the position and orientation according to the SfM model. The technology of navigation process is similar to scheme one, which mainly uses inertial tracking. It is worth mentioning that in this scheme, users can take almost any location as the starting point, and the more perfect the SfM model is, the closer the system is to achieve navigation in any location. The following figure is the schematic diagram of SfM model with different abundance (Fig. 3).

Fig. 3. On the left is the top view of the original 3D model, and as new images are added, the SfM model becomes more complete.

3.3   Map Based Navigation Scheme

Different from the former two schemes, the third scheme MB is mainly based on the real-time visual image captured by the camera to achieve continuous tracking in the navigation process. In the same way as scheme 1, the user needs to turn on the camera and scan the corresponding recognition image to obtain the real-time position at the beginning. After scanning, the corresponding small map and user's location will appear in the lower left corner of the screen. After the user selects the destination, he can view the corresponding route on the small map. At the same time, in the main area of the screen, the corresponding path is rendered in the real scene. Click the small map in the lower left corner to enlarge the map to the full screen. And in the full screen view mode, the user can view the whole map through double finger zooming and single finger moving. When the user moves according to the corresponding navigation route, the map control will update the user's location and route in real time, and render the path and the nearby POI in the main area of the screen in real time. When the user reaches the destination, the navigation ends. The scheme interface is as follows (Fig. 4):

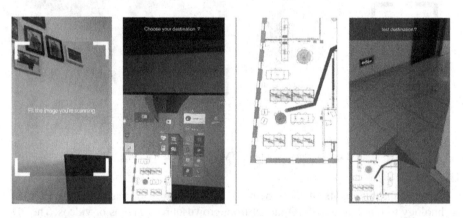

Fig. 4. Scheme MB: static recognition image, binocular camera, and inertial tracking.

It is worth mentioning that the scheme can obtain six degrees of freedom of the device in real time through the binocular camera, so the basis and accuracy of its continuous tracking depend on certain hardware conditions, such as iPhone 6S and above or some high-end Android phones. When there are few feature points in the navigation process (such as the white wall), the real-time tracking may fail. At this time, the system uses the inertial tracking mentioned in the previous two schemes as an alternative. The scheme also depends on the map corresponding to the actual scene, which can be a 3D map model with walls and POI models, or the 2D map plane added with walls and POI models. Different from scheme I, path generation is based on the RecastNavigation algorithm, which can generate the corresponding guide path in real time according to the starting point, destination and navigable area, as shown in the figure below. Using this algorithm, we only need to preset the navigable area and destination, so as long as the system obtains the user's real-time position, the user can switch the destination at any position during the navigation process and get the route in real time (Fig. 5).

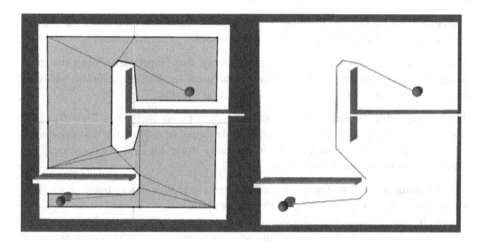

Fig. 5. Navigable area and planning path based on RecastNavigation algorithm.

4 Experiment and Results

4.1 Experimental Design

The main purpose of our experiment is to analyze the user experience of the three schemes and their performance in some important indicators (such as navigation accuracy, navigation time, etc.). We evaluate the user experience of the three schemes based on the best experience model (flow theory) proposed by psychologist Mihaly Csikszentmihalyi [23]. According to flow theory, when people are engaged in activities, if they devote themselves to the situation and filter out irrelevant intuition, they will enter an immersion state. The theory divides this state into the following parts:

A Challenging Activity That Requires Skills. Most of the best experiences happen in a series of activities. These activities are targeted and limited by the regular activities that need spiritual energy investment. It is impossible to achieve without appropriate skills.

The Merging of Action and Awareness. People become so focused on what they are doing that activities become spontaneous, almost automatic; they no longer realize that they are separate from the actions they are performing.

Clear Goals and Feedback. The reason for this full engagement in the process experience is that goals are usually clear and feedback is immediate. In the practical application of flow theory, these two indexes are often separated. The goal must be clear. The climber can see the summit of climbing and the chess player plays to win, which makes the participants more excited than sitting on the sofa aimlessly. At the same time, on a solo cruise, a person may sail in a small boat for weeks without seeing land. The importance of immediate feedback is illustrated by the excitement of finding a small island after crossing the ocean.

Concentration on the Task at Hand. The clearly structured demands of the activity impose order, and exclude the interference of disorder in consciousness.

The Paradox of Control. Activities that generate flow experiences, even the most dangerous ones, are designed to allow practitioners to develop sufficient skills to minimize the margin of error to as close to zero as possible.

The Loss of Self-consciousness. In flow, a person is facing challenges. To achieve the best, he must constantly improve his skills. At that time, he didn't have the opportunity to reflect on what it meant to him. If he really made himself self-conscious, the experience could not be very profound.

The Transformation of Time. One of the most common descriptions of the best experience is that time doesn't seem to pass as usual.

Finally, we selected five indicators including clear goals, instant feedback, concentration, potential sense of control and sense of time to design the questionnaire, as shown in the following Table 1:

Table 1. Questionnaire based on flow theory.

Theme	Index	Question
Clear goals	Clear position	I can easily know where I am
	Clear navigation	I can easily find and understand navigation information
Instant feedback	Interaction time	I get immediate and effective feedback when I interact (such as scanning pictures, selecting destinations)
	State changes	I can get immediate and effective feedback when the system state changes (for example, when moving)
Concentration	Immersion	I can always immerse myself in it
	Inattention (R)	I'm always distracted (R)
	Fascinated by the way	The way the system navigates fascinates me

(*continued*)

Table 1. (*continued*)

Theme	Index	Question
Potential sense of control	Control what I do	Control what I want to do well
	System instability (R)	Sometimes the system is unstable (R)
Sense of time	Time quickens	Sometimes time goes faster
	Time goes by	Time goes by at a different rate than usual

We recruited 24 volunteers to participate in our experiment. The volunteers are between 20 and 30 years old. And the ratio of men to women was 1:1. They had no experience of using AR indoor navigation before the experiment. We did the experiment in a building that none of these volunteers had ever been to. We designed three tasks A, B and C with the same number of turns and similar length. Before the task starts, we gave volunteers a simple training to understand the functions of the application and the tasks to be completed. Considering the possible impact of task sequence, we divided 24 volunteers into six groups and performed tasks in the order of ABC, ACB, BAC, BCA, CAB and CBA. After the task, we interviewed the volunteers and asked them to fill in the questionnaire. Finally, we collected the results of the questionnaire filled by volunteers and related qualitative indicators (distance difference, completion time and task completion rate).

4.2 Results and Analysis

The full score of our questionnaire is 10, and the minimum unit is 0.5. We calculated the median and interquartile range (IQR) of each question as follows (Table 2):

Table 2. Questionnaire results based on flow theory.

Index	IB		PCB		MB	
	Median	IQR	Median	IQR	Median	IQR
Clear position	5	1.5	8.5	1	8.5	1
Clear navigation	7	1.25	6	1.25	8	1.5
Interaction time	7.5	1	5	1.5	8	1.25
State changes	6	1.25	7	1.5	8.5	1
Immersion	5.5	1.5	7	1.25	8	1
Inattention(R)	3	1.5	4	1.5	4.5	1.75
Fascinated by the way	7.5	1.25	6	1.25	8	1.25
Control what I do	7.5	1.25	8	1	7.5	1
System instability(R)	5.5	1.75	3	1	3.5	1.25
Time quickens	4.5	2	6	1.25	6.5	1.5
Time goes by	6.5	1	6	1.5	6	1.5

Clear Position. IB scores low, probably because it cannot consistently display the user's location in the navigation. PCB and MB have similar results. The IQR of PCB is small, probably because it is always in large map mode.

Clear Navigation. PCB scores low, probably because of its single navigation way and no combination of virtual and real. MB has the highest score, which indicates that users prefer to have a small map widget in navigation.

Interaction Time. PCB scores low, mainly because it has to wait a few seconds to display the map and location after uploading the image. IB and MB scores are close to each other, and the instant feedback basically meets users' requirements.

State Changes. IB scores low, possibly because it disturbs the user during instruction switching. MB scores high, which indicates that the scheme can accurately reflect the user's movement on the mini-map, and provide more effective navigation information through a combination of various methods.

Immersion. IB scores low, possibly because it requires users to search for and scan new recognition image during navigation. The high score of MB indicates that it can provide a better sense of immersion.

Inattention(R). IB performs best in this category. MB may cause the user's attention to be distracted due to more information and the map has two modes of switching.

Fascinated by the Way. PCB scores low, indicating that users prefer the combination of virtual and real navigation.

Control what I do. There is no significant difference between the three schemes. PCB may give users a better sense of control because the scheme is relatively simple overall.

System Instability(R). IB performed poorly in this category, possibly because some users feel a lack of fault tolerance in the system when they deviate from the route.

Time Quickens. IB's poor performance may be due to the fact that it requires users to search and scan for new recognition images during navigation.

Time Goes by. There is no significant difference between the three schemes.

At the same time, we collected some qualitative data about these three schemes, including step deviation (which refers to the actual steps of the volunteer and the expected steps of navigation), task completion time and task completion rate, as shown in the following Table 3:

Table 3. Qualitative data.

	Step deviation	Time(s)	Completion rate (%)
IB	15.47	75.29	70.83
PCB	10.50	49.36	91.67
MB	7.75	36.20	83.33

From the qualitative data and our observation, we can see that the deviation step of MB is the smallest and the time is the shortest. IB requires the user to scan the recognition image in the navigation map, which increases the step deviation and time consumption. After the user deviates from the navigation map with IB, he may not be able to continue to complete the task because he cannot find the recognition image. PCB scheme can upload pictures anywhere to locate, so it has the best fault tolerance and the highest task completion rate, but uploading pictures takes time, so there is still a gap compared to MB in time.

After the task, we interviewed the volunteers and asked them how they felt about using the application, what problems they encountered and what suggestions they had.

In the interview results, in general, AR indoor navigation is considered to be attractive and practical. Many volunteers focus on the underlying principles and why there are three options. After we explained that there are differences among the three schemes in preparation, equipment performance and implementation principle, the volunteers understood and recognized the rationality of the three schemes.

From the perspective of using experience, volunteers prefer the MB scheme, and think that the IB scheme needs to scan the recognition map midway, which greatly affects the experience. There are also some volunteers who mentioned that they prefer to have a combination of virtual and real pages when using PCB.

From the perspective of the problems, the common problem of IB scheme lies in the fault tolerance of users after deviating from the path. Many volunteers find it difficult to find the recognition image after they deviate from the path in the middle, which leads to task failure. Some volunteers think that more recognition images can be added to the map as an optional middle point. Under the PCB scheme, users are satisfied that they can get location almost anywhere, but at the same time, it takes several seconds to upload the image to get the location. There are also some volunteers who did not complete the task in MB scheme. We observed that these volunteers tend to grasp the mobile phone at will, leading to the scheme entering the inertial tracking mode and thus increasing the navigation error.

In terms of suggestions, many volunteers think that the advantages of each scheme can be combined. For example, scheme 1 is compatible with more mobile phones, scheme 2 can get location anywhere, and scheme 3 has a better overall experience. Some volunteers mentioned the widget of path navigation, and they mentioned that the arrow can be placed on the ground according to their experience. Some volunteers suggested adding descriptions of surrounding objects in the navigation process, such as logos and names of shopping mall. Some volunteers raised concerns about the maintenance work after the scene change. They were worried that if the scene changed partially, our application might not be able to adjust flexibly.

4.3   Follow-up Experiments

We think about the suggestions put forward by the volunteers in the first experiment. As for the path widget, many volunteers tend to lay it on the ground. First, we need to verify whether this idea is more popular and whether it has practical help in the process of task. On the basis of the MB scheme, we carried out the secondary development, putting the path widget on the ground, taking the length of 4 m, and placing one unit every 0.1 m, as shown in the Fig. 6 below.

Fig. 6. New scheme: place path widget on the ground

We invited 12 of the original 24 volunteers (6 men and 6 women) to carry out follow-up experiments. We set tasks D and E in a building unfamiliar to 12 volunteers. Similar to the previous experiment, the two tasks have similar length and the same number of corners. Finally, we asked volunteers to give 0–10 scores for the two schemes and collect the time for them to complete the task, as shown in the Table 4 below.

Table 4. Results of follow-up experiment 1.

Index	OLD		NEW		P
	Median	IQR	Median	IQR	
Score	7.37	0.75	8.17	0.5	.001
Time(s)	22.30	4.15	20.71	5.30	.203

All volunteers successfully completed the task. It is not difficult to find that volunteers have higher scores for the new scheme, and the p value (<0.05) indicates that the statistical results are significantly different, indicating that the scheme of putting path widget on the ground is closer to people's mind. In terms of time, although the p value is 0.203 (>0.05), almost all volunteers' total time when using the new scheme is less than or equal to the old scheme, and the new scheme is 1.59 s faster in terms of average value, which shows that the new scheme can effectively accelerate the completion time of the task to a certain extent.

Next, we experimented the parameters of the path widget. We generated a version every 0.5 m for the experiment, and invited volunteers to score 0–10 points. We find that the path widget length is the most popular when the distance is 3.5 m–5 m. The experimental results are as follows (Fig. 7):

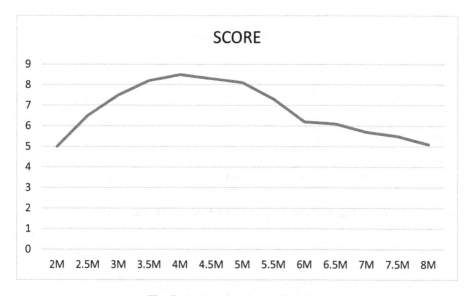

Fig. 7. Path widget length line chart.

We experimented the size and density of the widget when the length was 5 m. Slightly different, because the two parameters interact with each other, we allow volunteers to continuously adjust the two parameters and observe them in real time, stopping at the most appropriate position. Finally, we get a two-dimensional scatter diagram. The X axis in the figure represents the density of the widget. We can see that the basic distribution is 0.3 m–0.45 m, and the average value is 0.37 m. The Y axis in the figure represents the size of the widget, which is basically distributed in 0.15–0.3 m, with an average value of 0.24 m (Fig. 8).

We also did similar experiments on the size and distance (how far when appearing) of POI widget along the way, and finally we got a two-dimensional scatter diagram. The X axis represents the size of the widget, with an interval of 0.3–0.5 m and an average of 0.43 m. The Y axis represents the distance of the widget, with an interval of 3.5–5 m and an average of 4.22 m (Fig. 9).

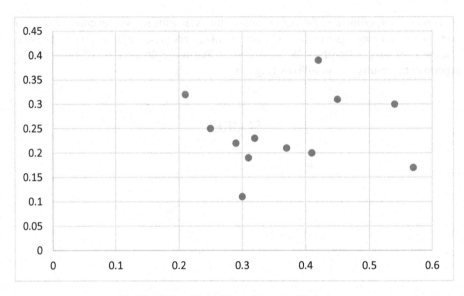

Fig. 8. Path widget size and density 2D scatter.

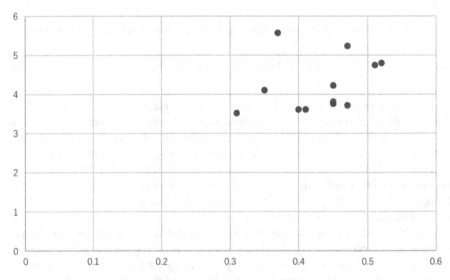

Fig. 9. POI widget size and distance 2D scatter.

5 Conclusions and Future Work

Starting from the existing navigation scheme, this paper analyzes the characteristics and advantages of augmented reality indoor navigation in indoor navigation. By combing the development process, characteristics and technical solutions of the existing solutions of augmented reality indoor navigation, we have finally summarized three solutions IB, PCB and MB. There are differences among the three schemes. IB supports more mobile phones. It needs to take multiple static pictures in the scene as recognition images. When the recognition is successful, the corresponding map will be displayed on the picture. The system provides continuous navigation through inertial tracking. PCB does not need to have a map in advance. Through collecting enough pictures or video information to build the point cloud model of the whole scene, users can scan and obtain location information and navigation in almost any place. The biggest difference between MB and IB is that the binocular camera is used for continuous tracking during navigation, while inertial tracking is only a supplementary means, which requires the hardware of mobile phone.

We optimized the three schemes to a certain extent, developed demo and carried out relevant experiments. In Experiment 1, we compared three schemes through subjective and objective indicators. Based on the flow theory, we know the advantages and disadvantages of the three schemes in terms of experience, and MB score is the highest overall. Based on the qualitative index, we find that MB has smaller error and faster time than the other two schemes, while PCB mode has the highest success rate because it can provide navigation in almost any position.

We observed and interviewed the volunteers, and carried out the follow-up experiments, and obtained the relevant parameters of path widget and POI widget.

The three schemes have practical application value from the results and analysis: when the system needs to be compatible with more devices and the investment is limited, we prefer IB. We tend to PCB when a higher success rate is needed. In the comprehensive aspect, MB performs the best, but also puts forward the requirements for the equipment. Of course, as some volunteers mentioned, we can combine three solutions at the same time when conditions permit.

We will continue to explore augmented reality indoor navigation on this basis in the future. On the one hand, with the progress of technology and hardware, there will be better solutions. On the other hand, we can also extract more user experience related indicators based on more in-depth experiments in more scenarios, and propose a better experience scheme.

References

1. Abowd, G.D., Atkeson, C.G., Hong, J., Long, S., Kooper, R., Pinkerton, M.: Cyberguide: a mobile context-aware tour guide. Wireless Netw. **3**, 421–433 (1997)
2. Addlesee, M., Curwen, R., Hodges, S., et al.: Implementing a sentient computing system. Computer **34**, 50–56 (2001)
3. Chittaro, L., Nadalutti, D.: Presenting evacuation instructions on mobile devices by means of location aware 3D virtual environments. In: Proceedings of the 10th International Conference on Human Computer Interaction with Mobile Devices and Services, pp. 395–398. ACM (2008)
4. LaMarca, A., Chawathe, Y., Consolvo, S., et al.: Place lab: device positioning using radio beacons in the wild. In: Pervasive Computing, pp. 116–133 (2005)
5. Hu, Y., Liao, X., Lu, Q., Xu, S., Zhu, W.: A segment based fusion algorithm of WiFi fingerprinting and pedestrian dead reckoning. In: 2016 IEEE/CIC International Conference on Communications in China (ICCC), pp. 1–6. IEEE (2016)

6. Huang, B., Qi, G., Yang, X., Zhao, L., Zou, H.: Exploiting cyclic features of walking for pedestrian dead reckoning with unconstrained smartphones, pp. 374–385 (2016). https://doi.org/10.1145/2971648.2971742
7. Gerstweiler, G., Vonach, E., Kaufmann, H.: Hymotrack: a mobile AR navigation system for complex indoor environments. Sensors 16(1), 17 (2015)
8. Gherghina, A., Olteanu, A.-C., Tapus, N.: A marker-based augmented reality system for mobile devices. In: 2013 11th Roedunet International Conference (RoEduNet), pp. 1–6. IEEE (2013)
9. Müller, H., Schöning, J., Krüger, A.: Mobile map interaction - evaluation in an indoor scenario. In: Workshop on Mobile and Embedded Interactive Systems, Informatik 2006 Gesellschaft für Informatike.V. (2006)
10. Reitmayr, G., Schmalstieg, D.: Location based applications for mobile augmented reality. In: Proceedings of the 4th Australian User Interface Conference on User Interfaces 2003, pp. 65–73. Australian Computer Society, Inc. (2003)
11. Höllerer, T., Hallaway, D., Tinna, N., Feiner, S.: steps toward accommodating variable position tracking accuracy in a mobile augmented reality system. In: Proceedings of AIMS 2001: Second International Workshop on Artificial Intelligence in Mobile Systems, pp. 31–37 (2001)
12. Wagner, D., Schmalstieg, D.: First steps towards handheld augmented reality. In: Proceedings of Seventh IEEE International Symposium on Wearable Computers 2003, pp. 127–135 (2003)
13. Mulloni, A., Seichter, H., Schmalstieg, D.: Handheld augmented reality indoor navigation with activity-based instructions. In: Proceedings MobileHCI 2011 (2011)
14. Kasprzak, S., Komninos, A., Barrie, P.: Feature-based indoor navigation using augmented reality. In: Proceedings - 9th International Conference on Intelligent Environments, IE 2013, pp. 100–107 (2013). https://doi.org/10.1109/ie.2013.51
15. Huang, J.-Y., Lee, S.-H., Tsai, C.-H.: A fast image matching technique for the panoramic-based localization. In: 2016 IEEE/ACIS 15th International Conference on Computer and Information Science (ICIS), pp. 1–6. IEEE (2016)
16. Dong, J., Xiao, Y., Noreikis, M., Ou, Z., Ylä-Jääski, A.: iMoon: using smartphones for image-based indoor navigation (2015). https://doi.org/10.1145/2809695.2809722
17. Noreikis, M., Xiao, Y., Ylä-Jääski, A.: SeeNav: seamless and energy-efficient indoor navigation using augmented reality, pp. 186–193 (2017). https://doi.org/10.1145/3126686.3126733
18. Gerstweiler, G., Vonach, E., Kaufmann, H.: HyMoTrack: a mobile AR navigation system for complex indoor environments. Sensors 16, 17 (2015). https://doi.org/10.3390/s16010017
19. Rustagi, T., Yoo, K.: Indoor AR navigation using tilesets, pp. 1–2 (2018). https://doi.org/10.1145/3281505.3281575
20. Becker, T., Nagel, C., Kolbe, T.H.: A multilayered space-event model for navigation in indoor spaces. In: Lee, J., Zlatanova, S. (eds.) 3D Geo-Information Sciences, pp. 61–77. Springer, Heidelberg (2009). https://doi.org/10.1007/978-3-540-87395-2_5
21. Goetz, M., Zipf, A.: Formal definition of a user-adaptive and length-optimal routing graph for complex indoor environments. Geo-Spatial Inf. Sci. 14(2), 119–128 (2011)
22. Krūminaitė, M., Zlatanova, S.: Indoor space subdivision for indoor navigation. In: GIS: Proceedings of the ACM International Symposium on Advances in Geographic Information Systems (2014). https://doi.org/10.1145/2676528.2676529
23. Csikszentmihalyi, M.: Flow: the psychology of optimal experience. Des. Issues 8(1), 80–81 (1991)

Study on User-Centered Usability Elements of User Interface Designs in an Augmented Reality Environment

Un Kim[1,2(✉)], Yaxi Wang[2(✉)], and Wenhao Yuan[2(✉)]

[1] Hubei Key Laboratory of Intelligent Robot (Wuhan Institute of Technology),
Wuhan 430073, China
[2] College of Art and Design, Wuhan Institute of Technology,
Wuhan, Hubei, China
tntno0l@naver.com, wangyaxi@wit.edub.cn,
whynotl99960l22@gmail.com

Abstract. In order to complete the augmented reality (AR) user interface (UI) design simply and quickly, the usable factors were studied in this work. The main focus of interface design is to increase usability. Various factors should be considered together when evaluating usability. An ideal usable model is usually user-centered, with the aim of perceiving the interests of users and easily completing targets. In order to cover all types of usable factors, the literature survey method had been used and a total of 85 usable factors had been collected by this survey. To make the usable factors adapt the augmented reality, the concept of factors is redefined. We extract the items which are adaptable and user-centered, combine or delete the items that have the same meanings and finally select 25 usable evaluative factors. The Human Computer Interaction professional is set as the target, and the related data is collected by Heuristic Evaluation. We are able to systematize the usable factors by principal component analysis, observe the correlation between the usable factors, and classify those with high correlation.

Keywords: User interface · Augmented reality · Usability · Heuristic evolution

1 Introduction

Virtual reality (VR) technology has been used since the 1960s, but it has been used only in certain areas due to technical problems and high costs. However, it has expanded into the personal domain through a number of factors, including the development of displays and 3D technologies and the miniaturization of hardware, lightening and falling costs [1]. With the recent development of augmented reality (AR) technology, it is being applied in various industries, and the basic technologies are being implemented in different forms [2]. Mobile devices provide users with

---

U. Kim—HBIR 201907.

J. Y. C. Chen and G. Fragomeni (Eds.): HCII 2020, LNCS 12190, pp. 97–106, 2020.
https://doi.org/10.1007/978-3-030-49695-1_7

different interactions and communications from other devices. In general, interaction is divided into person to person interaction and person to machine interaction [3], Mobile devices enable both types of interactions, as well as more and more interaction methods as seen in smartphones. However, there are a lot of wireless application protocol gateways in the study of user interface (UI) reflecting AR, in particular the tendency to focus on navigation. There exists a shortage of professional evaluation of UI design in the AR mobile environment.

With the trend of the times and the change of culture, the requirements of users are multidimensional and varied. The function of a product is different from the way it is used in a service environment, what should be paid attention to is that the rational consumption methods, such as price or function, are changing into the era of emotional service [4]. The perceptual service must respond positively and be applied according to the user's different request and has the connection with the interface in the process of analyzing and visualizing these requirements [5]. At the same time, an interface that can be close to the users Sensibility should be provided so that the user can experience usability simply and effectively [6], and the USABILITY of software quality, which has been mentioned for a long time, is the core principle of HCI (Human computer Interaction), now it has become a necessary factor [7]. In information appliances such as mobile devices and the Internet, usability is widely used as a means to improve the competitiveness of related products.

This is because usability-considering design can reduce both the physical and mental burdens on users, and improve workers' productivity and responsiveness [8]. In many cases, more effort is devoted to solving usability problems from the design phase than to post-usability evaluation [9]. It ultimately helps reduce the company's production and operating costs. Therefore, usability should be evaluated with a combination of different attributes. The ideal usability model is user-focused and friendly, and should easily get users interested in using it and achieving their intended goals [8]. The purpose of designers must be realized together to successfully implement usability. In this research, we examine the usage factors and analyze the linear combination of variable normalization to appraise the usability rapidly. The interface design of AR and the usage of Heuristic approach are studied and reported.

2 Methods

2.1 Heuristic Evaluation

Heuristics. Heuristics is an abbreviation of the Heuristic evaluation. The heuristic method is for the model solution method, is a method of successive approximation to the optimal solution. In this method, the obtained solution is repeatedly judged and modified until it is satisfied. It refers to the principles that estimators use in evaluating usability. Heuristics varied with the subjects to be evaluated, collated by Nielsen and Molich in 1990 [10].

Heuristic Evaluation. The heuristic evaluation aims to find the usability problems of the user interface and its advantage that can find problems in the shortest time.

Heuristic evaluation method is an expert evaluation method that applies the Heuristics, known as the USABILITY principles, to the interface to produce a usability checklist which was developed by Nielsen and Molich in 1990. It is learned that the Heuristic evaluation method is a relatively low-cost evaluation method that can be applied quickly and easily. Figure 1 is the result of a study conducted by Nielsen and Landauer on the effectiveness of identifying usability problems based on evaluators.
The result shows that the efficiency of finding usability problems is about 75% when there are 5 reviewers, but it will decrease sharply when there are more than 5 reviewers. Figure 2 shows the results of a survey on the efficiency of researchers and testing costs.

When there are five reviewers, the ration of benefits of cost was more than 60%. However [11], the ration will reduce with the increase of reviewers. In other words, heuristic evaluation is a method that produces a large number of important usability problems with relatively few expert evaluators, which can execute efficiently and fast.

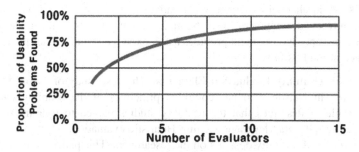

Fig. 1. Proportion of usability problems.

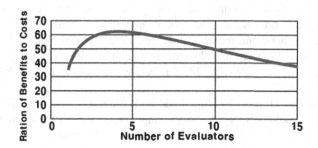

Fig. 2. Ration of benefits to costs.

The evaluation method is to describe the script of the project or to explore the system freely, and the professional estimators are used to judge the accuracy of the prototype design according to the usability principle. However, in an augmented reality environment where the technical environment is not yet mature, the form of interface usability cannot be determined. The existing usable and convenient evaluation methods are most suitable for the development process of software applied in the traditional GUI environments. If they are to be applied to augment reality environments that may not have clear goals, they need to be redefined based on the understanding of the nature of augmented reality.

2.2   Current Stage of Technology and Research

Current Stage of AR Technology. Augmented reality is a technology that seamlessly blends real-world and virtual world to provide users with a more advanced sense of engagement and reality [12]. Augmented reality has broader implications, especially for the visual basis, display technology, track technology, image integration technology, calibration technology, user interface, interaction, and visualization technology. According to GATTNET's 2019 trends report, immersive expertise including augmented reality and immersive experiences will change the way we view the digital world, from personal and simple UI technologies to multi-channel and multi-modal experiences. Multi-channel experiences take advantage of not only all human senses but also of advanced computers (heat, humidity, radar, etc.) in multi-mode devices. This multi experience environment provides a rich experience that defines the computer by the space around us [13].

Case Study on Usability Evaluation Elements. The case study of usability is gathered, centering in Nelson who has compiled principles of the usability evaluation elements. Table 1 describes that the usability studies related to user interfaces are largely based on GUI that leverage existing Heuristic evaluation.

The definition of usability depends on the researchers. This paper focus on the definitions of J. Nielsen and R. Mack, J. RoBIN, ISO 1942-11, ISO/IEC 9126, S. Lee, H. Jim, J. KIM.

Nielsen and R. Mack classified the elements of usability into Visibility of system status, Match between system and real world, User control and freedom, Consistency and standards, error prevention, Recognition rather than recall, Flexibility and efficiency of use, Aesthetic and minimalist design, Help users recognize, diagnose, and recover from error, 10. Help and documentation, Skills, Pleasurable and Respectful Interaction with the User, Privacy, 14. Subjective satisfaction, Memorability, Learnability, Efficiency [14].

J. Robin classified it into Core functionality, 1. Should be understandable within an hour, 2. System should be speak the user's language, 3. System should understand the user's language, 4. Feedback should be provided for all actions, Feedback should be timely and accurate, 5. UNIX concept should be minimized (ingeneral, minimize underlying system concept), 6. User sensibilities should be considered, 7. Functions should be logically grouped, 8. Interface should be logically ordered, 9. The core function should be clear, 10. The physical interaction whether the system should be natural the system should be efficient, reasonable defaults should be provided, accelerator should be provided, users should not have to enter system – accessible information.

Everything the user needs should be accessible through the GUI (or, in general, through whatever interface style is chosen fir the interface), the user interface should be customized, system should follow real-world conventions, system should follow platform interface conventions, system should be effectively integrated with the rest of the desktop, Keyboard core function should be supported, system should be designed to prevent error, undo and redo should be supported, Good visual design, there is no substitute for a good graphic arts [15]. ISO 1942-11classified it into Effectiveness, Efficiency, Satisfaction, Context of use [16]. While ISO/IEC 9126 classified it into Learnability, Operability, Understandability [17]. S. Lee classified it into Durability, Safety, Size, Familiarity, Arrangement, Attractiveness, Complexity, Simplicity [18].

H. Jim classified it into Effectiveness, Efficiency, Degree of satisfaction, Comprehensibility, Learning ability, Operating ability, Preference, Submissibility, Ease of learning, Empirient performance, System potential. Reuse options, Is it easy to use, Is it easy to learn and teach. Is it easy to learn again, Is it easy to learn or get rid of wrong habits, Is it easy to avoid inconveniences, Is it easy to support, Is it easy to appreciate, Is it easy to share in a group, Is it easy to integrate with traditional methods [19], and J. Kim classified it into Reactivity, Short-cutting, Developmental sensibility, Preventedness, Error repair, Predictability, Familiarity, Generalizability, User liquidity, Controllability, Public property, Multiple-handedness, Personalization, Re-time of change, Comprehensibility [20].

Through the research, the usability evaluation factors can be divided into three kinds. The first is a function-related factor, its purpose is to assess whether the retained functionality is important and whether it meets the user's requirements. The second is about the evaluation factors of user interaction. Among them, learning, satisfaction, emotional response and attractiveness are all factors. Finally, the third factor is to master the specific issues of design.

2.3   Redefinition of Evaluation Elements

The duplicate items in the survey were removed through the research. A total of 25 usability factors were finally screened out, which are Controllability, Direct Manipulation, Input method, Interaction, User Control, Efficiency, Feedback, Ease, Learnability, Simplicity, Predictability, Consistency, Familiarity, Visibility, Size, Attractiveness, Arrangement, Subjective satisfaction, Effectiveness, Tolerance Principle, Durability, Accuracy, Prevention, Error Indication and Congruity. The selected factors were specified and reinterpreted to suit the augmented reality environment.

According to the usage attributes obtained from the literature survey, the items suitable for augmented reality environment are selected.

Table 1. Reinterpretation of usability assessment elements

Elements	Reinterpretation
Arrangement	When designing physical object, the range of finger activity should be considered and each of the physical objects must not interfere with each other, when multiple physical objects are needed
Attractiveness	The operating mode and configuration of the system shall be designed to arouse the user's interest
Accuracy	In the process of using the system, the correctness of the operation of the design can be ensured
Consistency	A design that maintains the unity of functions within a system
Controllability	The user can operate the various functions of the system freely
Congruity	The language of the system and the method of the information prompt are different from the habits in real life, operation mode that is easy for users to familiar with should be provided
Durability	A design that makes a system less prone to failure or damage
Direct manipulation	The interface needs to give the user a sense of ease of operation
Effectiveness	A design that enables users to perform operations effectively
Efficiency	A design that enables users to understand and master how to use methods quickly
Error indication	The content and presentation of the error message needs to be made clear to the user
Ease	The task can be completed easily through the system
Feedback	The system needs to provide the user with the current task, future task and the correct feedback whether the task is completed or not
Familiarity	The interface design should be based on the user's existing knowledge and experience and design operation mode that users familiar with
Input method	Consider the added input way in an augmented reality environment
Interaction	Interactions should be taken into account for the user's sense of immersion in virtual reality
Learnability	Design a system that makes it easy to remember user habits
Prevention	When the user has performed the wrong operation, in order to prevent the wrong result to produce, the corresponding prevention method need to be prompted to users
Predictability	Design a user interface that is consistent with user predictions
Simplicity	The system should be simple and intuitive in design
Size	The size of the real environment should be considered
Subjective satisfaction	The use of the system should be able to induce subjective satisfaction from aspects such as fatigue, inconvenience, frustration and effort
Tolerance Principle	The system should allow multiple inputs and arrangements to prevent errors and reduce the cost of mistakes and operational errors
User Control	Users should be able to control the start and execution of system tasks autonomously
Visibility	All elements of the interface should be provided with clear visual prompts

For screening, 11 HCI related experts (master's degree, doctor's degree) took participated in the questionnaire survey. If the evaluation elements have relevance, they will be assessed with 2 points, if the relevance is not accurate, they will be assessed with 1 point, and if there is no correlation line, they will be assessed as 0 points.

In order to select the usability elements systematically, the statistical method of principal component analysis (PCA) is used.

$$
Z = \begin{pmatrix} x_{1_1} & \cdots & x_{1_o} \\ \vdots & \ddots & \vdots \\ x_{n_1} & \cdots & x_{n_o} \end{pmatrix} n \times p \left| F = \begin{pmatrix} f_{1_1} & \cdots & f_{1_c} \\ \vdots & \ddots & \vdots \\ f_{n_1} & \cdots & f_{n_c} \end{pmatrix} n \times c \right| \wedge_c
$$
$$
= \begin{pmatrix} \lambda_{1_1} & \cdots & \lambda_{1_c} \\ \vdots & \ddots & \vdots \\ \lambda_{p_1} & \cdots & \lambda_{p_c} \end{pmatrix} p \times c \left| \Delta = \begin{pmatrix} e_{1_1} & \cdots & e_{1_c} \\ \vdots & \ddots & \vdots \\ e_{n_1} & \cdots & e_{n_o} \end{pmatrix} \right| \tag{1}
$$

For the analysis, the following constraints are provided for the four variables Z (standardized observations), F (factor score Matrix), Λ (factor load), and Δ (specific factor), as shown in Eq. 1.

$\frac{1}{n-1}\left(f_{1_1}^2 + f_{2_1}^2 + \cdots + f_{n_1}^2\right) = 1$, The elements are standardized data, with an average of 0 and a dispersion of 1. On this basis, the sum of the squares is equal to n−1.

$f_{1_1}f_{1_1} + f_{n_1}f_{n_1} = 0$, the elements are independence.

$f_{1_1}e_{1_1} + f_{n_1}e_{n_1} = 0$, each factor and independent factor are mutually independent. Moreover, the independent factors are mutually independent. The correlation coefficient and commonness under this constraint are shown by the Eq. 2.

$$
Correlation_{i,j} = \sum_{k=1}^c \lambda_{i_1}\lambda_{j_1} = r_{i,j} \left| Commonity = \sum_{i=1}^c \lambda_1^2 = R^2 \right| \tag{2}
$$

Analysis of the results only selected the items with factor loading greater than 0.4. However, Feedback and Interaction consider the interaction to be appropriate and include it as the first factor. In addition, factors such as Learnability, Satisfaction, Uniformity, Consistency consider experience to be appropriate, so they are defined in the second factor. Grasp ability is a physical factor so that making it a third factor. Although it was finally classified as Attractive, it was classified as the fourth element with factor loading higher than 0.4.

The classification factors are shown in Table 2, and the reliability of the four factors is analyzed respectively. We have summarized that

1. Interaction support is the principle that must be provided in the Interaction between user and interface.
2. Experience support is the principle that users feel after Interaction.
3. Learning support is an understanding-related principle in user usage.
4. Emotional support is a principle related to the user's Emotional support.
5. Cognitive support is the principle that the user should provide in the Cognitive augmented reality UI Model.

Table 2. Principal component analysis

Variable	Component					
	1	2	3	4	5	6
Controllability	**.916**	.242	.074	.066	−.148	−.168
Direct manipulation	**.902**	.270	.115	.047	−.157	.057
Input method	**.744**	−.019	−.094	.003	−.032	.189
Interaction	**.718**	.231	−.187	.204	−.143	.406
User control	**.692**	.420	−.072	.246	.295	.359
Efficiency	**.614**	.384	−.043	.100	.506	.208
Feedback	.073	**.861**	.125	.006	.239	.223
Ease	.254	**.860**	−.039	.257	.145	−.036
Learnability	.360	**.857**	.092	.048	.193	−.104
Simplicity	.181	**.850**	−.066	.121	.067	−.242
Predictability	.138	−.010	**.897**	−.039	.267	.146
Consistency	−.337	.190	**.785**	.056	−.225	.143
Familiarity	−.141	−.286	**.778**	−.110	.336	−.086
Visibility	.009	.036	−.148	**.837**	−.091	.157
Size	.335	.101	.353	**.819**	−.206	.019
Attractiveness	.197	.236	−.122	**.778**	−.247	−.193
Arrangement	−.100	.105	.321	**.752**	.352	−.250
Subjective satisfaction	−.105	.264	.088	−.114	**.906**	−.153
Effectiveness	−.105	.264	.088	−.114	**.906**	−.153
Tolerance principle	.212	−.041	.426	−.008	−.065	**.743**
Durability	.266	−.035	−.362	−.085	−.205	**.713**
Accuracy	.001	.221	−.060	.414	.369	−.573
Prevention	.258	.020	−.343	−.103	.138	−.037
Error indication	.092	.052	−.294	.221	−.140	−.153
Congruity	.199	.179	**.683**	.297	−.116	−.117

Table 3. Reliability analysis of different factors

Cause	Element	Alpha of Cronbach
Interaction support	Controllability, Input method, Direct, Manipulation, User control, Interaction, Efficiency	.882
Learning support	Feedback, Ease, Learnability, Simplicity	.931
Experience support	Predictability, Consistency, Congruity	.757
Cognitive support	Visibility, Size, Attractiveness, Arrangement, Accuracy	.827
Emotional support	Effectiveness, Subjective satisfaction, Familiarity	.616

The results of reliability analysis were 0.882, 0.931 0.757, 0.827, 0.616. All of them were confirmed to be above 0.6 reliability (Table 3).

2.4   Discussion and Conclusion

The usability evaluation strategy in this study has reclassified and systematized the current evaluation indexes of GUI objects, focusing on the network and PC in the AR environments. The completed usability taxonomy has been developed as an evaluation system and can be used for both AR usability evaluation and UI design process research in an AR environment. However, up to now, most of the research about AR is technology-focused, but extensive research considering human factors is limited. Further development of the AR environment will require the development of specific evaluation plans that take into account actual users and evaluations of experts and general users.

We have studied and found that specific usability principles for UI in the augmented reality are different from the usability used in the current Interaction support, Learning support Experience, Cognitive support, and Emotional support based on the following principles,

It is essential that all illustrations are clear and legible. Vector graphics (rather than rasterized images) should be used for diagrams and schemas whenever possible. Please check that the lines in line drawings are not interrupted and have a constant width. Grids and details within the figures must be clearly legible and may not be written one on top of the other. Line drawings are to have a resolution of at least 800 dpi (preferably 1200 dpi). The lettering in figures should not use font sizes smaller than 6 pt (~ 2 mm character height). Figures are to be numbered and to have a caption which should always be positioned under the figures, in contrast to the caption be- longing to a table, which should always appear above the table. Figures and Tables should be cross referred in the text.

1. The element of Interaction support is the element of an application in an existing GUI, but it reflects the Input method feature of the augmented reality. Taking the Input method feature as an example, this study has identified the augmented reality factor for UI effects in a variety of hunting environments as a valid factor, which has not been well studied in depth in the existing GUI environment.
2. Regarding Learning support, simplicity is the specific factor that is reflected in the Learning support factor to prevent confusion from the varied input.
3. In the case of Cognitive support factors, the focus of the specific factor is the importance of natural interactions under augmented reality objectives.
4. If the existing heuristics evaluate the use of fast and simple systems, the concept of sensibility should be emphasized in augmented reality environments.

This work has studied usability elements to make it easy and fast to evaluate usability in the AR interface design. Based on the existing research in the augmented reality environment, the suitable items were extracted with users-focus. 25 items were finally selected with comprehensive statistics. In order to use the final selected usability elements in the augmented reality entity interface, the elements have been redefined. The original concept of the element is materialized to conform to the augmented reality environment. The usability elements were systematized and classified as Interaction support, Learning support, Experience support, Cognition support, Emotion support, etc. Reliability analysis has proved these factors.

References

1. Chung, W.: A study on usability evaluation tool in virtual reality platform. J. Korea Inst. Ind. Des. **13**(1), 117–126 (2019)
2. Lee, Y.: Development of outdoor augmented reality based 3D visualization application for realistic experience of structures. J. Korea Inst. Electron. Commun. Sci. **10**(2), 305–310 (2015)
3. Hoffman, D.L., Novak, T.P.: Marketing in hypermedia computer-mediated environments: conceptual foundations. J. Mark. **60**(3), 50–68 (1996)
4. Lee, S.: Study of User Interface Architecture Design for Augmented Display. Master's Thesis, Product Design, Department of Kookmin University (2012)
5. Jang, S.: The significance of semiology for visual web interface. J. Korea Inst. Electron. Commun. Sci. **13**(4), 795–802 (2018)
6. Kim, D.: Research on emotional experience-based UI design to improve use of weather applications. J. Korean Soc. Des. Cult. **25**(1), 29–38 (2019)
7. Jung, B.: The study of usability evaluation in the GUI of mobile computing-based on benchmark testing in the interface design of WIPI. J. Korean Des. Soc. **17**, 49–56 (2004)
8. Shi, W., Yang, X.: Usability of public terminal interface. Packag. Eng. **37**(6), 62 (2016)
9. Kies, J.K., Williges, R.C., Rosson, M.B.: Coordinating computer supported cooperative work: a review of research issues and strategies. J. Am. Soc. Inf. Sci. **49**, 776–791 (1998)
10. Young, I., Jeff, V.: Mental Models: Aligning Design Strategy with Human Behavior, p. 299. Rosenfeld Media, New York (2008)
11. Nielsen, J., Landauer, T.K.: A mathematical model of the finding of usability problems. In: Proceedings ACM/IFIP INTERCHI 93 Conference, Amsterdam, pp. 206–213 (1993)
12. Azuma, R.: Recent advance in augmented reality. IEEE Comput. Graph. Appl. **21**(6), 34–47 (2001)
13. Han, M.H.: Gartner Top 10 strategic technology trends for 2017. J. Korean Soc. Mech. Eng. **57**, 34–47 (2017)
14. Nielsen, J., Mack, R.L.: Usability Inspection Methods. Wiley, New York (1994)
15. Robin, J.: Usability Engineering: Improving customer Satisfaction While Lowering Development Costs. Sunsoft report (1993)
16. ISO/IEC 9241-11, Ergonomic requirements for office work with visual display terminals (VDTs) - Part11 Guidance on usability. ISO/IEC, Piscataway, N.J. (1998)
17. ISO/IEC 9126-1, Software engineering – Product quality –Part 1 Quality model. ISO/IEC, Piscataway, N.J. (2001)
18. Lee, S.: A Study on Satisfaction of User Interface Design for Social Network Game Usability Improvement-Focused on the Game between Kakao talk in Korea and wechat in China. Master's Thesis, Graduate School of Hanyang University (2017)
19. Jim, H.: (A) study on the free rail pass application GUI design through UI utility evaluation: focused on domestic youth pass Railro. Master's Thesis, Communication Design School of Sungkyunkwan University (2015)
20. Kim, J.: Introduction to HCI. Anti graphics, Seoul (2005)

Research on a Washout Algorithm for 2-DOF Motion Platforms

Zhejun Liu[1] , Qin Guo[1] , Zhifeng Jin[2(✉)] , and Guodong Yu[1]

[1] Tongji University, 1239 Siping Road, Shanghai 200092,
People's Republic of China
{wingeddreamer,1833496,1833497}@tongji.edu.cn
[2] Shanghai Academy of Spaceflight Technology, 3888 Yuanjiang Road,
Shanghai 201109, People's Republic of China
397446509@QQ.com

Abstract. This paper proposes a new washout algorithm optimized from those designed for 6-DOF Stewart platforms using the Human Vestibular Based Strategy. Its actual effect, from the perspective of user experience, was verified via a within-subject design experiment using a 2-DOF platform with limited rotation angles. The result showed that compared with the common 2-DOF algorithms using the Linear Shrinkage Ratio Strategy, our algorithm provided users with better immersion, presence and overall satisfaction, though no significant difference was found regarding simulator sickness. This positive result demonstrated the potential of the algorithm proposed here and may help to enhance the user experience of various kinds of motion platforms.

Keywords: Usability methods and tools · Vehicle simulation · Washout algorithm · Motion platform · 4D seat

1 Introduction

1.1 Background

Nowadays, motion platforms are widely used in the fields of entertainment, simulation, engineering and research. They have become important tools for training, product development and human-factors engineering all over the world [1–3]. As the demand for motion platforms keeps growing, there are increasingly higher standards for the fidelity of perceived motion. And therefore, advanced motion control techniques are getting more and more attention from researchers.

The motion of a real-life or simulated vehicle is very complex, but the possible movements of motion platforms are usually limited, making them impossible to copy the poses and motion of vehicles strictly. This brings forward the problem of how to convert the motion of a vehicle to motion platform control signals, which is the responsibility of a washout algorithm [4].

Defining the quality of experience and the flexibility of motion platforms, washout algorithms play critical roles in simulation systems. A poorly designed or implemented algorithm may lead to two bad consequences. First, it will affect the verisimilitude of a

J. Y. C. Chen and G. Fragomeni (Eds.): HCII 2020, LNCS 12190, pp. 107–122, 2020.
https://doi.org/10.1007/978-3-030-49695-1_8

simulation. More importantly, it may threaten the security of a motion platform, causing either mechanical damages when a hydraulic cylinder extends over its length limit or, in a worse case, injuries to its users or observers. Contrarily, a good washout algorithm not only ensures the safety and smoothness of a platform, but also makes full use of its ranges of motion.

Since six degree-of-freedom (abbr. 6-DOF) Stewart platforms are common in the industry, there are plenty of research papers based on it, in which the *Human Vestibular Based Strategy* (abbr. HVBS) is the latest trend. A 6-DOF platform might be suitable if the simulation target is a car, a tank or even a boat. But when it comes to aircrafts the limited rotation angles of it pose a big drawback. As a result, new equipment like the 2-DOF platform used in this research has been invented as a supplement. Contrast to 6-DOF platforms, there are very few studies on washout algorithms for 2-DOF ones, hence many of them just ended up using simple and inferior *Linear Shrinkage Ratio Strategy* (abbr. LSRS).

The purpose of this paper is to propose and evaluate a new algorithm for 2-DOF platforms optimized from 6-DOF ones using HVBS.

1.2   Equipment

The equipment used in this research was a 2-DOF platform in the *Immersive Simulation Lab* in the *College of Design and Innovation, Tongji University*, as shown in Fig. 1.

Fig. 1. The 2-DOF platform used in this research

It can rotate approximately from 0° to 40° on the X axis (pitch) and virtually unlimitedly on the Z axis (roll) as shown in Fig. 2.

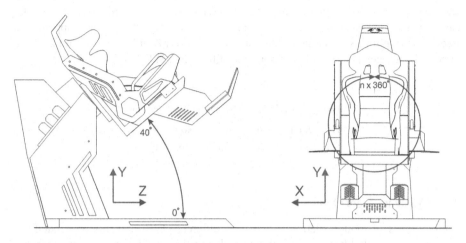

Fig. 2. The freedom of pitch (left) and roll (right)

2 Related Work

2.1 The Vestibular System

The human vestibular system, as shown in Fig. 3 [5], was suggested to be the base of wash algorithm design by Young, Oman and Mayne [6, 7]. It consists semicircular canals and otoliths and acts as human beings' primary organ that senses rotation and acceleration (semicircular canals for angular velocity and the otoliths for linear acceleration).

As far as velocity is concerned, vision is the only sense that provides a clue, which means that to create the illusion of speed, only images of moving environment are required and the platform may stay still [8–10].

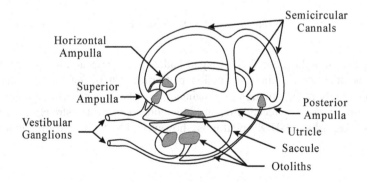

Fig. 3. The vestibular system of human beings

Otoliths work like a low-pass filter, which means that high frequency changes in specific force are not perceivable to human beings. Furthermore, otoliths keep us from sensing linear accelerations smaller than 0.17 m/s^2 in the horizontal directions (left-right and front-back) and 0.28 m/s^2 in the vertical direction (up-down). Similarly, semicircular canals work like a band-pass filter, allowing us to sense only the rotations happening at frequencies within a specific range. Agular velocity lower than 3.6°/s, 3°/s and 2.6°/s in pitch, roll and yaw respectively are not perceptible either [11, 12].

Table 1. Thresholds of human beings' sensation

Horizontal	Vertical	Pitch	Roll	Yaw
0.17 m/s^2	0.28 m/s^2	3.6°/s	3°/s	2.6°/s

2.2   Washout Algorithms

Various types of motion platforms and their different DOFs and motion capabilities must be coped with differently, which means there is no omnipotent washout algorithm suitable for all. Two commonly used strategies are briefly introduced below.

Linear Shrinkage Ratio Strategy (LSRS) is a strategy that simply scales the input rotation degree by a coefficient k and clamps the out-of-domain values as shown in Fig. 4 [13].

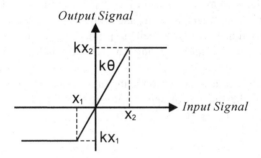

Fig. 4. The LSRS function curve

Being fast, straight forward and easy to understand, LSRS and its variants used to be quite popular for all kinds of motion platforms. But owing to its limitation in presenting widely ranged motion and maintaining sensory consistency (vision versus body motion), it has been recently replaced by more sophisticated strategies for 6-DOF platforms. Regarding 2-DOF platforms, however, LSRS is still the mainstream strategy.

Human Vestibular Based Strategy (HVBS)

There have been plenty studies on the HVBS for 6-DOF Stewart platforms, among which the classic algorithm introduced by Nahon et al. [14] was typical (Fig. 5).

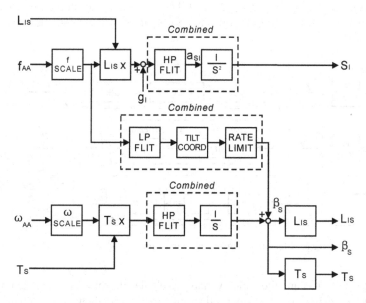

Fig. 5. The classic HVBS algorithm

The algorithm processes the input specific force (f_{AA}) with a high-pass filter (HP FLIT) and a low-pass filter (LP FLIT). The former keeps the high-frequency acceleration information, which is most perceptible to human beings, and converts it to minor linear movements of the platform. The longer, more consistent low-frequency acceleration was converted to platform rotation so that it can be mimicked with a gravity component.

For angular velocity (ω_{AA}), the algorithm keeps the most perceptible high-frequency part with a high-pass filter and discards the much less noticeable low-frequency part.

The processed data above was combined to determine the final orientation of the platform.

This strategy is broadly accepted thanks to its conciseness and high performance.

3 Our Algorithm

3.1 Overview

The differences between a 6-DOF Steward platform and the 2-DOF platform used in this study mainly include: 1) A 6-DOF platform can rotate on all three axes while the 2-DOF platform can only pitch and roll; 2) A 6-DOF platform can roll very limitedly, while the 2-DOF platform can roll freely by multiple 360° turns, making it possible to copy that rotation component of a simulated vehicle faithfully. 3) A 6-DOF platform may be manoeuvred to produce minor linear movements, while the 2-DOF platform can only rotate.

We modified and optimized the classic 6-DOF washout algorithm introduced above to accommodate the 2-DOF platform. Figure 6 is an overview of its mechanism.

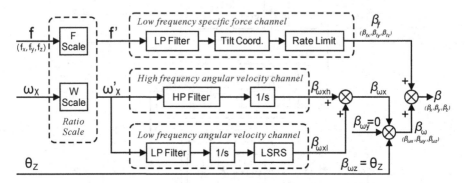

Fig. 6. Mechanism of our algorithm for the 2-DOF platform

On the left side are the input variables calculated from the simulated vehicle, including f, ω_x and θ_z. f is the calculated specific force exerted on the vestibular system. ω_x is the angular velocity on the X axis (pitch). θ_z is the angle on the Z axis (rol). f and ω_x are ratio scaled expand or shrink the value domain, yielding f' and ω_x'. In our case, the ratios equal 1 so f = f' and $\omega_x = \omega_x'$.

The low frequency part of f' was separated with a low-pass filter (LP Filter), and then converted to pitch or roll angles with the "Tilt Coordination" (Tilt Coord.) approach so that a component of gravity can be employed to simulate an acceleration not pointing downwards. Finally, the change rate of it must be controlled (Rate Limit) under a threshold value (see Table 1) to keep the semicircular canals from sensing it as an angular motion. As for the high frequency part of f', which is usually converted to linear motion of a 6-DOF platform, is discarded here because the 2-DOF platform doesn't support translation.

ω_x' is also separated into high and low frequency parts with filters (HP Filter and LP Filter). The high frequency part usually contains those quick and small turns most sensible to human beings. This information is converted to angle values by computing the first integral (1/s). The low frequency part, usually discarded by 6-DOF platforms, cannot be ignored in the case of 2-DOF platforms because an airborne or spatial vehicle usually have a much larger and unneglectable pitch angle than a ground vehicle, which is the first integral of these low frequency turns (1/s). Considering that our 2-DOF platform has limited pitch as shown in Fig. 2, we adopted the linear shrinkage ratio strategy (LSRS) to constrain its amplitude.

Eventually, the angular vector calculated from specific force (β_f) and the angular vector calculated from the orientation (β_ω) were added up as β to determine the final orientation of the motion platform.

The important parts of our algorithm are explained in more details below.

3.2 The Ratio Scale Functions

The ratio scale is done simply with two multipliers k_f and $k_{\omega x}$ as shown below:

$$f' = f \times k_f, \omega'_x = \omega_x \times k_{\omega x} \tag{1}$$

3.3 The Low Frequency Specific Force Channel

The low frequency specific force channel uses a second-order low-pass filter as shown below.

$$a_l^x = a_x \left(\frac{\omega_{lx}^2}{s^2 + 2\xi_{lx}\omega_{lx}s + \omega_{lx}^2} \right) \tag{2}$$

In this equation, ξ and ω are respectively the non-dimensional damping factor and the cut-off frequency (rad/s) of the low pass filter for specific force.

To simulate horizonal acceleration, the platform must be tilted to allow a component of gravity to create that illusion. This approach is called "tilt coordination". But since it's not possible to simulate vertical acceleration with a gravity component, tilt coordination is limited to work with accelerations in the front, back, left and right directions only [15, 16].

The pitch angle is calculated with the following equation.

$$\theta = -arcsin\left[a_y/(g \cos \emptyset)\right] \tag{3}$$

The roll angle is calculated with the following equation.

$$\emptyset = -arcsin(a_x/g) \tag{4}$$

3.4 The High Frequency Angular Velocity Channel

The equation used to perform high-pass filter is as follows.

$$\dot{\theta}_h = \dot{\theta} \left(\frac{s^2}{s^2 + 2\xi_{h\theta}\omega_{h\theta} + \omega_{h\theta}^2} \right) \tag{5}$$

In this equation, ξ and ω are respectively the non-dimensional damping factor and the cut-off frequency (rad/s) of the high pass filter for angular velocity.

3.5   The Low Frequency Angular Velocity Channel

The equation used to perform low-pass filter is as follows.

$$\dot{\theta}_l = \dot{\theta}\left(\frac{\omega_{l\theta}^2}{s^2 + 2\xi_{l\theta}\omega_{l\theta}s + \omega_{l\theta}^2}\right) \tag{6}$$

In this equation, ξ and ω are respectively the non-dimensional damping factor and the cut-off frequency (rad/s) of the low pass filter for angular velocity.

The linear shrinkage was performed using the following equation.

$$\dot{\theta} = \begin{cases} k\theta, & x_1 < \theta < x_2 \\ kx_1, & \theta \le x_1 \\ kx_2, & \theta \ge x_2 \end{cases} \quad (x_1 < x_2) \tag{7}$$

4   Experiment

4.1   Hypotheses

Hypothesis 1: Compared with the algorithm using LSRS (abbr. LSRS algorithm), ours shall prevail in immersion and presence thanks to the introduction of tilt coordination and the inclusion of the high-frequency rotational movements which would have been clamped by LSRS when the angular threshold is reached.

Hypothesis 2: Our algorithm shall have better simulator sickness (abbr. SS) level. This is because one of the causes of SS is sensory conflict [17] and our algorithm is expected to offer closer to real world and more consistent sensory experience.

Hypothesis 3: Our algorithm is expected to yield higher overall satisfaction because it has the capacity to present users with more acceleration and rotation information discarded by the LSRS algorithm, which tends to result in better realism and more excitement.

4.2   Material

To compare the LSRS algorithm with ours, we developed a VR flight simulator with the Unity engine. Users will enter a futuristic aircraft when they put on the head mounted display (abbr. HMD) and start their trip in a modern city. The aircraft accelerates gradually from a stationary status and gradually climbs up until it reaches a certain height. Then it decelerates and hovers there. Meanwhile, a ferry vessel approaches and pushes the aircraft horizontally from the left side to a huge mothership and docks it there (Fig. 7).

Fig. 7. Screenshot of the test material

The simulator has two versions using the LSRS algorithm and ours respectively. The LSRS version used these coefficients: Sx = 1, x ∈ [0°,40°]. The coefficients used in our algorithm are shown in Table 2, where LFSF means "low frequency specific force", HFAV means "high frequency angular velocity" and LFAV means "low frequency angular velocity".

Table 2. Coefficients used by our algorithm

Filter	ω	ζ	Ratio Scale Funtion		
LFSF	9.81	1	$K_f=1$		$K_{\omega x}=1$
HFAV	245.44	1	Linear Shrinkage Ratio		
LFAV.	245.44	1	$S_x=1$	$x_1=0$	$x_2=35$

The total length of the trip is 130 s. Because the two algorithms in many cases perform similarly, we carefully arranged 3 segments in order to reveal the differences.

Segment 1 is the accelerating phase when the aircraft thrusts forward. In this phase, our algorithm simulates the forward acceleration with tilt coordination and changes the pitch angle of the seat, while the LSRS algorithm does not. The acceleration and the pitch angle curves are shown in Fig. 8.

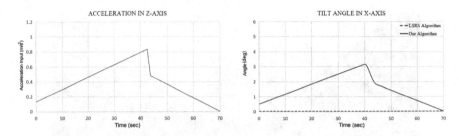

Fig. 8. Curves from the accelerating phase

Segment 2 is the bumpy phase when the aircraft climbs with its nose tilted upward. In this phase, our algorithm is still capable of representing the wavy rotation while the LSRS clamps this information because the pitch angle exceeds the 40° threshold. The rotation and the pitch angle curves are shown in Fig. 9.

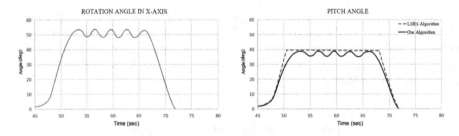

Fig. 9. Curves from the bumpy phase

Segment 3 is the dock-in phase when the aircraft is moved to the right by a ferry vessel and goes through an "accelerating > reaching max speed > decelerating process". In this phase, our algorithm simulates the horizontal acceleration and deceleration with tilt coordination and changes the roll angle of the seat, while the LSRS algorithm does not. The acceleration and the roll angle curves are shown in Fig. 10.

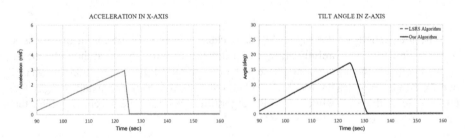

Fig. 10. Curves from the dock-in phase

4.3   Measures

Presence, immersion and simulator sickness were measured using the presence questionnaire by Martin Usoh et al. [18], the immersion questionnaire by Jennett C et al. [19] and the simulator sickness questionnaire by Kennedy et al. [20]. They were modified to suit the actual situation. See Table 3, Table 4 and Table 5.

The overall satisfaction was measured with two questions: "Which virtual experience gave you better experience?" and "Why do you prefer it over the other one?"

Table 3. Presence questionnaire

	Questions & Options
1	Did you have a sense of "being there" in the aircraft? (1: Not at all ~ 5: Very much)
2	To what extent were there times during the experience when the virtual space was the reality for you? (1: No time at all ~ 5: Almost all the time)
3	Do you think of the aircraft more as a miniature that you saw, or more as a real vehicle that you drove? (1: Miniature ~ 5: Real vehicle)
4	During the time of the experience, which was strongest on the whole, your sense of being in the aircraft, or of being elsewhere? (1: In the aircraft ~ 5: Elsewhere)
5	During the time of experience, did the motion of the chair feel realistic to you? (1: Very unrealistic ~ 5: Very realistic)
6	Consider your memory of being in the aircraft. How similar in terms of the structure of the memory is this to that of other transportation or entertaining vehicles you have used before? (1: Not similar at all ~ 2: Very similar)

Table 4. Immersion questionnaire

	Questions & Options
1	To what extent did you feel you were focused on the game? (1: Not at all ~ 5. Very Focused)
2	To what extent did you lose track of time? (1: No time at all ~ 5: Almost always)
3	To what extent did you feel as though you were separated from your real-world environment? (1: Not at all ~ 5: Very much)
4	To what extent did you enjoy the graphics and the imagery? (1: Not at all ~ 5: Very much)
5	To what extent did you enjoy the motion of the chair? (1: Not at all ~ 5: Very much)
6	How much would you say you enjoyed the experience? (1: Dislike it very much ~ 5: Enjoyed it very much)
7	Would you like to play the game again? (1: Not at all ~ 5: Very eager to)

Table 5. Simulator sickness questionnaire

	Question: To what extent did you suffer from the following symptoms during the experience you just had?	Options
1	General discomfort	1: Not at all
2	Fatigue	2: Slight
3	Headache	3: Moderate
4	Eyestrain	4: Severe
5	Difficulty focusing	
6	Salivation increasing	
7	Sweating	
8	Nausea	
9	Difficulty concentrating	
10	Fullness of the head	
11	Blurred vision	
12	Dizziness with eyes open	
13	Dizziness with eyes closed	
14	Vertigo	
15	Stomach awareness	
16	burping	

4.4 Subjects

22 subjects participated in the experiment. Their demographic data is shown in Table 6. There were inquiries about their health status before the experiment to make sure that they had normal vision and no potential physical or psychological problem of experiencing VR on a motion platform.

Table 6. Demographic data of the subjects

Gender		Age			Profession	
Male	Female	Average	Min	Max	Student	Designer
13	9	23.3	19	29	21	1

4.5 Apparatus

The experiment used high performance workstations running Windows 10 64bit version, as shown in Table 7. HTC Vive Pro, featuring a 110° viewing angle and a resolution of 1440 × 1600 pixels each eye, was used as the HMD device in the experiment. This guaranteed that user experience, especially in the HMD environment, would not be jeopardized by low framerate or poor visual quality.

Table 7. Hardware specification

CPU	Intel i7 9700	Graphic Card	NVIDIA Geforce 2070
Memory	16 GB	Harddrive	512 GB SSD
Display	65-inch LCD TV	HMD	HTC Vive Pro

The specification of the 2-DOF platform used in the experiment can be found in the introduction part at the beginning of this paper.

4.6   Procedure

The within-subject design experiment was carried out in the Immersive Simulation Lab in Tongji University. Subjects were asked to enter the lab one by one and went through the experimental procedure individually. They were randomly assigned to either group A (n = 12) or group B (n = 10) to minimize the bias caused by the carryover effect. The difference between them was that in Group A subjects experienced the LSRS algorithm first and then our algorithm followed, while Group B used a reversed order.

Figure 11 is a graphical description of the experimental procedure.

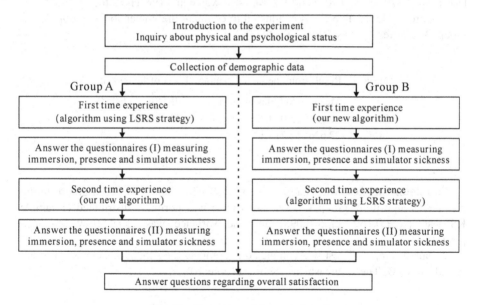

Fig. 11. Procedure of the experiment

5 Results and Discussion

5.1 Results

Presence was analyzed with SPSS v22. The data in each group (group A = LSRS algorithm, group B = our algorithm) was normally distributed (1-sample KS test, $p_A = 0.842$, $p_B = 0.939$) and the variance was equal (Levene's test, p = 0.478).

A paired samples T-test was conducted to compare the presence of group A and group B. The result is as follows (Table 8).

Table 8. Result from the paired samples T-test of presence

	Mean	Std. deviation	t	df	Sig. (2-tailed)
Group A	25.0000	6.00000	−3.440	21	0.002
Group B	27.5909	5.86888			

Immersion was analyzed with SPSS v22. The data in each group (group A = LSRS algorithm, group B = our algorithm) was normally distributed (1-sample KS test, $p_A = 0.979$, $p_B = 0.801$) and the variance was equal (Levene's test, p = 0.803).

A paired samples T-test was conducted to compare the immersion of group A and group B. The result is as follows (Table 9).

Table 9. Result from the paired samples T-test of Immersion

	Mean	Std. deviation	t	df	Sig. (2-tailed)
Group A	19.9545	5.00930	−4.557	21	0.000
Group B	22.6364	4.71619			

Simulator Sickness was analyzed with SPSS v22. The data in each group (group A = LSRS algorithm, group B = our algorithm) was normally distributed (1-sample KS test, $p_A = 0.169$, $p_B = 0.098$) and the variance was equal (Levene's test, p = 0.071).

A paired samples T-test was conducted to compare the simulator sickness of group A and group B. The result was as follows (Table 10).

Table 10. Result from the paired samples T-test of simulator sickness

	Mean	Std. deviation	t	df	Sig. (2-tailed)
Group A	95.2000	18.34860	−1.064	21	0.299
Group B	99.2800	29.93619			

Overall Satisfaction. 19 out of 22 subjects preferred our algorithm over the LSRS one, which is overwhelming. The reasons mentioned include: realism (n = 14), novelty (n = 2), excitement (n = 2) and less simulator sickness (n = 1).

5.2   Discussion

As expected, our algorithm performed better regarding presence and immersion. Many subjects reported they could clearly feel the acceleration and deceleration especially during the dock-in phase, which meant that tilt coordination worked pretty well and fulfilled its goal. On the contrary, the LSRS algorithm virtually kept the seat stationary during these phases and did not offer any sensation of body movement. The situation was similar for the bumpy phase where LSRS algorithm failed to present over-threshold rotation while our algorithm coped with it cleverly. All these advantages of our algorithm resulted in a better eye-body coordination, a stronger feeling of "being there", and thus a higher level of presence and immersion. And therefore, it's natural that most subjects thought our algorithm provided better overall satisfaction than the LSRS one.

As for simulator sickness, we expected our algorithm to yield better result but no significant difference was found. A reasonable conjecture is that too many factors, e.g. latency, field of view, resolution etc., influence SS and the difference between the two comparative algorithms was not big enough to cause significantly different performance. Another reason may be that the experimental material developed by us was meant to focus on handling acceleration and over-threshold rotation instead of SS. The whole experience was not likely to inflict strong SS, which further reduced the perceivable difference. It will be valuable to devise other experiments dedicated to the study of SS caused by both in the future.

6   Conclusion

This paper proposed a new washout algorithm optimized to suit the special characteristics of a 2-DOF platform based on the HVBS strategy for 6-DOF platforms. It was compared with the widely used LSRS algorithm for 2-DOF platforms via a within-subject design experiment and was proven to be significantly better regarding immersion and presence. It is reasonable to believe that our algorithm is capable of enhancing user experience from 2-DOF platforms. Though this research was based on the 2-DOF platform of a specific type, the findings and conclusions may very like be extended to other models.

Acknowledgement. This work is part of a joint research project hosted by the College of Design and Innovation, Tongji University and Shanghai Academy of Spaceflight Technology, with the help from Topow (Jiangsu) Research Institute of Virtual Reality Technologies Co., Ltd.

References

1. Kim, J.H., Lee, W.S., Park, I.K., et al.: A design and characteristic analysis of the motion base for vehicle driving simulator. In: Proceedings 6th IEEE International Workshop on Robot and Human Communication. RO-MAN 1997 SENDAI, Piscataway, Sendai, pp. 290–294 (1997)
2. Liao, C.S., Huang, C.F., Chieng, W.H.: A novel washout filter design for a six degree-of-freedom motion simulator. JSME Int. J. Ser. C Mech. Syst. Mach. Elem. Manuf. 47(2), 626–636 (2004)
3. Sivan, R., Ish-Shalom, J., Huang, J.K.: An optimal control approach to the design of moving flight simulators. IEEE Trans. Syst. Man Cybern. 12(6), 818–827 (1982)
4. Usman, M.: A novel washout algorithm for ground vehicles. In: 2013 3rd IEEE International Conference on Computer, Control and Communication (IC4), Piscataway, Karachi, pp. 1–6 (2013)
5. Ravichandran, K.: Driving simulator for tracked vehicles using Stewart platform manipulator. In: INTERACT-2010, N/A, Chennai, pp. 245–249 (2010)
6. Young, L.R., Oman, C.M.: Part II: a model for vestibular adaptation to horizontal rotation. In: Fourth Symposium on the Role of the Vestibular Organs in Space Exploration, Scientific and Technical Information Division, pp: 363. National Aeronautics and Space, Washington (1970)
7. Mayne, R.: A systems concept of the vestibular organs. In: Kornhuber, H.H. (ed.) Vestibular System Part 2: Psychophysics, Applied Aspects and General Interpretations. Handbook of Sensory Physiology, vol. 62, pp. 493–580. Springer, Heidelberg (1974). https://doi.org/10.1007/978-3-642-65920-1_14
8. Baseggio, M., Beghi, A., Bruschetta, M., et al.: An MPC approach to the design of motion cueing algorithms for driving simulators. In: 2011 14th International IEEE Conference on Intelligent Transportation Systems (ITSC), Piscataway, Washington, DC, pp. 692–697 (2011)
9. Chen, H.: Modeling, Prediction and Control. Ke xue chu ban she (2013)
10. Meiry, J.L.: The vestibular system and human dynamic space orientation. Man-Vehicle Control Laboratory (1966)
11. Rodenburg, M., Stassen, H.P.W., Maas, A.J.J.: The threshold of perception of angular acceleration as a function of duration. Biol. Cybern. 39(3), 223–226 (1981)
12. Pouliot, N.A., Gosselin, C.M., Nahon, M.A.: Motion simulation capabilities of three-degree-of-freedom flight simulators. J. Aircr. 35(1), 9–17 (1998)
13. Xiao, H.: A Study of the Algorithm for 6-DOF Platforms. Beijing Jiaotong University, Beijing (2014)
14. Nahon, M.A., Reid, L.D.: Simulator motion-drive algorithms-a designer'sperspective. J. Guid. Control Dyn. 13(2), 356–362 (1990)
15. Barbagli, F., Ferrazzin, D., Avizzano, C.A., et al.: Washout filter design for a motorcycle simulator. In: Proceedings IEEE Virtual Reality, N/A, Yokohama, pp. 225–232 (2001)
16. Yu, Z.: Automobile Theories. Machinery Industry Press, Beijing (2000)
17. Oman, C.M.: Motion sickness: a synthesis and evaluation of the sensory conflict theory. Can. J. Physiol. Pharmacol. 68(2), 294–303 (1990)
18. Usoh, M., Catena, E., Arman, S., et al.: Using presence questionnaires in reality. Presence Teleoper. Virtual Environ. 9(5), 497–503 (2000)
19. Jennett, C., Cox, A.L., Cairns, P., et al.: Measuring and defining the experience of immersion in games. Int. J. Hum. Comput. Stud. 66(9), 641–661 (2008)
20. Kennedy, R.S., Lane, N.E., Berbaum, K.S., et al.: Simulator sickness questionnaire: an enhanced method for quantifying simulator sickness. Int. J. Aviat. Psychol. 3(3), 203–220 (1993)

Usability of the Virtual Agent Interaction Framework

David Novick[(⊠)], Mahdokht Afravi, Oliver Martinez,
Aaron Rodriguez, and Laura J. Hinojos

University of Texas at El Paso, El Paso, TX 79968, USA
novick@utep.edu, mmafravi@gmail.com,
{omartinez14, aerodriguez14}@miners.utep.edu,
hinojoslj@gmail.com

Abstract. The Virtual Agent Interaction Framework (VAIF) is an authoring tool for creating virtual-reality applications with embodied conversational agents. VAIF is intended for use by both expert and non-expert users, in contrast with more sophisticated and complex development tools such as the Virtual Human Toolkit. To determine if VAIF is actually usable by a range of users, we conducted a two-phase summative usability test, with a total of 43 participants. We also tried porting to VAIF a scene from an earlier VR application. The results of the usability study suggest that people with little or even no experience in creating embodied conversational agents can install VAIF and build inter-action scenes from scratch, with relatively low rates of encountering problem episodes. However, the usability testing disclosed aspects of VAIF and its user's guide that could be improved to reduce the number of problem episodes that users encounter.

Keywords: Authoring systems · Virtual reality · Embodied conversational agents

1 Introduction

As embodied conversational agents (ECAs) in virtual reality become more ubiquitous, development of these applications becomes correspondingly burdensome. Authoring systems for ECAs hold the promise of making development of these applications simpler, faster, and more accessible. The Virtual Human Toolkit (VHT) [1] was the first publicly available development environment for ECAs; VHT is a collection of tools and resources intended for use by researchers and other sophisticated users. The Virtual Agent Interaction Framework (VAIF) [2] is a more recent authoring tool available on GitHub; VAIF is an asset for the Unity development platform and is intended for use by both expert and non-expert users.

Because VHT is a collection of advanced tools provided primarily for researchers, some people have found it difficult to use. And because VAIF is intended to support both experts and non-experts, it should be much easier to use. But is VAIF actually usable for developers? Or even for non-computer-science novice developers? This paper examines whether VAIF is, in fact, easy to use.

J. Y. C. Chen and G. Fragomeni (Eds.): HCII 2020, LNCS 12190, pp. 123–134, 2020.
https://doi.org/10.1007/978-3-030-49695-1_9

To determine VAIF's ease of use, we conducted a two-phase usability study, with a total of 43 participants. The first phase had 22 participants with technical backgrounds, and the second phase had 21 participants with non-technical backgrounds. The results of the study indicate that users of VAIF are able to complete representative tasks with low error rates.

2 Background

Designing human-virtual agent interactions is complicated, with many chances for errors. Some tools, such as the NPCEditor [3], enable developers to build interactions in a question-and-answer format. But the design of interactions involving only one agent is further complicated when we want to build interactions that are not limited to simple call-and-response systems, such as more natural conversations with a conversational agent (e.g., [4]). VHT, of which NPCEditor is a part, can handle multiparty interactions with several agents (e.g., [5]) but is really aimed at researchers rather than developers.

The Virtual Agent Interaction Framework was developed as an easy-to-use package for the Unity game engine that reduces the time required to build dyadic and multiparty interactions with virtual agents. VAIF is a Unity asset that is publicly available on GitHub and includes resources such as a user guide, tutorial videos published on YouTube, and a README. The VAIF Unity package is 72.8 MB, including the agent prefabs and code.

VAIF and its applications were developed to enable research into rapport between ECA and human, with particular emphasis on multimodal, multiparty, virtual or augmented reality interaction. VAIF provides an extensive array of features that enable ECAs to listen, speak, gesture, move, wait, and remember previous interactions. The system provides a library of sample characters with animations, facial expressions, phonemes for lip-syncing, and a configured test scene. In addition, characters can be assigned a personality and an emotional state to enable the creation of more realistic and responsive characters. Each character can appear in one or multiple timelines of events, and multiple characters can appear on the same timeline.

VAIF is open-source (https://github.com/isguser/VAIF), with a collection of short video tutorials (available at http://bit.ly/2FaL4bW). VAIF requires Unity 2017.1 or later (it is backwards compatible with other versions, but functionality is not guaranteed), and Windows 10 with Cortana enabled for speech recognition. It is also possible to create an interface to other speech-recognition platforms such as Google Speech. VAIF includes multimodal interaction functions such as LookAt, which can detect where the user is looking and InRange, which tracks the user's proxemics.

VAIF works by creating timelines of events. Each character can appear in one or multiple timelines, and multiple characters can appear on the same timeline. A timeline defines things happening in the virtual world, and agents' interactions. VAIF comes with a library of characters that can be used as-is with all of their features. Many developers will be able to build the systems they want with just these characters. Other developers may want to create new characters, and we encourage users of VAIF to contribute their characters to the library.

The agent's emotional state and personality are among the first things to configure. While personality is a read-only variable, as personalities typically should not change during short periods of time (cf., emotions), it can be used to affect agent behavior in conjunction with the character's emotional state. For example, a happy extroverted character will move differently than a happy introverted character. Agents' emotions in VAIF are based on Plutchik's wheel of emotions [6] but can be modified to fit other models of emotion. Likewise, personalities are based on the Myers-Briggs Type Indicator [7] but can be swapped out for other personality models.

Developing a fully working human-ECA interactive system in VAIF involves five steps:

- Choosing one or more agent models from VAIF's character gallery. If needed, developers can use tools outside VAIF, such as Fuse and Mixamo from Adobe, to create characters that can be used in VAIF.
- Integrating and configuring the agents, using VAIF's configuration screens.
- Writing the interaction in VAIF's interaction manager.
- Creating lip-synch for the agents. This is done through an external tool such as Oculus OVRLP.
- Putting the agents in a virtual-reality world. This can be done with an external tool such as VRTK, a Unity asset.

Once the initial emotion and personality have been set, the character status is displayed (see Fig. 1). Characters can be in any subset of the following states:

- Speaking: An audio file is playing and the character is lip-syncing. Animations and movements can be played while on this state.
- Listening: The character is waiting for a verbal response from the user. If this is enabled while the character is on the speaking state, the user can interrupt the character.
- Waiting: Similar to the listening state, the character is waiting for an environment response or user action, such as a visual queue or a script execution (e.g. waiting for the user to grab an item with VR controllers).
- LookAt: The agent is being looked at by the user.
- In-Range: The character is close enough to the user to initiate interaction.
- Moving: The agent is performing a translation in virtual space, such as walking or following another character.

The states are used internally by the system to detect different situations. For example, if the character is in the speaking state and the user talks, the character knows it is being interrupted and can react to it. If the character is waiting, nothing happens; but when the flags for being in-range and being looked-at turn true, the character will switch from waiting to speaking because it found an interlocutor. These states are calculated automatically depending on the interaction state.

The interaction manager is the central piece of the VAIF architecture. A manager is a script that requires no parameters but enables the characters to speak, move, gesture, remember, and look-at. It controls the flow of events across the interaction by creating a sequential timeline of events. VAIF's timelines contain all the events and control all characters' actions. In other words, the interaction manager enables developers to create events that are easy to configure and are applied automatically to the characters (see Fig. 2).

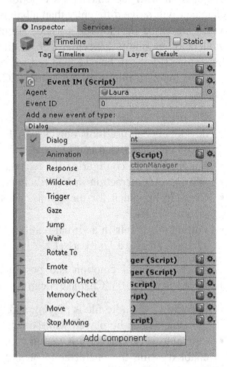

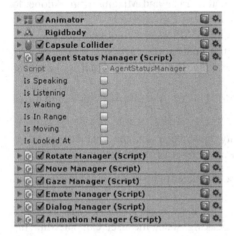

Fig. 1. VAIF controls for character status.   **Fig. 2.** VAIF controls for character events.

Figure 3 shows an example of a complex, multiple-agent scene implemented in VAIF, where the author is building a step in the dialogue for an agent named Laura.

3 Using VHT

Anecdotal reports suggested that even some experts in virtual reality and ECAs found VHT difficult to install and to use, perhaps reflecting VHT's research heritage. To assess this for ourselves, we asked a master's student in computer science, who was familiar with the Unity game engine, try to develop an application with VHT.

The installed VHT toolset was large, with a runtime image of about 10 gigabytes. The student made four attempts to get an agent to listen and talk; the fourth attempt was partly successful. To arrive there, though, the student had to deal with system internals to resolve errors and was unable, despite this, to get the application to work satisfactorily. For example, in Attempt 3, the student reported these actions:

- In Unity, after lots of file searching, I stumble across a prefab called "Globals" inside the Assets > Scripts folder
- I add the Globals prefab to the hierarchy
- I run the scene
- Agent Brad moves to idle position
  - Note: Brad moved to an idle animation
  - Note: I get warnings in the Unity console saying "Unknown actor id "Rachel""
  - I look for a Rachel in the project search bar and nothing was found

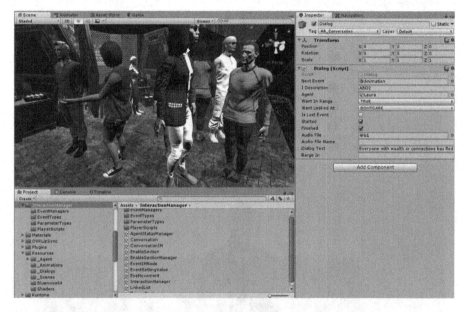

Fig. 3. Partial view of the VAIF interface, where the author is creating a step in the dialogue for an agent named Laura.

Figure 4 shows the part of the VHT interface during Attempt 3. Ultimately, the student reported that

> I did not enjoy spending so long trying to figure out why the tool did not work. I know the agent did not have the correct scripts attached to him, but as someone who doesn't know the inner workings of the tool it would take a very long time for me to figure it out. I write this out of the frustration of the fact that I couldn't use it.

Thus while VHT has a comprehensive set of sophisticated tools and resources, suitable for advanced development of VR-based ECAs, it has a correspondingly high level of difficulty.

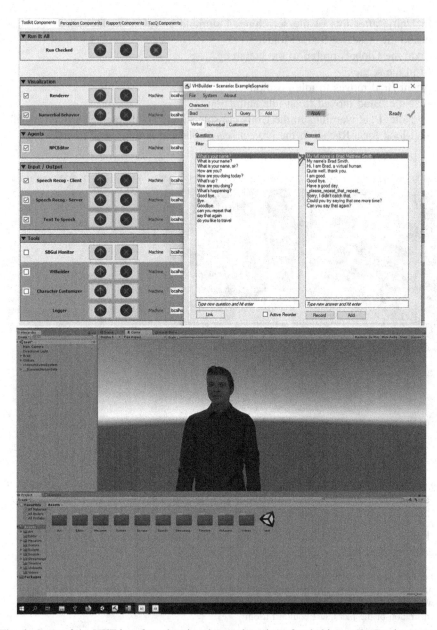

Fig. 4. Parts of the VHT interface showing the user's action of switching to the Brad agent and having the agent perform an action by double-clicking the "My full name is Brad Matthew Smith" answer. The user could see the agent moving and talking but could not hear any audio from the agent.

4   Methodology

To assess whether VAIF is usable in practice by developers of VR applications with ECAs, we conducted summative usability testing in two phases In Phase 1, the participants were students in UTEP's College of Engineering, many of whom were majors in Computer Science. For this phase, we categorized the participants into three groups (novice, intermediate, advanced), depending on their level of experience with the Unity game engine interface and their familiarity with Unity scripting or writing C# code. None of the participants had experience with VAIF. In Phase two, the participants were non-engineering majors, none of whom had experience with either Unity or VAIF.

We asked the participants to install VAIF and then to build, run, and test five agent-based scenes. For purposes of the summative analysis, the participants' activities were divided into five tasks, where Task 0 was the install/build. For each participant and each task, we measured the number of errors and the time taken. The total time for each participant was limited to one hour. If a task went uncompleted in the time allotted for that participant's skill level, the experimenters provided the participant with a new scene that contained all the completed work for the uncompleted task. For example, if a participant did not complete Task 2, the participant was provided with a Unity scene that contained the completed steps for Task 2 so that he or she could begin Task 3. For example, the start of Task 0 included the instructions shown in Fig. 4.

1.   Open Unity and import VAIF
           a.   Download VAIF from GitHub
           b.   Import VAIF
           c.   Use GitHubís README and QUICK HELP GUIDE to get familiari-
                 zed with VAIF
2.   Add the agent Laura (prefab) to the scene
3.   Create a Timeline

Fig. 5. Start of instructions to participants for first task.

Figure 5 shows one of the participants (with face obscured in this image) using the VAIF interface in Unity while working on Task 1. Figure 6 shows the final state of the interface after the participant (with face obscured in this image) completed Task 4.

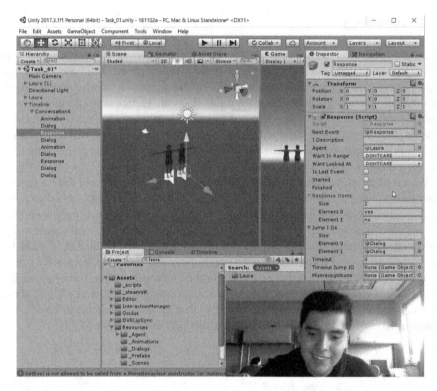

Fig. 6. Study participant using the VAIF interface in Unity while working on Task 1.

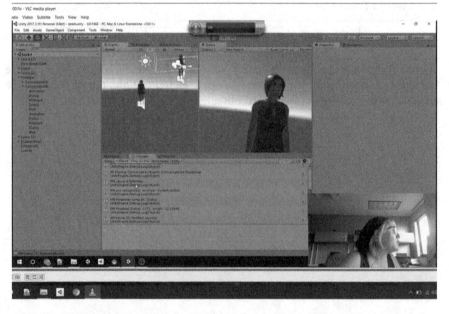

Fig. 7. Study participant using the VAIF interface in Unity while working on Task 1.

5 Results

Phase 1 of the usability study comprised 22 participants, all of whom were engineering majors, and of these most were computer science majors. Overall, these participants had low rates of problems in installing and using VAIF. As shown in Table 1, for four of five tasks, on average the participants encountered fewer that one problem episode per task. Task 1 had an average of 2.75 problem episodes, which could be expected because this was the first task in which the participants were actually implementing an application using VAIF. And, as could also be expected, the number of problem episodes fell sharply for the remaining tasks, as the participants had gained experience with VAIF.

We compared the rates of problem episodes as a function of participants' technical experience. As could be expected, the novice participants encountered more problems than did the intermediate and advanced participants. As shown in Table 2, on average the novice participants experienced about twice as many problems as did the intermediate and advanced participants.

Table 1. Total and mean number of problem episodes for Phase 1 participants using VAIF.

	Task 0	Task 1	Task 2	Task 3	Task 4
Total	19	55	19	19	19
Mean	0.95	2.75	0.95	0.95	0.95

Table 2. Comparison of novice vs. intermediate and advanced participants with respect to mean number of problems encountered.

	Mean
Novice	11.2
Intermed & Adv	5.4

Although most of the participants were introductory computer science students, some had little to no experience with basic functionality with computers, such as navigating through directories, downloading files, and switching between open programs. Nevertheless, two novice participants performed particularly well. One novice user never looked at the guide and only referred to the videos, stating disinterest in reading. This participant completed all tasks successfully, with only five errors across all five tasks. The other participant spent some time reading the guide independently, and then moving forward to complete the remaining tasks flawlessly and with time to spare.

Participants found some tasks easier than others. For example, for Task 0 one participant had no trouble downloading packages but then had some trouble following some of the guidelines in the "Quick Help Guide." In a later task, this participant had trouble with the steps on how to add events: instead of adding a Laura2 agent as instructed, the user added a completely different agent. Ultimately, though, this user mentioned that she found using VAIF a lot of fun because she was enrolled in a graphic design course. Another participant, on Task 1, tried clicking the Laura agent multiple times before just dragging the agent into the scene. On Task 3, this participant was not close enough to the microphone, so VAIF did not hear the participant's response. At the end of the session, this participant, who had never before used Unity, commented that with more practice everything in VAIF is self-explanatory.

Phase 2 of the usability study comprised 21 participants, all of whom were non-engineering majors. Table 3 shows the total and mean number of problem episodes for these participants. We expected that the non-engineering majors would encounter more problem episodes than the participants in Phase 1, and this was in fact the case for most tasks, as shown in Table 4.

Table 3. Total and mean problem episodes for Phase 2 participants using VAIF.

	Task 0	Task 1	Task 2	Task 3	Task 4
Total	15	50	80	35	31
Mean	0.71	2.38	3.81	1.67	1.48

Table 4. Comparison of mean number of problem episodes between Phase 1 and Phase 2.

	Phase 1	Phase 2
Mean	1.31	2.01

All of the Phase 2 participants completed all of the tasks but some needed guidance on the use of GitHub and Unity. Some participants also struggled with finding particular files in directories.

Overall, while many participants were able to successfully complete most or all tasks on their own, other participants had more difficulties. For example, one novice participant had a hard time knowing how to start building conversations. The user guide does cover this, and the participant later found it. The participant needed explanation of Unity functions and had difficulty creating events. The participant repeatedly dragged in animations like dialogues and did not know how to get past this. Similarly, the participant dragged in animations straight into the Laura agent when tasked to add events. However, by Task 3 the participant was getting more comfortable with Unity and was more confident as to what to do.

The Unity and VAIF interfaces could be more intuitive. For example, a participant had trouble with animations and audio files because the participant kept trying to do things on her own instead of following the user's guide. And even with the guide, problems could still occur. For example, the guide did not made it clear where Unity elements were located, and a participant attempted to click or drag events or folders with similar names to task targets.

We further tested VAIF's usability by asking a graduate student to port a scene into VAIF from a much more sophisticated VR application with ECAs, the Boston

Massacre History Experience [8]. The result is shown in Fig. 6. The student was familiar with VAIF and encountered no problems with the interface. However, the student's experience with porting the scene revealed a problem with VAIF's functionality that will be addressed in an update to the tool. Specifically, the Boston Massacre History Experience, like other VR applications developed at UTEP, consists of multiple scenes, but VAIF does not yet have the functionality of switching scenes in Unity. Thus while the first scene was successfully ported to VAIF, it would not be possible in the current version to transition to subsequent scenes.

Fig. 8. Partial view of VAIF interface after porting the first scene of the Boston Massacre History experience.

6   Conclusion

The results of this study suggest that people with little or even no experience in creating ECAs can install VAIF and build interaction scenes from scratch, with relatively low rates of encountering problem episodes. The number of problem episodes appears to decrease, as one would expect, as participants gain experience with Unity and VAIF. VAIF's usability is bounded by the characteristics of Unity's interface. Even so, aspects of VAIF's interface, and its companion user's guide, could be improved to help users avoid some of the problems encountered by participants in the usability study. And our experience in porting a scene to VAIF revealed that VAIF will have to be extended to enable transitions among scenes.

References

1. Gratch, J., Hartholt, A., Dehghani, M., Marsella, S.: Virtual humans: a new toolkit for cognitive science research. In: Proceedings of the Annual Meeting of the Cognitive Science Society, vol. 35, no. 35 (2013)

2. Gris, I., Novick, D.: Virtual Agent Interaction Framework (VAIF): a tool for rapid development of social agents. In: Proceedings of the 17th International Conference on Autonomous Agents and MultiAgent Systems. International Foundation for Autonomous Agents and Multiagent Systems, pp. 2230–2232 ((2018))
3. Leuski, A., Traum, D.R.: NPCEditor: a tool for building question-answering characters. In: LREC (2010)
4. Novick, D., Afravi, M., Camacho, A.: PaolaChat: a virtual agent with naturalistic breathing. In: Chen, J.Y.C., Fragomeni, G. (eds.) VAMR 2018. LNCS, vol. 10909, pp. 351–360. Springer, Cham (2018). https://doi.org/10.1007/978-3-319-91581-4_26
5. Hill Jr., R., Gratch, J., Marsella, S., Rickel, J., Swartout, W., Traum, D.: Virtual humans in the mission rehearsal exercise system. Kynstliche Intelligenz (KI) **17**, 5–12 (2003)
6. Plutchik, R.: A general psychoevolutionary theory of emotion. In: Theories of Emotion, pp. 3–33. Academic Press (1980)
7. Myers, I.B.: The Myers-Briggs Type Indicator: Manual. Consulting Psychologists Press, Palo Alto (1962)
8. Novick, D., et al.: The Boston massacre history experience. In: Proceedings of the 19th ACM International Conference on Multimodal Interaction, pp. 499–500 (2017)

Towards a Predictive Framework for AR Receptivity

Jennifer M. Riley[1] , Jesse D. Flint[1(✉)] , Darren P. Wilson[2] ,
Cali M. Fidopiastis[1] , and Kay M. Stanney[1]

[1] Design Interactive Inc., Orlando, Fl 32817, USA
Jesse.Flint@designinteractive.net
[2] U.S. Department of Veterans Affairs, Washington, DC, USA

Abstract. Given the sometimes disparate findings and the increasing application of AR in both training and operations, as well as increased affordability and
availability, it is important for researchers, user interface and user experience
(UI/UX) designers, and AR technology developers to understand the factors that
impact the utility of AR. To increase the potential for realizing the full benefit of
AR, adequately detailing the interrelated factors that drive outcomes of different
AR usage schemes is imperative. A systematic approach to understanding
influential factors, parameters, and the nature of the influence on performance
provides the foundation for developing AR usage protocols and design principles, which currently are few. Toward this end, this work presents a theoretical
model of factors impacting performance with AR systems. The framework of
factors, including task, human, and environmental factors, conceptualizes the
concept of "AR Receptivity", which aims to characterize the degree to which the
application of AR usage is receptive to the technology design and capabilities.
The discussion begins with a brief overview of research efforts laying the
foundation for the model's development and moves to a review of receptivity as
a concept of technology suitability. This work provides details on the model and
factor components, concluding with implications for application of AR in both
the training and operational settings.

Keywords: Extended reality · Virtual reality · Augmented reality · Receptivity

1   Introduction and Problem Statement

Augmented reality (AR) technologies augment the physical world by superimposing
computer graphics and relevant data points onto a user's natural world view and have
been purported to provide faster knowledge acquisition, improved retention, increased
motivation and engagement, and more hands-on and immersive learning [1–3]. In
operations, the technology is believed to provide visual supports that promote faster
performance and reduce errors [4]. Past research evaluating AR with novices in an
industrial context demonstrated that AR training produced faster learning of a memory-
based assembly routine as compared to a 3-D manual [5]. Jung [6] found that when
compared to the same 2D content, AR-based 3D projection mapping of a physical

© Springer Nature Switzerland AG 2020
J. Y. C. Chen and G. Fragomeni (Eds.): HCII 2020, LNCS 12190, pp. 135–151, 2020.
https://doi.org/10.1007/978-3-030-49695-1_10

environment significantly increased recognition memory accuracy for pattern locations, and led to greater spatial presence, and provided a 25% more "satisfying" experience.

While these studies speak to the benefits of AR training, other research points out potential limitations, including negative effects of AR cueing (i.e., attentional tunneling [7]), trainee dependency on AR-features and instructional components [8], which are effects that could potentially lead to lack of transfer of skill from AR to real world tasks. Past research using a reading task has demonstrated that the focal distance and context switching that occurs when using AR and integrating information from both virtual and real elements negatively impacts task performance and leads to eye strain and fatigue [9]. Furthermore, there are perceptual issues such as the characteristics of head-worn displays (HWDs) like AR headsets - mismatches between visually displayed information and other senses, restricted field of view (FOV) or mismatched inter-pupillary distance (IPD), which can result in physiological maladaptation. Physiological effects such as shifts in visual function, degraded proprioception, cyber or sim-sickness, and ataxia can compound concerns associated with human information processing and undesirable psychological effects that can significantly negatively impact learning and skill transfer to reality.

Given the sometimes disparate findings and the increasing application of AR in both training and operations, as well as increased affordability and availability, it is important for researchers, user interface and user experience (UI/UX) designers, and AR technology developers to understand the factors that impact the utility of AR. To increase the potential for realizing the full benefit of AR, adequately detailing the interrelated factors that drive outcomes of different AR usage schemes is imperative. A systematic approach to understanding influential factors, parameters, and the nature of the influence on performance provides the foundation for developing AR usage protocols and design principles, which currently are few. Toward this end, this work presents a theoretical model of factors impacting performance with AR systems. The framework of factors, including task, human, and environmental factors, conceptualizes the concept of "AR Receptivity", which aims to characterize the degree to which the application of AR usage is receptive to the technology design and capabilities. The discussion begins with a brief overview of research efforts laying the foundation for the model's development and moves to a review of receptivity as a concept of technology suitability. This work provides details on the model and factor components, concluding with implications for application of AR in both the training and operational settings.

2   Past AR Research

A number of empirical studies have evaluated the potential benefits of AR on human performance outcomes, some of which also assess user perceptions of AR usefulness to the context. The results of these studies provide evidence that variations of task type, differences among individual users, and environment of usage can drive whether AR outcomes are superior to or surpassed by traditional experiences. Given that purported benefits of AR are expected to increase some skill types and improve upon training experiences, it is important to understand the conditions under which positive effects are observed and those for which negative outcomes are possible.

2.1 Nature and Type of Task

Schmidt-Daly et al. [10] evaluated the utility of an AR-equipped sand table for enriching training of military map reading and land navigation planning tasks. The Augmented REality Sand table (ARES), developed by the U.S. Army Research Laboratory (ARL), provides a projection of graphical imagery or visual augmentations over physical sand that can be shaped to mirror real terrain [11]. The system-delivered AR can automatically present augmented overlays that match the dynamic manipulations of the physical (e.g., contours mapped to sand elevation), and can provide visual representation of variable terrain features (e.g., roads, vegetation). ARES has been reported to provide improved training of spatial skills and spatial reasoning competencies as compared to traditional, 2-D maps [10]. In a study allowing trainees to use all map media formats to complete map reading and basic route planning tasks, authors found the ARES training condition to produce better results for distance estimation tasks and landmark identification tasks when compared to use of a 2-D paper map and use of Google Earth© to present map data. Participants were more accurate on both tasks with using ARES than they were with either of the other map delivery mediums. This finding is in line with past research that has found AR to be helpful in learning spatial skills and spatial concepts [12, 13]. Evaluation of individual differences in this study, collected via demographic surveys of game play and familiarity, revealed that individuals who reported moderate to high game play proficiency perceived ARES to be more useful than the other map training tool types [14]. While these performance and perceived utility results are positive, the same study produced inconclusive data on the utility of the AR supported training on higher-order map-based tasks such as situational judgement and route selection. Though participants, in theory, would use the same lower-level information elements such as position, elevation, contour data, and other terrain features to complete the situational judgement tests, as they did for distance estimation and landmark identification tasks, their performance on the judgement tasks did not gain the same AR benefits, as Schmidt-Daly et al. [10] found no significant difference between the map presentation medium on this performance measure. Furthermore, while ARES received higher scores on perceived utility overall and individuals reporting more game experience provided high ratings on utility for the conditions, these participants actually performed better when using the other digital medium, Google Earth© [10].

In a study comparing AR to Virtual Reality (VR) in re-training of activities for daily living for stroke survivors, researchers found AR training to be superior [15]. The motivation for the AR-based training was to provide a more "natural way to maximize learning" of common daily activities for those suffering impact to their motor skills [16]. Khademi and colleagues [15] designed a pick-and-place task representative of daily activities that required trainees to pick up a virtual cylindrical object and "place" it inside a virtual square appearing at random locations within VR or AR. The VR environment was presented through a computer monitor. The AR was presented using a projection device providing a virtual overlay of the target square. The task included psychomotor elements such as reaching, tilting, grasping, and positioning. A score of object placement (i.e., total target placements achieved in a 30-s time limit) was calculated for each condition. Results indicated that the AR condition produced better performance than VR; that is, AR resulted in significantly more objects placed within the allotted time period as compared to the VR condition.

Other evaluations of AR for practice of psychomotor skills produced different outcomes, with AR performance falling below that of real-world training. Researchers exploring the potential application of AR for guiding precision actions found negative effects possibly related to challenges associated with a phenomenon termed "focal rivalry", the human limitations on simultaneously focusing visual attention on virtual and real objects [17]. The study investigated the impact of disparate focal cues on user performance and workload during an AR-guided task using the Microsoft HoloLens. The empirical task involved connecting dots, with and without AR support. Monocular (with one eye) and binocular (with both eyes) tests were performed and followed up with assessment of workload using the National Aeronautics and Space Administration Task Load Index (NASA-TLX). The results found no significant effects of the conditions on workload but did find better performance in the non-AR condition. When asked, participants reported feelings of comparable performance, however the data provide evidence of more errors with AR. On average the magnitude of error in lines drawn with AR guides was 2.3 mm in length, with the largest error at nearly 6 mm. Without AR, using just the naked eye, errors averaged about 0.9 mm. Errors in precision could be significantly detrimental to human performance outcomes in context such as AR-supported medical intervention, the context upon which this initial study of guided AR support was founded. Contrasting the study of AR benefitting the practice and execution of gross motor skills in a pick-and-place task [15], the results of this study indicates the influence of task type on AR utility. Such precision-based tasks may not be well-suited for AR application. This point is reiterated in an examination of studies evaluating AR for assembly-type tasks, which indicates training of complex and precise psychomotor skills may be limited in AR given the need to hone fine motor skills which are the result of years of practice [18].

Duration of the task will influence the duration of AR usage for either training or real task performance. Given the potential for visual discomfort, fatigue, headache, and nausea that has been observed in interactions with virtual environments and virtual content, longer exposures to AR to accommodate to task durations may be inadvisable. While research on aftereffects for AR are limited, past VR studies have demonstrated that the severity of psychological responses can be proportional to exposure duration [19]. Such effects may linger for hours or even days after exposure, which can impact user safety and the safety of others when symptomology influences user behaviors and performance outside of AR.

2.2 Individual Differences

In studies focused on individual differences, researchers have evaluated the potential for AR to attenuate the influence of individual differences on learning achievements. Zhang et al. [20] conducted research with elementary-aged students studying natural sciences. The research compared knowledge acquisition of natural science facts in AR supported training to learning achieved with traditional, non-AR supported training. Students using AR were able to download an AR application on their personal phones to use in the classroom. The application augmented their learning experience by providing additional information to them as they scanned their textbooks with the phones. The students in the non-AR group were provided supplemental information via traditional methods such as paper handouts and PowerPoint. The study results demonstrated that the non-AR group did not realize the learning gains observed with the AR-support group, which produced significantly better scores on an exam. Interestingly, the authors also reported that students in the AR-support group that were lower-performing in general, were able to perform closer to those considered higher-performing in general. These results provide evidence that AR-aided instruction can benefit the learning process and may help to lessen the impact of individual differences like proficiency levels. It should be noted that the quality of the instructional content might have some influence on the utility of the AR-supported approach.

Chen and Wang [21], also conducted research to evaluate the influence of individual differences, specifically on the impact of learning achievement in an AR-supported training protocol. The experimenters implemented a 3-part learning flow that moved from knowledge presentation with traditional methods, to learning with AR, to a reinforcement stage of learning during which students could elect to use AR while using a handout that guided reflection on their learning. They used questionnaires to evaluate two individual differences among the student-participants – learning style and competence with computer-based technologies. The researchers also assessed knowledge acquisition of the students comparing post-test results of knowledge with results obtained from a test administered prior to exposure to the training. The results of the study indicate that students were able to boost their knowledge of the science concepts covered during the 3-part training, with significant differences in the pre- and post-test scores. Evaluation of student perceptions of the AR training scheme indicated that the majority of participants preferred the AR portion of the learning protocol over the others. Over 90% of participants found the AR training "valuable" or "interesting". The effort to evaluate the influence of individual differences, however, produced unexpected results. The researchers found no significant influence of these individual differences. The authors state that the findings are not consistent with past research that has demonstrated supporting learning preferences and increased experience or familiarity with computer-based technologies adds to learning gains.

Stanney, Fidopiastis, and Foster [22] examined the impacts of physiological and biological individual differences on the occurrence of simulation sickness. The goal of the study was to determine the drivers of gender-based differences in the experience of simulation sickness. Across two experiments, male and female participants were exposed to a 20 min virtual rollercoaster using a VR headset or a flatscreen TV. In the first experiment, Inter Pupillary Distance (IPD) was found to account for 42% of variability in simulation sickness experienced. The second experiment demonstrated that when female participants were within the IPD accommodated by a VR headset, they experienced simulation sickness in a manner similar to male participants.

Individual differences with respect to psychological states such as the sense of presence may also impact the utility of AR. Research has reported relationships between immersive tendencies and presence experiences, noting that individuals producing high immersive tendencies scores also report high presence scores [23, 24]. This may have a significant impact on AR experiences given the potential for AR to result in symptoms of cyber- or simulator sickness. Research has reported a negative correlation between presence and cyber-sickness [25, 26]. Their data from multiple studies demonstrate a large negative correlation between sense of presence scores and self-reports on the severity of cyber-sickness symptoms. Research describing the interrelated constructs of immersion, presence, and cyber-sickness suggest that individual propensity toward immersion or lack thereof can influence AR experiences. Individuals more likely to be immersed, and thus "feel" present, may be less likely to suffer sickness which can negatively impact AR experiences.

2.3   Environmental Issues

Researchers examining use cases for AR are evaluating its application beyond controlled, indoor spaces. Azuma [27] discussed a number of environmental challenges in making AR work well outside. The author discusses general ergonomic issues with use in an uncontrolled environment, such as size, weight, power, and durability. A key environmental condition discussed is lighting, which is highly variable in outdoor spaces. Azuma [27] states that most AR displays are not able to achieve the brightness levels required to match the range of lighting conditions along the spectrum from bright sunlight to pitch-dark night. This results in significant issues in user capacity to recognize and identify virtual objects in the augmented space. Ultimately, the negative impact is observed as perceptual and human information processing issues that are compounded by the fact that the resolution of the displays also fails to match human vision capability.

Internal research by the authors and colleagues evaluating AR application across indoor and outdoor conditions has provided a number of insights. For marker based tracking systems, performance has been observed to be better in diffuse and stable lighting. Lighting that is not flickering and remains stable (e.g., does not change overly in terms of brightness) leads to better results with regard to system tracking of AR markers. This kind of consistency in lighting leads to consistency in marker registration of the AR system, which can improve application outcomes. For infrared Simultaneous Localization And Mapping (SLAM) based tracking AR, performance is best when there are no significantly dark or very bright areas in the environment. Performance has also been demonstrated as better when other infrared radiation sources are limited or avoided. In addition, solid white, solid black, reflective, and transparent materials have been observed to cause issues with tracking with infrared SLAM. In a proof-of-concept development effort toward applying AR for outside use with unmanned systems, the display issues created substantial concerns with respect to viewing critical robotic system data through the display, greatly impacting the ability to build situation awareness on the robot and other aspects of the operational task. The solution was to develop "shades" for the AR technology, which were 3-D printed and applied over the viewing goggles.

Beyond lighting, environmental elements such as heat and noise have been observed as problematic for AR technologies. Some systems (e.g., the Microsoft HoloLens) are not actively cooled and, as such, they can overheat in warm spaces. Others have integrated and active cooling capabilities (e.g., Magic Leap), which helps to ameliorate issues with overheating. Mobile Phones equipped with AR have been observed as quite versatile in this regard, and can operate in higher temperatures, despite being passively cooled. Voice commands are currently considered a primary source of input for AR systems. Noise, then, can be problematic for applications of AR. Most systems do not include noise-cancelling features, so noise can negatively influence user performance in training or operational settings. This can be a significant detriment in operations where gesture input is limited due to the need to use hands for other operational tasks.

3 AR Receptivity

Results from these various studies indicate a need for additional study of how the implementation of AR influences the quality of outcomes. That is, studies need to systematically evaluate how, where, for how long, and for whom AR is being applied. There are limited studies that look at the different factors influencing AR utility. Cheng and Tsai [13], for example, stress a need for exploring learner characteristics as "sparse studies" examine human factors involved in AR-related science learning. [18] list limitations in studies evaluating AR application to various kinds of assembly tasks, noting the number of other contexts in which AR can and should be studied given the variability of task types and complexities. The kinds of systematic reviews the research suggest adding to the overall body of work describing AR utility and offers results toward the development of AR usage guidelines. This kind of effort must begin with defining the important factors in AR implementation - human factors (individual differences), task factors (type, complexity, etc.), and environmental factors (physical attributes). Multiple parameters associated with each can work together to influence psychological and physiological experiences with AR. Maximizing effectiveness and reducing negative results requires ensuring the factors and parameters appropriately match to the AR technology and system capabilities. As such, the current work considers the concept of AR Receptivity. The term is used as a means of describing the "goodness of fit" or suitability of AR for a given application based on the receptivity of the individual user, the tasks for application, and the environment.

3.1 Technology Acceptance and Receptivity

The concept of AR Receptivity comes directly from past work on technology acceptance research. In the context of technology innovation, transfer and acceptance, receptivity has been defined as the "extent to which there exists not only a willingness (or disposition) but also an ability (or capability) in different constituencies (individuals, communities, organizations, agencies, etc.) to absorb, accept and utilize innovation options" [28]. Studies evaluating receptivity have used approaches such as the Technology Acceptance Model [29, 30] and the Technology Acceptance Scale [31] to assess technology suitability. The Technology Acceptance Model, for example has been used to assess technology receptivity in educational settings on the basis of the three primary model factors–perceived usefulness, perceived ease of use, and behavioral intentions [32]. The Technology Acceptance Scale, similarly presents queries to users related to perceived usefulness and perceived ease of use of technology and has been used to assess user receptivity of a robot-based coach for smoking cessation [31].

Both questionnaire-based methods produce scores on component scales and for the overall measure, with higher scores indicating high acceptance or receptivity. The component areas provide some starting point on technology use, acceptance, and adoption based on common aspects of usability, but they do not take other key factors into consideration. Consideration of these additional factors facilitate increased understanding of the conditions producing immediate and persisting effects of AR on human psychology (e.g., perception, attention, learning, memory), human cognitive-affective states (e.g., stress, engagement), and human physiology (e.g., ataxia, gut responses). An expanded model will highlight human factors (individual user differences), task factors (characteristics and work design), and environmental factors (physical elements), and relate the same understanding mediating or compounding influences of AR system design (e.g., optical, display, graphics capabilities) to characterize AR Receptivity [33]. Figure 1 presents a graphical depiction of the theoretical model.

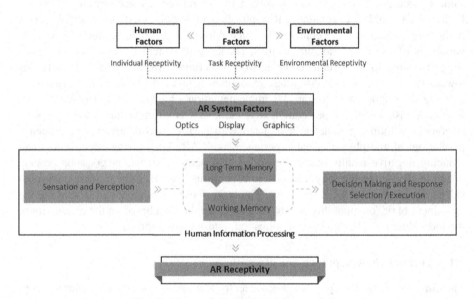

Fig. 1. Theoretical model of AR receptivity

3.2 Theoretical Model of AR Receptivity

The theoretical model includes three major "layers". The top layer presents three high-level factors that map to three proposed receptivity components. These components essentially describe the broad factor categories than can influence AR experiences, acceptance, and use. Human factors map to individual differences and Individual Receptivity. Task factors map to Task Receptivity, which focuses on the potential influence on task type and operational characteristics on AR outcomes. Environmental factors map to Environmental Receptivity, adding consideration for how the physical aspects of the environment impact ability to effectively use AR. For all three factors within the top layer of the model – human, task, and environment – receptivity is characterized by a willingness (of an individual) or inherent characteristic (of a task or environment), along with the ability (of an individual) or capability (of a task or environment) to absorb, convey, accept, implement, and/or effectively utilize AR technologies.

The three high-level factors in the top layer intersect with the AR system design factors, presented in the second layer. The way an AR technology is designed to work – its functional capabilities and limitation, its form factor, and the like – significantly influence the user's experience. Furthermore, as the system is applied to a specific user, for completing or learning a particular kind of task or competency, in a given application environment, the model must consider the influence of the system on overall outcomes. For AR, the system optics, display, and graphics are primary capability features that can present limitations to usage and utility. More specifically, system resolution, brightness, color fidelity, field of view, and capability for stereoscopy can influence the human perception and cognition when using AR. This leads to the intersection of the second layer of the model with the third layer which presents components of human information processing.

The quality of human information processing is critical to human performance in training or real-world operations. The degree to which a user can effectively and efficiently sense and perceive critical elements, comprehend and judge their meaning, encode relevant information in working and long-term memory, and further process the information for decision making directly impacts performance outcomes. The third layer of our theoretical model presents key aspects of human information processing – sensation, perception and attention, encoding into memory, decision making and response selection – as they are directly influenced by main and interacting effects related to human, task, environment, and system design factors. Theoretically, increasing receptivity associated with any factor would positively impact human information processing and performance, to the degree that the system capabilities do not degrade any receptivity element. There may, of course, be competing parameters or factors, as well as compounding and countering influences of each. The goal in AR application should be to provide the most advantageous conditions with respect to individual user, task application, and environment of use to optimize effectiveness of the selected AR technology. That is, the implementation and application should aim to optimize AR receptivity in order to maximize AR outcomes. Outcomes might be related to multiple aspects of overall system performance (e.g., objective task outcomes), training (e.g., efficacy, effectiveness, and transfer), acceptance (e.g., usage and adoption with the training or operational context), psychological responses (e.g., motivation, stress, engagement, task efficacy), or physical responses (e.g., sickness, dizziness, blurred vision). Designers, developers, and implementers may have differing goals with regard to which of the outcomes to prioritize for optimization. The authors contend, however, that consideration of the impact of all factors and how they interact to provide complementary benefits or compounding complaints is critical to understanding AR effectiveness.

3.3   Receptivity Factors: Human, Task, and Environmental

The theoretical AR Receptivity model can help guide considerations in regard to optimizing effectiveness of AR technology based on identified receptivity factors, as it links the AR system features and functional design capabilities to the deployment conditions of interest. Table 1, below, presents the factors impacting AR receptivity as outlines in the theoretical model. It should be noted, the list provides examples, and is not all-inclusive of the factor types or parameters.

Table 1. Human, task, and environmental factors impacting receptivity

Human factors	Task factors	Environmental factors
• Past experience • Mental models • Task proficiency • Perceptual and attentional skills and abilities (visual acuity, contrast sensitivity, color matching, stereo-acuity, dark focus, attention switching) • Cognitive, spatial, psychomotor skills • Personality traits and predispositions (engagement, self-efficacy, locus of control, immersive tendencies, mood, stress) • Attitudes and beliefs • Neural conditions	• Type of task (cognitive, psychomotor) • Duration • Complexity or level of difficulty • Sensory/perceptual needs (auditory, visual, haptic, etc.) • Psychomotor skill requirements (gross motor, fine motor and precision) • Cognitive skill requirements • Spatial skill requirements • Information requirements • Collaborative requirements • Temporal requirements • Task interface and interaction design	• Lighting • Noise • Temperature • Weather • Interference • Stability, vibration, perturbation • Complexity, distractions, dynamics

In general, human performance is affected by numerous user characteristics, at both the individual and the team level. Each human user has his or her own experiences, competencies and proficiency levels, aptitudes and attitudes, and personality traits and dispositions. Differences in motivation, capacity for engagement, ability to cope with stress, along with commonly considered characteristics such as age and gender can impact user learning and performance learning [34]. Attention allocation and capacity for switching attention between contexts and task elements, both AR and real-world, significantly affects user information processing and decision making [24]. It is, therefore, important to consider human factors inherent to the AR user when applying the technology and predicting the outcome of application. As an example, individuals with positive attitudes toward AR are more likely to be accepting of the technology and open to using AR when applied to work or training. Users with high quality perceptual, attention switching, or spatial skills might be expected to exhibit better task performance in AR than those lacking the same skills and abilities. In contrast, one might see negative AR acceptance, physiological responses, and task performance for persons, with low immersive tendencies, physical sensitivities to immersive technologies, or degraded perceptual skills. The key is that variable parameters or levels associated with human factors can directly influence AR experiences, usage, and utility. As such, human factors impact individual receptivity which is described as the willingness and ability of an individual to process information in, accept application of, and effectively use AR technologies.

- Individual Receptivity: The willingness and ability of an individual to process information in, accept application of, and effectively use AR technologies.

Task factors, both training-based and operational, influence user information processing and performance. Stanney [35] indicated that task characteristics affect user outcomes in AR applications. Task characteristics also determine the level of realism, immersion, and overall detail necessary to achieve the desired training or performance effect. Some task characteristics will be more or less suited to AR environments. The parameters of the task, the number and type of sensory cues and information elements that need to be represented or supported for the task, along with the variable cognitive or physical requirements and constraints of the context, are important to AR application. Task complexities can influence AR utility for learning. Long duration tasks may result in physiological aftereffects that are persistent and impact user safety. Poorly designed task interfaces may fail to provide needed sensory cues in the right formats which limits information processing performance. Tasks that are highly cognitive in nature, with little need for psychomotor skill or spatial reasoning, may result in low utility for AR. Tasks that rely on or prioritize sensory cues, knowledge, or skill sets that cannot be accurately represented, replicated, or completed in AR are not conducive to the application of the technology. As with human factors, implementers should aim to maximize utility of AR by applying it to tasks for which the characteristics of AR are highly suitable.

- Task Receptivity: The degree to which the characteristics, requirements, and constraints of tasks to be performed (in training or operations) can be effectively represented in AR technologies.

Many environmental factors directly relate to the reliability and durability of the AR technology. High temperature environments lead to low reliability in system performance in systems that rely on passive cooling. Noisy environments will result in poor voice input performance. Interference, lighting, and wet weather will all result in performance issues. In general, control of environments will increase control over reliability. That doesn't mean that all uncontrolled spaces should avoid AR usage. It means that implementers should consider the impact of environment when designing an application or implementation protocol. For example, if outdoor use is desire, timed exposure to heat or selection of cooler areas should be implemented. The goal is to optimize physical elements of the environment as much as possible to promote reliable system functioning.

- Environment Receptivity: The degree to which environment (training or operational) characteristics and constraints facilitate effective information delivery and AR utilization.

3.4   AR Technology Design Factors

One can easily conclude that increasing the match between AR capabilities and parameters of any single factor increases the potential for effective human information processing and performance with AR. However, assessment of receptivity and predicting the outcomes for AR receptivity go beyond single-factor assessment. It is highly probable and projected that factors and parameters of factors interact, given the nature of interrelationships among factors, to produce more complex outcome potentials. Some combinations are expected to produce better outcomes than others, but the specific effects of those combinations and the degree to which each factor and component influence and weigh on the outcomes are not well known. The theoretical model of AR Receptivity provides a foundation upon which to structure and roadmap a systematic empirical approach to examining these interrelated influences.

The review must consider the AR technology to be applied to the given context, as AR capabilities and features drive the level of immersion experienced and influences how and where the system can be applied for individual or collaborative tasks [36]. As such, the theoretical model presents the AR System Factors in the second layer of the model. Features and capabilities of the AR will either moderate or exacerbate the influence of the receptivity factors, in isolation or in combination, ultimately impacting the quality of human information processing and user experience in AR. As an example, the form factor (e.g., tablet, phone, or head display) is expected to influence overall AR Receptivity, with some forms projected to be better suited to some tasks than others. Task requiring hands to be free for completing task steps will be less receptive to tablet- or phone-based AR unless some device is applied to hold the platform for the user. Similarly, some forms will be better suited to some individual differences and environmental characteristics. Users that suffer negative physiological or psychological impacts from a high degree of immersion, may not be well-suited for head-worn displays, but better able to sustain performance with non-immersive AR. These same non-immersive deployment tools, like phones, may be best suited for use in uncontrolled environmental lighting and temperature when AR usage must be sustained for longer periods of time.

As another example, use cases for AR will require variable levels of or amounts of virtual content or assets to achieve specific experiential and functional goals. The amount of virtual content necessary to convey meaningful (context relevant) information for training or operational performance has been termed as the "weight" of the AR. Light AR conveys fewer virtual elements than "heavy" AR, which presents more virtual content as compared to real-world content. Mobile form factors may be best suited for light AR contexts, while head-mounted displays, which are more immersive, may be better for heavy AR contexts [37]. Researchers, such as Wu, Lee, Chian, and Liang [38] evaluating application of AR to training, suggest that the key is to implement the technology in such a way that it best supports meaningful use in context.

AR technical capabilities such as the quality of system optics, display, and graphics impact human visual perception in AR. Resolution, brightness, color fidelity, field of view, and stereoscopy capabilities vary across AR technologies. Mobile AR technologies for example typically provide good visual acuity, but lower stereo-acuity than head-worn technologies which are improving in the area of depth mapping, stereo-acuity and 3-D representation of information. It is important to note, however, that limitations in AR optics and graphics can result in image effects such as grainy or blurred images, limited visibility of various colors, and distortion of depth cues. Distorted scenes and misrepresented cues can impact information processing and cause immediate or persistent psychological effects, as well as physiological effects. Poor presentation can impact feelings of presence, perceptions of utility and task efficacy. Mismatches to the human visual system can lead to sickness. If the system capabilities are not adequate for the context (i.e., that is, the capabilities cannot provide meaningful information effectively and accurately), detection, recognition, and identification are hindered. This is highly detrimental when training in contexts where target/object detection are critical, as it may cause negative transfer or lead to reliance on false cues. These limitations and decrements would be compounded for users who have inherent limitations to perceptual systems, and environmental contexts that further degrade visuals.

4   Receptivity Use Case

The examination of the results from the authors' past and current efforts defines factors, examines relationships among factors, and devises a framework for examining AR technology receptivity. As an example, a specific AR platform might match all of the psychological sensation and perception requirements for a task yet misalign from a physiological perspective. Or, a platform might lead to few physiological effects, but misalign psychologically causing a mismatch between AR cues, multi-modal cues, and user interactions required for knowledge transfer or operational task performance. Additionally, an AR technology may simply fail in regard to the optics and graphics needed for accurate and precise visual perception and discrimination. A consideration of relevant receptivity factors and technology factors helps to lay the foundation for optimization. Consider the below use cases and relevance of AR Receptivity.

There is interest in applying Augmented Reality to medical training, in particular tactical combat casualty care (TC3). AR is expected to provide high-fidelity, hands-on training on battlefield injury states by presenting critical sensory cues and trainee task interactions for rapid repeated practice of trauma interventions. The application of use is intervention training for observed tension pneumothorax (TP), a condition in which air is moving into the space between the lungs and the chest wall. The trainee will use AR to practice needle decompression for releasing the pressure caused by the leaking air. As the training is for battlefield care, conditions should mimic that environment. A headset application is desired.

Individual receptivity should consider evaluations of conditions such as neural conditions and perceptual impairments that can exacerbate psychological or physiological effects. These individuals may need to be excluded from head-worn AR training. Psychological effects related to AR's capacity to influence human attention allocation should be considered in the training task design and interface design. Prolonged attention and required switching of attention between multiple AR elements and real-world element that drive decision making during the intervention could potential impact cognitive loading, as well as visual system aftereffects from long term exposure for an extended or repeated scenario. Similarly, as AR has been found to elicit higher cognitive activity (as compared to non-AR task situations) assessment of stress and engagement should be considered with human factors and individual differences, to ensure they don't persist following exposure. Trainees may need significant down time prior to returning to daily activities or normal duties. Individuals with lower skill levels might also experience higher loading as they are coping with using AR while also trying to learn skills. As such, their learning in AR headsets may need to be guided and focus on building of basic knowledge of TP to ensure they can absorb knowledge in AR and transfer that to future training or reality, before trying to integrate more complex skills.

Task receptivity can be linked to the task type. TP interventions requires fine motor skill application to place a needle in a specific location for relieving pressures in the chest cavity. Perceptual limitations can be caused when AR overlays don't correctly align with body landmarks and locations. Misperceptions of the correct location to place the needle and aligning with the intercostal space through the headset, can lead to negative transfer and impact real-world performance. Further, if there is not a one-to-one correspondence between such needle placement in the AR headset and the real world, this can lead to a shift in the kinesthetic position sense, which could lead to degraded hand-eye coordination in the real world. Prolonged exposure to perceptual mismatches can also lead to nausea, so exposure time should be evaluated.

Given the battlespace environment, implementers should consider where the training will occur, to avoid overly bright conditions and too-high temperatures. Shades, if available for the technology, might need to be applied during implementation to ensure the critical cues learned in the training are appropriately salient.

The training scenario implementation must ensure that the technological features of the AR headset that is selected can accurately convey critical multi-modal sensory cues. Depth cues relevant to the task (e.g., needle placement, needle depth, chest position and movement, etc.) should be adequately conveyed to ensure proper skill development. Technologies incapable of providing correct cues, including color, should be avoided.

This use case demonstrates a number of receptivity concerns that should be considered to promote effective human information processing and AR outcomes, including performance, psychological effects and physiological effects. So, while AR technology has the potential to advance the TC3 training, there is a critical need to identify any receptivity limitations that could compromise user states, training effectiveness and performance, and safety.

5   Implications for AR Usage Guidelines

Organizations interested in application of AR and realizing its full potential need to understand the human factors concerns with AR, the capacity to acquire and transfer skills in AR, and the ability to mediate negative effects of AR exposure for maximizing training and performance gains. The work presented here describes a theoretical model of AR Receptivity that can guide empirical studies systematically examining AR effects. The goal of the model is to define interrelated factors driving the suitability and utility of AR. Characterization of a receptivity construct will ultimately support stakeholders unfamiliar with AR platforms in moving beyond simple review of technical specifications and cost, to consider the relative "goodness of fit" or optimal implementation of the technology for the context and environment of use and the target user. It helps us better answer the questions around the best implementations for AR to promote acceptance, adoption, and effectiveness. Ultimately, the results of studies guided by and underlying framework provide evidence for development of implementation and usage protocols. Target areas that will benefit from usage and applications guidelines include, but are not limited to:

- Design guidelines of interfaces and interaction mechanisms to address task factors and AR system factors, including form factor and capabilities
- Implementation guidelines related to AR system selection addressing individual differences
- Implementation guidelines related to AR system selection and implementation to address task factors related to sensory cue needs and information presentation needs
- Implementation and usage guidelines relevant to environmental factors such as lighting, noise, temperature, size/space, when the environmental context for meaningful task application is critical to AR usage
- Implementation guidelines to address individual differences in contexts with important collaborative task requirements and/or team processing
- Application guidelines with respect to best fit of technology capabilities (i.e., optics and graphics) are critical to training or operational performance when paring those capabilities with the human visual system
- Usage guidelines on protocols for duration of usage to address physiological and psychological aftereffects
- Application guidelines on best fit of technology based on nature and type of tasks, including cognitive tasks (on continuum from basic to high-order decision making) and psychomotor tasks (ranging from gross motor skills to fine motor skills)
- Design and implementation guidelines for information presentation when context switching in AR is task driven; guidelines for appropriately balancing virtual and real objects in usage context.

References

1. Azuma, R.: A survey of augmented reality. Presence Teleoperators Virtual Environ. **6**(4), 355–385 (1997)
2. Lee, K.: Augmented reality in education and training. TechTrends **56**(2), 13–21 (2012)
3. Dunleavy, M., Dede, C., Mitchell, R.: Affordances and limitations of immersive participatory augmented reality simulations for teaching and learning. J. Sci. Educ. Technol. **18**(1), 7–22 (2009)
4. Sääski, J., Salonen, T., Hakkarainen, M., Siltanen, S., Woodward, C., Lempiäinen, J.: Integration of design and assembly using augmented reality. In: Ratchev, S., Koelemeijer, S. (eds.) IPAS 2008. IIFIP, vol. 260, pp. 395–404. Springer, Boston, MA (2008). https://doi.org/10.1007/978-0-387-77405-3_39

5. Hou, L.: Evaluating the use of augmented reality to facilitate assembly. Curtin theses (2013). https://espace.curtin.edu.au/bitstream/handle/20.500.11937/2125/190332_Hou2013.pdf? sequence=2&isAllowed=y

6. Jung, S., Lee, D., Biocca, F.: Psychological effects on 3 Dimensions projection mapping versus 2 dimensions: exploratory study. In: Proceedings of the International Society for Presence Research 2014, pp. 213–222 (2014)

7. Lambie, A.J.: Directing attention in an augmented reality environment: an attentional tunneling evaluation. Thesis, Rochester Institute of Technology (2015). https://pdfs. semanticscholar.org/2b60/6c3c0e1e8afe2cdb2456a61909451f6b544e.pdf

8. Webel, S., Engelke, T., Peveri, M., Olbrich, M., Preusche, C.: Augmented reality training for assembly and maintenance skills. In: BIO Web of Conferences, vol. 1, p. 97 (2011)

9. Gabbard, J.L., Mehra, D.G., Swan, J.E.: Effects of AR display context switching and focal distance switching on human performance. IEEE Trans. Visual Comput. Graphics 25(6), 2228–2241 (2018)

10. Schmidt-Daly, T.N., Riley, J.M., Hale, K.S., Yacht, D., Hart, J.: Augmented REality Sandtables (ARESs) Impact on Learning (No. ARL-CR-0803). Design Interactive, Inc. Orlando United States (2016)

11. Amburn, C.R., Vey, N.L., Boyce, M.W., Mize, J.R.: The augmented reality sandtable (ARES) (No. ARL-SR-0340). Army Research Lab Aberdeen Proving Ground MD, Human Research and Engineering Directorate (2015)

12. Juan, C., Beatrice, F., Cano, J.: An augmented reality system for learning the interior of the human body. In: 2008 Eighth IEEE International Conference on Advanced Learning Technologies, pp. 186–188. IEEE (2008)

13. Cheng, K.H., Tsai, C.C.: Affordances of augmented reality in science learning: suggestions for future research. J. Sci. Educ. Technol. 22(4), 449–462 (2013)

14. Schmidt-Daly, T.N., Riley, J.M., Amburn, C.R., Hale, K.S., David Yacht, P.: Video game play and effect on spatial knowledge tasks using an augmented sand table. In: Proceedings of the Human Factors and Ergonomics Society Annual Meeting, vol. 60, no. 1, pp. 1429–1433. SAGE Publications, Los Angeles (2016)

15. Khademi, M., Hondori, H.M., Dodakian, L., Cramer, S., Lopes, C.V.: Comparing "pick and place" task in spatial augmented reality versus non-immersive virtual reality for rehabilitation setting. In: 2013 35th Annual International Conference of the IEEE Engineering in Medicine and Biology Society (EMBC), pp. 4613–4616. IEEE (2013)

16. Mousavi Hondori, H., Khademi, M., Dodakian, L., Cramer, S., Lopes, C.: A spatial augmented reality rehab system for post-stroke hand rehabilitation. Stud. Health Technol. Inform. 184, 279–285 (2013)

17. Condino, S., Carbone, M., Piazza, R., Ferrari, M., Ferrari, V.: Perceptual limits of optical see-through visors for augmented reality guidance of manual tasks. IEEE Trans. Biomed. Eng. 67, 411–419 (2020)

18. Werrlich, S., Eichstetter, E., Nitsche, K., Notni, G.: An overview of evaluations using augmented reality for assembly training tasks. Int. J. Comput. Inf. Eng. 11(10), 1068–1074 (2017)

19. Kennedy, R.S., Stanney, K., Dunlap, W.P.: Duration and exposure to virtual environments: Sickness curves during and across sessions. Presence Teleoperators Virtual Environ. 9, 463–472 (2000)

20. Zhang, J., Liu, T.C., Sung, Y.T., Chang, K.E.: Using augmented reality to promote homogeneity in learning achievement. In: 2015 IEEE International Symposium on Mixed and Augmented Reality-Media, Art, Social Science, Humanities and Design, pp. 1–5. IEEE (2015)

21. Chen, C., Wang, C.-H.: Employing augmented-reality-embedded instruction to disperse the imparities of individual differences in earth science learning. J. Sci. Educ. Technol. **24**, 835–847 (2015). https://doi.org/10.1007/s10956-015-9567-3
22. Stanney, K.M., Fidopiastis, C., Foster, L.: Virtual reality is sexist: but it does not have to be. Front. Robot. AI **7**, 4. https://doi.org/10.3389/frobt.2020.00004011
23. Servotte, J.C., et al.: Virtual reality experience: immersion, sense of presence, and cybersickness. Clin. Simul. Nurs. **38**, 35–43 (2020)
24. Riley, J.M., Kaber, D.B., Draper, J.V.: Situation Awareness and attention allocation measures for quantifying telepresence experiences in teleoperation. Hum. Factors Ergon. Manuf. **14**(1), 51–67 (2004)
25. Witmer, B.G., Bailey, J.H., Knerr, B.W., Parsons, K.C.: Virtual spaces and real world places: transfer of route knowledge. Int. J. Hum. Comput. Stud. **45**(4), 413–428 (1996)
26. Witmer, B.G., Singer, M.J.: Measuring presence in virtual environments: a presence questionnaire. Presence **7**(3), 225–240 (1998)
27. Azuma, R.T.: The challenge of making augmented reality work outdoors. In: Mixed Reality: Merging Real and Virtual Worlds, pp. 379–390 (1999)
28. Jeffrey, P., Seaton, R.A.F.: A conceptual model of 'receptivity' applied to the design and deployment of water policy mechanisms. Environ. Sci. **1**(3), 277–300 (2004)
29. Weng, F., Rong-Jou, Y., Hann-Jang, H., Hui-Mei, S.: A TAM-based study of attitude towards use intention of multimedia among school teachers. Appl. Syst. Innov. **1**, 36 (2018). https://doi.org/10.3390/asi1030036
30. Davis, F.D.: Perceived usefulness, perceived ease of use and user acceptance of information technology. MIS Q. **13**, 319–340 (1989). https://doi.org/10.2307/249008
31. Patten, C., et al.: Survey of potential receptivity to robotic-assisted exercise coaching in a diverse sample of smokers and nonsmokers. PLoS ONE **13**(5), e0197090 (2018)
32. Jabeen, F., Khan, M., Ahmad, S.Z.: Understanding the technology receptivity in higher education: evidence from the UAE. Int. J. Technol. Hum. Interact. (IJTHI) **14**(3), 39–52 (2018)
33. Fidopiastis, C.: User-centered virtual environment assessment and design for cognitive rehabilitation applications. Electronic Theses and Dissertations, University of Central Florida (2006). https://stars.library.ucf.edu/etd/911/
34. Lu, H.P., Chiou, M.J.: The impact of individual differences on e-learning system satisfaction: a contingency approach. Br. J. Edu. Technol. **41**(2), 307–323 (2010)
35. Stanney, K.: Realizing the full potential of virtual reality: human factors issues that could stand in the way. In: Proceedings Virtual Reality Annual International Symposium 1995, pp. 28–34. IEEE (1995)
36. Broll, W., Lindt, I., Herbst, I., Ohlenburg, J., Braun, A.K., Wetzel, R.: Toward next-gen mobile AR games. IEEE Comput. Graphics Appl. **28**(4), 40–48 (2008)
37. Klopfer, E., Yoon, S.: Developing games and simulations for today and tomorrow's tech savvy youth. TechTrends **49**(3), 33–41 (2004)
38. Wu, H.K., Lee, S.W.Y., Chang, H.Y., Liang, J.C.: Current status, opportunities and challenges of augmented reality in education. Comput. Educ. **62**, 41–49 (2013)

Arms and Hands Segmentation for Egocentric Perspective Based on PSPNet and Deeplab

Heverton Sarah[✉], Esteban Clua[✉], and Cristina Nader Vasconcelos[✉]

Universidade Federal Fluminense, Niterói, Rio de Janeiro, Brazil
heverton.sarah@gmail.com, {esteban,crisnv}@ic.uff.br

Abstract. First person videos and games are the central paradigms of camera positioning when using Head Mounted Displays (HMDs). In these situations, the user's hands and arms play a fundamental role in self-presence feeling and interface. While their visual image is trivial in Augmented Reality devices or when using depth cameras attached to the HMDs, their rendering is not trivial to be solved with regular HMD, such as those based on smartphone devices. This work proposes the usage of semantic image segmentation with Fully Convolutional Networks for detaching user's hands and arms from a raw image, captured by regular cameras, positioned as a First Person visual schema. We first create a training dataset composed by 4041 images and a validation dataset composed of 322 images, both of them receive labels for an arm and no-arm pixels, focused on the egocentric view. Then, based on two important architectures related to semantic segmentation - PSPNet and Deeplab - we propose a specific calibration for the particular scenario composed of hands and arms, captured from an HMD perspective. Our results show that PSPNet has better detail segmentation while Deeplab achieves best inference time performance. Training with our egocentric dataset generates better arm segmentation than using images in different and more general perspectives.

Keywords: Egocentric skin image segmentation · Fully convolutional networks · Head mounted display · Self-presence

1 Introduction

According to [38], the degree of immersion on a Virtual Environment (VE) is related to the description of the technology, the realism that a display can show, the number of sensory types, the surrounding quality and how panoramic the virtual reality is. In particular, the immersion requires a Virtual Body (VB),

---

Supported by the Coordenação de Aperfeiçoamento de Pessoal de Nível Superior - Brasil (CAPES) - Finance Code 001. The authors also wish to thank Eder de Oliveira for giving the Egohand images, making possible our pixel label creation for training our models.

J. Y. C. Chen and G. Fragomeni (Eds.): HCII 2020, LNCS 12190, pp. 152–170, 2020.
https://doi.org/10.1007/978-3-030-49695-1_11

which represents the user location at the virtual environment, an essential aspect of the self-presence concept. One way to achieve this goal consists in the rendering of virtual representations of the human body, where the hands and arms play a fundamental role, due to its constant appearance in most of the first-person view shooting positioning.

Virtual Reality (VR) is currently present in many applications where the user experiences a sense of presence in a virtual environment. Nowadays, due to the increase of attention that different industries are giving to VR, it is very common to achieve and have HMD devices. Additionally, high quality and portable cameras are available at affordable prices, which are being used on the egocentric content recording, turning Augmented Reality (AR) applications easily configurable. This content can be used to train automatic detection techniques of users' arms.

Automatic detection and segmentation of human skin is a topic of broad interest due to a large amount of applications, such as detection of human faces [43], hand gestures [31], pedestrian detection [13], human pose detection to Virtual Reality environments [29], among many other examples. These applications are the result of applying distinct techniques, in which the process of separating skin image pixels from background pixels, called skin image segmentation, can be one of them. In this work, we intend to segment arms and hands, in real-time, from egocentric images perspectives.

Convolutional Neural Network (CNN) is a Deep Neural Network based approach that shows impressive results on processing visual signals [41]. Outputs of a layer are connected to inputs of others, where each layer may represent different features of the image. Typically, earlier layers detect simple patterns, while later layers describe more complex features. These feature detectors are only connected to a small region from the previous layer, reducing the number of parameters used by the network, in contrast with the fully connected networks, which is typically used in conventional neural networks.

To segment an image with a CNN, one can use convolutional layers from input to output, turning the network a Fully Convolutional Network (FCN) [24], in which upsampling layers enable pixelwise prediction when the network has subsampling layers, and skip architecture fuses information between layers that identify simple appearance patterns to ones which identify complex semantic patterns. Upsampling layers increase the size of a previous layer output, while the subsampling does the reverse.

Since the advent of FCN network, many researchers started to change other networks architectures to also be fully convolutional, by changing fully connected layers to convolutional ones. However, the process of applying convolutions decrease the spatial dimension of features, which is good to achieve better semantic features on deeper layers but reduces the quality of less semantic results which are done on earlier layers. This problem made different authors think in solutions to increase the spatial dimension of features or to take information from earlier layers to the latter one.

These networks were originally trained to segment various classes. To use them for a different problem, in which they were not trained, they must be trained again with another database which represents the new problem. To adapt them to human arms and hands segmentation in egocentric perspective, it is necessary more images of people in this perspective. Although exist some public dataset which contains this type of image for segmentation, the amount of images available is still much less than the available for image classification problems. Therefore, the construction of one more dataset can contribute to the emerging of more researches with a greater amount of images. Another problem is that these images must be captured by cameras positioned in the users' eyes to better represent the images that will be captured in the mixed reality application with visualization of users' arms. Another characteristic of this application is that the user will also move its head, generating camera movements, which means the training images should also simulate this situation.

The contribution of this paper is as follows: we first generate two datasets composed by egocentric images of human arms. We also use a third database, which is composed of images in different perspectives, to confirm if training with egocentric focused images improves egocentric segmentation; then we detach two relevant architectures for semantic segmentation - one based on the PSP network [46] and other based on Deeplabv3 with Mobilenet [8,20] and Xception [11]. Lastly, we propose configurations and parameters adjustments for hands and arms specific segmentation, focused on VR games and interactive experiences with First Person View paradigm of camera positioning.

In the next section, we show the related works. Following, we present our modeling for segmenting human skin image based on our detached architectures. Section 4 shows the specific configuration of our networks. Finally, we present our experiments and results, followed by summarization and future works descriptions.

2   Related Works

First Person Vision (FPV) presents multiple challenges: (1) Nonstatic cameras, (2) Variable illumination and background conditions, (3) Real-time processing, (4) Small video processing capabilities [3]. In order to segment hand images in these video situation, the segmentation technique must address those challenges. In this section, we present relevant works that approach human hand images in the egocentric view segmentation.

Based on traditional computer vision and machine learning techniques, [27] address the problem of segmenting human hands images in the egocentric view by developing a method which runs on Google cardboard/HMD application using a combination of histogram equalization, Gaussian blurring, and its proposed Multi Orientation Matched Filtering (MOMF). Although it achieves real-time inference, segmentation accuracy is 6.97% worse than SegNet [2]. [23] combines global appearance models with a sparse 50-dimensional combination of color, texture and gradient histogram features to segment hands under varying illumination and hand poses.

In the field of deep neural networks, [36] applies YOLO [33] convolutional neural network to detect hands in car driving scenario to recognize driver's grasp. Although the training was made using a large number of hand images, the focus was not the first person view.

Auto-Context [40] consists of a segmentation method where the segmenter is iterated, and each result from an iteration is used in the next iteration added to the original input. Another approach [44] develops a convolution neural network focused on segmenting egocentric images of hands in real time, which differentiates from Auto-Context by initially segmenting on a downscaled version of the input image, following by passing the result by the second iteration after upscaling. An image dataset, similar to ours (but smaller) was created with 348 images, 90% of them were used for training and the rest for testing.

DeepLabv3 [8] and PSPNet [46] were not created to work with the egocentric view. Nevertheless, in our research, they presented good results in semantic segmentation by deep neural networks. In this work, they are implemented to segment human hands images in egocentric view.

Depth cameras could also be used for the same purpose of our work. These data could be combined with pixels colors in conventional camera images in order to help pixel classifier algorithms to better split the interest objects [18,25,32,39].

3 Human Arms Segmentation in Egocentric View with PSPNet and DeepLab

In semantic segmentation, PSPNet [46] and DeeplabV3 [8] achieved state of the art on PASCAL VOC Challenge 2012 [14], a challenge that focuses on evaluating trained models on a dataset of many object classes related to realistic scenes, in which one of them is a person. The segmentation methods that achieve state of the art on this challenge may be a good classifier of pixels which represents humans or part of them.

PSPNet and DeeplabV3 also presented concepts that helped the evolution of segmentation using deep neural networks. Because of these achievements, we aim to fine tune these architectures in order to apply them in binary classification, that means, to separate pixels from an image that represents a human arm from pixels representing the background. We present an overview of these architectures and show how we adjusted them to achieve our particular objective.

3.1 PSPNet

Pyramid Scene Parsing Network (PSPNet) [46] aims to provide a global context prior. It is structured as a hierarchy of pooling which extracts features in different scales in order to be concatenated and to form a final feature map.

The overall architecture is shown in Fig. 1, where the input image pass through a pre-trained ResNet [19] with a dilated network strategy [6,45] to extract the feature map (Fig. 1(b)). It then goes to a pyramid pooling module (c), composed by 4-level pyramid kernels responsible for extracting feature maps in different scales. The result of each kernel has its depth dimension reduced by applying 1 × 1 convolution and its height and width upscaled by bilinear interpolation in order to make each feature map dimension the same as the pyramid input feature map. These feature maps are then concatenated to be merged with the previous one. The final step is to pass through a convolution layer, generating the prediction map.

In our implementation, the network layer "conv6" and all subsequent were set to be trained with an output size of 2, which represents the number of classes our problem needs: arm and no-arm. ResNet101 [19] (ResNet with 101 layers) was used to extract the feature map which is input for the pyramid pooling. This ResNet version has the last layers converted in dilated convolutions by [46] in order to upsample the final feature maps because ResNet is focused initially on classification and not segmentation.

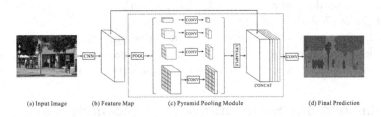

(a) Input Image   (b) Feature Map   (c) Pyramid Pooling Module   (d) Final Prediction

Fig. 1. PSPNet architecture [46]

3.2 Deeplab

The Deeplab version 3 (DeeplabV3) [8] uses Atrous Spatial Pyramid Pooling (ASPP) [7] and dilated convolutions [6,45] (or atrous convolutions) to transform ResNet [19] into a semantic segmentation neural network. The ASPP module is composed by dilated convolutions, which arranges features in different scales in order to better classify regions of various sizes. These features contain "holes", which is an amount r (atrous rate) of zeros that are put in every direction of a feature value, enabling to control how densely to compute feature responses without learning too many parameters. The final layers of ResNet are also composed by dilated convolutions to upscale the feature maps before the ASPP module.

Figure 3 shows ResNet [19] as a backbone network, modified to attend Deeplab V3 architecture, where the *output stride* is the amount of time the feature map is smaller than the input and *rate* is the atrous rate cited above. The ASPP (a) is composed by 1 × 1 convolution and three 3 × 3 dilated convolutions (all with 256 filters and bach normalization), where the three rate values are hyperparameters and can be adjusted for training and inference. Image pooling (b) operation is the result of applying global average pooling on the previous feature map, which passes through a 1 × 1 convolution with 256 filters and bach normalization, followed by bilinearly upsampling to the desired dimension.

DeepLabv3+ [9] (Fig. 2) is an Encoder-Decoder [16] version of DeepLabv3, where the encoder part consists of DeepLabv3 with ASPP module composed by atrous separable convolutions (the union of dilated convolution with depthwise separable convolutions [37]). The encoder's output is the last feature map before logits and is used as input to the decoder module. Before this feature map enters the decoder module, its spacial size is increased by bilinear interpolation with rate 4, and then it is merged with low-level encoder features (feature maps before ASPP and after applying 1 × 1 convolution to decrease channels). After merging, 3 × 3 convolutions are applied to improve results, and a bilinear interpolation of rate 4 is used to change the final spatial size. The best encoder using this architecture in [9] is a modified version of Aligned Inception [12] (or Aligned Xception).

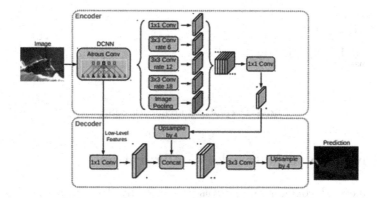

Fig. 2. DeepLabv3+ architecture (Source: [9])

The Xception version with DeepLabv3+ has more layers than the original [11], with the same entry flow structure and every max pooling operations replaced by depthwise separable convolution. There are also batch normalization and RELU activations after each 3 × 3 depthwise convolution. Our implementation of this Xception, composed by ASSP module and decoder, is called Xception X-65 [9]. MobileNetV2 [35] is focused on decreasing the number of parameters and operations in order to be possible for running through an environment with a low level of processing and memory, such as mobile devices. Its main components are the *inverted residuals* and the *linear bottlenecks*, which makes it better than the first version.

Unlike the residual modules of ResNet [19], MobileNetV2 modules first increase the input number of channels they receive as 1 × 1 convolutions. The result passes through a depthwise convolution, decreasing the number of parameters. Finally, a 1 × 1 convolution to turn the number of channels equal to the input is applied. This operation is called inverted residuals because it is the opposite of a standard residual [19].

Linear bottleneck consists in not doing non-linear activation before the addition operation between the block's output and the input activation with skip connections.

The MobileNetV2 with DeepLabV3 implementation was used in this work. Besides, MobileNet [35] detected that network version without ASSP module considerably decrease the number of operations. For this reason, we did not make use of the decoder.

In our implementation of these two encoders (Xception X-65 and MobileNetV2), the classification layer weights are not reused, and the last layer only has logits. Moreover, the trained model is exported to work with only two classes, unlike the standard 21 from the original implementation of the network.

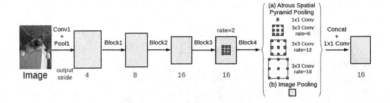

Fig. 3. Deeplab V3 architecture [8]

4 Convolutional Networks Configuration

For every network configuration, it was performed five training sessions in order to measure the evaluation metrics. Each PSPNet configuration was trained for 100K iterations (50 epoch of 2000 gradient passes) and each Deeplab for 30K iterations. Each of these configurations differs in hyperparameters and datasets.

4.1 Image Datasets

Four datasets were used in total, in which its image examples can be seen in Fig. 4. Two of them (ViolaSet [42] and SFA [5]) were merged to create another (Huskin), which is composed of images in various perspectives. The other two image datasets (Egohand and EgohandVal) were created from images we captured in the egocentric view:

- ViolaSet [42] (Fig. 4A), which contains 2922 images in various sizes (this is the number of images achieved from deleting GIFs and broken images from the total amount). It is composed of pictures of people (body and face) in different places and image sizes, with an uncontrolled background.
- SFA [5] (Fig. 4B), which contains 1118 images and is composed of pictures of human faces, with a less uncontrolled background.

Fig. 4. Dataset examples. (A) ViolaSet, (B) SFA, (C) Egohand, (D) EgohandVal.

- Egohand (Fig. 4C) is a dataset we created with 4041 images from [30], which contains 320 × 240 sized images of people in egocentric view performing a set of gestures in indoor environments. We generated masks for each image by applying segmentation with Grabcut [34].
- EgohandVal (Fig. 4D) is a dataset, also created in this work and composed by 322 640 × 360 sized images taken from different skin color individuals (4 individuals) and environments (indoor and outdoor) from Egohand. The gestures are similar to Egohand and other random ones. It is used as the validation set, with its labels also created by applying Grabcut [34].

Merging ViolaSet and SFA datasets, we composed the Huskin (human skin) dataset, resulting in 4040 images, in order to train with images of people in different perspectives and verify if it generates better models to segment egocentric images than training with a dataset composed of only egocentric images (which is the Egohand dataset). Furthermore, because datasets used to train deep neural networks are usually big (order of millions of images), and ours is way smaller than that, we also apply data augmentation techniques to verify if it improves training results.

Each network configuration was trained with Huskin and Egohand datasets, which results in two separate experiments. The trained models were validated with EgohandVal. That way we verify if training with Huskin is better than with Egohand.

4.2 Deeplab Training Configuration

PASCAL VOC 2012 [14] public available pre-trained weights were used to initialize the weights of our implementations of DeepLabv3+ with Xception as encoder and DeepLabv3 with MobileNetV2.

In order to train, the learning rate is maintained as the original paper and follows a "poly" policy, which is to multiply the learning rate started at 0.0001 by $\left(1 - \frac{iter}{max\_iter}\right)^{power}$ with $power = 0.9$, $iter$ representing the current iteration, max_iter the maximum iteration and $weight \; decay$ at $0,00004$.

Images and ground truth are resized to the crop size of 513×513 during training and evaluation.

The added blocks to the backbone networks were all trained with batch normalization, where $output\_stride$ is set to 16 in every deeplab network configurations. When Xception is used, the decoder output stride is set to 4, and ASPP module dilatation rates are set to 6, 12 and 18 for every training and evaluation. During training, we changed the batch sizes for the two encoders, leaving the other parameters as cited above, and the not mentioned are left as default:

MobileNetv2 - depth multiplier of 1; batch normalization with fine-tuning; output stride set to 16, since is the value that gave better results according to [35].

Xception - the encoder output stride is also set to 16 because it is the value that gives better results in processing and accuracy according to [9]; batch normalization fine-tuning is also used, with $decay$ of $0,9997$, $epsilon$ (variable used to avoid division by zero when normalizing activations and its variances) of 1e-3 using $gamma$ multiplier for scaling activations on batch normalization.

Data augmentation is applied by randomly scaling input images from 0.5 to 2.0 and randomly horizontal and vertical flipping during training.

As the original proposal of DeepLab [8] was made on Tensorflow [1], we also adopted this framework for the fine-tuning.

4.3   PSPNet Training Configuration

The fine-tuning was made using pre-trained weights with PASCAL VOC 2012 [14]. The learning rate was set fixed at 1e-10, momentum 0.99, batch size of one image and weight decay at 0.0005.

Images and its labels are resized to 473 × 473 during training and evaluation, which is the size of the network input.

Data augmentation is set to be the same as Deeplab. Hence, the Tensorflow operations were implemented in the Python programming language, in order to be used on Caffe [21], where the PSPNet network is originally implemented.

5   Results

In this section, we show the results of our performed experiments using different architecture configurations of DeepLab and PSPNet, described in Sect. 4. The experiments performance are measured by the metrics: average accuracy, F-Score [10] (harmonic average of precision and recall), Matthews correlation coefficient (MCC) [26], and its respective standard deviation resulted from five training sessions of each model.

We focused on comparing segmentation performance with MCC, although F-Score and accuracy were also captured in order to compare with other works. The best models from the two architectures, according to their MCC, will be used to test performance on GTEA public image dataset.

With our experiments, we show that models trained on the egocentric perspective have the best inference results when using egocentric images rather than the ones trained with images in different perspectives. Besides that, we show benefits on the segmentation performance, which makes possible inferences in real time. This hypothesis will show that our models can be used in VR applications that intend to show users' arms. At the end of the section, we will show images resulted from our segmentation with the best models and validated through the dataset and the GTEA.

The number of pixels which belongs to a background of an image or the ones which belongs to a human arm is naturally unbalanced, and for that reason, capturing segmentation accuracy may hide the real performance of a used model. This problem happens because human arms are usually not in a significant area of the captured image in the egocentric perspective. Therefore, the model may have more accuracy in background pixels rather than human arms pixels. This problem is widespread on binary classification, which makes necessary finding other metrics strategies to measure classification performance.

MCC [26] metric was initially created to measure secondary protein structures, where the value 1 represents an excellent performance, and -1 a bad one. Later, due to its focus on solving the unbalanced class problem, it was started to be used on measuring binary classification machine learning problems [4,17,22,28]. Another alternative to the use of accuracy is the F-Score [10] metric, which is also used to measure binary classification problems, where the value of 1 represents an excellent performance, and 0 is the contrary. These two metrics are used to measure the performance of models trained in this proposal. We focused on MCC because it is already used in problems with significant differences in classes distribution, as occur in our research. However, we also show accuracy and F-Score from models performance in order to expose our results for future comparisons and validations.

The training, evaluation and time inference tests were run on an NVIDIA GPU Tesla P100-SXM2-16 GB, Intel Xeon CPU E5-2698 v4 2.20 GHz, 528 GB of memory. The PSPNet was executed through Caffe NVIDIA Docker container 17.11. Deeplab used Tensorflow NVIDIA Docker container 18.04.

All the training and inference made with PSPNet were executed with only one GPU with the configurations cited above. In Table 3 we show PSP-Net training without data augmentation (we name it psp_huskin_no_aug or psp_egohand_no_ aug, according to which dataset was used to train it) results in better MCC on the validation set than with data augmentation (psp_huskin_aug or psp_egohand_aug).

Deeplab Mobilenet was trained with a batch size of 14 (we name it huskin_14b_ Mobilenet or egohand_14b_ Mobilenet) and Xception with a batch size of 4 (huskin_ 4b_Xception or egohand_4b_Xception) and 14 (huskin_ 14b_Xception or egohand_14b_Xception). When the training was executed with a batch of size 4, only one GPU was used. For batch size 14, two GPUs were used at the same time. When running inference, only one GPU was used for both cases of batch size.

Table 6 shows that Haskin Mobilenet version is better than Egohand one. However, the best Deeplab configuration is egohand_4b_Xception, with haskin_4b_ Xception very close to it. Additionally, as can be observed in Table 3, any version of PSP trained models have better MCC, where those trained with Egohand and no data augmentation had the best results, with values of 0.969 mean MCC.

By looking at Table 6, we also note that all Deeplab configurations have poor MCC, with its values very close to the 0, indicating that the models are not good binary classifiers, being almost random at predicting.

Qualitative results are shown in Fig. 5, in which (A) is the original image, (B) ground truth, (C) deeplab _egohand_14b_mobilenet, (D) deeplab_huskin_14b_ mobilenet, (E) deeplab_egohand_14b_xception, (F) deeplab _huskin_14b_xception, (G) psp_egohand_no_aug, (H) psp _huskin_no_aug. When can see PSP results have more fine details than Deeplab, although Huskin implementation (H) detects parts of a table as hand, and Egohand implementation (G) separates the table correctly from the hand (Tables 1, 2, 4 and 5).

This better quality in the PSP segmentation can be explained by its quantity of parameters and layers, which is higher than all the other cited implementations. This increase of parameters results in more significant results on the last layers. Its size is the result of merging 101 ResNet layers with the pooling pyramid at the end. Another fact which can contribute to this better performance is the output size of the feature map previous to applying the pooling pyramid,

Table 1. PSPNet Accuracy on Val set

	Mean accuracy	Standard deviation
psp_huskin_aug	96.39	1.463
psp_huskin_no_aug	97.50	0.423
psp_egohand_aug	99.05	0.113
psp_egohand_no_aug	**99.23**	0.074

Table 2. PSPNet F-Score on Val set

	Mean F-Score	Standard deviation
psp_huskin_aug	0.831	0.0870
psp_huskin_no_aug	0.893	0.0200
psp_egohand_aug	0.961	0.0073
psp_egohand_no_aug	**0.969**	0.0031

Table 3. PSPNet MCC on Val set

	Mean MCC	Standard deviation
psp_huskin_aug	0.826	0.0773
psp_huskin_no_aug	0.883	0.0208
psp_egohand_aug	0.957	0.0053
psp_egohand_no_aug	**0.965**	0.0035

Table 4. Deeplab accuracy on Val set

	Mean accuracy	Standard deviation
huskin_4b_Xception	81.75	0.156
huskin_14b_Mobilenet	**81.87**	0.164
huskin_14b_Xception	81.59	0.078
egohand_4b_Xception	81.71	0.120
egohand_14b_Mobilenet	**81.93**	0.117
egohand_14b_Xception	81.26	0.725

Table 5. Deeplab F-Score on Val set

	F-Score	Standard deviation
huskin_4b_Xception	0.140	0.0014
huskin_14b_Mobilenet	0.133	0.0019
huskin_14b_Xception	**0.142**	0.0010
egohand_4b_Xception	**0.141**	0.0011
egohand_14b_Mobilenet	0.130	0.0018
egohand_14b_Xception	0.138	0.0093

Table 6. Deeplab MCC on Val set

	MCC	Standard deviation
huskin_4b_Xception	0.043	0.0005
huskin_14b_Mobilenet	0.038	0.0005
huskin_14b_Xception	**0.043**	0.0002
egohand_4b_Xception	**0.044**	0.0003
egohand_14b_Mobilenet	0.036	0.0007
egohand_14b_Xception	0.037	0.0150

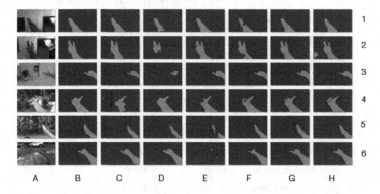

Fig. 5. Qualitative results. (A) is the original image, (B) ground truth, (C) deeplab_egohand_14b_mobilenet, (D) deeplab_huskin_14b_mobilenet, (E) deeplab_egohand_14b_xception, (F) deeplab_huskin_14b_xception, (G) psp_egohand_no_aug, (H) psp_huskin_no_aug.

which consists of 1/8 (that means output size of 8, with more details than the 16 from another network configurations cited) original input image size of the network. Besides that, even ResNet using DeepLab architecture, shown in [35], has fewer parameters (58.16M parameters and 81.0B multiplication-add operations) than original PSP, because it uses depthwise separable convolutions and dilated convolutions on ASSP module, which filters can have different scales without increasing the number of parameters.

The employment of data augmentation in every DeepLab configuration could have decreased its results because the images in which they were tested did not cover the situation where the user's arms are inverted upside down. These inverted images are part of one of the data augmentation applied to the training dataset. That may be one more reason PSPNet results were better, because data augmentation was not used on them.

The Xception implementation is smaller than PSP (54,17B mult-add operations) because it also uses dilated convolutions on its ASSP module. Besides that, the number of layers and the use of depthwise separable convolutions also decrease the number of parameters, making the network lighter, yet decreasing segmentation quality.

Table 7. Inference time test

	Mean time	Total time
PSP	21.997	7083.085
Mobilenet	0.026	8.577
Xception	0.076	24.475

Table 8. Tests on GTEA dataset

	MCC	Acurácia	F-Score
PSP	0.520	87.09	0.570
Xception	0.036	82.19	0.134

Our MobileNet implementation has substantially fewer parameters than Xception (2.11M parameters and 2.75B operations), being smaller and lighter than all cited network configurations, but also with worst MCC. Its size can be the result of not using an ASSP module (as mentioned before, using ASSP could increase the number of parameters and inference time). Besides that, it also does not have a decoder module, which is responsible for improving the feature map extracted from the encoder on Xception implementation; finally, its residual modules are inverted, helping to decrease more parameters because of the way it structures its operations.

Another interesting fact is the batch size used on Xceptions implementations. Using size 4 results in better MCC, that means, updating the weights faster, without looking to many training data gives a better model, which usually should not occur.

Concerning testing inference time, the 322 frames in 640 × 360 resolution from validation dataset were taken as input for the best network configurations. Segmentation time, measured by running the 322 frames, is shown in Table 7, where we can see Deeplab Mobilenet is better than the others, achieving 38 frames per second, while PSP cannot be used in real time application for segmenting every frame.

By looking at the number of parameters and operations from cited networks implementations, we can observe that MobileNet has better inference time because it is smaller than the other architectures, both in parameters and operations. PSP loses in inference time in comparison with all the other network configurations because it has more operations.

Tests on GTEA [15] public dataset were also performed. The dataset contains seven different types of daily activities made by four different individuals, all images captured in egocentric view. Table 8 shows MCC measures, accuracy, and F-Score for the best-trained network configurations (Deeplab egohand_4b_Xception and PSP egohand_no_aug) according to their MCC.

Figure 6 shows qualitative results from Table 8 tests, where we can see again that PSP (trained without data augmentation) has superior segmentation quality compared with DeepLab Xception trained with batch 4 and output stride 16. We also tested the output stride variation to 8 in MobileNet and Xception. As observed by the authors, the size 16 results in better segmentation quality, according to all metrics we used.

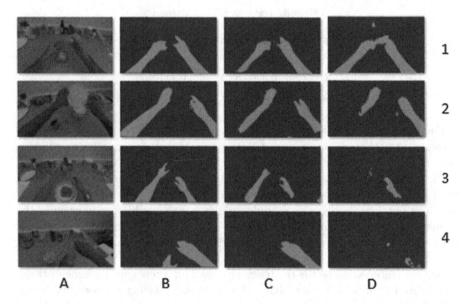

Fig. 6. Tests on GTEA. (A) original images for 4 subjects with different activities, (B) arms mask, (C) PSP, (D) DeepLab.

6 Conclusion

In this work, we proposed a human arms and hands segmentation strategy present in first person view images from Virtual Reality, Mixed Reality and Augmented Reality applications. Our method, when applied for fast execution, the segmentation quality drops compared to when focused on quality, which the reverse occurs. We also made publicly available all the source code and materials used for training[1].

---

[1] https://github.com/indexhever/ahsep.

In order to train egocentric human arms, it was first created a dataset of 4041 pixel masks, based on images from [30] dataset. These images generated our egocentric perspective dataset, called Egohand, focused on semantic segmentation of human arms. We also created another dataset for validation (EgohandVal), also in egocentric view. The first one has images captured in indoor environments. The second has images in indoor and outdoor environments with different skin color tone and illumination. Although the motivation for creating these datasets has been the application of mixed reality with the user's arm visualization, they can also be helpful for training networks that segment arms for another objective.

It was also presented fine tuning calibration and configuration of PSPNet and Deeplab network architectures, using our dataset for training and validation, in which DeeplabV3+ Xception trained using 4 batches on Egohand has shown the best result when considering inference time. In contrast, it does not represent a good pixel classifier by looking at its MCC value. PSP has presented the best MCC (0.969), although the inference time is not suitable for real-time segmentation, taking more than 20 s to segment one frame. Therefore, DeepLabV3+ Xception is the configuration that can be used in virtual or mixed reality application.

The DeeplabV3 Mobilenet configurations have presented the best results on inference time, making it possible to run 38 frames in one second.

The best training configurations were those trained with Egohand, which means that the results were better than training with a dataset with images in other perspectives (Huskin).

It was also verified that the PSPNet results were better when not using data augmentation. This could have damaged the DeepLab results, which have data augmentation in all configurations. In addition, one of Deeplab data augmentation consists in vertically inverting the images, resulting in inverted arms, which are not represented in the testing dataset. A future work can verify if training DeepLab configurations without this invertion can improve its results.

The main limitations of this work consist of the amount of GPUs used for training (only two for DeepLab and one for PSPNet) and capture of images for training. Training in more than one GPU on PSPNet was not possible due limitations of the frameworks optimizations for these scenarios. We limited the amount of GPUs when training DeepLab in order to try to match the training limitations, so that DeepLab uses batches of more than one image, which results in better training performance, while PSPNet has only one image per batch since it requires a significant amount of memory in one GPU.

For future works, Deeplab configurations should be trained for more iterations to see if MCC measure increases. Additionally, increasing the training dataset could also help. An application running on an HMD could also be created to test the whole system. [30] is a natural sequel to our research: after the user's arm rendering, the detection of different movements can be used for interaction inside a virtual environment.

References

1. Abadi, M., et al.: TensorFlow: large-scale machine learning on heterogeneous distributed systems. CoRR abs/1603.04467 (2016). http://arxiv.org/abs/1603.04467
2. Badrinarayanan, V., Kendall, A., Cipolla, R.: SegNet: a deep convolutional encoder-decoder architecture for image segmentation. arXiv:1511.00561 [cs], November 2015
3. Betancourt, A., Morerio, P., Regazzoni, C.S., Rauterberg, M.: The evolution of first person vision methods: a survey. IEEE Trans. Circuits Syst. Video Technol. 25(5), 744–760 (2015). https://doi.org/10.1109/TCSVT.2015.2409731
4. Boughorbel, S., Jarray, F., El-Anbari, M.: Optimal classifier for imbalanced data using Matthews Correlation Coefficient metric. PLoS ONE 12(6), e0177678 (2017). https://doi.org/10.1371/journal.pone.0177678. https://journals.plos.org/plosone/article?id=10.1371/journal.pone.0177678
5. Casati, J.P.B., Moraes, D.R., Rodrigues, E.L.L.: SFA: a human skin image database based on FERET and AR facial images. In: Anais do VIII Workshop de Visão Computacional. Rio de Janeiro (2013). http://www.sel.eesc.usp.br/sfa/
6. Chen, L.C., Papandreou, G., Kokkinos, I., Murphy, K., Yuille, A.L.: Semantic image segmentation with deep convolutional nets and fully connected CRFs. arXiv:1412.7062 [cs], December 2014
7. Chen, L.C., Papandreou, G., Kokkinos, I., Murphy, K., Yuille, A.L.: DeepLab: semantic image segmentation with deep convolutional nets, atrous convolution, and fully connected CRFs. arXiv:1606.00915 [cs], June 2016
8. Chen, L.C., Papandreou, G., Schroff, F., Adam, H.: Rethinking atrous convolution for semantic image segmentation. arXiv:1706.05587 [cs], June 2017
9. Chen, L., Zhu, Y., Papandreou, G., Schroff, F., Adam, H.: Encoder-decoder with atrous separable convolution for semantic image segmentation. CoRR abs/1802.02611 (2018). http://arxiv.org/abs/1802.02611
10. Chinchor, N.: MUC-4 evaluation metrics. In: Proceedings of the 4th Conference on Message Understanding, MUC4 1992, pp. 22–29. Association for Computational Linguistics, Stroudsburg (1992). https://doi.org/10.3115/1072064.1072067
11. Chollet, F.: Xception: deep learning with depthwise separable convolutions. CoRR abs/1610.02357 (2016). http://arxiv.org/abs/1610.02357
12. Dai, J., et al.: Deformable convolutional networks. CoRR abs/1703.06211 (2017). http://arxiv.org/abs/1703.06211
13. Dollar, P., Wojek, C., Schiele, B., Perona, P.: Pedestrian detection: an evaluation of the state of the art. IEEE Trans. Pattern Anal. Mach. Intell. 34(4), 743–761 (2012). https://doi.org/10.1109/TPAMI.2011.155
14. Everingham, M., Van Gool, L., Williams, C.K.I., Winn, J., Zisserman, A.: The PASCAL visual object classes challenge 2012 (VOC2012) results (2012)
15. Fathi, A., Ren, X., Rehg, J.M.: Learning to recognize objects in egocentric activities. In: CVPR 2011, pp. 3281–3288 (2011). https://doi.org/10.1109/CVPR.2011.5995444
16. Garcia-Garcia, A., Orts-Escolano, S., Oprea, S., Villena-Martinez, V., Garcia-Rodriguez, J.: A review on deep learning techniques applied to semantic segmentation. arXiv:1704.06857 [cs], April 2017
17. Gu, Q., Zhu, L., Cai, Z.: Evaluation measures of the classification performance of imbalanced data sets. In: Cai, Z., Li, Z., Kang, Z., Liu, Y. (eds.) ISICA 2009. CCIS, vol. 51, pp. 461–471. Springer, Heidelberg (2009). https://doi.org/10.1007/978-3-642-04962-0_53

18. Gupta, S., Arbeláez, P., Girshick, R., Malik, J.: Indoor scene understanding with RGB-D images: bottom-up segmentation, object detection and semantic segmentation. Int. J. Comput. Vis. **112**(2), 133–149 (2015). https://doi.org/10.1007/s11263-014-0777-6
19. He, K., Zhang, X., Ren, S., Sun, J.: Deep residual learning for image recognition. arXiv:1512.03385 [cs], December 2015
20. Howard, A.G., et al.: MobileNets: efficient convolutional neural networks for mobile vision applications. arXiv:1704.04861 [cs], April 2017
21. Jia, Y.,et al.: Caffe: convolutional architecture for fast feature embedding. arXiv preprint arXiv:1408.5093 (2014)
22. Koyejo, O.O., Natarajan, N., Ravikumar, P.K., Dhillon, I.S.: Consistent binary classification with generalized performance metrics. In: Ghahramani, Z., Welling, M., Cortes, C., Lawrence, N.D., Weinberger, K.Q. (eds.) Advances in Neural Information Processing Systems, vol. 27, pp. 2744–2752. Curran Associates, Inc. (2014). http://papers.nips.cc/paper/5454-consistent-binary-classification-with-generalized-performance-metrics.pdf
23. Li, C., Kitani, K.M.: Pixel-level hand detection in ego-centric videos, pp. 3570–3577 (2013)
24. Long, J., Shelhamer, E., Darrell, T.: Fully convolutional networks for semantic segmentation. arXiv:1411.4038 [cs], November 2014
25. Long, J., Shelhamer, E., Darrell, T.: Fully convolutional networks for semantic segmentation. CoRR abs/1411.4038 (2014). http://arxiv.org/abs/1411.4038
26. Matthews, B.W.: Comparison of the predicted and observed secondary structure of T4 phage lysozyme. Biochimica et Biophysica Acta (BBA) - Protein Structure **405**(2), 442–451 (1975). https://doi.org/10.1016/0005-2795(75)90109-9. http://www.sciencedirect.com/science/article/pii/0005279575901099
27. Maurya, J., Hebbalaguppe, R., Gupta, P.: Real time hand segmentation on frugal headmounted device for gestural interface. In: 2018 25th IEEE International Conference on Image Processing (ICIP), pp. 4023–4027 (2018). https://doi.org/10.1109/ICIP.2018.8451213
28. Menon, A., Narasimhan, H., Agarwal, S., Chawla, S.: On the statistical consistency of algorithms for binary classification under class imbalance. In: International Conference on Machine Learning, pp. 603–611, February 2013. http://proceedings.mlr.press/v28/menon13a.html
29. Obdržálek, S., Kurillo, G., Han, J., Abresch, T., Bajcsy, R.: Real-time human pose detection and tracking for tele-rehabilitation in virtual reality. Stud. Health Technol. Inform. **173**, 320–324 (2012)
30. de Oliveira, E., Clua, E.W.G., Vasconcelos, C.N., Marques, B.A.D., Trevisan, D.G., de Castro Salgado, L.C.: FPVRGame: deep learning for hand pose recognition in real-time using low-end HMD. In: van der Spek, E., Göbel, S., Do, E.Y.-L., Clua, E., Baalsrud Hauge, J. (eds.) ICEC-JCSG 2019. LNCS, vol. 11863, pp. 70–84. Springer, Cham (2019). https://doi.org/10.1007/978-3-030-34644-7_6
31. Phung, S.L., Bouzerdoum, A., Chai, D.: Skin segmentation using color pixel classification: analysis and comparison. IEEE Trans. Pattern Anal. Mach. Intell. **27**(1), 148–154 (2005). https://doi.org/10.1109/TPAMI.2005.17
32. Qi, X., Liao, R., Jia, J., Fidler, S., Urtasun, R.: 3D graph neural networks for RGBD semantic segmentation. In: 2017 IEEE International Conference on Computer Vision (ICCV), pp. 5209–5218, October 2017. https://doi.org/10.1109/ICCV.2017.556, iSSN 2380-7504
33. Redmon, J., Divvala, S., Girshick, R., Farhadi, A.: You only look once: unified, real-time object detection. arXiv:1506.02640 [cs], June 2015

34. Rother, C., Kolmogorov, V., Blake, A.: "GrabCut": interactive foreground extraction using iterated graph cuts. In: ACM SIGGRAPH 2004 Papers, SIGGRAPH 2004, pp. 309–314. ACM, New York (2004). https://doi.org/10.1145/1186562.1015720

35. Sandler, M., Howard, A.G., Zhu, M., Zhmoginov, A., Chen, L.: Inverted residuals and linear bottlenecks: mobile networks for classification, detection and segmentation. CoRR abs/1801.04381 (2018). http://arxiv.org/abs/1801.04381

36. Siddharth, Rangesh, A., Ohn-Bar, E., Trivedi, M.M.: Driver hand localization and grasp analysis: a vision-based real-time approach, February 2018. https://arxiv.org/abs/1802.07854v1

37. Sifre, L.: Rigid-motion scattering for image classification. Ph.D. thesis, Ecole Polytechnique, CMAP, October 2014

38. Slater, M., Wilbur, S.: A framework for immersive virtual environments (five): Speculations on the role of presence in virtual environments. Presence: Teleoperators and Virtual Environments 6(6), 603–616 (1997). https://doi.org/10.1162/pres.1997.6.6.603, https://doi.org/10.1162/pres.1997.6.6.603

39. Song, X., Herranz, L., Jiang, S.: Depth CNNs for RGB-D scene recognition: learning from scratch better than transferring from RGB-CNNs. CoRR abs/1801.06797 (2018). http://arxiv.org/abs/1801.06797

40. Tu, Z., Bai, X.: Auto-context and its application to high-level vision tasks and 3D brain image segmentation. IEEE Trans. Pattern Anal. Mach. Intell. 32(10), 1744–1757 (2010). https://doi.org/10.1109/TPAMI.2009.186

41. Vasconcelos, C.N., Clua, E.W.G.: Deep learning - Teoria e Prática. In: Jornadas de Atualização em Informática 2017. Sociedade Brasileira de Computação - SBC, Porto Alegre/RS, July 2017

42. Viola, P., Jones, M.: Rapid object detection using a boosted cascade of simple features. In: Proceedings of the 2001 IEEE Computer Society Conference on Computer Vision and Pattern Recognition. CVPR 2001, vol. 1, pp. I-511–I-518, vol. 1 (2001). https://doi.org/10.1109/CVPR.2001.990517

43. Viola, P., Jones, M.J.: Robust real-time face detection. Int. J. Comput. Vis. 57(2), 137–154 (2004). https://doi.org/10.1023/B:VISI.0000013087.49260.fb

44. Vodopivec, T., Lepetit, V., Peer, P.: Fine hand segmentation using convolutional neural networks. arXiv:1608.07454 [cs], August 2016

45. Yu, F., Koltun, V.: Multi-scale context aggregation by dilated convolutions. arXiv:1511.07122 [cs], November 2015

46. Zhao, H., Shi, J., Qi, X., Wang, X., Jia, J.: Pyramid scene parsing network. arXiv:1612.01105 [cs], December 2016

Virtual Scenarios for Pedestrian Research: A Matter of Complexity?

Sonja Schneider[(✉)] and Guojin Li

Department of Mechanical Engineering, Chair of Ergonomics, TU Munich,
Boltzmannstr. 15, 85748 Garching, Germany
sae.schneider@tum.de

Abstract. Virtual reality (VR) has become a popular tool to investigate pedestrian behavior. Many researchers, however, tend to simplify traffic scenarios to maximize experimental control at the expense of ecological validity. Multiple repetitions, facilitated by the brief durations of widespread crossing tasks, further add to predictability and likely reduce the need for cognitive processing. Considering the complexity inherent to naturalistic traffic, such simplification may result in biases that compromise the transferability and meaningfulness of empirical results. In the present work, we outline how human information processing might be affected by differences between common experimental designs and naturalistic traffic. Aiming at an optimal balance between experimental control and realistic demands, we discuss measures to counteract predictability, monotony, and repetitiveness. In line with this framework, we conducted a simulator study to investigate the influence of variations in the behavior of surrounding traffic. Although the observed effects seem negligible, we encourage the evaluation of further parameters that may affect results based on scenario design, rather than discussing methodological limitations only in terms of simulator fidelity.

Keywords: Pedestrian behavior · Virtual reality · Scenario design · Human information processing · Complexity

1 Introduction

During recent years, interest in pedestrian behavior has been fostered by demands to encourage eco-friendly, non-motorized modes of transportation as well as the fact that pedestrians are still at higher risk than other traffic participants in many countries [10, 33]. Reliably predicting their imminent actions is furthermore important to the successful implementation of vehicle automation [14], rendering them a focus for automotive engineers. Growing attention has led to the extension and refinement of methodological approaches to study the behavior of individual pedestrians. Many researchers appreciate the benefits of virtual reality (VR), which allows them to control and manipulate variables of interest in a nonetheless versatile and detailed environment. Providing high flexibility and experimental control at the same time, VR may – depending on the context – outperform some more conventional methods, including observations of naturalistic traffic and studies in physical laboratories.

J. Y. C. Chen and G. Fragomeni (Eds.): HCII 2020, LNCS 12190, pp. 171–190, 2020.
https://doi.org/10.1007/978-3-030-49695-1_12

Pedestrian simulators exist in various forms [36], with most of the more recent setups incorporating either head-mounted displays (HMDs) [9] or CAVE-like systems, i.e. several large screens between which participants can walk while visuals are adjusted to their perspective [8]. Although research objectives vary, many studies share a focus on street crossing [36]. The predominance of crossing scenarios may be explained by their relevance to safety, since they have repeatedly been linked to the risk of accidents [6]. Comparability with actual traffic, however, depends on the way such scenarios are implemented. In proposing a procedure to investigate gap acceptance in driving simulators, for example, Kearney et al. [18] suggest "presenting the same temporal gaps in each condition [to] facilitate comparison [...] to better understand how attentional demands and crossing strategies influence gap selection" (p. 178). The underlying rationale mirrors the (indispensable) goal of experimental research of ensuring sufficient experimental control. Nonetheless, we argue that one should be cautious about overemphasizing this objective without reflecting on the cost of repetition, monotony, and predictability.

Because individual crossings take little time, studies of pedestrian behavior often feature multiple repetitions [36]. Repeated measurements can thereby reduce statistical error arising from interpersonal variance and help to economize the comparison of numerous experimental conditions. On the other hand, recurrent crossings arguably lower scenario realism, since traversing the same street multiple times within minutes seems, at least outside an experimental setting, unfeasible. In addition, the presence of further traffic participants is often restricted to those immediately involved in the crossing task (i.e. approaching vehicles), and their direction of movement and acceleration profile may be oversimplified. Considering the complexity of real-world traffic, simulator studies may thus fail to capture the complexity and unpredictability that heighten the risk of accidents in naturalistic settings.

The present work aims to sensitize researchers to the question of ecological validity in simulated scenarios. Based on a model of human information processing, we discuss possible differences between experiments and the real world with regard to mechanisms of attention and expectation. Furthermore, we provide a summary of potential countermeasures, aiming at an optimal balance between experimental control and realistic demands. Finally, we present a simulator study involving 40 participants, in which the effects of variations in the surrounding traffic were investigated.

2   Experiments and Real World

In general, a simulation represents "an abstraction from reality" which "incorporates certain aspects [and] ignores others" [22] (p. 418). This idea applies not only to VR, but also to physical testbeds, which similarly replicate only those real-world aspects that are expected to influence the measure of interest. The challenge of creating a successful simulation thus lies in distinguishing necessary from irrelevant features. While such a distinction may be relatively obvious in some cases (e.g. the effect of visually representing an approaching object on the ability to locate its position is rarely questioned), others require more thorough consideration or empirical evidence.

In the field of pedestrian simulation, experimental studies have been conducted to investigate effects of stereovision [15] and the quality of auditory cues [4], to compare virtual and non-virtual environments [5, 38, 41] and to contrast different display types [20, 21, 39]. The complexity of traffic scenarios, on the other hand, has received surprisingly little attention, at least beyond differences between uni- and bidirectional traffic [8]. Nonetheless, it seems reasonable to expect that cognitive demands imposed by higher complexity may contribute to crash risk. Analyzing over 2000 accidents, for example, Otte et al. [27] found inappropriate attention allocation to be the most prominent cause for pedestrian injury, and Wells et al. [47] report distraction to frequently occur in real-world settings. If the cognitive processes evaluated in simulator studies fundamentally differ from the demands of naturalistic traffic, it may thus compromise the meaningfulness of experimental results.

2.1 Ecological Validity

The question of whether or not the demands imposed on human information processing match real-world contexts is linked to the concept of ecological validity. While validity in general refers to the extent to which a measure represents the value of interest, it encompasses a broad range of subordinate concepts, with partially inconsistent labeling across disciplines [25].

Ecological validity can be seen as a subtype of external validity, referring to the generalizability of results over different settings [25]. In traffic simulation, it thus relates to the extent to which simulated scenarios are consistent with the broad range of events occurring in naturalistic traffic. Although the competing goals associated with different facets of validity and the best way to reconcile them is vividly debated in other domains [17, 28], the question of whether scenarios adequately represent the setting of interest is rarely addressed in experimental pedestrian research. To ensure the usefulness of results, however, the representative selection of stimuli should be considered to be just as relevant as the elimination of confounding variables [28]. While representativeness depends on a number of factors, including the frequency of both critical and non-critical encounters, the present work concentrates on the cognitive demand associated with the mental processing of the given scenarios.

2.2 Human Information Processing

Over thirty years ago, Rumar [34] proposed a model of human information acquisition and processing in road traffic. Accordingly, information is construed as a combination of perception and expectation processes during mental operations rather than as a feature of the environment. Filters represent common limitations in human processing capacities: Perceptual filtering concerns physiological thresholds, whereas cognitive filtering depends on the motivational state and on expectation. Within this framework, expectation assumes a central role. While it is itself influenced by motivation and previous experience, expectation may not only determine whether attention is given to a particular stimulus, but also the way the input is subsequently interpreted.

Figure 1 displays a model adapted to the purpose of the present work. In contrast to Rumar [34], our objective is not primarily to illustrate limitations that may arise at different stages of mental operation, but to emphasize the interaction of internal states and processes such as motivation, expectation, and attention and their influence on observable human behavior.

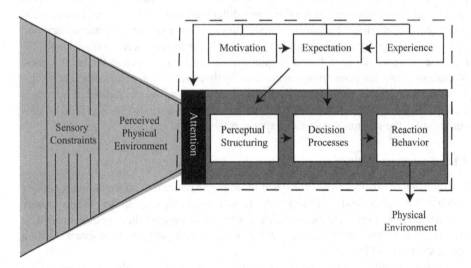

Fig. 1. Model of human information processing based on Rumar [34]. The processing of perceived stimuli depends on the allocation of attentional resources, which are themselves dependent on motivation, expectation and experience. Expectation further guides perceptual structuring and decision processes, which ultimately result in a behavioral response.

With regard to Rumar [34], we would like to add two assumptions. First, experience arises from a variety of sources. In pedestrian simulators, at least two types of experience can be distinguished, i.e. that of being a pedestrian in real-world traffic, and that related to previous experience within the experimental setting and familiarity with VR technology. While we would usually hope real-world experience to be most influential and thus the results to reflect what we would observe in naturalistic traffic, the relative importance of either source is hard to quantify. Second, we assume that expectations guiding attention allocation are affected by predictability, i.e. the ease and preciseness with which participants can foresee the timing and nature of future events, and that predictability itself partially depends on previous experience.

2.3   Information Processing in Experimental Research

Assuming that expectation is relevant to information processing, the generalizability of simulator studies may be compromised by high predictability. The latter is related to at least two task-dependent factors. On the one hand, it can be seen as a function of the time budget between the moment a future event can be anticipated and the moment it actually occurs. The longer this period, the higher the predictability [11]. More importantly, however, predictability is related to the perceived probability of events [7], which may be informed by previous experience. At high predictability levels, users may act in a routine manner [1], thus accelerating responses and reducing error rates [12]. If predictability is low, in contrast, more resources are required to continuously evaluate the appropriateness of actions and adjust one's behavior accordingly.

In experimental research, predictability has been linked to the variability of events. Petzoldt [30], for example, found performance in a lane-changing task to deteriorate if the timing and direction of an imminent lane-change was more variable. Green [12] reported that expectancy influenced brake reaction times, which doubled for surprising events. In comparison to the real world, he argues that in simulators, "there are fewer distractions, cognitive load is small, and the driver likely makes fewer eye movements to investigate objects in the peripheral field" (p. 202). He furthermore outlines that in "most simulator and controlled road studies [...] participants became highly practiced, which would reduce times compared to those likely in actual driving conditions" and that "simulator and controlled road studies put drivers on alert and probably switch them to a more conscious and controlled mode". While the assumption of increasing alertness competes with the idea of routine performance [1], both concepts may be relevant depending on the task. The existence of practice effects in pedestrian simulators is supported by accelerated responses in later trials [23].

In general, the repeated exposure to similar encounters and simplified surroundings may encourage participants to focus their attention in an unrealistic manner. Singh et al. [40] report vehicle detection to be delayed in the case of longer waiting times, possibly due to a decline in attention. Their findings suggest that in highly repetitive scenarios, participants may – consciously or subconsciously – make use of recurring patterns to economize their attention and accelerate their responses. If they are, for example, required to identify the first vehicle yielding for them to cross the road, they may focus their visual attention more strongly if all yielding vehicles start decelerating at the same position, knowing that outside a limited spatial zone, vehicles are likely to maintain their speed.

According to Bundesen et al. [7], visual attention results from the interaction of sensory evidence and attentional biases. In highly controlled detection-response tasks, perceptual processing is faster for expected stimuli. The same may apply to simulator studies in which detection refers to recognizing a specific behavior such as braking, and reactions consist in movements like initiating crossing. If participants expect that one of the vehicles is likely to brake within a certain time frame, it may thus accelerate behavioral responses.

Furthermore, visual attention is directional. Due to the physical boundaries of laboratories, but also in order to simplify the scenario, participants may be presented with unidirectional traffic. In this case, the spatial area of interest is severely restricted, minimizing the probability of missing events. Even if bidirectional traffic requires participants to divide their attention between opposite directions, objects of interest are typically limited in number and their trajectories restricted to straight movements, mainly at constant speed. Naturalistic traffic, in contrast, requires the dispersion of visual attention in order to continuously track a rapidly changing environment for potential hazards. The need to divide attention in dual-task conditions has been shown to impair pedestrian safety, resulting for example in a more variable trajectory and the failure to detect roadside events and identify crossing opportunities [13, 24]. In contrast to naturalistic traffic, however, the stimuli to which participants attended in the respective studies were both spatially restricted and predictable. Furthermore, a clear order of priority implied that performance in the secondary task was encouraged only on the precondition of collision avoidance. Hence, real-world traffic, in which simultaneous events can be equally relevant to traffic safety, may impose even higher demands.

3   Reducing Artificiality

Building on the previous section, the following paragraphs outline possible approaches to reduce the artificiality of experimental scenarios. It is important to note that empirical evidence regarding the effectiveness or possible side-effects of the proposed measures is missing. Furthermore, we are aware that for any specific application, our suggestions may be infeasible either for practical reasons or because they limit experimental control. With regard to the latter, however, we would like to stress once more that in applied research in particular, it may be inappropriate to disproportionally trade external for internal validity [28].

3.1   Avoiding Repetitions

If information processing is indeed altered by previous experience in the virtual environment, differences between simulated and real-world crossings likely arise from multiple repetitions, as is suggested by the evidence of learning effects [23]. Consequently, one may limit the number of trials to a single crossing per participant. If, however, the aim is for several conditions to be contrasted, such a procedure multiplies the resources which must be deployed for recruitment. Furthermore, measures under investigation are frequently subject to notable interindividual differences, fostering statistical noise in between-subject designs. Additional biases may result from unfamiliarity with the technical equipment: Particularly in HMDs, which prevent the vision of physical surroundings, motion may be affected by the fear of colliding and the limited cable length. If, on the other hand, practice trials are introduced to counteract such effects, they may cause similar adjustments as preceding experimental trials.

Alternatively, the repetitiveness of experimental designs may be addressed by embedding the actions of interest in a more realistic scenario. Instead of focusing on the act of street crossing, a cover story may be employed, according to which participants are instructed to perform a task that requires a change in location. With regard to designing an appropriate task, however, difficulties arise from the extended duration of the experiment and the limited space in current simulators, which prevents actions that cannot be performed close to the street. More importantly, the cover story itself may represent a confounding variable, altering the motivational state of participants [35, 37]. Finally, designing an appropriate task relies on relatively arbitrary estimates of what is deemed realistic and which time periods are feasible between individual crossings.

3.2   Environmental Distractors

A number of studies have focused on the effects of mobile devices [13, 23, 42, 43], whereas other sources of distraction have been evaluated to a lesser extent. Although certainly detrimental to pedestrian safety, concurrent tasks performed on handheld devices are mostly specified in advance and relatively predictable. Furthermore, their fulfillment is understood as subordinate to crossing success and the focus of attention is restricted. In the following we therefore concentrate on environmental distractors that form no part of an explicit dual-task condition, but may still compete for cognitive resources otherwise directed at crossing safely.

In general, one may distinguish static parts of the virtual scenery, such as infrastructure and neighboring buildings, from dynamic objects like surrounding traffic. Tapiro et al. [45] found smaller accepted gaps, delayed crossings, and a restricted gaze distribution in different age groups due to auditory and visual roadside distractors. A particularly large impact was observed for a group of passing cyclists, including sudden visual and auditory distractors, and the combination of multiple visual distractors and continuous background sound including speech. The authors explain these findings by the cyclists' travel direction being contrary to that of the motorized vehicles' and the human propensity to focus on natural speech, respectively. They conclude that visual distractors have a larger impact than auditory ones and that visually cluttered environments and sudden distractors are more detrimental than permanent stimuli. An enriched static scenery featuring a variable roadside appearance, in contrast, may even add to safety by attenuating signs of fatigue [46].

Particular considerations must be made with regard to surrounding traffic. Olstam [26] summarizes perceived intelligence, unpredictability resulting from variability, and virtual personalities that mimic cognitive states as three qualities that increase the realism of a traffic simulation. Scenario design, however, is restricted to avoid risky encounters unrelated to the research question and to support reproducibility [26]. In the scope of the present article, we distinguish between interacting agents, whose behavior is vital for task completion, and supplementary virtual humans and vehicles whose trajectory does not interfere with the participant's movements. In regard to the objective of counteracting artificiality, supplementary participants can be understood in terms of dynamic distractors. Varying the behavior of interacting agents, in contrast, typically affects the experimental design and will be discussed in the next paragraph.

Technically, external distractors are easy to implement in most street environments, whereas problems mainly concern experimental control. Unless their effect is explicitly part of the research question, external distractors must equally affect all experimental conditions. Universal and permanent distractors, however, not only restrict the range of possible events, but also facilitate compensatory techniques [45]. If, on the other hand, diverse and intermittent distractors are employed, their allocation to experimental conditions must be counterbalanced across participants to ensure internal validity. Further problems may arise as a result of the interaction between a particular distractor, condition, and individual.

3.3   Variability in the Behavior of Interacting Agents

Finally, repetitiveness can be diminished by variations concerning interacting agents and the experimental task itself. Obviously, the balance between external and internal validity is particularly delicate in this case. Randomization is typically restricted to factors that are no part of the research question, such as car models in studies that investigate crossing behavior as a function of gap size. Because multiple studies found effects of a vehicle's appearance [19, 29], comparability profits from a block-wise pseudo-randomization that ensures the same features for all experimental conditions. In general, parameters lacking immediate implications for the research question may be treated similarly to other environmental distractors. Factors more directly related to the research question, such as vehicle speed in gap acceptance scenarios, are typically kept constant for the sake of experimental control. To reduce predictability, however, one might shorten the time during which such parameters are stable. The later the final trajectory becomes obvious, the higher the uncertainty [11] and thus the presumable correspondence to real-world traffic.

With regard to the use case of street crossing, experimental conditions are mainly determined by the speed, acceleration, and physical appearance of approaching vehicles. Here, avoiding adjustments to result in confounding variance requires special care. However, balancing the need for internal and external validity [17, 28], researchers may decide in favor of a more realistic experimental environment and include variations in experimental conditions like the timing, number, and appearance of events. While varying vehicle behavior may compromise the categorization of experimental trials, statistical modelling can equally be applied to non-categorical variables [3, 31]. Since physical parameters such as velocities and distances naturally occur on a continuous scale, one may consider implementing them likewise in experimental designs. Variance can be generated by different approaches, e.g. by adding a random, normally distributed term to the target speed or distance, whose amplitude, variance, and update frequency may be informed by real-world observations. Alternatively, values observed in naturalistic traffic may directly be replicated in VR. Regardless of the method, the whole spectrum of expressions should be covered for all factor combinations, avoiding for example high speeds occurring predominantly with small gap sizes and vice versa.

Lastly, simulator studies may contain various types of scenarios. Particularly for non-continuous traffic and thus clearly separable trials, researchers may alternate between scenarios in which vehicles yield, and trials in which they do not. Even if the research question does not necessitate the inclusion of different scenario types, such variation may increase realism and lower predictability, albeit at the cost of longer studies and possible carry-over effects.

3.4   Summary

Table 1 summarizes the proposed measures, which are not mutually exclusive. Regardless of the method applied, we do not argue to trade internal for ecological validity, but to aim for an optimal balance between them.

Table 1. Overview of suggestions to reduce artificiality in simulator studies, including assumed advantages and expected challenges

	Advantages	Challenges
Avoiding repetitions		
Single-trial experiments	• No learning effects • Less expectation due to experiment-related experience	• Effortful recruitment • Unfamiliarity with the task and the technical equipment • Statistical noise due to interindividual differences
Cover stories	• Reduced repetitiveness • More natural situations, since crossing is typically goal-directed	• Design of an appropriate cover story • Motivational changes • Arbitrary estimates of e.g. realistic crossing intervals
Environmental distractors		
Environmental distractors	• Approaching the multi-task demands of real-world traffic • Attenuating effects of fatigue	• Selection of adequate distractors • Confounding effects if not equally distributed over experimental conditions • Habituation, in particular for permanent distractors • Statistical noise due to interactions between distractor, individual, and experimental condition
Variability in the behavior of interacting agents		
Variability unrelated to the research question	• Less obvious repetitions	• Possible side-effects on measures of interest that require adequate counterbalancing
Temporal variation in the behavior of interacting agents	• Reduced predictability	• Definition of optimal onset for constant behavior
De-categorization of independent variables	• More natural variation resulting in reduced predictability • No need for artificial classification	• Adequate mechanism to introduce variation • Efforts to ensure that similar expressions apply to all possible factor combinations • Alternative statistical modelling
Alternating trial types	• Reduced predictability	• Carry-over effects • Longer experimental durations if additional trials are introduced

Reducing the artificiality of experiments always bears the risk of compromising experimental control. A systematic discussion of the tension between reproducibility and realism is provided by Olstam [26]. While adjusting the behavior of interacting agents seems particularly challenging, other factors, such as the sudden appearance of distractors or a negligent selection of vehicle models, may equally affect the results.

Currently, however, virtual scenarios appear to be based on implicit assumptions that lack appropriate justification. Detailed static visuals, for instance, are typically considered desirable, whereas dynamic objects are excluded [42]. Repetitive and overly transparent scenarios may foster expectations that lead to changes in the allocation of attentional resources and reduce the extent of conscious decision-making in comparison to real-world traffic [12]. We thus hope that our work encourages the deliberate design of experimental scenarios, taking both internal and external validity into account.

4   Variability in Surrounding Traffic: A User Study

4.1   Research Question

As a first step towards evaluating the ideas outlined in the previous sections, a simulator study was designed to assess effects of variations in surrounding traffic. The presence of supplementary traffic, temporary variations in the behavior of interacting agents, and the alternation of trial types were manipulated simultaneously. Assuming that the simplifications inherent to many experimental designs may reduce the perceptual and cognitive demand in comparison with more realistic settings, our objective was to assess if such differences had an effect on common dependent measures.

Two virtual environments that varied in the degree of traffic complexity were compared, enabling an analysis of differences with regard to crossing decisions, crossing behavior, and the subjective agreement with real-world traffic. To alternate trial types, but also because effects may depend on the experimental task, we included scenarios both in which vehicles yielded and in which they did not.

4.2   Methodology

Experimental Design. In one group, a common, simplistic scenario was implemented, in which a row of vehicles approached from the left at a uniform speed of 30 km/h. Temporal gaps between the cars varied and participants were instructed to cross the street whenever they felt safe. In one of two blocks, one of the vehicles would always yield to the pedestrian. Whether vehicles should be expected to yield or not was announced at the beginning of the respective block. In the second group, in contrast, yielding and non-yielding trials alternated and approaching vehicles changed their speed and direction up to a distance of 40 m from the pedestrian's viewpoint. Supplementary traffic included virtual pedestrians walking on both sidewalks and additional vehicles that did not pass the pedestrian but drove on neighboring roads (Fig. 2). Background noise raised the overall sound volume in comparison to the simplistic scenario, in which the only sound resulted from passing vehicles. The static scenery and the vehicle behavior during the moment of passing was identical in both groups. Featuring environmental distractors, temporary variations in the behavior of interacting agents, and alternating trial types, the more complex environment thus included several of the proposed elements while maintaining relatively high experimental control.

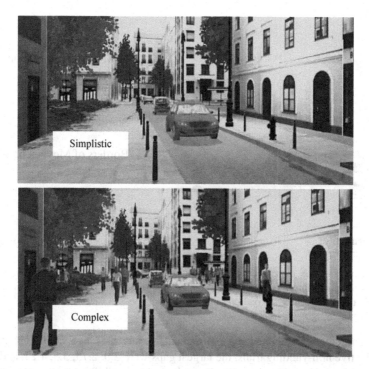

Fig. 2. Traffic scene in the simplistic and in the more complex environment. The latter featured additional traffic participants, auditory cues, and more variable driving behavior.

Participants. Forty participants were assigned to one of two groups, each comprising twenty people, with an equal share of males and females. Ages ranged between 19 and 33 years, with a mean of 23.2 years and a standard deviation of 3.5 years. Participants who experienced the complex environment were slightly younger (21.7 ± 2.6 years on average) than in the simplistic one (24.8 ± 3.8 years on average) and more likely to report previous VR experience (65% vs. 50%).

Apparatus and Scenario. The virtual environment was displayed via an HTC Vive Pro headset, offering a resolution of 1440×1600 pixels per eye at a refresh rate of 90 Hz and a nominal field of view of $110°$. Auditory cues were presented via integrated headphones. The simulation was created using the software Unity 3D version 2018.2.17f1 and run on a Hyrican Elegance 5701 equipped with an NVIDIA GeForce GTX 1080 Ti GPU.

To track the participants' movements, two base stations were placed in opposite corners of the experimental room (Fig. 3). The width of the virtual road corresponded to 3.5 m, whereas the total diagonal available for movements equaled approximately five meters.

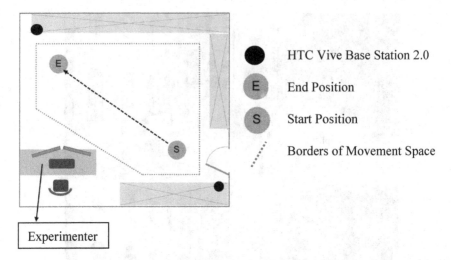

Fig. 3. Diagram of the experimental room. Participants could move freely within the area bounded by the green lines. The arrow between the positions marked by the letters "S" and "E" corresponds to the trajectory of road crossing.

Each participant completed ten experimental trials plus two additional practice runs. In the five non-yielding trials, the largest gaps were 2.0, 2.75, 3.5, 4.25, and 5.0 s, respectively. In order to more specifically address the possibility of delayed responses, each of these experimental gaps occurred twice per trial. In the five yielding trials, the distances at which the vehicles started braking matched the gaps in the non-yielding trials. Participants could cross the street any time after the first car had passed and were instructed to behave as they would in real life. In the complex setting, the order of trials was randomized, whereas in the simplistic environment, trials with and without yielding vehicles were summarized in blocks whose order was counterbalanced. Participants in this group were explicitly informed whether or not vehicles in the subsequent trials would yield.

Dependent Measures. Effects were analyzed with regard to both crossing decisions (i.e. acceptance of the first or second gap for a given gap size in the non-yielding trials) and crossing behavior (including the time needed to initiate and finish crossing as well as temporal safety margins). Furthermore, data on subjective impressions were collected by means of post-experiment questionnaires.

Crossing behavior was evaluated with regard to different segments of the crossing process. To limit the impact of differences in the starting position, all measures were calculated with regard to the middle part of the lane, excluding 0.25 m on either side. The initiation time (IT) describes the time between the moment the rear of a vehicle passes a pedestrian's theoretical crossing line and the moment this pedestrian enters the road. Negative ITs indicate that the pedestrian initiated walking before the vehicle had fully crossed the intersection line. The crossing time (CT) corresponds to the duration from leaving the pedestrian walkway on one side to arriving at the other. Average crossing speed was obtained by dividing the walked distance by the CT, taking all translations in the horizontal plane into account. Finally, the post encroachment time (PET) was defined as the time starting when the pedestrian leaves the part of the road that will be occupied by the dimensions of the following vehicle, and ending when the following vehicle reaches the pedestrian's crossing line. Since negative PETs indicate a virtual collision, it can be seen as a temporal safety margin.

After the experiment, participants rated the perceived predictability, complexity, and realism with respect to the vehicles' acceleration and trajectory as well as the scenario itself. A fourth category concerning the behavior of surrounding traffic was omitted from analysis, since - in particular in the simplistic group - this question seemed to be subject to ambiguous interpretation. All aspects were rated separately for yielding and non-yielding trials.

4.3   Analysis and Results

For one participant of each group, one of the yielding trials was excluded due to tracking failures. In 35% of the trials in which cars did not yield, participants did not cross. In 55.5% of those trials, they accepted the first and in 8.5% the second gap. One individual in the complex environment repeatedly crossed prior to the experimental gap or the yielding vehicle, accepting temporal intervals ranging between 1.44 and 1.79 s. These data points were excluded from further analysis.

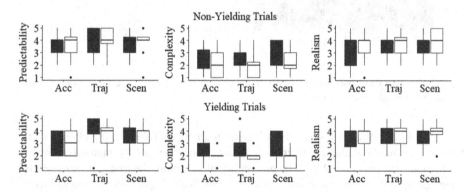

Fig. 4. Subjective ratings regarding the vehicles' acceleration (Acc) and trajectory (Traj) as well as the overall scenario (Scen) in the complex (blue) and the simplistic (white) environment (Color figure online)

Subjective ratings are displayed in Fig. 4. Overall, perceived predictability and realism appear relatively unaffected by variations in surrounding traffic, whereas more systematic differences occur for perceived complexity. However, due to the relatively small number of only twenty observations per group and the lack of a validated questionnaire, no inferential analyses were performed on these data.

Crossing decisions and crossing behavior were analyzed by means of mixed regression analyses. All models included a random intercept for the participant, reflecting the assumption that average values may vary between individuals.

Furthermore, all models included gap size as a second predictor along with the inter-action between gap size and complexity, since traffic complexity might be more decisive if crossing opportunities are ambivalent. Effects on the probability of accepting the first or second gap, respectively, were evaluated by means of mixed logistic regression. For the remaining measures, mixed linear regression was employed. All analyses were performed by means of the lme4 package [3] of the statistical software R [32].

Figure 5 pertains only to trials in which vehicles did not yield. Descriptively, participants in the complex environment crossed more often and more commonly chose the first rather than the second gap. Post encroachment times were relatively similar, although they seemed slightly more dependent on gap size in the simplistic environment.

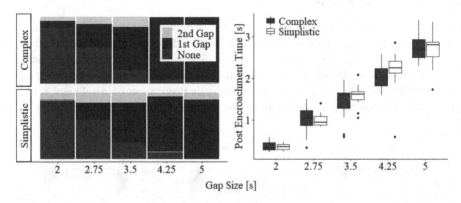

Fig. 5. Crossing decisions (left) and post encroachment times (right) as a function of gap size for the two virtual environments

According to the results of mixed logistic regression (Table 2), the chosen varia-tions in surrounding traffic influenced gap acceptance neither by themselves nor in interaction with gap size. While the probability of accepting the first gap increased for larger gaps, none of the predictors showed a significant impact on the probability of accepting the second gap.

Initiation times and crossing speeds were analyzed for all trials in which partici-pants moved to the opposite side of the street. Separate models were fitted for yielding and non-yielding trials. The analysis of post encroachment times, in contrast, was restricted to trials in which cars did not yield, because yielding cars were programmed to wait until crossing was completed. In line with Barr et al. [2], random slopes were included for gap size.

Again, the chosen manipulations of surrounding traffic did not cause significant differences (Table 3). Relatively large standard errors regarding the effect of complexity furthermore resulted in wide confidence intervals (Fig. 7). If vehicles did not yield and gaps were small, crossings were initiated earlier and participants walked faster (Fig. 6). Similarly, post encroachment times mainly depended on gap size (Fig. 5). The braking distance of yielding vehicles, in contrast, had no significant effect.

Table 2. Results of the logistic regression analyses performed to predict crossing decisions. Predictors that are significant at a level of $\alpha = .05$ are marked with an asterisk. (b: Unstandardized regression coefficient, SE: Standard error, CI: Confidence interval)

	b	SE	95% CI	z	Sig.
Model 1: probability of accepting the first gap					
(Intercept	−62.879	16.172	[−104.180; −32.822]	−3.888	*)
Complexity	15.653	13.281	[−9.146; 49.504]	1.179	
Gap size	20.144	5.128	[9.328; 32.959]	3.928	*
Interaction	−4.928	4.091	[−15.164; 2.786]	−1.205	
Model 2: probability of accepting the second gap					
(Intercept	−4.735	2.348	[−11.396; −1.987]	−2.016	*)
Complexity	−0.502	2.595	[−6.586; 4.691]	−0.193	
Gap size	1.199	0.734	[0.310; 3.170]	1.633	
Interaction	0.076	0.863	[−1.696; 2.061]	0.088	

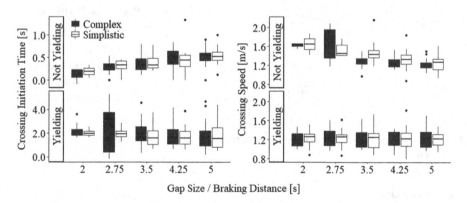

Fig. 6. Crossing initiation times (left) and average crossing speed (right) as a function of gap size and scenario for the two virtual environments. Note: In the yielding condition, the x-axis depicts the temporal gap at which the vehicle started decelerating.

Table 3. Results of the linear regression analyses performed to predict crossing behavior. Predictors that are significant at a level of α = .05 are marked with an asterisk. (*b*: Unstandardized regression coefficient, *SE*: Standard error)

	No yielding vehicles				Yielding vehicles			
	b	SE	t	Sig.	b	SE	t	Sig.
Model 1: post encroachment time								
(Intercept	−1.104	0.157	−7.030	*)				
Complexity	−0.246	0.218	−1.126					
Gap size	0.768	0.036	21.444	*				
Interaction	0.041	0.050	0.823					
Model 2: initiation time								
(Intercept	0.032	0.100	0.316		2.107	0.224	9.396	*)
Complexity	0.042	0.139	0.299		0.483	0.321	1.507	
Gap size	0.101	0.023	4.471	*	−0.080	0.072	−1.119	
Interaction	−0.009	0.317	−0.292		−0.071	0.102	−0.699	
Model 3: crossing speed								
(Intercept	1.958	0.120	16.331	*	1.250	0.048	25.81	*)
Complexity	−0.038	0.167	−0.229		−0.020	0.069	−0.286	
Gap size	−0.143	0.025	−5.722	*	−0.006	0.010	−0.626	
Interaction	−0.005	0.035	−0.150		0.010	0.014	0.737	

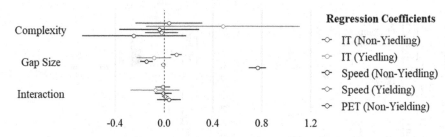

Fig. 7. Estimates and 95% confidence intervals for the fixed effect coefficients analyzed in linear regression

4.4   Summary

Based on the framework outlined in the previous sections, a simulator study was conducted to evaluate the effects of variations in surrounding traffic. Half of the participants experienced an environment in which supplementary virtual agents were present and the speed and direction of approaching vehicles varied up to a distance of 40 m. Neither crossing decisions nor crossing behavior were affected. In some cases, regression coefficients were numerically close to zero, which can be understood as a hint that effects were actually negligible. In other cases, however, regarding for example a descriptive tendency towards smaller post-encroachment times and delayed crossing initiation in yielding trials, possible differences might have been concealed by interindividual differences. Particularly wide confidence intervals (Fig. 7) can be explained by the fact that the virtual environment was, unlike gap size, varied between groups and effects of complexity were thus subject to interindividual noise. On the other hand, complexity also appears to result in larger differences within one group, in particular for the relatively small gap of 2.75 s (Fig. 6). Hence, some people might be more affected by distractors and reduced predictability than others.

Considering the overall pattern, there is little evidence for differences between the two groups in the present study. However, this must not be mistaken for a general lack of behavioral changes due to surrounding traffic. First, the participant sample was limited in size and in the range of personal characteristics. Other populations, such as children, may generally be more susceptible to environmental distractors [44]. Second, despite purposefully introducing additional variation, we aimed at maintaining maximal experimental control. To present equal gaps up to a size of five seconds, we restricted the zone in which the trajectory of approaching vehicles varied. Considering the limited resolution of VR applications and the fact that, driving at a speed of 30 km/h, vehicle behavior was identical in both groups during the last 4.8 s, one may conclude that rather than disproving an influence of predictability, the present results show that either this time was sufficient to predict future events or at least that participants in the simplistic group did not benefit from a longer time interval. After the first trials, it was also obvious that supplementary pedestrians would not interfere with the participants' task. Hence, the predefined and mostly straight pathways might have triggered similar compensatory measures as other permanent distractors, whereas virtual pedestrians may have a stronger effect if they change their trajectory, for example by crossing the street themselves [16]. Similarly, supplementary vehicles could be recognized as such at a relatively large distance (i.e. 40 m). Finally, trials in the present study were separated to facilitate the implementation of equal gap sizes, whereas continuous traffic might increase the overall demands on cognitive processing. Hence, although effects of the implemented measures seem negligible, investigating different options for surrounding traffic, also with regard to their potential in approaching real-world conditions, may be worthwhile.

5 Conclusion

Being simultaneously flexible and economic, detailed and controllable, virtual reality is a promising tool to study human behavior. A disproportionate focus on experimental control, however, may ultimately prevent researchers from utilizing the full potential of this technology. A major challenge concerns the reconciliation of traditional experimental paradigms, which are designed to test well-defined hypotheses originating from scientific theories, and more applied research, in which the accuracy of predictions may ultimately be more valuable than their agreement with a theoretical framework.

All simulation is associated with certain simplifications [22], but the extent to which they are justified depends on the research question. In traffic-related research in particular, which involves a complex and highly versatile environment, experimental results may be biased if scenarios resemble sophisticated detection-response tasks but fail to capture the cognitive demands related to naturalistic traffic – even if targets and distractors constitute visually detailed representations of complex real-world entities.

In the present work, we outlined how expectation and predictability may affect human information processing and presented some ideas on mechanisms to counteract possible side-effects of repetitions and overly transparent scenarios. While the evaluated variations in surrounding traffic seemed ineffective, alternative measures may better reflect the complexity encountered in real world. Future research is hoped to provide more evidence on whether and how changes in information processing influence the measures of interest, thereby supporting meaningful conclusions in an adjustable and risk-free experimental environment.

Acknowledgments. This research was supported by the German Research Foundation (Deutsche Forschungsgemeinschaft, project number 317326196).

References

1. Aarts, L., Davidse, R.: Behavioural effects of predictable rural road layout: a driving simulator study. Adv. Transp. Stud. **14**, 25–34 (2008)
2. Barr, D.J., Levy, R., Scheepers, C., Tily, H.J.: Random effects structure for confirmatory hypothesis testing. Keep it maximal. J. Memory Lang. **68**(3), 1–43 (2013)
3. Bates, D., Mächler, M., Bolker, B., Walker, S.: Fitting linear mixed-effects models using lme4. J. Stat. Softw. **67**(1), 1–48 (2015)
4. Bernhard, M., Grosse, K., Wimmer, M.: Bimodal task-facilitation in a virtual traffic scenario through spatialized sound rendering. ACM Trans. Appl. Perception **8**(4), 1–22 (2011)
5. Bhagavathula, R., Williams, B., Owens, J., Gibbons, R.: The reality of virtual reality: a comparison of pedestrian behavior in real and virtual environments. Proc. Hum. Factors Ergon. Soc. Ann. Meeting **62**(1), 2056–2060 (2018)
6. Blower, D.: Key Pedestrian Collision Scenarios in the U.S. for Effective Collision Avoidance Technologies (2014)
7. Bundesen, C., Vangkilde, S., Petersen, A.: Recent developments in a computational theory of visual attention (TVA). Vis. Res. **116**, 210–218 (2015)
8. Cavallo, V., Dommes, A., Dang, N.-T., Vienne, F.: A street-crossing simulator for studying and training pedestrians. Transp. Res. Part F Traffic Psychol. Behav. **61**, 217–228 (2019)
9. Deb, S., Carruth, D.W., Sween, R., Strawderman, L., Garrison, T.M.: Efficacy of virtual reality in pedestrian safety research. Appl. Ergon. **65**, 449–460 (2017)
10. European Commission: Road safety in the European Union. Trends, statistics and main challenges. Publications Office, Luxembourg (2018)
11. Gold, C., Naujoks, F., Radlmayr, J., Bellem, H., Jarosch, O.: Testing scenarios for human factors research in level 3 automated vehicles. In: Stanton, Neville A. (ed.) AHFE 2017. AISC, vol. 597, pp. 551–559. Springer, Cham (2018). https://doi.org/10.1007/978-3-319-60441-1_54
12. Green, M.: "How long does it take to stop?" Methodological analysis of driver perception-brake times. Transp. Hum. Factors **2**(3), 195–216 (2000)
13. Haga, S., Sano, A., Sekine, Y., Sato, H., Yamaguchi, S., Masuda, K.: Effects of using a smart phone on pedestrians' attention and walking. Procedia Manuf. **3**, 2574–2580 (2015)

14. Hartmann, M., Viehweger, M., Desmet, W., Stolz, M., Watzenig, D.: "Pedestrian in the loop": an approach using virtual reality. In: ICAT 2017. XXVI International Conference on Information, Communication and Automation Technologies, Proceedings, Bosnia & Herzegovina, 26–28 October 2017. IEEE, Piscataway, NJ1–8 (2017)
15. Jiang, Y., O'Neal, E.E., Franzen, L., Yon, J.P., Plumert, J.M., Kearney, J.K.: The influence of stereoscopic image display on pedestrian road crossing in a large-screen virtual environment. In: Proceedings - SAP 2017, ACM Symposium on Applied Perception (2017)
16. Jiang, Y., ONeal, E.E., Rahimian, P., Yon, J.P., Plumert, J.M., Kearney, J.K.: Joint action in a virtual environment: crossing roads with risky vs. safe human and agent partners. IEEE Trans. Vis. Comput. Graph. 25, 2886–2895 (2018)
17. Jimenez-Buedo, M., Miller, L.M.: Why a trade-off? The relationship between the external and internal validity of experiments. Theoria Int. J. Theory Hist. Found. Sci. 25(3), 301–321 (2010)
18. Kearney, J.K., Grechkin, T., Cremer, J.F., Plumert, J.M.: Traffic generation for studies of gap acceptance. In: Proceedings of the Driving Simulation Conference Europe, pp. 177–186. INRETS, Renault, Bron, Boulogne-Billancourt (2006)
19. Klatt, W.K., Chesham, A., Lobmaier, J.S.: Putting up a big front: car design and size affect road-crossing behaviour. PLoS ONE 11(7), 1–12 (2016)
20. Maillot, P., Dommes, A., Dang, N.-T., Vienne, F.: Training the elderly in pedestrian safety. Transfer effect between two virtual reality simulation devices. Accid. Anal. Prev. 99, 161–170 (2017)
21. Mallaro, S., Rahimian, P., O'Neal, E.E., Plumert, J.M., Kearney, J.K.: A comparison of head-mounted displays vs. large-screen displays for an interactive pedestrian simulator. In: Proceedings of the 23rd ACM Symposium on Virtual Reality Software and Technology - VRST 2017. ACM Press, New York, 1–4 (2017)
22. Molino, J.A., Opiela, K.S., Katz, B.J., Moyer, M.J.: Validate first; simulate later: a new approach used at the FHWA highway driving simulator. In: Proceedings of the Driving Simulation Conference 2005, pp. 411–420 (2005)
23. Neider, M., Gaspar, J., McCarley, J., Crowell, J., Kaczmarski, H., Kramer, A.: Pedestrians, automobiles, and cell phones; examining the effects of divided attention and aging in a realistic virtual reality street crossing task. J. Vis. 11(11), 98 (2011)
24. Neider, M.B., McCarley, J.S., Crowell, J.A., Kaczmarski, H., Kramer, A.F.: Pedestrians, vehicles, and cell phones. Accid. Anal. Prev. 42(2), 589–594 (2010)
25. Newton, P.E., Shaw, S.D.: Validity in Educational and Psychological Assessment. SAGE Publications Ltd., London (2014)
26. Olstam, J.: Simulation of surrounding vehicles in driving simulators. Doctoral thesis, Linköping University, Linköping (2009)
27. Otte, D., Jänsch, M., Haasper, C.: Injury protection and accident causation parameters for vulnerable road users based on German In-Depth Accident Study GIDAS. Accid. Anal. Prev. 44(1), 149–153 (2012)
28. Persson, J., Wallin, A.: Why internal validity is not prior to external validity. In: Philosophy of Science Association. 23rd Biennial Meeting, pp. 637–650 (2012)
29. Petzoldt, T.: Size speed bias or size arrival effect - how judgments of vehicles' approach speed and time to arrival are influenced by the vehicles' size. Accid. Anal. Prev. 95, 132–137 (2016)
30. Petzoldt, T., Krems, J.F.: How does a lower predictability of lane changes affect performance in the Lane Change Task? Appl. Ergon. 45(4), 1218–1224 (2014)
31. Pinheiro J., Bates, D., DebRoy, S., Sarkar, D., R Core Team: nlme: linear and nonlinear mixed effects models (2018)

32. R Core Team: R: a language and environment for statistical computing. R Foundation for Statistical Computing, Vienna, Austria (2018)
33. Retting, R.: Pedestrian Traffic Fatalities by State. 2018 Preliminary Data (2019)
34. Rumar, K.: The role of perceptual and cognitive filters in observed behavior. In: Evans, L., Schwing, R.C. (eds.) Human Behavior and Traffic Safety, pp. 151–170. Springer, Boston (1985). https://doi.org/10.1007/978-1-4613-2173-6_8
35. Sailer, M., Hense, J.U., Mayr, S.K., Mandl, H.: How gamification motivates: an experimental study of the effects of specific game design elements on psychological need satisfaction. Comput. Hum. Behav. **69**, 371–380 (2017)
36. Schneider, S., Bengler, K.: Virtually the same? Analysing pedestrian behaviour by means of virtual reality. Transp. Res. Part F Traffic Psychol. Behav. **68**, 231–256 (2020)
37. Schneider, S., Ratter, M., Bengler, K.: Pedestrian behavior in virtual reality: effects of gamification and distraction. In: Proceedings of the Road Safety and Simulation Conference (2019)
38. Schwebel, D.C., Gaines, J., Severson, J.: Validation of virtual reality as a tool to understand and prevent child pedestrian injury. Accid. Anal. Prev. **40**(4), 1394–1400 (2008)
39. Schwebel, D.C., Severson, J., He, Y.: Using smartphone technology to deliver a virtual pedestrian environment: usability and validation. Virtual Reality **21**(3), 145–152 (2017)
40. Singh, S., Payne, S.R., Jennings, P.A.: Toward a methodology for assessing electric vehicle exterior sounds. IEEE Trans. Intell. Transp. Syst. **15**(4), 1790–1800 (2014)
41. Singh, S., Payne, S.R., Mackrill, J.B., Jennings, P.A.: Do experiments in the virtual world effectively predict how pedestrians evaluate electric vehicle sounds in the real world? Transp. Res. Part F Traffic Psychol. Behav. **35**, 119–131 (2015)
42. Sobhani, A., Farooq, B.: Impact of smartphone distraction on pedestrians' crossing behaviour: an application of head-mounted immersive virtual reality. Transp. Res. Part F Traffic Psychol. Behav. **58**, 228–241 (2018)
43. Stavrinos, D., Byington, K.W., Schwebel, D.C.: Distracted walking: cell phones increase injury risk for college pedestrians. J. Saf. Res. **42**(2), 101–107 (2011)
44. Tapiro, H., Oron-Gilad, T., Parmet, Y.: Towards understanding the influence of environmental distractors on pedestrian behavior. Procedia Manuf. **3**, 2690–2697 (2015)
45. Tapiro, H., Oron-Gilad, T., Parmet, Y.: The effect of environmental distractions on child pedestrian's crossing behavior. Saf. Sci. **106**, 219–229 (2018)
46. Thiffault, P., Bergeron, J.: Monotony of road environment and driver fatigue: a simulator study. Accid. Anal. Prev. **35**(3), 381–391 (2003)
47. Wells, H.L., McClure, L.A., Porter, B.E., Schwebel, D.C.: Distracted pedestrian behavior on two urban college campuses. J. Commun. Health **43**(1), 96–102 (2018)

Comparative Study Design of Multiple Coordinated Views for 2D Large High-Resolution Display with 3D Visualization Using Mixed Reality Technology

Simon Su$^{(\boxtimes)}$ ⓘ and Vincent Perry

CCDC Army Research Laboratory, Aberdeen Proving Ground,
MD 21005, USA
simon.m.su.civ@mail.mil

Abstract. We present the design of our qualitative assessment of user interaction and data exploration using our hybrid 2D and 3D visual analytic application with 2D visual analytics application running on Large High-Resolution
Display (LHRD) and 3D visual analytics application running on mixed reality
immersive displays. The application used for the study visualizes our Monte
Carlo simulation over time showing topological, geospatial, and temporal
aspects of the data in multiple views. We assessed attitudinal responses on the
usefulness of visual analytics using 2D visualization on LHRD, and compare
that with visual analytics using 2D visualization on LHRD with 3D visualization
using mixed reality display. We first perform a usability test, where the participants complete a couple of exploratory tasks: one, identifying corresponding
assets in a visualization, and two, identifying patterns/relationships between
particular assets. Participants perform the same tasks using two different system
configurations: using 2D visualization on LHRD, using 2D and 3D visualization
together but as separate application, and using 2D visualization on LHRD and
3D visualization on Microsoft HoloLens with multiple coordinated views across
the two systems. A pilot study were conducted on the experimental design on
the relative effectiveness of the different setups towards accomplishing the given
tasks. We further discuss how the results of the pilot study confirm current
system design decisions, and also discuss additional user-centric characteristics
that must be considered to inform future design decisions.

Keywords: Mixed reality and non-immersive analytics · User study design

1 Introduction

The exploration, modeling and analysis of complex heterogeneous data require a vastly
different class of tools capable of supporting data-centric, user-centric, visualization
algorithm and systems agnostic visual analytics. Although the complexity of the data
increased dramatically, it is still crucial to be able to quickly analyze the datasets
generated to identify trends, anomalies, and correlations. Therefore, development of
novel visual analytics tools enabling real-time interactive data exploration can result in
the discovery of usable information for our user.

This is a U.S. government work and not under copyright protection in the U.S.;
foreign copyright protection may apply 2020
J. Y. C. Chen and G. Fragomeni (Eds.): HCII 2020, LNCS 12190, pp. 191–207, 2020.
https://doi.org/10.1007/978-3-030-49695-1_13

Various combinations of hardware and software platforms can be leveraged in the development of visual analytics tools. However, the most challenging design effort is to develop a visual analytics application for our requirements while considering the extensible and general-purpose aspect of the tool to support the next phase of the research. Specifically in our work, our goal is to support real-time interactive visualization of complex data through useful human-computer interaction on Large High-Resolution Display (LHRD) and 3D Mixed Reality systems. In addition, to address our need for faster prototyping and extensibility, we have taken advantage of a rich ecosystem of tools of the open source community in the development of our hybrid 2D and 3D data visualization application.

For complex heterogeneous data exploration, a visual analytics tool running on a LHRD and 3D Mixed Reality system opens up the possibility for the users to visualize and interact with the data using heterogeneous visualization hardware and software. This includes 2D data interaction on the LHRD and 3D data visualization using Mixed Reality system. Our complex Monte Carlo simulation data can unfold in many different ways, driving the need for a hybrid 2D and 3D visualization environment. Andrews et al. described the potential benefits of using LHRD for information visualization [1], which are in many ways applicable to our data analysis and visualization requirements.

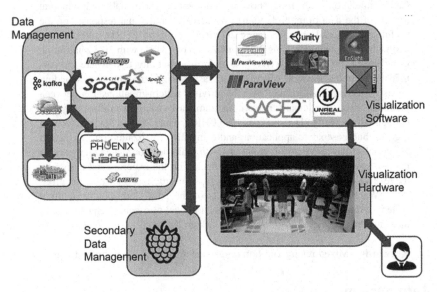

Fig. 1. System diagram for a dynamic visual computing framework for data intense analytics

The development of our LHRD visualization application took advantage of Scalable Amplified Group Environment2 (SAGE2) [2]. SAGE2 allows multiple displays to be used as a single large high-resolution multiuser workspace resulting in a low cost LHRD system. In our current development, we extended ParaViewWeb to run on SAGE2 to overcome the scalability limitation of our previous visualization framework [3] in the development of LHRD information visualization application targeting complex data visualization. For 3D data visualization, we also added a WebGL visualization component to our ParaViewWeb framework and also a Unity 3D application running on Microsoft HoloLens that receives synchronization data from a Unity Event Server to facilitate multi-coordinated views [4] between LHRD and Microsoft HoloLens visualization. The hybrid 2D and 3D Visual Analytics tool presented is also a part of our larger research effort in Dynamic Visual Computing Framework for Data Intense Analytics as shown in Fig. 1.

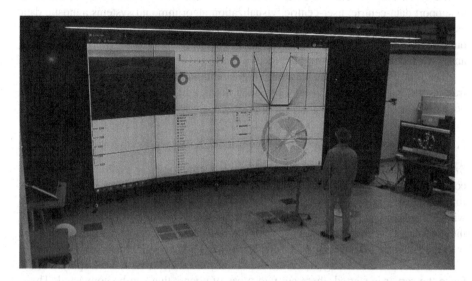

Fig. 2. Hybrid 2D and 3D visual analytics of our Monte Carlo simulation with the monitor to the right of the Large High Resolution Display system showing the view of the user on the Microsoft HoloLens Mixed Reality device.

The implementation of our visual analytics tools running across a LHRD and Microsoft HoloLens Mixed Reality system opens up the possibility for the users to visualize and interact with more of the data in its natural state. Our implementation supports multiple coordinated views across different visualization systems where user interaction with the data on the 24-tiled display system is also reflected on the data being displayed on the Microsoft HoloLens Mixed Reality system. Figure 2 shows the visualization of our Monte Carlo simulation data using our hybrid 2D and 3D visualization tool.

In the next section, we describe the related work of our paper. The following section describes the system architecture of our hybrid 2D and 3D visual analytics application to support heterogeneous data exploration. We then elaborate on the experimental design of our evaluation and then discuss the future work before we conclude.

2 Related Work

In the visualization of heterogeneous complex data, Reda et al. presented CAVE2 visualization system capable of 2D and 3D visualization [5]. Sommer et al. integrated 2D and 3D Visualization with a Semi-Immersive system for navigation [6]. Kerren et al. developed hybrid-dimensional approaches combining 2D and 3D visualization techniques in systems biology perspective [7]. However, our research involves using both a 2D display system and a Mixed Reality system for 3D immersive visualization to support data-centric, user-centric, visualization algorithm and systems agnostic data exploration. Furthermore, our current paper is a generalization with improvements over our previous work presented at SEARIS 2018 11th Workshop on Software Engineering and Architectures for Real-time Interactive Systems [8].

The following subsections describe in greater detail on the work related to SAGE2 framework and ParaViewWeb that provided the basic building blocks we used in the development of our 2D visualization application on our LHRD.

2.1 Scalable Amplified Group Environment2 Software Framework

SAGE2 software framework uses web-browser technologies to enable data-intensive collaboration across multiple displays acting as one large desktop workspace environment. In our setup, we have three client machines driving our 24-tiled display wall, with 8 displays per machine. The SAGE2 framework combines the multiple displays into one large workspace, allowing multiple users to connect via a modern browser over the network. SAGE2 software runs on the head node of our cluster, and launches a web server with the configuration of the client machines to host the display clients. Once the server is started, there are two types of clients that can be connected. These clients are the UI clients and the display clients. The UI clients are how the users connect to the environment, by typing the URL of the web server into a modern browser. The display clients are how the client machines of the cluster actually display what is to be shown on the wall. Multiple users can connect to a UI client on their own laptop or machine, with the ability to interact with what is displayed on the wall, as well as drag/drop files, or open SAGE2 applications on the wall. The server running on the head node is only aware of what applications and users are connected to the current SAGE2 session, but has no information about what is actually being displayed on the display clients.

The SAGE2 framework includes many applications that can be launched through a UI client and displayed across the wall. One such application is a WebView application that simulates a browser running within the multi-display workspace by embedding a web page via its URL into the application. The application may be resized, allowing viewing and interacting with web pages in a large display environment. It is the WebView SAGE2 application that we use to run our SyncVis visualization application showing various 2D and 3D visualizations of our Monte Carlo simulation data.

2.2   ParaViewWeb Framework

In the development of SyncVis, we utilized the JavaScript information visualization modules provided by the ParaViewWeb library for the multiple coordinated views capability. ParaViewWeb is a collection of visualization modules for web-based interactive rendering of potentially large scale scientific and information data. The library implements multiple views coordination, as well as coordination of the data through a provider system. Each provider module is responsible for managing a particular piece of data and/or part of the application state, and notifying the views when there is a change in state. For example, the FieldProvider keeps track of which data attributes are currently being visualized across all the views, and notifies when the list of attributes changes (due to user input).

Furthermore, the ParaViewWeb library implements a collection of visualization components that is responsible for rendering the views. They form the building blocks of the UI and are solely concerned with the rendering aspects of that particular component. In order to be a ParaViewWeb component, it must implement a small number of functions that provide the interface that ParaViewWeb expects, and so other charting libraries can be made into a component by creating this interface. As mentioned previously, they will receive events from the providers, and update their views appropriately.

In summary, we utilized some of the built-in data visualizations and provider modules that are provided to build SyncVis. To implement additional functionality not supported by the default ParaViewWeb modules, such as the visualization of temporal data and 3D scene rendering, we leveraged other existing visualization libraries by creating new ParaViewWeb compatible providers and visualization components expanding the capability of ParaViewWeb.

3   Hybrid 2D and 3D System Architecture Design

The visual information seeking Mantra described a typical analytical workflow involving an analyst first exploring the overview of the dataset, and then zoom and filter with details on demand [9]. However, in the process, it may be necessary for the user to explore the dataset using several different visualization techniques. For example, some 3D spatial data visualizations are more suitable using a 3D immersive visualization system, while feature extraction often is facilitated by 2D charts and infographics. To do this, the user may have to reformat the data and switch between different visualization techniques. In a typical visual analytics setup, the analyst has to switch between applications, languages, or libraries/toolboxes to iterate between visualizing and tweaking the parameters and/or querying a new subset of data. This workflow complicates the data analysis process, and also increases the cognitive load of the analyst.

Our visual analytics system architecture is designed to streamline the visual information seeking Mantra to allow for a much easier interoperability of visualization hardware and software to support unified data analysis tasks. This architecture can be used to create many custom hybrid data visualization systems. In the prototypes that we present here, we developed a hybrid 2D and 3D visualization application. The 2D visualizations are designed to run within a LHRD visualization environment, as this gives us the screen size to view a dataset from multiple different angles, across several charts, in a coordinated fashion. The 3D visualizations are designed to be deployed onto Mixed Reality system like the Microsoft HoloLens. The back-end of the system consists of a small collection of services that provide communication, data processing, and application state management. These components are designed to run within a High Performance Computing (HPC) environment to take advantage of its parallel data processing power. Our data-flow-oriented hybrid system gives users the ability to interact with the data in one system or application, and have the interactions affect correlated changes in other systems, supporting a unified data exploration experience. Figure 3 shows a schematic of the system components and how they are connected. In the next section, we illustrate the use of the system architecture with a network data visualization prototype and uses the 3D system as the main control, with interaction in VR updating the 2D visualizations to further inspect the data.

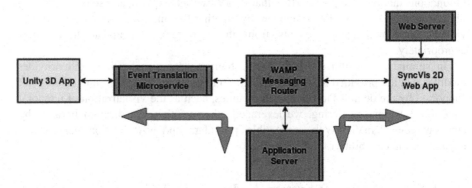

Fig. 3. Overall components of our hybrid visualization architecture. Visualization clients are in yellow, server components are in pink. The blue arrows represent the communication and data flow from the clients to the application server.

3.1   WAMP Messaging Router

A critical functionality of a visualization application that supports multiple distributed clients is efficient and flexible communication. As described in the previous sections, all visualization clients need to be updated automatically based on the user's interaction with any of the visualization clients. These can be accomplished through a message broker or middleware. For a message broker, the most fitting pattern to distribute messages here is through a publish-subscribe pattern in which connected clients subscribe to specific topics and receive the relevant message that has been published. This allows for messages to be pushed on demand, with appropriate granularity based on features subscribed by the client. This is an important feature for our data-centric and data-intensive visual analytics process to maintain an interactive workflow.

For the middleware method, a request-response pattern is most appropriate, as the client will directly signal the server to invoke the user action as a request. These patterns have complementary uses that have been combined into single integrated systems [10]. We use the Web Application Messaging Protocol (WAMP) for our system, because it offers precisely both of these communication patterns, in a simple, high level manner across a WebSocket. In particular, we use Crossbar.io's WAMP router/broker to provide the communication means for the hybrid 2D and 3D visualization application. The visualization clients, as well as the application server, will connect to the WAMP router using Crossbar.io's Autobahn WAMP client libraries for Python and JavaScript, which will then allow all connected components to communicate via the aforementioned patterns.

3.2 Application Server

For the Application Server component, we implemented a Python application server to be the "brain" of the distributed application. The Python application server is designed to be the single source of truth of the application state across all front-end clients and back-end services. This is important to ensure consistent maintenance of application state. With a visual analytic application, application state most often includes information such as variable selections that have been made, filters that have been applied to the data for drill downs, and what piece of data within a larger data store those selections and filters are associated with. This information is intended to be shared across all clients, and all clients can use the application server to coordinate changes to filters/actions applied across other system components. It also provides data in a granular fashion as needed by the clients. The communication itself uses the WAMP protocol as mentioned in the previous subsection.

The Autobahn client library is used to establish a WAMP based WebSocket connection from the application server to the WAMP router. With the WAMP architecture, any connected visualization clients will have bi-directional communication to the application server. Remote procedures are defined on the application server, which the clients can call. While communication in WAMP can be done in a fully distributed fashion across any two connected components, our system expects clients to communicate directly only to the application server.

In our development, we also compartmentalize application server logic into smaller protocol classes. The smaller protocol classes allows each protocol to be imported in a modular fashion, enabling development of flexible server applications. For example, there is a clear separation between the data protocol and filter protocol. Each new visualization prototype should implement custom version of these interfaces for their specific needs, though, especially for the filter and data protocols, default versions can be used. The protocols include Web Protocol, Filter Protocol, and Data Protocol. Web Protocol defines the interface that visualization clients can use to interact with the application server. Filter Protocol defines an internal API to maintain the logic for which pieces of data are being visualized, and how the data is currently sliced and drilled down. Data Protocol defines an internal API to access a data store.

For a custom web protocol implementation, we simply defined instances of the other protocols that is needed for a specific domain (i.e. filter protocol instance to manage specific types of data filtering) and define a WAMP based collection of RPCs. It is within those RPCs we applied the relevant server side logic using the APIs available in the other protocol instances. Data and state changes across the visualizations are communicated in a reactive way using publish-subscribe patterns. It is also at this point that relevant messages should be published to subscribing clients (i.e. the current state of the filter model after a change was made by a client).

In the present implementation, the data protocol contains a host of methods to pull data out of a large data store in a Pythonic interface, with functionality to iterate through entire rows of a specific data table; iterate through specific columns of a specific data table; iterate through select rows based on a filter function; get metadata about a given data table's variables, data types, and ranges, etc. By default, the data protocol utilizes ParaView's data table functionality, particularly through ParaView's 'simple' library. Using ParaView's DataTable functionality and API, we were able to access much of ParaView's ability to easily read from a variety of supported data formats and extract granular pieces of the data quickly. However, this interface can be extended to retrieve data using other sources.

It is also worth mentioning that, by the design of our protocol implementations, there is a decoupling of filter and state changes for data delivery to a given client. Filtering/state changes are communicated to the data server directly, but data updates are not directly requested and instead reacted to when the data update topic has been published by the data server. This results in additional logic that must be implemented for particular applications on the server, and also on the client, as it puts more responsibility on the clients to listen for filter changes and make appropriate data requests to the server based on those filter changes. However, the advantage with this approach is that it allows for quicker prototyping of specific reconfigurable visualization use cases, as data can be managed more flexibly. Refer to the prototype examples in the subsequent sections to see an illustration of how the application server can be utilized and extended for different hybrid, distributed visualization applications.

3.3   Unity for 3D Visualization Applications

For 3D assets with geospatial and temporal attributes, the most intuitive means to understand the data is through a 3D animation of the attributes. Unity development platform was used to develop our 3D visualization applications as it is a very powerful tool for creating high-end 3D graphics applications that can be deployed to various hardware platforms and devices. There is also a multitude of SDKs that may be imported into a Unity development environment to greatly speedup the application development. Therefore, Unity development platform is a very attractive option for creating interactive 3D visualization applications and simulations.

For data with temporal attributes, we can create an animation that plays out over the time steps of the data sets. For geospatial data, we can map the geospatial coordinates to Unity world space coordinates to correctly align the assets based off of the recorded geospatial data. In addition, we can load terrain directly into Unity that portrays the terrain at the desired geospatial coordinates. 3D assets can easily be brought into and removed from the scene as demanded by the specific application use case. Once the visual aspects of the Unity application are in place, we can then implement interaction capability for whatever hardware device we are targeting.

Since Unity has the ability to deploy to various platforms and devices, we choose to target the Microsoft HoloLens Mixed Reality device for our 3D Unity applications. Because the data sets contain 3D data, viewing the data on a 2D monitor limits the ability to really explore the geospatial data. Being able to immerse oneself in the data in the 3D environment and visualize the data in a 3D space allows for keener insights to be developed in the data analysis workflow. Through physical movement within the display environment, the user has the freedom to move around the mixed reality environment to further explore the data from different viewing angles and locations.

While 3D Unity applications provide insight into the 3D nature of the data, there is also a multitude of other data attribute that may describe the 3D assets in the mixed reality environment. For this information, there may be no way to display it within the 3D environment. Thus, this information is better displayed within a 2D application dedicated for information visualization. However, we still wish for this data to be coordinated among applications. Within Unity, we can integrate a web socket connection that allows for data to be communicated with other applications. This data transfer and communication requires the use of the event translation microservice, described in the next subsection.

3.4 Event Translation Microservice

As mentioned in the previous sections, we primarily utilize WAMP connections to pass information among separate system applications. Unfortunately, the current stable .NET version available for Unity does not support the desired WAMP libraries to establish bidirectional communication between our Unity application and the application server. If we had the ability to integrate WAMP directly into Unity applications, the normal messaging protocol we use could be extended from the application server to the Unity application directly. Due to this limitation, we designed the event translation microservice to map WAMP functionality over to Unity. This mapping enables communication and filtering of information to exist between the 3D Unity application and the application server such that the Unity application can interplay with the other visualizations connected to it, and have it work in a coordinated fashion.

In our implementation, the event translation microservice connects to the Unity application over a web socket connection. The microservice in turn connects to the application server using a WAMP connection. To communicate, the microservice will receive a payload from Unity specifying the RPC to call, as well as the argument inputs, and will forward this to the WAMP server by calling the corresponding RPC on it with the given inputs. In addition, the event translation microservice can subscribe to a topic published by the WAMP server with a corresponding event handler that pushes the published topic and payload to the Unity app as a serialized JSON message. At that point, the Unity app can respond to the message accordingly. Thus, the microservice acts as a hub to translate the events that occur in Unity to events recognized by the application server, and vice versa. With correct RPCs and parameter passing, the microservice facilitates the bidirectional communication between the 3D Unity application and 2D front-end data visualizations.

3.5 SyncVis for 2D Coordinated Views

As the exploratory data analysis involves many variables of heterogeneous types, it is useful to have several charts showing different angles of the overall data. Furthermore, creating a full visual analytic solution would involve the interoperation of a collection of charts and visualization that represents the same slice, combination, or configuration of data that the analyst wishes to see, and synchronization of each view such that any user action in one view changes all others, guaranteeing a unified representation. This is referred to as brushing and linking [11] as charts are "linked" because they are connected to the same dataset, and when that data set changes or is filtered, those changes are then "brushed" across all of the charts and graphs.

To accomplish the aforementioned visual analytics task, we developed a front-end application layer on top of the ParaViewWeb framework, which we named SyncVis [8]. We used ParaViewWeb because its InfoViz API supports interactive coordination across multiple views, and also supports linking of common data across multiple charts. Their provider modules can be used to facilitate data flow from data source towards visualizations. That is, each provider module is responsible for managing a particular piece of data and/or part of the application state, and interested visualization components are notified where there is a change in state through a publish-subscribe approach. In addition to the provider design, the InfoViz API also includes a collection of useful charts for visualizing more complex correlations between variables.

Besides managing the data, SyncVis also manages visualization component rendering by using the React framework. React makes it simpler to create composable UIs in a declarative fashion, and also allows us to use state of the art open source React based visualization components more easily. To create new web based visualization front ends, one would simply have to create a new provider module if we want to deliver new types of data to the visualizations. Existing React based visualization components can directly be used in SyncVis. ParaViewWeb composite providers are available throughout the React component hierarchy, hence individual visualization components can subscribe to provider events to retrieve new data and update the state of the visualization component, which triggers React to re-render the visualization automatically.

Although SyncVis applications are web-based application that can run in a normal browser, several UI decisions were made with the purpose of running the application on a LHRD to support a large number of coordinated visualizations. We utilize SAGE2 on our LHRD to run SyncVis applications, which supports running web applications through its WebView application as mentioned in the related work section.

4 Hybrid 2D and 3D Data Visualization of Monte Carlo Simulation

Our real-time interactive hybrid 2D and 3D visual analytics application allows the user to analyze and visualize the 3D Monte Carlo simulation. Our data centric design allows the user to set up the time period of interest and visualize the 2D and 3D data of the period on both the LHRD and Microsoft HoloLens Mixed Reality visualization systems. This gives the user the capability to visualize 2D data on a 2D LHRD platform and 3D data using 3D Mixed Reality technology.

We leveraged our hybrid 2D and 3D architecture to implement a visualization application for our Monte Carlo simulation [12]. The simulation generates both temporal and geospatial data for a variety of 3D assets. Using the visual analytics tool developed, the correlation between variables can be viewed using the different 2D charts and diagrams on the SyncVis application, and the corresponding 3D simulation can be viewed on the Mixed Reality system running on the Microsoft HoloLens device. The user will be able to perform relevant analysis of the data using both 2D and 3D visualization techniques. The user is able to interact with the dataset in the LHRD environment and have the simulation running on a mixed reality display updated in real time. Figure 4 shows the 3D animation based on the geospatial and temporal data generated by the simulation.

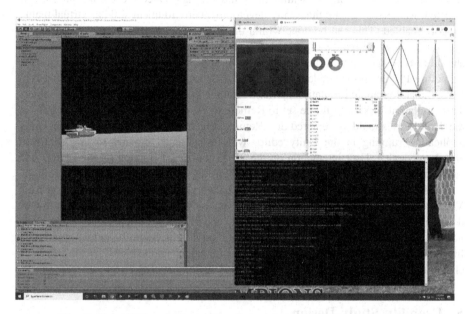

Fig. 4. Hybrid 2D and 3D visual analytics of our Monte Carlo simulation

4.1 Mixed Reality 3D Visualization Using Microsoft HoloLens

The hybrid 2D and 3D Monte Carlo simulation visualization application running on LHRD and Microsoft HoloLens Mixed Reality device is a continuation of our previous research into developing hybrid 2D and 3D visualization for LHRD and complete immersive HTC Vive device [8]. In order for the virtual reality (VR) Unity application to run in a mixed reality environment, a few changes need to be made to the actual client application environment [13]. First, the VR camera rig and controllers in the Unity scene to support VR application will need to be replaced with the default main camera which is used by the HoloLens. The camera background color should be set to black and the near clipping plane set to an appropriate distance. Furthermore, the scale of the user within the environment also needs to be adjusted accordingly. For the VR environment, the user was placed within the environment and could view the animation at life-size scale. However, in the mixed reality environment, it impedes the entire user's view to be engulfed in an immersive environment. Thus, the view we selected allows the user to take on a more omniscient view of the holographic environment at a viewing angle similar to that of a bird's-eye view. This view configuration allows the user to look around the area in front of the LHRD to view the 3D environment displayed on the Microsoft HoloLens device, and also observe the 2D visualization displayed on the LHRD without an obstruction of view.

Once the application environment is set up for viewing, a few more steps are necessary for the user to actually view the application within the HoloLens device. The Unity application's target platform needs to be switched from PC standalone to Universal Windows Platform within the build settings. Once the correct platform is targeted, we need to ensure that Unity development environment still has virtual reality support enabled. This can be done within the XR settings section of player setting by selecting the virtual reality supported checkbox. In addition, Windows Mixed Reality should also be specified as the Virtual Reality SDK. As the last step, the Holographic Remoting Player app is needed. For Unity to stream the 3D view to Microsoft Holo-Lens, the Holographic Emulation option within the Window menu bar must be enabled. The Emulation Mode should be set to Remote to Device and the current IP address of the HoloLens should be entered for Remote Machine. Once connected, the Unity application running in the Unity editor will be streamed directly to the Microsoft HoloLens device. User interaction on the 2D visualization running on the LHRD will cause the 3D visualization displayed on the Microsoft HoloLens to update accordingly.

While there are a few steps to follow to convert the Unity client application from VR mode to mixed reality mode, the steps are only specific to the actual hardware device intricacies. Due to the design of our 2D and 3D hybrid visualization framework, none of the underlying framework for message passing needs to be reconfigured. Our framework allows a plug-and-play workflow for client applications, as long as each client correctly implements publish/subscribe functions in response to interaction.

5   Usability Study Design

The ultimate goal of our usability study is to determine the effectiveness of using the multiple coordinated views across various 2D and 3D display devices in our visual analytics workflow. However, we want the users to have a fair and controlled study so as not to bias the responses in favor of the hybrid 2D and 3D multiple coordinated views system. Therefore, our usability study compared both multiple coordinated views in 2D visualization environment, as well as in a mixed reality and 3D visualization environment.

In running the experiment, we will only be testing the importance of 3D visualization environment for our visual analytics if we do not investigate running 3D visualization application on 2D visualization environment. We would minimize the relevance to multiple coordinated views and/or hybrid nature of the system components, since the 3D visualization would not be a constant factor for all tests. By bringing the 3D visualization into the 2D environment, we allow all environments to share the same components, but with different interaction capability. In addition, bringing the 3D visualization into 2D visualization environment allows the users to determine if there is a benefit of visualizing 3D data in a virtual environment, or if a 2D monitor is sufficient.

Fig. 5. Visualization Ecology with various display systems.

Figure 5 shows a visualization ecology with various 2D and 3D display systems that can be used to support exploratory data analysis. However, using a collection of loosely coupled heterogeneous display systems to support 2D and 3D data visualization can be counterproductive for a user. Without data coordination across heterogeneous display systems, the user is unable to gain much insight from the data shown in either visualizations without additional cognitive load. However, the multiple coordinated views of our hybrid 2D and 3D visualization application allows the user to interact with the 2D visualization on the LHRD and have the corresponding interaction updated on the 3D mixed reality display system. In doing so, the user will be able to decide if it is worthwhile to coordinate the 2D and 3D visualizations across display devices in our studies.

In this experimental design, we are also not considering the 2D visualization aspect in a 3D immersive environment. Similar to how we used 2D display environment for 3D visualization, we could implement the 2D visualization within a 3D immersive environment. However, we felt that this is unnecessary due to the nature of mixed reality environment. It does not matter whether the 2D is implemented with the Microsoft HoloLens device or not, as the view will be the same for the user regardless.

Therefore, we only base our usability study based on the two environments. In the first environment, we are running both the 2D and 3D visualization on our 2D LHRD device. The mouse and keyboard are used to interact with and move around the 3D visualization, where interaction with the temporal selection gadget updates both 2D and 3D visualization views. In the second environment, we have 2D visualization displayed on a monitor and the 3D visualization on the mixed reality environment. For both setups, no data is pre-populated and any interaction with the 2D visualization updates both the 2D and 3D visualizations.

5.1   Tasks

In our usability study, the users are asked to complete tasks solely to get them interacting with the environments. Although the answers do not matter, the users are asked to complete tasks in each environment as if they were the analysts using the setup to investigate the data set.

Our usability design has the ordering of the user assignment to different environment at random, and the given tasks are independent of the environment. However, only two tasks are assigned for each of the environment with specific purpose. For the two tasks, the users were asked to determine the path of an asset in the scene, and the other task involves determining the similarity of two events in the scene. In each environment, the user is required to interact differently to answer the posed question. By keeping the questions of similar nature, though not quite the same, we avoid preconditioning the users in any of the environments and are able to analyze the same data for the same purpose. Thus, the interaction and data analysis process is unique to the environment of the user, with all other factors being controlled. This allows the user to compare and contrast the data analysis process for each of the environments individually.

In interacting with the 2D only display environment, the user has to use the mouse to zoom, rotate, and pan the 3D scene in order to explore the data to accomplish the tasks on the user interface as shown in the Fig. 4. Once the data time frame is selected, the user can look to the 3D visualization to determine the path of the assets. For determining the similarity of the two events in the scene, the user compare the different views on the LHRD for a better situational awareness. However, this interaction requires the user to look to the different 2D visualization views after each selection for a better situational awareness from the dataset.

For the 2D visualization displayed on a monitor and the 3D visualization on the mixed reality environment with multiple coordinated view, the user can look around the 3D scene in mixed reality mode for a 3D immersive visualization. For this environment, the time slider interaction on the 2D view will update the data range for both 2D and 3D views.

5.2   Question and Analysis

For the questionnaire (as listed in the Appendix), we ask the users 10 questions total. For the first 8 questions, the users are asked to give their environment preference that they felt best answers the question. The answers were 2D, 2D/3D coordinated, or none. The final two questions we pose are to be answered on a Likert scale from 1 to 5, with 1 representing "strongly disagree" and 5 representing "strongly agree." In our pilot study, of the first 8 questions, all the users are in favor of 2D/3D coordinated.

For example, the majority of users prefer the 2D/3D coordinated environment for the question "Which mode did you feel allowed you to fully understand the data?" This shows that the combination of visualizations in their natural environment provides users with a deeper understanding. Another example includes the question "Which mode allowed for the most intuitive interaction with the data?" The majority of users voted that the 2D/3D coordinated allowed the most intuitive data exploration. It was commented that interacting with the 3D visualization in 2 dimensions using only a mouse was not as intuitive as 3D. However, 2D was still said to be faster and more convenient.

For the question "Which mode allowed for the quickest insights to be drawn from the data?", the majority of users voted that the 2D environment allows for the quickest insights to be drawn. Similar to the comment above, 2D is faster and more convenient considering the visualizations are side by side. With the mixed reality headset, there is no way to quickly analyze the data filtering and selection across visualizations. Thus, it is quicker for a user to interact with and quickly understand what is happening when looking at the same display.

In addition, the majority of users chose the 2D environment when asked "If you had to select one mode to use for data analysis, which would you select?" The main reasoning for selecting this mode is familiarity and quicker insights. Although the 3D representation may be a better way for the user to visualize the 3D data, there is overhead in getting comfortable with mixed reality setup when the user is used to using a mouse and keyboard on a 2D monitor. The first step is to show the overall benefit of viewing this data in 3D, then easing the interaction with that data for the user to make it as intuitive as possible.

The final two questions are answered on a Likert scale from 1 to 5. The purpose of the Likert scale is to quantify the user's opinion on using the hybrid system for data analysis. For the question "There is benefit in coordinating visualizations across 2D and 3D visualization systems?" all responses were on the upper ranges, 4s and 5s. For the question "There is benefit in viewing 3D visualizations in an immersive environment?", majority of the responses are in the upper ranges, 4s and 5s. In both cases, all users chose to agree with the statements posed. These responses show that the users do believe there is a benefit in viewing 3D visualizations in a 3D environment.

6   Discussion and Conclusion

In this paper, we described our interactive hybrid 2D and 3D visual analytics application that allows the user to analyze and visualize data from our Monte Carlo simulation. Our data centric design allows the user to visualize the 2D and 3D data of the data set on both the LHRD and Microsoft HoloLens Mixed Reality system. This gives the user the capability to visualize 2D data on a 2D LHRD platform and 3D data using 3D mixed reality technology.

We also described the data-flow-oriented architecture design that we used in the development of a hybrid 2D and 3D visual analytics tool. The architecture is used to develop an application demonstrating a viable real-time interactive hybrid 2D and 3D visual analytics application for a complex Monte Carlo simulation. The hybrid 2D and 3D application gives the user a better understanding of the outcome of their 3D simulations. The preliminary results of our usability survey show the benefit in using a hybrid 2D and 3D visual analytics application to support their data exploration. Furthermore, our mixed-reality setup could be the solution to ease the interaction between 2D and 3D systems while allowing the user to view the data in its natural environment using multiple coordinated views.

Acknowledgments.   This work was supported in part by the DOD High Performance Computing Modernization Program at The Army Research Laboratory (ARL), Department of Defense Supercomputing Resource Center (DSRC).

Appendix: Comparative Study Questionnaire

1. Which mode did you feel allowed you to fully understand the data? Why?
   2D   2D/3D coordinated   None
2. Which mode did you feel most appropriately represented the data? Why?
   2D   2D/3D coordinated   None
3. Which mode allowed for the most intuitive interaction with the data? Why?
   2D   2D/3D coordinated   None
4. Which mode allowed for the quickest insights to be drawn from the data? Why?
   2D   2D/3D coordinated   None
5. Which mode were you most likely to gain a better understanding of the data through interaction? Why?
   2D   2D/3D coordinated   None
6. Which mode was the most effective at updating the representation of data in response to interaction? Why?
   2D   2D/3D coordinated   None
7. Given the coordinated visualizations, which mode did you feel was easiest to understand how the data was filtered due to coordination? Why?
   2D   2D/3D coordinated   None
8. If you had to select one mode to use for data analysis, which would you select? Why?
   2D   2D/3D coordinated   None
9. There is benefit in coordinating visualizations across 2D and 3D visualization systems.
   (strongly disagree) 1   2   3   4   5 (strongly agree)
10. There is benefit in viewing 3D visualizations in a mixed reality environment.
    (strongly disagree) 1   2   3   4   5 (strongly agree)

References

1. Andrews, C., Endert, A., Yost, B., North, C.: Information visualization on large, high-resolution displays: issues, challenges, and opportunities. Inf. Vis. **10**(4), 341–355 (2011). https://doi.org/10.1177/1473871611415997
2. Marrinan, T., et al.: Sage2: a new approach for data intensive collaboration using scalable resolution shared displays. In: 10th IEEE International Conference on Collaborative Computing: Networking, Applications and Worksharing, pp. 177–186, October 2014. https://doi.org/10.4108/icst.collaboratecom.2014.257337
3. Su, S., Perry, V., Cantner, N., Kobayashi, D., Leigh, J.: High-resolution interactive and collaborative data visualization framework for largescale data analysis. In: 2016 International Conference on Collaboration Technologies and Systems (CTS), pp. 275–280, October 2016. https://doi.org/10.1109/cts.2016.0059
4. North, C.: Robust, end-user programmable, multiple-window coordination. In: CHI 98 Conference Summary on Human Factors in Computing Systems, CHI 1998, pp. 60–61. ACM, New York (1998). https://doi.org/10.1145/286498.286529
5. Reda, K., et al.: Visualizing large, heterogeneous data in hybrid reality environments. IEEE Comput. Graphics Appl. **33**(4), 38–48 (2013). https://doi.org/10.1109/mcg.2013.37
6. Sommer, B., Wang, S.J., Xu, L., Chen, M., Schreiber, F.: Hybrid dimensional visualization and interaction - integrating 2D and 3D visualization with semi-immersive navigation techniques. In: 2015 Big Data Visual Analytics (BDVA), pp. 1–8, September 2015. https://doi.org/10.1109/bdva.2015.7314295
7. Kerren, A., Schreiber, F.: Why integrate InfoVis and SciVis? An example from systems biology. IEEE Comput. Graphics Appl. **34**(6), 69–73 (2014). https://doi.org/10.1109/mcg.2014.122
8. Su, S., An, M., Perry, V., Chen, M.: Realtime interactive hybrid 2D and 3D visual analytics on large high resolution display and immersive virtual environment. Presented at SEARIS 2018 11th Workshop on Software Engineering and Architectures for Realtime Interactive Systems in Conjunction with IEEE Virtual Reality (2018)
9. Shneiderman, B.: The eyes have it: a task by data type taxonomy for information visualizations. In: Proceedings 1996 IEEE Symposium on Visual Languages, pp. 336–343, September 1996. https://doi.org/10.1109/vl.1996.545307
10. Rodrguez-Domnguez, C., Benghazi, K., Noguera, M., Garrido, J., Rodrguez, M., Ruiz-Lpez, T.: A communication model to integrate the request-response and the publish-subscribe paradigms into ubiquitous systems. Sensors **12**, 7648–7668 (2012)
11. North, C., Shneiderman, B.: Snap-together visualization: a user interface for coordinating visualizations via relational schemata. In: Proceedings of the Working Conference on Advanced Visual Interfaces, AVI 2000, pp. 128–135. ACM, New York (2000). https://doi.org/10.1145/345513.345282
12. Grahm, M.J.: Active protection system (APS) end-to-end modeling (EEM) animation and analysis tools. Aberdeen Proving Ground (MD): ArmyResearch Laboratory (US); 2018 January, Report No.: ARL-CR-0823 (2018)
13. Microsoft Homepage. https://docs.microsoft.com/en-us/windows/mixed-reality/unity-play-mode. Accessed 20 Feb 2020

Study on Assessing User Experience of Augmented Reality Applications

Lei Wang[1(✉)] and Meiyu Lv[1,2]

[1] School of Digital Media and Design Arts, Beijing University of Posts
and Telecommunications, Beijing 100876, China
wl_bupt@163.com
[2] Beijing Key Laboratory of Network and Network Culture, Beijing University
of Posts and Telecommunications, Beijing 100876, China

Abstract. With the development of the augmented reality technology and the popularisation of smartphones, the application of augmented reality based on mobile devices demonstrates an optimistic development prospect. The current development of mobile augmented reality is mainly technology-oriented, mostly emphasises on technology advancement as a basis of measure while placing insufficient emphasis upon user experience. User-centric design is increasingly important in the design of mobile applications. As it is crucial to quantify and evaluate user experiences of AR application to gain insight in pivotal areas for future development, which this research proposes that the application of the Delphi-AHP method is capable of identifying those areas via five first-level indicators and 20 second-level indicators. This method is tested and verified with six model display applications, which discovered the most important first-level indicators to affect user experience is a system's functionality and its display.

Keywords: Augmented reality · User experience · Evaluation method

1 Introduction

Human-computer interaction is changing drastically alongside the novel innovations and roles in computers and mobile devices. "Augmented reality is a cutting-edge technology that allows the user to observe real-world objects supplemented with computer-generated objects" [1]. By transforming visual interactions away from 2D to 3D, from point touch to gesture, human-machine interaction is converted to a fusion of human-machine-environment interaction, where the change of display and interaction bring new challenges to user experience (UX) design.

Ames et al. [2] define user experience as "a person's perceptions and responses that result from the use or anticipated use of a product, system or service". According to the same definition, UX includes the users' emotions, beliefs, preferences, perceptions, physical and psychological responses, behaviours and accomplishments that occur before, during and after use of a system. The term "user experience" is used along with "usability" with various degrees of relativity. We consider UX to be a larger entity,

J. Y. C. Chen and G. Fragomeni (Eds.): HCII 2020, LNCS 12190, pp. 208–222, 2020.
https://doi.org/10.1007/978-3-030-49695-1_14

encompassing usability and including both pragmatic and hedonic aspects of a system as UX is considered a significant factor for interactive products and services [3].

The gradual maturity of AR technology brought prosperity in the AR application market, particularly in the relatively matured smartphone industry where a large variety of applications based on AR interaction emerge constantly. As the market saturates, UX has become the main factor of competitiveness for interactive products and services [4]. The improvements and measures of user experience of a product is a continues process of iterative optimisation, where the necessity to have a clear assessment and cognition of the current user experience is essential. Therefore, the study on how to evaluate the user experience is critical at gaining the first-hand advantage within an increasingly competitive market environment.

Baidu AI Interaction Design Institute divides mobile AR application into three categories according to the distance between user and virtual model, and the differences between interactive contents in AR scenes: 1) Human-based AR, the user interacts with the face and human body; 2) Space-based AR, the user interacts with scenes and objects in the space in which they are located, such as placing objects such as furniture, models, people/animals on the ground and interacting with them; 3) Environment-based AR, the user can experience and interact with large scenes in the physical world [5]. Due to the diversity of applications and its potentials, space-based AR is the most widely used application. Therefore, this paper will use space-based AR as the research object as it has the capability to merge and interact with virtual displays with real-world environments.

The rest of this paper is as follows: Sect. 2 introduces the concept of the mobile augmented reality and an overview of the relevant studies. Section 3 constructs the user experience evaluation system of AR applications via the Delphi-AHP methodology. Section 4 applies the system to evaluate the six model display applications, which justifies the validity of the system. Section 5 concludes the research and suggests future research directions.

2   Study Basis

2.1   Mobile Augmented Reality

AR is a technology to superimpose the virtual information with reality while allowing interactions between the user and virtual information and to enhance people's perception of the real world through supplementing reality with additional information and data. In 1970, Professor Ivan Sutherland of the Massachusetts Institute of Technology first came up with the term "Augmented Reality." In 1997, Ronald Azuma [1] of the University of Northern Carolina proposed a clearer definition of the concept of AR, which is a more widely known definition that suggests that AR should have the following three characteristics:

1) Combination of virtuality and reality: Virtual object and real-world display and the same visual space.
2) Real-time interaction: The user can naturally interact with virtual objects and their real surroundings in real-time.

3) 3D registration: Calculate the location of the camera so that virtual objects are properly placed in the real-world perception.

Mobile AR is experienced via a smartphone or a handheld device [1]. In mobile AR, the "reality" is the camera view and the "virtual" is the superimposed enhanced graphics. For mobile AR in this article, we have added one more component [6]:

4) Complete accessibility via mobile devices (e.g. cellular phones, tablets, etc.).: The user can experience AR anywhere and interact in any environment.

With the advancement in relevant technologies, mobile AR has become the most prosperous field in AR application. AR not only delivers an enhanced visual sense but also the profound influence of cognitive understanding. Previous cognitive understanding of surroundings is achieved through a combination of traditional ways, such as dictionaries, maps, instructions or field trips. However, this information can be presented directly and naturally via the mobile AR application, overwhelmingly simplifies the procedures and reduces the opportunity cost for users.

2.2 Relevant Study Status

The study of mobile AR mainly focuses on the development of technology, such as a variety of output devices and interactive displayers, as well as the process of identifying and tracking tangible objects [4]. Although the general framework to assess user experience in other fields are robust, but the theoretical framework and research knowledge related to user experience within modern fields such as mobile AR are highly insufficient [6, 7].

Only less than 10% of AR literature discusses topics upon user-centric designs and the methodologies to assess user experience in AR application. Currently, literature mainly focuses on three aspects: Assessing the usability of augmented reality with human factors considered; User experience in augmented reality, concentrating on certain specific applications; Augmented reality design and evaluation methods.

Kalahti [9] proposed a heuristic algorithm to assess the usability of augmented reality applications. Based on the literature review, we developed a preliminary version of the heuristic algorithm and was evaluated by four experts. As a result, six evaluation criteria were formed: 1) Interaction methods and controls, 2) Display of virtual objects, 3) Relationship between virtual objects and the real-world setting, 4) Information related to virtual objects, 5) Ease of operation, and 6) Physical user comfort.

Li et al. [10] set up the evaluation criteria of VR/AR teaching experience according to three aspects: User interface, Usability and Interactive design. The indices of user interface include: Information display, Menu setting, Geographical location, Progress access, Operation, Input, Visual field, Customisation; the indices of usability include: Repetition strategy, Expectation, Entry strategy, Recognition ability, Consistency; the interactive design indices include: Initial experience, Operating environment, Goal, Task, Control, Feedback, Progress and plot.

Pribeanu et al. [11] proposed a multidimensional model to measure the perceived quality of AR applications. The model is specified by a second-order factor (perceived quality) and three dimensions: Ergonomic quality, Study quality, and Hedonic quality.

The purpose of this model is to introduce the previous research to a coherent framework of the AR-based educational platforms and to provide guidance for researchers and practitioners.

Dunser et al. [8] combined the particularity and the operating background of AR with the user-centric design principle and proposed that the design of augmented reality should consider the following eight aspects: Affordance, Reducing cognitive overhead, Low physical effort, Learnability, User satisfaction, Flexibility of use, Responsiveness and feedback, Tolerance to faults and unintended mistakes.

The current study on the assessment of AR mainly reflects the user-centric design and focuses on evaluating usability, with little emphasis on user experience and emotions [12], with no design evaluation system for mobile AR applications. Considering the different displaying methods and functions of AR across different applications, these applications cannot be evaluated by one system. Therefore, this paper focuses on the study of the model display applications.

3   Construction of User Experience Evaluation System

3.1   Determination of Evaluation Indexes

Many experts and scholars have paid attention to the importance of user experience in augmented reality and have made corresponding research on the application of AR in different fields. In this paper, through literature analysis on AR, study of AR industry specifications, user experience framework, collection of a large number of evaluation indices from existing research results in related fields, and in combination with real experience feedbacks from AR users, a set of indicators has been preliminarily determined, including 5 first-level indicators and 20 second-level indicators (as shown in Table 1).

Table 1. Preliminarily determined indicators set

First-level indicators	Display	Interaction	Performance	Function	Aesthetic experience
Second-level indicators	• Physical rationality • Intuitive visualization • Model quality • Virtual-real fusion	• Consistency • Feedback • Sense of control • Flexibility • Fault tolerance and error proof • Easy to learn • Novelty of interaction • Fluency • Clear operation • Status visibility • Humanized help • Guidance	• Stability • Response speed • Matching accuracy • Recognition ability	• Satisfaction of user's requirements • Efficiency improvement • Model richness • Cognitive improvement	• Immersion • Entertainment • Enjoyment • Novelty • Attractiveness • Gratification

On this basis, the expert consultation table is drafted, and the Delphi method is used to conduct two rounds of consultation for the selected discipline experts. Nine experts who are engaged in human-computer interaction, user experience, AR related work and research with rich theoretical knowledge are invited to consult on the above index set through Delphi method. Those experts first filled in the form of "judgment basis" and "familiarity level" to identify their authority in this field. Then they evaluated those indicators according to five levels: very important, important, average, unimportant and very unimportant, and give comments. The index is modified per expert's comments to further improve the index system.

The results of the first-round consultation are shown in Table 2, with multiple coefficients of variation >0.2, showing that experts differ greatly in their evaluation of the same index. According to the data analysis results of the first-round expert consultation and experts' comments, the following modification has been made: nine secondary indices (Intuitive visualization, Consistency, Novelty of interaction, Fluency, Efficiency improvement, Model richness, Entertainment, Novelty, Attractiveness) are deleted; two indexes (Sense of control and Flexibility, Feedback and Status visibility) are combined; the description of two indexes are modified (with "Stability" changed to "System stability", and "Recognition ability" to "Recognition rate"); and two indexes (Stability of synthetic environment, Detail presentation) are added.

Table 2. Delphi results of the first round

	Mean value	Standard deviation	Coefficient of variation	Median
C1-1	4.333	0.816	0.188	5
C1-2	4.556	1.257	0.276	5
C1-3	4.222	0.916	0.217	4
C1-4	4.222	0.786	0.186	4
C2-1	4.556	0.685	0.150	5
C2-2	4.889	0.314	0.064	5
C2-3	4.667	0.667	0.143	5
C2-4	4.444	0.685	0.154	5
C2-5	4.444	0.831	0.187	5
C2-6	4.667	0.667	0.143	5
C2-7	3.333	1.155	0.346	3
C2-8	4.556	0.685	0.150	5
C2-9	4.444	0.831	0.187	5
C2-10	4.889	0.314	0.064	5
C2-11	4.556	0.497	0.109	5
C2-12	4.333	0.816	0.188	5
C3-1	4.889	0.314	0.064	5
C3-2	4.778	0.416	0.087	5
C3-3	4.333	0.943	0.218	5
C3-4	4.111	1.197	0.291	5

(*continued*)

Table 2. (*continued*)

	Mean value	Standard deviation	Coefficient of variation	Median
C4-1	4.556	0.956	0.210	5
C4-2	4.222	0.786	0.186	4
C4-3	3.222	1.227	0.381	3
C4-4	3.556	1.343	0.378	4
C5-1	4.778	0.416	0.087	5
C5-2	4.556	0.685	0.150	5
C5-3	4.444	0.831	0.187	5
C5-4	4.111	1.100	0.268	5
C5-5	4.444	0.956	0.215	5
C5-6	4.111	0.994	0.242	4

Table 3. Concordance coefficient of expert consultation opinions

	First round	Second round
Number of indexes	30	20
Concordance coefficient	0.401	0.629
Chi-Square	102.004	32.096
P	0.000	0.000

While the results of the first-round consultation are communicated back to the experts, the second round consultation is carried out. In the second round, the average number of secondary indicators is more than 4 points, and the full score ratio is more than 0.5. The expert concordance coefficient increased from 0.4 in the first round to 0.63 (as shown in Table 3), indicating that in the second round of expert consultation, the experts' opinions are more unified, and the degree of concordance is higher. Through the non-parametric test, the results show that there is a significant difference between the two rounds of expert consultation results. Therefore, experts have a high degree of concordance on the structure and indicators of the evaluation system, and the results are effective. Thus, the index system structure is determined, as shown in Fig. 1.

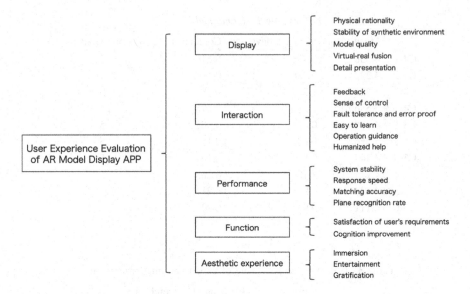

Fig. 1. Index system structure

3.2   Determination of Index Weight

The weight of the index is a representation of the importance of the index. The weight is calculated by comparing the importance of each index and then attaching the weight to it. Analytic Hierarchy Process (AHP) is a statistical system method proposed in the 1970s by Thomas L. Saaty, an American operational research scientist. It combines qualitative method with a quantitative method. AHP relies on the judgment of experts to obtain the priority scale [13], which uses the absolute judgment scale to compare. The absolute scale defines the relative importance of one indicator over another to a given objective (as shown in Table 4). Seven experts in the fields of augmented reality and human-computer interaction were invited to participate in the evaluation of the importance of those indicators.

Table 4. AHP scoring scale and meaning

Relative importance	Definition	Meaning
1	Equally important	Two goals are equally important
3	Slightly more important	one goal is slightly more important than the other
5	Quite more important	one goal is quite important than another
7	Obviously more important	one goal is obviously more important than another
9	Absolutely more important	one goal is absolutely more important than another
2, 4, 6, 8	Intermediate value of two adjacent judgments	Used during compromise

In this paper, the weight of the five first-level indicators of the display, interaction, performance, function and aesthetic experience is taken as an example of AHP calculation method. The specific steps are as follows:

① According to the scoring scale table of AHP, the comparison matrix A is formed by pairwise comparison of relevant elements.

$$A = \begin{bmatrix} 1 & 3 & 5 & 1 & 2 \\ 1/3 & 1 & 2 & 1/3 & 1/2 \\ 1/5 & 1/2 & 1 & 1/5 & 1/3 \\ 1 & 3 & 5 & 1 & 2 \\ 1/2 & 2 & 3 & 1/2 & 1 \end{bmatrix}$$

② Calculate the maximum eigenvalue and weight vector.

Set A = (aij) be n-order matrix, normalise each column of A to get B = (bij), and use formula (1) to calculate.

$$\bar{a}_{ij} = a_{ij} / \sum_{k=1}^{n} a_{kj}, i, j = 1, 2, \ldots, n. \tag{1}$$

$$B = \begin{bmatrix} 0.330 & 0.316 & 0.313 & 0.330 & 0.343 \\ 0.110 & 0.105 & 0.125 & 0.110 & 0.086 \\ 0.066 & 0.053 & 0.063 & 0.066 & 0.057 \\ 0.330 & 0.316 & 0.313 & 0.330 & 0.343 \\ 0.165 & 0.211 & 0.188 & 0.165 & 0.171 \end{bmatrix}$$

$$\tilde{w}_i = \sum_{j=1}^{n} \bar{a}_{ij}, i = 1, 2, \ldots, n. \tag{2}$$

Use formula (2) to obtain the sum of lines:

$$C = \begin{bmatrix} 1.630 \\ 0.536 \\ 0.304 \\ 1.630 \\ 0.899 \end{bmatrix}$$

$$w_i = \tilde{w}_i / n. \tag{3}$$

Use formula (3) to normalize C to obtain:

$$\begin{bmatrix} 0.326 \\ 0.107 \\ 0.061 \\ 0.326 \\ 0.180 \end{bmatrix}$$

Calculate the maximum eigenvalue:

$$\lambda_{max} = \frac{1}{n}\sum_{n=1}^{n}\frac{(AW)_i}{W_i} = \left(\frac{1.630}{0.326} + \frac{0.536}{0.107} + \frac{0.304}{0.061} + \frac{1.630}{0.326} + \frac{0.899}{0.180}\right)/5 = 5.051$$

③ Calculate consistency index (CI): $CI = \frac{\lambda_{max}-n}{n-1} = \frac{0.051}{4} = 0.004$

④ By comparing the random consistency index table, RI = 1.12 is obtained by n = 5.

⑤ Calculate CR: $CR = \frac{CI}{RI} = \frac{0.004}{1.12} = 0.0034 < 0.1$

Seven experts conducted a consistency analysis on the comparison results of the first-level indicators. The CR values were all less than 0.1, so the consistency test was all passed. Seven experts take the weighted average value of each indicator's weight (as shown in Table 5) to obtain the comprehensive weight of the first level indicators. In view of the above method, data analysis is made on each influencing factors of the secondary indicators. After the weight of each index is obtained, the total weight is then calculated. The specific method is to multiply the judgment matrix of each index by the weight of its upper layer. The results are shown in Table 6.

Table 5. Weight results of first-level indicators

First level weight	Expert 1	Expert 2	Expert 3	Expert 4	Expert 5	Expert 6	Expert 7	Weight
Display	0.3263	0.3103	0.5883	0.3600	0.4691	0.4030	0.3263	0.3103
Interaction	0.3263	0.2414	0.1491	0.2800	0.2010	0.2444	0.3263	0.2414
Performance	0.1799	0.1724	0.1491	0.2000	0.2010	0.1367	0.1799	0.1724
Function	0.1068	0.1724	0.0585	0.1200	0.0862	0.1367	0.1068	0.1724
Aesthetic experience	0.0607	0.1034	0.0549	0.0400	0.0427	0.0791	0.0607	0.1034
CR	0.3263	0.3103	0.5883	0.3600	0.4691	0.4030	0.3263	0.3103

It can be concluded from the index weight result that the "function" (0.3156) is the most important one in the first level index, and the "practicability of the product" is the aspect that users consider more. Besides, users are prone to use products that have practical functions, and the practicability will also affect whether users to use the product again. Even if the experience of augmented reality is good, users will still consider whether it is necessary to apply AR technology on a certain product and whether it can meet users' needs or improve their efficiency and cognition.

The "display" effect of the model (0.2443) is also an important dimension in the evaluation. The location, size, light and shadow effect, degree of refinement, stability, floating sensation and degree of integration with the environment all affect users' realistic sense of the model.

The experience immersion is also the aspect that users pay much attention to. The introduction of sound and the sound effect of feedback make the interaction more

Table 6. Index weight and meaning

First level index	Weight	Two level indexes	Explanations	Weight	Total weight
Display	0.2443	Physical rationality	The position where the model is placed. The shape, size, shadow, action and feedback of the model conform to the physical reality	0.2471	0.0604
		Stability of synthetic environment	The synthetic environment will not change physically with the change of time and space	0.2491	0.0609
		Model quality	The model style, level of sophistication, and the expected style of application are consistent	0.2965	0.0724
		Virtual-real fusion	The virtual scene and the real scene are well combined, and the light effects, shadows, and occlusion are properly handled	0.0787	0.0192
		Detail presentation	Provides a way to view model details	0.1286	0.0314
Interaction	0.1545	Feedback	Timely and obvious feedback, consistent with cognition	0.1959	0.0303
		Sense of control	Flexible and controllable operation, interactive operation is efficient and easy to control	0.2695	0.0416
		Fault tolerance and error proof	The bearing capacity of the wrong operation, e.g. the function of deletion and reset is provided in case where model is misplaced or cannot be recovered	0.0827	0.0128
		Easy to learn	Interactive operation conforms to cognition, and the interactive mode is easy to learn and remember	0.2049	0.0317
		Operation guidance	Provide guidance on operation in time	0.1925	0.0298
		Humanized help	Provide timely and visible help center, and provide operable improvement suggestions in case of abnormality	0.0546	0.0084
Performance	0.1359	System stability	The system can complete the task smoothly and stably	0.4056	0.0551
		Response speed	Including environment identification, loading speed of model, and adopting appropriate strategies to reduce users' perception of loading time	0.1171	0.0159
		Matching accuracy	The accuracy of position matching between virtual object and real space	0.2585	0.0351
		Plane recognition rate	Horizontal Plane recognition success rate	0.2188	0.0297
Function	0.3156	Satisfaction of user's requirements	The extent to which the function meets the user's needs	0.6513	0.2056
		Cognitive improvement	Enhance users' cognition after use	0.3487	0.1100
Aesthetic experience	0.1498	Immersion	To focus on the task in the current target situation	0.4087	0.0612
		Entertainment	Interesting and entertaining in terms of user experience	0.2724	0.0408
		Gratification	Satisfaction with senses and information	0.3189	0.0478

interesting and enhance the user's immersion. The stronger the sense of reality, the better the user's immersive experience.

4 Experimental Design

4.1 Methodology

Taking the existing AR model display products on the market as an example, user experience evaluation is conducted with the above evaluation index system to verify the rationality of model construction and the effectiveness of the practical application. According to the AR ranking, two categories of six AR applications in the top, middle and bottom of the ranking are selected as the evaluation objects, which are "education" apps (Assemblr, JigSpace, Homebrew Club) and "furniture" apps (Housecraft, IKEA Place, Chuangzaojia).

The experiment is divided into two parts: product experience and rating scale. First, the main test personnel introduced the experiment, showed the task scene and task content to the test subjects before experiencing each app. After understanding the task, the test subjects completed the task in order according to the task table. The experiment used an in-group design and in order to avoid the influence of learning effect on scores, the sequence of experimental products was processed according to Latin square design. After experiencing all the apps, the test subjects rate the six apps according to the indicators constructed above. To ensure that users understand the meaning of indicators, a specific explanation is made to each indicator. The score table uses a Likert 5-point scale to obtain users' experimental experience.

Experiment task: the experience of AR model display products mainly includes the following aspects: initial startup, scene building, model interaction and abnormal conditions. Five experiment tasks are designed to correspond to these four aspects (Table 7).

Table 7. Experimental tasks

Task number	Task content	Focus of test
1	Start the application, browse the app homepage and operation guide, and select a model	Initial startup (application startup, content guidance, model loading, technical preparation)
2	Identify the surrounding environment and place the model	Scene Building (environment identification and model placement)
3	Interact with the model, including displacement, scaling, rotation, selection, deletion	Model interaction
4	Greatly enlarge, reduce and move the model, and then restore it to its original position and state as much as possible	Abnormal status (model lost, model out of screen)
5	Get up and walk around the house, scan around with the camera and focus on the model again	Stability of synthetic environment

Subjects: after screening and invitation confirmation, a total of 14 users participated in the experiment, including 7 males and 7 females. The age is between 20 and 30. In order to ensure consistency of AR understanding among subjects, users who have not used AR-related products in their previous experience are selected as test subjects.

Device: the experimental device is an iPhone XR with the system of IOS 12.3.1. The experiment is conducted indoors under a Wi-Fi network.

4.2   Result

By scoring six AR products, six groups of data of display, interaction, performance, function, and aesthetic experience are obtained by synthetic weight. According to the results of variance analysis of each group of data (Table 8), the two-tailed significance of display, interaction, performance, function, and aesthetic experience are 0.000, 0.000, 0.013, 0.003, and 0.000 respectively, all less than 0.05, indicating that the five main evaluation indexes in the evaluation system can effectively distinguish the experience of different AR products, and further indicating that the evaluation indexes analysed in this paper have certain reference value and practical significance.

Table 8. Results of variance analysis

	Score						F	P
	Assemblr	JigSpace	Homebrew club	IKEA Place	Housecraft	Chuangzaojia		
Display	3.64	4.28	3.03	4.40	4.40	3.62	5.722	0.000**
Interaction	3.14	3.81	1.86	3.11	3.49	3.04	5.700	0.000**
Performance	3.95	4.13	3.10	4.04	4.27	3.43	3.327	0.013*
Function	3.21	4.21	2.58	3.87	4.29	3.17	4.310	0.003**
Aesthetic experience	2.91	3.89	1.73	3.66	4.06	3.20	3.327	0.000**

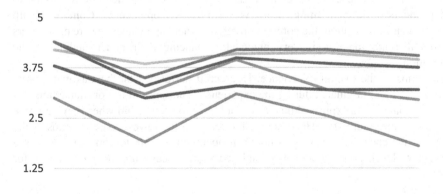

Fig. 2. Scoring results of six apps

In terms of display, Housecraft, IKEA Place, JigSpace perform well. Housecraft handles the textures and details of the models very well, and the models are solid, allowing for home furniture stacking. The effect of collision is also designed, and the sense of reality is better (Fig. 2).

In terms of interaction, there is a large gap between scores. JigSpace performed best because the interaction was cognitive, natural and controlled. In the case of model abnormality, it provides users with reset buttons. Bounds are set for zooming. However, the existing problems are that when the screen is out or the model is lost, there is no guide to retrieve them. Moreover, no operation guide or tutorials are provided during the process of scanning the plane and users are confused about what to do. Although Assembler gives a graphical representation of the operation in the interface, many users feel that the description is ambiguous, and the interaction cannot be successfully completed after attempts made in accordance to the guidelines. The lowest score was given to the Homebrew Club as interaction is slow, unstable and inconsistent with the cognition. Users expressed that they could not control it well after multiple and stressful attempts. The model can be added infinitely but cannot be deleted in the scene as the operational icons are too ambiguous.

In terms of performance, Housecraft scored the best, with faster speed in the process of identifying the environment and more accurate plane recognition. It provides operational guidance for identifying the plane, and gives feedback on the identification progress, reducing the user's perception of the loading time. In the experience process, it rarely shows an abnormal state and the test subject can successfully complete the given task, indicating a highly satisfying system stability.

In terms of functions, Housecraft scored well in furniture applications. It displays the projection of the furniture on the ground while placing the furniture. It well reflected the width, height and floor area of the furniture and helped users make purchase decisions. With strong practicability, it is well in line with the scene of the user's home design. Among educational applications, JigSpace allows users to understand how different things work via step-by-step procedures. Combined with animation and explanation, the complex structure is clear at a glance, where many users express that the function is very practical, enhancing their understanding of the application.

In terms of the overall experience, Housecraft performed the best as many users were amazed and fascinated during the experience. The sense of fun or immersion was good and many users expressed that they would like to use it again when they purchase furniture in the future. The Homebrew Club received the lowest score in terms of the overall experience, as it was not smooth in operation, unable to complete tasks at a satisfactory level, poor functionality, and had no practical value or value-adding for users.

5   Conclusions

This paper constructs the user experience evaluation system for the AR model display applications. Firstly, it collects the evaluation indices through analysing previous literature, initially establishing the hierarchical evaluation system. Through exercising the

Delphi method, 5 first-level indicators (Display, Interaction, Performance, Function and Aesthetic experience) and 20 second-level indicators are obtained. The index weight is then quantified by the analytic hierarchy process. After which, the system and its indicators are robustly tested through applying it to six mobile AR products in the market, verifying the validity of the main evaluation indices. The results suggest that function (0.32) and display (0.24), two second-level indices, have a greater influence over the user experience. Firstly, designers of relevant applications should prioritise its practicality, whether the use of AR technology is necessary, and whether the use of such technology can efficiently and effectively resolve challenges or result in cognitive improvement. Functional practicality affects the user's willingness to use and future possibility to reuse the application. Secondly, the display of the model is also an important dimension of evaluation. The location of the model, the size of the model, the light and shadow effects, the quality of the model, the stability of display, and the degree of virtual-real fusion with the environment will affect the sense of the reality of the model. By constructing a user experience evaluation system for the AR model display applications, the design elements and weights that affect the AR user experience are defined, providing informative insights to application designs of related applications. In addition, it can help the designer to adjust the design and evaluate each design's impact upon user experience. According to the conclusion of this paper, the goal of the augmented reality system design needs to be clear and precise. By considering the influence of various factors on the user experience, the user experience level of augmented reality applications will be comprehensively promoted, and the development of mobile augmented reality products is further initiated.

References

1. Azuma, R.T.: A survey of augmented reality. Teleoperators Virtual Environ. **6**(4), 355–385 (1997)
2. Ames, S., Wolffsohn, J., Mcbrien, N.: The development of a symptom questionnaire for assessing virtual reality viewing using a head-mounted display. Optom. Vis. Sci. **82**(3), 168–176 (2005)
3. Olsson, T., Saari, T., Lucero, A., Arrasvuori, J., Vaananen, K.: Reflections on experience-driven design: a case study on designing for playful experiences. In: DPPI, pp. 164–174 (2013)
4. Irshad, S., Rambli, D.: User experience of mobile augmented reality: a review of studies, pp. 125–130. IEEE (2014)
5. Baidu Al Interaction Design Lab: A guide to Mobile terminal space level AR interaction design. https://mp.weixin.qq.com/s/2vZBuCxxPz_yJxu38PO45g. Accessed 12 Sept 2019
6. Keating, G., Guest, D., Konertz, A., Padovani, N., Villa, A.: Design, User Experience, and Usability, Theory, Methods, Tools and Practice, pp. 135–141. Springer, Heidelberg (2011). https://doi.org/10.1007/978-3-642-21708-1
7. Olsson, T., Kärkkäinen, T., Lagerstam, E., Ventä-Olkkonen, L.: User evaluation of mobile augmented reality scenarios. J. Ambient Intell. Smart Environ. **4**(1), 29–47 (2012)
8. Dünser, A., Grasset, R., Billinghurst, M.: A survey of evaluation techniques used in augmented reality studies, pp. 123–145. ACM (2008)

9. Kalalahti, J.: Developing usability evaluation heuristics for augmented reality applications. Lutpub.lut.fi. (2015). https://lutpub.lut.fi/handle/10024/103081
10. Li, X.P., Zhao, F.N., Zhang, S.G.: Research on the design and application of VR/AR teaching experience. In: China Educational Technology, p. 10 (2018)
11. Pribeanu, C., Balog, A., Iordache, D.: Measuring the perceived quality of an AR-based learning application: a multidimensional model. Interact. Learn. Environ. **25**(4), 482–495 (2016)
12. Zhou, G.Z.: Research on the construction and application of mobile AR user experience model. In: PLA Information Engineering University (2013)
13. Saaty, T.L.: Decision making with the analytic hierarchy process. Serv. Sci. **1**(1), 83–98 (2008)

How Interaction Paradigms Affect User Experience and Perceived Interactivity in Virtual Reality Environment

Duo Wang[1]([⊠]) [iD], Xiwei Wang[1] [iD], Qingxiao Zheng[2] [iD],
Bingxin Tao[1] [iD], and Guomeng Zheng[1] [iD]

[1] Jilin University, Changchun 130022, Jilin, China
2228927617@qq.com
[2] University of Illinois at Urbana-Champaign, Champaign, IL 61820, USA

Abstract. Interactivity is one of the major features of virtual reality (VR) comparing with traditional digital devices. Many virtual reality devices and applications provide more than one input instruments for users to experience VR content. This study compares user behavior and perceived interactivity with three interaction paradigms to investigate the influence of interaction paradigms on user experience in virtual environment. An experiment of 36 participants was conducted to measure three factors of user experience and three factors of perceived interactivity. An ANOVA test was conducted and the results show that interaction paradigms have significant influence on user total interaction frequency, playfulness of interactivity and controllability of interactivity. Results did not show significant difference on total experience time between groups, which indicates that how long time the users spent in experiencing VR were not significantly affected by what type of interaction paradigms they used. This study has theoretical and practical implications on designing and developing virtual reality user experience.

Keywords: Interaction paradigm · Virtual reality · User experience · Interactivity

1 Introduction

The emergence of virtual reality (VR) technology has gained enormous attention in recent years. VR technology provides an immersive experience to the users by generating various types of interactive activities through multiple sensory such as visual, auditory, and tactile perceptions (Guttentag 2010). Interactivity is one of the major features of VR devices comparing with traditional digital devices. User experience not only contain physical interactions, but also related to user Interactivity which can be seen as reactions of an embodied human with the world, including the environment, objects, and humans (Heeter 2000). This is consistent with the interactivity effects model (Shin et al. 2013), which revealed positive effects of interactivity on engagement, attitude, and behavioral intention. Many virtual reality devices and applications provide more than one input instruments for users to experience VR content. Users

© Springer Nature Switzerland AG 2020
J. Y. C. Chen and G. Fragomeni (Eds.): HCII 2020, LNCS 12190, pp. 223–234, 2020.
https://doi.org/10.1007/978-3-030-49695-1_15

behave differently and have different perceptions when experiencing VR with different interaction paradigms (Ferguson et al. 2020).

Pausch (1993) obtained that compared HMD and joystick as input devices for locating targets in a virtual world are different. Previous study also showed that the perceived difficulty in controlling a smartphone with one hand varied significantly according to the range of thumb movement required for the manipulation (Shin et al. 2016). Interactivity is achieved by the presentation of information through different combinations of modalities, including visual, auditory, and other sensory modalities (Li et al. 2019). As a new type of digital reading, VR reading provides multisensory experience by allowing users to gain multiple types of information such as text, image, video, narrative audio and 360 virtual environment.

There are many advantages of digital reading over printed text include interactivity, nonlinearity, immediacy in accessing information, and the convergence of text, images, audio, and video (Chih-Ming and Fang-Ya 2014). Comparing to traditional reading, one of the purposes of VR reading is to enable users to gain information with an interactive and fun way (Rau et al. 2018). Investigating how user behave and perceive when reading in virtual environment is important to researchers and developers to understand VR users' intentions (Kim et al. 2014). Thus, this study trys to understand user experience and perceived interactivity in VR reading experience, which are considered to be crucial to not only designing virtual reality user experience, but also research in VR user behavior.

2 Method

2.1 Participants

As college students are one of the user groups who have the most interest and experience of using VR devices, thirty-six college students were recruited as participants from Jilin University. As the demographic characteristics of participants shown in Table 1, 17 (47.2%) participants are male and 19 (52.8%) participants are female. The overall age of participants is around 18, where 50% of the sample is under 18 years old. Almost a half of the participants (47.2%) are interested in VR technology, and only 8.3% of the participants are uninterested in VR, which is predictable because the young generation were born with digital devices and have the ability of learning and accepting new technology in a relatively short time. However, over a half of the participants don't have basic knowledge about VR technology such as what platforms VR applications use and what components VR devices have. In terms of experience of using VR, 58.3% of the participants have experienced VR regardless of what scenario they were in.

Table 1. Demographic characteristic of participants

Characteristic	Group	Number of participants (%)
Sex	Male	17(47.2%)
	Female	19(52.8%)
Age	<=18	18(50.0%)
	>=19	18(50.0%)
Interest	Uninterested	3(8.3%)
	Normal	16(44.4%)
	Interested	17(47.2%)
Knowledge	Unknown	20(55.6%)
	Normal	8(22.2%)
	Known	8(22.2%)
Experience	Experienced	21(58.3%)
	Inexperienced	15(41.7%)

2.2 Apparatus and Stimuli

In this research, we conducted an experiment to examine how interaction paradigms affect user interactive behavior and perceived interactivity. In this experiment, participants were asked to read a virtual reality interactive magazine through a VR reading application called VIVE Paper, which provides three interaction paradigms to interact in the virtual environment, which are: 1) interaction paradigm 1 allows user to experience VR reading by using two motion controllers; 2) interaction paradigm 2 allows user to experience VR reading by using a printed book tracker and hand gesture; 3) interaction paradigm 3 allows user to experience VR reading by using the printed book tracker and a motion controller instead of hand gesture. Figure 1 illustrates the printed book tracker and a hand gesture. The greed dots on the right side of Fig. 1 represent the current position of the user's finger top.

Fig. 1. Demonstration of interaction paradigm with hand and book tracker.

2.3   Measurement

To evaluate the user perceived interactivity, three dependent variables of interactivity were assigned and measured. The interactivity was measured through a questionnaire which consists of 14 items. Five questions were to test the controllability of interactivity; another five questions were to test the playfulness of interactivity; the other four questions were to test the user's behavioral intentions. On the other hand, this study also measured three factors of user's physical interaction behavior to evaluate the difference of user experience between groups.

Controllability of Interactivity. The first one is controllability of interactivity which refers to the degree of control that users have over the objects they see, the content they experience in virtual environment (Park et al. 2020), as well as to what extent the user can control their behavior in the VR specific interaction methods. It is worth to note that users who perceive high controllability may not have a good control in action.

Playfulness of Interactivity. Users could get entertained through experience VR content and interacting with virtual environments. Previous study showed that playfulness would also impact user's sense of interactivity (Park et al. 2020). Thus, the second one is playfulness of interactivity which reflects the degree of enjoyment that users perceive when interacting with VR technology.

Behavioral Intentions. Behavioral intensions refer to whether the user have favorable and unfavorable behavioral intentions in the context of retail (Zeithamal et al. 1996). In this study, favorable behavioral intentions includes willingness to acquire knowledge through this VR interaction experience frequently in the future, willingness to use the VR device later and so on (Table 2).

Table 2. Questionnaire items of user perceived interactivity

Variable	Measurement scales
Controllability of interactivity	1. I think I have a lot of control over the experience of using VR function 2. When I use VR, I am free to choose what I want to see 3. When using VR, I have no control over what I can do in this experience 4. It's easy for me to interact with VR devices 5. I can learn VR devices in a short time
Playfulness of interactivity	1. I think it's really interesting to use VR devices 2. I think my mood is very relaxed and comfortable when I use VR equipment to acquire knowledge 3. Using VR devices makes my reading very interesting, and I am interested in the reading form 4. I don't think it's boring to use the VR device 5. In general, I think I enjoy the whole use process
Behavioral intentions	1. I will recommend reading or experience of this VR device to my friends in the future 2. I would like to acquire knowledge through this VR interaction experience frequently in the future 3. I will share this VR experience form with others in the future 4. I will tend to use the VR device later

Learning Time. As none of the participants have experienced the VR reading application before the experiment, each participant would have to go through the tutorial section until he or she confidently feel being able to operate all three interactive functions. Learning time refers to the duration of each participant's tutorial section. Since each interaction paradigm has different input devices, the material of each tutorial section vary. Thus, difference of interaction paradigm may affect how long time participants spend.

Experience Time. Experience time refers to the duration of the participant's formal test. How long time the participants would like to spend in a particular VR experience could be influenced by multiple factors, in which interaction paradigm is a considerable factor. Participants experience VR application with different interaction paradigm may have different willingness of continuing the current experience.

Interaction Frequency. Interaction frequency refers to the total number of interaction that a participant executes during the entire formal test through the interaction device. In this particular case, as mentioned above, VR reading experience provides user three different type of interactive functions, which are button pressing, page turning and video controlling. Although the difference of interaction paradigms would not affect the content that participants see, it is still considered that participants with different interaction paradigms would behave differently in terms of how frequently execute the three interactive functions in VR.

2.4   Procedure

After entering the laboratory, each participant was asked to answer a questionnaire including basic information and experience of using virtual reality. All participants were sequentially numbered beforehand and randomly assigned to three groups associated with three interaction paradigms. After answering the questionnaire, each participant put on HMD and headphone with the help of experimenters. The first section of the VR experience is a step by step tutorial which contains information of how to operate the virtual book with input devices associated with each interaction paradigm. The participants were asked to confirm whether they successfully learned the operations of each interaction function and the manipulations of corresponding input device. Then the formal experiment was conducted until the participant fully finished the tutorial section. Participants was asked to answer a questionnaire of perceived interactivity as soon as they finish the formal experiment.

Fig. 2. Participant of group 2 using book tracker to experience VR reading.

2.5 Data Collection

The questionnaires were originally answered in printed paper. Thus all data were manually collected by experimenters. A screen recording software OBS Studio was used to record each participant's entire VR experiment including tutorial section and formal test. Then data of the three physical interaction - experience duration, learning duration and total interaction frequency - was manually coded. The data about different tested measurements came from different groups of participants, meaning that the experiment is not a repeated measure design. Moreover, since the interaction paradigm was an independent variable, it became the dependent samples of the measure design. In order to evaluate whether or not the different interaction paradigms have impact on users VR reading experience and interactivity, an one-way ANOVA test was conducted with interaction paradigm as the dependent variable, and six measurements introduced above as the independent variables. In addition, a Tukey's HSD post hoc test was performed to investigate which groups are different from others specifically. Finally, the statistical software, SPSS 25.0, was used to analyze the results, with $p < 0.05$ set as the level of a significant difference.

3 Results

3.1 User Experience ANOVA Result

This study was designed to explore the effect of interaction paradigm types on user experience and perceived interactivity. As shown in Fig. 3, group 1 has the overall longest experience time, longest learning time and highest interaction frequency among the three groups. In contrary, group 2 has the overall shortest experience time, shortest learning time and lowest interaction frequency. Among the three physical interaction measurements, experience time has relatively the largest standard deviation in all three groups than the other two factors. In particular, group 1 has the largest standard deviation of experience time, which indicates that the range of experience time of participants in group 1 is wide and the distribution is not centralized. Besides, the mean value of experience time with three interaction paradigms were 691.417(SD = 313.816), 558.917(SD = 221.703), 593.917(SD = 282.655) seconds respectively. Result did not show statistically significant difference of experience time ($F_{(2,33)}$ = 0.684, p > 0.05) between three groups. Table 3 shows the result of ANOVA with experience time, learning time and interaction frequency.

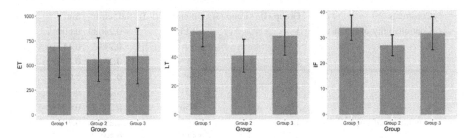

Fig. 3. Result of experience time, learning time and interaction frequency of three groups.

As shown by the result of ANOVA concerning learning time in Table 3, the difference of learning time between groups with different interaction paradigms is statistically significant (F(2,33) = 6.296, p < 0.01). After being analyzed through Tukey' s HSD multiple range test, it was discovered that learning time of group 1, group 2 and group3 are 58.333(SD = 10.957), 41.000(SD = 11.612), 55.000(SD = 13.730) respectively, as shown in Table 4. In terms of learning time, group 2 has a significant difference from the other two groups, where the other two groups don't have significant difference from each other.

Table 3. ANOVA results of user experience

Constructs	Groups	N	Mean	Std. deviation	F	Sig.
Experience time	1	12	691.417	313.816	0.684	0.512
	2	12	558.917	221.803		
	3	12	593.917	282.655		
Learning time	1	12	58.333	10.957	6.296	**0.005**[**]
	2	12	41.000	11.612		
	3	12	55.000	13.730		
Total interaction frequency	1	12	33.917	4.924	4.97	**0.013**[*]
	2	12	27.000	4.143		
	3	12	31.750	6.457		

Note: *p < 0.05. **p < 0.01. ***p < 0.001.

Also, the effect of interaction paradigm types on total interaction frequency reached a significance level (F(2,33) = 4.97, p < 0.05), as shown in Table 3. After being analyzed through Tukey's HSD multiple range test, it was discovered that the difference of total interaction frequency between group 1 (two controllers interaction) and group 2(gesture interaction) is statistically significant, group 1 has a mean of 33.93(SD = 4.924) times and group 2 has a mean of 27.0(SD = 4.143) times respectively, as shown in Table 4.

Table 4. Tukey's HSD results of user experience and perceived interactivity

Constructs	Group (I)	Group (J)	Difference (I–J)	Std. error	Sig.
Controllability of interactivity	1	2	−0.15	0.24089	0.809
		3	0.5	0.241	0.111
	2	1	0.15	0.241	0.809
		3	**.650***	0.241	0.029
	3	1	−0.5	0.241	0.111
		2	**−.650***	0.241	0.029
Playfulness of interactivity	1	2	−0.233	0.293	0.707
		3	0.533	0.293	0.178
	2	1	0.233	0.293	0.707
		3	**.767***	0.293	0.034
	3	1	−0.533	0.293	0.178
		2	**−.767***	0.293	0.034
Behavioral intentions	1	2	−0.133	0.338	0.918
		3	0.15	0.338	0.897
	2	1	0.133	0.338	0.918
		3	0.283	0.338	0.682
	3	1	−0.15	0.338	0.897
		2	−0.283	0.338	0.682
Total interaction frequency	1	2	**6.917***	2.244	0.011
		3	2.167	2.244	0.603
	2	1	**−6.917***	2.244	0.011
		3	−4.75	2.244	0.102
	3	1	−2.167	2.244	0.603
		2	4.75	2.244	0.102
Learning time	1	2	**17.333****	5.184	0.006
		3	3.333	5.184	0.798
	2	1	**−17.333****	5.184	0.006
		3	**−14.000***	5.184	0.028
	3	1	−3.333	5.184	0.798
		2	**14.000***	5.184	0.028
Experience time	1	2	132.5	117.429	0.504
		3	97.5	117.429	0.687
	2	1	−132.5	117.429	0.504
		3	−35	117.429	0.952
	3	1	−97.5	117.429	0.687
		2	35	117.429	0.952

Note: *p < 0.05. **p < 0.01. ***p < 0.001.

3.2   Perceived Interactivity ANOVA Result

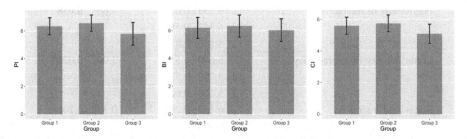

Fig. 4. Result of playfulness of interactivity, behavioral intention and controllability of interactivity of the three groups.

Table 5 shows the result of ANOVA with such perceived interactivity evaluation as playfulness of interactivity, behavioral intention and controllability of interactivity. The effect of interaction paradigm types on playfulness of interactivity reached a significance level ($F_{(2,33)}$ = 3.603, p < 0.05). After being analyzed through Tukey's HSD multiple range test, it was discovered that the mean score of playfulness of interactivity is significantly different between group 2 and group 3, where group 2 has a mean of 6.567(SD = 0.582) and group 3 has a mean of 5.800(SD = 0.816) respectively, as shown in Table 4. This also indicates that participants in group 2 perceived higher playfulness of interactivity than participants in group 3.

Besides, ANOVA results shows that the effect of interaction paradigm types on controllability of interactivity reached a significance level (F(2,33) = 3.992, p < 0.05), as shown in Table 5. After being analyzed through Tukey's HSD multiple range test, it was discovered that the mean score of controllability of interactivity is significantly different between group 2 and group 3, where group has a mean of 5.750(SD = 0.530) and group 3 has a mean of 5.100(SD = 0.603) respectively, as shown in Table 4. Namely, in terms of controllability of interactivity, the participants in group 2 perceived more freely and smoothly control in VR reading experience than participants in group 3 (See Fig. 4).

However, the interaction paradigm types did not produce a statistically significant effect on behavioral intensions (F(2,33) = 0.352, p > 0.05). The mean score of behavioral intensions of group 1, group 2 and group 3 are 6.167(SD = 0.752), 6.300 (SD = 0.794) and 6.017(SD = 0.802) respectively, as shown in Fig. 2. Table 5 shows the result of ANOVA with behavioral intensions.

Table 5. ANOVA results of perceived interactivity

Constructs	Groups	N	Mean	Std. deviation	F	Sig.
Playfulness of interactivity	1	12	6.333	0.614	3.603	**0.038***
	2	12	6.567	0.582		
	3	12	5.800	0.816		
Controllability of interactivity	1	12	5.600	0.538	3.992	**0.028***
	2	12	5.750	0.530		
	3	12	5.100	0.603		
Behavioral intentions	1	12	6.167	0.752	0.352	0.706
	2	12	6.300	0.794		
	3	12	6.017	0.802		

Note: $*p < 0.05$. $**p < 0.01$. $***p < 0.001$.

4   Discussion

4.1   User Experience

Both learning time and total interaction frequency have a statistically significant difference between the three groups. Prior to the formal experiment, hand gesture interaction was considered, to some extent, harder to learn than the other interaction paradigms with traditional VR motion controllers, because users would be more familiar with traditional motion controllers. Regarding learning time, group 2 with hand gesture interaction and group1 with two controllers interaction spent relatively shorter time to finish the tutorial section than group 3 with one controller interaction. Results indicate that participants in group 2 have the shortest mean of learning time, which means they learned how to operate VR reading with hand gesture even faster than participants learning how to user motion controller. This finding has considerable implication on interaction design of VR experience, where we usually think that motion controllers would be one of the most common and easiest way to interact in VR.

On the other hand, as indicated in this study, group 1 with two controller interaction has the highest total interaction frequency, followed by group 3 with one controller interaction, and then group 2 with gesture has the lowest total interaction frequency. The effects of different interaction paradigm types on total interaction frequency reached a significance level. The participants would click the button on the controller to interact with the virtual reality environment when using two controllers interaction or one controller interaction. Clicking the button may strengthen the feeling of interaction. Thus, participants tend to interact with the controller rather than the gesture in the virtual reality environment. Even though hand gesture interaction is relatively easy to learn, participants with motion controllers still interacted more frequently than those with hand gesture.

Concerning the experience time, there was no significant difference found between the three interaction paradigm types. One potential reason is that the difference of interaction paradigm do not affect how long the participants would like to spend in experiencing VR application. Participant's experience time may be related to the contents of experience rather than the interaction paradigm.

4.2   User Perception

The results of perceived interactivity indicate that interaction paradigm types are the major factor affecting how user perceive interactivity. The above results correspond with those of playfulness of interactivity and controllability of interactivity. Regarding interaction paradigm types, participants with hand gesture interaction have overall higher score on perceived interactivity than participants with one controller interaction. And the participants with two controller interaction are similar to participants with hand gesture interaction.

Concerning results of user perceived interactivity, participants in group 2 and group 3 have a higher score than participants in group 3, which indicates participants in group 3 may perceive the least playfulness during the VR experience. This may due to the interaction paradigm they use in that some participants met difficulties with the way combining printed book and motion controller. On the other hand, participants in group 1 and group 2 may be less constrained and more attracted to the virtual reality environment, which makes it more interesting.

Additionally, with the scores of controllability of interactivity compared, group 2 with hand gesture interaction gets the highest score; group 1 with two controllers interaction ranks the second, and group 3 with one controller interaction gets the lowest score. There are two potential reasons for this result, as described below. First, because of the device itself, when the participants use hand gesture to interact with the virtual reality environment based on infrared sensor, hand gesture interaction is more sensitive than the others. Therefore, the participants would feel more comfortable when interacting with hand gesture. Second, hand gesture interaction is a more similar paradigm comparing with the hand movement of turning pages of real books in everyday life. Participants were unfamiliar with motion controllers prior to this experiment even though some of whom had VR experiences.

Besides, Results did not show significant difference of behavioral intentions between the three groups, which indicates that participants' behavioral intentions are mainly determined by the virtual reality environment provided by VR equipment instead of what type of interaction paradigm they use. On the other hand, it is worth to note that even though participants in group 2 have the lowest score in all three measurement of physical interactions, conversely, they have the highest scores in all three measurements of perceived interactivity. The design of interaction paradigm with printed book tracker and hand gesture is a novel attempt in VR reading, which provides users a better perception of interactivity in experiencing VR. However, novel interaction paradigms sometimes may cause difficulties to user's physical interaction.

5   Conclusion

This study explored how interaction paradigm types in the virtual reality affect users experience and perceived interactivity. While the interaction paradigms were being independent variable, the participants' experience time, learning time and total interaction frequency were recorded through screen recording; meanwhile a questionnaire was used to carry out subjective evaluation of users' perceived interactivity. In this way, the effects of interaction paradigm types on perceived interactivity have been investigated. The findings suggest that the interaction paradigm has an effect on users' experience and perceived interactivity. Specifically, participants using interaction paradigm with hand gesture have the smallest mean of learning time and total interaction frequency. Moreover, participants with two controller interaction and hand gesture interaction have higher score than participants with one controller interaction in terms of playfulness of interactivity and controllability of interactivity. The above findings can be used as a reference by VR designers to design the interaction paradigm.

Acknowledgment. This research is sponsored by the International Innovation Team of Philosophy and Science of Jilin University and Major Project of the National Science Foundation (No. 71673108).

References

Chih-Ming, C., Fang-Ya, C.: Enhancing digital reading performance with a collaborative reading annotation system. Comput. & Educ. **77**, 67–81 (2014)

Ferguson, C., van den Broek, E.L., van Oostendorp, H.: On the role of interaction mode and story structure in virtual reality serious games. Comput. Educ. **143**, 103671 (2020)

Kim, S.Y., Prestopnik, N., Biocca, F.A.: Body in the interactive game: how interface embodiment affects physical activity and health behavior change. Comput. Hum. Behav. **36**, 376–384 (2014)

Rau, P.-L.P., Zheng, J., Guo, Z., Li, J.: Speed reading on virtual reality and augmented reality. Comput. Educ. **125**, 240–245 (2018)

Guttentag, D.: Virtual reality: applications and implications for tourism. Tourism Manage. **31**(5), 637–651 (2010)

Heeter, C.: Interactivity in the context of designed experiences. J. Interact. Advertising **1**(1), 1–17 (2000)

Li, Y., Huang, J., Tian, F., Wang, H.-A., Dai, G.-Z.: Gesture interaction in virtual reality. Virtual Reality Intell. Hardware. **1**, 84–112 (2019)

Shin, D., Choi, M., Kim, J.H., Lee, J.-G.: Interaction, engagement, and perceived interactivity in single-handed interaction. Internet Res. **26**(5), 1134–1157 (2016)

Shin, D.: User experience in social commerce: in friends we trust. Behav. Inf. Technol. **32**(1), 52–67 (2013)

Pausch, R., Shackelford, A., Proffitt, D.: A user study comparing head-mounted and stationary displays. In: Virtual Reality, pp. 41–45 (1993)

Park, M., Yoo, J.: Effects of perceived interactivity of augmented reality on consumer responses: a mental imagery perspective. J. Retail. Consum. Serv. **52**, 101912 (2020)

Zeithamal, V.A., Berry, L.L., Parasuraman, A.: The behavioral consequences of service quality. J. Mark. **60**(4), 31–46 (1996)

MRCAT: In Situ Prototyping of Interactive AR Environments

Matt Whitlock[1]([✉]), Jake Mitchell[1], Nick Pfeufer[1], Brad Arnot[1], Ryan Craig[1], Bryce Wilson[1], Brian Chung[1], and Danielle Albers Szafir[1,2,3]

[1] Department of Computer Science, University of Colorado Boulder, Boulder, CO 80309, USA
{matthew.whitlock,jake.mitchell,nicholas.pfeufer, bradley.arnot,ryan.craig,bryce.d.wilson,brian.chung, danielle.szafir}@colorado.edu
[2] Department of Information Science, University of Colorado Boulder, Boulder, CO 80309, USA
[3] ATLAS Institute, University of Colorado Boulder, Boulder, CO 80309, USA

Abstract. Augmented reality (AR) blends physical and virtual components to create a mixed reality experience. This unique display medium presents new opportunities for application design, as applications can move beyond the desktop and integrate with the physical environment. In order to build effective applications for AR displays, we need to be able to iteratively design for different contexts or scenarios. We present MRCAT (Mixed Reality Content Authoring Toolkit), a tool for *in situ* prototyping of mixed reality environments. We discuss the initial design of MRCAT and iteration after a study ($N = 14$) to evaluate users' abilities to craft AR applications with MRCAT and with a 2D prototyping tool. We contextualize our system in a case study of museum exhibit development, identifying how existing ideation and prototyping workflows could be bolstered with the approach offered by MRCAT. With our exploration of *in situ* prototyping, we enumerate key aspects both of AR application design and targeted domains that help guide design of more effective AR prototyping tools.

Keywords: Augmented reality · Prototyping · Multimodal interaction

1 Introduction

Many display media have established iterative design workflows, where designers prototype at increased levels of fidelity to elicit feedback before the application is developed [18]. To elicit early feedback, designers will often employ simple sketch-based prototyping, but with continued iteration and increased fidelity, prototypes increasingly look as they will appear in the target display media (i.e., in a browser window for a web application or on a touchscreen for a mobile application). Despite notable research in AR content creation [25,29,38,42], AR

© Springer Nature Switzerland AG 2020
J. Y. C. Chen and G. Fragomeni (Eds.): HCII 2020, LNCS 12190, pp. 235–255, 2020.
https://doi.org/10.1007/978-3-030-49695-1_16

application prototyping lacks support for higher fidelity prototypes that allow designers to experience and refine prototypes in the target display.

Prototypes of AR applications typically come in the form of sketches and descriptions of how the environment should look. The practice of sketching and writing is accessible to designers and domain experts, relative to the alternative of developing the entire application in code. However, these sketches offer low fidelity representations of the idea in the designer's mind. Game engines such as Unity afford prototyping on a 2D display, but decontextualize virtual content from the real world. If designers were to instead prototype AR applications in AR, they could place virtual content in tandem with the physical environment. This *in situ* approach to prototyping AR environments allows designers and domain experts to truly express and experience their ideas as they become a reality, However, *in situ* AR prototyping tools do not yet support the needs of designers, in part due to lack of guidance on how to design effective *in situ* prototyping tools. With this paper, we address the benefits of an *in situ* approach to AR prototyping, discussing usability of prototyping tools and key aspects of environment design for AR prototyping tools to address going forward.

We introduce a tool for AR *in situ* prototyping called the Mixed Reality Content Authoring Toolkit (MRCAT) and discuss how our work with the tool elicited the needs for prototyping AR applications. We present a workflow for AR prototyping where designers can create, save, share and load AR experiences, placing, manipulating and annotating virtual models directly in the environment to craft mixed reality experiences *in situ*. We discuss the design of MRCAT in the context of common guidelines for prototyping tools and the results of a preliminary study exploring the needs of *in situ* prototyping tools compared to AR application prototyping in 2D. Through these efforts, we enumerate ways to increase the usability of AR prototyping tools and key aspects of *in situ* environment design for future prototyping tools.

2   Related Work

AR prototyping systems often either remove virtual content from physical context [29] or use an adapted form of sketching with ubiquitous materials like cardboard and glass [6], limiting the fidelity to the intended AR experience. Alternatively, prototypes offering higher fidelity often require programming knowledge in order to build [37]. As AR technology becomes more accessible, domain experts will increasingly need to be part of application design. Participatory design allows for ideation within a "third space" between technologists and domain experts that includes ideas novel to both fields through co-creation [31]. Within AR, previous systems have explored prototyping tools for domain experts such as educators [23] and museum exhibit curators [45] by editing video streams in a 2D AR browser. With our work, we explore how *in situ* prototyping can allow users to build high fidelity prototypes directly in the target environment using intuitive WYSIWYG tools. We build on past work in AR content creation and user interfaces (UIs) that will make AR prototyping workflows feasible to a broad range of users.

2.1   AR Content Creation

Research in AR content creation tools has explored different approaches to more intuitively create mixed reality experiences. Tools like DART [29] and ComposAR [38] allow users to augment video and picture representations of the physical environment with virtual content. Other content creation tools allow users to customize which 3D models are associated with different fiduciary markers in tangible AR applications [5, 25, 42]. With headsets having six degree-of-freedom tracking to localize within a room, markerless AR content creation tools allow users to place virtual objects in the room to change the appearance *in situ* [49].

In situ prototyping tools allow users to create and edit applications directly in the application's target environment. This approach is of particular interest as AR applications typically rely on blending virtual content and the physical space. For example, SceneCTRL allows users to edit arrangements of physical and virtual objects both by placing new objects and visually deleting existing physical objects. [49]. Built on the AMIRE content authoring framework, work on assembly tutorial authoring allows users to build AR tutorial components as they assemble the physical object [50]. Work in AR museum presentation authoring explores scene editing on a web browser [42] and is then extended to use a mobile phone to create and edit virtual models for a museum exhibit directly in the space [36]. While these use cases provide examples where designers can build with the display medium directly in the target environment, little is know about what exactly are the benefits to AR prototyping *in situ* or how to design applications that optimize for these benefits. Through our work with MRCAT, we propose design guidelines for AR prototyping tools and discuss scenarios in which *in situ* AR prototyping could improve existing design workflows.

2.2   AR Multimodal Interaction

UIs for prototyping tools must support a number of tasks. Effective UI design for *in situ* AR prototyping is further complicated by the fact that there are not standard interaction metaphors and best practices for AR UI design. Fluid interaction is critical to the success of prototyping AR applications. AR systems commonly make use of freehand gestures to manipulate object transforms [7, 17] since the metaphor to grab and manipulate a virtual object maps to manipulation of physical objects. Freehand gestures have also been used to annotate [11, 26], sketch [1, 46], navigate menu systems [13, 32] and update descriptive characteristics such as color [34]. Alternatives to gestural interaction include using mediating devices such as tangible markers [25], secondary tablet/phone displays [1, 30] and video game controllers [43, 44]. This disparate exploration of different modalities for interaction in AR makes it difficult to identify specific best practices when crafting an AR interface. However, performance differences across tasks indicate that multimodal interaction may provide more intuitive means for supporting the array of capabilities necessary to prototype AR experiences.

Research in multimodal interaction considers how input modalities can complement one another. For example, gaze plus gestural interaction typically utilizes the user's gaze for object specification and a hand gesture to perform object manipulation [9,12,41]. Voice is often used in tandem with gaze or freehand gestures. Users can use a gesture to specify an object to move and a voice command such as "move behind the table" to indicate where to move it [21,33] or to change the color or shape of an object [28]. Multimodal interactions can also provide *mutual disambiguation*, where input from multiple modalities probabilistically provides greater precision than either input on its own [24]. In AR prototyping, these multimodal approaches could provide greater accuracy and speed in interactions than individual modalities could achieve on their own, leading to more efficient design of high quality prototypes.

The target design tasks can also guide the best ways to interact with a system. For example, picking items in a data visualization may be well-suited to gestural interaction while higher-level commands like creating a new visualization would be well-suited to voice interaction [2]. High agreement scores in elicitation of translation, rotation and scaling gestures suggest that freehand gestures are intuitive for transform manipulations [34]. However, the low agreement scores for interface-level commands and descriptive characteristics suggest that a different modality should be employed for these tasks. To support fluid, interactive design *in situ*, we build on findings in multimodal interaction, utilizing gestural interaction to manipulate object transforms [7,9,17,40] and voice commands for descriptive characteristics [27,28] and interface-level commands [41,49].

3   Design Guidelines

We reviewed literature on prototyping methods and commercial prototyping tools to better understand limitations in current approaches and how these guidelines might extend to *in situ* approaches. We used these guidelines to create a preliminary version of MRCAT, grounded in prototyping best practices. MRCAT offers an extended suite of prototyping functionality, including directly placing/manipulating virtual objects and saving and loading scenes. While a complete survey of prototyping best practices is beyond the scope of this work (see Carter & Hundhausen [8] for a survey), we synthesized three guidelines from prior literature and our own experiences that extend these practices to the unique needs of *in situ* prototyping in AR:

D1: Full Experience Prototyping. To effectively create design artifacts, prototyping tools should allow designers to capture the intended experience and different application designs [3]. Traditional tools give designers the ability to design on a blank slate, adding GUI elements such as menus, text boxes and buttons. On the other hand, AR prototyping tools need to consider interactions of physical and virtual elements—both 2D and 3D—by giving designers the ability to enumerate relationships. For example, when prototyping an AR museum exhibit, designers should be able to place exhibit pieces on tables, floors and walls as they see fit. Considering that not all information may be represented by placement and manipulation of virtual models in the environment (e.g., the proposed interactive nature of the virtual object), AR prototyping tools should also consider methods to describe these additional needs. In MRCAT, we implement this guideline through combined model integration, transformation and text-based annotation.

D2: Intuitive UI. Creating interactive AR applications requires disparate design tasks (e.g., positioning models, mocking interactions, annotating models). While mouse and keyboard interactions would be efficient and familiar for these tasks in 2D prototyping tools such as proto.io[1], we need to consider task mappings for novel AR interfaces. Deeply nested menu structures common to 2D prototyping tools do not translate well to AR. In MRCAT, we guided interaction mappings with prior literature (Sect. 2.2), using freehand interactions for model manipulation, and voice commands for abstract operations such as deleting objects, changing color and saving.

D3: Constrained Interactions. Users should clearly understand how their input will change the environment. If the system does not clearly and efficiently convey how the interaction will affect the environment, users will be frustrated by unexpected outputs and will need to spend additional time correcting. We provide simple, understandable interactions by constraining the degrees of freedom manipulated at one time. For example, users can either be moving, scaling or rotating an object—but not more than one of these operations—at a time. This strategy is employed in common 3D modeling tools such as Unity[2] and Sketchup[3]. In MRCAT's implementation, we build on prior AR research that achieves this by mapping the same gesture to different functionalities [39]. Explicit mode switching—implemented via voice commands and menu options— ensures users know what manipulation they are performing (e.g. translation, rotation, scaling).

We combine these design guidelines with ideas from 2D prototyping tools and previous AR literature to implement a system for *in situ* AR prototyping.

4   MRCAT Preliminary Design

We built MRCAT to allow users to create and edit prototypes *in situ*. This system instantiates the design guidelines laid out in Sect. 3, providing full experience prototyping *(D1)*, an intuitive UI *(D2)* and constrained interactions *(D3)*.

4.1   System Overview

MRCAT is a prototyping tool built for the Microsoft HoloLens[4] that allows users to place and manipulate objects in the environment. Users can first copy desired prefabricated element (prefabs) or custom 3D models into the project folder to tailor the initial models to their target application. MRCAT starts by loading a billboarded main menu showing the functionality available to the user, including

---

[1] https://proto.io.
[2] https://unity.com.
[3] https://sketchup.com.
[4] https://docs.microsoft.com/en-us/hololens/hololens1-hardware.

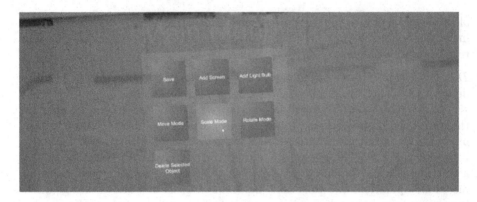

Fig. 1. MRCAT's main menu. Users can enter different interaction modes through the menu interface or through equivalent "MRCAT `mode`" commands. For example, the user can select "Scale Mode" from the menu, or say "MRCAT Scale."

a list of models extracted from the project folder (Fig. 1). MRCAT allows users to enable different modes that determine how their interaction will affect the selected objects: "Move", "Rotate", "Scale", "Annotate (Note)" and "Color".

To enter an interaction mode, the user can either select the mode from the set of options on the main menu or use a voice command (i.e. "MRCAT `mode`"). Users select menu options through the built-in gaze-tap gesture, where a cursor raycasted from the center of the user's gaze indicates which item to select with and a freehand tap gesture acts as a click. To engage with 3D models, the user selects an object with the same gaze-tap gesture, and subsequent interactions will affect all selected objects. Users can move, rotate or scale objects, depending on what interaction mode they have selected. This manipulation is done with the gaze-drag gesture, similar to the gaze-tap, but rather than a tap, the user presses down their finger to hold, moves their hand in front of the headset and finishes the interaction by releasing their finger back up.

After completing a prototype, the user can export the prototyped application as an XML file containing all relevant information about objects created. Files are relatively small (1.6 MB on average in the study, Sect. 5), and can be loaded into MRCAT to recreate and edit the scene. By changing the headset camera prefab prior to loading MRCAT, users can view the prototype in any headset, such as the GearVR, or on the desktop.

4.2   System Functionality

MRCAT enables users to interact with virtual content by moving between different interaction modes. To ensure that novice users are only able to perform one action at a time ($D3$), MRCAT employs voice commands and redundant menu options to allow the user to enter each interaction's mode. The user selects all objects they want to manipulate, rendering a red border around those objects to indicate engagement. The user can then either give the voice command "MRCAT

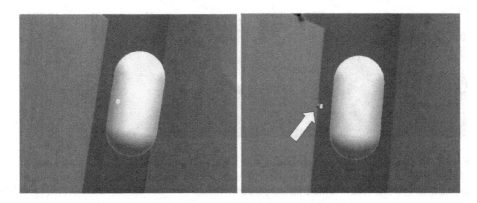

Fig. 2. When moving objects, a small yellow sphere (right) indicates attempted displacement. Here the user is trying to move the virtual capsule through a wall, but the capsule collides with and renders against the wall (arrow added for emphasis). (Color figure online)

mode" to enter that mode (e.g., "MRCAT Rotate") or select the corresponding menu option. This "MRCAT" initiation is similar to familiar voice-interaction with assistants such as Apple's Siri[5] and Amazon's Alexa[6] *(D2)*. Then the user performs the appropriate gesture to change all selected objects.

Object Placement/Translation: Users can add and reposition objects throughout the environment using MRCAT. To add an object, the user selects a menu item or says "Add `item name`". The user can then control the placement of a virtual object, moving the object with their gaze. The object sits 2 m in front of the middle of the user's gaze and a small yellow sphere appears in the middle of the object transform to indicate where the user is placing or attempting to place the object (Fig. 2). If the object collides with another virtual object or physical surface such as a floor, wall or table (as detected using the HMD's depth camera), the object temporarily rests on the surface it collided with. The yellow sphere visually cues that there has been a collision and that the user may need to move the object elsewhere. Once the user is satisfied with an object's location, they select the object again to finalize its position.

Users can also move objects already placed in the environment, entering "Move" mode with a "MRCAT Move" command. To move objects, users first select the object, outlining it in red. They can then use hand gestures to move the object to different points in the environment. We employ only gestures for position refinement to allow for more precise object placement, rather than coarse-grain object placement that allows users to quickly get the desired objects into the environment before fine-tuning the positioning. The user can freely position objects in the environment rather than having objects locked 2 m from their forward gaze, which may require them to crane their neck to precisely move

---
[5] https://apple.com/siri/.
[6] https://developer.amazon.com/en-US/alexa.

Fig. 3. Rotating a virtual screen about the Y axis. When the user begins dragging, a virtual joystick appears (right) to give the user an interaction metaphor of pulling a joystick to the left (label added for emphasis).

an object. Using the gaze-drag gesture, users can grab and move all selected objects, such that displacement of the hand along the X, Y, and Z axes maps proportionally to displacement of the selected objects. As with initial object placement, objects cannot be moved through a surface or another object. To end translation, the user releases the gaze-drag gesture.

Rotation: MRCAT allows users to rotate virtual objects placed in the environment. To rotate an object, the user says "MRCAT Rotate" and enters a rotation mode. As with translation, the user presses and holds their hand to begin rotating selected objects. In piloting, we found that users preferred to rotate objects about one axis at a time for better control and precision *(D3)*. MRCAT then processes whether the user's initial hand movement is primarily along the X, Y or Z axis, and locks the object to rotate about one axis. If the initial hand displacement is to the left or right relative to the user, the object rotates about the Y axis (yaw). Similarly, hand displacement up and down maps to rotation about the X axis (pitch), and hand displacement along the Z axis maps to rotation about the Z axis (roll). To provide a visual indicator of the rotation control, a stick with a ball at the end appears in the middle of the object's transform, inspired by the metaphor of pushing and pulling a joystick (Fig. 3).

Scale: MRCAT also allows users to resize placed objects, entering this mode through the "MRCAT Scale" command. To begin scaling, the user presses and holds their hand, establishing the hand position as the initial grab point. Displacement of the hand along both the X and Y axes corresponds to uniform scaling of the object along all axes simultaneously. Grabbing and dragging either up or to the right increases object size, while dragging either down or to the left decreases size. As with scaling functionality of popular 3D modeling software (such as Unity and SketchUp), scaling an object to a negative number results in a mirrored positive scaling. To finish scaling, the user releases their finger.

Change Material: Users can change object appearance through voice commands. To change the appearance of selected objects, the user says "MRCAT material name," and all selected objects will change to have that material. For simplicity, we limited materials to the colors of the rainbow, black, white and ghost (transparency).

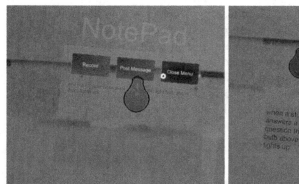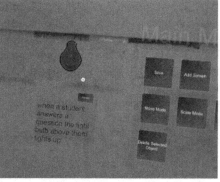

Fig. 4. Interface for recording user dictation as a note (left) and posting it to a virtual object (right). After pulling up the Notepad interface with the "MRCAT Note" command, users select the "Record" button to begin recording. Recording ends after two seconds of silence, at which point users can select the "Post Message" button to post the note to highlighted objects.

Annotation: MRCAT allows users to textually annotate objects in the scene to note additional ideas the designer has in mind or provide feedback on an element of the design *(D1)*. These annotations can indicate relationships between objects, fill in gaps where the 3D model design may fall short or allow for prototype feedback *in situ*. Users can annotate an object by first entering annotation mode by saying "MRCAT Note." An annotation interface then appears with buttons for recording, posting and closing (Fig. 4). As with the main menu, the annotation interface and the notes placed in the environment are billboarded to always face the user. To record a text annotation, the user says "MRCAT Note," and MRCAT plays a short "listening" audio clip to indicate that recording has begun. The user then dictates the note and the recording ends when the user stops speaking for 2 s. The user says "MRCAT Post" to render the note as a sticky-note style panel with a "Remove" button. The note appears above the object and moves with the object. To avoid occlusion, the note renders above its associated object if the user is looking down at the object and will render below the object if the user is looking up or directly at the object.

We employed basic dictation recognition for text entry, as text entry remains an open problem in AR and VR research [16,47,48]. Voice dictation is relatively fast but inaccurate, whereas use of a gesture-enabled virtual keyboards are slow but accurate [19]. Due to the already prominent use of voice interaction in MRCAT and a prioritization of speed over accuracy, we chose dictation for freeform text input, likened to post-it notes. The primary limitation of this approach is that mistakes result in a re-recording, rather than editing individual words. We anticipate annotations being fairly brief as designers typically prioritize visual depictions over long descriptions when building prototypes [3]. The brief nature of these annotations mitigates this limitation, as re-recording the intended text is generally inexpensive.

System-Level Interactions: Saving and loading prototypes is implemented using voice commands. Users can export prototyped scenes to XML files using the command "MRCAT Save" or by selecting the "Save" item on the main menu. MRCAT then plays the "listening" sound to indicate recording has begun, and the user says the name of the target XML file. The file is saved as the name specified by the user with spaces as underscores. MRCAT then plays audio "Space saved as `file name`." To load a saved file, the user says "MRCAT Load," followed by a file name.

5   Evaluation

To identify the benefits of prototyping *in situ*, we evaluated MRCAT against a 2D prototyping alternative built in Unity. We conducted a 2 (prototyping tool) × 2 (scenario) mixed factors study with 14 participants (12M, 2F). The study asked participants to prototype two IoT configurations with smart devices: a conference room and a classroom. In each scenario, participants completed four tasks: create a preliminary design, illustrate an example use case, integrate a new design constraint, and propose an alternative design.

5.1   Desktop Prototyping

For our user study, we use a subset of functionality from Unity to parallel the functionality of MRCAT. Desktop content creation tools [38,42] typically use a hierarchical view of objects, available to Unity users in a "Hierarchy" view pane. Unity provides icons in the top left part of the UI that allow the user to switch between rotation, translation and scaling modes. Unity also has built-in functionality to allow users to drag pre-built objects into the scene, and to change their materials. Using a prefabricated Note element, we also allow users to drag annotations onto objects to label them To begin study tasks, we provide an initial mock-up of the target environment's furniture arrangement to start.

5.2   Scenarios

We described two IoT-based scenarios to participants that would be relatively familiar, but also required similar considerations to effectively prototype in AR. We chose these IoT-based scenarios for two reasons. First, prototyping interactive AR applications may be a foreign concept so asking participants to prototype something like an AR game may be a challenging task to understand. With smart devices becoming increasingly ubiquitous, building an IoT application provides participants with a more familiar set of tasks. Additionally, a key aspect of prototyping interactive environments is designing for the interplay of physical and virtual content *(D1)*. We conducted the study in a conference room with tables and chairs, and both scenarios require that participants utilize the layout of the space in the design of the interactive environment. Each participant completed both scenarios: one with MRCAT and one with Unity. Scenarios were counterbalanced between participants.

The smart conference room scenario required participants to prototype a network of connected smart devices that would improve collaborative screen sharing in meetings in the conference room. The four required tasks in this scenario were: *Initial Design:* Add primary and secondary displays to the room with smart light bulbs for each of the four people in the room to later associate users with displays. *Example Use Case:* Illustrate usage of the smart conference room where meeting members connect to the smart displays. *New Design Constraint:* Prototype what it would look like if light bulbs needed to hang from the ceiling. *Alternative Configuration:* Change the displays to be on different walls and resize them to be of equal priority, rather than a primary and secondary.

In the learning room scenario, we gave participants tasks to prototype a room that facilitates learning through a collaborative tabletop display and quiz questions. The four required tasks in this scenario were as follows: *Initial Design:* Prototype using the table as a tabletop display for all students to use and smart light bulbs at each seat for the four individual students. *Example Use Case:* Illustrate usage of the prototyped environment where students in the room are answering an administered quiz question. *New Design Constraint:* Prototype a similar environment where each student has a tablet-sized display at their seat. *Alternative Configuration* The table may be too small for a dedicated display, so explore an alternative where the screen is wall-mounted instead.

5.3 Procedure

After signing a consent form and being briefed on the study, participants were shown how to use prototyping tool, walking through the interactions and allowing them to practice. We then instructed participants on the scenario's tasks one at a time, exiting the environment while participants completed each task. After all tasks in the scenario, we administered a questionnaire to elicit feedback through the System Usability Survey (SUS) and 17 additional Likert-scale questions measuring the perceived efficacy and usability of the tool followed by open-ended feedback. Participants repeated the process with the second scenario and second prototyping tool before completing a 24 Likert-scale question survey with open-ended feedback asking participants to directly compare the two methods for accomplishing particular tasks. Participants then completed a demographics questionnaire and were compensated with a $10 Amazon gift card.

5.4 Results

We collected objective and subjective measures related to the usability of each paradigm for effective prototyping. We measured time to completion and questionnaire responses, using open-ended feedback to contextualize our results.

Overall, the objective measures pointed to significant limitations of MRCAT in comparison with Unity. Participants generally took longer with MRCAT ($\mu = 28.3$ min) than with Unity ($\mu = 25.78$ min). Participants reported higher

System Usability Score (SUS) for Unity ($\mu = 72.1$) than for MRCAT ($\mu = 51.9$). Participants also typically preferred Unity when asked to directly compare the two for particular tasks. Specifically, they preferred the Unity for object placement, translation, rotation, scaling and annotating, while preferring MRCAT only for object recoloring.

Despite objective limitations, open ended feedback pointed to significant opportunities for *in situ* prototyping, offering potential improvements to system design and hardware limitations that help us reason about displays and interaction modalities. Participants responded positively to editing and navigating the virtual and physical environment in parallel. They noted positive aspects of being "able to interact with the world in 3D and to be able to see what [they are] trying to do in real time. "*(P10)* and to "see what [they] built from multiple angles easily." *(P3)*. Participants also identified that "working the actual room was useful...to get a better sense of scale" *(P1)* and saw value in "getting a true feel for environment" (P5). This heightened sense of scale enabled them to prototype to higher fidelity. Participants stated that MRCAT "definitely allowed for the user to better visualize how the room would look in reality, which is a pretty significant advantage over Unity. Seeing exactly where everything would theoretically go in person is a much different experience than exploring a room through a computer." *(P9)* and that a prototype built with MRCAT "could be much closer to a convincing prototype" *(P14)*.

The most negative feedback for MRCAT and in favor of the 2D prototyping tool related to the inefficiencies of transform manipulations in MRCAT. Participants felt like "[users] can be a lot more precise using a mouse and keyboard" *(P6)* and that "the HoloLens tool wasn't as accurate with the placement of the objects, so [they] couldn't get things to look exactly how [they] wanted." *(P12)*. Among the specific operations, object rotations were most often noted as problematic (6 our of 14 participants). We built on feedback provided by participants to revise our transform manipulation model (Sect. 6).

Another salient theme from open-ended feedback was frustration with the headset itself. Responses indicated that the hardware likely contributed to higher frustration and lower usability scores in the Likert and SUS measures. One participant noted that "the weight of the HoloLens on my head...discouraged me from looking upwards" *(P7)*. Limited field of view was also cited as a possibly confounding factor, with a participant pointing out that the "HoloLens was...difficult to use, not because of the complexity, but because of the limited vision" *(P14)*. Though these factors are difficult to disentangle from inefficiencies in MRCAT and will likely be mitigated with future AR headsets, they are worth considering in design of AR prototyping tools going forward.

6 Design Iteration

Open-ended feedback illuminated several opportunities to improve the design of MRCAT. We specifically identified issues participants had with understanding the system's current state for object interaction and their mental model of how

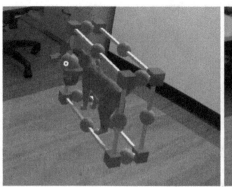

Fig. 5. The revised MRCAT interface uses wireframe cubes for transform manipulation. These cubes allow for continuous translation (dragging the object), scaling (dragging a corner cube), and rotation (dragging a sphere on an edge). When the user first engages with a rotation sphere, two sets of arrows indicate which axes the user can rotate (left). An initial movement to the left begins rotation about the vertical y-axis (right).

their input affects the prototype. In light of the feedback on transform manipulations with MRCAT, we add an additional design guideline to those in Sect. 3:

D4: Visual and Continuous Transform Manipulation. Though 2D prototyping tools make use of explicit mode-switching to map multiple functions to mouse dragging in 2D, our study found that this paradigm did not work as well in AR. AR prototyping tools should consider how 3D visual interfaces can provide users with an intuitive interface to manipulate objects continuously, without explicitly stating which mode they wish to be in. This increased continuity and system transparency should help reduce frustration and time to perform multiple transform manipulations. Iterating on MRCAT's UI design, we focused on allowing users to navigate to different perspectives and manipulate objects with more visual guidance on how their gestures will impact the selected objects.

To address this, we implement a 3D wireframe cube (Fig. 5) explored in prior AR studies [9,10]. Selecting an object with the gaze-tap toggles the wireframe cube around that object. Like the red outline in the previous iteration of MRCAT, the wireframe cube indicates engagement with objects for transform manipulations, color changes, and annotations. Performing a gaze-drag on the object translates all selected objects. Grabbing and dragging a blue box on the wireframe's corner uniformly scales all selected objects. Grabbing and dragging a sphere on one of the wireframe's edges allows the user to rotate the selected objects along one axis at a time. As with the preliminary implementation's "Rotation" mode, initial hand displacement determines which direction the object rotates. Engaging with one of the wireframe's 12 spheres provides users arrows indicating two possible rotation directions.

To mitigate issues with the HoloLens' gaze-drag gesture and limited field of view when manipulating objects, we added visual feedback to indicate lost

Fig. 6. Example usage of MRCAT in prototyping an interactive dinosaur exhibit. Here the designer prototypes proxemic interactions that trigger audio clips (left) and proto-types gestural interaction to trigger animations (right).

hand-tracking. An inherent limitation of freehand gestures relative to mouse-and-keyboard ones is that the user does not necessarily know when the their hand is outside of the headset's tracking area. In the preliminary evaluation, this lost hand-tracking caused participants to sometimes "[drag their] hand outside the screen several times on accident" *(P1)*. Since freehand gestures cannot provide any haptic feedback like a vibration or the sensation of a released button, we supplement MRCAT with a subtle visual flash when hand-tracking is lost. When the user moves their hand outside the field of view while manipulating an object, MRCAT tints the scene to a dark gray. The gray tint slowly fades away over the next two seconds. This visual feedback on system state is employed rather than audio because the user is engaging with a visual interface to manipulate objects, rather than audio feedback used when saving and loading scenes. This capability allows the user to understand that the headset is no longer processing their input and that they will need to restart the gaze-drag in order to continue.

Informal user feedback from MRCAT's revised design suggests that the updated UI significantly improves several usability issues from our study. This feedback provides promising evidence that many of the usability drawbacks in our initial study reflect a lack of design knowledge for effective *in situ* AR pro-totyping tools rather than limitations of *in situ* approaches generally. While we hope to elicit additional insight into these challenges in future studies, we evaluated our revised MRCAT approach through a case study in museum studies.

7   Case Study: Museum Exhibit Prototyping

We anticipate that AR prototyping will bolster AR integration into a number of domains. However, AR has not gained traction in many domains at least in part due to the lack of tools for domain experts to develop applications. We see *in situ* prototyping as a key component of overcoming this limitation and demonstrate the utility of *in situ* AR prototyping through museum exhibit development. We worked with an exhibit developer at a Natural History museum to build grounded insight into how *in situ* prototyping may benefit domain experts.

We worked with the exhibit developer to build foundational knowledge of existing ideation, collaboration, and prototyping workflows used to create new exhibits through a series of discussions about the potential for technology to support exhibit development and how MRCAT could support these practices. We began by characterizing existing workflows in museum exhibit development, followed by a brief demonstration of MRCAT, and concluded with how *in situ* AR prototyping may supplement existing practices. Most of the discussion centered around an in-progress exhibit at a heritage center, where the exhibit's design challenges were in utilizing a historic building to share contemporary and historic perspectives in accessible ways for diverse audiences.

Ideation: The initial ideation phase consists of brainstorming possible solutions and aggregating to common themes. Exhibit development teams typically brainstorm ideas on post-it notes, which then required clustering, organizing and digitizing. The museum team typically wants to first brainstorm design ideas then critically reflect on their options conceptually and graphically. For example, teams could test possible configurations to get at questions of intended experience: Is it hands-on? Are there videos? Is it a sensory experience? Fluid AR prototyping would enable them to try different experiences quickly and at minimal time and material cost. The ability to rapidly edit and reload scenes in MRCAT could enable curators to quickly explore these different representations.

Building Prototypes: The exhibit developer saw the most notable value of *in situ* prototyping as enabling people to visually communicate exhibit ideas more concretely to allow stakeholders to more accurately respond the approaches the exhibit development team is exploring. Currently, to move towards a final design, the exhibit team will create sketches, blueprints, CAD renderings, color and font palettes, and preliminary graphics and labels. The exhibit team may print prototype materials on cardboard to build physical prototypes. Relative to this approach, MRCAT would allow for higher fidelity prototypes that are significantly closer to what the end experience may look like.

Collaboration: Collaborating on museum exhibits requires input from a number of key stakeholders. In this case, the stakeholders included tribal leaders, University students, teachers, anthropologists, and a core group of museum employees including our expert. While some collaboration is in-person, a majority is done over phone calls. In both scenarios, higher fidelity prototypes built in AR would likely scaffold conversations better than sketches and descriptions. Even with a greater initial investment of time, our expert mentioned that they could communicate their entire vision to large groups of people at once, but that any such system would require technological training. With MRCAT's ability to save and load XML prototypes, users can review, build on and annotate prototypes for a more collaborative design workflow.

Our demonstration of MRCAT for museum exhibit development provided exciting opportunities for future systems. Our expert envisioned that AR prototyping done correctly could allow developers to explore a wide range of ideas, populating virtual galleries to reflect a diversity of options but requiring models that span diverse possible content. Our interviews revealed that *in situ* prototyping workflows could enable more rapid exploration of different designs, increased fidelity and improved local and remote collaboration.

8 Discussion

MRCAT explores how *in situ* prototyping can positively impact design workflows for AR. We derive and refine guidelines for building *in situ* prototyping tools and show in a use case how these tools could benefit a broad set of domains.

8.1 Key Aspects for AR Prototyping

Our discussions with a museum exhibit developer exemplifies how *in situ* AR prototyping could immediately benefit design workflows. Pairing these discussions with study feedback suggests two key benefits for in situ prototyping tools.

Constraints of the Physical Environment: *In situ* AR prototyping emphasizes the importance of environmental constraints. Our participants and domain expert noted that an idea that proposes virtual augmentations in tandem with the physical environment itself is better represented by a prototype built *in situ* than one made through decontextualized techniques. In designing museum exhibits, prototyping *in situ* gives designers the ability to understand the scale of the proposed exhibit and the interplay with existing infrastructure, while more traditional techniques like sketching do not allow for high fidelity illustration of the proposed exhibit and do not consider the environmental constraints.

In cases where the look, feel and scale of the virtual objects in the target space are critical, *in situ* AR prototyping can provide a means to design for the interplay of the physical and virtual environment. In the preliminary study, users could directly manipulate virtual objects in the real world and leverage interactions between virtual and physical objects. For example, users would place virtual lightbulbs directly in the physical space and resize virtual screens such that they were positioned on the physical tables and walls. In designing exhibits, developers wanted to test out configurations for the allotted space. Prototypes built directly in the target environment enable designers to seamlessly blend physical and virtual content.

Co-located and Remote Collaboration: *In situ* prototyping can enable new means of collaboration. By saving and loading XML representations of scenes within the target environment, multiple designers can iterate on prototypes by adding, reconfiguring and annotating saved arrangements. Extending MRCAT to allow multiple AR headsets to view the same scene would allow for synchronous, multi-user editing and design review within the environment.

Collaboration was identified as a significant potential benefit of AR prototyping in our discussions with museum experts. The higher fidelity prototype built *in situ* would provide collaborators a better sense of the idea in each designer's mind. MRCAT allows prototypes to be loaded into VR headsets or 2D displays, making prototypes more portable, but removing virtual content from its physical context. By extending MRCAT's XML files with depth and RGB camera capture, prototypes could be exported with a representation of the physical environment for remote viewers in VR or on a desktop to view the prototype in reconstructed contexts.

In addition to museum exhibit development, *in situ* prototyping may also benefit a number of other domains. For example, prior work has explored AR as a UI for connected smart environments [14,22]. AR prototyping would allow designers to propose configurations of integrated smart environments and craft integrated device interfaces. AR has also shown promise for improving education [4,15,20]. However, successfully integrating these platforms into classrooms requires empowering educators with control over interface design to engage more fluidly with lesson plan design and educational content. This would allow educators to understand holistically how students may interact with the technologies to facilitate better educational outcomes. Theater sets increasingly integrate technologies to deliver unique performances [35]. *In situ* prototyping allows set designers and directors to more fluidly integrate novel interactive components and experience different designs from a variety of perspectives.

8.2 Usability and Longitudinal Study

Our preliminary study of MRCAT revealed the need for thorough consideration of effective multimodal interaction in AR. After our preliminary study, we prioritized increased visual feedback to enable fluid transform manipulation *(D4)*. Use of the 3D wireframe cube instead of explicit mode switching allowed for more fluid object manipulation and increased understanding of how exactly the performed gesture will affect virtual objects. Continued study of these interactions will improve interface efficiency for MRCAT and other AR prototyping tools.

Another important consideration for AR prototyping is how particular modalities map to different design tasks. We designed our interface based on mappings commonly used in prior literature (Sect. 2.2), but continued study of which tasks will be better suited to different interaction modalities will improve the usability of *in situ* prototyping tools. For example, while freehand gestures are commonly used for transform manipulations [7,9,17], they should be evaluated against multimodal gaze plus voice interactions [21,33] or video game controllers [43,44] to empirically confirm the decision. We employed voice for text entry, prioritizing speed over accuracy [19]. This decision matched participants' desires to use the annotation interface for relatively short, post-it style annotations, such as "the screen does not have to be a smart table. It can also be a secondary wall screen" *(P6)* and "the question gets displayed on all of the tablets in the students input their answers" *(P7)*. With continued research on HMD text entry, the basic dictation recognition used in MRCAT should be substituted with future work on text entry optimized for HMDs.

Longitudinal study of AR prototyping tools will be critical to effective adoption of *in situ* prototyping workflows. Our discussion of museum exhibit development identified the potential for developers to employ AR when prototyping exhibits. However, integration of *in situ* AR prototyping into museum design workflows and observing how the tools shape design practices usage will reveal further guidelines for effective AR prototyping tools.

Longitudinal study could also reveal how to best extend the breadth of prototyping features available to designers. For example, MRCAT currently does not integrate interactive components such as responsive objects as there are not well-documented standards for prototyping rich interactions without scripting or complex menu structures. In the preliminary study, users employed annotations to describe interactivity and in Fig. 6, we demonstrate how virtual models can visually depict interactivity. Further extensions of MRCAT could enable designers to mock the interactions to build fully interactive prototypes, allowing them to conduct user studies with interactive AR prototypes. With increased comfort from continued use of AR prototyping tools, we could test this extended functionality to make interactive prototypes better than with a usability study.

9   Conclusion

In situ prototyping allows designers to build and ideate on interactive mixed reality applications within a target environment. We implement a tool for building *in situ* prototypes called MRCAT, through which we identify guidelines for design of such prototyping tools. Through a preliminary user study, we identify trade-offs between *in situ* and decontextualized 2D prototyping. We consider several aspects of *in situ* prototyping: system design, multimodal user interaction and key domains that may benefit from an *in situ* approach. This work provides a roadmap for *in situ* AR prototyping research, such that AR prototyping tools could enable higher fidelity and more collaborative design in AR.

Acknowledgements. We thank the CU Senior Projects program for facilitating development of MRCAT. This work was supported by NSF Award #1764092.

References

1. Arora, R., Habib Kazi, R., Grossman, T., Fitzmaurice, G., Singh, K.: SymbiosisSketch: combining 2D & 3D sketching for designing detailed 3D objects in situ. In: Proceedings of the 2018 CHI Conference on Human Factors in Computing Systems. Association for Computing Machinery, New York (2018)
2. Badam, S.K., Srinivasan, A., Elmqvist, N., Stasko, J.: Affordances of input modalities for visual data exploration in immersive environments. In: 2nd Workshop on Immersive Analytics (2017)
3. Beaudouin-Lafon, M., Mackay, W.E.: Prototyping tools and techniques. In: Human-Computer Interaction, pp. 137–160. CRC Press (2009)
4. Beheshti, E., Kim, D., Ecanow, G., Horn, M.S.: Looking inside the wires: understanding museum visitor learning with an augmented circuit exhibit. In: Proceedings of the 2017 CHI Conference on Human Factors in Computing Systems, pp. 1583–1594. Association for Computing Machinery, New York (2017)

5. Billinghurst, M., Kato, H., Poupyrev, I.: The magicbook - moving seamlessly between reality and virtuality. IEEE Comput. Graph. Appl. **21**(3), 6–8 (2001)
6. Broy, N., Schneegass, S., Alt, F., Schmidt, A.: Framebox and mirrorbox: tools and guidelines to support designers in prototyping interfaces for 3D displays. In: Proceedings of the SIGCHI Conference on Human Factors in Computing Systems, pp. 2037–2046. Association for Computing Machinery, New York (2014)
7. Buchmann, V., Violich, S., Billinghurst, M., Cockburn, A.: FingARtips: gesture based direct manipulation in augmented reality. In: Proceedings of the 2nd International Conference on Computer Graphics and Interactive Techniques in Australasia and South East Asia, pp. 212–221. Association for Computing Machinery, New York (2004)
8. Carter, A.S., Hundhausen, C.D.: How is user interface prototyping really done in practice? a survey of user interface designers. In: IEEE Symposium on Visual Languages and Human-Centric Computing, pp. 207–211, September 2010
9. Chaconas, N., Höllerer, T.: An evaluation of bimanual gestures on the Microsoft hololens. In: IEEE Conference on Virtual Reality and 3D User Interfaces (VR), pp. 1–8 (2018)
10. Chakraborty, A., Gross, R., McIntee, S., Hong, K.W., Lee, J.Y., St. Amant, R.: Captive: a cube with augmented physical tools. In: Extended Abstracts on Human Factors in Computing Systems, CHI 2014, pp. 1315–1320. Association for Computing Machinery, New York (2014)
11. Chang, Y.S., Nuernberger, B., Luan, B., Höllerer, T.: Evaluating gesture-based augmented reality annotation. In: IEEE Symposium on 3D User Interfaces (3DUI), pp. 182–185 (2017)
12. Chang, Y.S., Nuernberger, B., Luan, B., Höllerer, T., O'Donovan, J.: Gesture-based augmented reality annotation. In: IEEE Virtual Reality (VR), pp. 469–470 (2017)
13. Dachselt, R., Hübner, A.: Three-dimensional menus: a survey and taxonomy. Comput. Graph. **31**(1), 53–65 (2007)
14. Garcia Macias, J.A., Alvarez-Lozano, J., Estrada, P., Aviles Lopez, E.: Browsing the internet of things with sentient visors. Computer **44**(5), 46–52 (2011)
15. Giraudeau, P., et al.: Cards: a mixed-reality system for collaborative learning at school. In: Proceedings of the 2019 ACM International Conference on Interactive Surfaces and Spaces, pp. 55–64 (2019)
16. Grossman, T., Chen, X.A., Fitzmaurice, G.: Typing on glasses: adapting text entry to smart eyewear. In: Proceedings of the 17th International Conference on Human-Computer Interaction with Mobile Devices and Services, MobileHCI 2015, pp. 144–152. Association for Computing Machinery, New York (2015)
17. Ha, T., Feiner, S., Woo, W.: WeARHand: Head-worn, RGB-D camera-based, bare-hand user interface with visually enhanced depth perception. In: IEEE International Symposium on Mixed and Augmented Reality (ISMAR), pp. 219–228 (2014)
18. Hall, R.R.: Prototyping for usability of new technology. Int. J. Hum. Comput. Stud. **55**(4), 485–501 (2001)
19. Hoste, L., Dumas, B., Signer, B.: SpeeG: a multimodal speech- and gesture-based text input solution. In: Proceedings of the International Working Conference on Advanced Visual Interfaces, pp. 156–163. Association for Computing Machinery, New York (2012)
20. Ibáñez, M.B., Di Serio, Á., Villarán, D., Kloos, C.D.: Experimenting with electromagnetism using augmented reality: impact on flow student experience and educational effectiveness. Comput. Educ. **71**, 1–13 (2014)

21. Irawati, S., Green, S., Billinghurst, M., Duenser, A., Ko, H.: "Move the couch where?": developing an augmented reality multimodal interface. In: IEEE/ACM International Symposium on Mixed and Augmented Reality, pp. 183–186 (2006)
22. Jahn, M., Jentsch, M., Prause, C.R., Pramudianto, F., Al-Akkad, A., Reiners, R.: The energy aware smart home. In: 5th International Conference on Future Information Technology, pp. 1–8 (2010)
23. Jee, H.-K., Lim, S., Youn, J., Lee, J.: An augmented reality-based authoring tool for E-learning applications. Multimedia Tools Appl. **68**(2), 225–235 (2011). https://doi.org/10.1007/s11042-011-0880-4
24. Kaiser, E., et al.: Mutual disambiguation of 3D multimodal interaction in augmented and virtual reality. In: Proceedings of the 5th International Conference on Multimodal Interfaces, pp. 12–19. Association for Computing Machinery, New York (2003)
25. Lee, G.A., Nelles, C., Billinghurst, M., Kim, G.J.: Immersive authoring of tangible augmented reality applications. In: Third IEEE and ACM International Symposium on Mixed and Augmented Reality, pp. 172–181 (2004)
26. Lee, G.A., Teo, T., Kim, S., Billinghurst, M.: Mixed reality collaboration through sharing a live panorama. In: SIGGRAPH Asia 2017 Mobile Graphics and Interactive Applications. Association for Computing Machinery, New York (2017)
27. Lee, M., Billinghurst, M.: A wizard of Oz study for an AR multimodal interface. In: Proceedings of the 10th International Conference on Multimodal Interfaces, pp. 249–256. Association for Computing Machinery, New York (2008)
28. Lee, M., Billinghurst, M., Baek, W., Green, R., Woo, W.: A usability study of multimodal input in an augmented reality environment. Virtual Reality **17**(4), 293–305 (2013)
29. MacIntyre, B., Gandy, M., Dow, S., Bolter, J.D.: Dart: a toolkit for rapid design exploration of augmented reality experiences. In: Proceedings of the 17th Annual ACM Symposium on User Interface Software and Technology, pp. 197–206. ACM (2004)
30. Millette, A., McGuffin, M.J.: DualCAD: integrating augmented reality with a desktop GUI and smartphone interaction. In: IEEE International Symposium on Mixed and Augmented Reality (ISMAR-Adjunct), pp. 21–26 (2016)
31. Muller, M.J.: Participatory design: the third space in HCI. Chapter. In: The Human-computer Interaction Handbook, pp. 1051–1068. L. Erlbaum Associates Inc., Hillsdale (2003)
32. Ni, T., Bowman, D.A., North, C., McMahan, R.P.: Design and evaluation of freehand menu selection interfaces using tilt and pinch gestures. Int. J. Hum. Comput. Stud. **69**(9), 551–562 (2011)
33. Piumsomboon, T., Altimira, D., Kim, H., Clark, A., Lee, G., Billinghurst, M.: Grasp-shell vs gesture-speech: a comparison of direct and indirect natural interaction techniques in augmented reality. In: IEEE International Symposium on Mixed and Augmented Reality (ISMAR), pp. 73–82 (2014)
34. Piumsomboon, T., Clark, A., Billinghurst, M., Cockburn, A.: User-defined gestures for augmented reality. In: Kotzé, P., Marsden, G., Lindgaard, G., Wesson, J., Winckler, M. (eds.) INTERACT 2013. LNCS, vol. 8118, pp. 282–299. Springer, Heidelberg (2013). https://doi.org/10.1007/978-3-642-40480-1_18
35. Ponto, K., Lisowski, D., Fan, S.: Designing extreme 3D user interfaces for augmented live performances. In: IEEE Symposium on 3D User Interfaces (3DUI), pp. 169–172, March 2016

36. Rumiński, D., Walczak, K.: Creation of interactive AR content on mobile devices. In: Abramowicz, W. (ed.) BIS 2013. LNBIP, vol. 160, pp. 258–269. Springer, Heidelberg (2013). https://doi.org/10.1007/978-3-642-41687-3_24
37. de Sá, M., Churchill, E.: Mobile augmented reality: exploring design and prototyping techniques. In: Proceedings of the 14th International Conference on Human-Computer Interaction with Mobile Devices and Services, pp. 221–230. Association for Computing Machinery, New York (2012)
38. Seichter, H., Looser, J., Billinghurst, M.: ComposAR: an intuitive tool for authoring AR applications. In: 7th IEEE/ACM International Symposium on Mixed and Augmented Reality, pp. 177–178 (2008)
39. Smith, J., Wang, I., Woodward, J., Ruiz, J.: Experimental analysis of single mode switching techniques in augmented reality. In: Proceedings of the 45th Graphics Interface Conference on Proceedings of Graphics Interface 2019. Canadian Human-Computer Communications Society, Waterloo (2019)
40. SyafiqahSafiee, N., Ismail, A.W.: Ar home deco: virtual object manipulation technique using hand gesture in augmented reality. In: Innovations in Computing Technology and Applications, vol. 3 (2018)
41. Turini, G., et al.: A Microsoft hololens mixed reality surgical simulator for patient-specific hip arthroplasty training. In: De Paolis, L.T., Bourdot, P. (eds.) AVR 2018. LNCS, vol. 10851, pp. 201–210. Springer, Cham (2018). https://doi.org/10.1007/978-3-319-95282-6_15
42. Walczak, K., Wojciechowski, R.: Dynamic creation of interactive mixed reality presentations. In: Proceedings of the ACM Symposium on Virtual Reality Software and Technology, pp. 167–176. Association for Computing Machinery, New York (2005)
43. Walker, M.E., Hedayati, H., Szafir, D.: Robot teleoperation with augmented reality virtual surrogates. In: 14th ACM/IEEE International Conference on Human-Robot Interaction (HRI), pp. 202–210 (2019)
44. Whitlock, M., Harnner, E., Brubaker, J.R., Kane, S., Szafir, D.A.: Interacting with distant objects in augmented reality. In: IEEE Conference on Virtual Reality and 3D User Interfaces (VR), pp. 41–48 (2018)
45. Wojciechowski, R., Walczak, K., White, M., Cellary, W.: Building virtual and augmented reality museum exhibitions. In: Proceedings of the Ninth International Conference on 3D Web Technology, pp. 135–144. ACM, New York (2004)
46. Wolf, D., Dudley, J.J., Kristensson, P.O.: Performance envelopes of in-air direct and smartwatch indirect control for head-mounted augmented reality. In: IEEE Conference on Virtual Reality and 3D User Interfaces (VR), pp. 347–354 (2018)
47. Xu, W., Liang, H., Zhao, Y., Zhang, T., Yu, D., Monteiro, D.: RingText: dwell-free and hands-free text entry for mobile head-mounted displays using head motions. IEEE Trans. Visual Comput. Graphics 25(5), 1991–2001 (2019)
48. Yu, C., Gu, Y., Yang, Z., Yi, X., Luo, H., Shi, Y.: Tap, dwell or gesture? Exploring head-based text entry techniques for HMDs. In: Proceedings of the 2017 CHI Conference on Human Factors in Computing Systems, pp. 4479–4488. Association for Computing Machinery, New York (2017)
49. Yue, Y.T., Yang, Y.L., Ren, G., Wang, W.: SceneCtrl: mixed reality enhancement via efficient scene editing. In: Proceedings of the 30th Annual ACM Symposium on User Interface Software and Technology, pp. 427–436. ACM, New York (2017)
50. Zauner, J., Haller, M., Brandl, A., Hartman, W.: Authoring of a mixed reality assembly instructor for hierarchical structures. In: Proceedings of the Second IEEE and ACM International Symposium on Mixed and Augmented Reality 2003, pp. 237–246 (2003)

Augmented Reality for City Planning

Adam Sinclair Williams[1]([⊠]), Catherine Angelini[2], Mathew Kress[2],
Edgar Ramos Vieira[2], Newton D'Souza[2], Naphtali D. Rishe[2], Joseph Medina[2],
Ebru Özer[2], and Francisco Ortega[1]

[1] Colorado State University, Fort Collins, CO 80523, USA
{AdamWil,fortega}@colostate.edu
[2] Florida International University, Miami, FL 33199, USA
{cange017,mkres006,evieira,ndsouza,rishe,jmedi145,eozer}@fiu.edu

Abstract. We present an early study designed to analyze how city
planning and the health of senior citizens can benefit from the use of
augmented reality (AR) with assistance of virtual reality (VR), using
Microsoft's HoloLens and HTC's Vive headsets. We also explore whether
AR and VR can be used to help city planners receive real-time feedback from citizens, such as the elderly, on virtual plans, allowing for
informed decisions to be made before any construction begins. In doing
so, city planners can more clearly understand what design features would
motivate senior citizens to visit or exercise in future parks, for example.
The study was conducted on 10 participants 60 years and older who live
within 2 miles from the site. They were presented with multiple virtual options for a prospective park, such as different walls for cancelling
highway noise, as well as benches, lampposts, bathroom pods, walking
and biking lanes, and other street furniture. The headsets allowed the
participants to clearly visualize the options and make choices on them.
Throughout the study the participants were enthusiastic about using the
AR and VR devices, which is noteworthy for a future where city planning
is done with these technologies.

Keywords: Human-centered computing · Visualization design and
evaluation methods · Augmented and virtual reality

1 Introduction

There is a novel and rapidly expanding phenomenon taking place as augmented
reality (AR) and virtual reality (VR), henceforth referred to by their acronyms,
are rapidly taking over a myriad of sectors from the entertainment and game
industry to architecture and medical training. According to the International
Data Corporation, worldwide spending on AR and VR is projected to increase
by 68 percent in 2019 from 2018 [10]. Another area which could greatly benefit
from the introduction of these technologies is city planning, in particular when
it comes to catering to the needs of senior citizens. By 2030, there will be 72.1
million elderly Americans over the age of 65, with 750,000 of them residing
in Miami, FL, which is known to have the highest percentage in the entire

© Springer Nature Switzerland AG 2020
J. Y. C. Chen and G. Fragomeni (Eds.): HCII 2020, LNCS 12190, pp. 256–271, 2020.
https://doi.org/10.1007/978-3-030-49695-1_17

US [2]. According to the Center for Disease Control (CDC), seven out of ten deaths among Americans are from chronic diseases, and nearly one out of every two adults has at least one chronic illness, many of which are preventable. The National Prevention Strategy proposed by the CDC recognizes that good health comes not solely from receiving quality medical care but also from mitigating a disease before it starts, such as through healthy exercise in open areas and parks, provided by effective city planning.

We present an early study designed to analyze how city planning will benefit from the use of AR and VR, making it more efficient and accurate in catering to the needs of people such as senior citizens. In the study, AR and VR help to understand what elements would make the participants more willing to exercise in a specific area of Miami, if such elements were to be constructed. This area is referred to as "M-path," which is an underutilized zone in Miami, FL, that lies under Miami's elevated Metro-rail transit system and passes through several inner-city neighborhoods, where a large population of senior citizens is located and is known for its heavy vehicular traffic.

1.1 Contribution

Improving the health of senior citizens is a pressing issue, with cities needing to adapt and plan adequately to cater to their growing needs. This study introduces a novel way to address this issue by introducing a groundbreaking technology to enhance a city's planning efforts. As far as we were able to search, no work has combined city planning with AR at full scale, let alone to use it to influence planning decisions to improve the health and accommodation of citizens. Most importantly, the biggest contribution is that this type of study with these technologies is feasible and provides a path forward for other researchers to pursue similar avenues of study.

2 Related Work

2.1 Health and Safety

While there is no direct research that has explored city planning to improve senior citizens' health, there have been similar attempts to improve health in general through AR and VR. For example, Ha-na et al. performed a study to improve balance while walking and running to help avoid falls for 21 elderly women with 10 doing the Otago Exercise Program with VR and 10 doing it without the VR [12]. The study found that the women that completed the exercise program with the VR increased their mobility and physical activity more than without it. Hence, it provides some initial insight as to how these enhanced reality technologies can improve health instead of harming it. Basing it upon Microsoft's Kinect software, virtual reality has also been used to make the RemoviEM system and has proven to be successful for rehabilitation for people with multiple sclerosis as seen in [9], using aerobics and strength training. The personalized rehabilitation exercises the software included with the VR proved to help the patients more than the traditional exercises, which corroborates with Ha-na et al on the fact that VR/AR can be an effective option in improving health.

AR technology has also been used to increase outside physical activity. The software called "HybridPLAY" [5] is a prime example of this. With this application, users could attach a sensor to playground equipment to be able to use the equipment as an input to their phone to complete mini-games. They found that the use of such games increases the likelihood of users going to a park or outside to exercise. Another example can be seen in a 2019 study using "Pokemon go", a mobile AR game where users walk around outside trying to capture small creatures which can be found at various locations throughout a city. Hino et al. found that older users of this game had much higher step counts at the end of 7 months than non-users [7]. Furthermore, Yang et al. conducted a survey of apps that implemented behavioral change techniques specifically for physical activity [11]. They found that the most successful apps used a combination of social support, demonstrations of the physical activities, and instructions on how to perform the activity which can suggest that these apps can provide a low-cost intervention that could help increase a user's physical activity. If people have easy and quick access to ways in which they can be more active, then the probability of them engaging in this lifestyle increases.

Additionally, VR and AR technologies have been shown to improve overall safety as noted in the study by Schall Jr. et al. [8]. They studied how to evaluate the effectiveness of AR cues in improving driving safety among 20 elderly drivers with cognitive impairments [8]. This system provided cues as the subjects drove with primary targets such as cars or pedestrians and secondary targets such as dumpsters or barrels. Drivers responded favourably when pedestrian and walking signs where shown with the AR technology as it made it much more clear to them, decreasing their risk of getting into an accident.

2.2   City Planning

Due to how recently the AR technology has been adopted, limited research has supported city viewing or planning in this way. For example, Zhang et al. used the Microsoft HoloLens to visualize the City of Toronto, Canada [13]. Even though the visualization was of a miniature model on top of a table, it shed light on the potential of applying AR to city planning, as entire buildings, roads, parks and more could be visualized and modified before actually being constructed. On the other hand, Claes and Moore used AR to increase awareness about local issues around a city [6]. Their study, while limited to a single location, did provide interesting reactions by the locals, such as curiosity, personal reflections, social interactions, and perceptional changes, among others [6]. In a sense, the novelty of AR on its own helps to increase interest and public engagement when it comes to city planning and other applications.

3   System Design

3.1   First Iteration with VR

Fig. 1. Virtual reality environment (first iteration)

In the first iteration of our testing environment, we created a VR space that simulated the future park, as shown in Fig. 1. While this was a great way to design and test in the lab, it was difficult to have senior citizens come and experience the site with the modifications that were made. The participants would have needed to travel to the lab to see the VR mock-up before going to the site, which would have a large time-gap in between and would defeat the purpose of real-time feedback from the participants. The environment only being available in the lab also meant that the participants could forget or misremember what they saw afterwards, skewing their opinions on the different elements for the park. In addition, given the participants' age group, additional precautions needed to be taken in order to simulate walking through the park's path, which had the consequence of making the walk feel less natural for them. While this may still be a possibility in the future, we decided to use a different approach.

3.2   Second Iteration with AR

Our second iteration consisted of an augmented reality environment with the use of the Microsoft HoloLens headset. In order to understand what future elements would take for senior citizens to exercise in an area with heavy bicycle and car traffic, we decided to analyze how AR could be used for them to see the changes superimposed directly on the site and give real-time feedback on said changes. In particular, we decided to focus on receiving feedback on three different types of walls for the future park. The Microsoft HoloLens was selected due to its transparent and holographic features that allow users to see virtual objects, while simultaneously being able to see the real environment around them. Note that we are using the term "holographic" loosely here to indicate virtual objects in an augmented reality environment which can only be seen through the headset. We received positive feedback regarding the HoloLens itself, with the participants being quite enthusiastic in using it. The use of AR allowed the participants to walk through, see and experience the site with all the virtual modifications, giving them a detailed look at how the environment could look in the future. In order to create the environment, we used the Unity Game Engine developed by Unity Technologies [4], which provided a streamlined and powerful toolset to develop projects for AR applications. In addition, we used 2D and 3D modeling software, such as Adobe Photoshop [1], Paint 3D, and Google SketchUp [3], as well as incorporating Microsoft's Mixed Reality Toolkit with settings that are designed specifically to support the HoloLens.

Prior to calculating the correct measurements of the site, we began to build a draft of the park design in Unity and started to create the 3D models. However, it was crucial that we understood who our targets were, which in this case were the senior citizens. In this iteration, the augmented reality environment we created included several extra models that were soon taken out, such as exercise equipment, water fountains, palm trees, rocks, bushes and decorations which made the virtual environment more appealing. However, we found that the large amount of virtual objects tended to be overwhelming to the HoloLens wearer. When using the AR headset at the site with all the elements, it became evident that there were too many real objects already surrounding the area, and the participants could get confused or distracted from focusing mainly on the three different types of walls and main street furniture. Our goal was to make the interface and experience as user-friendly as possible, which is why we decided to mark their gaze with a purple dot to make it clear to the participants where they were focusing (see Fig. 3). This design tactic as well as physically going to the site allowed us to gain the necessary insight for our next iteration.

The more detailed virtual environment we created in Unity was based upon actual measurements collected on site and the problem areas that were identified by the city and researchers, which included the following: lack of places to sit, lack of safety, noise from the highway, no clear path for walking or cycling, darkness at night, no nearby places to use the restroom and the overall unsafe atmosphere of the area. We had several meetings with people from Florida International University's School of Architecture and School of Physical Therapy to help us finalize the street furniture that would address those problem areas. We built three separate scenes in Unity, with each including lamp posts by the path to help illuminate it, separate pedestrian and cyclist lanes, signage/way finding, either a small wall, a tall wall, or a glass wall to separate and minimize highway noise, benches to rest, and bathroom pods as seen in Figs. 2 and 7. All of the distances and positioning of the elements relative to each other were accurate to the measurements we took, with the elements being placed relative to the real path in the site. This allowed for the objects to remain accurately fixed in their spatial location as the participants moved around and walked by them, being able to see them from several angles, such as how the post signaling the bike and walking line is seen from different distances in Figs. 5 and 3. The final environment can be seen in Fig. 4. Note that the wall seems to be floating above the ground as the image was taken using the HoloLens capture software, which has a different perspective than the headset's wearer. However, to the participants the objects appeared in their correct locations, allowing them to experience the wall and surrounding street furniture as intended in real-life scale and distance.

Fig. 2. Lamppost in AR

After the deployment of the three different scenes to the HoloLens and the testing done on site it was found that some of the models had colors that were too dark. An example of this was the benches that had a dark brown color which had to be adjusted to brighter and lighter colors so that the holograms were more visible in daylight with the headset. The current iteration of the HoloLens thus seems to have issues rendering dark objects in a well-lit environment, but it is very likely that this will be corrected or improved in subsequent versions (Fig. 6).

Fig. 3. View from AR with gaze tracking purple cursor

Fig. 4. Environment in AR showing the glass wall scene

Fig. 5. Biking and walking sign in AR

Fig. 6. Walking and biking lane separator in AR

Fig. 7. Floor signs in AR

3.3   Third Iteration with AR

Our third and final iteration had finalized scenes for both AR and VR environments. In order to address visibility concerns due to the limited field of view of the HoloLens, along with some participants having difficulty seeing, we used the HTC Vive VR headset, which would allow the participants to become more immersed into the fully virtual environment and understand all of the new elements that would be added without interference from existing objects in the site. Note that we added the HTC Vive in addition to the Microsoft HoloLens to add another dimension to the visualization of the park. The VR headset was only used from a stationary viewpoint and not to walk through the environment. This is explained further in the next section.

4   Experiment Design

For this pilot study, 10 elderly adults who live within 2 miles of the "M-path" near the Miami Metro-rail Station participated. The participants were required to be at least 60 years old, be English or Spanish speakers, be able to walk independently without any walking aids, have no lower limb surgery or injuries from falls during the previous 6 months, and pass the Mini-Cog test[1]. The study took place at the "M-path". All participants received an explanation about the study's goals and procedures and were given the opportunity to ask and receive answers to any questions they had. After the explanations, they were asked to read and sign the informed consent form in their preferred language and were given thirty dollars for their time and contribution.

---

[1] See https://mini-cog.com/.

4.1   Preparation

The participants were fitted with Inertial Measurement Units (IMUs), from the MTw Awinda system from Xsens Technologies, to assess their gait and balance during testing. This was done to ensure the AR or VR headsets would not have a negative impact on their mobility. The IMUs were attached using Velcro tape to the participant's legs, torso, arms, and head through a headband. During testing, the participants walked along the existing path on the site with the equipment. A control experiment was also conducted as a simple walk-through without the headsets (neither the HoloLens or Vive). The first part of the experiment involved assessing their balance while standing still and getting accustomed to the AR and VR experience. Hence, after confirming that the IMUs were not disrupting the participants mobility, they were asked to stand on a force plate for 30 s to measure their balance, cross-referencing the force plate with the MTw Awinda system for calibration. The HoloLens was then placed on the subject powered off and their balance was measured for 30 s, as seen in Fig. 8. Following this, the HoloLens was turned on and prepared for the participant with the tall wall scene and the participants balance was taken again. Then, the Vive was used with the participant standing to allow them to first fully see the entire virtual environment with no external distractions. This way they would know what new elements were going to appear on the AR environment mixed in with the real world (e.g., lamp posts, benches, bike lanes, line separations, and more). While they were using the VR headset, the balance was also recorded for 30 s. Note that at this point of the experiments, subjects were not walking.

4.2   Walk-Through

After the previous steps mentioned above were completed, the participant walked four times in the given path using the HoloLens headset with someone following right behind them for safety purposes. It was of particular importance to maintain a natural walking condition while having someone close to the subjects in case they fell due to loss of balance, especially as the AR experience was completely new to most participants. While the participant was walking, measurements were taken with the IMU's software. The experiment began with the HoloLens placed on participant's head while turned off and included the following conditions with each condition being randomized.

- HoloLens on with short wall scene.
- HoloLens on with tall wall scene.
- HoloLens on with glass wall scene.

4.3   Participant Response

At the end of the experiment, the participants were asked to rate how much each wall contributed to the environment on a Likert scale (1–5), with 1 being "Dislike very much" and 5 being "Like very much". Most responses about the virtual

Fig. 8. Balance test with the HoloLens

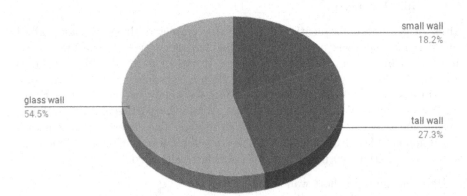

Fig. 9. Percentage of participants that gave the wall a rating of 5/5 with 5 being the highest score.

objects were favorable, as shown in Fig. 9 and 10. However, the results should be taken as a simple guide, as the users had to not be exposed to others and wanting to please the researchers could have been a factor in the questionnaire. Nevertheless, we think it is important to report that the participants felt that

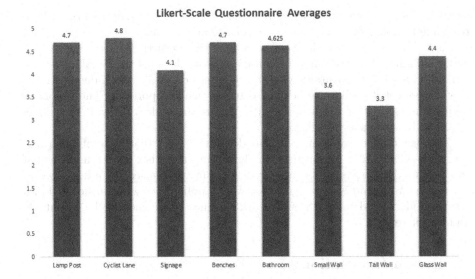

Fig. 10. Likert-Scale Questionnaire about the virtual objects using AR

those objects were well placed for this particular part of the city. Another potential influence on their responses may have been previous exposure to pictures by the city officials. In addition to those questions, they were asked "Are there any other features that you would like to see in place in the "M-path" that would further encourage you to use the space?" and their response was audio-recorded and noted down. For example, one subject mentioned that additional exercise equipment, water fountains, and more trees would benefit the space around them and encourage them more to exercise in it.

5   Discussion

As noted by the data collected from the 10 participants, seen in Fig. 9, it was clear that AR made a difference in their understanding of how the area could look in the near future. Several of the participants had attended previous city meetings where there were talks about the "M-path" and pictures were shown of how it could potentially look like. However, the subjects still had questioned whether themselves or other people in their community would actually use the park as they could not visualize it easily. Informally, we were told by the participants that it was not until they saw and experienced the actual virtual environment while using the HoloLens that they were able to internalize the changes proposed by the city. This response is highly encouraging as it highlights the strength of AR in city planning, allowing citizens to see first-hand what development proposals would look like and how they could impact the environment within the city. As a result, being able to personally experience a virtual design superimposed onto a real location will undoubtedly increase the quality of future designs due to the real-time feedback city planners can receive from citizens.

As for the participants themselves, none of them lost their balance or experienced motion sickness or any other impairment while using the HoloLens. They were all able to walk naturally with the HoloLens on or off, which demonstrates how convenient it is that the headset is hands-free and portable. The HoloLens permits users to wear the headset with glasses on, while VR headsets such as Vive had limited space for glasses.

The participants were amazed that despite the fact that none of them had ever tried on an AR or VR headset, the holograms that they saw around them of the benches, lampposts, and other street furniture, immersed them into a world where the unsafe and isolated park they were familiar with was transformed into a safe, modern, and elderly-friendly park that motivated them to be go outside and be active.

6   Design Implications

After the experiment was completed, we were able to analyze how AR and VR can work outside to re-imagine areas by blending the real and virtual world together to create an immersive and realistic experience for users. Likewise, we were able to examine how AR and VR can make an impact in the architecture, health, and engineering fields. There is an up and coming reality where the construction of a home for a family could take place with a virtual model being shown to them through AR to gauge their response. They could walk through the house in scale and make decisions on each element before any of it has even been constructed. Similarly, city planners and architects will be able to build shopping centers, buildings, and anything that they can think of. In this experiment, we have seen that this is not far from becoming reality with all the recent advancements in AR technology.

Nevertheless, some recommendations on designing these virtual spaces are needed. For instance, the 3D space should be built with bright and light colors if using the current incarnation of the HoloLens as they will appear less transparent when rendering the holograms. Due to the effect of bright sunlight on the headset, it is also recommended that the experiments be done at night or somewhere with adequate shade to also prevent the HoloLens from heating up, which provides for a more immersive experience. Due to the HoloLens' low field of view of 35 degrees in the current version, the use of the Vive VR headset, with its larger field of view of 110 degrees, not only blocked the daylight and made the holograms more visible but it allowed the users to see the entire area without having to move their head or walk around. However, it should still only be used as a supplementary visualization tool to the AR headset as it requires large amounts of external hardware and a battery. However, the upcoming Oculus Go and Oculus Odyssey headsets may address these issues or the Microsoft HoloLens 2 might be enough, which was just recently announced on February, 2019. At the site, we had to use a battery to power the laptop running the VR application, base stations that track hand movements and have to be mounted above head height and the Link Box connecting the Vive to the laptop. Hence, the headset was also connected via cable, unlike the HoloLens which had the advantage of having no external hardware apart from the headset itself. While we understand this is only a technical difficulty which will be eventually addressed with technological development, it points to the importance of the portability of headsets and, in particular, the need to design headsets that can be used in everyday tasks regardless of the environment or time of day. Another important consideration is to try to rely on applications that do not require internet connectivity or at the very least, little connectivity. For example, there may be areas where connectivity is not ideal. In our particular case, we made sure that the Microsoft HoloLens application did not need any internet connectivity, but this may not always be possible in some potential applications.

The implications that this research may have for city planning and health promotion have direct impacts in architecture, construction, and other areas. There are cases, such as the one presented in this work, where constructing different options is either unfeasible or economically counterproductive. We have shown how virtual environments such as those made possible through AR headsets can have an impact in making these decisions easier. AR can make city planning extremely intuitive and integrated with the general public, especially in an area as critical as our elderly and their health.

7   Future Work

From the data collected and the results gathered, there are several next steps that need to be completed. After taking into consideration the participants' requests or concerns for street furniture outside of what they had seen on the AR and VR headsets and their choice of wall, we will share our results with the City of Miami and add the suggested models to the applications to create a final AR environment with the participants' choices included. This design was given to city for consideration of a new "M-Path" to be built in the near future. Ideally, with the cooperation of the City of Miami and others, we are planning to conduct a larger experiment with over 30 participants with the new recommendations. This larger sample size will help to determine if the headsets cause any mobility issues.

8   Conclusion

We conducted a user study to see the feasibility of using AR to enhance city planning and cater to a specific demographic's needs, in this case, the elderly and their health. While it is too early to tell and more research is needed, there are clear indications that this technology can provide a real benefit to accessible city planning and directly improve the health of senior citizens as a result. While the sample size of the experiment was admittedly small, the participants were able to visualize the three possible configurations for the future park, and make a decision based on what they observed. In addition, the participants expressed great satisfaction and enthusiasm with respect to wearing the AR headset and how immersive the experience felt for them. Finally, we have also shown that this technology can be safely used by senior citizens.

The future of accessible city planning can be done with AR, thus fully realizing what the name actually entails. Creating a reality for anyone that augments their current reality. This is an example of an area where AR has a societal impact and can benefit senior citizens on top of the benefits to city planning. We focused on seniors to demonstrate how city planners could accommodate a specific demographic. However, everyone could benefit from AR by directly being able to visualize the future of their cities and living spaces. Families could see their future home before it is built, the elderly could experience their future parks before they are developed and developers could envision future skyscrapers before they dot the skyline. With this technology, cities can cater to the needs of their citizens by being able to see and analyze in advance when planning for smarter, better and more accessible environments.

References

1. Adobe. https://www.adobe.com/. Accessed 22 Mar 2019
2. Quickfacts Florida. https://www.census.gov/quickfacts/geo/chart/fl/AGE775217. Accessed 22 Mar 2019
3. Sketchup. https://www.SketchUp.com/. Accessed 22 Mar 2019
4. Unity. https://www.unity.com/. Accessed 22 Mar 2019
5. Boj, C., Díaz, D.J., Portalés, C., Casas, S.: Video games and outdoor physical activity for the elderly: applications of the HybridPLAY technology. NATO Adv. Sci. Inst. Ser. E Appl. Sci. **8**(10), 1912 (2018)
6. Claes, S., Vande Moere, A.: Street infographics: raising awareness of local issues through a situated urban visualization. In: Proceedings of the 2nd ACM International Symposium on Pervasive Displays, PerDis 2013, pp. 133–138. ACM, New York (2013). https://doi.org/10.1145/2491568.2491597
7. Hino, K., Asami, Y., Lee, J.S.: Step counts of middle-aged and elderly adults for 10 months before and after the release of pokémon GO in Yokohama, Japan. J. Med. Internet Res. **21**(2), e10724 (2019)
8. Schall Jr., M.C., et al.: Augmented reality cues and elderly driver hazard perception. Hum. Fact. **55**(3), 643–658 (2013). https://doi.org/10.1177/0018720812462029
9. Pedraza-Hueso, M., Martín-Calzón, S., Díaz-Pernas, F.J., Martínez-Zarzuela, M.: Rehabilitation using kinect-based games and virtual reality. Procedia Comput. Sci. **75**, 161–168 (2015). 2015 International Conference Virtual and Augmented Reality in Education
10. Torchia, M., Shirer, M.: Worldwide spending on augmented and virtual reality expected to surpass $20 billion in 2019. https://www.idc.com/getdoc.jsp?containerId=prUS44511118. Accessed 22 Mar 2019
11. Yang, C.H., Maher, J.P., Conroy, D.E.: Implementation of behavior change techniques in mobile applications for physical activity. Am. J. Prev. Med. **48**(4), 452–455 (2015)

12. Yoo, H.N., Chung, E., Lee, B.H.: The effects of augmented reality-based Otago exercise on balance, gait, and falls efficacy of elderly women. J. Phys. Ther. Sci. **25**, 797–801 (2013). https://doi.org/10.1589/jpts.25.797

13. Zhang, L., Chen, S., Dong, H., Saddik, A.E.: Visualizing Toronto city data with hololens: using augmented reality for a city model. IEEE Consum. Electron. Mag. **7**(3), 73–80 (2018). https://doi.org/10.1109/MCE.2018.2797658

Gestures and Haptic Interaction in VAMR

Assessing the Role of Virtual Reality with Passive Haptics in Music Conductor Education: A Pilot Study

Angelos Barmpoutis[1]([⊠]), Randi Faris[2], Luis Garcia[2], Luis Gruber[2], Jingyao Li[1], Fray Peralta[3], and Menghan Zhang[1]

[1] Digital Worlds Institute, University of Florida, Gainesville, FL 32611, USA
angelos@digitalworlds.ufl.edu,
{jingyaoli, zhangmenghan}@ufl.edu
[2] Computer and Information Science and Engineering, University of Florida, Gainesville, FL 32611, USA
{randi.faris, luis.garcia104, luisgruba}@ufl.edu
[3] School of Music, University of Florida, Gainesville, FL 32611, USA
fray.peralta@ufl.edu

Abstract. This paper presents a novel virtual reality system that offers immersive experiences for instrumental music conductor training. The system utilizes passive haptics that bring physical objects of interest, namely the baton and the music stand, within a virtual concert hall environment. Real-time object and finger tracking allow the users to behave naturally on a virtual stage without significant deviation from the typical performance routine of instrumental music conductors. The proposed system was tested in a pilot study (n = 13) that assessed the role of passive haptics in virtual reality by comparing our proposed "smart baton" with a traditional virtual reality controller. Our findings indicate that the use of passive haptics increases the perceived level of realism and that their virtual appearance affects the perception of their physical characteristics.

Keywords: Virtual reality · Passive haptics · Music conductor education

1 Introduction

The use of computer systems in instrumental music conductor education has been a well studied topic even outside the area of virtual reality [1]. Several systems have been proposed that offer targeted learning experiences [2, 3] which may also combine gamified elements [6]. In the past decades, several visual interfaces have been designed using the available technologies at each given period of time [4, 5, 7], which most recently included eye tracking [8] and augmented and virtual reality platforms [3].

Recent advances in real-time object tracking and the availability of such systems as mainstream consumer products has opened new possibilities for virtual reality applications [13, 14]. It has been shown that the use of passive haptics in VR contribute to a sensory-rich experience [15, 16], as users have now the opportunity to hold and feel the main objects of interaction within a given immersive environment, such as tools, handles, and other instruments. For example, tracking the location of a real piano can

© Springer Nature Switzerland AG 2020
J. Y. C. Chen and G. Fragomeni (Eds.): HCII 2020, LNCS 12190, pp. 275–285, 2020.
https://doi.org/10.1007/978-3-030-49695-1_18

help beginners learn how to play it using virtual reality [20]. However, the use of passive haptics in virtual environments for music education is an understudied area, because it requires precise real-time tracking of objects that are significantly smaller than a piano, such as hand held musical instruments, bows, batons, etc.

In this paper, we present a novel system for enhancing the training of novice instrumental music conductors through a tangible virtual environment. For the purposes of the proposed system a smart baton and a smart music stand have been designed using commercially available tracking sensors (VIVE trackers). The users wear a high-fidelity virtual reality headset (HTC VIVE), which renders the environment of a virtual concert hall from the conductor's standpoint. Within this environment, the users can feel the key objects of interaction within their reach, namely the baton, the music stand, and the floor of the stage through passive haptics. A real-time hand and finger motion tracking system continuously tracks the left hand of the user in addition to the tracking of the baton, which is usually held in the right hand. This setup creates a natural user interface that allows the conductors to perform naturally on a virtual stage, thus creating a highly immersive training experience.

The main goals of the proposed system are the following: a) Enhance the traditional training of novice instrumental music conductors by increasing their practice time without requiring additional space allocation or time commitment from music players, which is also cost-effective. b) Provide an interface for natural user interaction that does not deviate from the traditional environment of conducting, including the environment, the tools, and the user behavior (hand gesture, head pose, and body posture), thus making the acquired skills highly transferable to the real-life scenario. c) Just-in-time feedback is essential in any educational setting, therefore one of the goals of the proposed system is to generate quantitative feedback on the timeliness of their body movement and the corresponding music signals. d) Last but not least, the proposed system recreates the conditions of a real stage performance, which may help the users reduce stage fright within a risk-free virtual environment [9–12].

A small scale pilot study ($n = 13$) was performed in order to assess the proposed system and particularly the role of passive haptics in this virtual reality application. The main focus of the study was to test whether the use of passive haptics increases the perceived level of realism in comparison to a typical virtual reality controller, and whether the virtual appearance of a real physical object, such as the baton, affects the perception of its physical characteristics. These hypotheses were tested using A/B tests followed by short surveys. The statistical significance of the collected data was calculated, and the results are discussed in detail. The reported findings support our hypotheses and set the basis for a larger-scale future study.

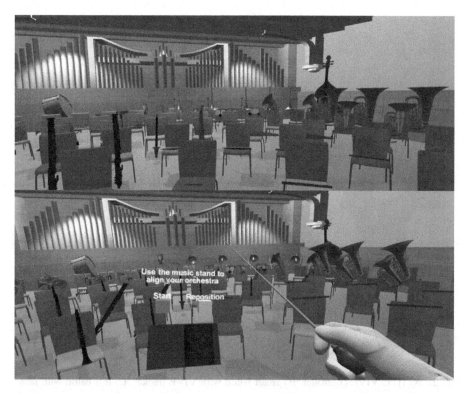

Fig. 1. Top: screenshot of the virtual reality orchestra, bottom: screenshot of the virtual reality graphical user interface with the smart music stand and the smart baton.

2 Methods

A virtual reality orchestra environment was developed by imitating the architectural design of the University of Florida Auditorium (Fig. 1 top). The virtual environment featured a large instrumental ensemble arranged in a typical semi-circle layout with 5 rows of chairs. In order to minimize the 3D modeling and animation needs for this project, avatars of music players were not included in this environment. Instead, the instruments were animated using a motion sequence that approximated the expected motion pattern for each type of instrument during performance [19]. By default, the instruments were in a resting position on their respective chairs (except for percussion instruments), as shown on the top panel of Fig. 1. In the main activity of this simulation the virtual band performed the 1st suite in E flat for military band op. 28 no. 1 by the British composer Gustav Holst. During the performance the instruments were animated right above their respective chairs as shown on the bottom panel of Fig. 1.

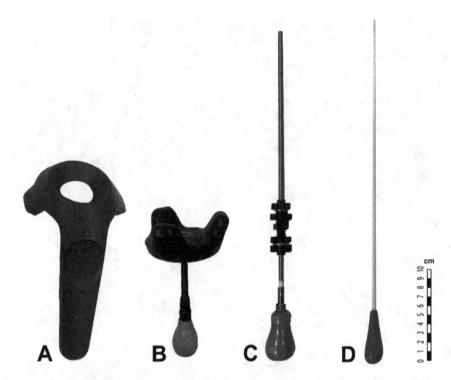

Fig. 2. A) HTC VIVE controller, B) smart baton with VIVE tracker, C) test baton with same weight as B, D) real conductor's baton.

The system allowed the user to interact with the virtual environment using a virtual reality headset and controllers (HTC VIVE), which were tracked in real time (6 DOF for each device). In addition, two VIVE trackers were firmly attached to two real physical objects, a music stand and a wooden handle, in order track the position and orientation of these objects. A virtual representation of these objects was rendered within the virtual environment at their corresponding locations, thus allowing the user to hold and interact with these physical objects while observing their virtual image in real time.

More specifically, a VR-tracked baton with passive haptic feedback, dubbed here "smart baton," was created by attaching a wooden handle to a VIVE tracker with a ¼ in. bolt as shown in Fig. 2B. The total weight of this smart baton was 130 g (88 g tracker and 42 g handle with bolt), which was 64% of the weight of the HTC VIVE controller (203 g). The texture, size, and shape of the handle was selected so that its overall haptic feedback resembles that of a real baton (Fig. 2D). The user could hold the smart baton in a natural way without obstructing the tracker, while observing the 3D model of a real conductor's baton, which was rendered at the corresponding position within the virtual reality environment. Similarly, the user could touch the music stand or even reposition it on the virtual stage by interacting with the corresponding real physical object. The bottom panel of Fig. 1 demonstrates the use of the smart baton and the music stand within the virtual environment.

One of the features that were implemented in the proposed smart baton was real-time beats-per-minute (BPM) estimation by analyzing the motion pattern of the baton and identifying the local extrema of the baton's tip trajectory. The rolling BPM estimate was used to modify the playback speed of the music performance, thus providing the user-conductor with the ability to control the tempo of the performance in a natural way. Furthermore, the user could cue specific instruments by looking towards them (implemented using head tracking) or gesturing with their left hand (implemented using hand tracking with Valve Index controller).

A graphical user interface within the virtual environment provided instructions to the users as well as feedback with regards to their tempo and cuing. Additional features of the implemented system include: a) turning the pages of the score on the music stand by naturally using the left hand to perform a page-turning motion, b) repositioning the entire orchestra by moving the real music stand, so that it is better oriented within the user's physical space, and c) recording the complete data transcripts of a session, including the motion of the user (head, baton, and left hand), the detected cues, and the estimated tempo.

Although this virtual reality application was designed as an early prototype of an experiential learning system for novice instrumental music conductors, this paper does not focus on assessing its learning features. The main focus of the user study presented in the next section is to assess the role of passive haptics in this application and how their use may affect a user's perceptions.

3   User Study

A pilot study was conducted in the Reality Lab of the Digital Worlds Institute at the University of Florida, in order to assess the effect of passive haptics in the proposed virtual reality application (IRB 201902916). The study was designed to test the following hypotheses:

- The use of passive haptics increases the perceived level of realism in a virtual reality application.
- The virtual appearance of a real physical object affects the perception of its physical characteristics, such as weight and size.

During this study the subjects were presented with two sets of A/B tests that targeted the aforementioned hypotheses. In the first test, the users were asked to mimic conducting a virtual orchestra using our virtual system with two different types of batons: a) a virtual baton that was controlled by the HTC VIVE controller (Fig. 2A), and b) a virtual baton that was controlled by our smart baton (Fig. 2B). Both controllers were visualized in VR with the same 3D model of a real conductor's baton (Fig. 3 top).

In the second test, the users were asked to perform a similar task using two different versions of our smart baton: a) our smart baton visualized with the 3D model of a real conductor's baton (Fig. 3 top), and b) our smart baton visualized with the 3D model of its real appearance (Fig. 3 bottom). This was followed by an additional test that contrasted two similarly weighted but differently shaped controllers (B and C).

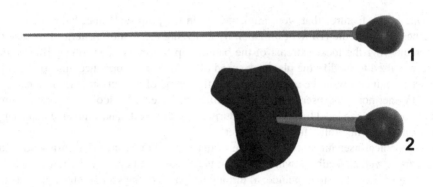

Fig. 3. The virtual baton models used in our user tests: 1) 3D model of a real conductor's baton, which was used in conjunction with the controllers A and B (Fig. 2) as test cases A1 and B1 respectively, 2) 3D model of the actual physical shape of our smart baton, which was used in conjunction with the controller B (Fig. 2) as test case B2.

In order to limit bias in this study the following measures were taken:

- The description of the study that was communicated with the subjects did not reveal the details of the hypotheses made in this study.
- The subjects did not have visual contact with the controllers/batons they were holding for the entire duration of the study session.
- The order of the two versions of controllers in each A/B test was randomized.
- The duration of exposure of the subjects to each controller was fixed.

Each A/B test was immediately followed by a survey conducted verbally, while the subject was still wearing the VR headset. The survey included the questions listed in Table 1. In each question, the subjects were given the following possible responses: 1) clearly the first controller, 2) slightly the first controller, 3) about the same, 4) slightly the second controller, 5) clearly the second controller. Finally, the subjects were asked to complete a short demographic questionnaire at the end of the session.

Table 1. The bank of questions we used in our A/B tests.

Q1	Did the 1st or the 2nd controller you held feel more like a real baton?
Q2	Did the 1st or the 2nd controller you held feel lighter?
Q3	Did the 1st or the 2nd controller you held feel bulkier?
Q4	Was the 1st or the 2nd controller you held more appropriate for this use?
Q5	Was the 1st or the 2nd controller you held clearer on how to operate?
Q6	Was the 1st or the 2nd controller you held more comfortable to use?
Q7	Was the 1st or the 2nd controller you held easier to move?
Q8	Could the 1st or the 2nd baton improve someone's skills in conducting?

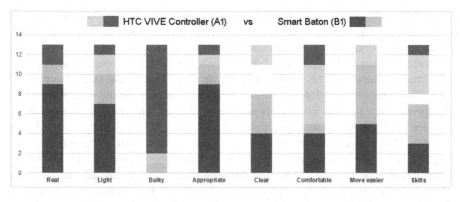

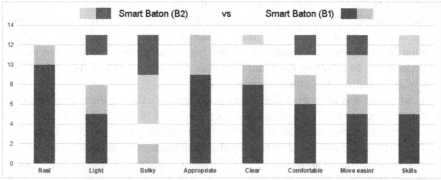

Fig. 4. The results from the A/B tests between the HTC VIVE controller and the smart baton (top) and between the two virtual representations of the smart baton (bottom). Red and green indicate responses in favor of the respective cases A and B, while darker and lighter shades indicate strong and weak responses respectively. (Color figure online)

In total, 13 subjects were enrolled in this study in the age group between 19–23. None of the subjects had used VR more than once, and the majority of the subjects did not have any prior experience in VR. Since this pilot study did not assess the educational aspect of our prototype application, the subjects were not required to have any level of instrumental music conductor training.

In the next section we present and analyze the collected data and discuss the key findings from this study.

4   Results

The data collected from the two main A/B tests in our study are shown in Fig. 4. The order of the metrics in the horizontal axis of this figure corresponds to the order of questions in Table 1. In each test, the A and B cases are denoted by a letter that indicates a hardware controller from Fig. 2 followed by a number that indicates a virtual appearance from Fig. 3. For example, "B1" denotes our proposed smart baton visualized in VR using the 3D model of a real conductor's baton. According to the responses, our proposed smart baton felt more real, lighter, less bulky, easier to move, and more appropriate for this application compared to the HTC VIVE controller. In addition, more than 60% of the users felt that it was clearer how to operate the proposed smart baton, which could be attributed to the simpler interface and lack of buttons.

A chi-square test of independence was performed to examine the relation between the type of controller and the perceived level of realism. The relation between these variables was found to be significant, χ^2 (1, N = 13) = 12.46, p < .001. Users responded that our smart baton felt more real compared to the baton that was operated using the HTC VIVE controller, easier to move, and more appropriate for this application. It should be noted that in this test both controllers were visualized with the same 3D model in the virtual environment, and the only variable was the hardware controller. These findings support the first hypothesis of this study.

With regard to the second hypothesis, according to Fig. 4 (bottom) the users found that our smart baton felt less bulky, more comfortable, and more real when visualized using the 3D model of a real conductor's baton compared to using it while observing its real appearance. In addition, the same controller felt lighter to more than 60% of the users when visualized with the thinner 3D model.

A chi-square test of independence was performed to examine the relation between the virtual appearance of a controller and its perceived physical characteristics. The relation between these variables was found to be significant, χ^2 (1, N = 13) = 7.53, p < .01. It should be noted that in this test the same hardware controller was used, and the only variable was its appearance in the virtual environment. These findings support the second hypothesis of this study.

When comparing our smart baton with a same weight but differently shaped test baton (Fig. 2C), we found that the small length of the baton in our proposed design reduces the torque applied to the handle as the user moves the baton. As a result, the subjects found that the proposed smart baton was lighter than the same weight test baton, χ^2 (1, N = 13) = 12.4, p < .001. The detailed results of the χ^2 tests of significance for each question and each A/B test in our study are reported in Table 2.

Table 2. The results of the χ^2 test of significance. Each cell contains the dominant choice in the respective A/B test, the χ^2 value, and the probability value.

More real	**B1**, 12.4, p < .001	**B1**, 22.1, p < .001	B, 2.46, N/S
Lighter	**B1**, 7.53, p < .01	**B1**, 5.53, p < .02	**B**, 12.4, p < .001
Bulkier	**A1**, 18.6, p < .001	**B2**, 7.53, p < .01	B, 2.46, N/S
Appropriate	**B1**, 12.4, p < .001	**B1**, 26.0, p < .001	**B**, 9.84, p < .0025
Clear to operate	**B1**, 5.53, p < .02	**B1**, 12.4, p < .001	B, 1.38, N/S
Comfortable	A1, 1.38, N/S	**B1**, 7.53, p < .01	**B**, 12.4, p < .001
Easy to move	**B1**, 12.4, p < .001	B1, 0.61, N/S	**B**, 15.3, p < .001
Improve skills	B1, 0.65, N/S	**B1**, 9.84, p < .0025	**B**, 9.84, p < .0025

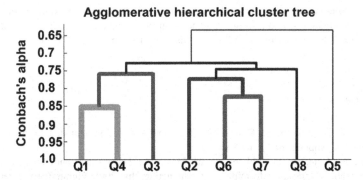

Fig. 5. Hierarchical clustering of the questions based on their internal consistency. Two clusters were found (shown here in green and red). Brighter colors indicate stronger connection. (Color figure online)

Furthermore, the internal consistency of the 8 metrics that we used in our questionnaire was assessed by calculating Cronbach's alpha [17] from the responses of each individual A/B test ($\alpha = 0.86$, 0.85, 0.90) as well as from the cumulative responses across tests ($\alpha = 0.86$). In all cases, the calculated values exceeded the reliability estimates ($\alpha = 0.70$) recommended by Nunnally [18].

Finally, an agglomerative hierarchical cluster tree was created by computing the linkage between the questions using the largest affinity between two single elements from the respective clusters of questions (see Fig. 5). In our case, we employed Cronbach's alpha as the measure of affinity, which indicates the internal consistency between a pair of questions. According to Fig. 5, questions 1 and 4 were linked together at consistency level $\alpha = 0.85$ and were joined by question 3 at $\alpha = 0.75$. Similarly, questions 6 and 7 were also linked together at $\alpha = 0.82$ and joined by question 2 at $\alpha = 0.77$. This indicates that the questions about "how real" and "how appropriate" are associated with "less bulky", and the questions about "how comfortable" and "easy to move" are associated with "lighter." It should be noted that the questions about "easy to operate" and "improve skills" were connected with weaker links to the rest of the clusters ($\alpha < 0.75$).

5 Conclusions

In this paper we demonstrated how passive haptics can be used to enhance the user experience in a virtual reality application for instrumental music conductor training. A set of metrics was developed to assess various aspects of the user's experience after holding and using a baton within a virtual environment. The users in our pilot study found that our proposed smart baton felt more real, lighter, easier to move and operate, and more appropriate for this application. Our findings set the basis for a larger-scale future study that can be further developed in order to assess the educational aspects of this virtual reality application in terms of its learning outcomes as a tool that can supplement the traditional methods for instrumental music conductor training.

Acknowledgements. The authors would like to thank the anonymous volunteers who participated in this study. We would also like to express our appreciation to the University of Florida College of the Arts for providing funding for this project through the 2020 Research Incentive Award.

References

1. Morita, H., Hashimoto, S., Ohteru, S.: A computer music system that follows a human conductor. Computer **24**(7), 44–53 (1991)
2. Nijholt, A., Reidsma, D., Ebbers, R., ter Maat, M.: The virtual conductor: learning and teaching about music, performing, and conducting. In: 2008 Eighth IEEE International Conference on Advanced Learning Technologies, pp. 897–899. IEEE (2008)
3. Orman, E.K., Price, H.E., Russell, C.R.: Feasibility of using an augmented immersive virtual reality learning environment to enhance music conducting skills. J. Music Teach. Educ. **27**(1), 24–35 (2017)
4. Schertenleib, S., Gutiérrez, M., Vexo, F., Thalmann, D.: Conducting a virtual orchestra. IEEE Multimedia **11**(3), 40–49 (2004)
5. Argueta, C.R., Ko, C.-J., Chen, Y.-S.: Interacting with a music conducting system. In: Jacko, Julie A. (ed.) HCI 2009. LNCS, vol. 5611, pp. 654–663. Springer, Heidelberg (2009). https://doi.org/10.1007/978-3-642-02577-8_72
6. Dillon, R., Wong, G., Ang, R.: Virtual orchestra: an immersive computer game for fun and education. In: Proceedings of the 2006 International Conference on Game Research and Development, pp. 215–218. Murdoch University (2006)
7. Segen, J., Gluckman, J., Kumar, S.: Visual interface for conducting virtual orchestra. In: Proceedings 15th International Conference on Pattern Recognition. ICPR-2000, vol. 1, pp. 276–279. IEEE (2000)
8. Orman, E.K.: Effect of virtual reality exposure and aural stimuli on eye contact, directional focus, and focus of attention of novice wind band conductors. Int. J. Music Educ. **34**(3), 263–270 (2016)
9. Akay, M., Marsh, A.: The use of virtual reality technology in the treatment of anxiety disorders. In: Information Technologies in Medicine, Rehabilitation and Treatment, pp. 19–37. IEEE (2001). https://doi.org/10.1002/0471206458.ch2
10. Tudor, A.-D., Poeschl, S., Doering, N.: Virtual audience customization for public speaking training procedures. In: 2013 IEEE Virtual Reality (VR), pp. 61–62. IEEE (2013)
11. Heuett, B.L., Heuett, K.B.: Virtual reality therapy: a means of reducing public speaking anxiety. Int. J. Humanit. Soc. Sci. **1**(16), 1–6 (2011)
12. Stupar-Rutenfrans, S., Ketelaars, L.E.H., van Gisbergen, M.S.: Beat the fear of public speaking: mobile 360 video virtual reality exposure training in home environment reduces public speaking anxiety. Cyberpsychol. Behav. Soc. Netw. **20**(10), 624–633 (2017)
13. Harley, D., Tarun, A.P., Germinario, D., Mazalek, A.: Tangible VR: diegetic tangible objects for virtual reality narratives. In: Proceedings of the 2017 Conference on Designing Interactive Systems, pp. 1253–1263. ACM (2017)
14. Siqueira de, A.G., Bhargava, A.: Tangibles within VR: tracking, augmenting, and combining fabricated and commercially available commodity devices. In: IEEE Conference on Virtual Reality and 3D User Interfaces, Reutlingen, Germany, March 2018
15. Han, D.T., Suhail, M., Ragan, E.D.: Evaluating remapped physical reach for hand interactions with passive haptics in virtual reality. IEEE Trans. Visual. Comput. Graph. **24**(4), 1467–1476 (2018)

16. Harley, D., Verni, A., Willis, M., Ng, A., Bozzo, L., Mazalek, A.: Sensory VR: smelling, touching, and eating virtual reality. In: Proceedings of the Twelfth International Conference on Tangible, Embedded, and Embodied Interaction, pp. 386–397. ACM (2018)
17. Cronbach, L.: Coefficient alpha and the internal consistency of tests. Psychometrika **16**, 297–334 (1951). https://doi.org/10.1007/BF02310555
18. Nunnally, J.: Psychometric Theory. McGraw-Hill, New York (1967)
19. Visi, F., Coorevits, E., Schramm, R., Miranda, E.: Musical instruments, body movement, space, and motion data: music as an emergent multimodal choreography. Hum. Technol. **13**, 58–81 (2017)
20. VRtuos: Learn how to play your real piano with a virtual application. https://sidequestvr.com/#/app/494. Accessed 20 Feb 2020

FingerTac – A Wearable Tactile Thimble for Mobile Haptic Augmented Reality Applications

Thomas Hulin[1,2(✉)], Michael Rothammer[1], Isabel Tannert[1],
Suraj Subramanyam Giri[1], Benedikt Pleintinger[1], Harsimran Singh[1,2],
Bernhard Weber[1], and Christian Ott[1,2]

[1] Institute of Robotics and Mechatronics, German Aerospace Center (DLR),
82234 Wessling, Germany
Thomas.Hulin@dlr.de
[2] Centre for Tactile Internet with Human-in-the-Loop (CeTI),
Cluster of Excellence at TU Dresden, Dresden, Germany

Abstract. FingerTac is a novel concept for a wearable augmented haptic thimble. It makes use of the limited spatial discrimination capabilities of vibrotactile stimuli at the skin and generates tactile feedback perceived at the bottom center of a fingertip by applying simultaneous vibrations at both sides of the finger. Since the bottom of the finger is thus kept free of obstruction, the device is well promising for augmented haptic applications, where real world interactions need to be enriched or amalgamated with virtual tactile feedback. To minimize its lateral dimension, the vibration actuators are placed on top of the device, and mechanical links transmit the vibrations to the skin. Two evaluation studies with N=10 participants investigate (i) the loss of vibration intensity through these mechanical links, and (ii) the effect of lateral displacement between stimulus and induced vibration. The results of both studies support the introduced concept of the FingerTac.

Keywords: Augmented haptics · Tactile feedback · Wearable devices

1 Introduction

Compared to pure cutaneous haptic feedback on the skin, kinesthetic feedback provides forces and torques. Such feedback is essential for delicate tasks that occur e.g. in telerobotic applications, where a user is required to intuitively control the forces applied by the remote robot. However, this benefit comes

Funded by the German Research Foundation (DFG, Deutsche Forschungsgemeinschaft) as part of Germany's Excellence Strategy – EXC 2050/1 – Project ID 390696704 – Cluster of Excellence "Centre for Tactile Internet with Human-in-the-Loop" (CeTI) of Technische Universität Dresden.

J. Y. C. Chen and G. Fragomeni (Eds.): HCII 2020, LNCS 12190, pp. 286–298, 2020.
https://doi.org/10.1007/978-3-030-49695-1_19

at the price of complex mechanical hardware systems. While a couple of well-developed kinesthetic devices for force and torque feedback for the hand exist, the situation is different for fingers. Hand exoskeletons are often obstructive and have limited force capabilities. In comparison, tactile feedback can be realized by much leaner and lighter devices.

A lot of research was conducted towards incorporating several types of strategies into delivering tactile feedback to the user. Pin-arrays use dense arrangements of skin contactors that exert pressure onto the skin to display tactile information. Such pin-arrays can be actuated using electromagnets [28], piezoelectric crystals [27], shape memory alloys [26] and pneumatic systems [13]. They can be used to provide braille dot patterns and virtual surface texture, among others, to the user. Although such devices are very effective in conducting tactile information via spatially sampled approximation, they are not mobile or wearable since they usually need a significantly large separate actuation system. Some tactile displays use the principles of electrovibration and electrical stimuli to provide vibrational friction, pressure and vibration at the same time [9].

Certain tactile devices apply multi-DoF force vectors on the user's fingerpad at one or multi contact points. Minamizawa et al. [12] proposed a wearable device comprised of two motors and a movable belt in contact with the user's finger, designed for generating normal and shear stress to deform the fingerpads which simulates a weight sensation of a virtual object. The "hRing" proposed by Pacchierotti et al. [16], is another 2-DoF cutaneous device based on the same principle as [12], and is used to provide normal and tangential stimulus to the proximal phalanx of the index finger. Schorr and Okamura [21] presented an approach that uses a pair of finger mounted devices that deforms the fingerpads to convey interaction information such as grasping, squeezing, pressing, lifting, and stroking. Prattichizzo et al. [17] developed a miniature device with parallel mechanism that applies 3-DoF force onto the fingerpad through a rigid platform which is actuated using cables and miniaturized motors. Leonardis et al. [10], developed a wearable haptic device modulates the contact forces, in 3-DoF, by stretching the skin. Solazzi et al. [23] designed a portable interface with fast transient that could display contact and orientation information to the user. The device was later upgraded by adding a voice coil, enabling it to simultaneously deliver the virtual surface's orientation and a wide frequency bandwidth of tactile stimulation [5]. A ferro-fluid based tactile device was fabricated by Singh et al. [22], that can also transmit both orientation and texture information at the same time. Although such devices are wearable, the overall structure is not compact enough to be worn on more than a couple of fingers as it obstructs the user's natural workspace.

By far, vibrational feedback has outnumbered other forms of tactile feedback due to its advantages of being compact, lightweight, wearable and portable. Voice coil motors and piezoelectric materials are some of the common actuators used to generate non-directional feedback, such as vibration patterns, for wearables [6], VR [15] or video games. They can also be used to transmit directional cues through a wearable belt [25], vest [3] of wristband [18], or for communicating emotions [1]. Some researchers also use other actuation technologies to generate vibrotactile feedback, for instance shape memory alloys [20] or electro-active polymers [2,14].

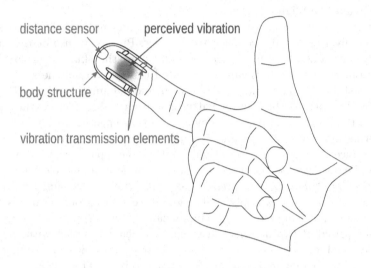

distance sensor   perceived vibration

body structure

vibration transmission elements

Fig. 1. Conceptual sketch of the FingerTac.

While most of the above mentioned devices only work with virtual reality, there are others that can be used for augmented reality as well, as these devices interfere only minimally when interacting with real objects. Fani *et al.* [4] presented the Wearable-Fabric Yielding Display which can convey softness information for passive and active haptic exploration. It was also shown that by controlling the volumetric distribution of acoustic field through a two-dimensional phased ultrasound array, volumetric haptic shapes can be rendered in mid-air [7,11]. One of its shortcomings is the limited workspace, where the ultrasound arrays must create a shape within the functional volume of the device, and is therefore not wearable. Taking the research forward in the direction of wearablity, Spelmezan *et al.* [24] showed that by placing an array of ultrasound emitters on the back of the hand and timing the pulses, a tactile sensation on the palm due to constructive interference can be created. However, ultrasonic emitters are not small enough to make such a technology wearable at the moment.

This paper follows a different approach and introduces FingerTac, a novel concept for a tactile thimble. While various approaches exist to generate tactile feedback at a fingertip, the unique feature of our concept is that it generates tactile feedback at the bottom side of a fingertip and at the same time keeps this bottom side unobstructed. This is achieved by inducing vibrational feedback at both sides of a finger and making use of the limited spatial discrimination capabilities of vibrotactile stimuli at the skin. Thus, our device generates perceived vibration in-between the two contact areas where the stimuli are applied.

This unique property makes the device well suited for augmented haptic applications, where both real and virtual objects need to be touched and manipulated.

The remainder of this document discusses the conceptual idea of the Finger-Tac in more detail, describes two demonstrators, and presents evaluation studies as proof of concept.

2 Concept and Functional Demonstrators

The conceptual sketch of the FingerTac is illustrated in Fig. 1. The device induces vibrational feedback via two contact areas that are located on both sides of a fingertip. Vibrational stimuli are applied simultaneously on both contact areas at similar frequencies, such that the perceived vibration lies in-between the two areas at the fingertip's bottom side. At the same time, this central fingertip area is kept uncovered to enable unobstructed interactions with real objects.

To minimize the lateral dimensions of the device, the actuators are located on its top side above the fingernail, and the vibrations are transferred from the actuators to the skin via two vibration transmission elements. Vibrations between these elements and the body structure are mechanically decoupled through a flexible vibration isolation structure. The body structure may also hold different sensors. In particular, a distance sensor at the front of the fingertip would allow for measuring and feeding back the distance of surrounding objects and could thereby extend the possible fields of application of such device. For instance, visually impaired people could benefit from this additional information, which has recently been shown in a pilot study with a vibrotactile wristband [19].

The following sections discuss design criteria that were considered for the FingerTac, and describe the functional demonstrators that were built and used for the conducted user studies.

2.1 Design Considerations

Several design criteria are of importance for the FingerTac in order to achieve clear tactile feedback, high wearing comfort, and unhindered natural interaction with the environment. While a wide range of objectives for designing tactile devices are known [8], the following aspects are of particular relevance for the FingerTac due to its nature as wearable augmented haptic device:

Unobtrusive Shape: A wearable device needs to ensure kinematic compatibility with the human body movements. Compared to classical tactile devices that are made for interaction in virtual environments, this objective is of high importance for the FingerTac, as the device should be used while interacting with both virtual and real environments. The device should minimally interfere with the fingerpad, so that the user can grasp or interact with real objects.

Low Inertia: Minimizing the overall mass of the device is one of the most important design goals for a wearable haptic interaction device. Apart from the overall mass, the distribution of masses also plays an important role especially during rotational movements of the hand. Components with a higher mass should be placed as close as possible to the pivot point or center of the fingers. Heavier components such as the battery can be separated from the device and placed on rather stronger body parts, i.e. on the hand instead of the finger.

High Comfort: A wearable haptic device should be comfortable and easily adaptable to the user's finger. High contact pressure and sharp edges should be avoided and a wide range of finger sizes should be covered.

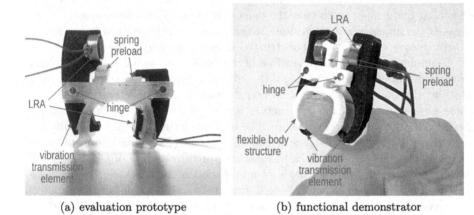

(a) evaluation prototype   (b) functional demonstrator

Fig. 2. Evaluation prototype and functional demonstrator to evaluate the FingerTac concept.

These objectives highly influenced the design of the functional demonstrators of the FingerTac as described below in the next section.

2.2   Functional Demonstrators

Figure 2 shows two different devices that were developed to evaluate the principal idea of our concept and to compare how much signal strength is lost if vibration is transmitted via vibration transmission elements. The evaluation prototype of Fig. 2(a) was developed first to evaluate the effect of the transmission elements compared to direct contact between actuator and skin. It has two different transmission elements, with the actuator placed on the top and bottom side respectively.

The functional demonstrator shown in Fig. 2(b) has two identical vibration transmission elements. They allow for placing the vibrotactile actuators on the top side of the device (i.e. on the fingernail side). Hence, they make it possible to reduce the device's dimensions on the bottom and the sides of a finger.

While the vibration transmission elements are 3d-printed out of traditional PLA (polylactic acid), a flexible material is used for the body structure such that the device can be used on fingers of different dimensions. The vibration actuators are linear resonant actuators (LRA) that provide high oscillation amplitudes and fast response dynamics. Their nominal operating frequency is 235 Hz and hence in the range in which the skin has high sensitivity. The technical system specifications of the built demonstrator are summarized in Table 1.

Table 1. System specifications of the FingerTac.

System specifications	
Size	16 mm × 24 mm × 31 mm (l × w × h)
Weight	Approx. 6 g (+ cables 3 g)
Supported diam. range	11 mm–18 mm
Actuators	2 LRAs, ⌀8 mm × 3.2 mm, 2 V
Rated frequency	235 Hz
Microcontroller	ESP32, Espressif systems, 2.4 GHz

3 Evaluation Studies

In order to evaluate the suitability of the concept and to determine the reduction of tactile stimulus due to the transmission of vibrations through the vibration transmission elements, studies were conducted on the evaluation prototype and the functional demonstrator with N = 10 subjects each.

3.1 Study on the Evaluation Prototype

The first study investigates the influence of the vibration transmission element. The evaluation prototype of Fig. 2(a) was used for this purpose.

Sample: Nine right-handed and one left-handed employees and students (9 males and 1 female) from DLR took part in this study (age = 26.3 ± 2.83 years, ranging from 23–32). Four of these participants had previous experience with haptic feedback systems.

Experimental Task and Design: The device was put on the index finger of the participant. Rectangular vibration patterns were activated subsequently in random order on each actuator (see Fig. 3). Three different time periods for the patterns were used (t_{on} = 50 ms, t_{off} = {20, 100, 200} ms). After each pattern, the participant had to repeat the experiment with changed direction of the device, i.e. the device was rotated by 180° such that the short and long transmission elements exchanged their positions.

Procedure: After a short introduction and signing informed consent, the evaluation prototype was put on the index finger of the participant's dominant hand. After the experiment, each participant was asked to fill out a questionnaire.

Results: The participants rated the experiments on a 7-point Likert-type scale ("Which actuator has the better localizable vibration?", 1 = direct contact with skin; 7 = vibration transmission element, and "How is the intensity of vibration?", 1 = very low; 7 = very high). The vibration transmission element resulted in a better score for localized vibration (M = 4.75, SD = 1.7). The obvious reason for the higher localization ratings for the vibration transmission element is because the vibration is applied over a smaller skin area compared to the actuator that is in direct contact with the skin.

For the intensity, both actuators obtained similar scores (M = 4.7, SD = 0.9 for the vibration transmission element vs. M = 4.4, SD = 1.2 for direct contact). These results indicate that the vibration transmission element is a suitable alternative to actuators in direct contact with the skin.

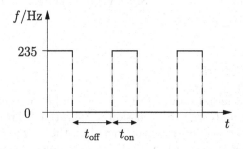

Fig. 3. Vibration pattern used in the studies. The nominal vibration frequency for the actuators was 235 Hz.

3.2   Study on the Functional Demonstrator

The goal of the second study was to show that by providing stimulus to the sides of a fingertip, the vibrations can be felt in-between at the fingerpad, and that participants are able to discriminate between different vibration patterns.

Sample: Ten participants (8 males and 2 females, 9 right-handers and 1 left-hander) were recruited from the student and staff population of the DLR (age = 25.6 ± 7.15 years, ranging from 18–44). All participants read and signed a consent form.

Experimental Task and Design: The participants executed two different tasks.

Task 1 – Localization of Vibrations: During the first task, the participants were asked to touch an external actuator in such a way that the actuator was located directly between the two vibration contact areas of the FingerTac (see Fig. 4). The actuator was placed on a scale. Participants were advised to keep the weight on the scale between 400 to 600 g, only with their index finger. In this range the vibration intensity of the external actuator is comparable to that of the demonstrator. To improve the participants' mobility and their view on the scale, the cable mounting direction of the FingerTac was modified compared to the original design of Fig. 2(b). In a random order, ten vibrations were presented,

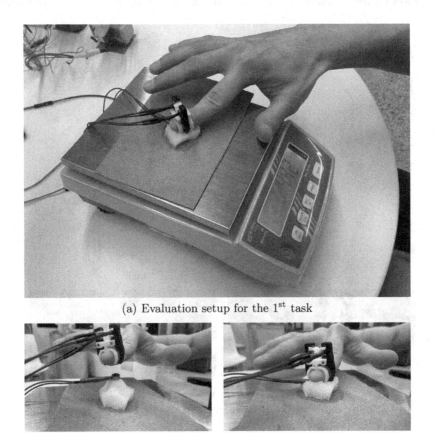

(a) Evaluation setup for the 1st task

(b) Close-up view on the index finger before and while pressing on the external actuator

Fig. 4. 1st task: localization of vibrations. The participants wore the FingerTac on the index finger of their dominant hand and pressed against an external vibration actuator with a force between 3.92 and 5.89 N (resp. 400 to 600 g).

some coming from the external actuator, some from the FingerTac itself. After each vibration, the participant had to indicate the origin of the vibration.

Task 2 – Discrimination of Frequencies: The second task investigated the discrimination capability with regard to different vibration patterns (see Fig. 5). It consisted of a familiarization period and two subtasks. First, four bricks with different colors were placed in front of the participants. Each color represented a different frequency of vibrations (red: 13.33 Hz, yellow: 8.00 Hz, blue: 3.63 Hz and green: 1.38 Hz). These frequencies were implemented as vibration patterns in the form of a rectangular function with fixed activation periods of $t_{on} = 50$ ms and different pause times of $t_{off} = \{25, 75, 255, 675\}$ ms (see Fig. 3). During the training, participants touched and held the bricks and feeling the different vibration patterns. They were asked to touch each brick at least twice to assure

(a) Evaluation setup for the 2nd task

(b) Close-up views on the index finger illustrating the two subtasks on frequencies discrimination

Fig. 5. 2nd task: discrimination of frequencies. Four different bricks representing four different vibration patterns were used during this subtask. The participants were blindfolded during the task and asked to find a brick with a specific color (respectively vibration pattern) by comparing it to the other bricks' vibration patterns (subtask 1), or to absolutely identify the color respectively pattern of a brick without being able to compare it to the other bricks (task 2). (Color figure online)

that they are able to recall the patterns during the experiment. As soon as they felt ready, participants were blindfolded.

Frequency detection subtask 1: Next, all bricks were placed in front of them and they were asked to identify a specific color, just by feeling the vibration pattern while grasping and touching the brick. After selecting one, the participants were asked to rate the difficulty of identifying the brick on a 7-point Likert-type scale ("Please rate the difficulty of identifying the color", 1=very low; 7=very hard). This was repeated six times with a systematic variation of the colors; each color appeared at least once.

Frequency detection subtask 2: For the second subtask, the experimenter handed the participant one brick and s/he had to identify the color. The participant was asked to rate the difficulty of identifying the color for all six repetitions. Each subject conducted both tasks subsequently.

Procedure: After a short introduction and signing informed consent, FingerTac was carefully placed on the first phalanx of the index finger of the dominant hand. Participants wore an ear protection to avoid them hearing the vibrations during all experiments. During the second task, the participants were blindfolded after the familiarization period. One experimenter wrote down the answers given by the participants.

Results: The N = 10 subjects detected the external system in 84.2% of the cases (significantly more often than guess probability, i.e. 50%, $p < .001$), while the detection rate for the functional demonstrator was 53.8%, which is not significantly different from guess probability. This means that the subjects were not able to tell the origin of vibration if the functional demonstrator was active (Table 2).

Table 2. Localization of vibrations

		Detected		Binomial test
		"External tactor"	"FingerTac"	results
Activated	"External tactor"	84.2%	15.8%	$p < .001$
	"FingerTac"	46.2%	53.8%	n.s

Frequency detection subtask 1: All frequencies were detected correctly in 100% of the cases. Accordingly, subjects indicated that it was rather easy to detect these frequencies with ratings ranging from M = 1.6 to 2.2 (M(1.38 Hz) = 1.6; M(3.63 Hz) = 2.1; M(8 Hz) = 2.2; M(13.33 Hz) = 1.6).

Frequency detection subtask 2: We found detection rates above 90% for the both lower frequencies (92.3% for 1.38 Hz and 100% for 3.63 Hz) while detection rates for the both higher frequencies reached 83.3% (8 Hz) and 85.7% (13.33 Hz) (Table 3).

Table 3. Frequency detection subtask 2

			Detected			
			Green	Blue	Yellow	Red
Activated	Green	1.38 Hz	**92.3%**	7.7%	..	
	Blue	3.63 Hz	..	**100%**	..	..
	Yellow	8.00 Hz	..	16.7%	**83.3%**	..
	Red	13.33 Hz	..	..	14.3%	**85.7%**

The interrelation between activated and detected frequency was analyzed with Goodman und Kruskal's Lambda and showed a significant relation ($\lambda = .87$; $p < .001$). Although the difficulty ratings were higher compared to Task 1 they all ranged below the scale mean of M = 4 (M(1.38 Hz) = 2.1; M(3.63 Hz) = 2.9; M(8 Hz) = 3.6; M(13.33 Hz) = 3.3).

4   Conclusion

This paper introduced FingerTac, which is a novel concept for a wearable tactile device for mobile augmented haptic applications. Its uniqueness is that it combines, for the first time, augmented haptics on a wearable light-weight device. As a result, it makes possible simultaneous tactile interaction with virtual and real objects.

A set of two evaluation studies was conducted to evaluate the effectiveness of the approach. It was observed that vibration transmission over a mechanical link is expedient when compared to a vibration actuator in direct contact with the skin, because it can result in better localized tactile feedback and slimmer device design. It was observed from the second study that by providing stimulus to the sides of a fingertip, the vibrations were felt in-between at the fingerpad. Furthermore, it could be verified that such device may be used to distinguish between various objects by providing different vibration patterns. In particular, a relative discrimination and assignment of four vibration patterns with different pause periods was easy with a detection rate of 100%. An absolute mapping was still possible for more than 90% of all cases.

The next technological step is to design and build an integrated battery-powered version of the FingerTac device. This version may also contain enhancements, particularly with regard to additional sensors. It is also up to future work to investigate the relevance of the device for different mobile haptics applications. Since finger usage is task-dependent, using more than two fingers may be required for certain tasks. Thus, it would be essential for the user to get tactile feedback displayed on several fingers, which can be achieved using several FingerTac devices simultaneously.

References

1. Culbertson, H., Nunez, C.M., Israr, A., Lau, F., Abnousi, F., Okamura, A.M.: A social haptic device to create continuous lateral motion using sequential normal indentation. In: IEEE Haptics Symposium, pp. 32–39 (2018)
2. De Rossi, D., Carpi, F., Carbonaro, N., Tognetti, A., Scilingo, E.P.: Electroactive polymer patches for wearable haptic interfaces. In: International Conference of the IEEE Engineering in Medicine and Biology Society, pp. 8369–8372 (2011)
3. van Erp, J.B., van Veen, H.A.: A multi-purpose tactile vest for astronauts in the international space station. In: EuroHaptics, pp. 405–408. ACM Press, Dublin (2003)
4. Fani, S., Ciotti, S., Battaglia, E., Moscatelli, A., Bianchi, M.: W-FYD: a wearable fabric-based display for haptic multi-cue delivery and tactile augmented reality. IEEE Trans. Haptics 11(2), 304–316 (2017)
5. Gabardi, M., Solazzi, M., Leonardis, D., Frisoli, A.: A new wearable fingertip haptic interface for the rendering of virtual shapes and surface features. In: IEEE Haptics Symposium, pp. 140–146 (2016)
6. Gemperle, F., Ota, N., Siewiorek, D.: Design of a wearable tactile display. In: IEEE International Symposium on Wearable Computers, pp. 5–12 (2001)
7. Inoue, S., Makino, Y., Shinoda, H.: Active touch perception produced by airborne ultrasonic haptic hologram. In: IEEE World Haptics Conference (WHC), pp. 362–367 (2015)
8. Jones, L.A., Sarter, N.B.: Tactile displays: guidance for their design and application. Hum. Fac. 50(1), 90–111 (2008)
9. Komurasaki, S., Kajimoto, H., Ishizuka, H.: Fundamental perceptual characterization of an integrated tactile display with electrovibration and electrical stimuli. Micromachines 10(5), 301 (2019)
10. Leonardis, D., Solazzi, M., Bortone, I., Frisoli, A.: A 3-rsr haptic wearable device for rendering fingertip contact forces. IEEE Trans. Haptics 10(3), 305–316 (2016)
11. Long, B., Seah, S.A., Carter, T., Subramanian, S.: Rendering volumetric haptic shapes in mid-air using ultrasound. ACM Trans. Graph. (TOG) 33(6), 1–10 (2014)
12. Minamizawa, K., Fukamachi, S., Kajimoto, H., Kawakami, N., Tachi, S.: Gravity grabber: wearable haptic display to present virtual mass sensation. In: ACM SIGGRAPH Computer Graphics (2007)
13. Moy, G., Wagner, C., Fearing, R.S.: A compliant tactile display for teletaction. In: IEEE International Conference on Robotics and Automation (ICRA), vol. 4, pp. 3409–3415 (2000)
14. Mun, S., et al.: Electro-active polymer based soft tactile interface for wearable devices. IEEE Trans. Haptics 11(1), 15–21 (2018)
15. Nara, T., Takasaki, M., Tachi, S., Higuchi, T.: An application of saw to a tactile display in virtual reality. IEEE Ultrason. Symp. 1, 1–4 (2000)
16. Pacchierotti, C., Salvietti, G., Hussain, I., Meli, L., Prattichizzo, D.: The hRing: A wearable haptic device to avoid occlusions in hand tracking. In: IEEE Haptics Symposium, pp. 134–139. IEEE (2016)
17. Prattichizzo, D., Chinello, F., Pacchierotti, C., Malvezzi, M.: Towards wearability in fingertip haptics: a 3-dof wearable device for cutaneous force feedback. IEEE Trans. Haptics 6(4), 506–516 (2013)
18. Schätzle, S., Ende, T., Wuesthoff, T., Preusche, C.: VibroTac: an ergonomic and versatile usable vibrotactile feedback device. In: IEEE International Symposium in Robot and Human Interactive Communication (Ro-Man), Viareggio, Italy, pp. 705–710 (2010)

19. Schätzle, S., Hulin, T., Pleintinger, B.: VibroTac S: an electronic assistive device for blind and visually impaired people to avoid collisions. In: Ahram, T., Karwowski, W., Taiar, R. (eds.) IHSED 2018. AISC, vol. 876, pp. 613–619. Springer, Cham (2019). https://doi.org/10.1007/978-3-030-02053-8_94
20. Scheibe, R., Moehring, M., Froehlich, B.: Tactile feedback at the finger tips for improved direct interaction in immersive environments. In: IEEE Symposium on 3D User Interfaces (3DUI) (2007)
21. Schorr, S.B., Okamura, A.M.: Fingertip tactile devices for virtual object manipulation and exploration. In: CHI Conference on Human Factors in Computing Systems, pp. 3115–3119 (2017)
22. Singh, H., Suthar, B., Mehdi, S.Z., Ryu, J.H.: Ferro-fluid based portable fingertip haptic display and its preliminary experimental evaluation. In: IEEE Haptics Symposium, pp. 14–19 (2018)
23. Solazzi, M., Frisoli, A., Bergamasco, M.: Design of a cutaneous fingertip display for improving haptic exploration of virtual objects. In: International Symposium in Robot and Human Interactive Communication, pp. 1–6. IEEE (2010)
24. Spelmezan, D., González, R.M., Subramanian, S.: Skinhaptics: ultrasound focused in the hand creates tactile sensations. In: IEEE Haptics Symposium, pp. 98–105 (2016)
25. Tsukada, K., Yasumura, M.: ActiveBelt: belt-type wearable tactile display for directional navigation. In: Davies, N., Mynatt, E.D., Siio, I. (eds.) UbiComp 2004. LNCS, vol. 3205, pp. 384–399. Springer, Heidelberg (2004). https://doi.org/10.1007/978-3-540-30119-6_23
26. Velázquez, R., Pissaloux, E.E., Wiertlewski, M.: A compact tactile display for the blind with shape memory alloys. In: IEEE International Conference on Robotics and Automation (ICRA), pp. 3905–3910 (2006)
27. Yang, G.H., Kyung, K.U., Srinivasan, M.A., Kwon, D.S.: Quantitative tactile display device with pin-array type tactile feedback and thermal feedback. In: IEEE International Conference on Robotics and Automation (ICRA), pp. 3917–3922 (2006)
28. Yang, T.H., Kim, S.Y., Kim, C.H., Kwon, D.S., Book, W.J.: Development of a miniature pin-array tactile module using elastic and electromagnetic force for mobile devices. In: IEEE World Haptics Conference (WHC), pp. 13–17 (2009)

WIKNECTVR: A Gesture-Based Approach for Interacting in Virtual Reality Based on WIKNECT and Gestural Writing

Vincent Kühn[✉], Giuseppe Abrami, and Alexander Mehler

Texttechnology Lab, Goethe University Frankfurt, Robert-Mayer-Strasse 10,
60325 Frankfurt am Main, Germany
vincent.kuehn@stud.uni-frankfurt.de, {abrami,mehler}@em.uni-frankfurt.de,
https://www.texttechnologylab.org

Abstract. In recent years, the usability of interfaces in the field of *Virtual Realities* (VR) has massively improved, so that theories and applications of multimodal data processing can now be tested more extensively. In this paper we present an extension of VANNOTATOR, which is a VR-based open hypermedia system that is used for annotating, visualizing and interacting with multimodal data. We extend VANNOTATOR by a module for *gestural writing* that uses data gloves as an interface for VR. Our extension addresses the application scenario of WIKINECT, a museum information system, and its gesture palette for realizing gestural writing. To this end, we implement and evaluate seven gestures. The paper describes the training and recognition of these gestures and their use within the framework of a user-centered evaluation system for virtual museums as exemplified by WIKINECT.

Keywords: Gestural writing · WikiNect · VAnnotatoR · Multimodal annotation · Virtual Reality

1 Introduction

Recent developments of 3D glasses and other interfaces to *Virtual Realities* (VR) has enabled theories [11,12] and implementations of corresponding applications [15]. Such applications allow users to immerse themselves in virtual action contexts and scenarios. To achieve this immersion, the corresponding interfaces must be as intuitive as possible. This is no trivial task, as Erra et al. [3] make clear given the 3D glasses currently available. These glasses are controlled by hand controls, whose buttons can be assigned various functions. However, the use of such controllers leads to a limitation of the learning curves of users (due to a lack of intuitive handling) and the number of executable controls is limited by

© Springer Nature Switzerland AG 2020
J. Y. C. Chen and G. Fragomeni (Eds.): HCII 2020, LNCS 12190, pp. 299–312, 2020.
https://doi.org/10.1007/978-3-030-49695-1_20

the hardware. While such controllers may be sufficient for common applications, they are largely unsuitable for immersive control that requires the free use of hands for gesture formation.

A more realistic perspective is achieved by evaluating gestures or body movements to control applications. In this paper we present such a gestural control in the area of VR systems. More specifically, we describe an extension of VANNOTATOR [1,10,14] by means of a gesture-based control that uses data gloves as an interface for VR. VANNOTATOR is an open hypermedia system designed for annotating, visualizing and interacting with multimedia content (texts, images, their segments and relations, videos, audios, 3D objects, 3D buildings, etc.). Starting from the notion of *gestural writing* as introduced in [12] we develop a writing system that allows users to navigate and interact with objects in VANNOTATOR just by using gestures. Gestural writing means to use only indexical or iconic gestures to gesture parts of propositional acts and thus to make assertions about the reference objects involved. Analogous to pictograms, Mehler et al. [12] call such gestures *gestograms*. That is, gestograms are iconic or indexical gestures with a referential or predicative meaning. In this paper, we implement and test a subset of the gestures proposed in [12] for gestural writing. We describe the training and recognition of these gestures and their use within the framework of a user-centered evaluation system for virtual museums. This application scenario is based on WIKINECT [11], a museum information system that here is reimplemented in VR.

The paper is organized as follows: Sect. 2 gives a brief overview of related work. Sect. 4 describes the architecture of our implementation of gestural writing. Sect. 6 provides an evaluation of our system. Finally, Sect. 7 gives a summary and an outlook on future work.

2   Related Work

The gesture-based control of software is not a new topic. In this area there are a number of projects as described by Xue et al. [18]. Several of these projects use *Kinect* (c.f. [19]). Jambursia et al. [6], for example, describe a system for recognizing hand signs with *Kinect*. An alternative is proposed by Drossis et al. [2] who describe a system for navigating in virtual environments by the help of *Leap Motion*. Marin et al. [9] present a combination of *Leap Motion* and *Kinect*. It utilizes a multi-class SVM classifier without using 3D glasses. However, detection is not limited to data gloves or sensors such as those provided by Leap Motion. Ghosh and Ari [4] use image recognition techniques to detect gestures. The use of data gloves as hand-related data input for neural networks is described in [13,17]. As far as we know, there is no implementation yet that supports gestural writing in virtual environments, so it is worth taking this step, as explained in the next sections.

3   Application Context

The application scenario on which our implementation of gestural writing builds is WikiNect [12]. WikiNect is a museum information and annotation system that helps museum visitors to document and evaluate or even recommend their museum visit on site. WikiNect serves, among other things, to replace analog, usually offline communication in this area by digital online communication. In this context, Mehler et al. [12] developed a theory for the formation of gestures on the basis of Lakoff's theory of image schemata [8]. These gestures serve to implement gestural writing with the task of enabling the latter type of online communication. While WikiNect is designed as an information system that is used on site with *Kinect*, we opted for VAnnotatoR as the environment for transferring WikiNect to VR, henceforth called WikiNectVR. For this extension of VAnnotatoR, seven gestures were selected and implemented using data gloves (*Hi5*[1]). By the use of these gloves a more exact assignment of hand positions is possible. Compared to visual recognition systems such as *Kinect* and *Leap Motion*, these positions can also be recognized without direct visual contact. The usage of gestures is promising in several respects:

1. The control of software can be made more flexible and intuitive through gestures. Whether you need to navigate in a virtual browser, select, segment or link objects, all these operations can be simplified by gestures: selections are then made by indexical gestures, links are established by drawing edges from the respective source to the target, segmentations by drawing polygons or ellipses etc.
2. Even the input and use of linguistic information can be accelerated. In WikiNectVR, users can trigger Natural Language Processing (NLP) gesturally. For this purpose, WikiNectVR uses the NLP interface of VAnnotatoR for TextImager [5] to preprocess text input in a variety of languages. As a consequence, users may gesturally refer to a visual depiction of a discourse referent (e.g. a person) in order to automatically select all text segments referring to it.

As a result of these enhancements, WikiNectVR as a prototype allows its users to annotate, segment, link and evaluate virtualized museum tours and their virtualized artifacts and finally to network in online social communities for this purpose. As a special application scenario for testing gestural writing in WikiNectVR, we focus on the evaluation and rating system of WikiNect: The evaluation system in WikiNect allows users to rate a picture given one or two categories (e.g. emotions or style). In comparison to other ratings systems the results are displayed in a different way and show up as a new picture. The style is based on the paintings of Piet Mondrian. A picture is vertically and horizontally divided with black lines and each of the resulting rectangles is filled with a color. The rectangles may vary in size depending on the salience of the underlying evaluation. In WikiNect the size and the color of a rectangle is

---

[1] https://hi5vrglove.com/.

given through the user's answers in the rating system. The implementation of WIKINECTVR is realized with Unity3D[2] as described in the following section.

4 Implementation

A first implementation and evaluation of WIKINECTVR's gesture palette is described in [7]. The implementation contains two parts: gesture learning and gesture recognition. We start with explaining the second step.

4.1 Gesture Recognition

We use a feed-forward neural network based on [16] for gesture recognition. It uses all information collected from data gloves to recognize the corresponding gesture based on hand positioning data. In order to generalize input data, we perform preprocessing. To this end, we represent each finger by two vectors: The first one starts at the wrist, the second one at the basal finger joint, both vectors end at the fingertip. By these two vectors, we represent and distinguish the different finger orientations. In addition to the fingers' individual positions, the position and rotation of the respective hand is processed. Rotation data is represented in the normal vector of the hand. The vectors are collected by an agent as the binding element between the neural network and the rest of the gesture recognition system. Since learning is done with policy optimization, the agent/network is rewarded or punished with the same value as it has shown for the best results.

When a gesture is generated by the user, it is recognized by the network and the result is transmitted to WIKINECTVR's *GestureController*. Since the gesture recognition takes place in real time, the controller is constantly confronted with new gestures. In order to prevent a gesture from being triggered unintentionally, the controller verifies whether or not past decisions contained the same gesture. In this way, we reduce the probability of false positives.

4.2 Gesture Learning

Since neural networks can hardly be trained in real time, the gestures to be learned must be collected in a training corpus. For this purpose, we generated the so-called *Frankfurt GESTural writing corpus* (FGEST) which is available via GitHub[3].

It stores each individual gesture token together with its hand and finger orientation and rotation data as required by our neural network for training. FGEST recorded and represented 300 tokens for each gesture to be learned where these tokens have been generated by five different persons. In principle, this approach makes it possible to calculate different models or classifiers for

---

[2] https://unity.com.
[3] https://github.com/texttechnologylab/FGEST.

the same or different gestures. We used a learning rate of $3e - 4$ as the policy optimization showed the best results compared to a smaller one (e.g. $1e - 5$) An LSTM was also used, but did not achieve as good learning outcomes as the Feed Forward network. This may be because the LSTM takes more time to perform a step and therefore requires longer training times (Fig. 1).

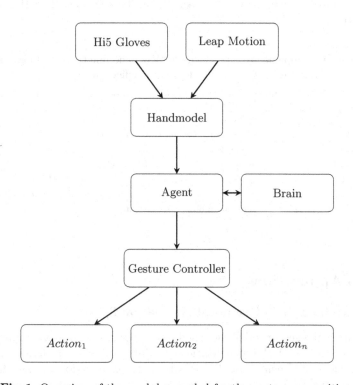

Fig. 1. Overview of the modules needed for the gesture recognition.

Gestures. Starting from the gesture palette described in [12], we trained and evaluated seven gestures (Table 1). First of all, this relates to the POINT gesture (henceforth denoted by →) that is implemented to allow for selecting objects. To gesturally indicate a user's wish to go forward or backward within the rating system of WIKINECTVR, and, thus, to enter the rating of the next or the last object, we introduce two gestures: the GREATERTHAN (>) and the SMALLERTHAN (<) gesture. Both are created in front of the user's torso where the SMALLERTHAN gesture inverts the direction into which the GREATERTHAN gesture is created (Fig. 2).

The search function requires two gestures to trigger searches in a search context. To this end, we implement the so-called ISEQUAL (==) and the ISUNEQUAL (!=) gesture. The ISEQUAL gesture is formed with both hands, which iconically represent an equal sign. The ISEQUAL gesture is performed by positioning the flat palms orthogonally to each other (Fig. 3).

With these gestures a (museum) visitor of WIKINECTVR can select pictures
(P), artists (A) or museums (M) by means of the POINT gesture and the gestures
described before. Reference objects of a pointing gesture can denote classes (e.g.
the class of paintings $\mathbb{P}$) or single entities (e.g. a concrete person such as an
artist A_i). As there are different application scenarios which the user can select
he needs a possibility to switch between them. This is done with the so called
AND gesture.

Table 1. Gestures implemented in WIKINECTVR. The functions in italics have been
implemented only in the WIKINECTVR for the specified purpose.

Gesture	Notation	Function
GREATERTHAN	>	go forward (rating system scenario)
SMALLERTHAN	<	go backward (rating system scenario)
NEGATION	!	*deselect the active rating field (rating system)*
ISEQUAL	==	*search the cutting quantity of objects*
ISUNEQUAL	!=	*search the symmetric difference of the objects*
AND	∧	*switch between the museum graph and the search interface*
POINT	→	click on an object or select it

5   Two Applications

5.1   WIKINECTVR's Graphical Navigation System

For evaluating the gestures distinguished so far, two use cases were implemented.
As described in Sect. 1 the visualization and interaction with virtual objects is
evaluated and tested using VR. For this purpose, a scenario was used from the
museum context. To this end, museum content was visualized as a graph in VR
(*museum graph*). The data refers to paintings, their artists, current exhibition
venues and data about artists and their paintings. In this simplified virtual
museum, visitors can view paintings and associated information, such as *label*,
the *year of creation* and *artist* (Fig. 6).

At the same time, pictures of single artists can be selected. By visiting the
virtual museum, a graph is created that enables various possibilities of interaction
with the images. On the one hand, all functionalities described in [10], such as
image segmentation and annotation, can be performed. On the other hand, the
virtual paintings, based on WIKINECT, can be rated along different categories.
The latter is described in Sect. 5.2. The interface is controlled by gestures that
are listed in Table 1 and can be assigned to various operations. In accordance
with the implemented gesture set, various operations were defined.

As a visitor of this virtual museum, the user is positioned within the virtual
museum graph, in which he or she can switch back and forth between individual
nodes. The graph itself is projected onto the virtual museum floor, where neighboring nodes at a distance of 2 are displayed as shown in Fig. 5. By selecting a

node using the GREATERTHAN gesture, the user moves to the target node. At the same time, it is possible to search within the graph using the AND gesture.

Fig. 2. Visualization of the GREATERTHAN gesture.

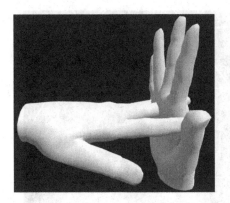 

Fig. 3. Visualization of the IsUNEQUAL gesture.   **Fig. 4.** Visualization of the AND gesture.

The search interface is also represented through a graph structure. When a search is initialized, representations of searchable objects types (e.g. images or painters) show up around the user as nodes (Fig. 7). Afterwards there are several possibilities to use this view: The user can select certain objects for which additional information is to be displayed. Or a class of object is referred to, e.g. artists, so that all instances of this class are selected. After selecting a group objects (see Fig. 6) it is possible to make further selections in the resulting context by means of corresponding search gestures (Fig. 4).

5.2 WIKINECTVR's Rating Interface

In addition to being able to obtain information about paintings, users can also rate them. The rating interface, which can be used for any object in the virtual museum (and not only for images), basically implements the interface model of [12]. The rating interface utilizes three gestures. The first one is the POINT gesture for object selection. The next two gestures are the GREATERTHAN and the SMALLERTHAN gesture. They allow users to move forward or backward. Before rating an object, the user has to select it together with at least two rating categories for spanning a matrix (see Fig. 8). Each rating is visualized through a cube showing a Mondrian-style painting on its surface. They are placed in front of a partially transparent image of the object to show the link between an object and its rating. The ratings are made visible by the color and size of the fields on the surface of the cube (for example, a larger field in the upper right area means that more good ratings were given).

When the user has made his or her choice, the valuation interface appears together with a row or matrix showing the valuation gradations (see Fig. 10). The Mondrian-style painting on the right-hand side (see Fig. 9) gets updated and the next evaluation criterion is displayed. If the user needs to review or change his previous ratings, he can return to the relevant criterion and update it. Once

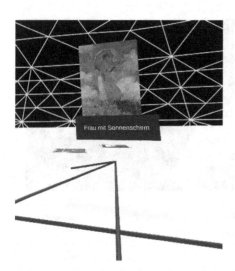

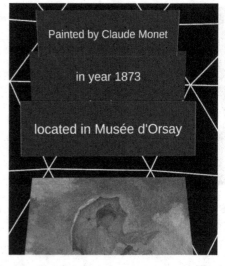

Fig. 5. Visualization of the virtual museum. The user is located relative to the node as part of the virtual museum graph representing an artist and can see one of his paintings.

Fig. 6. Further information about the selected painting can be displayed; in this case, the artist, the year of creation and the museum in which the painting is exhibited are shown. Red highlighted attributes were selected using the POINT gesture and joined as described in Sect. 5 using the EQUAL gesture. (Color figure online)

the evaluation is complete, the user has the possibility to see his results or get an overview of all evaluations.

6   Evaluation

We evaluate our gesture recognition tool in the context of gestural writing. To this end, the test persons had to write five test sentences gesturally using our gesture palette. In this case, the gestures are used to connect objects with each other. There are sentences which concern the gestural connection of two objects, and sentences in which three objects are affected. Therefore, the user annotates three sentences with two objects and two sentences with three different objects in the evaluation. For this purpose, the objects must be selected by the annotator and linked with a gesture of our gesture palette.

All objects represented in the annotation scenario can be annotated using the sentences in Table 2.

For illustration we look at the following example: "The armchair is bigger than the chair" (see Fig. 11). The annotators are now requested to select the objects *armchair* and *chair* and link them using the GREATERTHAN gesture. The user input is displayed in three blue input fields, with a gesture expected in every second field. The input is only changed when the user looks at the specific field to prevent side effects such as incorrectly selected objects or gestures. After the annotator has selected the objects and the gesture, the input is evaluated and visual feedback is given: A correct annotation is visualized in green, a wrong in red.

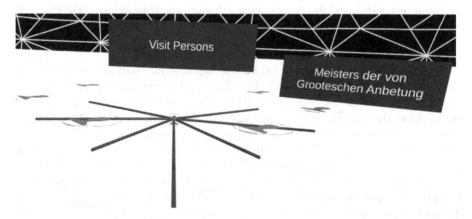

Fig. 7. A view on painters mapped by the *museum graph*. The user initialized the search layout while looking on the painters section.

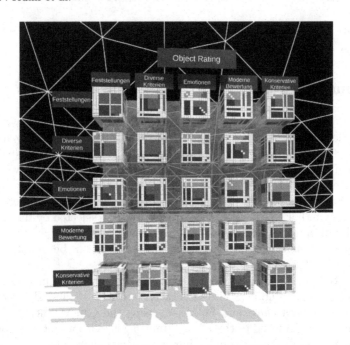

Fig. 8. To rate a picture it has to be selected using the GREATERTHAN gesture. The resulting rating view shows the image (transparent) in the background with the available category matrix in the foreground. In this example, five evaluation categories connected with 10 questions, each of which can be used individually or in combination with another categories, are distinguished. The fields in the evaluation matrix are filled with the results of previous evaluations. The results are represented in Mondrian style. A new rating is performed simply by selecting the corresponding element. The diagonal items represent the one-dimensional evaluation categories.

In total, the evaluation included 12 participants, all studying computer science, nine of whom were male and three female. The evaluated parameters are the time it takes for the test person to manifest the sentence and whether he has selected the correct gestures and objects. This distinction is important in order to differentiate whether the selection was wrong or whether the target gesture was not recognized. For result No. 2 (Table 3), it should be noted that not all gestures have the same recognition rate. In addition, for result No. 3, some gestures were not separate enough, so that wrong objects were selected. The best gesture has a rate higher than 92%. The EQUAL gesture is the one with the lowest rate. This variance between the gestures may result from the training data. Since the EQUAL gesture is a static gesture, we assume that there was not enough accurate training data. To minimize this type of error, the neural network needs more training data to better distinguish the gestures.

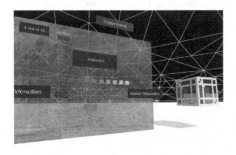

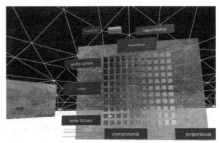

Fig. 9. The visualization of a one-dimensional rating category. The painting to be rated is transparent in the background and the current question is shown in the foreground. Below the rating scale one finds descriptions of the maximums. The scale covers a range from −5 to +5 including zero. A progress bar is displayed at the top. On the right side of the rating panel is a Mondrian visualization of the result, which changes with each rating.

Fig. 10. The rating panel with two categories. The structure is similar to the panel with only one category. The difference, however, is the expansion from one to two scales. On the left side, the image is displayed non-transparent. Not visible, but still present is the result as a Mondrian-style visualization on the right side of the rating panel.

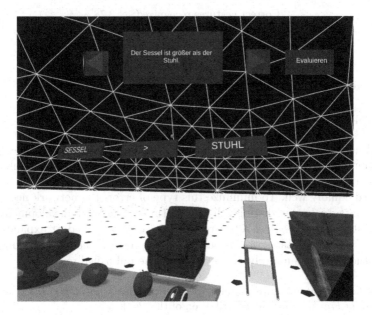

Fig. 11. An example sentence of the evaluation (in German language). Translation: "The armchair is bigger than the chair" and it is written on the big blue panel at the top. Below it, one sees three blue boxes that visualize the selected objects and the gestures of the evaluators. It means that *Armchair > Chair*. (Color figure online)

Table 2. Evaluation sentences and the corresponding objects to be selected with the linking gesture.

Sentence	Relation
The *chair* is smaller than the *armchair*	chair < armchair
The *plant* is more expensive than the *mouse*	plant > mouse
The *armchair* is bigger than the *chair*	armchair > chair
The *apple* and the *kiwi* are different	apple ≠ kiwi
The *kiwi* tastes as good as the *apple*	kiwi = apple
The *chair* is not an *armchair*	chair ≠ armchair
The *sofa* is not only larger than the *chair*, but also larger than the *armchair*	sofa > chair & sofa > armchair
The *armchair* is larger than the *chair*, but it is smaller than the *sofa*	sofa > armchair > chair

Table 3. Evaluation results based on 12 participants.

No.	Category	Result
1	Correct sentences reconstructed	70%
2	Correct gestures recognized	78%
3	Correct objects selected	82%

7 Conclusion and Future Work

In this paper, we presented a gesture-based, virtual approach to WIKINECT by means of the VANNOTATOR. For recognizing our gesture alphabet, we trained a neural network by using a corpus of 400 data units per gesture. The gesture recognition was then evaluated by means of 12 test persons. As a result of our evaluation, promising results were achieved, although the gestures were not all recognized equally well. To minimize this type of error, the network needs more training data to better distinguish the gestures. The next development steps of our gesture-based control software will therefore be aimed at expanding the amount of training data as well as our gesture alphabet. The corresponding data of this study and the underlying software will be published on GitHub.

Acknowledgement. We are grateful to the *Scholarship Fund for Teaching at the University of Frankfurt* for the contribution of this work.

References

1. Abrami, G., Mehler, A., Spiekermann, C.: Graph-based format for modeling multimodal annotations in virtual reality by means of VAnnotatoR. In: Stephanidis, C., Antona, M. (eds.) HCII 2019. CCIS, vol. 1088, pp. 351–358. Springer, Cham (2019). https://doi.org/10.1007/978-3-030-30712-7_44
2. Drossis, G., Birliraki, C., Margetis, G., Stephanidis, C.: Immersive 3D environment for data centre monitoring based on gesture based interaction. In: Stephanidis, C. (ed.) HCI 2017. CCIS, vol. 713, pp. 103–108. Springer, Cham (2017). https://doi.org/10.1007/978-3-319-58750-9_14
3. Erra, U., Malandrino, D., Pepe, L.: Virtual reality interfaces for interacting with three-dimensional graphs. Int. J. Hum.-Comput. Interact. **35**(1), 75–88 (2019). https://doi.org/10.1080/10447318.2018.1429061
4. Ghosh, D., Ari, S.: A static hand gesture recognition algorithm using k-mean based radial basis function neural network (2011)
5. Hemati, W., Uslu, T., Mehler, A.: Textimager: a distributed UIMA-based system for NLP. In: Proceedings of the COLING 2016 System Demonstrations. Federated Conference on Computer Science and Information Systems (2016)
6. Jambusaria, U., Katwala, N., Kadam, M., Narula, H.: Finger writing in air using kinect. Int. J. Comput. Sci. Inf. Technol. (IJCSIT) **5**(6), 8119–8121 (2014)
7. Kühn, V.R.: A gesture-based interface to VR. Bachelor Thesis, Goethe University of Frankfurt (2018). http://publikationen.ub.uni-frankfurt.de/frontdoor/index/index/docId/50915
8. Lakoff, G.: Women, Fire, and Dangerous Things. University of Chicago press, Chicago (1987)
9. Marin, G., Dominio, F., Zanuttigh, P.: Hand gesture recognition with leap motion and kinect devices. In: 2014 IEEE International Conference on Image Processing (ICIP), pp. 1565–1569 (2014). https://doi.org/10.1109/ICIP.2014.7025313
10. Mehler, A., Abrami, G., Spiekermann, C., Jostock, M.: VAnnotatoR: a framework for generating multimodal hypertexts. In: Proceedings of the 29th ACM Conference on Hypertext and Social Media, Proceedings of the 29th ACM Conference on Hypertext and Social Media (HT 2018). ACM, New York (2018). https://doi.org/10.1145/3209542.3209572
11. Mehler, A., Lücking, A.: WikiNect: Towards a gestural writing system for kinetic museum wikis. In: Proceedings of the 2012 ACM Workshop on User Experience in e-Learning and Augmented Technologies in Education, UXeLATE 20(2012). https://doi.org/10.1145/2390895.2390899
12. Mehler, A., Lücking, A., Abrami, G.: WikiNect: image schemata as a basis of gestural writing for kinetic museum wikis. Univ. Access Inf. Soc. **14**(3), 333–349 (2014). https://doi.org/10.1007/s10209-014-0386-8
13. Murakami, K., Taguchi, H.: Gesture recognition using recurrent neural networks (1991)
14. Spiekermann, C., Abrami, G., Mehler, A.: VAnnotatoR: a gesture-driven annotation framework for linguistic and multimodal annotation. In: Proceedings of the Annotation, Recognition and Evaluation of Actions (AREA 2018) Workshop. AREA (2018)
15. Tecchia, F., Avveduto, G., Brondi, R., Carrozzino, M., Bergamasco, M., Alem, L.: I'm in vr!: using your own hands in a fully immersive MR system. In: Proceedings of the 20th ACM Symposium on Virtual Reality Software and Technology, VRST 2014, pp. 73–76. ACM, New York (2014). https://doi.org/10.1145/2671015.2671123, http://doi.acm.org/10.1145/2671015.2671123

16. Unity Technologies: Unity ML-Agents Toolkit Documentation (2018). https://github.com/Unity-Technologies/ml-agents/blob/master/docs/Readme.md

17. Weissmann, J., Salomon, R.: Gesture recognition for virtual reality applications using data gloves and neural networks (1999)

18. Xue, L., Parker, C.J., McCormick, H.: A virtual reality and retailing literature review: current focus, underlying themes and future directions. In: tom Dieck, M.C., Jung, T. (eds.) Augmented Reality and Virtual Reality. PI, pp. 27–41. Springer, Cham (2019). https://doi.org/10.1007/978-3-030-06246-0_3

19. Zhang, X., Ye, Z., Jin, L., Feng, Z., Xu, S.: A new writing experience: finger writing in the air using a kinect sensor. IEEE MultiMedia **20**(4), 85–93 (2013). https://doi.org/10.1109/MMUL.2013.50

An Empirical Evaluation on Arm Fatigue in Free Hand Interaction and Guidelines for Designing Natural User Interfaces in VR

Xiaolong Lou[1,2(✉)], Xiangdong Li[3], Preben Hansen[4],
and Zhipeng Feng[1]

[1] School of Digital Media and Design, Hangzhou Dianzi University,
Hangzhou, People's Republic of China
{xlou, fengzhipeng}@hdu.edu.cn
[2] State Key Lab for Novel Software Technology,
Nanjing University, Nanjing, People's Republic of China
[3] College of Computer Science and Technology, Zhejiang University,
Hangzhou, People's Republic of China
axli@zju.edu.cn
[4] College of Computer Science and Management, Stockholm University,
Stockholm, Sweden
preben@dsv.su.se

Abstract. This research had a systematic study on arm fatigue issue in free hand interaction in VR environment and explored how arm fatigue influenced free hand interaction accuracy. A specifically designed target-acquisition experiment was conducted with 24 volunteered participants (7 left-handedness, 17 right-handedness) recruited. The experiment results indicated that (1) arm fatigue resulted in short durations of hand operation, or frequent alternations of operating hand. The user's dominant hand had a more durable operation than the non-dominant one; (2) hand operate position had a significant effect on arm fatigue level, a bent arm posture was found to be more labor-saving than an extended arm posture, (3) hand operation at a higher position (e.g., at the head height) perceived arm fatigue more easily than that at a lower position (e.g., at the waist height); and (4) arm fatigue impact hand interaction accuracy negatively.

Keywords: Free hand interaction · Arm fatigue · Handedness · Interaction accuracy

1 Introduction

The popularity of virtual reality (VR) has benefited a wide range of fields, such as education [1], sports training [2], rehabilitation [3] and entertainments [4]. Especially in recent years, due to a rapid development of sensing technologies, VR has become the most representative platform for conducting natural human-computer interaction tasks [5]. In these tasks, users directly acquire and operate with virtual objects as if in the real world. Therefore, object acquisition by free hand is the most fundamental operation in

© Springer Nature Switzerland AG 2020
J. Y. C. Chen and G. Fragomeni (Eds.): HCII 2020, LNCS 12190, pp. 313–324, 2020.
https://doi.org/10.1007/978-3-030-49695-1_21

VR applications. It is of great significance to investigate such a basic operation and based on this to develop guidelines for designing more efficient natural user interfaces (NUIs) in VR.

In physical world, free hand operation is intuitive and labor-saving. For example, when a user acquires and manipulates a mouse on a desk, he or she can put the arm on the desk without having the arm raised. In a VR environment, however, free hand operation is more labored and less natural. The most important reason is that physical support and haptic feedback are often lacking in such an environment [6]. In performing free hand interaction tasks in VR, the user needs to keep the arm raised in mid-air all the time. From this perspective, operation unsustainability and arm fatigue are obvious usability deficiencies in free hand interaction that need to be considered and alleviated in future VR applications.

In this paper, we conducted an object-acquisition experiment to investigate the arm fatigue problem and its effect on interaction task efficiency, and based on these to conclude guidelines for building more efficient and easier-to-use NUIs in VR. We investigated the relationship between arm posture and arm fatigue level, and proved that hand operation height, angle and distance had respective influences on arm fatigue level. Arm posture the user performs in target acquisition is relevant to the spatial position of the target. For example, when the target is located at a near and high position, the user raises the hand to acquire the target through a bent arm posture; but when the target is located at a far and low position, the user puts the hand down and stretches the arm to acquire it, as shown in Fig. 1.

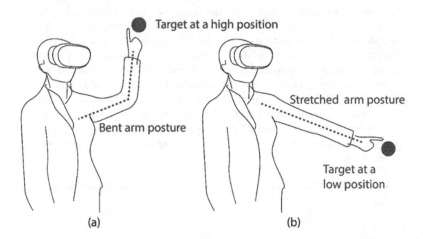

Fig. 1. User's arm postures and target positions in target acquisition tasks.

To the best of our knowledge, this research is the precedent work which systematically investigates free hand operation fatigue in VR environment. More specifically, this paper presents the relationship between arm posture and arm fatigue level in free hand interaction and summarizes guidelines for designing more usable and efficient natural user interfaces (NUIs) in VR. The main contributions of this paper can be summarized as follows:

1) This is the first work to differentiate arm postures in terms of hand operation height, angle and distance, which provides a novel framework for analyzing arm posture and arm fatigue level.
2) This work proved that UI layout and target position in VR not only influenced free hand interaction accuracy and efficiency but also had a close correlation with arm fatigue level, which suggested strategies for improving usability of UIs in VR.

2 Related Work

Free hand interaction, i.e., a natural interaction modality through arm movements and bare hand gestures, has been broadly researched over the last decades. Compared to mouse- and Wii controller- mediated interactions, hand direct interaction has advantages in higher intuitiveness and convenience [7]. In temporary interaction with interactive advertisings in shopping malls, for instance, it is inconvenient for passers-by to take out phones or pick up specific devices to interact with the digital content on a display; but direction interaction by free hand is more acceptable and preferred in such situations.

In addition to the advantages, free hand interaction also has deficiencies, such as ambiguity of hand gestures and inaccuracy in arm movements [8]. Quite a few technologies have been proposed to address these deficiencies. For example, Vogel and Balakrishnan [7] have proposed to adopt a high-precision motion-tracking system, i.e., Vicon system, to make gestural interaction more accurate. But Haque et al. [9] had taken use of an EMG sensor worn on the user's arm to implement a precise hand interaction.

Arm fatigue is another common problem in free hand interaction. Hincapié-Ramos et al. [10] have proposed a metric – *consumed endurance (CE)* – to quantitatively measure arm fatigue level and proven that the arm posture, e.g., bent and extend, and the hand operating height, e.g., shoulder height and waist height, are two critical factors in free hand interaction fatigue. More specifically, hand interaction at a lower height of the waist with the arm bent is more labor-saving than that at the shoulder height with the arm extended. But in practical free hand interaction tasks such as target acquisition in VR, hand gesture variations not only refer to hand operating height and arm bend posture, but also include arm operation angle in relative to the body which has seldom been concerned in previous research. This paper deemed that it is necessary to systematically evaluate arm fatigue level in different conditions of hand operation height, angle and distance. The arm fatigue problem has been pointed out to cause spontaneous alternation of the operating hand [11]. From this perspective, we support that hand operate duration can be used to measure arm fatigue level, a more durable operation indicates that the arm perceives fatigue less easily, or a lower fatigue level.

3 Methodology

This research designed and conducted a target acquisition experiment in a specifically designed VR application and evaluated hand operation fatigue level in different conditions of target height, angle and distance in relative to the user's operating hand. Task performance, such as error rate of target acquisition, operating hand duration and post-task user assessment on fatigue level were collected and analyzed.

3.1 Participants

Twenty-four volunteered participants (15 males and 9 females) aged from 19 to 33 were recruited. All the participants had normal or corrected-to-normal vision, without self-reported physical impairments. Seven of them were left-handedness while other seventeen were right-handedness. Through the measurement tool of the VR HMD's configuration utility, the inter-pupillary distance (IPD) of the participants were measured, ranging from 6.90 cm to 7.60 cm (M = 7.05, SD = 0.48). Given the IPD data, the HMD was tuned to provide a correct perspective and stereoscopic rendering for each participant.

3.2 Apparatus

The experiment was conducted in a VR laboratory. An Oculus Rift HMD (developer kit) with two Touch controllers were used, and the HMD was connected to a workstation computer (Win10, 64 GB memory, and 4.0 GHz Intel 32-core processor) through a 5-meter-long cable. The workstation was also connected to a monitor in 40 in., which was provided for supervising visual field in VR scene. The Oculus HMD offers a nominal diagonal field of vision (FOV) of approximately 100° at a resolution of 1920 * 1080 pixels (960 * 1080 pixels for each eye). Two IR cameras were respectively mounted on a desk to track spatial positions and movements of the HMD and the Touch controller. A motion-sensing camera of ASUS Xtion PRO^{TM} was mounted on the desk to recognize and track the user's operating hand.

3.3 Procedure

The experimenter used the Unity3D engine in C# to develop a specific target acquisition VR application. In this application, a stereoscopic scene was rendered and a yellow-colored target appeared at random positions in field of vision (FOV). A virtual hand was rendered to represent the operator's working hand. Each participant was required to complete 12 task blocks. Each block consisted of 300 target acquisition trials. In each trial, a yellow-colored sphere (i.e., a target with a diameter of 3.0 cm) was presented at a random position. The participant was required to move the controller to touch the target and then the target turned to a blue color (to give a visual cue), the participant pressed the button on the controller to complete a target acquisition trial.

After each trial, the target disappeared and a new one showed at another random position. From one to another, the participant needed to continuously complete 300 acquisition trials until the application program terminated automatically. During each block, once the participant perceived arm fatigue, he or she could report to the experimenter and alternate the hand. The moments of hand alternation were identified and recorded by the experimenter as well as the program. When acquiring a target, if the participant triggered the controller button without touching the target, an error was identified. The error times and related target positions were recorded by the program.

Before the formal blocks, the participant was given an introduction about the research purpose and task requirements. They were also given enough time to practice and get familiar with the experiment tasks. In formal blocks, the participants were required to continuously complete all trials. All participants adopted the operating hand alternately, for example, in the first block used the left hand firstly while in the second block used the right hand firstly. Hand adoption order was count balanced among participants, namely a half of participants firstly used their left hand in the first block; but the other half of participants firstly used their right hand in the first block. Between two blocks, each participant was given 5 min to relax arms and eyes.

3.4 Experimental Design

In this research, a 2 (hand orientation) × 2 (target distance) × 2 (target direction) × 3 (target height) repeated-measures within-participant design was adopted. Every participant completed 12 task blocks, and each block is a combination of different target distance, direction and height. Hand orientation, target distance (or hand operate distance), target direction (or hand operate direction) and target height (or hand operate height) were chosen as independent variables. Hand orientation refers to the choice of operating hand in interaction. Figure 2 gives an illustration about the arm posture variations in different conditions of target direction, distance and height in relative to the center of the body.

As shown in Fig. 2(a), target direction or hand operate direction was classified into 2 categories: at left-sided direction and at right-sided direction; as shown in Fig. 2(b), different target distances correspond to different arm bend levels. A large distance corresponds to an extended arm posture, but a close distance corresponds to a bent arm posture; as shown in Fig. 2(c), the user either raises the hand up to acquire the target over the head or puts the hand down to catch the target at the waist height.

In this research, 2 target directions, 2 target distance (large and close distance) and 3 target heights were chosen. Table 1 presents a summary about the independent variables, experimental design and measurement metrics. Quantitative performance data, such as error rate of target acquisition and hand duration in different combinations of independent variables were collected and analyzed. In addition, one 7-point Likert scale of NASA-TLX [12] was adopted to measure the user's assessment on fatigue level, plus user's subjective feedback after the task blocks.

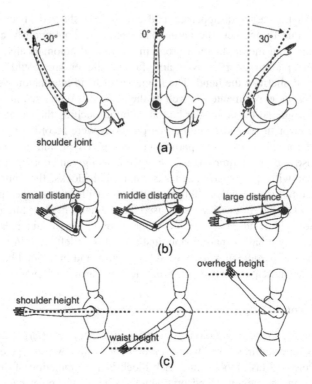

Fig. 2. An illustration of arm posture variations: (a) target direction in relative to the body center, e.g., at the left-sided and right-sided directions; (b) target distance, different distances result in different arm bend level; (c) target height, or hand operate height.

Table 1. Independent variables, experimental design and measurement metrics.

Independent variables	Experimental design	Measurement metrics	
• Hand orientation: (1) Left hand (2) Right hand	Within-participant	Quantitative	• Target acquisition error rate • Hand duration
• Target direction: (1) Left-sided direction (2) Right-sided direction			
• Target distance: (1) 25 cm (2) 50 cm		Qualitative	• NASA-TLX scale assessment • Post-task feedback
• Target height: (1) Head (2) Shoulder (3) Waist			

4   Analyses and Results

Each participant completed 12 task blocks and each block generated one task log file, thus a total of 288 (24 participants × 12 blocks per participant) log files were collected. Each log file recorded error times of target acquisition and related target direction, distance and height information, as well as moments of hand alternation. All results were analyzed by repeated-measures ANOVA with post-hoc Tukey HSD test, and two-tailed dependent T-test for paired comparisons. All reported results were significant at least at the $p < 0.05$ level.

4.1   Hand Interaction Duration and Accuracy

As interpreted in previous, hand operation fatigue has a close correlation with hand operate duration. A shorter duration or a more frequent alternation of operating hand represents that the user perceives arm fatigue more easily. Based on this, this research chose hand interaction duration to quantitatively evaluate arm fatigue level. Besides, hand interaction accuracy (i.e., accuracy of target acquisition) and its correlation with arm fatigue level were measured. To evaluate the handedness effect on hand duration result, this paper comparatively analyzed the performance data of the left-handed and right-handed participants. Table 2 presents a summary about the hand interaction duration result in different conditions of handedness, operating hand orientation, target distance, direction and height.

Table 2. A summary about the hand interaction duration results.

Handedness	Operating hand	Target distance	Target height	Mean hand duration (second)	Std. dev.
Left-handed	Left hand	25 cm	Overhead	270.8	37.86
			Shoulder	294.1	42.55
			Waist	326.5	52.48
		50 cm	Overhead	221.4	33.83
			Shoulder	253.9	34.62
			Waist	289.2	45.59
	Right hand	25 cm	Overhead	211.9	26.66
			Shoulder	242.9	36.57
			Waist	265.5	35.18
		50 cm	Overhead	152.7	21.54
			Shoulder	195.8	24.59
			Waist	226.3	37.44

(continued)

Table 2. (*continued*)

Handedness	Operating hand	Target distance	Target height	Mean hand duration (second)	Std. dev.
Right-handed	Left hand	25 cm	Overhead	213.8	30.44
			Shoulder	230.2	31.74
			Waist	277.7	38.57
		50 cm	Overhead	142.5	26.31
			Shoulder	208.8	26.41
			Waist	232.3	29.39
	Right hand	25 cm	Overhead	266.1	38.48
			Shoulder	284.6	47.79
			Waist	337.6	52.37
		50 cm	Overhead	240.2	37.81
			Shoulder	244.5	35.11
			Waist	295.3	43.82

A repeated measures ANOVA analysis of handedness (2) $\times$ hand orientation (2) $\times$ target distance (2) $\times$ target height (3) was conducted and proved that handedness factor had a significant influence on hand interaction duration result ($F(1, 23) = 121.07$, $p < 0.05$). More specifically, for left-handedness, left-hand interaction resulted in a longer hand duration than right-hand interaction (*two-tailed T-test*, $t(11) = 62.11$, $p < 0.05$); but for the right-handedness, the result was converse ($t(11) = -75.20$, $p < 0.05$). In addition, there were also significant effects of target distance ($F(1, 23) = 97.34$, $p < 0.05$) and height ($F(1, 23) = 150.22$, $p < 0.05$). Figure 3 below presents a clearer comparison about hand duration result in different conditions of handedness, operating hand orientation, target distance and height. As shown, there was an obvious interaction effect of handedness $\times$ operating hand orientation ($F(2, 46) = 82.15$, $p < 0.05$). In acquiring targets at a distance of 25.0 cm, the user performed interaction tasks through a bent arm posture, which resulted in a mean hand working duration of 268.48 s ($SD = 39.23$). But in acquiring targets at a larger distance of 50.0 cm where the user completed the tasks through an extended arm posture, the hand working duration became significantly shorter ($M = 225.24$, $SD = 33.04$), indicating that arm posture had a close correlation with free hand interaction fatigue level, a bent arm posture was proved to be more labor-saving than an extended arm posture. In target height effect analysis, it was proved that a lower target height (or a lower hand operate position) generated a longer duration result. In another word, hand operation at a lower position of waist is more labor-saving than that at a higher position of shoulder or head.

This paper further explored the relationship between arm fatigue and hand interaction accuracy. Given target acquisition error trials and related information records in task log files, target acquisition error rates in different conditions of handedness, operating hand orientation, target distance and target height were calculated, as shown in Table 3.

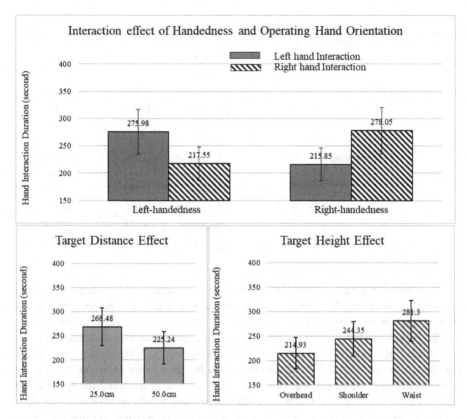

Fig. 3. Hand duration result comparisons in different conditions of handedness, operating hand orientation, target distance and target height.

Table 3. A summary about target acquisition error rate results.

Handedness	Operating hand	Target distance	Target height	Mean error rate	Std. dev.
Left-handed	Left hand	25 cm	Overhead	0.040	0.008
			Shoulder	0.034	0.006
			Waist	0.037	0.011
		50 cm	Overhead	0.048	0.011
			Shoulder	0.035	0.003
			Waist	0.049	0.014
	Right hand	25 cm	Overhead	0.046	0.007
			Shoulder	0.036	0.006
			Waist	0.045	0.009
		50 cm	Overhead	0.054	0.010
			Shoulder	0.042	0.007
			Waist	0.051	0.010

(continued)

Table 3. (*continued*)

Handedness	Operating hand	Target distance	Target height	Mean error rate	Std. dev.
Right-handed	Left hand	25 cm	Overhead	0.043	0.009
			Shoulder	0.032	0.005
			Waist	0.042	0.011
		50 cm	Overhead	0.053	0.013
			Shoulder	0.038	0.009
			Waist	0.048	0.009
	Right hand	25 cm	Overhead	0.036	0.010
			Shoulder	0.029	0.008
			Waist	0.029	0.005
		50 cm	Overhead	0.043	0.007
			Shoulder	0.034	0.004
			Waist	0.041	0.010

A repeated measures ANOVA analysis of handedness (2) × hand orientation (2) × target distance (2) × target height (3) on target acquisition error rate result showed that there were significant effects of target distance ($F(1, 23) = 112.15$, $p < 0.05$) and height ($F(1, 23) = 39.68$, $p < 0.05$), and there was a significant interaction effect of handedness × operating hand orientation ($F(2, 46) = 36.57$, $p < 0.05$). For the left-handedness, left hand interaction resulted in a lower error rate; but for the right-handedness, the result was converse. This paper also analyzed the relationship between hand duration and target acquisition error rate result, as shown in Fig. 4. It clearly showed that a longer duration generated a higher acquisition error rate, indicating that arm fatigue had a significantly negative effect on hand interaction accuracy.

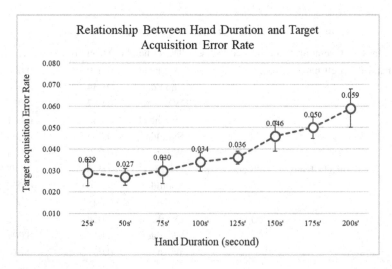

Fig. 4. An illustration about the relationship between hand interaction duration and target acquisition error rate.

4.2   Arm Fatigue Assessment

As interpreted in previous, this research also adopted the 7-pointer Likert NASA-TLX scale [12] to measure perceived arm fatigue level in different conditions of hand orientation, target distance and target height. Assessment results were generally consistent with hand duration performance. In a summary, the left-handedness and the right-handedness perceived arm fatigue differently. For the left-handedness, left-hand interaction resulted in a longer hand interaction duration than in right-hand interaction. But for the right-handedness, the left arm perceived fatigue more easily than the right arm. And target position was found to have a close correlation with perceived arm fatigue level: in acquiring target at a higher position, the user's perceived arm fatigue was more obvious. An extended arm posture generated arm fatigue more easily than a bent arm posture.

5   Discussion and Conclusion

Through a free hand target acquisition experiment in VR, this research proved that hand operation fatigue is an important factor which not only influenced hand operate duration in interaction tasks but also impacted hand interaction accuracy significantly. Based on the experiment findings, implications and suggestions are discussed for developing more efficient and user-friendly interaction techniques and user interfaces in VR.

First, it has been demonstrated that the user's dominant hand interacted more accurately and durably than the non-dominant hand. From this perspective, the user's dominant hand is more skilled at and should be assigned to completing efficient interaction tasks, e.g., moving a controller to alternate viewing angle and moving an object to a faraway destination. But the non-preferred hand is more adapted to and should be assigned to performing aiding operations, such as drawing a graphical stroke and inputting texts. Second, in natural hand operation tasks, arm fatigue is a universal and inevitable issue, which resulted in non-persistent interaction or a short task duration. It implies that user's perceived arm fatigue should be concerned and if possible, should be alleviated in natural hand interactive applications. Strategies and optimizations, e.g., designing breaks in hand interaction tasks, can be considered in VR applications. Last, this research systematically revealed the motor ability differences between the dominant hand and the non-dominant hand, in terms of movement agility, precision and task duration. Such findings imply that the user's operating hand should be identified and tracked in real time; and based on these, hand-adaptive user interfaces can be developed to make hand interaction more efficient and comfortable. For example, when the user is identified to be interacting by the left hand, interactive targets show at left side of visual field to have them acquired more efficiently.

Acknowledgments. This work was supported by the National Natural Science Foundation of China under the grant number of 61902097; the Natural Science Funding of Zhejiang Province under the grant number of Q19F020010; and the Research Funding of State Key Laboratory of Novel Software Technology under the grant number of KFKT2019B18.

References

1. Kaufmann, H., Schmalstieg, D., Wagner, M.: Construct3D: a virtual reality application for mathematics and geometry education. Educ. Inf. Technol. **5**(4), 263–276 (2000). https://doi.org/10.1023/A:1012049406877
2. Gallagher, A.G., Ritter, E.M., Champion, H., Higgins, G., Fried, M.P., Moses, G.: Virtual reality simulation for the operating room. Ann. Surg. **241**(2), 364–372 (2005)
3. Cao, S.: Virtual reality applications in rehabilitation. In: Kurosu, M. (ed.) HCI 2016. LNCS, vol. 9731, pp. 3–10. Springer, Cham (2016). https://doi.org/10.1007/978-3-319-39510-4_1
4. Zyda, M.: From visual simulation to virtual reality to games. Computer **38**(9), 25–32 (2005)
5. Jetter, H.C., Reiterer, H., Geyer, F.: Blended interaction: understanding natural human - computer interaction in post-WIMP interactive spaces. Pers. Ubiquit. Comput. **18**(5), 1139–1158 (2014)
6. Burdea, G.C.: Force and Touch Feedback for Virtual Reality. Wiley, New York (1996)
7. Vogel, D., Balakrishnan, R.: Distant freehand pointing and clicking on very large, high resolution displays. In: Proceedings of the 18th Annual ACM Symposium on User Interface Software and Technology, pp. 33–42. ACM, New York (2005)
8. Sagayam, K.M., Hemanth, D.J.: Hand posture and gesture recognition techniques for virtual reality applications: a survey. Virt. Real. **21**, 91–107 (2016)
9. Haque, F., Nancel, M., Vogel, D.: Myopoint: pointing and clicking using forearm mounted electromyography and inertial motion sensors. In: Proceedings of the 33rd Annual ACM Conference on Human Factors in Computing Systems, pp. 3653–3656. ACM, New York (2015)
10. Harrison, C., Ramamurthy, S., Hudson, S.E.: On-body interaction: armed and dangerous. In: Proceedings of the Sixth International Conference on Tangible, Embedded and Embodied Interaction, pp. 69–76. ACM, New York (2012)
11. Tanii, K., Kogi, K., Sadoyama, T.: Spontaneous alternation of the working arm in static overhead work. J. Hum. Ergol. **1**(2), 143–155 (1972)
12. Hart, S.G.: Development of NASA-TLX (task load index): results of empirical and theoretical research. Hum. Ment. Workload **52**(6), 139–183 (1988)

Design and Validation of a Unity-Based Simulation to Investigate Gesture Based Control of Semi-autonomous Vehicles

Brian Sanders[1]([✉]), Yuzhong Shen[2], and Dennis Vincenzi[3]

[1] Department of Engineering and Technology, Embry-Riddle Aeronautical University, Worldwide, Daytona Beach, USA
sanderb7@erau.edu
[2] Department of Computational Modeling and Simulation Engineering, Old Dominion University, Norfolk, VA, USA
yshen@odu.edu
[3] Department of Graduate Studies, Embry-Riddle Aeronautical University, Worldwide, Daytona Beach, USA
vincenzd@erau.edu

Abstract. The objective of this investigation is to explore the use of hand gestures to control semi-autonomous vehicles. This was achieved through the use of simulations built in Unity and real-life demonstrations. Screen-spaced simulations modeled the control of a recreational quadcopter while Virtual Reality simulations followed by actual demonstrations used a small ground vehicle. The purpose of the actual demonstrations was to validate observations and lessons learned about vehicle control and human performance from the simulations. The investigative process involved identifying natural gestures to control basic functions of a vehicle, matching them to the selected gesture capture technology, developing algorithms to interpret those gestures for vehicle control, and arranging the appropriate visual environment using the Unity game engine to investigate preferred use of those gestures. Observations and participant feedback aided in refining the gesture algorithms for vehicle control and visual information, indicated the simulations provided suitable learning experiences and environments from which to assess human performance. Results indicate that the gesture-based approach holds promise given the availability of new technology.

Keywords: Hand gestures · Unity · Simulation · Semi-autonomous systems

1 Introduction

Drones (aka, unmanned aerial systems or UAS) are used for a variety of purposes including aerial videography, photography, and surveillance. Successful accomplishment of these tasks requires the execution of a series of basic maneuvering functions (i.e., take off, acceleration, point-to-point navigation) that, when combined, contribute to a mission capable system. Commercially available small unmanned aerial systems (sUAS) have traditionally been designed and controlled using legacy interface

© Springer Nature Switzerland AG 2020
J. Y. C. Chen and G. Fragomeni (Eds.): HCII 2020, LNCS 12190, pp. 325–345, 2020.
https://doi.org/10.1007/978-3-030-49695-1_22

approaches to control the remote vehicle. These traditional control interfaces are typically one dimensional (1D) or two dimensional (2D) devices that allow the user to interact with a system in a limited manner [1]. For example, keyboards are 1D input devices that allow for text input and activation of preprogrammed functions via a sequence of key/text inputs. Mice have expanded input capabilities into a 2D framework, but input is still limited to menu item selection or "hotspots" on a graphical user interface. Both of these control devices, while functional and useful, are limited in nature and not very intuitive in terms of control movement, input, and function, and they are often slow and time consuming as control through these devices often requires a series or sequence of inputs to achieve the desired end state.

Other legacy control devices, such as those that are joystick based are better, but still an attempt to translate 2D input into movement through a three-dimensional (3D) space or environment. Integration with touch-sensitive devices such as phones and tablets are beginning to emerge on the market to replace or augment discrete physical controls and information displays [1]. However, these devices are, in many cases, simply electronic or digital versions of the same 2D legacy control devices. These devices typically combine electronic visual displays with touch input, and sometimes electronic input (GPS, accelerometers, and automation for example).

An alternative to these traditional command and control approaches is via the use of gestures. Development of a gesture-based approach for sUAS operation may be a viable alternative for implementation into command and control interfaces using technology that is designed to recognize gestures. A gesture-based approach can free the operator from having to hold and operate a multi-joystick, multi-button-based controller by correlating the UAS operations to a set of fluid, intuitive, natural, and accepted set of hand gestures. This in combination with new visual displays can create an entirely new command and control structure. Design of these systems will require careful investigation of human factors issues to populate gesture libraries that are natural and intuitive, as well as cognitive loading considerations due to the easy availability of a vast amount of visual information. The initial investigation of these factors can be accomplished via the use of basic simulations.

2   Background

2.1   Is It Science Fiction or Is It Real?

The concept of a reality-virtuality continuum was first introduced by Paul Milgram in 1994. In that paper, Milgram and Kishino (1994) [2] discussed the concept of a reality-virtuality continuum with the real world environment on one end of the continuum and a totally virtual computer generated environment on the other end of the continuum. Between the two ends of the continuum is a wide range of mixed reality variations between total real environment and total virtual environment. Most advanced interfaces today fall somewhere in the mixed reality section of the reality-virtuality continuum.

Although Virtual Reality (VR) and Mixed Reality (MR) type displays have been available since the 1980s and 1990s, MR interfaces that include control components have not. Interactive, MR display and control interfaces have only recently appeared on the consumer market in a usable and affordable form. Typically, a combination of technology can be integrated and utilized to create an inclusive human-machine interface that can be used to both display information in a VR environment while designing a control interface which can be used to manipulate objects in the real or virtual worlds. This combination of technology provides the means to design a MR display and a VR control interface for use in a real or virtual world.

For purposes of this research the one-dimension spectrum view is expanded to three-dimensions (3D) as shown in Fig. 1. It includes the visual interface spectrum, the interaction spectrum, and the mixed reality spectrum, where the visual interface spectrum is defined to span the range of 3D images on a two-dimensional (2D) space (aka, screen space), mixed reality in the form of handheld devices (such as tablets) and head mounted augmented reality (AR) devices to fully immersive VR headsets. The interaction spectrum includes human-machine interfaces such as the mouse, touch screen, handheld controllers, and gestures. This chart can be populated with technology examples such as that shown in the figure, so this indicates the proposed research topic is feasible. Albeit, the utility of it is still unanswered. Further, to fully answer the question requires investigations across each of the spectrums. This study focuses primarily on a component at the far end interaction spectrum, which can be considered to include gestures, and along the visual interface spectrum to include the screen space and VR headsets.

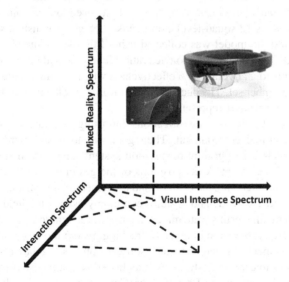

Fig. 1. 3D virtual technology spectrum

2.2 Gestures and Gesture Capture Technology

Gesture-based control, as well as traditional control technology, pose a unique challenge to remote operations of unmanned vehicles. To begin with, the term "unmanned system" is a misnomer at this point in time; since there is a human operator present in the system, the system will always be "manned" in some way. The only difference in the case of unmanned systems is that the operator is not collocated with the vehicle. Thus, placing the operator in a unique position and providing a different operational perspective since many of the environmental cues normally present in manned scenarios are no longer present and available to the human operator.

Research has suggested that while separated from the vehicle gestures can help mentally connect with it. Cauchard et al. [3] investigated how to interact with flying robots (aka drones). They conducted a study to learn how to naturally interact with drones. In this investigation gestures were made by a participant even though actual vehicle control was achieved by a remote operator in a separate location. Results show strong agreement between participants for many interaction techniques, such as when gesturing for the drone to stop. They discovered that people interact with drones as with a person or a pet, using interpersonal gestures, such as beckoning the drone closer.

Some previous related research centered around development of computer algorithms that would allow robotic systems to recognize gesture commands in the field as part of military teams. Other research has focused on virtual reality environments integrated with optical sensors to recognize and measure movement, velocity, and patterns of movement, of fingers and hands, and then translates those gestures into commands. Hamilton, et al. [4] conducted research that focused on developing the ability for robotic systems to understand military squad commands. The long-term goal was to develop the capability to integrate robots with ground forces as seamless teammates in combat operations. Their research focused on creating a recognition model that understands 12 squad-level commands, such as rally, listen, stop, and come here. The input into the model was collected using Microsoft Kinect's skeletal model and processed with a logistic regression activation function to identify the gesture. The logistic model showed an overall 97% effectiveness when discriminating if the datasets are from a given member set. The decision model was 90% effective in determining the gesture class a given dataset represents.

Lampton et al. [5] conducted investigations into using a gesture recognition system integrated with a virtual environment. Their goal was to measure the accuracy and effectiveness of a VR based gesture recognition system. The system consisted of two video cameras, software to track the positions of the gesturers hands, and software to recognize gestures by analyzing the position and movement of the hands. The researchers selected 14 basic and accepted hand gestures commonly used in the field by U.S. Army personnel. In general, the results were mixed in terms of recognition and accuracy. Many of the gestures were problematic in terms of tracking, recognition, or both.

Recent advancements in hardware and software processing has resulted in large strides in the ability to capture gestures. As mentioned above the Microsoft Kinect's is one example. Another one is the Leap Motion Controller (LMC) [6]. It is a relatively recent technology that can capture and track hand motion with a sensor just slightly bigger than a standard USB flash drive. It is the selected technology for this study, so it warrants a detailed discussion on previous work to support this decision.

Being a new technology, limited literature is available on the LMC performance. But a few studies have emerged over the last few years. For example, Weichert et al. [7] evaluated the reported accuracy and repeatability of the LMC. A novel experimental setup was developed making use of an industrial robot with a reference pen allowing a position accuracy of 0.2 mm. A deviation between a known 3D position and the average LMC measured positions below 0.2 mm was obtained for static setups and of 1.2 mm for dynamic setups.

Guna et al. [8] investigated the performance of the LMC with a professional grade, high-precision, fast motion tracking system. A set of static and dynamic measurements were performed with different numbers of tracking objects and configurations. For the static measurements, a plastic arm model simulating a human arm was used and measurements were made at 37 reference locations covering the controller's sensory space. For the dynamic measurements, a special V-shaped too was created to simulate two human fingers. In the static scenario, the standard deviation was less than 0.5 mm. The results of the dynamic scenario revealed inconsistent performance of the controller, with a significant drop in accuracy for samples taken more than 250 mm above the controller's surface. These two studies suggest that the LMC is a highly accurate system. While it may have some limitations of sensory space it is considered a good model technology to use for the current investigation.

In another validation effort Smeragliolo et al. [9] compared the LMC with an accepted markered motion capture technology. Their goal was to assess the use of the LMC for possible health care applications. Participants were instructed to perform three clinically relevant wrist (flexion/extension, radial/ulnar deviation) and fore arm (pronation/supination) movements, which were tracked with each technology and compared results by performing Pearson's correlation and root mean square error. Wrist flexion/extension and radial/ulnar deviation showed good overall agreement between the two approaches. However, when tracking forearm pronation/supination, there were serious inconsistencies in reported joint angles. Hand posture significantly influenced the quality of wrist deviation and forearm supination/pronation, but not wrist flexion/extension. They concluded the LMC is capable of providing data that are clinically meaningful for wrist flexion/extension, and perhaps wrist deviation, but not for measuring forearm pronation/supination. In additional to another validation of the LMC performance this investigation also provides meaningful insight into the range of physical motion applicable for gesture library development since it showed some natural limitations of hand motions.

As suggested by Wigdor and Wixon [10], new touch and gesture devices may require new interface designs. It appears that the LMC falls under that basic premise. Following this line of thought, Scicali and Bischof [11] argue that a 2D mouse is not very useful in a 3D environment and that the LMC may be a better fit. They developed several games to gauge user performance in different 3-D environments. They obtained excellent general information about several usable gestures and information feedback such as auditory and visual features that accompany desired gesture interaction with the virtual environment.

A few actual applications have been reported too. Staretu and Moldovan [12] used the LMC to control an anthropomorphic gripper with five fingers. Following the creation of the prototype, performance tests were conducted under real conditions to evaluate the recognition efficiency of the objects to be gripped and the efficiency of the command and control strategies for the gripping process. It was found that the command and control system, both in terms of capturing human hand gestures with the Leap Motion device and effective object gripping, is operational.

There has also been documented efforts to control drones with the LMC and multi-modal approaches. Sarkar et al. [13] used the LMC to control some basic motions of a UAV. They present the implementation of using the LMC to control an off the shelf quadcopter via simple human gestures. The drone was connected to a ground station via Wi-Fi and then the LMC was connected to the ground station via USB port. The LMC recognized the hand gestures and relayed it on to the ground station. Some basic tests were accomplished to document the feasibility of the LMC based system to control the vehicle motion.

There have been reported efforts to extend the application of gesture-based control to include other modalities too. Chandarana et al. [14] explored a multimodal natural language interface that uses a combination of speech and gesture input modalities to build complex UAV flight paths by defining trajectory segment primitives. Gesture inputs (measured with the LMC) were used to define the general shape of a segment while speech inputs provide additional geometric information needed to fully characterize a trajectory segment. They observed that the interface was intuitive, but the gesture module was more difficult to learn than the speech module. This, and the other studies cited above, highlight the possibilities of alternative command and control approaches with the emergence of new technology.

2.3   Cognitive Loading Considerations

An example of what is possible for a command and control system, and in particular methods to reduce cognitive loading, was discussed by Zollman et al. [15]. They investigated the application of micro aerial vehicles (MAVs) equipped with high-resolution cameras to create aerial reconstructions of selected locations. They identified that a challenge is that automatic flight path planning and autonomous flying is often applied but so far cannot fully replace the human in the loop for supervising the flight on-site to assure that there are no collisions with obstacles. They went on to discuss that this workflow yields several issues in cognitive loading, such as the need to mentally transfer the aerial vehicle's position between 2D map positions and the physical environment, and the complicated depth perception of objects flying in the distance. They presented an AR supported navigation and flight planning of micro aerial vehicles by augmenting the user's view with relevant information for flight planning and live feedback for flight supervision. Additionally, they introduced depth hints supporting the user in understanding the spatial relationship of virtual waypoints in the physical world and investigated the effect of these visualization techniques on the spatial understanding. So, the investigated highlighted the possibilities of an AR system and specific challenges related to cognitive processing.

Zollman et al. [15] highlighted a few of the cognitive loading issues related to the design of an AR based command and control system. There are several more that need to be considered [16, 17]. For example, Dodd et al. [18] investigated touch screen capability in aircraft cockpits and stated that as elements and workload increase in number and complexity, increased cognitive loading will follow. For the current effort this will drive the number and complexity of gestures we expect a participant to initiate for controlling the vehicle. As the research progresses beyond the flat screen additional factors come in to play. As AR capability is added, issues of switching views between the operator real-world view and a virtual framework need to be considered. Recent evidence indicates that very different brain processes are involved in comprehending meaning from these sources [19].

The above discussion highlights some of the complexities that can quickly emerge in a command and control system. So careful consideration must be given to the design of the simulation and real-life demonstration. The approach taken in this investigation is to minimize the load on the working memory. This will result in limiting the information transmitted to the user to include basic vehicle status (i.e., speed, altitude) and visual information to improve perception and vehicle component control. Taking this approach will keep the focus on the control aspect and suitability of the basic simulation environment.

2.4 Contributions of this Work

Developing this next generation of command and control systems will require codification of effects across a spectrum of technologies, such as that illustrated in Fig. 1, and human factors and limitations. This investigation will add to the somewhat limited literature on gesture-based control of drones by developing suitable gesture-based libraries and mechanisms (i.e., hand positions and virtual visual aids) suitable for command and control of semi-autonomous systems, and also the applicability of a commercially available game engine to develop simulations with interactive interfaces for which to observe human performance, use as a training aid, and communicate with a remote vehicle.

3 Approach, Implementation and Results

3.1 Approach

There are two research objectives for this project. One is related to the human factors aspect while the second addresses the suitability of a simulated environment as an assessment and training tool. They are stated as follows:

- Investigate the application of gesture-based control of semi-autonomous systems to identify capability, challenges, and limitations to assess the feasibility (can you do it) and viability (does it add value) of the approach.
- Assess suitability of a simulation environment to (1) support assessment of human performance and interface preferences for vehicle control and (2) provide a training environment for transition to a real-world system.

A two-phase approach is taken to address the objectives. Phase 1 involved simulation only. It centered around the idea of observing a user's ability to control a recreational quadcopter. The steps in this phase start with the identification of hand gestures to control the vehicle and the selection and accuracy validation of a gesture capture technology. With these fundamental building blocks in place the simulation development follows an evolutionary approach where participants are brought in periodically to exercise the simulation and provide feedback on the basic gesture-based concept and simulation features. Modifications and additions were made after each of these events. The objective of Phase 2 is to add validity to the findings from the pure simulated environment. In this phase a small ground vehicle was selected as the control model. This phase included a virtual reality simulation to train and familiarize the participant with the controls and vehicle performance. It was then followed by a physical demonstration of navigating an actual vehicle around a room. Details of the simulation development are presented in the next section.

3.2   Implementation and Results: Phase 1

Gestures and LMC Measurements. The first step in the task breakdown and gesture matching is to identify the functions associated with flying and operating the representative recreational hovercraft (aka., quadcopter). These are then matched to the LMC capability. This task breakdown is shown in the first column of Table 1. It is partitioned into categories of flight control and camera control. There are 7 potential actions in the flight control category related to the movement of the vehicle in the airspace. While the camera actions refer to the view (i.e., a first-person view from the operator or vehicle) and direction (pitch and yaw). The description of the flight control is an abstraction and describes what the operator wants to make happen rather than how the vehicle does it. For example, the desired action is for the vehicle to climb or descend, translate in a horizontal plane, or yaw around its vertical axis. This motion is enabled through the application forces and torques on the vehicle. Those forces and torques in turn are determined by the internal control logic of the air vehicle, or in this investigation a C# script, and are transparent to the operator.

Table 1. Quadcopter control actions and corresponding gestures

Vehicle action	Gesture
Flight control	
Climb/descend	Left hand pitch
Translate left/right	Right hand roll
Translate forward/aft	Right hand pitch
Yaw	Left hand yaw or roll
Increase/decrease speed	Controlled by vehicle pitch and roll
Stop	Fist/remove hands from control environment
Control initiation	Open hand
Camera control	
Switch view	Tapping motion
Pitch	Right and left index finger
Yaw	Left hand yaw

It was desired to build on previous investigations performed using mechanical systems [7] and assess how smoothly the human performed gestures described in Table 1 are captured by the LMC. Figure 2 is a representative example of the hand angle vs sample number captured by the LMC. In this case a left-right rotation of the hand. It was produced by performing the gesture with the right hand at a natural speed so as not be excessively slow or fast. It can be observed that the LMC captured the gesture with a high degree of fidelity. The slope variations are a result of minor changes in rotational speed of the hand, indicating again the highly accurate nature of this sensor. This exercise demonstrated the precise results produced by the LMC algorithms used to processes the captured images and also indicates the necessity of data smoothing in the gesture interpretation algorithms, which is discussed.

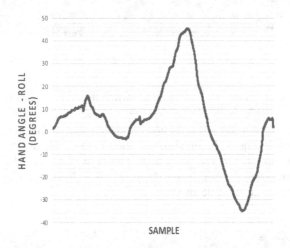

Fig. 2. Representative gesture capture using LMC

Virtual Environment Development. Figure 3 shows a screen capture of the initial virtual environment. The drone is a generic representation of a recreational quadcopter. It models a 1 kg drone with nominal dimensions of 30 cm × 30 cm × 10 cm and has red lights indicating the forward part of the drone and blinking green lights in the rear of the unit. The arrow in the left-hand corner serves as an orientation aid for users to determine the vehicle direction when it is too far away to clearly distinguish the lights. This is best understood by rotating the arrow 90° so it is on a parallel plane with the vehicle. For the case shown in the figure the arrow indicates it is coming at the user from the right. The vehicle information displayed is altitude, speed, and range to vehicle and is shown in top left of the figure. An alternative concept for the vehicle data was to have it follow the vehicle in a fixed position. However, it would tax working memory unnecessarily and so not implemented since this was not a focus of the research at this point in time. Therefore, the side position was decided so the user could quickly glance at the data when needed.

Fig. 3. Initial simulation screen design (Color figure online)

A dynamic user interface (UI) was used to switch the camera view using gestures. It is a capability available in the Orion Version of the LMC API [6]. In this case a dynamic UI is attached to the left hand and is visible when that hand is rotated toward the user as shown in Fig. 4. It contains two buttons to enable the user to switch the view between the operator or vehicle camera. This type of dynamic UI is an attractive feature for the proposed system. It has the potential to lower working memory load since it is not always in the field of view.

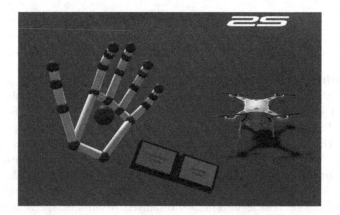

Fig. 4. Dynamic UI to control view perspective

Now that the visual component of the VE has been described let us dive into some of the mechanics that made it work starting with a discussion of how the vehicle motion was controlled. Unity provides a physics engine to apply forces and torques to an object via its Rigidbody class, which controls the object's linear motion via forces and angular motion via torques. Figure 5 shows two free body diagrams of the model vehicle. The left one shows the four forces produced by each propeller. By adjusting individual propeller forces a force-torque combination will be applied to the actual vehicle to produce the desired flight behavior. For this simulation the vehicle was modeled with a rigidbody component attached to it. This enables the application of a single 3D force vector and a single 3D torque vector to the vehicle. For the simulated vehicle, the four propeller forces are then modeled as single force in y-direction relative to the orientation of the vehicle (i.e., perpendicular) and a single torque vector as shown in freebody diagram on the right. Maximum forces and torques values applied to the vehicle were adjusted so that the simulated vehicle performance closely approximated that of the real vehicle.

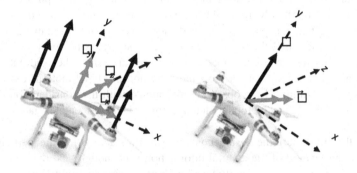

Fig. 5. Modeling the vehicle forces and torques

As an initial step, a linear relationship was used to interpret the data from the control source in determining the applied force and torque. A limit on the hand rotation was based on the observations on the range of motion of natural hand gestures discussed previously. For example, the maximum wrist rotation was set to 30°. Even though the user may rotate the hand to a larger angle the control input was maxed out at this condition. One last component of the UAV class to discuss was the application of a control loop. The control technique implemented was a proportional-integral-derivative (PID) controller. For the initial simulation the PID controller was implemented to control hover and limit the vehicle pitch and roll angle.

User Testing: The purpose of the first round of tests was to make a comparative assessment between a joystick/button device (the Xbox 360) and gesture-based control. Four participants took part in the testing. Each participant engaged in two scenarios with each control approach. The first was play time and the second was a search mission. In the first activity the users were not asked to do anything specific. It was just meant to give them time to explore the response of the vehicle to the flight control inputs via the two techniques and also become familiar with operation of the dynamic UI for controlling the camera view. In the second scenario they were asked to locate and navigate the vehicle to a location. There was no prescribed path at this point but rather just a destination. After this the participants were asked to engage in a short post-test interview. The total time to complete the test and post-test interview typically took just under an hour per participant.

In general, the participants preferred the Xbox controller over the gesture-based control system. Several observations and comments support this position. For example, on average twice as much time (11 min vs 22 min) was spent in play mode with the gesture-based system. This is an indication that the users felt more comfortable with the Xbox controller. A typical user's ability to control the vehicle significantly improved over the play period, but they still did not feel as comfortable with gesture system as compared to the joystick device at the end of the play session. Finally, mission times when using the Xbox were on the order of three minutes while the missions using gesture control were rarely completed due to fatigue and frustration with the system.

In the post-test interviews participants reported feeling fatigued, mostly due to using the gesture system. This is most likely from a combination of physical and mental fatigue. Even though only minimal hand movement is required to control the vehicle, it was observed that the participants used large hand gestures requiring more energy compared to the small thumb motions that can be used with the joystick. Also, the vehicle did not respond as accurately to these gestures since they did not fall into the detection region (i.e., the green box) and were not the subtle motions expected by the processing algorithm. These observations coupled with the consideration that gesture control is a new approach probably led to a higher level of mental engagement and thus fatigue.

For the most part the visual content was satisfactory for the participants. The location and amount of the textural information was enough, and the user's responses did not indicate they were overly taxed with processing that information. In fact, they were typically so focused on the vehicle that they needed to be reminded this information was available. On the other hand, the virtual hands were distracting.

Other comments and observations centered around the use of the dynamic UI and visual aids. Participants could not consistently produce the menu and often could not make the selection once the menu was available. Restricting the region where the vehicle control was activated received unfavorable comments too. The control box made them feel constricted, and it led to lack of control because they frequently had to check where they were in the field of view. Finally, they had difficulty processing vehicle orientation using the arrow. One final observation that all of the participants made was that they liked how the gesture-based system made them feel more connected to the vehicle response.

The comments and observations from this set of tests led to several modifications of the simulation. First, the idea of introducing an unconstrainted play environment did not result in effective condition for the participants to learn the new gesture interface. A building block training environment was implemented to address this shortfall. Second, participants had a difficult time processing the correlation of the vehicle orientation with the 2-D direction indicator. In the updated version of the simulation a 3D representation of the vehicle was included. This is shown in the bottom of Fig. 6 as a semitransparent sphere containing a small-scale version of the drone model. This drone matches the pitch and roll orientation as well as the direction the vehicle is flying. It is anticipated that this will reduce the cognitive loading and thus fatigue since it is a more direct representation of the vehicle's orientation and will require minimum processing to understand the vehicles position.

Components of the user interface (UI) were also updated. A neutral command was programmed into the simulation. If a hand was detected to be in the shape of a fist then no control command would be transmitted to the vehicle. Also, the virtual hands were made out of clear material, so it was less distracting to the user but still available for reference. Next, the dynamic UI was hard for participants to control. So, this was replaced by simply performing a task that appears as if the user was touching the vehicle to change the camera view. When viewing from the camera a small semi-transparent square in front of the viewer is the target interface. In addition to being a bit more intuitive it is also a simpler technique. A command (rotating the index finger) was also added to rotate the camera pitch angle 90°. This let the users scan from a position parallel to the flight path and straight down, which was useful for searching an area and landing.

Fig. 6. Modified simulation screen design

To assess the effectiveness of these modifications, two participants from the previous test were brought back. It was conceded that the joystick approach far exceeded the gesture-based control at this time, so the users were asked only to engage in the gesture-based control approach. Each participant was first led through the training environment. As anticipated, this aided in helping them develop a feel for the limited range of motion required to control the vehicle. Then they again went into the play and mission scenarios. In general, the feedback from the users was much more positive and it was observed that they had better control of the vehicle, able to complete the requested missions, and switch camera views. They also demonstrated a lower level of fatigue and frustration.

Algorithm Redesign. Previous implementation of the PID controller was limited to transiting to hover mode and ensuring the vehicle did not exceed its maximum rotation angle in pitch and roll. This approach was expanded to include more control setpoints. These setpoints include the vertical climb rate, yaw rate, and the pitch and roll angle. Having this structure results in the hand gestures determining the setpoint and then the PID controller determines the required force and torque vector to maintain the vehicle in this condition until an additional command is given. So, it is still a kinetic based simulation.

The setpoint is determined based on a cubic relationship using the normalized change in hand orientation. This approach can be clarified by studying Fig. 7. This figure illustrates a cubic relationship between the normalized gesture command and a control parameter. For this illustration the maximum value of the control parameter is set to three. Assume that the vehicle is on the ground waiting for takeoff. This condition then defines the initial setpoint shown in the figure. A change in hand orientation from the reference orientation, such as positive pitch rotation, is then normalized and the new setpoint is determined based on a cubic function. Once this command is set the user can then return their hands to the neutral (e.g. resting) position and the vehicle will continue to follow that last input command by virtue of the PID controller. Note that returning the hands to the reference orientation does not affect the setpoint. Incremental changes to this updated setpoint are made again following the cubic function shown above, so a small change in hand orientation will result in a small change in the setpoint while a larger change will increase it more but not beyond its maximum. Finally, an additional state was added to the system, so in this version there were three: active control, hover, and cruise. Switching between the states was achieved by touching the thumb and index finger. After a change in state the reference hand position can be reset based on the user's preference. Finally, data smoothing was implemented to remove the jitter resulting from the captured hand gestures. This approach provides the operator with a wide range of control and flexibility anywhere in the flight envelop.

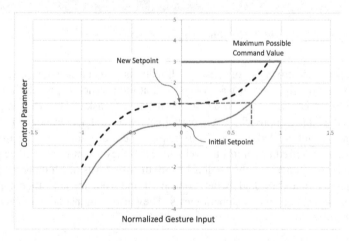

Fig. 7. Redesigned gesture interpretation algorithm

Several tests by the developer and a complete novice demonstrated that these changes resulted in a significantly improved command and control system. First, the vehicle is easier to control and is more stable in flight. More precise control of performance parameters and vehicle positioning is enabled too by the new control algorithm. Further, the updated gesture interpretation algorithm combined with the implementation of the state machine resulted in the user being able to keep a lower level of physical stress on the hands and wrist. This is a positive consequence of not requiring the user to maintain off-neutral, fixed hand positions for the vehicle to maintain its current flight trajectory.

3.3   Implementation and Results: Phase 2

VR Simulation. A VR simulation was built to provide the training and observation environment for this phase. The VR environment was designed to represent the geometry of a room with dimensions of 5 m × 10 m × 3 m. Figure 8 shows the simulated environment with the model car in it. It contained a few obstacles such as pillars and tables that provided targets when directing test participants to navigate around. Hardware used in this experiment include the Leap Motion Controller (LMC) and Oculus Rift Headset. The LMC generates the operational gesture recognition environment while the Oculus Rift provides an immersive display environment.

Fig. 8. Virtual environment with model car

Figure 9 shows the virtual trackball concept introduced in Phase 1. The virtual trackball and the new visual component, a 2D disk with a crossbar (aka command indicator), work in a coordinated manner. The trackball itself has a diameter of 0.1 m, which is about the size of a softball. The intent is to provide the user with an anchor for the hand to rotate around. Erratic readings can result from the LMC if the hand gets too close it. This distance is approximately 2.5 cm above the LMC. An alert range is conservatively set to 5 cm. At this point the trackball turns yellow.

The control indicator is composed of a cross bar each with a disk that moves either vertically or horizontally. The vertical component is tied to the pitch of the right hand and the forward and backward motion of the vehicle. The horizontal motion is tied to roll of the right hand, which is used to control the steering angle. The maximum motion of these gestures is set to 30°. Control of the vehicle based on these gestures is made through the use of a wheel collider and will be discussed a little later. To further support muscle memory training users are positioned in a chair with the LMC just below and in front of the right arm rest. While not practical for an actual application it helps to provide an anchor for the arm. This in turn lets the user focus on the small hand motions required for vehicle control.

Keeping with the forced based simulation approach the Wheel Collider capability in Unity is applied to each wheel. This is a collider-based capability with application to ground vehicles [20]. It is built upon a collider, wheel physics and a slip-based friction model. Figure 10 shows a picture of the simulated vehicle in the VR environment with the wheel collider visible. The key parameters are contained in the slip model, suspension system components, and ability to apply torque to the wheels and also control their direction. For the current model steering was applied to the front wheels, while motor torque was applied to the rear wheels.

Fig. 9. Trackball and control indicator (Color figure online)

Fig. 10. Wheel collider

Virtual and Real-Life Demonstrations. The purpose of these tests was to see if the human performance observations from the simulation environment transfer to a real-life demonstration. Adding validity to the lessons learned and observations from Phase 1 and supporting the realism of the simulation. There were two rounds of testing conducted. In the first round the initial, linear control algorithm was implemented, so this was a direct control of the vehicle motor torque and steering using a linear gesture interpretation algorithm. The second round of testing implements most but not all of the modified control algorithm. This is due to the face that feedback parameters (i.e., vehicle speed) are not always available. For example, vehicle speed is available in the VR simulation but not in the actual vehicle. The following features are included: cubic interpretation of gestures, incremental command inputs, commands based on a neutral reference position. So, this still captures some of the foundational elements of the control approach related to lowering the physical stress on user.

First Round of Testing. Two sessions were conducted in the first round. One a high participation count (around 15 participants) but informal activity and one a more formal but lower participation count (2 participants). In either case there was a training period followed by a play time in the VR environment, followed by an event where the user controlled the model vehicle shown in Fig. 11. The initial training mode involved no vehicle movement, but the indicator was free to move. This enabled the user to become familiar with the hand position and the small range of motion required for vehicle control. After that forward and backward motion was enabled to allow the user to become familiar with the visual effect of the moving car. Finally, the car steering was enabled. This step-by-step training process was inspired from the findings of Phase 1.

Fig. 11. Adeept smart car [21]

Informal observations of approximately 15 people took place. During these engagements it was observed that within about 20 min the majority of the participants were able to reasonably control the vehicle in both virtual and real-life scenarios (10 min in each environment). Further, the large gestures from previous testing were not observed and the participants used small, relaxed gestures. So, it appears that the combination of the virtual visual aids and anchoring of the arm produced the desired results. One issue that was observed is that the turning performance was a little unstable. More like seeing someone ride a wobbly bicycle rather than the smooth, consistent motion.

Two additional but more formal tests were conducted. In this case, each participant was processed through the same rigorous training process before enabling the play mode. Similar observations were made to the informal test described above about had motions and vehicle control. It was further observed that users became more confident in their ability to control the car in around 10 min. As described above in the informal test session, speed control was smooth but the turning was still a bit unstable. This is something that the latest control algorithm corrected.

Second Round of Testing. Participation in the second round of tests was limited to the developer. In this round the developer implemented and exercised the new control scheme in both the VR environment and with the remote-control car. The main differences in implementation between car-based scenarios and the UAV simulation is in selection and implementation of setpoints. For the VR simulations vehicle speed and wheel angle were the setpoints used with PID controller scheme. These setpoints are not available with the remote-control car. That would require additional vehicle sensors to provide feedback, so the active PID controller is not implemented. Other features, such as the cubic gesture interpretations and data smoothing, are integrated into the control methods.

After some initial testing it was decided to slightly modify the control algorithm to more smoothly control the car. In the UAV control a performance parameter is set such as climb rate or desired roll angle to achieve the desired speed. Then the PID controller maintains that condition. In the case of the car controller this worked well for the speed control. In the VR simulation the user could adjust desired speed and then the PID controller would determine the required torque to apply to the wheel. In the remote-control car case the user torque is directly linked to the cubic gesture function. In each of these scenarios the user can still return their hand to the neutral position and the car will continue at that speed.

To stabilize the steering required returning to a more rudimentary approach. This is due to the fact that steering, especially in confined venues, is a more dynamic event requiring constant adjustments. It was found that the best way to steer the car was to maintain the hand in a rotated position while turning but release it once the target direction was achieved. The wheel position would in turn then return to a zero angle. It was also decided to implement a three-to-one steering ratio. For example, the maximum recognized hand rotation angle was set to $\pm 30°$ while the maximum steering angle of the car was set to $\pm 10°$. This is another feature that translates the less accurate human performance to more precise control of the car. These adjustments made executing basic maneuvering such as ovals and figure eight's more manageable. This final exercise illustrates the complexity of the control process and several of the features that need to be considered in the design of such a system.

4 Summary and Conclusions

The ability to control vehicles via gesture-based control is achievable. Additionally, with the emergence of head mounted, augmented reality technology it may make it preferable. However, at this point there is still a strong preference for the joystick approach. This maybe the result of a combination of familiarization and maturity of the technology. The joystick-based controller has been around for a number of years, its basic design is well tailored, and its functions are well developed. The gesture-based system is still new and can be intuitive, but it is not so yet. While care was taken in this effort to implement natural gestures, they were still new ideas. However, participants learned the new system quickly (on the order of minutes) to achieve a moderate level of vehicle control and stated they felt more connected to the vehicle using this approach.

Another conclusion is that the available gesture capture systems are highly accurate and capable of detecting a wide range of hand motions. These hand motions can subsequently be transformed into control commands. However, the human is not as precise. To make these systems more useable data processing and control systems need to be implemented that smooth out the variations in human performance and thus stabilize the vehicle control. Also, being a new interface will require training environments to familiarize the user with the range of motion required since it is basically unlimited by any mechanical constraints. For example, a joystick is a mechanical based system and it has motion limits. A hands-free gesture system is wide open and limited only by the physical makeup of the operator. Establishing proper training environments showed that this motion can be easily learned. Further, the research has revealed other subtilties on motion that were not originally considered. For example, the original gesture concept was to simply rotate flat hands via a pitch and roll motion of the wrist. Observations showed the preferred neutral position of a hand was slightly offset and semi-rounded making it more suitable for a virtual track ball concept. Testing on a larger scale is required to further investigate human performance and preferences for this control idea. The system developed in this research is now setup to conduct these larger scale tests.

References

1. Balog, C.R., Terwilliger, B.A., Vincenzi, D.A., Ison, D.C.: Examining human factors challenges of sustainable small unmanned aircras systems (sUAS) operations. In: Savage-Knepshield, P., Chen, J. (eds.) Advances in Human Factors in Robots and Unmanned Systems. AISC, vol. 499, pp. 61–73. Springer, Cham (2016). https://doi.org/10.1007/978-3-319-41959-6_6
2. Milgram, P., Kishino, F.: A taxonomy of mixed reality visual displays. IEICE Trans. Inf. Syst. **E77-D**(12), 1321–1329 (1994)
3. Cauchard, J.R., Jane, L.E., Zhai, K.Y., Landay, J.A.: Drone & me: an exploration into natural human-drone interaction. In: Proceedings of the 2015 ACM International Joint Conference on Pervasive and Ubiquitous Computing, Osaka, Japan (2015)
4. Hamilton, M.S., Mead, P., Kozub, M., Field, A.: Gesture recognition model for robotic systems of military squad commands. In: Interservice/Industry, Training, Simulation and Education Conference, Orlando, FL (2016)
5. Lampton, D.R., Knerr, B., Clark, B.R., Martin, G., Washburn, D.A.: ARI Research Note 2306-6 - Gesture Recognition System for Hand and Arm Signals. United States Army Research Institute for Behavioral Sciences, Alexandria (2002)
6. Leap Motion: Leap Motion. https://www.leapmotion.com/. Accessed 16 Sept 2019
7. Weichert, F., Bachmann, D., Rudak, B., Fissler, D.: Analysis of the accuracy and robustness of the leap motion controller. Sensors **13**(5), 6380–6393 (2013)
8. Guna, J., Jakus, G., Pogacnik, M., Tomazic, S., Sodnik, J.: An analysis of the precision and reliability of the leap motion sensor and its suitability for static and dynamic tracking. Sensors **14**(2), 3702–3720 (2014)
9. Smeragliuilo, A.H., Hill, N.J., Disla, L., Putrino, D.: Validation of the leap motion controller using markered motion capture technology. J. Biomech. **49**(9), 1742–1750 (2016)
10. Wigdor, D., Wixon, D.: Brave NUI World Designing Natural User Interfaces for Touch and Gesture. Morgan Kaufmann, Burlington (2011)
11. Scicali, A., Bischof, H.: Useability study of leap motion controller. In: Proceedings of the International Conference on Modeling, Simulation and Visualization Methods (MSV), Athens, Greece (2015)
12. Staretu, I., Moldovan, C.: Leap motion device used to control a real anthropomorphic device. Int. J. Adv. Robot. Syst. **13**(3), 113 (2016)
13. Sarkar, A., Ganesh Ram, R.K., Patel, K.A., Capoor, G.K.: Gesture control of drone using a motion controller. In: International Conference on Industrial Informatics and Computer Systems (CIICS), Sharjah, pp. 1–5 (2016)
14. Chandarana, M., Meszaros, E.L., Trujillo, A., Allen, B.D.: Natural language based multimodal interface for UAV mission planning. In: Proceedings of the Human Factors and Ergonomics Society 2017 Annual Meeting, Los Angeles, CA (2017)
15. Zollman, S., Hoppe, C., Langlotz, T., Reitmayr, G.: FlyAR: augmented reality supported micro aerial vehicle navigation. IEEE Trans. Vis. Comput. Graph. **20**(4), 560–568 (2014)

16. Givens, A., et al.: Monitoring working memory load during computer-based tasks with EEG pattern recognition methods. Hum. Factors: J. Hum. Factors Ergon. Soc. **40**(1), 79–91 (1998)
17. Rorie, C., Fern, L.: UAS measured response: the effect of GCS control model interfaces on pilot ability to comply with ATC clearances. In: Proceedings of the Human Factors Ergonomics Society 58th Annual Meeting (2014)
18. Dodd, S., Lancaster, J., Miranda, A., Grothe, S., DeMers, B., Rogers, B.: Touch screens on the flight deck: the impact of touch target size, spacing, touch technology and turbulence on pilot performance. In: Proceedings of the Human Factors and Ergonomics Society Annual Meeting, Chicago, Illinois (2014)
19. Ravassard, P., et al.: Multisensory control of hippocampal spatiotemporal selectivity. Science **340**(6138), 1342–1346 (2013)
20. Unity: Unity Documentation. https://docs.unity3d.com/Manual/. Accessed 19 Sept 2019
21. Adeept: Adeept. https://www.adeept.com/. Accessed 18 Sept 2019

Hand Gesture Recognition for Smartphone-Based Augmented Reality Applications

Eric Cesar E. Vidal Jr.$^{(\boxtimes)}$ ⓘ and Ma. Mercedes T. Rodrigo ⓘ

Ateneo de Manila University, Katipunan Avenue, 1108 Quezon City, Philippines
ericvids@gmail.com

Abstract. Hand Gesture Recognition (HGR) is a principal input method in head-mounted Augmented Reality (AR) systems such as HoloLens, but the high cost and limited availability of such systems prevent HGR from becoming more prevalent. Alternatively, smartphones can be used to provide AR experiences, but current smartphones were not designed with HGR in mind, making development of HGR applications more challenging. This study develops a software-based framework that implements HGR as a principal input method for smartphone AR applications. This framework assumes a contemporary smartphone with dual back-facing cameras, which enable stereo imaging and thus allow extraction of limited depth information from the environment. Several image processing techniques, derived and improved from previous work, were used to filter the noisy depth information to segment the user's hand from the rest of the environment, and then to extract the pose of the hand and fingers in real-time. The framework additionally facilitates the development of cross-platform AR applications for both head-mounted (HoloLens) and smartphone configurations. A user experiment is held to determine whether a smartphone-based AR application developed using our HGR framework is comparable in usability to the same application on the HoloLens. For each device, participants were asked to use the application and fill out a usability questionnaire. They were also asked to compare the two systems at the end. This experiment shows that, despite the current limitations of smartphone-based HGR, the smartphone system's usability is competitive with that of the HoloLens. This study ends with recommendations for future development.

Keywords: Augmented Reality · Hand Gesture Recognition · Image processing · Usability

1 Introduction

Augmented Reality (AR) layers virtual objects on the real world, typically by rendering these objects over a live video feed or by using see-through displays. AR is billed as a compelling technology for educational applications [1] and was originally expected to have an adoption time of 2–3 years as of 2016. However, AR has not achieved expected mainstream usage as of 2019 [2], due in part to the high cost and challenging ergonomics of head-mounted displays (HMDs) used to display traditional AR.

An important input method in HMD-based AR, such as Magic Leap 1 and Microsoft HoloLens, is Hand Gesture Recognition (HGR). HGR allows the user to use

© Springer Nature Switzerland AG 2020
J. Y. C. Chen and G. Fragomeni (Eds.): HCII 2020, LNCS 12190, pp. 346–366, 2020.
https://doi.org/10.1007/978-3-030-49695-1_23

hand movements and positions to control an application: one can form and move a fist to drag virtual objects around, or select an object by directly gazing at it through the HMD's display while bringing one finger up, then quickly bringing the finger down ("air-tap") [3].

HGR technology in head-mounted AR platforms is currently in active development, as evidenced by the increasing number and complexity of recognized hand poses on the Magic Leap 1 [4] and the latest iteration of HoloLens [5]. This suggests that HGR is currently being considered as a preferred method for interacting with AR applications alongside other established input methods (game controllers, touchscreens, etc.).

The theoretical basis for this suggestion is embodied cognition (EC), which assumes that sensory perceptions, motor functions, and sociocultural contexts shape the structure and development of thinking skills, including mathematical abilities and higher-order abstract reasoning as well as sense-making in general [6, 7]. Human beings are better able to construct meaning and understanding when using their technological devices within physical and social environments rather than in more detached information-processing contexts [8]. Additionally, [8] asserts that direct-hand interaction enables users to move beyond the traditional WIMP (windows, icons, menus and pointers) interface's gestural input metaphors (point-and-click, drag-and-drop, scroll-wheel-to-zoom) or their equivalents as used on touchscreens (tapping, tap-and-drag, pinch-to-zoom). The two-dimensional nature of these metaphors is not naturally suited for manipulating 3D objects. In contrast, hand-based interactions enable users to physically reach for a virtual object and use natural hand gestures to perform WIMP-style interactions (e.g., air-tap, grab-to-drag, pull-closer/farther-to-zoom-in/out) while potentially enabling more interactions that don't have any natural mapping in WIMP (e.g., rotating/scaling around any arbitrary axis by rotating/pinching three fingers at any 3D orientation).

Mobile devices such as tablets and smartphones can be used in place of HMDs to minimize costs for the deployment of AR applications. In fact, smartphones are noted to have singlehandedly caused a boom in the popularity of AR [9], incentivized by the recent development of two standard application programming interfaces (APIs): Google's ARCore [10] and Apple's ARKit [11]. However, these APIs, at the time of this writing, have a major disadvantage compared to HMDs: they assume a minimum smartphone specification of a single back-facing RGB (red-green-blue) camera and a digital gyroscope, which provides only limited information to the application developer (specifically, the position and orientation of the device with respect to the environment, as well as rudimentary surface detection on which to anchor virtual objects). Current HMDs feature a dedicated environment-facing depth sensor, which does not only allow the proper display of occluded 3D graphics (e.g., displaying virtual objects behind a desk or other real-world object), but also enables the detection of the user's hand and its current pose. While it is possible to extract the depth information of the environment through other means, such as employing dual back-facing cameras [12], fundamental problems still exist (as will be discussed shortly in this paper), and the resulting development complexity meant that very few smartphone AR applications currently feature HGR as an input method.

The lack of progress in this subject area also means that it is currently unknown whether an AR-HGR (Augmented Reality with Hand Gesture Recognition) application on the smartphone is comparable, in terms of usability, with the same application on an HMD device. Answering this question has two major implications: First, having an AR-HGR implementation on a smartphone that is at least nearly comparable with that of a head-mounted device would mean that the barrier to entry into AR-HGR experiences would be considerably lowered, allowing for users with cheaper devices to have similar AR experiences with the same levels of interaction, and ultimately reducing development and deployment costs for low-budget scenarios such as educational apps and games. Second, proving that AR-HGR is viable on a smartphone may entice smartphone hardware and API developers to make substantial improvements in order to better support AR-HGR (e.g., by adding/supporting hardware that can help with the AR-HGR experience, such as ultra-wide-view camera lenses and/or native back-facing depth sensors).

This study attempts to address the two aforementioned issues (namely, the availability of AR-HGR on smartphones, and its usability) via a two-step process: first, an application framework is developed in order to simplify the development of smartphone-based AR applications that feature HGR, and second, a sample smartphone application is developed using this framework and is evaluated for usability vis-à-vis the same application running on a head-mounted device.

The rest of this paper is structured as follows: The second section details the development process of the framework, identifying major problems and the methods that were implemented to solve these problems, as well as to enumerate the remaining issues and limitations of the framework. The third section describes the usability evaluation process, first by describing the test application and then outlining the evaluation procedure. The fourth section discusses the results of the evaluation. Finally, the paper concludes with plans for further improvement and real-world usage of the software framework as well as recommendations for future hardware support.

2   Framework Development

This section describes the architecture of our AR-HGR application framework, along with major design decisions and a discussion of the framework's limitations.

An existing game engine, Unity, is used as a base system due its wide platform support, including Universal Windows Platform or UWP (used by Microsoft Holo-Lens) as well as Android and iOS (for smartphones) [13]. Unity can be extended with native code and third-party plugins, e.g., OpenCV [14], which will be used extensively by our framework. On top of this base system, we build our own custom hand gesture recognition module, which we call AR Mobile Device Gestures (AMDG). In order to enable the device comparison and usability evaluation tasks at the end of this study, AMDG is designed as a high-level, cross-platform API for providing AR and HGR functionality to any generic Unity application; internally, it uses the UWP's XR camera and input providers when building for the HoloLens platform, and acts as its own camera and input provider when building for the iOS platform (Android support is planned for later). Note, however, that the handheld nature of the smartphone system fundamentally limits AMDG's support to one hand only (as opposed to XR input's support for two hands; inputs from the other hand are ignored).

Figure 1 shows the AMDG process pipeline when serving as the Unity application's gesture input provider. As with other contemporary hand gesture systems [15], we identify four major phases: image capture/preprocessing, hand segmentation, feature detection, and gesture classification/rendering. These phases will be described in detail in the next four subsections.

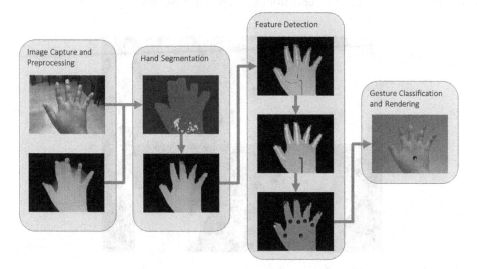

Fig. 1. AR Mobile Device Gestures (AMDG) process pipeline.

2.1 Image Capture and Preprocessing

Image capture is provided by the dual back-facing cameras of the phone. Dual camera feeds enable the creation of a stereo image from which depth information can be extracted. For our framework, a design decision was made to use back-facing cameras exclusively (both for environment display and gesture input) because smartphone-based AR applications are usually designed for back-facing cameras (i.e., displaying the user's environment is essential to the AR experience), and because iOS 12, the current version during development time, does not allow for simultaneous front and back camera streams [16]. This is a substantial limitation because the iPhone X series' front-facing depth sensor cannot be used for gesture input while the back-facing cameras are active. However, this design decision makes our framework potentially compatible with all contemporary dual-back-facing camera phones.

Note that iOS 12 also does not provide separate raw image feeds for each camera in the back-facing pair; instead, it provides a proprietary algorithm that computes and delivers a depth map to the application [17]. Otherwise, if separate left and right stereo images are natively available, the depth map can be computed using other well-known methods, e.g., [12].

2.2 Hand Segmentation

The depth map produced from a stereo-camera system is of lower quality than that produced from a dedicated depth sensor. Since stereo depth map algorithms typically rely on correct matching of feature points between a pair of images [12], artifacts are introduced due to matching errors or insufficient matches. In the case of iOS's depth map matching, these artifacts are manifested as noise clouds between fingers (see Fig. 2, lower left). In extreme cases, some edge details (such as fingernails or highly reflective skin patches) disappear from the depth map entirely.

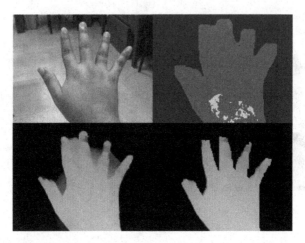

Fig. 2. Left: raw RGB and depth maps. Upper right: classification into sure-foreground (yellow), background (gray) and unknown (purple) pixels. Lower right: final filtered depth map. (Color figure online)

Some depth-sensor-based HGR systems designed for older depth sensors (such as Kinect) isolate the user's hand from the rest of the environment by matching the depth map with the color (RGB) map taken at the same time frame, then eliminating depth pixels that do not match the skin color of the user [18]. While modern depth-sensor-based HGR systems do not require this technique (such as HoloLens), we revisit this idea in order to eliminate the noise clouds from our depth map, in order to achieve acceptable hand-segmentation accuracy for the later HGR phases.

Previous systems assumed a static hand color model using either Gaussian mixture or elliptical boundaries in the 3D color space [19]. This required online training to find the color space boundaries of the user's hand, and while the method is effective for static backgrounds and a fixed camera, the mobility of our AR camera setup renders this technique impractical due to the need to constantly retrain the model under fluctuating lighting conditions. Instead, we use the following real-time algorithm:

- The original RGB map is converted to a CIE-Lab map. This is for computational convenience, since human-perceptual differences between two colors is approximately represented as a Euclidean distance between the colors' corresponding vectors in CIE-Lab color space. Each color vector contains three components: L (lightness), a* (green-to-red hue shift), and b* (blue-to-yellow hue shift) [20].

- A minimum *reference depth value* is found, where the total number of depth pixels that are less than or equal to this reference value covers at least 10% of all pixels in the depth map. (In our implementation, the reference depth value is measured in meters from the camera sensor plane and is capped to a maximum value of 0.6 m).

- In addition, a *maximum depth threshold* is found by adding a constant value to the reference depth value (empirically set to 0.2 m in our implementation). The maximum depth threshold represents a depth cut-off value; depth values greater than this threshold are processed with morphological dilation [21] (to account for the depth map cutting off some edge details), and the pixels that remain are marked as "sure-background" pixels.

- All depth values nearer or equal to the reference depth value are processed with morphological erosion [21] (to discard pixels that are potentially near the hand's edges, whose original colors may be bleeding into the surrounding environment), then the remaining depth pixels is used as a mask for computing a histogram of the CIE-Lab map. The peak of this histogram is assumed to be the predominant skin color of the user and are thus "sure-foreground" pixels.

- Pixels that are drastically different in hue from the predominant skin color (computed by taking the pixel's a* and b* components and finding their Euclidean distance from the predominant skin color's a* and b*) are marked as additional background pixels. See Fig. 2, upper right, where background pixels due to depth or hue are marked as dark gray or light gray, respectively.

- A flood-fill operation is performed (again, see Fig. 2, upper right), starting from sure-foreground pixels (yellow) and expanding into the remaining unmarked pixels (purple). The flood-fill considers both differences in depth and luminance of neighbor pixels before expanding to these pixels. This results in a substantial reduction of noise clouds in the depth map.

- At the end of the procedure, a final morphological dilation is performed with all pixels visited by the flood-fill operation (in order to cover some remaining small holes), and these pixels retain their original depth value while all other pixels have their depth values changed to infinite (represented as black in Fig. 2, lower right).

2.3   Feature Detection

For our framework, it is determined that a relatively simple set of features is required to accommodate the user interface gestures that are already available on the HoloLens 1 [3] and 2 [5]. These features include: the position and orientation of each of the five fingers, as well as a centroid hand position (palm).

A fast method for determining these features is desirable due to the substantial amount of processing power already being used by the phone for depth map processing as well as rendering an AR environment. Significant progress has been made in developing machine-learning models for hand gesture recognition that run on smartphones, such as Google's MediaPipe [22]; such a model may be used as a drop-in option for our framework in the future. However, architectural complexity and limitations in processing power prevent the use of this method for the time being.

Instead, an existing, fast method for determining the position of fingertips [23] is adapted for use with our framework. This method employs the use of the *distance transform* algorithm, described as follows: a distance map is initialized where all pixels with a corresponding depth map value of infinite (black) is marked as 0, and the rest of pixels are unmarked. Then, any unmarked pixel directly adjacent to a 0 pixel in any direction (horizontal, vertical, and diagonal) will be marked 1 (diagonal moves are capped to 1 to enhance the algorithm's speed). Afterwards, any unmarked pixel adjacent to a 1 will be marked 2, and so forth until all pixels are marked. This results in each pixel in the distance map being labeled with the distance to the closest 0 pixel.

Fig. 3. Left-to-right: local maxima after distance transform; dilation to find connected pixels; result after finding extents of connected regions. (Color figure online)

A local maximum pixel in the distance map (i.e., a pixel with no adjacent pixels that has a higher-valued label) corresponds to a "distance-based feature pixel", useful for detecting fingers [23]. However, unlike the suggestion in [23] to use simple threshold values to identify fingers, we instead combine this with the depth value of each local maximum to estimate a *blob radius:* that is, assuming that a given local maximum is the center of a circular blob whose radius is given by its label, we can compute the physical radius of the blob from its depth value. This is given by:

$$r = d * \frac{2z \tan\left(\frac{f}{2}\right)}{h} \tag{1}$$

where r is the blob radius, d is the label value (i.e., minimum distance to a 0 pixel), z is the depth value in meters, f is the vertical field-of-view angle of the camera, and h is the height of the camera in pixels (assuming a standard camera perspective transformation). Essentially, the label value is multiplied by the height of a square box that is z meters away from the camera plane and completely filling a single pixel. The result, expressed in meters, is then compared with a minimum and maximum "finger radius" (empirically set to 0.006 m and 0.015 m, respectively). In Fig. 3, left, each maximum pixel with a blob radius between the minimum and maximum finger radius is marked yellow. These local maxima pixels form rough "finger lines" (actually curves) that correspond to the center lines of the user's actual fingers.

While [23] suggests a different method to find the hand "centroid", i.e., the rough center of the hand, we instead reuse the above distance transform results to find a "hand line". In Fig. 3, left, pixels that are between the maximum finger radius and a maximum "hand radius" (set to 0.06 m) are marked purple.

It is observed that the local maxima pixels are rarely physically connected, therefore, morphological dilation [21] is necessary (see Fig. 3, middle) to connect these pixels. Once connected, we can use the standard connected component labeling algorithm to label the finger and hand lines: two similarly marked pixels belong to the same label if they are directly adjacent or if there exists a path between them passing through pixels of the same label. After determining all labels ("lines"), all but the longest "hand line" and the first five longest "finger lines" are discarded.

The extents of each labeled line correspond to the final set of features that we want to track (see Fig. 3, right). The hand centroid is determined by finding each finger line's centroid (a simple average of all (x, y) coordinates of the finger line's pixels) and then finding the point in the hand line where the sum of the distances from each finger line's centroid is minimized. This usually (but not always) corresponds to one of the extremum points of the hand line. Finally, each finger's tip and base point is determined by finding, for each finger line, the pixel that is farthest and closest to the hand centroid, respectively.

2.4 Gesture Classification and Rendering

For the purposes of direct comparison with HoloLens, a simple pose classification system is devised to identify four basic poses: open hand, closed hand, two fingers, and one finger (see Fig. 4). The "two-finger" pose was originally planned for implementing the HoloLens 2 "pinch" gesture. Implementation difficulties (discussed in the next subsection) forced this pose to be dropped; however, the "pinch" gesture is functionally equivalent to the "grab" gesture, which uses open and closed hand poses [5].

Each pose is easily identified by simply counting the number of fingers (with one special case: the "one-finger" pose will only register when the finger is fully pointed upwards, similar to HoloLens). In terms of gesture classification, the transition from one pose to another determines the type of gesture. To this end, the framework tracks the current hand pose in a simple state machine in order to determine whether the next pose is in a valid state. For example, an "air-tap" may be registered only if the previous pose is "one-finger" and the current pose is "closed-hand", and a subsequent "tap-release" may be registered only if the sequence of poses started with "one-finger" (and not "open-hand"). The sequence of poses is critical for distinguishing certain interface actions: for example, the air-tap gesture remembers the initial "hotspot" position of the user's fingertip, and subsequent dragging of the closed-hand pose moves the hotspot relative to this initial position rather than using the absolute hand centroid. (Note that our system's air-tap hotspot differs from the HoloLens: in HoloLens, the user is asked to "gaze" at the object they want to interact with before performing the air-tap, whereas in our system, the user hovers their finger above it.)

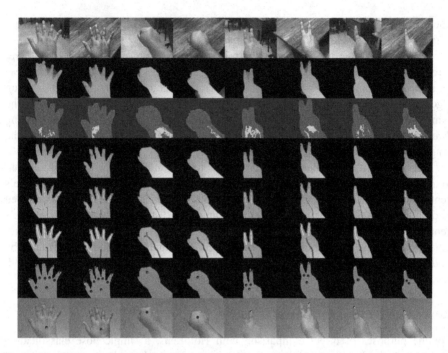

Fig. 4. Hand poses under alternating lighting conditions. Left-to-right: open hand, closed hand, two fingers, one finger (selection phase of air-tap).

For final rendering, the segmented hand image (as determined by the depth map) is rendered on top of the final AR image with a constant, non-opaque alpha transparency value. This is done in order to allow the virtual AR scene to partially show through the user's hands. While fully occluding AR objects behind the user's hand may be deemed more realistic, AR objects are only visible in the phone's screen, and fully obscuring them will result in the complete loss of visual cues pertaining to AR object locations, which may translate to a bad user experience.

2.5 System Limitations

This section briefly discusses our HGR framework's current limitations, as noted through empirical testing.

Unlike previous methods with a training procedure to calibrate the system with the user's skin color [18, 19], our method works without pre-training and is fairly robust to real-time variations in lighting conditions and skin colors (as seen in Fig. 4). However, since only the predominant hand color is accounted for, the method sometimes fails to find fingers with significant color variations (e.g., skin folds, shadows) or depth changes (e.g., angled fingers). This problem becomes especially severe when one tries to implement the "pinch" gesture (see Fig. 5, top) where fingers can occasionally get cut off. Fingernails also tend to get cut off, but this usually results in a slight offset to the finger's hotspot and is normally not noticed by users, who are usually focusing at the virtual object being manipulated and not on their own fingers.

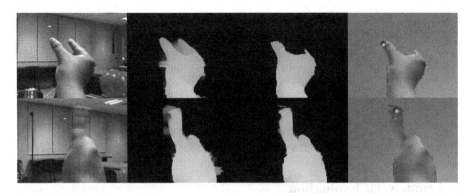

Fig. 5. Finger cut-off (top) and depth map desynchronization due to fast motion (bottom). Left-to-right: raw RGB, raw depth, filtered depth, blended result.

Gestures performed with very fast motion exhibit a different issue (see Fig. 5, bottom): the apparent desynchronization of the computed depth map from its paired RGB map at the same time frame. This is due to the depth map being computed from two asynchronously running cameras, resulting in a delay between the RGB frame that is shown to the user and the RGB frame from the other camera (used in conjunction with the first RGB frame to calculate the depth map). This results in garbage depth frames during fast motion. For this reason, the framework implements a pose-smoothening filter where a new hand pose is identified only if the pose appears in the majority of the last 5 frames (similar to the method used in [24]).

A full view of the user's hand is needed in order to identify a hand pose (see Fig. 6). This may become problematic for usability as this requires users to keep their hand within the limited field-of-view of the phone. For iPhone X, the field-of-view is measured to be 37.72° horizontally, limited by the telephoto field-of-view angle of the second camera lens used for computing depth. The iPhone X also does not report depth information that is less than 0.2 m away from the camera, requiring users to significantly extend their hand behind the phone while bringing the phone closer to their eyes in order for their hand gesture to be visible. This is in contrast to the HoloLens 1, whose depth sensor has a 120° field-of-view, 4 times wider than its display's 30° field-of-view. This design is partly why HoloLens requires users to gaze directly at a virtual object that will be the target for gestures such as air-tap; the air-tap itself is allowed to be performed outside of the display's extents, which incidentally aids in user comfort. This limitation may be partly remedied with the iPhone 11, which features a dual camera setup with both wide-angle lenses.

Finally, Apple's ARKit is unfortunately not supported by the current framework due to API restrictions built into iPhone X and iOS 12. This means that support for tracking of planar surfaces (which aids in localizing the phone's position relative to the world) is currently not possible. Thus, for this framework, the phone's gyroscope sensor is accessed directly in order to provide an AR experience equivalent to ARKit's orientation tracking mode (which only accounts for a user staying at the same position while being able to rotate the phone). This problem should be remedied in iPhone 11 with iOS 13 and above.

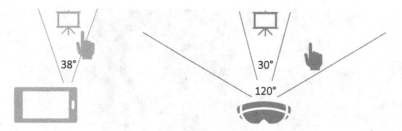

Fig. 6. Gesture area visualization on iPhone X vs HoloLens 1.

3 Framework Evaluation

Our AR-HGR application framework is used for the development of a sample application that features all of the framework's supported gestures. This application is described in the next subsection. This app is then subjected through a usability evaluation procedure to determine whether smartphone-based AR-HGR is a viable alternative to head-mounted AR-HGR, which is described in the succeeding subsection.

3.1 Description of Application

The sample application (see Fig. 7) is similar in design to other educational games, with extensive use of on-screen instructional text and images to guide the user through the AR content.

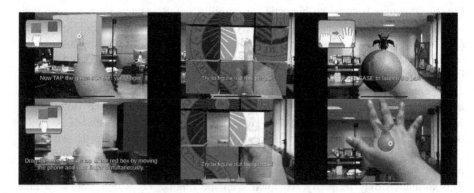

Fig. 7. Sample app. Left-to-right: onboarding tutorial; puzzle game; ball-throwing game.

The application starts with an onboarding tutorial similar to the HoloLens first-use tutorial, since users are expected to have never previously used hand gestures for application input. This is followed by two mini-games: a jumbled picture puzzle, and a ball-throwing game that expects the user to use physics principles to successfully pass the ball to a virtual character. An application session takes roughly 5–10 min.

The devices used for the evaluation procedure are a HoloLens 1 and an iPhone X (2017 release). The HoloLens 1 does not support the 5-finger "grab" and "release" gestures, so these were replaced with the 1-finger "air-tap" and "tap-release" gestures for the HoloLens app. In turn, the iPhone X app was also relaxed to allow the 1-finger gesture to be used for cases where the 5-finger version is preferred, although the on-screen instructions heavily recommend using the 5-finger version instead.

3.2 Usability Evaluation Protocol

A total of 24 study participants were recruited. All participants are female high school students with an average age of 17 (±1) years old, matching the target audience of our educational-game-style application. Participants were divided into two groups, wherein the first group uses the HoloLens 1 version of the app first before the iPhone X version, and vice versa for the second group. This is done to discover potential differences due to *anchoring bias* [25]: testers may be influenced by the order of usage of the two devices, that is, their experience with the first device may shape their opinion of their experience with the second device.

Pre-test. A 4-question, 7-point Likert-style test is given to each participant before the actual experiment, for the purpose of self-assessing their familiarity with the following technology topics: Augmented Reality, Hand Gesture Recognition, HoloLens, and Phone-Based AR (e.g., Pokémon GO). This is done as an informal measure of the participants' likelihood to be influenced by the *novelty effect*: perceived usability is increased for a given technology on account of its newness, and gradually normalizes as the technology becomes more commonplace [26].

Application Testing. Participants are asked to use each device, one after the other, under the supervision of a test facilitator. The test facilitator notes down the progress of each participant in each device and assists with any difficulties. Due to time constraints, not all participants are able to finish using the application on one device in the allotted time of 5 min; the participants were gently asked to stop once time is up. They are also allowed to stop on a voluntary basis.

Per-Device Usability Evaluation. After using each device, participants are asked to fill out a Handheld Augmented Reality Usability Scale questionnaire (HARUS) [27] specifically for that device. HARUS is a 7-point Likert-style questionnaire with 16 questions. Since the HoloLens is technically not a handheld device, the questions are adapted to better reflect the hardware's usage, and care is taken in wording to ensure that the original intention of each question is not lost (See Table 1). In addition, question #4, which originally pertains to the general ease in performing user input, is adjusted to specifically focus on the hand gesture input aspect of the application.

Table 1. Paired evaluation questions for HoloLens and iPhone versions.

	HoloLens question	iPhone question
1	I think that interacting with the HoloLens application requires a lot of body muscle effort	I think that interacting with the phone application requires a lot of body muscle effort
2	I felt that using the HoloLens application was comfortable for my arms, hands and head	I felt that using the phone application was comfortable for my arms and hands
3	I found the HoloLens difficult to carry while operating the application	I found the phone difficult to carry while operating the application
4	I found it easy to perform hand gestures for the HoloLens	I found it easy to perform hand gestures for the phone's back-facing camera
5	I felt that my arm/hand/head became tired after using the HoloLens application	I felt that my arm/hand became tired after using the phone application
6	I think the HoloLens application is easy to control	I think the phone application is easy to control
7	I felt that I was losing control and dropping the HoloLens at some point	I felt that I was losing control and dropping the phone at some point
8	I think the operation of this HoloLens application is simple and uncomplicated	I think the operation of this phone application is simple and uncomplicated
9	I think that interacting with this HoloLens application requires a lot of mental effort	I think that interacting with this phone application requires a lot of mental effort
10	I thought the amount of information displayed on the HoloLens screen was appropriate	I thought the amount of information displayed on the phone screen was appropriate
11	I thought that the information displayed on the HoloLens screen was difficult to read	I thought that the information displayed on the phone screen was difficult to read
12	I felt that the information display was responding fast enough	I felt that the information display was responding fast enough
13	I thought that the information displayed on the HoloLens screen was confusing	I thought that the information displayed on the phone screen was confusing
14	I thought the words and symbols were easy to read	I thought the words and symbols were easy to read
15	I felt that the HoloLens display was flickering too much	I felt that the phone display was flickering too much
16	I thought that the information displayed on the HoloLens screen was consistent	I thought that the information displayed on the phone screen was consistent

Post-test Device Survey. After each participant has evaluated the usability of each device, they are asked to answer a device survey, adapted from an existing hand-held vs. hands-free AR device study [28]. Participants may choose one device, both, or neither. The results are later tallied in order to discover the participants' preferred devices, both in the current context (i.e., the application they just used) and in forward-looking applications. Note that while this study focuses on comparing only the hand-gesture-recognition aspect of each device, a question related to the quality of AR visuals is also included, on the suspicion that other aspects of the hardware technology influence the participants' ultimate preference. Participants are also encouraged to write additional comments on their device preference, though this is optional (Table 2).

Table 2. Device preference questions.

Shorthand (as used in charts)	Preference question
For Current App	Which device would you prefer for this specific AR application?
For General Apps	Which device would you use for using other AR applications in general?
For Educ. Apps	Which device would you use for educational apps to learn about sciences, history, or other subjects?
For Visualization	At which device is the graphical visualization of the AR world more appealing to you?
For Hand Gestures	Which device would you prefer to use for efficient input of hand gestures?
For Short-Term Use	Which device would you use for short amounts of time?
For Long-Term Use	Which device would you use for long amounts of time?

4   Results and Discussion

This section discusses the results of the aforementioned usability evaluation protocol. An analysis of these results will help us answer the question of whether AR-HGR on smartphones is a viable alternative to AR-HGR on head-mounted displays, specifically in the context of educational use (which is the target of our sample application).

4.1   Pre-test Results

The self-assessment pre-test, on a Likert scale from 1 to 7, reveals the following participants' average familiarity with the given technology topics:

- 3.00 ($\pm$1.38) = slight familiarity with Augmented Reality
- 3.25 ($\pm$1.77) = slight familiarity with Hand Gesture Recognition
- 1.13 ($\pm$0.45) = close to no familiarity with HoloLens
- 4.21 ($\pm$1.41) = average familiarity with Phone-based AR (e.g., Pokémon GO)

The participants' non-familiarity with HoloLens, coupled with pre-existing familiarity with phone-based AR, indicates that the usability evaluation will be partly influenced by the novelty effect. That is, usability results will likely be skewed in favor of HoloLens on account of its newness to the participants, relative to phone AR. That said, the rest of this discussion will compare the usability of each device via quantitative measures and shall emphasize other identified factors over the novelty effect.

4.2 Application Testing Results

During application testing, the test facilitators noted down the progress of each participant, as well as other notable observations.

It was found that all users successfully completed the tutorial on both devices. However, while all users were able to finish the puzzle game on the HoloLens, one user did not finish the puzzle on the iPhone. This is due to a hand-detection issue that went undiagnosed at testing time. Informal diagnosis after the user test reveals that smaller hand sizes (similar to that of the reported user) were not being consistently detected by the system because the allowed hand radius range was set at compile time to (0.015 m, 0.06 m]. Apart from needing to account for the small hand size, this hand radius range also has to consider the non-visibility of parts of the hand during motion; thus, a smaller minimum value was needed for this user's case. Making this range a run-time option is considered for future testing.

All users who reached the ball-throwing mini-game on a given device were able to successfully execute the ball-throwing gesture, on command and on intention. (5-finger grab-and-release on iPhone, 1-finger tap-and-release on HoloLens.) However, only a handful of users were able to successfully pass the ball to the virtual character within the testing time limit. The total number of successes was unfortunately not noted down, as it was initially expected that all users will eventually succeed. The difficulty was likely due to the game itself: the users were expected to discover the successful solution on their own (i.e., the ball needs to be thrown at a high angle). The choice of device was not a factor: notably, 3 users successfully passed the ball on their second device in exactly one throw, and 2 of these users actually failed to pass the ball on their first device (2 users succeeded on iPhone, 1 on HoloLens).

Another notable observation is that some participants were wearing bracelets or long-sleeved cuffs, and this initially prevented the iPhone from detecting their hands. (The bracelet/cuff was incorrectly detected as the predominant skin color, cutting off the hand prematurely.) When the said participants removed their bracelets or brought their cuffs up to their elbow, they were able to continue with no further issues.

4.3 Post-test Device Survey Results

Figure 8 depicts the result of the post-test device survey. Assuming the null hypothesis of an equal preference likelihood for either device, we apply a Pearson chi-square test of independence on the HoloLens-only and iPhone-only answers for each question. This test reveals that, for 3 out of 7 scenarios, there is no observed significant difference ($P > 0.05$) in preference for either device: for general apps ($\chi^2 = 1.6363...$), for educational apps ($\chi^2 = 0.6$), and for short-term use ($\chi^2 = 2.33...$). This means that the differences observed in the chart, while appearing to be slightly significant (particularly, for general apps and for short-term use), are not sufficiently large to disprove the null hypothesis due to the small number of participants in the survey (24). Participant comments with regards to these items also substantiate this finding (e.g., "both devices help get the children's attention", "phone is similar to the HoloLens and would help more 'cause it's portable", "both devices are very fun and visually interactive").

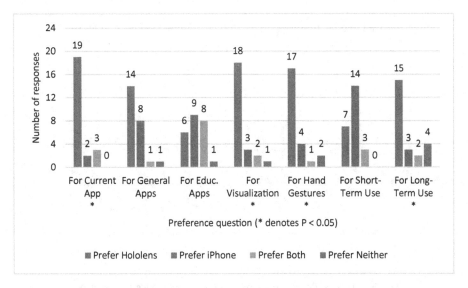

Fig. 8. Post-test device comparison (all users).

However, the same chi-square test reveals that the null hypothesis is disproven ($P < 0.05$) for the remaining questions: preference for current app ($\chi^2 \approx 13.762$), for visualization ($\chi^2 \approx 10.714$), for hand gestures ($\chi^2 \approx 8.048$), and for long-term use ($\chi^2 = 8.0$). This means that the participants significantly prefer the HoloLens for these four questions. This result is substantiated by the amount of participant comments favoring the HoloLens related to these questions (e.g., "HoloLens is easier and fun", "HoloLens movements are more natural", "calibration for hand gestures was amazing [for HoloLens]", "phone was tiring to use after a long time", "phone makes both arms tired", "phone does not detect hand gestures as efficiently"). Nevertheless, the existence of comments that are contrary to this result (e.g., "[HoloLens is] difficult to keep in head", "can't see in [HoloLens] app", "I got dizzy using HoloLens", "phone was easier to use compared to HoloLens") show that these preferences are still subjective on a person-to-person basis and the phone app's usability is not absolutely discredited compared to the HoloLens version. A total of 13 participants had written comments that overall favor the HoloLens over the iPhone, and 6 participants had written comments favoring the iPhone over the HoloLens.

When separating the groups according to their first device used (see Fig. 9), a chi-square goodness-of-fit test ($\chi^2 \approx \{0.386, 5.143, 2.278, 3.556, 4.529, 4.286, 5.067\}$ for each paired column, respectively) reveals no significant differences ($P > 0.05$) between each group's preferences compared to the combined population's preferences; that is, no anchoring-bias-like effects were observed for the post-test device survey.

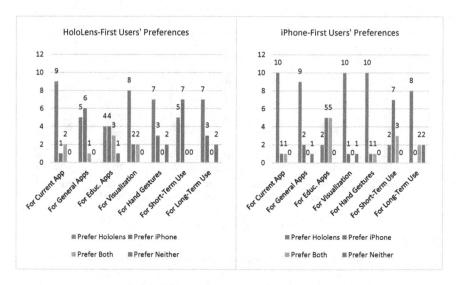

Fig. 9. Post-test device comparison, grouped by device-use recency.

4.4 Per-Device Usability Evaluation Results

In order to compare the relative perceived usability of the HoloLens and the iPhone on the same application, we use a paired two-sample Student's t-test on the HARUS usability questionnaire results (see Fig. 10). For 9 out of 16 usability questions, we find significant differences ($P < 0.05$) between the participants' experience with the HoloLens compared to their corresponding experience with the iPhone. We list these questions down in Table 3 to diagnose the differences, and it is revealed that all of these differences favor the HoloLens over the iPhone. Moreover, for 2 of the 9 questions ("Comfortable for the arms, hand, & head", and "Arm/hand/head became tired"), extreme differences in averages of up to 2.17 points are noted. This echoes an earlier-identified system limitation (discussed in Subsect. 2.5), where the iPhone application is significantly hampered by the need to keep the whole hand visible to the phone's dual-back-facing cameras in order to perform hand gestures. Thus, we can conclude that, unless the iPhone's dual-back-camera design is altered to accommodate a wider field-of-view and a closer depth map minimum (to allow for a shorter camera-to-hand distance), user comfort over prolonged periods of time will suffer in comparison with HoloLens.

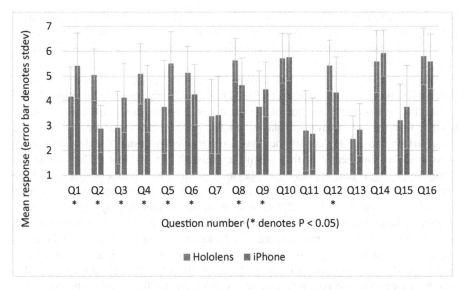

Fig. 10. Perceived usability differences between HoloLens and iPhone.

Table 3. Usability questions with significant differences between HoloLens and iPhone.

Question	HoloLens mean	iPhone mean	Difference
Q1. Requires a lot of body muscle effort	4.17 (neutral)	5.42 (slightly agree)	**1.25**
Q2. Comfortable for arms, hand & head	5.04 (slightly agree)	2.88 (slightly disagree)	**2.17**
Q3. Difficult to carry device	2.92 (slightly disagree)	4.13 (neutral)	**1.21**
Q4. Easy to perform hand gestures	5.08 (slightly agree)	4.08 (neutral)	**1.00**
Q5. Arm/hand/head became tired	3.75 (neutral)	5.50 (agree)	**1.75**
Q6. Easy to control app	5.13 (slightly agree)	4.25 (neutral)	**0.88**
Q8. App operation is uncomplicated	5.63 (agree)	4.63 (slightly agree)	**1.00**
Q9. Interaction requires mental effort	3.75 (neutral)	4.46 (neutral)	**0.71**
Q12. Information display is fast enough	5.42 (slightly agree)	4.33 (neutral)	**1.08**

For the other questions in the table, only small average differences are found (1.25 points or less). Closer inspection reveals that these differences are all slight perception changes that pushes the comparative usability from slightly positive to neutral (except in Q1, from neutral to slightly negative, and Q8, from positive to slightly positive); that is, the perceived usability changes are not major. Given that the rest of the questions show no significant differences in usability, it may be concluded that, barring the hardware field-of-view issue, the HGR technology developed in this study is already very close in usability to that found in HMD-based devices, but that there are still slight usability differences specifically in ease of control, muscle and mental effort, and the speed of information display. These remaining issues may be alleviated with a faster, more accurate software implementation.

When separating the groups according to their first device used and applying a paired *t*-test on all 32 questions (see Fig. 11), we find a significant perception change on the iPhone's usability for one of the questions, possibly due to anchoring bias: "I thought that the information displayed on the phone screen was consistent". The perceived iPhone display consistency has a better average result (6.08) when participants used the HoloLens first than when they used the iPhone first (5.08), which is a mildly surprising result. A possible explanation is: since the HoloLens-first users have already used the HoloLens app by the time they use the iPhone app, they may have found that the latter is not too different in terms of information display consistency (this notably includes the display of the user's real hand on top of virtual AR objects); in contrast, iPhone-first users have not seen the HoloLens app in action and would rate the display's consistency on its own (with the lower rating probably due to prior experience in previous smartphone AR apps). While this result is inconclusive for now, this may be a variant of the novelty effect and might merit further study (Table 4).

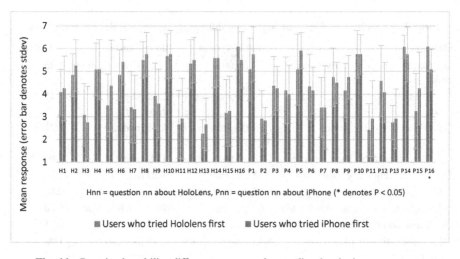

Fig. 11. Perceived usability differences, grouped according by device-use recency

Table 4. Usability questions with significant differences depending on device-use recency

Question	HoloLens-first users	iPhone-first users	Difference
P16. I thought that the information displayed on the phone screen was consistent	6.08 (agree)	5.08 (slightly agree)	**1.00**

5   Conclusion

This study explored the feasibility of using a dual-back-camera smartphone to develop Augmented Reality (AR) applications that feature Hand Gesture Recognition (HGR), and whether such a system is comparable in usability to the same application running on a head-mounted system such as HoloLens. The foregoing framework development study and subsequent usability evaluation concludes that AR-HGR is indeed possible on smartphones, and an AR-HGR application on such a device is fairly competitive in usability with its HMD-based counterpart despite several hardware and implementation limitations.

We have identified the small field-of-view of current dual-camera smartphones such as that found on iPhone X as the main hindering limitation, which may likely be solved with future hardware improvements (particularly, the addition of wide-view camera lenses or back-facing depth sensors to phones). Further improvements to the reliability and speed of the software-based HGR solution would also help in usability.

Future work includes the development of full-fledged educational AR applications using the framework developed in this study, and usability evaluation over prolonged time periods (which may exhibit a reduced novelty effect and permit better comparisons). Using machine-learning-based pose identification may further increase gesture vocabulary and allow support for sign language as an AR interaction possibility.

References

1. Johnson, L., Adams Becker, S., Cummins, M., Estrada, V., Freeman, A., Hall, C.: NMC Horizon Report: 2016 Higher Education Edition. The New Media Consortium, Austin, Texas (2016)
2. Alexander, B., et al.: EDUCAUSE Horizon Report 2019 Higher Education Edition. EDU19 (2019)
3. Microsoft: Getting around HoloLens (1st gen). https://docs.microsoft.com/en-us/hololens/hololens1-basic-usage. Accessed 19 Feb 2020
4. Magic Leap: Hand Tracking. https://developer.magicleap.com/learn/guides/lumin-sdk-handtracking. Accessed 19 Feb 2020
5. Microsoft: Getting around HoloLens 2. https://docs.microsoft.com/en-us/hololens/hololens2-basic-usage. Accessed 19 Feb 2020
6. Hornecker, E., Buur, J.: Getting a grip on tangible interaction: a framework on physical space and social interaction. In: Proceedings of the SIGCHI Conference on Human Factors in Computing Systems, pp. 437–446. ACM, New York (2006)
7. Redish, E.F., Kuo, E.: Language of physics, language of math: disciplinary culture and dynamic epistemology. Sci. Educ. 24, 561–590 (2015)
8. Li, N., Duh, H.B.-L.: Cognitive issues in mobile augmented reality: an embodied perspective. In: Huang, W., Alem, L., Livingston, M.A. (eds.) Human Factors in Augmented Reality Environments, pp. 109–135. Springer, New York (2013). https://doi.org/10.1007/978-1-4614-4205-9_5
9. IQUII: From Augmented Reality to Mobile Reality: it's the smartphone that drives augmented reality. https://medium.com/iquii/from-augmented-reality-to-mobile-reality-its-the-smartphone-that-drives-augmented-reality-31ae65b44958. Accessed 19 Feb 2020

10. Google Developers: ARCore overview. https://developers.google.com/ar/discover. Accessed 19 Feb 2020
11. AppleInsider: ARKit Overview. https://appleinsider.com/inside/arkit. Accessed 19 Feb 2020
12. Kaushik, V., Lall, B.: Fast hierarchical depth map computation from stereo (2019). http://arxiv.org/abs/1901.09593
13. Unity: Multiplatform. https://unity3d.com/unity/features/multiplatform. Accessed 19 Feb 2020
14. OpenCV: About. https://opencv.org/about/. Accessed 19 Feb 2020
15. Cheok, M.J., Omar, Z., Jaward, M.H.: A review of hand gesture and sign language recognition techniques. Int. J. Mach. Learn. Cybernet. (2017). https://doi.org/10.1007/s13042-017-0705-5
16. Apple Developer Documentation: Choosing a Capture Device. https://developer.apple.com/documentation/avfoundation/cameras_and_media_capture/choosing_a_capture_device. Accessed 19 Feb 2020
17. Apple Developer Documentation: AVDepthData – AVFoundation. https://developer.apple.com/documentation/avfoundation/avdepthdata. Accessed 19 Feb 2020
18. Shih, H., Ma, C.: Hand segmentation with skin color fine-tuning using Kinect depth sensor. In: 2017 IEEE 6th Global Conference on Consumer Electronics (GCCE), pp. 1–2 (2017)
19. Lee, J.Y., Yoo, S.I.: An elliptical boundary model for skin color detection. In: Proceedings of the 2002 International Conference on Imaging Science, Systems, and Technology (2002)
20. Wikipedia contributors: CIELAB color space. https://en.wikipedia.org/wiki/CIELAB_color_space. Accessed 19 Feb 2020
21. OpenCV 2.4.13.7 documentation: Eroding and Dilating. https://docs.opencv.org/2.4/doc/tutorials/imgproc/erosion_dilatation/erosion_dilatation.html. Accessed 19 Feb 2020
22. Google AI Blog: On-Device, Real-Time Hand Tracking with MediaPipe. https://ai.googleblog.com/2019/08/on-device-real-time-hand-tracking-with.html. Accessed 19 Feb 2020
23. Le, D., Mizukawa, M.: Fast fingertips positioning based on distance-based feature pixels. In: International Conference on Communications and Electronics 2010, pp. 184–189 (2010)
24. Sato, Y., Saito, M., Koike, H.: Real-time input of 3D pose and gestures of a user's hand and its applications for HCI. In: Proceedings IEEE Virtual Reality 2001, pp. 79–86 (2001)
25. Cho, I., Wesslen, R., Karduni, A., Santhanam, S., Shaikh, S., Dou, W.: The anchoring effect in decision-making with visual analytics. In: 2017 IEEE Conference on Visual Analytics Science and Technology (VAST), pp. 116–126 (2017)
26. Koch, M., von Luck, K., Schwarzer, J., Draheim, S.: The novelty effect in large display deployments–experiences and lessons-learned for evaluating prototypes. In: Proceedings of 16th European Conference on Computer-Supported Cooperative Work-Exploratory Papers. European Society for Socially Embedded Technologies (EUSSET) (2018)
27. Santos, M.E.C., Taketomi, T., Sandor, C., Polvi, J., Yamamoto, G., Kato, H.: A usability scale for handheld augmented reality. In: Proceedings of the 20th ACM Symposium on Virtual Reality Software and Technology, pp. 167–176. ACM, New York (2014)
28. Riedlinger, U., Oppermann, L., Prinz, W.: Tango vs. HoloLens: a comparison of collaborative indoor AR visualisations using hand-held and hands-free devices. Multimodal Technol. Interact. 3, 23 (2019)

User-Centric AR Sceneized Gesture Interaction Design

Xin-Li Wei[1(✉)], Rui Xi[1], and Wen-jun Hou[1,2]

[1] School of Digital Media and Design Arts, Beijing University of Posts
and Telecommunications, Beijing 100876, China
Shirley_Musen@163.com
[2] Beijing Key Laboratory of Network Systems and Network Culture, Beijing
University of Posts and Telecommunications, Beijing 100876, China

Abstract. With the rapid development of AR technology, the interaction between humans and computers has become increasingly complex and frequent. However, many interactive technologies in AR currently do not have a very perfect interaction mode, and they are facing huge challenges in terms of design and technical implementation, including that AR gesture interaction methods have not yet been established. There is no universal gesture vocabulary in currently developed AR applications. Identifying appropriate gestures for aerial interaction is an important design decision based on criteria such as ease of learning, metaphors, memory, subjective fatigue, and effort [1]. It must be designed and confirmed in the early stages of system development, and will seriously affect each aerial application project development process as well as the intended user of the user experience (UX) [2]. Thanks to user-centric and user-defined role-playing method, this paper set up a suitable car simulation scenarios, allowing users to define the 3D space matches the information exchange system under AR design environment based on their habits and cultural backgrounds, in particular, It is a demanding gesture during the tour guide and proposes a mental model of gesture preference.

Keywords: Gesture interaction · Guessability · AR

1 Introduction

1.1 Augmented Reality (AR)

Augmented reality is a technology that seamlessly fuses real-world information with virtual information [3]. It can bring physical information (visual, sound, taste, touch, etc.) that is difficult to experience in a certain space and time range in the real world. Through computer and other scientific technologies, virtual information is superimposed on the real world after simulation and is perceived by human senses, thereby achieving a sensory experience beyond reality. AR technology realizes the real-time overlay of real information and virtual information on the same screen or space at the same time. The integration of virtual and real is the key content of AR technology [4]. Integration of the actual situation makes the AR technology to achieve the extension of enhanced reality environments, seamless integration of virtual information with the real

© Springer Nature Switzerland AG 2020
J. Y. C. Chen and G. Fragomeni (Eds.): HCII 2020, LNCS 12190, pp. 367–378, 2020.
https://doi.org/10.1007/978-3-030-49695-1_24

environment, to achieve integration is to focus on the actual situation on the track identification markers, related to the complex coordinate conversion information, requiring real-time mapping The position of the virtual information in the 3D space is displayed on the screen.

1.2 Mid-Air Gesture Interaction

Mid-air gesture interaction has evolved into a feasible human-computer interaction (HCI) interaction. As an auxiliary interaction mode, it has been applied in many fields, such as home entertainment [5], in-vehicle systems [6], and human-computer interaction [7]. Although the AR/VR glasses break device for air gesture interaction in the air is closer to the way of natural interaction, it is still not ideal. The problems of low recognition efficiency [8] and insufficient function mapping design [9] have not been completely solved. Although existing designs focus on specific scenarios, they ignore their spatiotemporal characteristics. The application of the interaction system is single [10] and the interaction dimension is relatively simple [11]. Moreover, improper design of the mapping between gestures and interaction functions will make the user's cognitive burden relatively heavy, especially in 3D scenes such as information communication, virtual assembly, etc., the systematicity of interactive system design still needs to be improved [12].

1.3 Scene-Based Interaction

The original meaning of the scene refers to the scenes that appear in dramas and movies. Goffman proposed the pseudo-drama theory, which explained the behavior area: all the places that felt to some extent restricted [13]. Merovitz extended the concept of "scene" from Goffman's "simulation theory" [14]. Robert Scoble proposes the "five forces" of the mobile Internet: mobile devices, social media, big data, sensors and positioning systems [15].

With the development of information technology, scenes are states where people and behaviors are connected through network technology (media), and this scene creates unprecedented value and also creates a new and beautiful experience that guides and standardizes the user's Behavior has also formed a new lifestyle. The development of augmented reality technology and the use of fusion between virtual scenes and physical scenes become possible, and the scenes interact with each other and restrict each other. Scene interaction design is the design to improve the user experience for each scene. Therefore, based on the scene-based interaction, the development of augmented reality interaction design is focused on the interaction relationship between specific scenes and behaviors. Based on the time, place, person or other characteristics in the scene, it quickly searches and explores relevant information, and outputs content that meets the needs of users in specific situations. To construct specific experience scenarios, pay attention to the experience and perceptibility of design results, establish a connection between users and products, achieve a good interaction between the two, give users an immersive experience or stimulate user-specific behaviors [16]. In a word, the scene-based design is based on a specific scenario and through experience to promote events that are sufficient to balance the value relationship between the subject and the object [17].

1.4 Predictability Studies

In the user-centric design concept, intuitive design is the most important part. Cognitive psychology believes that intuitive design is the process by which people can quickly identify and handle problems based on experience. This process is unwise, fast and easy. Blackler's research also confirms this process [18]. Cooper also mentioned that the intuitive interface design allows people to quickly establish a direct connection between functions and tasks based on interface guidance [19]. With the continuous development of gesture recognition devices, the main design problem turns to gesture-induced research, the purpose of which is to trigger gestures that meet certain design standards, such as learnability, metaphors, memory, subjective fatigue, and effort. One of the methods with the highest user adoption is the "guessability" study, which was first introduced as a unified method for assessing the ergonomic characteristics of a user's mental model and gestures [20]. In general, predictability research refers to the cognitive quality of input actions and is performed by having participants present a gesture that can better match the task without any prior knowledge. Gesture sets are derived from data analysis using various quantitative and qualitative indicators and then classified [21]. Other studies have enriched demand gestures by applying other metrics for analysis, and further extended them to specific application systems [22]. Selection-based heuristic research is used as a variant of predictable research [23]. By establishing levels of predictability and protocol metrics, the results of user experience can be quantified, and they can be used to assess the degree of intuition in action design [24]. At present, there are researches based on guessability, such as interaction on large touch screens [25], Smartphone gesture interaction [26], Hand-foot interaction in the game [27], VR gesture interaction [28], etc. The User-defined method is a good method to study gesture interaction based on augmented reality, and it is worth further research.

1.5 Role-Playing

The role-playing method is mainly proposed by interaction designer Stephen P. Anderson. It is mainly used in the early stage of interactive prototyping during system development. The user's interaction is elaborated, and the user's interaction process and details are recorded, including the user's mood and emotions during the process. Researchers need to control the user's choices at all times during the experiment to streamline unnecessary choices [29]. By completing the entire test, it helps to adjust and make decisions in the preliminary design.

2 The User - Defined Gesture Set Is Established Under Guessability

2.1 Participants

A total of 12 volunteers (6 women, 6 men) were recruited. Participants were all undergraduates from Beijing university of posts and telecommunications, ranging in age from 20 to 23 (mean: 21.6, SD = 0.76). All participants have no experience in using 3D interactive devices such as Leap Motion and Xbox, so they can be regarded as novice participants. All users have no use of hand disorders and visual impairment and are right-handed. This experiment followed the ethics of each psychological society, and all participants obtained informed consent.

2.2 Tasks

In order to find the interactive command of visit guide class gesture that is consistent with users' habits, and ensure the usability of gestures in the daily visits. We first listed 21 operating instructions of the 3D spatial information interaction system in the tour guide scene. Invited four familiar Leap Motion gestures of related experts (use Leap Motion at least three hours a day), through expert evaluation scenario task difficulty can be divided into level 3. Besides, an online questionnaire was conducted among 24 people who were familiar with gesture interaction in the past three months, and they scored the importance of the third-level difficulty task respectively. Finally, they selected 6 operation instructions of the first-level difficulty, 1 operation instruction of the second-level difficulty, and 3 operation instructions of the third-level difficulty. To visit the bootstrap class scene found in the process of collecting the 4S shop visit guide scene can cover screen instructions. Therefore, the scene of 4S shop car purchase is taken as an example to carry out the scenario-based command design (see Table 1).

Table 1. Six typical augmented reality scenarios with 10 corresponding instructions

Scene description	Command	Description
Change the size of the 3D model	Zoom in	Geometric magnification of the XYZ direction of a three-dimensional object
	Zoom out	Geometric reduction of the XYZ direction of a three-dimensional object
Change the angle of the 3D model	Rotate	Rotate the three-dimensional object at any angle in the XYZ direction
Operate the menu in three - dimensional space	Wake-up	Renders the file or menu interface
	Hide-out	Hide the file or menu interface
	Switch over	Switch the display content in the interface
Change the appearance of a 3D object	Change color	Change the color of a 3D object by using a texture ball
Multiple people collaborate to view the edited 3D model	Trigger	Live synchronous shared signal excitation
	Share	Real-time information sharing on site
Virtual space message	Space tag message	Place the virtual tag in three dimensions

2.3   Experiment Setup

The experimental Settings are shown in Fig. 1. The relevant 3D materials of the experiment were placed on a platform with a height of 130 cm, and participants were required to stand 60 cm away from the platform to perform relevant operations according to the instructions. In the experimental setting, the test subjects were deemed to have successfully triggered the function after making two different (less similar) gestures. Role-playing and interactive methods were used to give the subjects relevant information feedback.

During the formal experiment, users were asked to wear transparent glasses and told that the scene required a certain degree of imagination. It also prompts the user to allow any contact with the model material in the scene during the experiment. Participants were asked to make at least two gestures for each task to avoid lingering biases. The corresponding materials of role-playing props in the experiment are shown in Fig. 2 and the feedback Settings are shown in Table 2.

Fig. 1. The experimental scene

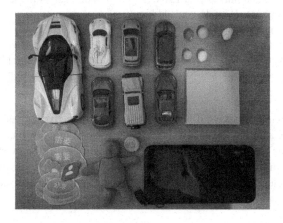

Fig. 2. Role-playing props

Table 2. Commands & words & feedback

Command	Words	Feedback
Zoom in	"Now you need to zoom in on the model of the car, what gestures or actions do you use to make this command to the system"	Replace the small car model with the large car model
Zoom out	"What if I wanted to shrink this model"	Replace the small car model with the large car model
Rotate	"What if I wanted to rotate this model"	The vehicle model was changed to a certain angle following the direction of rotation of the subject
Wake-up	"In fact, there are many interactive menus in this system, just like buttons in the phone. You need to wake up (activate them) by a gesture or action. What would you do?"	The paper menu icon was placed in front of the subjects
Hide-out	"If you can't use these menus, how do you hide them"	Put away the paper menu icon
Switch over	Now, the model of the car has a virtual display next to it, but the content on it is not complete, the rest is on another screen, how do you get another screen to appear?	Replace a convenience note with something else
Change color	Now you're still in this mixed reality scenario, and these little balls of different colors are the mediators that can trigger the change in the color of the car, what do you do?	According to the choice of the subject, the car model is changed to the corresponding color
Trigger	Now that you've changed the color of the car, you want to show this effect to your fellow driver, add him to your LAN, how do you trigger this action?	"You have now activated the Shared signal" voice-over prompt
Share	A dot appears on his head. Now you need to add him to your LAN via your phone. How do you add him to your phone list?	"Your friend can already see your color changes to the car," the voice-over prompts
Space tag message	Now that you've written a message on your phone, how do you post it in this virtual space?	The post-it notes, which represent the virtual labels, were placed where the subjects wanted to put them

Based on previous studies [30], we collected the subjective scores of the proposed gestures from five aspects: learnability, metaphor, memorability, subjective fatigue, and effort. Participants were asked to use a 5-point Likert scale for every two gestures (1 = completely disagree, 5 = completely agree). To evaluate the five aspects: the gesture is easy to learn, the interactive gesture exists naturally in the scene, my gesture is easy to remember, the movement I perform is not easy to fatigue, I do not feel the exertion of this gesture.

2.4 Data Analysis

A total of 76 gestures, 163 different gestures, were collected.

The two experts first classified gestures based on video and verbal descriptions of the participants. A gesture is the same gesture if it contains the same movement or gesture. Movement is mainly the direction of the knuckle movement, including horizontal, vertical and diagonal; A pose is a position at the end of the body, such as an open or kneaded hand. The differences between two experts in the classification process need to be determined by a third expert. We ended up with 76, 163 gestures, five of which were excluded because participants confused the meaning of the task or because the gesture was hard to recognize.

Then according to the consistency calculation formula proposed by Vatavu and Wobbrock (see Fig. 3) [31], the consistency of each command gesture was calculated. The experimental data are shown in Table 3.

$$AR(r) = \frac{|P|}{|P|-1} \sum_{P_i \subseteq P} \left(\frac{|P_i|}{|P|} \right)^2 - \frac{1}{|P|-1}$$

Fig. 3. The formula for calculating the value of AR

Table 3. Agreement score

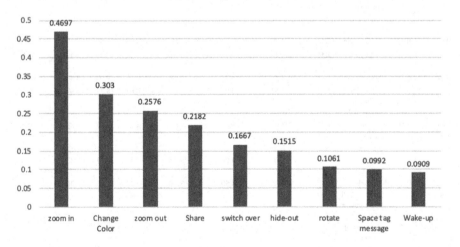

Where P is the total number of gestures for command r, and Pi is the number of the same gesture subset I in command r [31]. The distribution of AR values is from 0 to 1. In addition, according to the explanation of Vatavu and Wobbrock: a low agreement is implied when AR $\leq$ 0.100, a moderate agreement is implied when 0.100 < AR $\leq$ 0.300, a higher agreement is implied when 0.300 < AR $\leq$ 0.500, and AR > 0.500 signifies very high agreement. By the way, when AR = 0.500, the agreement rate is equal to the disagreement rate, which means the low agreement rate [31].

Table 4. Experimental group and control group score results

Command	AR	Gesture	Learnability	Metaphorical	Memorability	Subjective fatigue	Effort	Overall score	Average	Accuracy
Zoom in	0.4697	The distance between the palms of the hands varies greatly	5.00	3.83	4.50	3.17	3.50	20.00	4.00	83.00%
		One finger of both hands changes dramatically	4.33	3.83	3.83	3.17	**3.83**	19.00	3.80	100.00%
Zoom out	0.2576	The distance between the palms of the hands varies slightly	4.83	3.83	4.33	3.83	4.00	20.83	4.17	83.00%
		One finger of both hands changes dramatically and straightly	4.17	3.83	3.83	3.16	3.67	18.67	3.73	100.00%
Roate	0.1061	The wrist turns the palm	4.50	4.17	4.50	3.33	3.33	19.83	3.97	100.00%
		Under the car give a rotating wheel	4.00	4.00	3.83	**3.50**	**4.17**	19.50	3.90	100.00%
Wake-up	0.0909	Finger snap	3.83	4.00	4.83	3.83	4.00	20.50	4.10	67.00%
		Clap your hands	**4.33**	3.33	3.33	3.33	3.33	17.50	3.50	83.30%
Hide-out	0.1515	Finger snap	3.83	3.50	4.33	3.67	3.66	19.00	3.80	100.00%
		The hands are in the shape of X	**4.00**	**3.67**	3.00	3.67	**4.00**	18.33	3.67	66.67%
Switch over	0.1667	Sweep your palms vertically	4.83	4.83	5.00	4.67	4.83	24.17	4.83	83.00%
		Hands pointing	4.33	4.00	4.00	3.33	3.50	19.17	3.83	100.00%
Change color	0.303	Grab the material ball and throw it in the direction of the model	4.67	4.33	4.50	3.83	4.17	21.50	4.30	100.00%
		I'm gonna hit hte texture ball	4.67	3.83	4.33	3.50	3.50	19.83	3.97	100.00%

(*continued*)

Table 4. (*continued*)

Command	AR	Gesture	Learnability	Metaphorical	Memorability	Subjective fatigue	Effort	Overall score	Average	Accuracy
Trigger	0.0636	Click on the side of the glasses frame	5.00	4.00	4.50	4.83	4.83	23.17	4.63	100.00%
		Wave hand	3.50	3.00	3.00	4.00	3.50	17.00	3.40	83.30%
Share	0.2182	Grab the dot and put it in your phone list	4.33	4.00	4.33	3.50	3.67	19.83	3.97	100.00%
		Click on the dot	4.33	3.83	3.83	2.83	3.33	18.17	3.63	83.30%
Space tag message	0.0992	Grab the phone's tag and stick it in the virtual space	3.83	4.67	4.67	3.50	3.67	20.34	4.07	100.00%
		Click on the tab on your phone	4.17	3.00	4.17	3.00	3.67	18.01	3.60	83.30%

2.5 Subjective Rating of the Proposed Gestures

Although the user-defined method is effective in revealing the user's mental model of gesture interaction, it has some limitations [1]. User subjectivity may affect the accuracy of experimental results. An effective way to overcome this disadvantage is to show the user as many gestures as possible [32]. And re-check the most appropriate gesture.

2.6 Methods

According to the score of the subjects in experiment 1, two experts selected a group of high-grouping gesture sets from the gestures with scores in the first 50% of each instruction, and a group of low-grouping gesture levels from the last 50% of the gestures as the control group.

The new 12 students (1:1 male to a female) took part in the second experiment, which was set up in the same way as above. The 12 students were randomly divided into two groups, each with a 1:1 male to female ratio. The two groups of subjects did not conduct experiments in the same experimental environment at the same time. The subjects were required not to communicate with each other about the experimental contents during the experiment.

The actions corresponding to each instruction were repeated three times. After each command action, the subjects were given unlimited time to understand the intention behind the command. Once the participants understood the instructions, they were asked to rate the usability of the gestures based on ease of learning, metaphor, memorability, subjective fatigue and effort. After finishing all the actions for 10 min, the subjects need to recall the relevant actions according to relevant instructions, and the staff will record the error rate of the subjects.

3   Results and Discussion

As can be seen from Table 4, the average value of the high group is generally larger than that of the low group.

In the score of a single index, the gesture of the "hidden" menu at the AR glasses end showed a lower score of "hands over X" gesture than a higher score of "snapping fingers" gesture. However, in the subsequent test, it was found that only 66.67% of the participants in the lower group were correct. Finally, "snapping fingers" was included in the final gesture set.

It can also be seen from the data in Table 4 that for a pair of opposite operation instructions: the "wake up" and "hide" of the high group both adopted the operation instructions of snapping fingers, but when the subjects scored the "hide", the score was lower than that of the "wake up". Feedback from thinking out loud suggests that users prefer differentiated gestures.

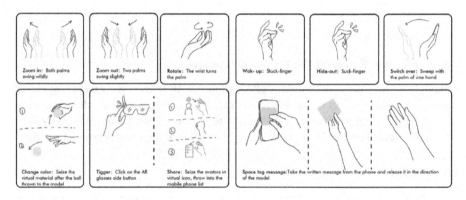

Fig. 4. User-defined gestures

Finally, it is concluded that gestures with high grouping can all be included in the final gesture set, which is shown in Fig. 4. In order to further reduce the experimental error, the gender of the subjects was analyzed by one-way ANOVA and no gender difference was found.

3.1   Mental Model Observations

According to the results of user-defined experiments, the characteristics of user psychological model can be obtained:

- Users prefer gestures that are tightly tied to the real world.
- For a pair of opposite operation instructions, such as "on-off" and "zooming in and out", users prefer those gestures with obvious differences.
- Users prefer to use dynamic gestures, and the interaction is not limited to the palm.
- In the face of complex scenes, users will choose multiple actions to complete the interaction.

4 Results and Discussion

In this paper, taking the 4S shop buying scene as an example, the most basic and common set of interactive commands and gestures in the scene of the tour guide is proposed. The goal is achieved by combining the method of guesswork, role play and scene interaction. The results were verified by newly recruited experimenters using the method of guessability. Combined with the two experimental data and the feedback of users' loud thinking, the user psychological model of gesture interaction in the AR scene was proposed. The resulting gesture set fits the scene of tour guide, which conforms to the user's cognition and usage habits, and provides some enlightenment for the design of 3D information interaction in the scene of the tour guide.

References

1. Hou, W., Feng, G., Cheng, Y.: A fuzzy interaction scheme of mid-air gesture elicitation. J. Vis. Commun. Image Represent. **64**, 102637 (2019)
2. Nair, D., Sankaran, P.: Color image dehazing using surround filter and dark channel prior. J. Vis. Commun. Image Represent. **50**, 9–15 (2018)
3. Graham, M., Zook, M., Boulton, A.: Augmented reality in urban places: contested content and the duplicity of code. Trans. Inst. Br. Geogr. **38**, 464–479 (2013)
4. Zhang, S., Hou, W., Wang, X.: Design and study of popular science knowledge learning method based on augmented reality virtual reality interaction. Packag. Eng. **20**, 60–67 (2017)
5. Lea, R., Gibbs, S., Dara-Abrams, A., Eytchison, E.: Networking home entertainment devices with HAVi. Computer **33**, 35–43 (2000)
6. Basari, Saito, K., Takahashi, M., Ito, K.: Measurement on simple vehicle antenna system using a geostationary satellite in Japan. In: 2010 7th International Symposium on Communication Systems, Networks & Digital Signal Processing (CSNDSP 2010), pp. 81–85 (2010)
7. Hancock, P., Billings, D., Schaefer, K., Chen, J., de Visser, E., Parasuraman, R.: A meta-analysis of factors affecting trust in human-robot interaction. Hum. Factors **53**, 517–527 (2011)
8. Atta, R., Ghanbari, M.: Low-memory requirement and efficient face recognition system based on DCT pyramid. IEEE Trans. Consum. Electron. **56**, 1542–1548 (2010)
9. Ben-Abdennour, A., Lee, K.Y.: A decentralized controller design for a power plant using robust local controllers and functional mapping. IEEE Trans. Energy Convers. **11**, 394–400 (1996)
10. Pramanik, R., Bag, S.: Shape decomposition-based handwritten compound character recognition for Bangla OCR. J. Vis. Commun. Image Represent. **50**, 123–134 (2018)
11. Bai, C., Chen, J.-N., Huang, L., Kpalma, K., Chen, S.: Saliency-based multi-feature modeling for semantic image retrieval. J. Vis. Commun. Image Represent. **50**, 199–204 (2018)
12. Han, J., et al.: Representing and retrieving video shots in human-centric brain imaging space. IEEE Trans. Image Process. **22**, 2723–2736 (2013)
13. Goffman, E.: The Presentation of Self in Everyday Life. Doubleday, Oxford (1959)
14. Asheim, L.: Libr. Q.: Inf. Commun. Policy **56**, 65–66 (1986)
15. Robert, S.: Age of Context: Mobile. Sensors, Data and the Future of Privacy (2013)

16. Liang, K., Li, Y.: Interaction design flow based on user scenario. Packag. Eng. **39**(16), 197–201 (2018)
17. Wei, W.: Research on digital exhibition design based on scene interaction. Design **17**, 46–48 (2018)
18. Blackler, A., Popovic, V., Mahar, D.: Investigating users' intuitive interaction with complex artefacts. Appl. Ergon. **41**, 72–92 (2010)
19. Cooper, A., Reimann, R., Cronin, D.: About Face 3: The Essentials of Interaction Design. Wiley, Indiana (2007)
20. Xu, M., Li, M., Xu, W., Deng, Z., Yang, Y., Zhou, K.: Interactive mechanism modeling from multi-view images. ACM Trans. Graph. **35**, 236:201–236:213 (2016)
21. Han, J., Zhang, D., Hu, X., Guo, L., Ren, J., Wu, F.: Background prior-based salient object detection via deep reconstruction residual. IEEE Trans. Circuits Syst. Video Technol. **25**, 1309–1321 (2015)
22. Xu, M., Zhu, J., Lv, P., Zhou, B., Tappen, M.F., Ji, R.: Learning-based shadow recognition and removal from monochromatic natural images. IEEE Trans. Image Process. **26**, 5811–5824 (2017)
23. Xu, M., Li, C., Lv, P., Lin, N., Hou, R., Zhou, B.: An efficient method of crowd aggregation computation in public areas. IEEE Trans. Circuits Syst. Video Technol. **28**, 2814–2825 (2018)
24. Wobbrock, J.O., Aung, H.H., Rothrock, B., Myers, B.A.: Maximizing the guessability of symbolic input. In: CHI 2005 Extended Abstracts on Human Factors in Computing Systems, pp. 1869–1872. ACM, Portland (2005)
25. Wobbrock, J.O., Morris, M.R., Wilson, A.D.: User-defined gestures for surface computing. In: Proceedings of the SIGCHI Conference on Human Factors in Computing Systems, pp. 1083–1092. ACM, Boston (2009)
26. Ruiz, J., Li, Y., Lank, E.: User-defined motion gestures for mobile interaction. In: Proceedings of the SIGCHI Conference on Human Factors in Computing Systems, pp. 197–206. ACM, Vancouver (2011)
27. Silpasuwanchai, C., Ren, X.: Jump and shoot!: prioritizing primary and alternative body gestures for intense gameplay. In: Proceedings of the 32nd Annual ACM Conference on Human Factors in Computing Systems, pp. 951–954. ACM, Toronto (2014)
28. Leng, H.Y., Norowi, N.M., Jantan, A.H.: A user-defined gesture set for music interaction in immersive virtual environment. In: Proceedings of the 3rd International Conference on Human-Computer Interaction and User Experience in Indonesia, pp. 44–51. ACM, Jakarta (2017)
29. Anderson, S., Heartbeat-A Guide to Emotional Interaction Design, Revised edn. (2015)
30. Chen, Z., et al.: User-defined gestures for gestural interaction: extending from hands to other body parts. Int. J. Hum.-Comput. Interact. **34**, 238–250 (2018)
31. Vatavu, R.-D., Wobbrock, J.O.: Formalizing agreement analysis for elicitation studies: new measures, significance test, and toolkit. In: Proceedings of the 33rd Annual ACM Conference on Human Factors in Computing Systems, pp. 1325–1334. ACM, Seoul (2015)
32. Dim, N.K., Silpasuwanchai, C., Sarcar, S., Ren, X.: Designing mid-air TV gestures for blind people using user- and choice-based elicitation approaches. In: Proceedings of the 2016 ACM Conference on Designing Interactive Systems, pp. 204–214. ACM, Brisbane (2016)

Cognitive, Psychological and Health Aspects in VAMR

Towards the Specification of an Integrated Measurement Model for Evaluating VR Cybersickness in Real Time

Ahlem Assila[1]([⊠]) [iD], Taisa Guidini Gonçalves[2]([⊠]) [iD],
Amira Dhouib[3]([⊠]), David Baudry[1]([⊠]) [iD], and Vincent Havard[1]([⊠]) [iD]

[1] LINEACT, CESI Engineering School, Reims, France
{aassila,dbaudry,vhavard}@cesi.fr
[2] Federal University of Rio de Janeiro – PESC/COPPE, Rio de Janeiro, Brazil
taisa@cos.ufrj.br
[3] National Engineering School of Saint-Etienne (ENISE), LTDS,
CNRS UMR 5513, Saint-Etienne, France
amiradhouib@live.fr

Abstract. Cybersickness (CS) is an affliction that limits the use of virtual reality (VR) applications. For decades, the measurement of cybersickness has presented one of the most challenges that have aroused the interest of VR research community. Having strong effects on users' health, cybersickness causes several symptoms relating to different factors. In most cases, the literature studies for VR cybersickness evaluation adopt the questionnaire-based approaches. Some studies have focused on physiological and postural instability-based approaches, while others support the VR content. Despite the attention paid to define measurements for assessing cybersickness, there is still a need for a more complete evaluation model that allows measuring cybersickness in real time. This paper defines a conceptual model that integrates subjective and objective evaluation of CS in real time. The proposed model considers three CS factors (i.e. individual, software and hardware). The aim is to consider the heterogeneous findings (subjective and objective measures) related to the selected CS factors that define integrated indicators. The theoretical part of the model was initially validated by researchers who have comprehensive knowledge and skills in VR domain. As a research perspective, we intend to evaluate the proposed model through a practical case study.

Keywords: Cybersickness · Virtual environment · Measurement · Evaluation · Integration

1 Introduction

Thanks to the digital revolution, virtual reality (VR) has been gaining popularity due to its capacity to immerse users into virtual environments (VE) [1]. This technology has been widely used in many fields, such as industrial maintenance, learning, healthcare, entertainment, and scientific visualization [2, 3]. However, the VR immersion may induce different undesirable side-effects for the users, such as cybersickness (CS) [4].

© Springer Nature Switzerland AG 2020
J. Y. C. Chen and G. Fragomeni (Eds.): HCII 2020, LNCS 12190, pp. 381–396, 2020.
https://doi.org/10.1007/978-3-030-49695-1_25

This latter exhibits similarities to motion sickness[1] and simulator sickness[2], and it's often categorized as a form of motion sickness [5]. In this way, different symptoms can be produced by CS like eyestrain, nausea, vertigo, disorientation, etc. [6]. These symptoms are essentially related to different factors, such as visual/no visual factors, tracking factors, simulator, task, and individual factors [3, 7, 8].

Previous cybersickness research have been proposed several evaluation methods; some are related to specific factors [9], while others consider more general solutions [10]. To the best of our knowledge, no work has defined a more complete approach that considers cybersickness factors with an integrated and complementary manner. We argue that the integration of these factors when evaluating cybersickness are essential to obtain better measures.

In this context, we are interested to define an integrated cybersickness measurement model that combines CS factors, in order to measure this effect in real time. This research introduces the first step towards the conceptual definition of an integrated model to aid the evaluation of cybersickness in real time. Towards this objective, different well-known evaluation methods will be used in conjunction with CS measures and factors.

This article is organized as follows: Sect. 2 introduces a brief background about VR and CS concepts and the previous works about cybersickness evaluation. Section 3 describes our proposed model for measuring cybersickness in real time. Section 4 presents a first validation of the model followed by a discussion that highlights some limits of our proposal, in Sect. 5. Finally, Sect. 6 concludes the paper and outlines some future perspectives.

2   Background

This section presents the background of our research. First of all, we define the concepts related to virtual reality and cybersickness. In the following, we present a set of measures that can be used to evaluate the cybersickness and the existing factors that cause it. Finally, we present recent research works proposed for the measurement of cybersickness in VR.

2.1   Virtual Reality and Cybersickness Concepts

As stated earlier, virtual reality represents a computer technology that allows users to feel present in a virtual environment through Head-Mounted Displays (HMD). In some cases, the use of VR may cause users an undesirable side-effect called cybersickness. Throughout the years, different definitions have been proposed in order to describe this effect in VR [11–13]. Nevertheless, there is a consensus that cybersickness consists of the emergence of a set of symptoms of discomfort by exposure to a VE. Such symptoms can occur during or after a VR immersion and can include, for example, eye strain, nausea, and headache [14]. In many cases, CS's symptoms can persist for hours

---

[1] Motion sickness can be defined as any sickness endured by observation of visual motion [5].

[2] Simulator sickness describes the sickness produced by vehicle simulators [5].

and, sometimes, for days [15, 16]. For these reasons, CS can be one of the main aspects to make people reject VR technology [17]. In order to measure the undesirable effects of CS, different measurements were used over the last years. The next section presents some of the most well-known measures of cybersickness along with the main factors that can cause it.

2.2 Cybersickness Measures and Factors

A number of different measures are provided in the research field to evaluate cyber-sickness in VE. These measures may be classified into two main types, namely objective and subjective measures. *Subjective measures* can be collected through multi-item questionnaires such as the Simulator Sickness Questionnaire (SSQ) [18], Cybersickness Questionnaire (CSQ) [19], and Virtual Reality Sickness Questionnaire (VRSQ) [20]. *Objective measures* involve the analysis of physiological measures. These latter can be obtained, for example, from heart rate [21], skin conductance [22] and respiration rate [23]. Objective measures may involve also analysis of behavioral measures like task competence [21], and early finalization of a VR experience [24].

Different factors exist in the literature aiming to contribute to CS in virtual environments. Based on Rebenitsch's classification [8], three categories of factors can be distinguished. These include: (1) *individual* which are related to the information concerning the user who interacts with the VR environment; (2) *hardware* related to the VR device and its configuration; and (3) *software* which concerns the VR content. Each factor can be further broken down into different sub-factors.

2.3 Related Work

Cybersickness effects can be measured and detected using a wide variety of approaches. According to Rebenitsch [8] three categories of approaches can be defined: (1) the *questionnaire-based approaches* which aim to perform subjective evaluation using specific cybersickness questionnaires (post or pre-immersion test such as SSQ [18]; (2) the *postural instability-based approaches,* which aim to evaluate the ability of an individual to maintain balance and postural control [8]; and (3) *the physiological/biometric-based approaches* which aim to measure different psychological signals like skin conductance and heart rate. In the following, these categories of approaches will be explained in detail.

Questionnaire-Based Approaches. Several questionnaires for evaluating cybersickness in VR are available in the literature. From the most used and known questionnaires, we quote SSQ [18], CSQ [19] and VRSQ [20].

The SSQ is a standard questionnaire and the most frequently used in assessing cybersickness, especially physiological status and comfort degree of subjects [18]. It consists of 16 items representing side effects emerging from interaction with virtual environments. This questionnaire distinguishes three main dimensions. These latter concern nausea (e.g. stomach awareness, increased salivation, etc.), oculomotor (e.g. eyestrain, difficulty focusing, blurred vision, etc.), and disorientation (e.g. vertigo) on a scale of 0–3 [9].

CSQ represents a variant of SSQ which emphasizes the symptoms in SSQ that would appear to clearly indicate cybersickness [19]. It retained nine symptoms and focused on the two dimensions: dizziness and difficulty in focusing.

Another variant of SSQ, called Virtual Reality Sickness Questionnaire (VRSQ), was proposed recently by Kim et al. [20]. This variant considers nine symptoms of the original SSQ and focuses only on oculomotor and disorientation dimensions.

Several studies have used other questionnaires to evaluate cybersickness. For instance, Liu et al. [9] have proposed a study to compare three methods of acustimulation approach[3] when evaluating cybersickness. They used Motion Sickness Susceptibility Questionnaire (MSSQ) [25] before the experiment to measure the history of motion sickness. Then, they used SSQ before and after VR video watching to measure physiological status, disorientation, oculomotor and comfort degree. Finally, they used Nausea Rating Test (NRT) questionnaire [26] to measure nausea symptoms during and after VR video watching.

Sevinc and Ilker [10] presented a comparison of different questionnaires to evaluate cybersickness effects in virtual environments. This study reports a psychometric evaluation of the SSQ and its variants, which are CSQ, VRSQ and FSSQ (French translation of SSQ). The results have shown that CSQ and VRSQ revealed better indicators of validity than the SSQ and FSSQ questionnaires. Moreover, this study indicated that the psychometric qualities of CSQ and VRSQ questionnaires are quite similar.

Postural Instability-Based Approaches. In most cases, these approaches are used in conjunction with questionnaires or physiological based approaches. Arcioni et al. [27] reported about postural instability theory and its proposals. This study shows that individual differences in postural activity can predict which people are more likely to experience visually induced motion sickness. The cybersickness was induced via multisensory stimulation combined head-and-display motion when participants continuously turn their head from left to right. It was subjectively evaluated by SSQ questionnaire. In [28], Wu et al. use an objective measurement of posture through the unbalanced analysis of variation (ANOVA) test. Their goal was to measure the presence and motion sickness of participants. In addition, the experiment includes subjective ratings of the VR experience, based on Motion Sickness Assessment Questionnaire (MSAQ) and Igroup Presence Questionnaire (IPQ). The postural data was included because it can be more sensitive to the immersion change compared to subjective measurements.

Physiological/Biometric-Based Approaches. The aim of physiological (also referred to as biometrics) approaches is to develop objective cybersickness measurements [8].

Guna et al. [22] examine the influence of content type (omnidirectional video) as well as of the video playback device (TV, 4x VR HMD) on the users in terms of VR sickness. To evaluate the VR sickness effects, both subjective (SSQ and SUDS (Subjective Units of Distress Scale [29]) and objective measures have been used. Questionnaires have been combined with the measurement of the physiological

---

[3] It represents a medical approach that presents a form of alternative therapy [9].

parameters (i.e. electrodermal activity and skin temperature, respiratory frequency, and heart rate), as objective measures. SSQ questionnaire could be the most important subjective tool when assessing the VR sickness effects. While, for the physiological parameters, electrodermal activity is the most correlated with VR sickness effects.

In [30], Kim et al. have proposed a cybersickness predictor based on electroencephalogram (EEG) measurement during VR simulation and a Recurrent Neural Network (RNN) prediction model.

Gavgani et al. [31] examined the use of tonic and phasic forehead skin conductance level before and during the immersion. Apart from the use of physiological measures, they recorded subjective symptoms post-experiment using MSAQ. Then, they compared subjective symptoms and physiological effects of motion sickness produced by physical motion and by immersion in VR in the same subjects. The results show that symptoms and physiological changes induced during CS and motion sickness are quite similar.

Summary. From the literature review, we noted that *questionnaire-based approaches* represent the most widely used approaches for the evaluation of VR cybersickness. According to Davis et al. [32], the questionnaire is popular since it represents an easy and cheap to do approach. However, it cannot provide in any way a real time data while the participant is in the virtual environments. Therefore, this approach is not useful to measure cybersickness in real time, but it can collect *individual information* about users before the test. It can be noted also that the use of objective measures from *postural instability and psychological approaches* would provide real time and accurate data about cybersickness. In addition, different approaches have been presented that include questionnaires, physiological and postural instability measures in a separate way. The integration of these aspects makes the analysis and interpretation phases complicated given the heterogeneity of the measures used.

3   Proposed Measurement Model for Evaluating Cybersickness in Real Time

In this research, we argue that the definition of a model to evaluate cybersickness in real time, by considering CS factors is very promising. For this purpose, an integrated model that supports subjective and objective CS evaluation in real time is proposed in this paper. The aims of our model consist of:

- Measuring VR cybersickness in real time by considering three CS factors;
- Ensuring a complete assessment by integrating subjective and objective evaluation findings related to the CS factors;
- Providing many CS measures that correspond to each factor and sub factor;
- Presenting indicators to integrate subjective and objective measures of CS.

For the proposed model, we decided to consider three cybersickness factors as defined by [8], namely: *individual*, *hardware*, and *software* (details about these factors can be found in Sect. 2.2). As shown in Fig. 1, the integrated CS measurement model includes four components: (1) cybersickness factors and sub factors; (2) cybersickness measures; (3) cybersickness evaluation tools; and (4) indicators.

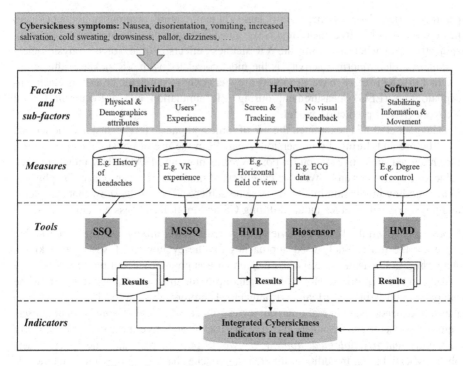

Fig. 1. Integrated cybersickness measurement model

The first component includes the *factors* and *sub factors* of CS. It aims to identify the source of cybersickness issues. For the proposed model, three cybersickness factors are considered: (i) **individual** – this factor is related to two sub factors which concern *users' experience* and their *physical and demographics attributes*.; (ii) **hardware** – it depends on two sub factors (i.e., *no visual feedback* and *screen and tracking movement*) due to the use of VR device; and (iii) **software** – this factor concerns the VR application content and more specifically the two sub factors: *stabilizing information* and *movement* [3, 8].

The second component of our model concerns *cybersickness evaluation measures* associated with each selected sub factor. As mentioned in Sect. 2.2, a variety of cybersickness measures are proposed in the literature. In this research, the selection process of measures is based essentially on the works of [3, 6–8].

Table 1 synthesizes the selected measures along with their associated factors, sub factors, and used tools.

Table 1. Factors, measures and tools for cybersickness evaluation

Factors	Sub-factors	Measures	Tools
Individual	Demographics and Physical attributes	History of motion sickness	MSSQ
		History of headaches/migraines	SSQ
	Experience	VR experience	MSSQ
		Postural stability[a]	
		Duration	Timer
Hardware	Screen & Tracking	Horizontal field of view	Head-Mounted Display
		Calibration	
		Head movements	
	Nonvisual Feedback	Electrocardiogram (ECG)[b] data	Biosensor tools
		Electrogastrogram (EGG)[c] data	
		Electroencephalogram (EEG)[d] data	
		Skin temperature	
Software	Stabilizing Information & Movement	Sitting versus standing	Head-Mounted Display
		Independent visual backgrounds[e]	
		Self-movement speed	
		Degree of control[f]	

[a]Postural instability is the ability of an individual to maintain balance and postural control [3].
[b]Electrocardiogram monitors the heart rate [6].
[c]Electrogastrogram detects stomach movement and strength [6].
[d]Cybersickness Predictor Based on Brain Signal Analysis [30].
[e]Independent Visual Backgrounds (IVB) are elements of the visual field that remain stable relative to the user [8].
[f]The degree of control allows to check if the users control their movements in a virtual environment [3].

The third component includes the *tools* used to extract the subjective and objective measures (see Table 1). In order to capture the essential measures of **individual** factors, we considered questionnaire tools. Regarding the evaluation of *physical and demographic attributes*, we adopted the Motion Sickness Susceptibility Questionnaire (MSSQ) [25]. The SSQ questionnaire is generally used to evaluate the history of headaches/migraines.

Regarding **hardware** factor, we proposed HMD to capture *screen and tracking measures* [3]. Apart from the use of subjective measures, we used the biosensors tools (e.g., ECG sensor, EGG sensor, EEG sensor, chest belt transducer, etc.) [22] to capture *physiological and biometric* measures. Concerning **software** factor, we considered HMD [3].

Different heterogeneous findings are captured from these CS evaluation tools. However, the interpretation of these results makes the evaluation very complicated, especially when they are presented separately. In order to facilitate the interpretation phase, we propose the integration of specific measures, called *indicators,* in the fourth component. The objective of this integration is to present the evaluation findings in a more consistent way.

As defined by ISO/IEC 15939 standard, an *indicator* represents "a measure that provides an estimation or evaluation of specified attributes derived from a model with respect to defined information needs" [33]. This concept has been applied in the Human-Computer Interaction field to define usability evaluation indicators that combine subjective and objective evaluation findings for user interfaces [34]. Evenly, it has been applied in the field of virtual reality [35] to define an indicator for navigation performance measurement in a VE.

A general process to define indicators [34] was the base of this work. The first step concerns the identification of information needs, in our case VR *cybersickness factors evaluation* (see Table 1). The second step involves identifying the *measures* to be used when specifying the *indicator* (see Table 1). To facilitate the next steps we named the measures according to each factor (**individual** factor - Individual Measure (IM); **hardware** factor - Hardware Measure (HM) divided on Hardware No Visual Measure (HNVM) or Hardware Screen Tracking Measure (HSTM); **software** factor - Software Measure (SM)).

The third step aims to interpret each measure through a set of defined rules. Each rule consists of checking whether the results of the measurements are acceptable (i.e. 1) or not (i.e. 0) according to predefined thresholds. For example, the Simulator Sickness Questionnaire (SSQ) returns as results a total score which is defined as the sum of all 16 SSQ items. Each item is based on a four-point likert scale ranging from 0 (the symptom does not exist) to 3 (very severe symptom). Small values are better, since score 0 indicate that the CS symptoms does not exist. To check if the returned SSQ total score is acceptable, a threshold X should be specified by an evaluator. Thus, SSQ total score returned acceptable results for values ϵ [0, X[and not acceptable for values ϵ [X, Y] (where Y is the maximum value of the total score).

The fourth step involves the definition and analysis of the *indicator* itself. As already explained, the latter represents the integration/combination of selected *measures.* The *indicators* are instantiated as a combination of a minimum of three *measures* previously defined (IM, HNVM, HSTM and SM). In this way, one cybersickness indicator i (CS_i) is the combination of one IM, one HM, and one SM. The analysis of the indicator, which is based on the predefined decision criteria, allows to identify the level of cybersickness present in a virtual environment.

In the case where the indicator is composed of three measures, our model generates eight possible decision criteria since each measure can return either an acceptable (1) or unacceptable (0) results. For example, the decision criterion *C1* represents: *if* IM return 0 and HM return 0 and SM return 0 (i.e. there have not acceptable results) *then* CS = 100%. Table 2 shows the possible combinations of three measures that instanced the indicators in conjunction with the level of CS.

Table 2. Decision criteria for cybersickness indicators combined three measures

	C1	C2	C3	C4	C5	C6	C7	C8
IM	0	0	1	1	0	0	1	1
HM	0	1	0	1	0	1	0	1
SM	0	1	1	0	1	0	0	1
CS	100%	66%	66%	66%	33%	33%	33%	0%

In summary, we have four possible cases:

1) There is a **severe cybersickness** problem (100%) in the case where all measures return not acceptable results associated to the three cybersickness factors.
2) There is a **moderate cybersickness** problem (66%) if three measures return not acceptable results associated to two cybersickness factors.
3) There is a **mild cybersickness** problem (33%) in the case where only one measure returns not acceptable results associated to one cybersickness factor.
4) There is **none cybersickness** problem (0%) if all measures return acceptable results associated to the three cybersickness factors.

Further, in the case where the indicator is composed of four measures, our model generates 16 possible decision criteria. For example, the decision criterion *C16* refers to: *if* IM return 1 and HSTM return 1 and HNVM return 1 and SM return 1 (i.e. there have acceptable results) *then* CS = 0%. Table 3 shows the possible combinations of the four measures that instanced the indicators and the level of CS.

Table 3. Decision criteria for cybersickness indicators combined four measures

	C 1	C 2	C 3	C 4	C 5	C 6	C 7	C 8	C 9	C 10	C 11	C 12	C 13	C 14	C 15	C 16
IM	0	0	0	0	1	0	0	0	1	1	1	0	1	1	1	1
HSTM	0	0	0	1	0	0	1	1	0	0	1	1	0	1	1	1
HNVM	0	0	1	0	0	1	0	1	0	1	0	1	1	0	1	1
SM	0	1	0	0	0	1	1	0	1	0	0	1	1	1	0	1
CS	100 %	75 %	75 %	75 %	75 %	50 %	50 %	50 %	50 %	50 %	50 %	25 %	25 %	25 %	25 %	0 %

In summary, we have five possible cases:

1) There is a **severe cybersickness** problem (100%) in the case where all measures return not acceptable results associated to three cybersickness factors.
2) There is a **moderate cybersickness** problem (75%) if three measures return not acceptable results associated to two/three cybersickness factors.

3) There is a **mild cybersickness** problem (50%) in the case where only two measures return not acceptable results associated to one/two cybersickness factors.
4) There is a **very mild cybersickness** problem (25%) in the case where only one measure returns not acceptable results associated to one cybersickness factor.
5) There is **none cybersickness** problem (0%) if all measures return acceptable results associated to the three cybersickness factors.

4   Model Evaluation

The first version of the model was evaluated by four researchers who have comprehensive knowledge and skills in VR domain. In this way, we have defined a questionnaire (see Fig. 2) inspired by the work of [36].

It consists of eight questions (likert scale) concerning the *understandability, ease of use*, and *usefulness and practicality* of the model; and three open questions that aim to collect information to improve the model. Analyzing the results of the eight likert scale questions and the three open questions (see Fig. 3), we can note that:

1) Concerning the *understandability,* the model structure and components are understandable for all researchers. In addition, many users (75%) agrees that the model content and rules are understandable. Analyzing the answers of the first open question, we identified that the researchers have suggested to include eventually examples of rules which would make the measures interpretation easier for users.
2) Regarding the *ease of use*, 50% of the researchers are slightly agree with the selected measures and the first version of rules. The second half of researchers have a neutral response. Based on the user's answers to the second open question, more information (such as the form of frame rate) about measures can be added to make the model more precise.
3) Concerning the *usefulness and practicality* of the model, many users (75%) slightly agrees for an experimental study. However, only 50% of the researchers agree that the model can be useful and practical in the industry. Some suggestions and notes have been proposed by researchers to make the model more practical. The first suggestion is to simplify the rules and to provide recommendations on the employability of this model. A second suggestion consists of specifying a weight of these measures according to their influence on cybersickness, which can be more appropriate since the proposed measures do not reflect cybersickness in the same way. For example, the RV content/application has a prominent role to the feeling of discomfort in a VE.

Model evaluation questionnaire					
Appraiser information					
Date					
Name (Optional)					
Organization/Institute					
Position					
Experience with virtual reality and cybersickness					
Email					

Part 1 - Likert scale questions

Criteria	Strongly Disagree	Slightly Disagree	Neither Disagree Nor Agree	Slightly Agree	Strongly Agree
Understandability					
The model structure is understandable					
The model components are understandable					
The model content is understandable					
The rules are understandable					
Ease of Use					
The measures are easy to use					
The rules are easy to use					
Usefulness and Practicality					
The model is useful conducting case studies (experimental study)					
The model is practical for use in industry					

Part 2 - Open questions

Question 1 - Could the model be made more understandable? How?

Question 2 - Could the model be made more useful? How?

Question 3 - Could the model be made more practical? How?

Fig. 2. Evaluation questionnaire

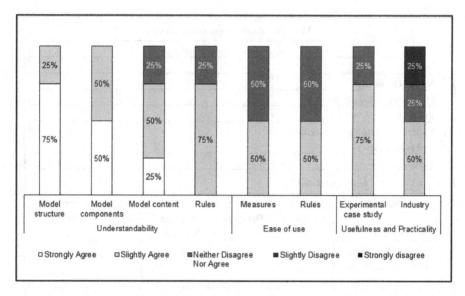

Fig. 3. Results for likert scale questions

5   Discussion and Limitations

In general, the evaluation shows that the first version of the proposed model is *understandable, ease of use*, and *useful and practical*. Many of the suggestions are integrated into the proposed model generating the version here presented (version 2.0). For example, in the version 1.0 we have used the term "rule" for the interpretation of measures and indicator results. This causes a lack of understandability about the proposed rules. Thus, in the version 2.0 of our model, we have defined two terms. A rule allows interpreting the results of a predefined measure to check if the results are acceptable or not according to predefined thresholds. While, decision criteria allow interpreting the results of the indicator itself based on a set of rules consisting on interpreting the values related to the selected measures of the indicator.

Although the obtained results are promising, there exist some limitations. The first one concerns the proposed model which focuses only on three factors based on the classification of [8]. It should be noted that other factors exist in the literature, like the environmental factors that include temperature, relative humidity, light, air quality, ambient noise, etc. [6]. Taking into consideration this limitation, we suggest including other factors in the proposed model in future work.

Another limitation is related to the no exhaustiveness of the used lists of measures and tools. Additional ones can be integrated then on our proposed model. Further, while physiological measures provide more detailed and precise data about cyber-sickness, those are usually more expensive to perform and the results are more complex to analyze [32].

The third limitation concerns the interpretation of cybersickness indicators. We are not concerned with the combinations of measures. Furthermore, only a "theoretical" evaluation of the proposed model was performed. It will be beneficial to consider different cases studies for a practical validation in the future.

As future work, we envisage the evaluation of the model through a practical case study based on an industrial virtual reality learning environment (VRLE) [37]. The VR application allows simulating, in a collaborative VRLE, an industrial assembly process composed of 43 assembly steps containing 150 parts to assemble spread on up to 6 manual workstations (Fig. 4(a) and (b)). It also allows the simulation of a robotic workstation to train for assembly tasks assisted by a robotic arm (Fig. 4(c) and (d)).

In order to evaluate the integrated cybersickness measurement model, experiments will be conducted within a virtual reality experimentation platform allowing real time acquisition of VR simulation data and Human physiological signals. For the model evaluation, the first considered measurements will be the session duration, head movements, electrocardiogram and electroencephalogram data and HMD VR simulation data like movement and interactions in VR session. Complementary data will be also recorded during the VRLE session in order to have complementary indicators on the performance and behavior. It will include eye tracking measurement, skeleton (posture) and localization data, galvanic skin response data and task progression and errors during the training scenario. Pre and post session questionnaire on user experience will be also deployed.

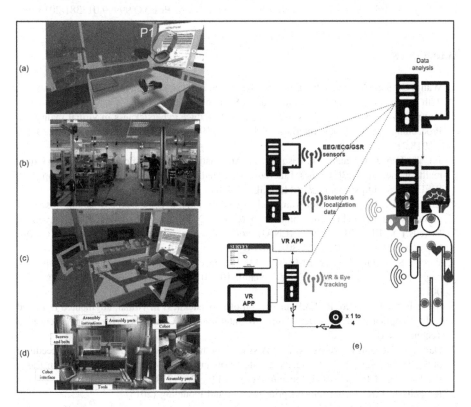

Fig. 4. Virtual reality learning environment of an industrial assembly process and (e) Virtual reality experimentation platform with real time data acquisition

6   Conclusion and Perspectives

This paper has presented a conceptual model for supporting subjective and objective cybersickness evaluation in real time. The model integrated three main factors (i.e. individual, software and hardware), sub factors, measures, tools and indicators related to cybersickness (i.e. individual, software and hardware). The main goal consists on considering the subjective and objective measures related to the selected CS factors.

Our proposal was initially validated the model by researchers who have a comprehensive knowledge and skills in VR domain. The first results show that our model must be enhanced in terms of the experiments by considering different practical cases studies. This point will be one of the research perspectives. Also, we intend to define a new way to interpret the different combinations of measures.

Future work will also investigate the integration of other factors (sub factors), measures, tools and indicators related to CS in the proposed model. In the hope that our proposal can help the researches and industrials in cybersickness evaluation.

Acknowledgments. The authors would like to acknowledge the researchers who evaluate the model presented in this study. LINEACT authors thanks the financial support granted by the Europe (FEDER), region Grand Est and region Normandie through the NumeriLab project and the Industrial Chair CISCO – VINCI Energies. Taisa Gonçalves thanks the financial support granted by CAPES – Science without Borders Program (DOC-PLENO 99999.013381/2013-00).

References

1. Wang, G., Suh, A.: User adaptation to cybersickness in virtual reality: a qualitative study. In: 27th European Conference on Information Systems (ECIS) (2019)
2. Farmani, Y., Teather, R.: Viewpoint snapping to reduce cybersickness in virtual reality. In: Proceedings of Graphics Interface 2018, pp. 159–166 (2018). https://doi.org/10.20380/gi2018.21
3. Jin, W., Fan, J., Gromala, D., Pasquier, P.: Automatic prediction of cybersickness for virtual reality games. In: IEEE Games, Entertainment, Media Conference (GEM), Galway, pp. 1–9. IEEE (2018). https://doi.org/10.1109/GEM.2018.8516469
4. Choroś, K., Nippe, P.: Software techniques to reduce cybersickness among users of immersive virtual reality environments. In: Nguyen, N.T., Gaol, F.L., Hong, T.-P., Trawiński, B. (eds.) ACIIDS 2019. LNCS (LNAI), vol. 11431, pp. 638–648. Springer, Cham (2019). https://doi.org/10.1007/978-3-030-14799-0_55
5. Weech, S., Kenny, S., Barnett-Cowan, M.: Presence and cybersickness in virtual reality are negatively related: a review. Front. Psychol. **10** (2019). https://doi.org/10.3389/fpsyg.2019.00158
6. Silva, B.M., Fernando, P.: Early prediction of cybersickness in virtual, augmented & mixed reality applications: a review. In: 5th International Conference for Convergence in Technology (I2CT), India (2019)
7. Davis, S., Nesbitt, K., Nalivaiko, E.: A systematic review of cybersickness. In: Proceedings of the 2014 Conference on Interactive Entertainment – IE 2014, Newcastle, NSW, Australia, pp. 1–9. ACM Press (2014). https://doi.org/10.1145/2677758.2677780
8. Rebenitsch, L.R.: Cybersickness prioritization and modeling (2015)

9. Liu, R., Zhuang, C., Yang, R., Ma, L.: Effect of economically friendly acustimulation approach against cybersickness in video-watching tasks using consumer virtual reality devices. Appl. Ergon. **82**, 102946 (2020). https://doi.org/10.1016/j.apergo.2019.102946

10. Sevinc, V., Berkman, M.I.: Psychometric evaluation of Simulator Sickness Questionnaire and its variants as a measure of cybersickness in consumer virtual environments. Appl. Ergon. **82**, 102958 (2020). https://doi.org/10.1016/j.apergo.2019.102958

11. McCauley, M.E., Sharkey, T.J.: Cybersickness: perception of self-motion in virtual environments. Presence Teleop. Virt. Environ. **1**, 311–318 (1992). https://doi.org/10.1162/pres.1992.1.3.311

12. Stanney, K.M., Kennedy, R.S., Drexler, J.M.: Cybersickness is not simulator sickness. In: Proceedings of the Human Factors and Ergonomics Society Annual Meeting, pp. 1138–1142 (1997). https://doi.org/10.1177/107118139704100292

13. Rebenitsch, L., Owen, C.: Review on cybersickness in applications and visual displays. Virtual Reality **20**, 101–125 (2016). https://doi.org/10.1007/s10055-016-0285-9

14. LaViola, J.J.: A discussion of cybersickness in virtual environments. ACM SIGCHI Bull. **32**, 47–56 (2000). https://doi.org/10.1145/333329.333344

15. Kellog, R.S., Castore, C.H., Coward, R.E.: Psychophysiological effects of training in a full vision simulator. In: Annual Scientific Meeting of the Aerospace Medical Association (1980)

16. Gower, D.W., Fowlkes, J.E.: Simulator Sickness in the UH-60 (Black Hawk) Flight Simulator. Army Aeromedical Research Laboratory, U.S. (1989)

17. Fernandes, A.S., Feiner, S.K.: Combating VR sickness through subtle dynamic field-of-view modification. In: IEEE Symposium on 3D User Interfaces (3DUI), Greenville, SC, USA, pp. 201–210. IEEE (2016). https://doi.org/10.1109/3DUI.2016.7460053

18. Kennedy, R.S., Lane, N.E., Berbaum, K.S., Lilienthal, M.G.: Simulator sickness questionnaire: an enhanced method for quantifying simulator sickness. Int. J. Aviat. Psychol. **3**, 203–220 (1993). https://doi.org/10.1207/s15327108ijap0303_3

19. Stone III, W.B.: Psychometric evaluation of the Simulator Sickness Questionnaire as a measure of cybersickness. Graduate Theses and Dissertations, 15429 (2017). https://lib.dr.iastate.edu/etd/15429

20. Kim, H.K., Park, J., Choi, Y., Choe, M.: Virtual reality sickness questionnaire (VRSQ): motion sickness measurement index in a virtual reality environment. Appl. Ergon. **69**, 66–73 (2018). https://doi.org/10.1016/j.apergo.2017.12.016

21. Nalivaiko, E., Davis, S.L., Blackmore, K.L., Vakulin, A., Nesbitt, K.V.: Cybersickness provoked by head-mounted display affects cutaneous vascular tone, heart rate and reaction time. Physiol. Behav. **151**, 583–590 (2015). https://doi.org/10.1016/j.physbeh.2015.08.043

22. Guna, J., Geršak, G., Humar, I., Song, J., Drnovšek, J., Pogačnik, M.: Influence of video content type on users' virtual reality sickness perception and physiological response. Future Gener. Comput. Syst. **91**, 263–276 (2019). https://doi.org/10.1016/j.future.2018.08.049

23. Dennison, M.S., Wisti, A.Z., D'Zmura, M.: Use of physiological signals to predict cybersickness. Displays **44**, 42–52 (2016). https://doi.org/10.1016/j.displa.2016.07.002

24. Kinsella, A.J.: The effect of 0.2 Hz and 1.0 Hz frequency and 100 ms and 20–100 ms amplitude of latency on simulatory sickness in a head mounted display (2014)

25. Golding, J.F.: Motion sickness susceptibility questionnaire revised and its relationship to other forms of sickness. Brain Res. Bull. **47**, 507–516 (1998). https://doi.org/10.1016/S0361-9230(98)00091-4

26. Lo, W.T., So, R.H.Y.: Cybersickness in the presence of scene rotational movements along different axes. Appl. Ergon. **32**, 1–14 (2001). https://doi.org/10.1016/S0003-6870(00)00059-4

27. Arcioni, B., Palmisano, S., Apthorp, D., Kim, J.: Postural stability predicts the likelihood of cybersickness in active HMD-based virtual reality. Displays **58**, 3–11 (2019). https://doi.org/10.1016/j.displa.2018.07.001

28. Wu, T.L.Y., Gomes, A., Fernandes, K., Wang, D.: The effect of head tracking on the degree of presence in virtual reality. Int. J. Hum.-Comput. Interact. **35**, 1569–1577 (2019). https://doi.org/10.1080/10447318.2018.1555736

29. Milosevic, I., McCabe, R.E. (eds.): Phobias: The Psychology of Irrational Fear. Greenwood, an imprint of ABC-CLIO, LLC, Santa Barbara (2015)

30. Kim, J., Kim, W., Oh, H., Lee, S., Lee, S.: A deep cybersickness predictor based on brain signal analysis for virtual reality contents. In: IEEE International Conference on Computer Vision (ICCV), pp. 10580–10589 (2019)

31. Gavgani, A.M., Walker, F.R., Hodgson, D.M., Nalivaiko, E.: A comparative study of cybersickness during exposure to virtual reality and "classic" motion sickness: are they different? J. Appl. Physiol. **125**, 1670–1680 (2018). https://doi.org/10.1152/japplphysiol.00338.2018

32. Davis, S., Nesbitt, K., Nalivaiko, E.: Comparing the onset of cybersickness using the Oculus Rift and two virtual roller coasters. In: Pisan, Y., Nesbitt, K., Blackmore, K. (eds.) 11th Australasian Conference on Interactive Entertainment (IE 2015), Sydney, Australia (2015)

33. ISO/IEC: Systems and software engineering – Measurement process (ISO/IEC 15939:2007) (2007)

34. Assila, A., Oliveira, K.M., Ezzedine, H.: Integration of subjective and objective usability evaluation based on IEC/IEC 15939: a case study for traffic supervision systems. Int. J. Hum.-Comput. Interact. **32**, 931–955 (2016). https://doi.org/10.1080/10447318.2016.1220068

35. Assila, A., Plouzeau, J., Merienne, F., Erfanian, A., Hu, Y.: Defining an indicator for navigation performance measurement in VE based on ISO/IEC15939. In: De Paolis, L.T., Bourdot, P., Mongelli, A. (eds.) AVR 2017. LNCS, vol. 10324, pp. 17–34. Springer, Cham (2017). https://doi.org/10.1007/978-3-319-60922-5_2

36. Salah, D., Paige, R., Cairns, P.: An evaluation template for expert review of maturity models. In: Jedlitschka, A., Kuvaja, P., Kuhrmann, M., Männistö, T., Münch, J., Raatikainen, M. (eds.) PROFES 2014. LNCS, vol. 8892, pp. 318–321. Springer, Cham (2014). https://doi.org/10.1007/978-3-319-13835-0_31

37. Havard, V., Jeanne, B., Lacomblez, M., Baudry, D.: Digital twin and virtual reality: a co-simulation environment for design and assessment of industrial workstations. Prod. Manuf. Res. **7**, 472–489 (2019). https://doi.org/10.1080/21693277.2019.1660283

Cognitive Workload Monitoring in Virtual Reality Based Rescue Missions with Drones

Fabio Dell'Agnola[(✉)][iD], Niloofar Momeni[(✉)][iD], Adriana Arza[(✉)][iD], and David Atienza[(✉)][iD]

Embedded Systems Laboratory of Swiss Federal Institute of Technology Lausanne, Lausanne, Switzerland
{fabio.dellagnola,niloofar.momeni,adriana.arza,david.atienza}@epfl.ch, https://www.epfl.ch/labs/esl

Abstract. The use of drones in search and rescue (SAR) missions can be very cognitively demanding. Since high levels of cognitive workload can negatively affect human performance, there is a risk of compromising the mission and leading to failure with catastrophic outcomes. Therefore, cognitive workload monitoring is the key to prevent the rescuers from taking dangerous decisions. Due to the difficulties of gathering data during real SAR missions, we rely on virtual reality. In this work, we use a simulator to induce three levels of cognitive workload related to SAR missions with drones. To detect cognitive workload, we extract features from different physiological signals, such as electrocardiogram, respiration, skin temperature, and photoplethysmography. We propose a recursive feature elimination method that combines the use of both an eXtreme Gradient Boosting (XGBoost) algorithm and the SHapley Additive exPlanations (SHAP) score to select the more representative features. Moreover, we address both a binary and a three-class detection approaches. To this aim, we investigate the use of different machine-learning algorithms, such as XGBoost, random forest, decision tree, k-nearest neighbors, logistic regression, linear discriminant analysis, gaussian naïve bayes, and support vector machine. Our results show that on an unseen test set extracted from 24 volunteers, an XGBoost with 24 features for discrimination reaches an accuracy of 80.2% and 62.9% in order to detect two and three levels of cognitive workload, respectively. Finally, our results are open the doors to a fine grained cognitive workload detection in the field of SAR missions.

Keywords: Cognitive Workload Monitoring · Physiological signals · Machine learning · Search and rescue missions · Simulator · Drones

---

This work has been partially supported by the NCCR Robotics through the Symbiotic Drone project, and by the ONR-G through the Award Grant No. N62909-17-1-2006.

© Springer Nature Switzerland AG 2020
J. Y. C. Chen and G. Fragomeni (Eds.): HCII 2020, LNCS 12190, pp. 397–409, 2020.
https://doi.org/10.1007/978-3-030-49695-1_26

1   Introduction

The use of drones in search and rescue (SAR) missions can be very cognitively demanding. Rescuers often operate in extreme conditions, under time pressure, and dealing with the scarcity of human resources. Moreover, they have to find strategies to face all types of unexpected events that a SAR mission may hide. Since high levels of cognitive workload can negatively affect human performance [10,13], there is a risk of compromising the mission and leading to failure with catastrophic outcomes. Therefore, a Cognitive Workload Monitoring (CWM) system that detects elevate workload levels could be used to notify the rescues and prevent them from taking dangerous decisions.

Nowadays, there are three main methods to measure cognitive workload; that is, subjective surveys, performance metrics, and assessing the human physiological response [3,6]. Due to the needs of a continuous monitoring and the unpredictability of SAR missions, neither surveys nor performance metrics can be used for cognitive workload monitoring of rescues. In contrast, the cognitive workload monitoring from physiological signals, which can be acquired with wearable sensors, is suitable for this application.

Continuous workload monitoring is a challenging task because is a multi-dimensional problem. Many factors affect cognitive workload; that is mental, physical, and temporal demands, the overall performance, the frustration level, and the effort [5]. The perceived workload is both environmental and subjective dependent, it changes among individuals according to their learning skills and their ability to address and perform a particular task. Despite that, state-of-the-art studies that target cognitive workload detection from physiological signals showed promising results [3,4,9,12].

The objective of this work is to detect cognitive workload levels from physiological signals in the field of SAR missions with drones. However, due to the unpredictable conditions and the difficulties of having a cognitive workload reference value during real SAR missions, the data collection becomes really difficult. Therefore, we rely on Virtual Reality (VR) to emulate immersive SAR mission. Our main contributions are as follows:

- We induce three levels of cognitive workload using a VR simulator for SAR missions with drones.
- We detect high and low levels of cognitive workload with an accuracy, precision and recall of 80.2%, 79.6%, 71.7%, respectively on an unseen dataset, which prove the generalization of our model.
- We explore a three-class cognitive workload detection, thus identifying high, medium, and low levels of cognitive workload with an accuracy of 62.9%, which is a promising results considering the complex identification of cognitive workload levels generated in our virtual SAR mission.

The rest of the paper is organized as follows. Section 2 describes the methods applied to induce and detect different levels of cognitive workload. Section 3 describes the setup of the experiment and Sect. 4 reports our results. Finally, in Sect. 5 we draw the main conclusions of this work.

2   Cognitive Workload Characterization and Detection Methods

The general idea of the method applied for estimating cognitive workload, including sensor placement, is show in Fig. 1. A VR based simulator is used to induce different levels of cognitive workload by changing the difficulty of the tasks [4]. Then, the cognitive workload is detected from physiological signals by following a standard methodology, which includes signals acquisition, preprocessing, feature extraction, and classification. Finally, an elicitation technique based on a multidimensional assessment tool, the NASA Task Load Index (NASA-TLX) [6], and a questionnaire to evaluate the difficulty of the tasks are used to label the different levels of induced cognitive workload.

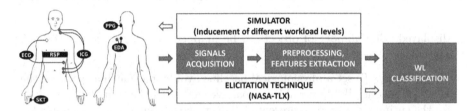

Fig. 1. Cognitive workload (WL) estimation from physiological signals, such as Electrocardiogram (ECG), Respiration (RSP), Impedance Cardiogram (ICG), Skin Temperature (SKT), Photoplethysmography (PPG), and Electrodermal Activity (EDA).

2.1   Simulator for Search and Rescue Mission with Drones

The proposed VR based simulator emulates a simplified SAR mission, where the pilot needs to fly a drone through a pathway and map a damage situation of a disaster area. The simulator was implemented with Unity3D [15] and used to track the workload influence on SAR missions with drones in [4]. In the simulator, the flight pathway is shown by 90 waypoints (black rings) distributed every 20 m along a randomly generated trajectory over a village. The speed of the drone is fixed at 6 m/s for all the tasks. The damage situation is represented by cubes that randomly appear over the flying pathway, as shown in Fig. 2. The colors of the cubes are chosen according to the regulation of the Swiss Firefighters; that is, yellow to indicate rescue situations, red for fire, blue for water damages, and green for the accidents.

To induce different levels of workload, both flying and mapping activities are combined yielding in the following tasks:

– *Training (T):* A training sequence is proposed to let the user familiarize himself with the simulator. The training sequence has a combination of both flying and mapping activities. The user is asked to fly as close as possible through the center of the waypoints. In addition, the user needs to press the button of the controller relative to the color of the objects that are randomly

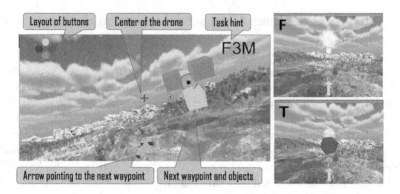

Fig. 2. Simulator for search and rescue mission with drones. Overview of different conditions: flying and mapping (F3M), flying (F), and training (T). (Color figure online)

displayed. The number of objects to be mapped are 60 per session, i.e., 15 per color.

- *Baseline (B):* To set a physiological baseline avoiding as much as possible the effect of uncontrollable variables, a passive task with the same framework as for the entire experiment is presented. This task is a flying sequence controlled by an auto-pilot. During this task, the user just needs to watch the sequence presented to him without any other additional activity.

- *Flying (F):* Flying task is considered as a medium level of cognitive workload. During this task, the subject solely needs to fly the drone as close as possible to the center of the waypoints.

- *Mapping 3 object (3M):* This task is also considered as a medium level of cognitive workload. During this task, the subject has to identify three objects of different color that appear at the same time on the screen and has to press the button of the controller corresponding to the color of the object. The number of objects to be mapped are 240 per session, i.e., 60 per color.

- *Flying and Mapping 3 objects (F3M):* This task is considered as a high level of the cognitive workload. It is the same as training, including the same combination of both the flying and mapping activities but with a more demanding mapping activity. The objects displayed simultaneously on the screen are three as in 3M task, and not only one as in the training phase.

2.2   Cognitive Workload Classification

The proposed methodology to build a model for CWM has three main steps. The first step is the acquisition of different signals, such as Electrocardiogram (ECG), Respiration (RSP), Impedance Cardiogram (ICG), Skin Temperature (SKT), pulse wave through Photoplethysmography (PPG), and Electrodermal Activity (EDA), as selected in [4, 9].

The second step is the preprocessing and feature extraction, where we filter the physiological signals and we extract several features to capture the functionality of the human physiology as we did in [1,9]. For the feature extraction we use a 1-minute sliding window without overlap. Then, we apply a Recursive Feature Elimination with Cross Validation (RFECV) to select the most important physiological features that better characterize different levels of cognitive workload. Our RFECV is based on the eXtreme Gradient Boosting (XGBoost) algorithm and uses the SHapley Additive exPlanations (SHAP) framework for a more detailed prediction interpretation [8].

Finally, the third and last step is the cognitive workload classification. In this step, we first investigate several machine learning algorithms to select the model that best fits our classification problem. To this aim, we compare XGBoost, Random Forest (RF), Decision Tree (DT), k-Nearest Neighbors (kNN), Logistic Regression, Linear Discriminant Analysis (LDA), Gaussian Naïve Bayes (GNB), and Support Vector Machine (SVM).

Both RFECV and the machine learning algorithms are trained and validated on the training set using a shuffled Leave-P-Groups-Out Cross-Validation (LPGOCV) with five iterations considering each time 20% of the groups as validation set. Each group is composed of all observations recorded in one day that belong to one subject. If not otherwise specified, the machine learning algorithms are trained and tested with [11] using default parameters.

Thus, we have applied the same procedure to address both binary and three-class classification problems. Finally, to prove the generalizability of our model, a final test is done on an unseen test set, which includes data from 30% of the groups, that was initially putted apart for this purpose only.

3 Experimental Study

To build a database and investigate the cognitive workload characterization and detection from physiological signals, we perform an experimental study applied a designed protocol as in Fig. 3 using the VR simulator for SAR mission with drones. To control the simulator it was used a Gamepad from Logitech [7]. We recorded the physiological signals with the Biopac acquisition set [2], which is CE certified for medical monitoring.

3.1 Study Protocol

Our study protocol starts with a setup phase, where we provide information about the experiment and we place the sensors. Additionally, we propose a training sequence to let the participant get familiar with the simulator. Then, we proceed with two phases of data collection, as shown in Fig. 3.

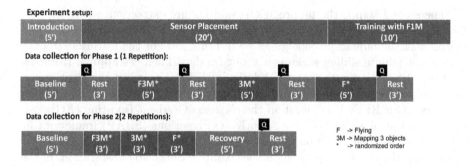

Fig. 3. Protocol of the experiment, which includes different conditions, such as base-line (B), mapping activity (3M), flying activity (F), flying and mapping performed simultaneously (F3M), and filling a questionnaire (Q) to evaluate the NASA-TLX.

Phase 1 is composed of four different tasks (i.e., B, F, 3M, and F3M), where the order of F, 3M, and F3M is randomized to avoid any bias related to the order of these activities. Before each resting period, the subjects were asked to rate the perceived level of cognitive workload by evaluating the NASA-TLX. The time duration for each task in Phase 1 is five minutes.

Phase 2 consists of a concatenated sequence of the tasks presented in Phase 1 (i.e., B, F, 3M, and F3M). As in Phase 1, the order of F3M, 3M, F is randomized. However, in Phase 2 there is no resting period between the tasks. Phase 2 is executed twice in a row, and the NASA-TLX is evaluated only at the end of each sequence. The tasks duration in Phase 2 is limited to three minutes. Except the data collected from the second repetition of Phase 2 that is kept apart for testing our final machine-learning algorithm, the rest of the data is selected only for training the machine-learning algorithms.

Participants were asked not to talk, and to avoid as much as possible any kind of unnecessary movements during the main tasks, but they were free to rest and move otherwise.

3.2   Participants

In our study participated 24 volunteers (6 females and 18 males), aged between 21 and 39 years old (27.7 ± 4.8). All but one participated twice in two different days. The participants were healthy, free of any cardiac abnormalities and were receiving no medical treatment. The ethical approval for this study was obtained from the Cantonal Ethics Commissions for Human Research Vaud and Geneva; namely, ethical approval application number PB2017-00295.

3.3   Database

From the 47 experimental sessions performed, we build our datasets based on the workload reported by the participants in the NASA-TLX questionnaire. Values higher than 55% and lower than 5% are labeled as low and high workload, respectively. Following this criteria, 259 observations are labeled as low workload and 249 are labeled as high, which makes a dataset of 508 observations. By including the medium level of workload, we extend our dataset to 748 observations.

Both datasets are split into two subsets of 70% and 30% of groups of observations for both training and testing, respectively. Thus, the test set includes all the observation of 14 groups randomly selected from the second day, while the training set includes all the remaining groups of observations acquired the first day.

4 Results

Our results include the cognitive workload perceived by the volunteers and used as reference. Moreover, we provide results of a binary CWD and results of a three-class CWD.

4.1 Cognitive Workload Reference

Both the tasks' difficulty perceived by the participants and the cognitive workload level reported with the NASA-TLX procedure after each task are shown in Fig. 4. Each box includes 144 data points, which were averaged across all the trials.

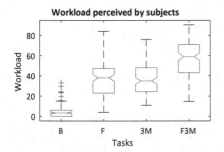 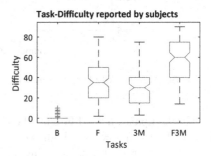

Fig. 4. Perceived workload per task. Different conditions: baseline (B); mapping (3M); flying (F); and flying and mapping (F3M).

Both cognitive workload and tasks' difficulty show an increasing trend in the order of B, 3M, F and F3M. Then, a two-tail t-tests yielded a significant difference between most of the tasks (p-value < 0.001, n = 47), except for the cognitive workload between 3M and F where the difference is not significance. The significance difference of the difficulty between tasks 3M and F is limited to a p-value < 0.05. A significant Pearson's correlations between cognitive workload and tasks' difficulty is observed (p-value < 0.001, n = 47). The high correlation confirms the validity of the assumption that cognitive workload increases with the difficulty of the tasks.

4.2   Binary Cognitive Workload Detection

Following our methodology to develop a model for cognitive workload monitoring (see Sect. 2) we first process the physiological signals. In particular we consider in this study the RSP, ECG, PPG and SKT from where we extracted 156 features as in [9]. Then, we performed the feature selection step.

The result of the RFECV based on SHAP values and using a XGBoost model is shown in Fig. 5. The score increases by adding features until it reaches its maximum with 24 features. Then, it decreases and reaches a plateau if more than 45 features are used. Finally, we selected 24 features to train an XGBoost classifier, which reaches a LPGOCV accuracy of 79.5%. The 24 most important physiological features characterizing high levels of cognitive workload level of the participants are shown in Table 1.

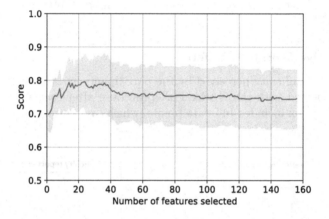

Fig. 5. SHapley Additive exPlanations (SHAP) score used for feature selection.

The comparison of different classification algorithms for the binary classification between low and high workload levels are summarized in Table 2. In particular, we report both training and LPGOCV accuracy before and after feature selection. As expected, considering the large amount of features compared with the limited size of our dataset, the models trained with all the features show an important gap between train and LPGOCV accuracy, which is a clear sign of overfit. This overfitting problem was addressed by using simplest models (e.g., linear instead of non-linear models) and models with less parameters (i.e., lower capacity). Indeed, the use of LDA drastically reduces the gap between training and LPGOCV accuracy, especially when a limited amount of features are used. Although the training data is not sufficient to find an optimum, the highest LPGOCV accuracy is given by XGBoost (79.5%). Thus, the results provided next are based on XGBoost only.

Finally, in order to minimize the errors, we fine tuned the decision threshold of our model on cross-validation. A plot of precision, recall, and accuracy as a function of different decision thresholds is shown in Fig. 6.

Table 1. Description of the selected features.

Features	Description
RR_{CSI}[a]	Cardiac Sympathetic Index, L/T ratio of the RR Lorenz plot [14]. L and T are the longitudinal and transverse axis' lengths, respectively
RR_{Lnz2L}[a,b]	Longitudinal axis length of the second-order RR difference Lorenz plot
RR_{Lnz2LoT}[a,b]	L/T ratio of the second-order RR difference Lorenz plot
$RR_{\text{Lnz2log}_{10}\text{LT}}$[b]	$\log_{10} LT$ of the second-order RR difference Lorenz plot
RR_{HFpond}[a,b]	Mean of the HF band frequencies weighted by their corresponding power
PP_{LnzT}[b]	Length of the transverse axis T of the PP Lorenz plot
PA_{Std}[a]	Standard deviation of the pulse amplitude
PA_{Median}[b]	Median value of the pulse amplitude
PRT_{Mean}[b]	Mean value of the pulse wave rising time
PRT_{Median}[b]	Median value of the pulse wave rising time
PRT_{Std}[a,b]	Standard deviation of the pulse wave rising time
k_{Median}[b]	Median value of the pulse rise speed
k_{Std}[a]	Standard deviation of the pulse rise speed
$Inh_{\text{Time Median}}$[a,b]	Median value of the inspiration time from RSP
$Exh_{\text{Time Median}}$[a,b]	Median value of the expiration time from RSP
$Inh_{\text{Time RMS}}$[a]	RMS value of the inspiration time from RSP
$Exh_{\text{Time Mean}}$[a]	Mean value of the expiration time from RSP
$Inh_{\text{Amp Median}}$[a,b]	Median value of the inspiration amplitude from RSP
$Exh_{\text{Amp Median}}$[a,b]	Median value of the expiration amplitude from RSP
$RSP_{\text{Prd Mean}}$[a,b]	Mean value of respiration period
$RSP_{\text{Prd Median}}$[b]	Median value of respiration period
$RSP_{\text{Rate Median}}$[b]	Median value of respiration rate
$RSP_{\text{Rate Mean}}$[b]	Mean value of respiration rate
$RSP_{\text{Rate Std}}$[a]	Standard deviation of respiration rate
$RSP_{\text{Rate RMS}}$[a,b]	RMS value of respiration rate
RSP_{PSD2n}[a,b]	Normalized Power Spectral Density (PSD) of RSP in the second frequency band (i.e., 0.25–0.5)
RSP_{PSD3}[a,b]	PSD of RSP in the third frequency band (i.e., 0.5–0.75 Hz)
RSP_{PSD3n}[b]	Normalized PSD of RSP in the third frequency band
$NN50$[b]	Number of interval differences of successive NN-intervals greater than 50 ms
$RSA_{\text{Shift Rad}}$[a,b]	Phase shift between RSP and RR
$RSA_{\text{R0 Mean}}$[a]	Mean value of the Respiration Sinus Arrhythmia (RSA) curve
$RSA_{\text{Rn Std}}$[a]	Standard deviation of RSA curve
SKT_{Power}[a]	Total Power of the SKT
SKT_{Gradient}[a,b]	Gradient of the SKT

[a] and [b] refer to the binary and three-class problems, respectively.

Table 2. Comparison of different classification models in term of accuracy.

Model	All features		24 features	
	Training	LPGOCV	Training	LPGOCV
XGBoost	100%	74.5% (0.09)	100%	79.5% (0.08)
Random Forest	100%	73.3% (0.08)	100%	76.8% (0.08)
Decision Tree	100%	68.1% (0.09)	100%	73.2% (0.07)
k-Nearest Neighbors	92.35%	71.4% (0.06)	90.7%	76.5% (0.08)
Logistic Regression	86.89%	74.7% (0.07)	83.3%	76.1% (0.05)
Linear Discriminant Analysis	95.9%	71.6% (0.06)	86.6%	78.7% (0.05)
Gaussian Naïve Bayes	81.6%	70.4% (0.09)	82.7%	76.3% (0.06)
Support Vector Machine	89.6%	72.8% (0.07)	84.4%	75.4% (0.04)

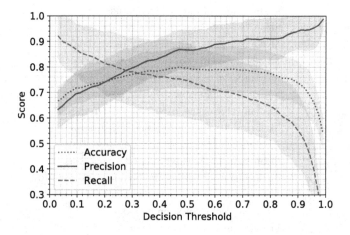

Fig. 6. Decision threshold as function of precision, recall, and accuracy.

Although the higher CV accuracy is reached with a threshold around 0.5, which is the default decision threshold in binary classification, the recall is poor. However, by choosing a threshold equal to 0.27 (where precision almost equals recall), we have an equal error rate and the accuracy is still acceptable. A detailed comparison between the use of a threshold at 0.5 and one at 0.27 is reported in Table 3.

The results on an unseen test set of the workload detection based on XGBoost with 24 selected features and a threshold at 0.27 that shows the generalization power of the final workload detection model are reported in Table 4.

Although results obtained in CV suggest the use of an XGBoost with the 24 selected features and a threshold of 0.27, as a comparison we also report in Table 4 the results of an XGBoost before and after feature selection and a decision threshold at 0.5. As on the test set, an increase of accuracy exists and, as a result, a reduction of the difference between precision and recall after

Table 3. LPGOCV performance of XGBoost with different decision thresholds.

Model	Features	Threshold	Accuracy	Precision	Recall
XGBoost	24	0.5	79.5%	86.5%	74.6%
		0.27	76.5%	78.4%	78.6%

Table 4. Generalization power of the workload detection model (XGBoost) on the unseen test set.

Model	Features	Threshold	Accuracy	Precision	Recall
XGBoost	All	0.5	79.6%	94.3%	55.0%
	24	0.5	76.8%	84.6%	55.0%
	24	0.27	80.2%	79.6%	71.7%

applying both feature selection and threshold tuning. Overall, these results show that our model generalizes well for cognitive workload detection.

4.3   3-Class Cognitive Workload Detection

As explained in Sect. 2, we also explore the three-class detection problem using the same procedure that we applied for the binary problem. The applied RFECV technique with XGBoost algorithm based on SHAP values also selected 24 features with a maximum accuracy of 54.7%, which is still clearly better than random (33%). The selected physiological features characterizing low, medium, and high levels of cognitive workload are reported in Table 1.

From the comparison of the different classification methods reported in Table 5, we can see that XGBoost is again slightly better than the others. The important difference between training and CV accuracy clearly indicates an overfitting problem. Acquiring more data will probably solve this problem

Table 5. Comparison of different three-class models in term of accuracy.

Model	All features		24 features	
	Training	LPGOCV	Training	LPGOCV
XGBoost	100%	53.5% (0.04)	98.7%	54.7% (0.04)
Random Forest	100%	52.9% (0.06)	100%	54.6% (0.07)
Decision Tree	100%	41.9% (0.07)	100%	45.9% (0.06)
k-Nearest Neighbors	69.8%	35.2% (0.08)	77.6%	53.4% (0.04)
Logistic Regression	74.2%	53.2% (0.05)	65.5%	54.4% (0.06)
Linear Discriminant Analysis	86.5%	53.5% (0.07)	69.3%	54.0% (0.05)
Gaussian Naïve Bayes	61.5%	49.3% (0.04)	62.5%	52.9% (0.05)
Support Vector Machine	75.7%	52.9% (0.05)	66.4%	54.3% (0.05)

and increase the performance of some models, such XGBoost, random forest, and decision tree. However, our results suggest to select again the XGBoost with 24 features to address our three-class problem.

Finally, on an unseen test set, the cognitive workload detection based on the 3-class XGBoost with 24 selected features shows an accuracy and both averaged precision and recall of 62.9%.

5   Conclusion

The goal of this work was to detect cognitive workload levels from physiological signals in the field of SAR missions with drone. Although the volunteers were not exposed to the same stressful conditions as they would be in the case of a real SAR mission, with augmented reality we were able to inducing different level of cognitive workload that are related to SAR mission with drones. From the collected dataset we compared different machine-learning algorithms and we found that an XGBoost with only 24 features is enough to address both a binary and a three-class problem. The two class XGBoost was able to detect high and low levels of cognitive workload with an accuracy of 80.2%. The three-class XGBoost was able to detect high, medium, and low levels of cognitive workload with an accuracy of 62.9%. Considering the little difference between the levels of induced workload our results are promising and open the doors to a fine grained cognitive workload detection in the field of SAR missions.

References

1. Arza, A., et al.: Measuring acute stress response through physiological signals: towards a quantitative assessment of stress. Med. Biol. Eng. Comput. **57**(1), 271–287 (2018). https://doi.org/10.1007/s11517-018-1879-z
2. Biopac: MP160 Data Acquisition Systems. https://www.biopac.com/product/mp150-data-acquisition-systems/
3. Cain, B.: A Review of the Mental Workload Literature. Defence Research and Development Toronto, Canada (2007). http://www.dtic.mil/dtic/tr/fulltext/u2/a474193.pdf
4. Dell'Agnola, F., Cammoun, L., Atienza, D.: Physiological characterization of need for assistance in rescue missions with drones. In: IEEE International Conference on Consumer Electronics (ICCE), pp. 1–6, January 2018. https://infoscience.epfl.ch/record/261415
5. Evans, D.C., Fendley, M.: A multi-measure approach for connecting cognitive workload and automation. Int. J. Hum.-Comput. Stud. **97**, 182–189 (2017). https://www.sciencedirect.com/science/article/pii/S1071581916300623
6. Hart, S.G., Staveland, L.E.: Development of NASA-TLX (task load index): results of empirical and theoretical research. In: Hancock, P.A., Meshkati, N. (eds.) Human Mental Workload, Advances in Psychology, vol. 52, pp. 139–183. North-Holland (1988). http://www.sciencedirect.com/science/article/pii/S0166411508623869
7. Logitech: Gamepad F130. http://support.logitech.com/en/product/gamepad-f310

8. Lundberg, S.M., Lee, S.I.: A unified approach to interpreting model predictions. In: Guyon, I., et al. (eds.) Advances in Neural Information Processing Systems 30, pp. 4765–4774. Curran Associates, Inc. (2017). http://papers.nips.cc/paper/7062-a-unified-approach-to-interpreting-model-predictions.pdf
9. Momeni, N., Dell'Agnola, F., Arza, A., Atienza, D.: Real-time cognitive workload monitoring based on machine learning using physiological signals in rescue missions. Technical report, EPFL, April 2019. https://infoscience.epfl.ch/record/265352
10. Moray, N.: Mental Workload : Its Theory and Measurement. Published in coordination with NATO Scientific Affairs, Plenum Press (1979). https://books.google.ch/books?id=SP3lBwAAQBAJ&lr=&source=gbs_navlinks_s
11. Pedregosa, F., et al.: Scikit-learn: machine learning in Python. J. Mach. Learn. Res. **12**, 2825–2830 (2011)
12. Ranchet, M., Morgan, J.C., Akinwuntan, A.E., Devos, H.: Cognitive workload across the spectrum of cognitive impairments: a systematic review of physiological measures. Neurosci. Biobehav. Rev. **80**, 516–537 (2017). https://linkinghub.elsevier.com/retrieve/pii/S0149763416305413
13. Teigen, K.H.: Yerkes-Dodson: a law for all seasons. Theory Psychol. **4**(4), 525–547 (1994). https://doi.org/10.1177/0959354394044004
14. Toichi, M., Sugiura, T., Murai, T., Sengoku, A.: A new method of assessing cardiac autonomic function and its comparison with spectral analysis and coefficient of variation of R-R interval. J. Auton. Nerv. Syst. **62**(1), 79–84 (1997). http://www.sciencedirect.com/science/article/pii/S0165183896001129
15. Unity Technologies, I.: Unity3D. https://unity3d.com/

Negative Effects Associated with HMDs in Augmented and Virtual Reality

Charles R. Descheneaux[1]([envelope]), Lauren Reinerman-Jones[1],
Jason Moss[2], David Krum[3], and Irwin Hudson[2]

[1] University of Central Florida,
3100 Technology Pkwy, Orlando, FL 32816, USA
cdeschen@ist.ucf.edu
[2] U.S. Army Combat Capabilities Development Command-Soldier Center,
12423 Research Parkway, Orlando, FL 32826, USA
[3] Mixed Reality Lab, University of Southern California,
12015 Waterfront Drive, Playa Vista, CA 90094, USA

Abstract. Head mounted displays (HMD) are becoming ubiquitous. Simulator sickness has been an issue since the first simulators and HMDs were created. As computational power and display capabilities increase, so does their utilization in technologies such as HMDs. However, this does not mean that the issues that once plagued these systems are now obsolete. In fact, evidence suggests that these issues have become more prevalent. Whether the system is Augmented Reality (AR), Virtual Reality (VR), or Mixed Reality (MR) the issues associated with simulator sickness or cybersickness have become more widespread. The reasons are uncertain, but probably multiple. One possible reason is the concept of vection, which is the illusion of movement to the participant where there is none physically. Vection plays a vital role in immersion and presence, however; it is also integral in simulator sickness. Another potential reason is the availability of HMDs. Traditionally a tool used in military training or laboratory settings, HMDs have now become a consumer item. This work reviews the current state of HMD issues such as simulator sickness or cybersickness. It reviews the similarities and differences of the sickness states that are commonly found with HMDs. Also, terms such as presence and immersion are delineated so they are used appropriately. The current theories on simulator sickness and cybersickness are reviewed. Further, the measurement and mitigation strategies currently being employed to reduce sickness are reviewed. Lastly, suggestions for more accurate measurement are recommended.

Keywords: Head mounted displays · Augmented reality · Virtual reality · Immersion · Presence · Vection

1 Introduction

In 2003, 36 junior high school students were hospitalized after watching a movie in the auditorium. The movie was shot with a handheld camera that was shaky and jittery. The movie was projected on a large screen for 294 students to watch. Six students had symptoms after 10 min, three vomited and one had symptoms of headache and nausea

© Springer Nature Switzerland AG 2020
J. Y. C. Chen and G. Fragomeni (Eds.): HCII 2020, LNCS 12190, pp. 410–428, 2020.
https://doi.org/10.1007/978-3-030-49695-1_27

with a decrease in blood pressure. More students were sent to the school nurse with similar symptoms. After a brief rest, 22 students were transported to the local hospital for treatment. After an hour, another 14 students with similar symptoms were sent to the hospital. Overall 36 out of 294 (12.24%) students were treated for nausea, headache, cold clammy sweat, and decreased blood pressure. The students with the most symptoms were the ones seated closest to the screen with the largest field of view (FOV) and near the middle [1].

Although this was a very simplified virtual environment (VE), this incident demonstrates the power of VEs. Virtual environments come in a variety of modes; however, the two most pertinent to this effort are virtual reality (VR) and augmented reality (AR). Virtual reality occurs when the environment that the participant views is entirely computer-generated. Most of the time the participant wears a head mounted display (HMD), which is a head worn device that includes a visual display for the participant to see the VE. Usually there are two screens, one in front of each eye. The screens are separated in space to create the illusion of depth [2]. Augmented reality occurs when the true setting of the space is augmented with some virtual objects. This can be done monocularly or binocularly. AR systems can be either video see through or optical see through [3, 4]. Video see through has a video feed from cameras mounted on the HMD; while optical see through devices usually use a half silvered or semi-transparent mirror so the augmented image can be projected onto the mirror with the real world still in view [3]. AR video see through is sometimes referred to as VR video pass through, but this is a misnomer. The defining distinction between AR and VR is the view of reality; AR uses the real world and VR uses a computer-generated world. However, when evaluating many systems that are in use, one will find a blend of technologies. There are AR systems that use some attributes from the virtual world and some VR systems than contain AR components. Thus, there is a continuum between the strict AR and VR systems [5] (Fig. 1).

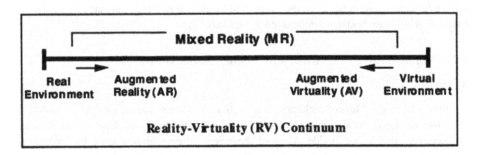

Fig. 1. Mixed reality continuum [5]

1.1 The User

The above technology has shown tremendous advances as computing power has evolved. However, the technology is only beneficial if the intended user can properly utilize the benefits. In this case the user is the human. Therefore, it is prudent to review the anatomy, physiology and limitations of the human systems that are used to create their effects. These systems are the human visual system and human vestibular system.

The Visual System. The normal human visual system has two eyes separated by approximately 65 mm in the skull. The reason for the displacement of the eyes is to create disparity that is used later in the visual system to create binocular vision and therefore the possibility of depth perception. Light is focused on the human retina which contain cells called rods and cones. There are approximately 120 million rods and 6–7 million cones in the human retina. The cones are concentrated in the central retina and are responsible for our fine visual acuity and color vision. The cones dissipate in population from the visual axis to the peripheral retina. The peripheral retinal is made of rods which are responsible for night vision and movement. After the retina is stimulated, the visual signal travels to the optic nerves and then through the brain to terminate at the occipital (visual) cortex of the brain. From there, other neurons are sent to visually associated areas for color vision and depth perception. There are also connections between the visual pathway and the vestibular system [6].

The Vestibular System. The human vestibular system is part of a multi-sensory organ system that coordinates postural control and spatial orientation. Postural control implies balance. Balance is a complex system that relies on input from the visual system, vestibular system, autonomic, and proprioceptive receptors. The vestibular system is made up from the semicircular canals (SSC), the utricle, and the saccule. The SSC sense angular acceleration of the head, while the utricle and saccule sense linear acceleration of the head. The vestibular system also has input into the cardiovascular system and visceral activity. Irritants or irregularities to the vestibular system can cause heart palpitations and an upset stomach. The vestibular system and visual system create the vestibulo-ocular system. This system helps with balance along with input from the cerebellum. The vestibulo-ocular system is a feedback loop coordinated by the visual and vestibular systems that controls sense of head position and relative eye position. Discordant information between the visual and vestibular systems can cause issues with balance, heart rate, and gastrointestinal symptoms [7].

1.2   Negative Effects of Virtual Environments and Symptoms

Sickness

Motion Sickness. Motion sickness is a well know nauseous or emetic (vomiting) response to riding in a motor vehicle. It is also seasickness, airplane sickness, and sickness due to a carnival ride. Most of the scientific community agree the hallmark signs of motion sickness are: nausea (possibly leading to emesis), increased salivation, pallor, cold sweating, and drowsiness [8, 9]. Simulator Sickness (SS) was first seen in pilots during training in flight simulators in the 1960's [9]. Simulator sickness shares much of the same symptomatology as motion sickness: dizziness, fatigue, drowsiness, nausea, headache, and general discomfort. However, SS is heavily visually induced due to the visuo-vestibular interaction [8, 9]. Cybersickness refers to visually induced motion sickness caused by some inadequacy from the simulator, but not the simulation element itself [8, 9].

Simulator Sickness/Cybersickness. Simulator sickness or cybersickness has been an issue since the first HMD was created by Sutherland in 1968 [8]. Simulator sickness was first noticed in military flight simulators. Symptoms of apathy, sleepiness, disorientation, fatigue, vomiting, and general discomfort are commonly seen. Cybersickness is experienced by participants in virtual environments that are stationary, but produce a compelling sense of motion, called vection. Usual symptoms of cybersickness are nausea, eye strain, and dizziness [10]. Simulator sickness and cybersickness are used interchangeably in the literature. In fact, there is a debate whether there is a real difference between the two terms from motion sickness due to the overlapping symptomology [11]. It is not within the scope of this paper to reduce the semantics over whether a negative effect should be labeled simulator sickness or cybersickness. For the sake of simplicity, simulator sickness (SS) will be used throughout. The emphasis will be on the negative effects of VR and AR in HMDs. It has been shown that up to 80% of participants will experience some sort of SS while engaged in a VE. Somewhere between 25% and 34% will be nauseous and up to 17% will be unable to continue the simulation due to the negative effects [12]. Most of these adverse symptoms are seen with VR, as it has dominated the scientific literature in the past twenty years. Even though AR environments may imply the same issues, the experiments to prove the same effects have not been completed [8]. Geyer and Biggs [13] point out that they were not able to find any research that compares sickness levels between AR and VR HMDs.

Susceptibility

Gender Differences. It is usually assumed that females are more susceptible to SS when compared to males. Using an evolutionary point of view, this theory is supported by the fact that females have a wider visual field when compared to their male counterparts [14]. Therefore, the female experience of vection may be greater. Many studies show a slight difference between the two genders [15–17]; however, some studies do not show a significant difference [18]. Even though SS was not different in this study, postural instability was significantly more pronounced in women, although women recovered quicker than men [19]. Another study points out that 78% of participants that complain of SS are women. In some studies, SS symptoms are twice that in the female population when compared to the male population and with higher severity, although others have found that symptoms of nausea are about the same when the two genders are compared [17]. It is likely that some of the differences in these studies vary due to the nature of the simulation and the amount of vection that was induced.

Individual Differences. There is a vast array of the susceptibility of humans to motion sickness. As seen above, it may depend on gender; however, individual variation does occur. There have been screening tools to determine the preponderance to motion sickness. The first tool was a two-page questionnaire, the Motion Sickness Susceptibility Questionnaire (MSSQ) [20]. Based on their work, Golding [21] created the MSSQ-Short, referring to the original by Reason and Brand as the MSSQ-Long. Golding's version of the MSSQ-Short was a single page with a zero to three rating system. It was created to be shorter and easier to administer. Golding validated his shortened version against the long version [21]. Recently, Georgia Tech produced the Georgia Tech Simulator Sickness Screening Protocol (GTSSSP), which is a computer administered pre and post drive screening tool used mostly for driving simulators [22]. However, there is agreement between all three of the questionnaires with a previous history of motion sickness providing a reliable metric for SS.

After Effects

Cognitive Effects. Cognitive deficits are a potential side effect of experiencing a VE, although the complete effect is not known. Individual differences are a factor in any human experiment or experience. Also, each VE is slightly different, making a one to one comparison difficult. In a study using a car simulator, participants' performance was not statistically significant; however, there was a significant difference in driving style after the VE. Participants drove slower, more cautiously, and made fewer steering maneuvers after experiencing a VE [23]. The UH-60 is a flight simulator for the UH-60 Black Hawk helicopter. It is not recommended to pilot for at least 6 h after using the flight simulator and if there are any symptoms, an overnight waiting period is recommended [24]. Even an off the shelf VR HMD company, the Oculus company, recommends that if there are any negative effects from the VE, the participant should not operate machinery or drive until after all negative symptoms have subsided [23]. However, in another study using the Oculus Rift HMD (VR) and a flat screen TV, there was mild to moderate SS, but only a mild decrease in cognitive performance [25]. Some of the first reports of SS after effects were significant. In one instance a gentleman had to pull over from driving, get out of the car, and walk around after spending time in a VE. Other lasting potential effects are: postexposure ataxia, disorientation, disorientating flashbacks, and negative adaptation behaviors [13]. Vestibulo-ocular reflex gain may be reduced following exposure to a VR environment. This would lead to a reduction in coordination between eyes, hands, and head. Vestibular-evoked myogenic potentials (VEMP) are a way of measuring vestibular processing. VEMP uses small electrodes on the sternocleidomastoid muscles to measure potentials. Although results of a study using VEMP was not conclusive, it was shown that there was VEMP asymmetry and amplitude changes following just one minute of VR vection [26]. According to one author, directly following a military flight simulation 60.4% of the participants experienced post exposure ataxia. Over 14.6% lasted 30 min to ten hours after experiencing the VE. Ataxia has been reported in 34% of post exposure effects that lasted up to one hour. While 6% lasted four hours, 4% lasted six or more hours. Approximately 1% had spontaneous post exposure flashbacks [27]. Pilots already have a high tolerance for physiological changes associated with motion and visual dynamics. Therefore, if an aviator is showing SS, then that technology will likely be amplified for the majority of other individuals. However, experienced pilots sometimes show increased SS when visual and physics models of a simulator are not matched to each or to reality because their bodies and brain are trained to expect certain forces and dynamics [28, 29]. Also, while these percentages might seem inconsequential, even one pilot operating a high-value aircraft on a high-risk mission could be devasting.

Avoidance. Negative effects from VEs can lead participants to avoid using the device if the participant had a negative experience. The HTC Vive is a consumer VR HMD. In one experiment participants using the HTC Vive avoided highly concentrated object areas during the simulation. When asked why, all responded that it felt more comfortable to be away from a more complex screen with multiple objects within the visual field. Participants specifically complained of eyestrain, focusing problems, and nausea [30]. This is just one instance of a negative experience causing changes in behavior during the simulation. Further, Fernandes and Feiner [31] state that people will avoid using a VE if they have had a poor experience.

Discontinuity of Training/Negative Transfer. Simulator sickness can be detrimental to training. First, if a number or percentage of subjects cannot finish the simulation, they cannot complete the training [32]. This leaves those subjects out of synch with the rest of the platoon, squadron, or company. Second, symptoms of SS may persist for 6 to 24 h after the VE is experienced. In the case of a pilot, this would ground them for a day, keeping them from their flight training or duties. Further, if the participant produces protective behavior either physically or cognitively, there is the possibility of negative transfer. In this case the simulation caused the participant to become worse at the task or at a minimum produce behavior that can negatively impact the real-world situation.

1.3   Accepted Theories of Simulator Sickness

There are a few accepted theories on SS. These include the sensory conflict theory, postural instability theory, and poison theory. The sensory conflict theory, Reason and Brand [20], is based on the visual system and the vestibular system. In this situation, the visual flow of the world that is seen is unequal to the vestibular systems input creating a situation of visual-vestibular discrepancies. The discrepancy is the cause of the symptoms [10, 20]. The postural instability theory states that humans want to maintain a stable posture. Simulator sickness results in the perception of an unstable posture. These perceptions in the VE visually show changes that are not equivalent to the current or normal body position and therefore lead to a conflict. The longer one is in a VE, the worse the conflict becomes [33]. This theory is controversial, as it was shown by Warwick-Evans, Symons, Fitch and Burrows [34] that postural instability did not correlate with SS in their study comparing sensory conflict to postural instability. Further, Dennison and D'Zmura [35], showed that SS occurred without significant postural instability. The poison theory, Treisman [36] originates in our evolution. We as humans have some defensive mechanisms for self-protection and preservation. If we ingest something that is poisonous, some symptoms are hallucinations and dizziness. This would induce an attempt to void our stomach of the offending item in order to protect ourselves. Along a similar line of thought, when one gets dizzy from a VE, the automatic sense of self-preservation creates an emetic response. This theory fails on many levels and therefore, has not seen wide acceptance [10, 36].

1.4   Measurement of Simulator Sickness

There are three categories of ways to measure SS: direct observation, objective, and subjective. The direct observation method relies on watching for signs and symptoms directly from the participant. Motion sickness tends to be gastrointestinal in nature, however SS is more visual. Symptoms of eyestrain, difficulty focusing, nausea, headache, and general feeling of uneasiness are usually associated with SS [8].

Objective Methods. Objective methods of measuring SS are relatively new and therefore, not widely accepted yet. However, they do show promise in their correlations with well-known questionnaires, which have been the standard measure of SS. Due to their limited acceptance they will be simply stated, rather than completely reviewed. Some of the promising objective measures of SS are: heart rate variability, respiration rate, electrogastrogram [8, 37], blood pressure [38], electroencephalogram (EEG) [39], eye blink, skin conductance, respiration, skin temperature, photoplethysmorgram [40], vestibular-evoked myogenic potentials (VEMP) [26], transcranial doppler ultrasound (TCD), near infrared spectroscopy (NIRS) [41], and measuring postural stability [42].

Subjective Methods. The most accepted way to measure SS is via questionnaire. There are three that have been the most accepted. The Fast Motion Scale (FMS) is a one question scale administered throughout the time in the VE. This is a verbal scale that was validated against the Simulator Sickness Scale (SSQ) nausea subscale. The power of this scale is in its simplicity of a one number answer about the feeling of nausea. It ranges from zero (no sickness) to twenty (frank sickness) [43]. The Misery Scale (MISC), is another verbal one number answer scale. This scale has been validated against the Motion Sickness Susceptibility Questionnaire (MSSQ) by Golding [44]. The reference points range from zero to ten [45]. The Simulator Sickness Questionnaire (SSQ) is the oldest and most utilized scale for SS. It was based on the Pensacola Motion Sickness Questionnaire (MSQ). Over 1,100 participants in a series of factory analyses were used to create the scale. It is a written scale that derives one number from three weighted subscales: nausea, oculomotor, and disorientation. After the subscales are calculated, a weighted final number is calculated [8, 46]. However, this scale is not without controversary. Opponents argue that it was designed and intended for a specific simulation – naval aviation within a flight simulation and any other use is improper [37]. Further, many researchers try to correlate the subscales with a single metric. This, by definition, is improper. The scale has three subsets that are weighted and then a final number that is weighted, resulting in a single number. Extracting out a single subscale is improperly using the scale.

1.5   Negative Characteristics of Virtual Environment Platforms (HMD)

Vection. Vection is an illusion created by the VE that produces the sense of movement while the participant is stationary. Vection is more prevalent in people who experience SS while engaged in a VE, especially HMDs. An example of this is a study comparing an Oculus Rift (VR) version 1 to a flat screen TV. Four out of 60 (6.7%) participants did not complete the study due to intense nausea [25]. In another study, vection was seen more when the scene was compensated for by head tracking. Again, the Oculus Rift HMD (VR) was used with three conditions: non-compensated, compensated and inversely compensated. The most SS was seen with the inversely compensated trial, however there was little difference between the compensated and non-compensated trials [47].

Field of View. While HMDs and VEs have been created, there was a trend towards larger field of view (FOV) to enhance the experience and decrease SS. However, it has been shown that as the FOV was increased, so did the postural instability. This simple study was shown using a Box-light projector, 3-foot dome and 180-degree FOV [48]. The graphics of the computer generates an internal FOV, while the screen on the VE produces an external FOV. Bos et al. [45] that found increasing the ratio between the real and virtual FOV decreases SS [45]. The useable FOV is also been studied as a potential SS instigator. Moss and Muth [49], found that occluding the peripheral vision in a HMD caused more SS then when the external environment was viewable in the periphery. They recommend further research in this area to determine the impact on realism and presence when the peripheral vision is not occluded (Moss and Muth) [49].

Time in Simulator. Time in simulator is a factor in SS. It has been shown that the longer duration in the VE, the greater the SS [15, 50, 51]. In one study 61% of participants complained of symptoms within the 20-min virtual environment. A total of 5% could not complete the study due to severe symptoms [52]. In another study, SS increased with exposures longer than 30 min [53]. Also, a study that looked at image delay on SS showed no significant effect of the delay, however it was noted that participants symptoms of SS increased with increasing time in the VE [54]. Although there is a discord between time in VE and SS, there is agreement that longer exposure usually leads to increased symptoms.

Image Lag and Latency
Early computing power was greatly limited when compared to today. Image lag and latency was thought to contribute to the SS issue. It was simply stated that SS is caused by the lag of the user's head movements and the computer/HMDs ability to stay coincident due to processing time, however this was from the early 1990's [55]. Recently, Moss and Muth [49] showed a non-significant difference with visual display latency up to 200 ms. However, there is disagreement in the latency area. The peripheral visual field can appreciate flicker much better than central vision; therefore, one must be cognoscente whether it is central or peripheral latency. In a 2017, a review of SS stated that 30 ms is the minimum for central acuity. They further point out that the peripheral latency should be less due to the peripheral retinas ability to perceive flicker [56]. Another study using and HTC Vive (VR) HMD with a 9.5-min presentation task, it was noted that latency jitter was significant at 46.67 ms [57]. This difference between 30 ms and 200 ms shows the vast discrepancies between studies. Another issue is individual ability. Not all humans are created equal regarding peripheral flicker perception. Individual variation is an area that has yet to be explored in VEs and flicker frequency perception. It has been estimated that up to 43% of the variance could be attributed to individual variation when comparing VEs [37].

Recently, the Oculus company has published that frame rate should be no less than 60–90 fps when using their HMD [58].

Image Scale Factor. The image scale has also shown some interesting findings in SS. Image scale factor is the difference between the geometric field of view (GFOV) and the display field of view (DFOV). Geometric field of view is the viewable size of the HMD. Display field of view is the size of the image that is displayed in the HMD. If GFOV is equal to DFOV, then there is a one to one ratio, however if they are not coincident, then there is a minification or magnification factor [53]. Simulator sickness was shown to be greater when the image scale from the HMD was greater or less than 1:1. This study was completed with a HMD and Virtual i/o glasses in a VR environment [53]. In contrast, another study looking at the image scale showed when the two were congruent, SS with worse than when the two were not congruent [59]. Moss and Muth [49], showed image scale was not a significant issue. In their study, a HMD with live video from digital cameras and bi-ocular displays were used as the VE [49].

Balance. Balance is an important aspect of human nature. When we are in balance, our world seems right, when out of balance, it seems very disturbing. This was shown in a study using the HTC Vive (VR) and comparing eyes open and closed. Participants were asked to stand in a slightly off-balance stance with eyes open, closed, and with the Vive. Balance was the worst with the Vive, followed by eyes closed then the best balance was eyes open [60].

Immersive Effect and Presence. Some have suggested that if a VE is immersive enough, the experience will negate any SS effects while the participant is actively engaged in the environment. Unfortunately, this relationship is poorly understood and often stated as fact rather than having scientific background. Many state that this concept should be explored further [61–63]. Conversely, a study by Yildirim [64], found SS to negatively effect the VE experience [64]. This is an issue that is controversial, with some studies showing the effect and others negating the effect. Whitmer and Cellary [65], showed a negative correlation of SS to presence, while others showed a positive correlation [66–68]. Theoretically a greater sense presence will produce a feeling of enjoyment. A negative effect will be felt as an undesirable experience. In fact, Lin, Duh, Parker, Abi-Rached and Furness [69], showed a negative correlation between SS and enjoyment, while they showed a positive correlation between SS and presence. The implication is that the more presence is felt, the increased effect of SS and the more negative the experience. It is obvious that this issue is still unresolved.

Head Movement. Head movement is another issue in the VE arena, especially with VR HMDs. While wearing an Oculus DK1 HMD (VR), Arcioni, Palmisano, Apthorp and Kim [70] showed that participants had less SS when head motion was at a minimum. Also, it was noted that participants using the HMD moved their head less within the VE than if they were not wearing the HMD [70]. This may work well as a strategy to reduce SS; however, if the VR system is to be used in a practical manner, head movements are essential.

Velocity of Navigation. Speed while traversing through a VE has been studied as a potential SS issue. It has been suggested that faster navigation speeds produce more SS. In a study that compared a CAVE (C-Automatic Virtual Environment) to a HTC Vive (VR) with navigation speeds of 10 m/s and 24 m/s, no difference was seen between the CAVE and the HMD; however, higher speeds did lead to more SS [71]. The same issue was seen with the Samsung Gear HMD (VR) used in an exploration of tourist areas of Rio de Janeiro. They traveled at 0.5 m per frame up to 2.5 m per frame. Participants kept reporting they felt uncomfortable because the movement was too fast [56].

Realism. Realism is becoming a more important issue as computing power and graphics capabilities increase. The possibility to make an artificial scene look real is becoming reality. However, this realism theoretically causes more vection and there-fore more SS. Although this has been reported previously [10], one study failed to show a difference between a realistic scene and a bland shadowed scene. This study used the HTC Vive HMD (VR) in each scenario. The common significant factor between the realistic scene and bland scene was more reported nausea while traversing stairs in the simulation [72].

Binocular Occlusion Effect. The human eyes are separated to create retinal disparity and allow binocular vision. The Binocular Occlusion Effect is when the digital image is presented to one eye then presented to the other eye to create the perception of depth. When this occurs, the fellow eye is blocked temporarily. Theoretically, this happens so quickly than the participant cannot perceive the change. However, if the participant can perceive the change it would be quite distracting and has the potential to cause conflict and consequently SS [56]. True depth perception is difficult to simulate binocularly, to compensate for this dilemma monocular cues are used to help induce depth perception [27].

Accommodation and Convergence Conflict. In human vision, accommodation and convergence are coincident. They are autonomically linked. Often in VR displays, the image is always in focus, at a fixed point in space a specific distance from the par-ticipant. This creates a conflict of the accommodation and convergence system such that it can cause eye strain and other oculomotor symptoms [13, 37].

1.6 Mitigation Strategies

Participant

Medication. Medication and homeopathic options have been attempted to mitigate SS. Antihistamines (meclizine, cyclizine) and anticholinergics (scopolamine) are common medications, while ginger is a common homeopathic agent [52, 73]. One can clearly see the commonality between motion sickness and SS with the types of treatments attempted.

Schedules and Adaptation/Habituation. Habituation is a decrease in behavioral response to a stimulus occurring after repeated exposures to the stimulus. Adaptation is a change in sensory receptors that has occurred after chronic exposure to a stimulus [13, 74]. However, these terms are often used interchangeably. Participation schedules in VE has also been used to mitigate SS. Adaptation has been shown to decrease SS. Also, repeated exposure using a smaller version, a simplified version or repeated exposure to the simulation has shown to decrease SS [73, 75]. An experiment with 70 participants wearing a HMD showed that habituation occurred in all trials. No significant difference was seen on time between trials, however the number of exposures was significant [76]. Habituation was seen in another study using the Oculus Rift HMD (VR) for three consecutive days. Participants were able to use the device from approximately 1.3 min the first day up to twelve minutes on the third day [41]. Previous experience is a similar factor. If a participant has had previous experience in a simulated environment analogous to what they are about to experience, their chance of SS is usually less than those who are novices. Adaptation occurs while the participant is engaged in the simulator. With time, adaptation occurs in those individuals where it is possible. However, there is another adaptation period that the individual goes through after the VE. They must re-adapt to the real world. In this instance, there are sometimes issues with re-adaptation that can take minutes to hours. Although adaptation seems to be the most promising mitigating factor, it is estimated that 3–5% will never adapt [13, 77].

Vestibular Stimulation. Vestibular stimulation is a way to subject the vestibular nerve (eight cranial nerve) to stimulation in order to prevent SS. The eight cranial nerve is responsible for hearing and balance along with the visual system and the cerebellum. Vestibular stimulation can come in two forms; motion platform or indirect electrical stimulation. A motion platform is a moveable platform the participant stands on and helps keep the visual cues aligned with what the vestibular system is experiencing. The platform usually moves synchronously with the visual scene that is being simulated. Alternatively, the vestibular nerve can be stimulated via an electrical signal on the mastoid bone called galvanic vestibular stimulation (GVS). This bone is behind and just under the ear. The correct amount of electrical stimulation on the bone causes stimulation of the vestibular nerve and coordinates the visual and vestibular systems [32, 78]. In one study comparing the display HoloStation, a 3-dimensional projection system (Christie Digital Systems, Inc., Cypress, CA) and the HMD Oculus DK2 (VR), GVS decreased SS in both environments. It was especially useful when the stimulation occurred during the faster speeds and with acceleration [79].

Galvanic Cutaneous Stimulation. Galvanic Cutaneous Stimulation (GCS) utilizes electrodes on the sternocleidomastoid muscles which are neck muscles just under the mastoid process. GCS effects the cardiovascular autonomic response and in this study reduced SS. The impulses are under the motor threshold, so no movement was induced with stimulation. Although, GCS did not totally alleviate SS, it did help lower the percentage of SS according to the SSQ [80].

Proprioceptive Feedback. Proprioception is the brains ability to know where the limbs are in space and allow us to feel touch and pressure. Via the visual system, it also allows us to know what orientation objects are in space compared to our existence in the environment. One study looked at using vibrating sensors on the back of the thighs in order to provide proprioceptive feedback and decrease SS. The HMD was and Oculus Rift DK1 (VR) and a joystick navigation system. There was a decrease in SS for each participant that received the cutaneous stimulation. The author's estimate that there was a 47% overall decrease in SS with the use of the cutaneous stimulation [81].

Time in Simulator. It has been eluded to above, however it was seen in many studies that time in simulator or VE greatly correlated with SS. The longer time in the VE the greater the SS and severity [15, 50, 51]. One study shows how this concept can be used to decrease SS. The Oculus Rift DK2 (VR) was compared to a 3-dimensional television and the Google cardboard. The Oculus Rift created a greater sense of immersion compared to the other two items and SS was not an issue; however, the trials were kept very short. Each participant used the VE for anywhere from 50 s to just under two minutes [60]. While this decreased SS in the study, realistically a military simulation is going to be much longer than two minutes, so the practicality is limited.

Rest Frames and Independent Visual Backgrounds. It has been suggested that because the human visual system can identify stationary objects along the visual axis better than moving targets that 'rest' frames be utilized in the VE [78]. The rest frames would allow the user to become grounded again, although it does have the potential to disrupt the VE experience. Within this line of thought is the idea of an independent visual background (IVB). In this study participants wore Crystal Eyes shutter glasses, which are stereo 3-dimensional liquid crystal display glasses. The glasses were used while looking at a video display. In the background was a grid overlaid onto the entire field of view. The presence of the IVB helped reduce balance disturbances when compared to those cases where the IVB was not used [82]. Another potential way to help the user gain a point of reference is using a focal point in the visual field. This gives a fixed frame of reference and helps reduce some SS. One study simply used a virtual nose in the central visual field that reduced SS [58].

Virtual Environment

Postural Stability. Postural stability or grounding is another method to help reduce or prevent SS. In this scenario, the participant is offered a handle, table, or even a chair with a headrest which seems to help the chance of SS [73]. Position and control work together to affect SS. Users that are in control of the simulation have less SS than participants that are in the simulation but are not in control. This is analogous to someone who gets car sick, except when they are driving. Also, position has an effect. Sitting is better than standing and having a stability point is better than standing alone [78]. This strategy supports the postural instability theory.

Field of View. Field of view is thought to be a significant factor in SS. It has been shown that the wider the FOV, the greater incidence of SS and negative effects. Some show an almost linear effect. When the FOV is doubled, so is the incidence of SS [37]. Therefore, decreasing FOV decreases SS, but at the expense of presence. However, one study looked at dynamically changing FOV in instances where there would be a greater chance of SS. This study used the Oculus Rift DK2 HMD (VR) with a gaming controller while the participant was seated. The initial FOV was 120°, however it was decreased to 90° and 80° dynamically based on the information seen by the participant. Overall, there was a very low incidence of SS using the dynamic peripheral occlusion method [31].

Optical Flow. Optical flow, especially in the peripheral visual field has been a potential reason for SS. Some ways to reduce this flow, is occlusion or independent visual background. Another way that was recently tried was peripheral visual cues. These cues were in the form of either white dots or an iris effect with the peripheral area slightly greyed out. This study used the HTC Vive HMD (VR) and controllers for navigation. The results were in significant; however, the authors suggest a trend in the data and that modifying the type of peripheral cues may help with SS [83].

Vection. Vection can also be used to counteract SS. A decrease in the amount of vection causes a decrease in immersion, however it does seem to help with SS. A first person shooter game was created using the Oculus Rift DK2 (VR). The image was limited to horizontal plane movements only. When the head was rotated, the image was blurred. This limited blur seemed to help those that experienced acute symptoms of SS. It overall helped the feeling of nausea [84].

1.7   Augmented Reality vs. Virtual Reality

It has been suggested that AR systems are more advantageous than VR due to their innate ability to coordinate the visual and vestibular systems. There seems to be less SS when AR systems are compared to VR systems [85, 86]. In other words, AR provides a more realistic scenario to the participant. This realism relies on the fact that part of their view involves the real world [87]. Unfortunately, this is mostly speculation as no formal metric to determine or define simulator sickness has been used. It has further been stated that "… we are unable to identify any research explicitly comparing sickness levels between AR and VR HMD" [13, p. 402]. Others have simply proclaimed that SS is not present in AR without a formal study to determine that statement [88]. One potential reason for AR having less SS is vection. In the real environment, vection is not present since movement is real and not virtual. There is no lag or latency and the background is properly located according to the participant. Visual and sensory systems are coincident providing no sense of conflict. All these factors favor the sensory conflict theory and give a rationalization behind why there is more SS in VR when compared to AR.

There has been an extremely small amount of studies done on AR and SS, however one study, using the Microsoft HoloLens (AR), reported no nausea at all. The most common symptoms were difficulty focusing (24% slight to moderate) and blurred vision (21% slight to moderate). Study participants were able to move their head freely in space. All participants stated they would use AR again. This study involved aviation, medicine and space environments [8]. The Microsoft HoloLens (AR) was used in another experiment that contained intellectual tasks as well as manual tasks. Each participant went through three experiments of 30 min with a short break in between. The Microsoft HoloLens (AR) did not show an alteration of memory, attention or energy. No significant SS was reported, and all participants completed the tasks. The only complaint was the fitment of the HMD [89]. Another study used the Microsoft Hololens (AR). Over 142 participants were used to determine their level of simulator sickness. Of the symptoms reported, 19% reported slight eyestrain, and 3% reported moderate eyestrain. Post experiment symptoms were eyestrain, headache and general discomfort. No one reported nausea [8].

There are very few studies that compare SS in AR and VR systems. One study compared AR and VR with a 3 D input device and a simple desktop mouse. In general, the AR participants outperformed the VR participants when using the 3 D input device. The authors suggest the increased engagement between the user's hand and the virtual images may have contributed to the AR being more positive. Also, the AR scene was less complex when compared to the VR scene since AR utilizes the actual background, while VR completely creates the entire image and background [90]. Another study compared the Microsoft Hololens (AR) to the Oculus Rift (VR). The VR group showed, elevated heart rate, skin conductance and higher level of overall arousal vs the AR system. The AR participants adapted more rapidly than the VR participants [91]. The easier and more rapid acceptance of AR systems could be due to the spatial orientation of objects in space. In AR systems, the user has a real time, real vs virtual, view of the space around them. This is probably the reason AR systems show less sickness and overall better acceptance [92]. The Microsoft Hololens (AR) was compared to the HTC Vive (VR) in a military simulation first person shooter task. The AR and VR scenarios used the same setting with synchronized and asynchronized motion of a moveable platform. The participant was located on the bow of an Arleigh-Burke class destroyer and was asked to use a M2 Browning .50 caliber machine gun. The gun was realistic and mounted; however, the trigger was replaced with a button for the simulation. The goal was to shoot an enemy target. The participant was standing on a moveable platform that was stationary, moving synchronously with the view and asynchronously with the view. Ten shots destroyed the target. The HTC Vive (VR) had a display resolution of 1080 × 1200 per eye, 110° field of view and a refresh rate of 90 Hz. The AR condition was projected onto three screens that measured 65 in × 48.5 in each. The screens were joined at 45° angles and were placed to provide 110° visual field. The Microsoft Hololens (AR) projected commands at 2.3 megapixels. Commands were shown in the top and bottom of the participants field of view for 'destructive free fire' and 'cease'. The study looked at the accuracy of the shooter in each scenario as well as the sickness levels for each. The study consisted of two, fifteen-minute sessions, stopping to administer a simulator sickness questionnaire. Each consecutive session was at least 24 h apart. Although sickness symptoms increased with time, there was no significant difference in the SSQ between the AR and VR systems. It was also noted that shot accuracy was better for the VR system than the AR system, however it was also stated that the AR system was at a different perspective than the VR, so shooters had to adjust their aim and learn where to shoot [93].

In summary, AR is considered easier to adapt to and produces less SS, however the research to support this claim is scarce. AR research is minimal compared to its prevalence. Even VR applications, which have been studied more widely, studies show a drastic disagreement in SS. Much of the literature simply talks about virtual environments, without stating whether the study is VR or AR. Therefore, it would seem prudent to investigate the incidence of simulator sickness and its relationship to AR platforms as well as investigate VR and simulator sickness. With a better understanding of the incidence, more complete theories on origin and mitigation strategies can be formulated.

References

1. Ujike, H., Ukai, K., Nihei, K.: Survey on motion sickness-like symptoms provoked by viewing a video movie during junior high school class. Displays **29**, 81–89 (2008)
2. Cruz-Neira, C., Sandin, D.J., DeFanti, T.A.: Surround-screen projection-based virtual reality: the design and implementation of the CAVE (1993). ResearchGate, Chicago
3. Carmigniani, J., Furht, B.: Handbook of Augmented Reality. Springer, New York (2011). https://doi.org/10.1007/978-1-4614-0064-6
4. Cutolo, F., Ferrari, V.: The role of camera convergence in stereoscopic video see-through augmented reality displays. Int. J. Adv. Comput. Sci. Appl. **9**(8), 12–17 (2018)
5. Milgram, P., Takemura, H., Utsumi, A., Kishino, F.: Augmented reality: a class of displays on the reality-virtuality continuum. In: Proceedings of SPIE, pp. 282–292 (1995)
6. Williamson, S.J., Cummins, H.Z.: Light and Color in Nature and Art. Wiley, New York (1983)
7. Balban, C.D., Black, R.D., Silberstein, S.D.: Vestibular neuroscience for the headache specialist. Headache Currents **59**, 1109–1127 (2019)
8. Vovk, A., Wild, F., Guest, W., Kuula, T.: Simulator sickness in augmented reality training using the Microsoft hololens. In: CHI, Montreal, Quebec, Canada (2018)
9. Stanney, K.M., Kennedy, R.S., Drexler, J.M.: Cybersickness is not simulator sickness. In: Proceedings of the Human Factors and Ergonomics Society, Santa Monica (1993)
10. Davis, S., Nesbit, K., Nalivaiko, E.: A systematic review of cybersickness, Newcastle (2014)
11. Dennison, M.S., Krum, D.M.: Unifying research to address motion sickness. In: IEEE Conference on Virtual Reality and 3D User Interfaces, Osaka, pp. 1858–1859. IEEE (2019)
12. Lawson, B.: Motion sickness symptomatology and origins. In: Hale, K.S. (ed.) Handbook of Virtual Environments, 2nd edn. CRC Press, Boca Raton (2015)
13. Geyer, D.J., Biggs, A.T.: The persistent issue of simulator sickness in naval aviation. Aerosp. Med. Hum. Perform. **89**(4), 396–405 (2018)
14. Parnell, S.E.: How a Man's Mind Really Works!. http://www.dulcimermedicalcenter.org. Accessed 05 Sep 2019
15. Jaeger, B.K., Mourant, R.R.: Comparison of simulator sickness using static and dynamic walking simulators. In: Proceeding of the Human Factors and Ergonomics Society 45th Annual Meeting, pp. 1896–1900 (2001)
16. Stanney, K.M., Hale, K.S., Nahmens, I., Kennedy, R.S.: What to expect from immersive virtual environment exposure: influences of gender, body mass index, and past experience. Hum. Factors **45**(3), 504–520 (2003)
17. Shafer, D., Carbonara, C., Korpi, M.: Modern virtual reality technology: cybersickness, sense of presence, and gender. Media Psychol. Rev. **11**(2), 1–13 (2018)
18. Melo, M., Vasconcelos-Raposo, J., Bessa, M.: Presence and cybersickness in immersive content: effects of content type, exposure time and gender. Comput. Graph. **71**, 159–165 (2018)
19. Harm, D.L., Taylor, L.C., Bloomberg, J.J.: Adaptive changes in sensorimotor coordination and motion sickness following repeated exposures to virtual environments (2007)
20. Reason, J.T., Brand, J.J.: Motion Sickness. Academic Press, Oxford (1975)
21. Golding, J.F.: Predicting individual differences in motion sickness susceptibility by questionnaire. Personality Individ. Differ. **41**, 237–248 (2006)
22. Gable, T.M., Walker, B.N.: Georgia tech simulator sickness screening protocol. Georgia tech school of psychology, Technical report, Atlanta (2013)
23. Mittelstädt, J.: Factors and cognitive impairments of cybersickness in virtual reality, Hamburg (2019)

24. Gower, D.W., Fowkles, J.: Simulator sickness in the UH-60 (Black Hawk) flight simulator, USAARL, Orlando (1989)
25. Mittelstaedt, J.M., Wacker, J., Stelling, D.: VR aftereffect and the relation of cybersickness and cognitive performance. Virtual Reality 23(2), 143–154 (2018). https://doi.org/10.1007/s10055-018-0370-3
26. Gallagher, M., Dowsett, R., Ferrè, E.R.: Vection in virtual reality modulates vestibular-evoked myogenic potentials. Eur. J. Neurosci. 50, 3557–3565 (2019)
27. Kolaninski, E.: Simulator sickness in virtual environments. U.S. Army Research Institute for the Behavioral Sciences, Alexandria
28. Stanney, K., Kennedy, R., Drexler, J.: Cybersickness is not simulator sickness. In: Proceedings of the Human Factors and Ergonomics Society Annual Meeting, vol. 42, no. 2, pp. 1138–1142 (1997)
29. Pausch, R., Thomas, C., Conway, M.: A literature survey for virtual environments: military flight simulator visual systems and simulator sickness. Presence 1(3), 344–363 (1992)
30. Wang, G., Suh, A.: User adaptation to cybersickness in virtual reality: a qualitative study. In: Twenty-Seventh European Conference on Information Systems, pp. 1–15, Stockholm-Uppsala (2019)
31. Fernandes, A.S., Feiner, S.K.: Combating VR sickness through subtle dynamic field-of-view modification, pp. 201–210. IEEE (2016)
32. Cevette, M.J., et al.: Oculo-vestibular recoupling using galvanic vestibular stimulation to mitigate simulator sickness. Aviat. Space Environ. Med. 83(6), 549–555 (2012)
33. Riccio, G.E., Stoffregen, T.A.: An ecological theory of motion sickness and postural instability. Ecol. Psychol. 3, 195–240 (1991)
34. Warwick-Evans, L.A., Symons, T., Fitch, T., Burrows, L.: Evaluating sensory conflict and postural instability. Theories of motion sickness. Brain Res. Bull. 47(5), 165–469 (1998)
35. Dennison, M.S., D'Zmura, M.: Cybersickness without the wobble: experimental results speak against postural instability theory. Appl. Ergon. 58, 215–223 (2017)
36. Treisman, M.: Motion sickness: an evolutionary hypothesis. Science 197, 493–495 (1977)
37. Rebenitsch, L., Owen, C.: Review on cybersickness in applications and visual displays. Virtual Reality 20(2), 101–125 (2016). https://doi.org/10.1007/s10055-016-0285-9
38. Kiryu, T., Uchiyama, E., Jimbo, M., Iijima, A.: Time-varying factors model with different time-scales for studying cybersickness. In: Shumaker, R. (ed.) ICVR 2007. LNCS, vol. 4563, pp. 262–269. Springer, Heidelberg (2007). https://doi.org/10.1007/978-3-540-73335-5_29
39. Sollins, B., Chen, D., Reinerman-Jones, L., Tarr, R.: Truck driving distractions: impact on performance and physiological response. In: Proceedings of the Human Factors and Ergonomics Society 58th Annual Meeting, pp. 2171–2175 (2014)
40. Kim, Y.Y., Kim, H.J., Kim, E.N., Ko, H.D., Kim, H.T.: Characteristic changes in the physiological components of cybersickness. Psychophysiology 42, 616–625 (2005)
41. Gavgani, A.M., Nesbitt, K.V., Blackmore, K.L., Nalivaiko, E.: Profiling subjective symptoms and autonomic changes associated with cybersickness. Auton. Neurosci. Basic Clin. 203, 41–50 (2017)
42. Villard, S.J., Flanagan, M.B., Albanese, G.M., Stoffregen, T.A.: Postural instability and motion sickness in a virtual moving room. Hum. Factors 50(2), 332–345 (2008)
43. Keshavarz, B., Hecht, H.: Validating an efficient method to quantify motion sickness. Hum. Factors 53(4), 415–426 (2011)
44. Golding, J.F.: Motion sickness susceptibility questionnaire revised and its relationship to other forms of sickness. Brain Res. Bull. 47(5), 507–516 (1998)

45. Bos, J.E., de Vries, S.C., van Emmerick, M.L., Groen, E.L.: The effect of internal and external fields of view on visually induced motion sickness. Appl. Ergon. **41**, 516–521 (2010)

46. Kennedy, R.S., Lane, N.E., Berbaum, K.S., Lilienthal, M.G.: Simulator sickness questionnaire: an enhanced method for quantifying simulator sickness. Int. J. Aviat. Psychol. **3**, 203–220 (1993)

47. Palmisano, S., Mursic, R., Kim, J.: Vection and cybersickness generated by head-and-display motion in the Oculus Rift. Displays **46**, 1–8 (2017)

48. Duh, H.B., Lin, J.J., Kenyon, R.V., Parker, D.E., Furness, T.A.: Effects of field of view on balance in an immersive environment. In: Proceedings of the Virtual Reality 2001 Conference (2001)

49. Moss, J.D., Muth, E.R.: Characteristics of head-mounted displays and their effects on simulator sickness. Hum. Factors **53**(3), 308–319 (2011)

50. So, R.H., Lo, W.T., Ho, A.T.: Effects of navigation speed on motion sickness caused by an immersive virtual environment. Hum. Factors **43**(3), 452–461 (2001)

51. Lo, W.T., So, H.Y.: Cybersickness in the presence of scene rotational movements along different axes. Appl. Ergon. **32**, 1–14 (2001)

52. Regan, C.: Human factors. An investigation into nausea and other side-effects of head-coupled immersive virtual reality. Virtual Reality **1**(1), 17–31 (1995). https://doi.org/10.1007/BF02009710

53. Draper, M.H., Viirre, E.S., Furness, E.S., Gawron, V.J.: Effects of image scale and system time delay on simulator sickness within head-coupled virtual environments. Hum. Factors **43**(1), 129–146 (2001)

54. Moss, J.D., Austin, J., Salley, J., Coats, J., Williams, K., Muth, E.R.: The effects of display delay on simulator sickness. Displays **32**, 159–168 (2011)

55. Hettinger, L.J., Riccio, G.E.: Visually induced motion sickness in virtual environments. Presence Teleoper. Virtual Environ. **1**(3), 306–310 (1992)

56. Carvalho, P., Miyagawa, T., Maciel, F., Melo, P.: VR Rio 360: the challenges of motion sickness in VR environments. In: Lackey, S., Chen, J. (eds.) VAMR 2017. LNCS, vol. 10280, pp. 495–504. Springer, Cham (2017). https://doi.org/10.1007/978-3-319-57987-0_40

57. Stauffert, J.P., Neibling, F., Latoschik, M.E.: Effects of latency jitter on simulator sickness in a search task. In: IEEE Conference on Virtual Reality and 3D User Interfaces, pp. 121–127 (2018)

58. Clift, L.: Novel control systems for virtual reality, and their effects on cyber sickness. University of Birmingham, Birmingham (2018)

59. Toet, A., de Vries, S.C., van Emmerik, M.L., Bos, J. E.: Cybersickness and desktop simulations: field of view effects and user experience, vol. 6957, pp. 1–11 (2008)

60. Kelly, J.W., Klesel, B.C., Cherep, L.A.: Visual stabilization of balance in virtual reality using the HTC vive. ACM Trans. Appl. Percept. **16**(2), 1–11 (2019)

61. Nichols, S., Haldane, C., Wilson, J.R.: Measurement of presence and its consequences in virtual environments. Int. J. Hum. Comput. Stud. **52**(3), 417–491 (2000)

62. Tan, C.T., Leong, T.W., Shen, S., Dubravs, C., Si, C.: Exploring gameplay experiences on the Oculus Rift. In: Proceedings of the 2015 Annual Symposium on Computer-Human Interaction in Play, pp. 253–263 (2015)

63. Von Mammen, S., Edenhofer, S.: Cyber sick but still having fun. In: Proceedings of the 22nd ACM Conference on Virtual Reality Software and Technology, pp. 325–326 (2016)

64. Yildirim, C.: Cybersickness during VR gaming undermines game enjoyment: a mediation model. Displays **59**, 35–43 (2019)

65. Witmer, B.G., Cellary, W.: Measuring presence in virtual environments: a presence. Presence **7**(3), 225–240 (1998)

66. Slater, M., Steed, A., Usoh, M.: The virtual treadmill: a naturalistic metaphor for navigation in immersive virtual environments. In: First Eurographics Workshop on Virtual Environments, pp. 71–83 (1993)
67. Liu, C.-L., Uang, S.-T.: Effects of depth perception cues and display types on presence and cybersickness in the elderly within a 3D virtual store. J. Ambient Intell. Human. Comput. 7(6), 763–775 (2015). https://doi.org/10.1007/s12652-015-0317-4
68. Seay, A.F., Krum, D.M., Hodges, L., Ribarsky, W.: Simulator sickness and presence in a high field-of-view virtual environment. In: CHI, pp. 784–785 (2002)
69. Lin, J.J., Duh, H.B., Parker, D.E., Abi-Rached, H., Furness, T.A.: Effects of field of view on presence, enjoyment, memory, and simulator sickness in a virtual environment. In: Proceedings of the IEEE Virtual Reality (2002)
70. Arcioni, B., Palmisano, S., Apthorp, D., Kim, J.: Postural stability predicts the likelihood of cybersickness in active HMD-based virtual reality. Displays 58, 3–11 (2019)
71. Kwok, K.K., Ng, T.A., Lau, H.Y.: Effect of navigation speed and VR devices on cybersickness. In: IEEE International Symposium on Mixed and Augmented Reality Adjunct, pp. 91–92 (2018)
72. Pouke, M., Tiiro, A., LaValle, S., Ojala, T.: Effects of visual realism and moving detail on cybersickness. In: IEEE Conference on Virtual Reality and 3D User Interfaces, pp. 665–666 (2018)
73. Keshavarz, B.: Exploring behavioral methods to reduce visually induced motion sickness in virtual environments. In: Lackey, S., Shumaker, R. (eds.) VAMR 2016. LNCS, vol. 9740, pp. 147–155. Springer, Cham (2016). https://doi.org/10.1007/978-3-319-39907-2_14
74. Balter, S.G., Stokroos, R.J., Eterman, R.M., Paredis, S.A., Orbons, J., Kingma, H.: Habituation to galvanic vestibular stimulation. Acta Otolaryngol. 124, 941–945 (2004)
75. Kim, S., Lee, J.H., Park, J.H.: The effects of visual displacement on simulator sickness in video see-through head-mounted displays. In: ISWC, pp. 79–82 (2014)
76. Howarth, P.A., Hodder, S.G.: Characteristics of habituation to motion in a virtual environment. Displays 29, 117–123 (2007)
77. Johnson, D.M.: Introduction to and review of simulator sickness research. U.S. Army Research Institute, Arlington (2005)
78. LaViola, J.J.: A discussion of cybersickness in virtual environments. SIGCHI Bull. 32(1), 47–56 (2000)
79. Weech, S., Moon, J., Troje, N.F.: Influence of bone-conducted vibration on simulator sickness in virtual reality. PLOS one (2018)
80. Gálvez-García, G., Gabaude, C.: Alleviating simulator sickness with galvanic cutaneous stimulation. Hum. Factors 57, 649–657 (2015)
81. Plouzeau, J., Paillot, D., Chardonnet, J., Merienne, F.: Effect of proprioceptive vibrations on simulator sickness during navigation task in virtual environment. In: International Conference on Artificial Reality and Telexistence (2015)
82. Duh, H.B., Abi-Rached, H., Parker, D.E., Furness, T.A.: Effects on balance disturbance of manipulating depth of an independent visual background in a stereographic display. In: Proceedings of the Human Factors and Ergonomics Society 45th Annual Meeting, pp. 1882–1885 (2001)
83. Buhler, H., Misztal, S., Schild, J.: Reducing VR sickness through peripheral visual effects. In: IEEE Conference on Virtual Reality and 3D User Interfaces, Reutlingen, pp. 517–518 (2018)
84. Budhiraja, P., Miller, M.R., Modi, A.K., Forsyth, D.: Rotation blurring: use of artificial blurring to reduce cybersickness in virtual reality first person shooter (2007)
85. Slay, H., Phillips, M., Vernik, R., Thomas, B.: Interaction modes for augmented reality visualization. In: Australian Symposium on Information Visualisation, Sydney (2001)

86. Gregory, R.: Eye and Brain: The Psychology of Seeing. Mcgraw-Hill Book company, Toronto (1973)
87. Alkahamise, A.O., Monowar, M.M.: Rise of augmented reality: current and future application areas. Int. J. Internet Distrib. Syst. **1**, 25–34 (2013)
88. Duh, H.B., Parker, D.E., Furness, T.A.: An "independent visual background" reduced balance disturbance evoked by visual scene motion: implication for alleviating simulator sickness. In: CHI, pp. 85–89 (2001)
89. Cometti, C., Païzis, C., Casteleira, A., Pons, G., Babault, N.: Effects of mixed reality head-mounted glasses during 90 minutes of mental and manual tasks on cognitive and physiological functions. PeerJ (2018)
90. Krichenbauer, M., Yamamoto, G., Taketom, T., Sandor, C., Kato, H.: Augmented reality versus virtual reality for 3D object manipulation. IEEE Trans. Vis. Comput. Graph. **24**(2), 1038–1048 (2018)
91. Keighrey, C., Flynn, R., Murray, S., Murray, N.: A QoE evaluation of immersive augmented and virtual reality speech & language assessment applications. IEEE (2017)
92. Ma, M., et al.: Personalized augmented reality for anatomy education. Clin. Anat. **29**, 446–453 (2016)
93. Pettijohn, K.A., Peltier, C., Lukos, J.R., Norris, J.N., Biggs, A.T.: Comparison of virtual reality and augmented reality: safety and effectiveness. Naval Medical Research Unit Dayton (2019)

Mixed Mock-up Meets ErgoCAM: Feasibility Study for Prospective Ergonomic Evaluation of Manual Assembly Processes in Real-Time Using Augmented Reality and Markerless Posture Analysis

Tobias Dreesbach[1], Alexander Mertens[1,2(✉)], Tobias Hellig[1],
Matthias Pretzlaff[3], Verena Nitsch[1], and Christopher Brandl[1,2]

[1] Institute of Industrial Engineering and Ergonomics,
RWTH Aachen University, Bergdriesch 27,
52062 Aachen, Germany
a.mertens@iaw.rwth-aachen.de
[2] ACE GmbH, Charlottenstraße 14, 52070 Aachen, Germany
[3] HELLA GmbH & Co. KGaA, Beckumer Straße 130,
59552 Lippstadt, Germany

Abstract. The sustainable planning of production systems and processes requires a high degree of flexibility in the processes, both in terms of the production methods used and scalability, in order to be able to react to changing requirements at short notice. These requirements often hamper companies' efforts to guarantee health-promoting working conditions and systems as the workload involved in a correspondingly short-cycle analysis and evaluation of stressors would be too great. As a result, the individual needs of employees, such as adapting the workplace to suit personal constitutional traits, are often not taken into account sufficiently. In order to address this problem, two prototypical systems for digitally supported workplace design are tested in this paper. The focus lies on a mixed mock-up demonstrator, which combines classic mock-up planning with augmented reality technology and enables the generation of individualized manual assembly workstations. This demonstrator is used and examined in conjunction with ErgoCAM, a prototype of a markerless system, to evaluate individual postures in real time. The aim is to ascertain which benefits the combination of the systems offers with regard to the flexible and early ergonomic evaluation of assembly workstations in practice. Specifically, in a feasibility study, it is examined to which extent a reliable ergonomic evaluation of assembly operations is possible by combining the two prototypes.

Keywords: Manual assembly workstations · Posture analysis · Mixed mock-up · ErgoCAM · Augmented reality · Stress

© Springer Nature Switzerland AG 2020
J. Y. C. Chen and G. Fragomeni (Eds.): HCII 2020, LNCS 12190, pp. 429–439, 2020.
https://doi.org/10.1007/978-3-030-49695-1_28

1 Introduction

Due to the increasing demand for customer-specific technical products, both products and production systems are becoming increasingly more complex [1, 2]. With recent advances in the development of products and production processes, companies can use resources more efficiently as well as increase performance, flexibility and speed for the new production processes [1]. At the same time, when designing industrial workplaces, companies must also ensure that the physical fitness of the workforce is maintained, which is becoming increasingly important, especially in countries with aging work-forces. An ergonomic design of age(ing)-appropriate workplaces would prevent poor posture. However, such design is usually difficult using conventional methods in the early planning phase because the actual behaviour that workers exhibit when per-forming the activity can usually only be estimated. Augmented reality applications may support ergonomic workplace design, for example by depicting the new workplaces in what is known as a mixed mock-up and simultaneously ergonomically evaluating the resulting work performance.

1.1 Mixed Mock-up Demonstrator

A mixed mock-up may be used as a planning method to design production systems. A conventional method of planning, production systems such as assembly worksta-tions, entails the use of a mock-up that schematically maps the layout using cardboard boxes. Cutter knives, hot glue guns, adhesive tape, jigsaws, pins and measuring tapes serve as tools for the setup [3]. With classic mock-ups, however, there is a need to provide physical work equipment belonging to the new work system in a suitable form so that its use in the fulfilment of the work task can be explored. As creating corre-sponding work equipment can be time-consuming and costly, there is always the risk that it is not possible to work with the current mock-up version or that there is not a sufficient number of parts available. With a mixed mock-up, manual assembly work-stations and steps can be created individually at an early stage using virtual elements, e.g. the work equipment, and reconfigured flexibly. The working environment is depicted using augmented reality. Virtual objects are thus added to the real environ-ment. The characteristic features of an augmented reality system are a combination of the real and virtual world, interactivity as well as real-time capability [4]. The tech-nology is increasingly used in industrial production to support the handling of complex or difficult tasks [5].

Figure 1 shows the reality-virtuality continuum, which classifies the technology on a spectrum between the real and a purely virtual environment.

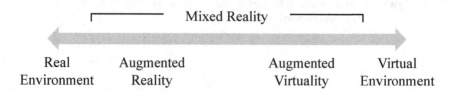

Fig. 1. The reality-virtuality continuum according to MILGRAM and KISHINO (based on [6])

Using augmented reality, the mixed mock-up demonstrator considered in this paper not only simulates the equipment but also includes the material and the manual assembly process. The demonstrator provides information about the height of the workbench, the accessibility of components, tools and the assembly object during the assembly operation, and a possible implementation of material provision. A new workstation can be created via a provision mode. Construction data for components can be utilized and digitalised standard equipment such as boxes, shelves and roller conveyors are available. In an assembly mode, it is also possible to simulate an initial manual assembly with the virtual components, in which the two working steps "placing" and "screwing" can be carried out. To simulate different assembly operations, the components can be replaced by other design data. A reference point on the physical mock-up table is used for the geometrically correct superimposition of the virtual space with the physical mock-up. Based on this anchor point, the coordinate system for the virtual elements is superimposed on the physical space.

Figure 2 shows the assembly operation for a headlight. For this purpose, augmented components are placed in a housing and screwed together. Initially, the components on the shelves, a housing receptacle, a screwdriver and a screw container can be seen virtually.

Fig. 2. Assembly operation with the mixed mock-up [7]

Previously, it was only possible to examine ergonomic aspects on the basis of visually recognisable features when creating a station layout with the mixed mock-up. A zone system referencing height and width contains four ergonomic gripping areas as a supporting tool for workplace design. As shown in Fig. 3, the optimal case for material placement is the central zone between elbow and shoulder height. In this area, an activity is enabled without the displacement of a body axis and short gripping distances are realised. The outermost area of the zone system is outside the ergonomic area and should be omitted for material placement where possible.

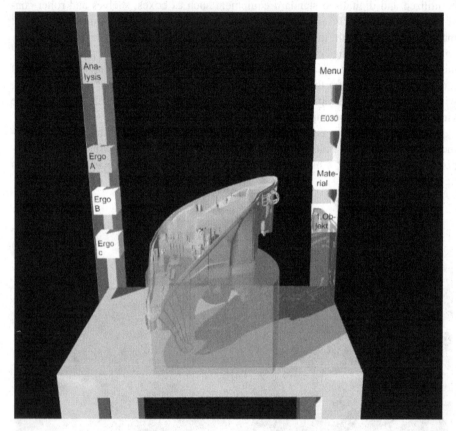

Fig. 3. Example illustrating the zone for optimal material placement (greens zone) using the mixed mock-up (Color figure online)

The early visualisation of future planning statuses and planning results by means of elements virtually superimposed in the field of vision facilitates the understanding of complex processes and creates a common knowledge base of all areas involved in the planning process [8]. Compared to the creation of parts e.g. in 3D printing for the classic mock-up, the mixed mock-up also offers a significant time and cost advantage, as the current data status of design data or equipment can be made available virtually within minutes.

1.2   ErgoCAM

The ergonomic design of a work task entails the adaptation of technology to the needs of the human being in order to facilitate work. The aim is to bring the stressors acting on the working person to a level that will not impair their health. Designing work tasks in accordance with ergonomic principles is necessary in order to maintain an acceptable work performance in the long term without damaging health [9]. In order to design a harm-free and executable work activity, physiological factors must be taken into account in addition to socio-psychological influencing variables, the latter of which are not the focus of this paper. The limits for the physiological factors are usually set by human biomechanics [10]. The level of physical stress in the performance of assembly activities can be quantified mainly using three dimensions: the intensity of the force, the frequency with which the force is applied and the duration over which the activity is performed. Other influencing factors can be posture, speed of movement, vibrations, and various other physical, psychological and organisational factors.

A wide variety of methods for studying physical work activities exist, that can quantify some of the factors related to physical stress. These methods differ in terms of their focus and the employed data collection method. Depending on the requirements, a suitable method must therefore be selected for a particular application. When selecting a method, there are usually the two conflicting requirements in operational practice: the lowest possible data collection effort vs. the highest possible data accuracy [11]. In order to classify the methods according to their advantages and disadvantages, they can be assigned to the three categories self-assessment, observational methods and direct measurements of stress conditions [12]. Self-assessment requires a low data collection effort, but is typically also afflicted by low data accuracy because the information is based on a subjective assessment. Observational methods are a frequently used approach in operational practice in order to identify hazards at work and evaluate physical work activities [13]. Measurement methods, however, offer the advantage that a large amount of data can be obtained with a high degree of accuracy. On the other hand, measurements require a comparably large amount of time and data processing effort. A large investment in the equipment is also often necessary at the beginning [12]. However, the technology-driven transition from manual assessment procedures to digitalised and networked measuring systems makes it possible to resolve the compromise between a low data collection effort and high data accuracy for a class of observational methods known as stress assessment methods [11].

One promising approach when it comes to analysing occurring stresses is the digital recording and evaluation of postures by cameras with integrated depth sensors. During this, depth information is measured by a camera system and transferred by software into a skeleton model with articulation points. Above all, articulation points such as the knees, hips and elbows are recorded for this purpose. Conditions such as joint angles, forces acting on joints, posture and movement speeds can be calculated using biomechanical models of the muscular and skeletal system. The calculation is performed either automatically using integrated algorithms to calculate the skeleton model or by post-processing the data using a software package provided to match the camera system.

The digital recording and evaluation of posture is researched and implemented in the form of ErgoCAM [14]. ErgoCAM supports ergonomic postures in the performance of work tasks by analysing human activities and movements without markers and in real time, as well as visualising the results of the stress assessment in a generally comprehensible format. It consists of a measuring system comprised of motion detection sensors in combination with evaluation systems (Fig. 4). An optical sensor is used for the non-invasive and continuous detection of articulation points. ErgoCAM includes a didactic communication concept to provide visualisation that can be interpreted easily by most users. In this way, ErgoCAM supports the development of ergonomic improvement measures and facilitates testing and discussion. Thus, even people without specialist training can interactively engage in the ergonomic design of activities and movements [11].

Fig. 4. Concept of ErgoCAM for markerless posture analysis e.g. during assembly

1.3 Combination of the Mixed Mock-up Demonstrator with ErgoCAM

It is necessary to consider ergonomic aspects in the planning of production systems as workplaces that are inadequately ergonomically designed can both hinder the efficient use of employees and have a negative impact on health. The first ergonomic assessment of a work activity in assembly takes place in order to create the assembly process structure. The assembly process structure represents the logical and chronological sequence of assembly work tasks and determines which subtasks must be performed one after the other or can be performed independently of each other. Based on the assembly process structure, an overall planning alternative can be developed from several alternative technical solutions in the next planning phase [15].

Even during the planning of the assembly process structure, a combination of the mixed mock-up demonstrator and ErgoCAM makes it possible to design the assembly processes flexibly and evaluate them with regard to a human-compatible design of the workplace. In the future, interdisciplinary project and method teams should create an assembly process with the mixed mock-up demonstrator in order to discuss options with customers as well as suppliers. ErgoCAM is to be used here to show, by means of a process-accompanying analysis, whether there is potential for ergonomic optimisation in the planned assembly operations. In particular by recording the individual postures of people, added value is to be created by identifying more than just one area of the workplace as ergonomic. It will be analysed how the necessary movements are expressed in different individuals, for example in the case of tall, short or older people. In the conception and development phase of a new production system, different setup scenarios are to be tested on the basis of the results. Using the ErgoCAM communication concept for knowledge transfer, the planners should be able to discuss the ergonomic design of activities and movements even without expert knowledge and include an initial ergonomic assessment of the respective assembly operation in the planning.

1.4 Objective

The present article describes a feasibility study that explores the potential of utilizing the described mixed mock-up demonstrator in conjunction with ErgoCAM for the prospective ergonomic evaluation of an assembly workstation.

2 Methodology

In a feasibility study, it was exploratively examined whether ErgoCAM recognises the assembly process with the mixed mock-up demonstrator similarly to a real assembly situation. The test setup includes several assembly stations. The assembly sequence had been pre-determined and information about the planned material provision and assembly operations was available. The design data for the components were available and, with the demonstrator, it was possible to carry out the necessary assembly steps for the stations under consideration. In addition, physical components, which were printed in 3D, were already available. The test person wore the Meta2 augmented reality glasses and SenseGlove data gloves. In addition, HTC Vive position trackers were attached to the glasses and gloves. The depth sensor built into ErgoCAM detected the users independently of this. ErgoCAM was first placed in front of the assembly station and analysed the movements made by a test person during the assembly operations. In a first run, the assembly operations were performed without the mixed mock-up demonstrator. The results of the ErgoCAM analysis of the first run served as reference results. In a second run, the assembly operations were performed with the mixed mock-up demonstrator.

The first research question posed was: (1) To what extent is it possible to evaluate assembly operations using a combination of the mixed mock-up and ErgoCAM? In this context, two influencing variables were considered, which change during the analysis when using the mixed mock-up demonstrator. Firstly, the additionally required hardware and, secondly, the pure virtual nature of the components shown on the AR-glasses. Hereby it was examined whether the glasses, the gloves and the position trackers influence the interpretation of the test subjects' contours and their movements by ErgoCAM. It was also examined whether the virtual components allow the feasibility of the analysis with ErgoCAM or whether real components still have to be used for an analysis. In a second research question, the potential and challenges of the interaction of both prototypes through the virtual elements will be investigated. In contrast to the purely physical setup, the ratio of physical and virtual elements can be adjusted as desired with the mixed mock-up demonstrator. It must be verified which elements should be mapped virtually and which elements in reality. The second research question (2) is therefore: To what extent does the quality of the ergonomic evaluation vary with the ratio of virtual to real elements when performing the operations?

3 Results

With regard to research question (1), it was possible to establish during the field investigation that, despite components worn close to the body, the contours of the test subjects were recorded sufficiently accurately to parameterise the skeleton model required for the evaluation of the assembly operations. In the context of addressing research question (1), the effects of the virtual components on the feasibility of the analysis were also investigated in the test setup. On a physical level, the hands of the test person are empty throughout the entire assembly operation. Only the test person himself can see whether the virtual components are gripped correctly. It was shown that ErgoCAM correctly records the movements of the test person even when using virtual components and performs an evaluation of the assembly operations. The different ratio of physical to virtual elements has not led to any restrictions in the handling of the components. Consequently, it can be concluded that, despite the additional hardware and virtual components, an evaluation of the assembly operations can be successfully performed with the combination of the mixed mock-up and ErgoCAM.

To investigate research question (2), identical test runs were carried out with the mixed mock-up demonstrator, each with real and virtual objects. It proved to be advantageous to display the assembly station as a virtual element in the mixed mock-up because ErgoCAM is positioned in front of the assembly station. In this way, Ergo-CAM can track the movements of the test person without physical objects covering the view of the test person. The challenge is that the virtual representation of the components can influence the measurement result, as the motion sequences of the test person may deviate slightly from reality as the virtual elements lack weight. Although the weight of the components can be stored in the analysis tool to calculate the occurring stress, the evaluation, however, refers to the movements actually performed. In contrast to physical objects, heavy components can be handled as virtual objects without any effort and thus influence the performed motion sequence. As long as only small weights are associated with the components, the analysis process has only a minor effect on the results. If work equipment and components have a higher dead weight or are more difficult to handle, it cannot be ruled out that the movement patterns during handling may deviate from those under real conditions. For this reason, critical compensation strategies that occur in practice, for example, cannot be prospectively identified.

The measurement curves for the compressive stress on the test subject's spine during the assembly operations with the mixed mock-up demonstrator (yellow) and without corresponding hardware worn close to the body (blue) typify the two runs from the test setup and are shown in Fig. 5. The compressive forces determined by Ergo-CAM show that the peaks of the loads are reached at different times. A slight time offset for the measurement curves can be traced back to a different time span between the start of the measurement and the start of the performance of work. In the recorded data, however, it can be seen that, in addition to the slight offset, the measurement curves do not run parallel. From this, it can be concluded that the work processes are influenced by the additional hardware and the transferability of the results is subject to limitations. The data suggest that the motion sequences in the second run were performed more slowly and deliberately. The maxima of the deflections of both curves, however, differ only slightly from each other, meaning that the interpretation with regard to the ergonomic potential for action is similar in both cases.

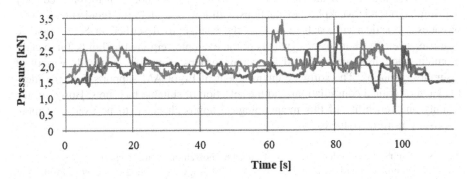

Fig. 5. Measurement curves for the stress on a test person (compressive force on the lumbosacral transition in kN) during assembly operations with a mixed mock-up demonstrator (yellow) and without (blue) (Color figure online)

4   Limitations

The test setup refers to a project in the company HELLA GmbH & Co. KGaA. The project thus comprises several assembly stations for manual assembly in series production. Within the project, individual assembly stations, which can be mapped by the mixed mock-up, are investigated. In the entire production system, there are also assembly stations that could not be mapped by the mixed mock-up so far, such as stations with robot use. The implementation itself is subject to the limitation that it was not carried out by an experienced worker due to the redesign of the work system. It must therefore be assumed that the postures of the test persons during the assembly operations do not always correspond to the posture of an experienced worker. In addition, the exploration was only carried out with a small sample without measurement repetition, which means that inter- and intra-individual deviations can only be taken into account to a limited extent.

5 Discussion and Conclusion

An ergonomic evaluation of postures and movements during the redesign of an assembly workstation was performed using a combination of a mixed mock-up demonstrator and ErgoCAM. It has thus been shown that a combination of both digital technologies is fundamentally feasible and that there is great potential for synergy effects. However, it could not be conclusively clarified to what extent the use of the mixed mock-up demonstrator would affect the validity of the measurement results of ErgoCAM. In particular, it was not possible to determine the situations in which the "missing" influence of dead weight and manageability of the work equipment conceals possible risks conclusively. However, it has been shown that the maximum level of deflection is similar in both runs and that the evaluations lead to a similar interpretation despite the varying timing.

The integrated use of the two technologies thus shows potential for prospectively realising ergonomic workplace evaluations with low cost and time requirements. This provides a practical approach to address the challenges described in Sect. 1 and to evaluate, even in short cycles, whether, for example, ergonomic limits for health-promoting activities are exceeded for certain groups of people in a wide variety of assembly scenarios. The software environment of ErgoCAM supports both the identification of critical constellations and the selection of suitable measures. However, the validity and reliability of this methodological approach needs to be examined more rigorously in further studies.

Acknowledgements. Funded by the Deutsche Forschungsgemeinschaft (DFG, German Research Foundation) under Germany's Excellence Strategy – EXC-2023 Internet of Production – 390621612.

References

1. Deuse, J., Weisner, K., Hengstebeck, A., Busch, F.: Gestaltung von Produktionssystemen im Kontext von Industrie 4.0. In: Botthof, A., Hartmann, E.A. (eds.) Zukunft der Arbeit in Industrie 4.0, pp. 99–109. Springer, Heidelberg (2015). https://doi.org/10.1007/978-3-662-45915-7_11
2. Westkämper, E.: Der Produktentstehungsprozess. In: Einführung in die Organisation der Produktion. Springer, Berlin (2006)
3. Bertagnolli, F.: Lean Management. Springer, Wiesbaden (2018). https://doi.org/10.1007/978-3-658-13124-1
4. Azuma, R.T.: A survey of augmented reality. Teleoperators Virtual Environ. 6(4), 355–385 (1997)
5. Steiger, L., Mehler-Bicher, A.: Augmented Reality. Theorie und Praxis. Walter de Gruyter GmbH & Co KG, Berlin (2014)

6. Milgram, P., Kishino, F.: A taxanomy of mixed reality visual displays. IEICE Trans. Inf. Syst. **77**(12), 1321–1329 (1994)

7. Fraunhofer Institut: InnoVisions: Mit der Zukunft hantieren. Mixed Mock-Ups erleichtern die Planung von Montagearbeitsplätzen. Fraunhofer-Verbund IUK-Technologie, Berlin (2018)

8. Reinhart, G., Zäh, M.F., Patron, C., Doil, F., Alt, T., Meier, P.: Augmented Reality in der Produktionsplanung. In: VDI-Fachmedien, Düsseldorf 651–653 (2003). wt-online (Ausgabe 09-2003)

9. Lotter, B., Wiendahl, H.-P.: Montage in der industriellen Produktion, 2nd edn. Springer, Berlin (2012)

10. Bullinger, H.-J.: Ergonomie. Produkt- und Arbeitsplatzgestaltung, 1st edn. Vieweg+Teubner Verlag, Stuttgart (1994)

11. Johnen, L., Brunner, O., Hellig, T., Nitsch, V., Mertens, A., Brandl, C.: Interaktives Erleben und Erlernen von Ergonomie mit ErgoCAM. In: Dachselt, R., Weber, G. (eds.) Mensch und Computer 2018, pp. 989–993. Gesellschaft für Informatik e.V., Bonn (2018)

12. David, G.C.: Ergonomic methods for assessing exposure to risk factors for work-related musculoskeletal disorders. Occup. Med. **55**(3), 190–199 (2005)

13. Takala, E.P., Pehkonen, I., Forsman, M., Hansson, G.A., Mathiassen, S., Neumann, W.: Systematic evaluation of observational methods assessing biomechanical exposures at work. Scand. J. Work Environ. Health **36**(1), 3–24 (2014)

14. Brandl, C., Bonin, D., Mertens, A., Wischniewski, S., Schlick, C.M.: Digitalisierungsansätze ergonomischer Analysen und Interventionen am Beispiel der markerlosen Erfassung von Körperhaltungen bei Arbeitstätigkeiten in der Produktion. Zeitschrift für Arbeitswissenschaften **70**, 89–98 (2016)

15. Bullinger, H.-J.: Planung der Materialbereitstellung in der Montage. Springer Fachmedien, Wiesbaden (1994)

Fake People, Real Effects

The Presence of Virtual Onlookers Can Impair Performance and Learning

Wouter Durnez[1]([✉]) [iD], Klaas Bombeke[1] [iD], Jamil Joundi[1] [iD],
Aleksandra Zheleva[1] [iD], Emiel Cracco[2] [iD], Fran Copman[2], Marcel Brass[2] [iD],
Jelle Saldien[1] [iD], and Lieven De Marez[1] [iD]

[1] imec-mict-UGent, Department of Communication Sciences, Ghent University,
Miriam Makebaplein 1, 9000 Gent, Belgium
wouter.durnez@ugent.be

[2] Department of Experimental Psychology, Ghent University, Henri Dunantlaan 2,
9000 Gent, Belgium

Abstract. Can effects of social influence be elicited in virtual contexts, and if so, under which conditions can they be observed? Answering these questions has theoretical merit, as the answers can help broaden our understanding of the interaction mechanisms described by social psychology. The increasing popularity of immersive media in training applications, however, has made these questions of practical significance. Virtual reality (VR), in particular, is a weapon of choice in designing training and education simulations, as it can be used to generate highly realistic characters and environments. As a consequence, it is key to understand under which circumstances virtual 'others' can facilitate or impede performance and – especially – learning. In this study, we investigated the impact of virtual onlookers on an adapted Serial Reaction Time (SRT) task that was presented in VR. In each trial, participants responded to a series of spherical stimuli by tapping them with handheld controllers when they lit up. Depending on the experiment block, the sequence order was either the permutation of a *fixed* order (and therefore predictable given the first stimulus), or fully *random* (and therefore unpredictable). Participants were divided into three groups (*audience* variable), depending on the environment in which the task was set: a group without onlookers (*none* condition), a group with a computer-generated audience (*CGI* condition), and a group being watched by a prerecorded audience (*filmed* condition). Results showed that the presence of a virtual audience can hamper both overall performance and learning, particularly when the audience appears more realistic. This study further reinforces the notion that the effects of social influence transcend the physical presence of others, but rather extend to virtual audiences.

Keywords: Social inhibition · Social facilitation · Learning · Virtual reality

---

W. Durnez, K. Bombeke and J. Joundi–These authors contributed equally to this work.

J. Y. C. Chen and G. Fragomeni (Eds.): HCII 2020, LNCS 12190, pp. 440–452, 2020.
https://doi.org/10.1007/978-3-030-49695-1_29

1   Introduction

In the presence of others, we behave differently [12]. Consider the following scenarios. In the first, a musician puts on the recital of a lifetime, encouraged by the opportunity to showcase his skills in front of admiring spectators. In the second, the mind of a young researcher goes blank as he – in spite of his numerous flawless repetitions the day before – stumbles his way through a conference presentation. These so-called audience effects are examples of what Zajonc [15] called "the oldest experimental paradigm of social psychology" - *social facilitation.*

The *social facilitation effect* (SFE) refers to the finding that, when observed by other people, an individual's performance will be better on simple and well-trained tasks, yet worse on complex and new tasks [2,15]. Several theories have attempted to explain this phenomenon, of which Zajonc's social facilitation theory (or generalized drive hypothesis) sparked the most interest [15,16]. The theory argues that the mere presence of others will increase arousal, facilitating dominant responses or automatic reflexes. In simple, well-learned tasks, these dominant responses will enhance performance (i.e., social facilitation), whereas in complex, novel tasks, they need to be overruled by more appropriate responses, impairing performance (also called "social inhibition") [15,16].

Social facilitation has since been the focus of many research endeavors [12,13]. With the rapid progression of computers and computer-generated images (CGI), however, an interesting new research angle presented itself. What if the 'other' was no longer physically present, but represented through a virtual avatar? What if the virtual avatar was controlled, not by another human being, but by a simple computer program? A study by Rickenberg and Reeves [11] suggested that the psychology of human-human relationships translates to how people react to virtual agents, as the visual properties of these avatars automatically trigger social responses. With respect to the SFE, however, the evidence has been largely inconsistent [1,8,10,17].

Hoyt and colleagues [8] conducted a study in which participants performed two categorization tasks of different difficulty levels. They either did so alone, or in front of a virtual audience. Participants in the latter condition were either led to believe that the audience were human-controlled avatars, or computer-controlled agents. Interestingly, the experimenters only found evidence for *social inhibition* in the *avatar* condition, suggesting that the driving force in the effect was not the puppet, but who (or what) the participants believed to pull its strings. No other social facilitation (or inhibition) effects were found. A similar result was obtained by Zanbaka and colleagues [17]. They found evidence for social inhibition only when female participants performed novel categorization and pattern recognition tasks in the presence of a virtual human. No such effects were found among the male participants.

More recent studies have failed to paint a clearer picture. In 2007, Park and others [10] found evidence for both social facilitation and social inhibition for a variety of tasks that were performed in the presence of a virtual agent. Notably, these effects were found in spite of informing participants that the virtual deuteragonist was an artificial intelligence, and therefore not human-controlled. A 2010 study by Hayes and colleagues [6] found trends towards social facilitation and inhibition in performance of simple and complex math tasks. However, none of the effects reached significant levels. Furthermore, they showed that the gender of the observer impacted the participants' sense of presence ratings. Nonetheless, no straightforward explanation was offered regarding this effect. Baldwin and colleagues, finally, conducted three different experiments that were specifically geared towards replication of the SFE, and failed to find any evidence [1].

Why does it seem so hard to converge on a set of replicable results? Although there can be many possible explanations, these mixed findings can arguably be attributed – in part – to problems with the design and difficulty level of different experimental tasks. More specifically, a common problem in social facilitation research relates to the ceiling effect present in the simple task (see also [17]) but absent in the complex task. Typically, participants first undergo a practice phase, after which they have to meet a certain accuracy criterion before they move on to the main blocks. As a result, participants are already highly skilled at the onset of the actual experimental phase, leaving little to no room for improvement. In other words, the simplicity of the task makes it impossible to detect additional effects of the presence of an audience. A second problem relates to the difference in task difficulty between the simple and the complex task itself. By only having the rather arbitrarily chosen dichotomy between simple and complex tasks, it is possible that previous studies failed to observe more subtle social facilitation and inhibition effects.

Furthermore, the aforementioned research efforts neglected to take the level of realism of their avatars into account, using virtual entities ranging from Microsoft Word's Clip (e.g., [5]) to more realistic models of human beings (e.g., [1,17]). To the best of our knowledge, there has been no previous research comparing the effects that virtual avatars of different levels of realism have on behavior. Given today's technology, however, virtual humans in three-dimensional environments can be made very similar to real humans. 360° video, for instance, makes it possible to use actual humans as observers in the virtual environment by using prerecorded footage. Comparing the effects of a virtual audience consisting of real (albeit filmed) people with an audience of artificially crafted 3D avatars would help elucidate the role of the audience's visual credibility. Is it enough that we are being watched by other 'agents', or is it necessary that we – on some level – perceive the audience as 'realistic human beings'?

In this study, we aimed to address the shortcomings of earlier research by introducing a VR-tailored serial reaction time (SRT) task. In this task, participants had to respond to a sequence of illuminated spheres as quickly and accurately as possible. Depending on the condition participants were assigned to, they performed this task in front of a CGI audience, a filmed audience, or in an empty room. In addition, in half of the experimental blocks the sequence was made predictable given the first lit up sphere. Participants could learn an underlying sequence, which enabled them to anticipate the illumination of the next sphere, allowing them to (potentially) respond more quickly and more accurately.

This task has two main advantages compared to the studies discussed earlier. First, it is less likely that we come across a ceiling effect, given the main dependent measure: reaction time. Second, by introducing a memory element, we are able to – for the first time – investigate the effects of (virtual) onlookers on learning speed. If participants succeed in memorizing the underlying sequence in fixed order blocks, this should be reflected in lower response times and higher accuracy scores. In doing so, we avoid the typical (and somewhat arbitrary) dichotomy between a simple and a complex task, focusing on learning performance instead. Besides the aforementioned methodological advantages, the focus on learning processes instead of final performance makes findings with regard to social facilitation and inhibition effects more ecologically valid and more informative for real-world applications, given the increasing ubiquitousness of immersive media in the fields of training and education. For example, in the manufacturing industry, virtual and augmented reality are increasingly used to train new employees, with employers trying to find the most efficient and effective ways to do so. Our study thus aims to inform developers of such training environments on the impact of the virtual 'people' they populate their simulators with.

2   Method

2.1   Participants

For this study, 60 participants with normal or corrected eyesight were recruited through online sampling. Due to technical difficulties at the onset of the experiment, the first participant's data were omitted from the dataset. Our participant pool consisted of more women (76.3%; M = 26.2 years old; SD = 8.9 years old) than men (23.7%; M = 31.4 years old; SD = 13.9 years old). Almost all of them were highly educated or still attending university (52.5% had a bachelor's degree, and 22% had a master's degree). All subjects participated on a voluntary basis and signed an informed consent with ethical approval from the university's ethical committee.

2.2   Design and Stimulus Material

Using Unity (version 3.5), we constructed a custom-made environment in which our SRT task was performed. Participants were assigned to one of three groups (*audience* variable): a group performing the task in an empty (virtual) room (*none* condition), a group performing the task in the presence of a CGI audience (*CGI* condition), and a group performing the task in the presence of a filmed audience (*filmed* condition). They were sat down in our lab and the experimenter put on the head-mounted display (HMD). Doing so, each participant found themselves in the same (virtual) room: a co-creation space that was recorded using a 360° video camera. In the *none* condition, this room was empty (Fig. 1a). Participants in the *CGI* condition were placed across four 3D-rendered virtual characters (Fig. 1b). These characters were superimposed on the room in such a manner that their presence seemed natural (i.e., they were scaled appropriately and appeared to stand on the floor, rather than float). People in the *filmed* condition, finally, saw four 'real' people in front of them – their 360° backdrop video was one of the same room, yet now containing four actual people looking at the camera (Fig. 1c). Importantly, we made sure that each audience contained an equal number of male and female onlookers, so effects could not be attributed to gender differences between them [6]. Each video only lasted about 10 s, but was looped in such a way that they contained no video glitches (e.g., abrupt changes in movement or facial expressions caused by cutting the original video). To achieve this fluency, the videos were copied, reversed, and concatenated, resulting in a video that could be repeated indefinitely.

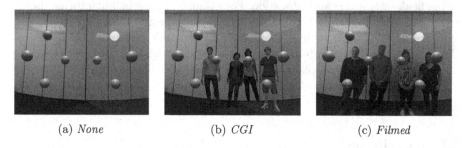

(a) *None*   (b) *CGI*   (c) *Filmed*

Fig. 1. Snapshot of the virtual environments corresponding to each of the *audience* conditions. (Color figure online)

In our experiment, we used an adapted version of the serial reaction time task (SRT). In front of each participant, 8 grey spheres floated in the air. They were positioned in two diamond formations, 4 on the left and 4 on the right of the participant. We made sure that the spheres were spread out in order to minimize the chance of accidentally hitting the wrong sphere. The formation of the spheres, in turn, was chosen in an effort to contain all spheres within the participant's (HMD-imposed) field of view. In other words, if a participant was looking straight ahead, all spheres were visible. To ensure this was the case for each participant, the experimenters made sure that everyone sat in exactly the same spot and did not move their chair. A single trial in the task was as follows: 8 spheres lit up (turned fluorescent green, see Fig. 1) in a certain sequence. Participants were asked to tap the illuminated sphere using one of two controllers, one of which was placed in each hand. Tapping a sphere caused it to extinguish (turn grey again), and the next sphere to illuminate. Participants felt a vibration in the respective controller when tapping a sphere, irrespective of whether they tapped the correct (green) sphere. Each illumination lasted for 5 s or until a response was registered, giving participants ample time to respond. However, participants were asked to respond as fast and as accurate as possible. Participants were given no instructions on which controller to use for which of the spheres, and were free to choose their approach. When piloting, we noticed that some responses were incorrectly registered as 2 separate taps, due to the irregular geometry of the controller meshes colliding with the spheres. These 'double taps' had unrealistically fast response times (i.e., under 100 ms). To mitigate this issue, we set an inactivation period of 150 ms after each tap. Spheres could already illuminate in this window, but responses were not registered. Piloting confirmed that the response time of intentional reactions always exceeded this window, leaving participants oblivious to this technical restriction.

All data was logged in the Unity application. For each trial, we recorded *audience* (none, CGI, or filmed), *order* (random or fixed), trial number, block number (both overall and within each level of the *order* variable, e.g., the 3th random block), the exact order in which the 8 spheres were illuminated during that trial, and the reaction time (RT) to respond to each single sphere illumination. Accuracy was also logged on a sphere-level – if a participant erroneously tapped a sphere that was not illuminated, this was counted as an incorrect response. A correct trial consisted of 8 correct responses (tapped spheres). Any mistake caused the trial to be labeled as incorrect.

2.3   Procedure and Technical Set-Up

Upon arrival in the lab, participants were briefed on the experiment and what was expected of them. They signed an informed consent and were asked to take place on a chair in the middle of the room, next to a large television screen on which the experimenter could see what the participant observed in VR. Next, the experimenter carefully put the HTC Vive HMD on the participants' head and two HTC Vive controllers in their hands. The HTC Vive HMD offers a resolution of 2160×1200 (with 1080×1200 per eye), global lighting and AMOLED-displays of 90 Hz. After making sure the participants' vision was not blurry because of incorrect placement, the experiment started with an instruction screen.

Participants were first presented with a practice block of 14 trials. In this block, the sequences were completely random – the illumination pattern could thus not be predicted. Next, participants completed 8 blocks of 14 trials, resulting in a total of 112 trials. In half of these blocks, the sequence was random. In the other half, the sequences were permutations of a fixed base sequence (e.g., given the base sequence of 1-2-3-4-5-6-7-8, a first sequence could be 3-4-5-6-7-8-1-2, followed by 5-6-7-8-1-2-3-4, etc.). In other words, participants could *learn* the underlying sequence, after which all sphere illuminations were predictable given the first illuminated sphere. Importantly, participants were informed of this mechanism, allowing them to try and learn the pattern from the start. Block order alternated, and was balanced (i.e., the first block was fixed or random an equal number of times over all participants). Participants were also informed about the block type (*order*: random vs. fixed) at the start of each block.

2.4   Analysis

We analyzed response time (RT) and (trial) accuracy using linear mixed-effects models with a Gaussian link function and a binomial link function, respectively. All statistical modeling consisted of the following steps. First, we entered the between-subject variable *audience*, the within-subject variables *order* and *block number* as well as all interactions (to the third degree) in the model as fixed factors. We also added a random effect to reflect adjustments to the intercept, conditional on the subject variable. We then verified whether the addition of a random effect for the *order* and *block number* variables, conditional on *subject*, increased the model's goodness of fit. If this was the case, the random effect was retained in the next modeling steps. In a second step, we sought out the most parsimonious model to fit the data, by systematically omitting non-significant fixed effects from the model. Models were compared using likelihood-ratio tests. The third and final step consisted of inspecting the best model's analysis of variance table and evaluating specific hypotheses. Significant interactions were investigated using post-hoc contrast analyses, which were corrected for multiple testing according to the Holm-Bonferroni method [7]. See [3,4,14] for a similar approach.

3   Results

3.1   Reaction Time

To analyze the RT data, we first omitted all incorrect trials from the data set (i.e., trials where one or more of the spheres were not tapped in time, or where a wrong sphere was tapped instead). We then filtered the data by applying the interquartile range criterion to the RT data distribution. More explicitly, we calculated the interquartile range ($IQR = Q_3 - Q_1$) and removed RTs below $Q_1 - (1.5 \times IQR)$, as well as RTs over $Q_3 + (1.5 \times IQR)$. This resulted in a removal of 0.036% of all trials. Overall RT performance is visualized in Fig. 2, whereas the evolution of RT over time is shown in Fig. 3.

The model that best described the RT data contained all fixed effects and interactions, as well as a subject-based random intercept, a random effect of *block number*, and a random effect of *order*. In it, 2 main effects were significant (*order*: $\chi^2(1) = 32.886; p < 0.001$, and *block number*: $\chi^2(3) = 66.769; p < 0.001$), as well as 2 two-way interaction effects (*audience* x *block number*: $\chi^2(6) = 16; p < 0.001$, and *order* x *block number*: $\chi^2(3) = 208,842; p < 0.001$).

Since it contained a significant three-way interaction effect ($\chi^2(6) = 41.229; p < 0.001$), the model was not restricted further. However, in order to disentangle this complex interaction, the data was split up according to the levels of the *audience* variable. Statistical modeling was then reapplied to each subset.

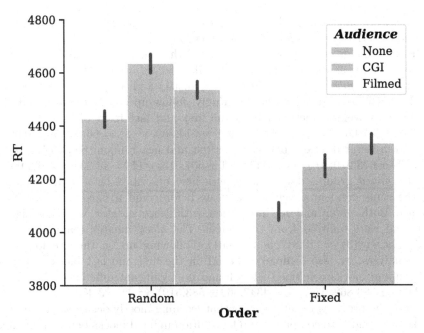

Fig. 2. Mean RT for blocks with random order sequences (left) and blocks with fixed order sequences (right). Bars reflect 95% confidence interval.

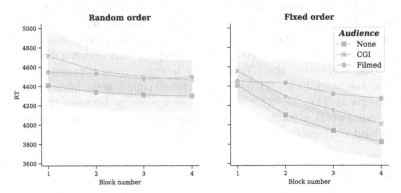

Fig. 3. Evolution of RT for blocks with random order sequences (left) and blocks with fixed order sequences (right). Bands reflect 95% confidence interval.

For the *none* group, the best model contained a subject-based random intercept, a random effect of *block number*, and a random effect of *order*. The model showed two significant main effects (*order*: $\chi^2(1) = 13.341; p < 0.001$; *block number*: $\chi^2(3) = 31.609; p < 0.001$), as well as a significant interaction ($\chi^2(3) = 41.229; p < 0.001$). Follow-up contrast analysis showed no significant improvement between the first and fourth random block. In the fixed blocks, however, RTs significantly decreased ($M_{block1} = 4410.509 \pm 534.726, M_{block4} = 3831.206 \pm 491.945, \chi^2(1) = 74.826, p < 0.001$).

In the *CGI* group, the best fit contained the same random and fixed effect structure. It too showed two significant main effects (*order*: $\chi^2(1) = 28.954; p < 0.001$; *block number*: $\chi^2(3) = 50.788; p < 0.001$) and a significant interaction ($\chi^2(3) = 56.797; p < 0.001$). Interestingly, follow-up contrasts suggested significant improvement between both the first and last fixed block ($M_{block1} = 4564.087 \pm 670.601, M_{block4} = 4018.998 \pm 614.880, \chi^2(1) = 66.961, p < 0.001$), and – to a lesser degree – between the first and last random block ($M_{block1} = 4713.209 \pm 673.210, M_{block4} = 4463.901 \pm 567.516, \chi^2(1) = 14.234, p < 0.001$).

The *filmed* group's data, finally, was best described by a model containing the same random effect structure as before, and a fixed term for *block number*. Both *order* and its interaction with *block number* were not significant, and were omitted from the model. The *block number* main effect was significant ($\chi^2(3) = 20.012, p < 0.001$). Following up on the previous contrast analyses, we also compared the RT in the first and last blocks (of fixed and random blocks combined), but found no significant difference ($M_{block1} = 4473.089 \pm 583.862, M_{block4} = 4347.862 \pm 583.519), \chi^2(1) = 3.400, p = 0.065$).

Since the previous results suggest that learning mostly occurred in the fixed blocks, we decided to compare the RT evolution in fixed blocks between different *audience* groups. To this effect, we restricted the data to contain only fixed blocks, and fit a separate model. This model contained a random subject-based intercept and a random effect of *block number*, as well as fixed factors for *audience* and *block number*, and their interaction. In the model, the interaction effect was significant ($\chi^2(6) = 15.111, p = 0.019$). We further explored this interaction through contrast analysis by comparing the difference between the first and fourth blocks (reflecting the RT gain – or learning rate) between groups. We found that the block-based RT evolution differed significantly between *CGI* and *filmed* groups ($\chi^2(1) = 7.737, p = 0.011$), and more so between the *none* and *filmed* groups ($\chi^2(1) = 9.139, p = 0.008$). The difference in learning rate between the *none* and *CGI* groups was not signficant.

3.2   Accuracy

The accuracy measure – reflecting whether all spheres were tapped in the right order (correct), or whether one or more mistakes were made (incorrect) – was modeled using the same approach (see Fig. 4). In this case, however, the best model contained a single fixed effect for the *audience* variable, a random subject-based intercept, and a random effect for the *order* variable. The effect of *audience* was significant ($\chi^2(2) = 6.343, p = 0.042$), showing higher accuracy for the *none* ($M = 0.926 \pm 0.262$), and *CGI* ($M = 0.937 \pm 0.243$) groups compared to the *filmed* group ($M = 0.882 \pm 0.262$).

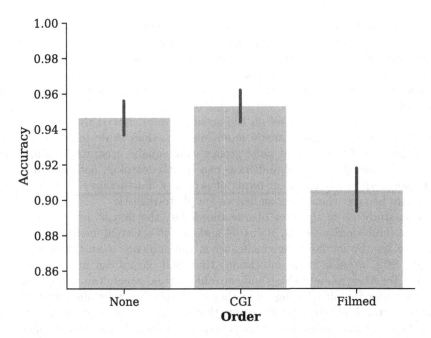

Fig. 4. Mean accuracy for *audience* conditions. Bars reflect 95% confidence interval.

4 Discussion

The aim of this study was to investigate the impact of virtual onlookers on performance and learning. To this effect, we designed a virtual environment in which participants performed an adapted SRT task by responding to a sequence of illuminating spheres. In half of the experimental blocks, the presented sequences were strictly random. In the other blocks, the sequences were – given the first illuminated sphere – predictable. In these blocks, participants could attempt to remember the underlying activation pattern, allowing them to anticipate the illumination of the next spheres and, thus, to perform better (i.e., faster reaction time, higher accuracy). As such, we were able to quantify each participant's learning rate, apart from overall performance.

Analyzing the participants' reaction time data clearly indicated that our adapted paradigm was effective, as participants were able to improve their response times on predictable (fixed) trials in both the *none* group (no audience) and the *CGI* group (artificially generated audience). Interestingly, the performance of participants in the *filmed* audience group did not improve significantly between the first and last fixed block, suggesting that their learning rate was hampered by the presence of the audience. In addition, the gain in response time was larger in the *none* group compared to the *CGI* group. This suggests that social inhibition may also have been at work in the *CGI* group, although we were unable to demonstrate this on a statistically significant level. Curiously, participants in the CGI group seemed to improve their response time to random trials over the course of the experiment, which could reflect increasing skill in the motor aspect of our task (e.g., handling the controllers with increasing precision). Further inspection of the data suggested that this was due to an especially poor performance in the first block (see Fig. 3), rather than an increased learning speed. As such, we are hesitant to attribute these observation to a potential effect of the *CGI* audience.

The results of our analyses on the accuracy data showed that, on average, people in the *filmed* group made more mistakes than those in other groups. Participants in the *CGI* and *none* groups were equally accurate. Again, these results indicate that virtual audiences can inhibit learning, not only in terms of response speed, but also in terms of accuracy. Furthermore, this seems to especially be true when these audiences are photo-realistic.

This study is, to the best of our knowledge, the first to present evidence of social inhibition caused by a virtual audience in a virtual environment. This evidence was by far most convincing when the audience consisted of recorded people. Still, we also found indications that CGI agents can influence performance. Together, these findings indicate that virtual agents can affect behavior – in this case: impair learning – but that the level of visual realism matters. In that respect, it is also interesting to note that participants were at all times aware that the environments and the characters therein were not human-controlled, but were either computer-generated or prerecorded. As such, our findings can hardly be attributed to their belief in human-controlled avatars, contrasting our results with those of Hoyt and colleagues [8].

This study has clear practical relevance in this era of immersive media, where VR-based training applications are increasingly prevalent. As computer graphics become more photo-realistic, social effects are more likely to arise. Specifically, our study predicts that photo-realistic audiences are likely to impair the performance and learning rate of those who attempt to execute tasks in virtual training environments. In that regard, two additional remarks present themselves.

First, it is likely that the correlation between the strength of a social effect and the visual realism of the virtual agents is not strictly linear. Earlier research by Mori and colleagues [9] uncovered the existence of the so-called 'uncanny valley effect': the observation that highly realistic yet imperfect human-like avatars are appraised more negatively compared to their ostensibly less realistic counterparts. In other words, unless the CGI representation is absolutely "perfect", people will notice subtle abnormalities in the representation which might result in an adverse response. Readers should thus be cautioned in extrapolating our findings to different degrees of 'realism'.

Second, it may be tempting to interpret the results of this study as a warning not to include realistic 'others' in virtual training environments. Indeed, doing so might impair the user's performance and learning speed, which at first glance may seem undesirable. However, it is important to note that our study did not evaluate performance beyond the contexts participants were assigned to. What would happen to task performance when people who previously practiced the task in an empty environment are made to execute it in front of an audience?

Could it be that they will be less capable to deal with the effect of the audience? Conversely, are people who trained in front of an audience better armed to deal with their influence? It is conceivable that, while training in front of (virtual) audiences slows down learning, it also prepares the trainees to handle the social impact of onlookers. A surgeon who only practices a procedure in an empty virtual environment may feel daunted having to perform it in front of fellow surgeons for the first time, partially negating the training effects of the simulation. Future experiments should be conducted to evaluate the cross-over effects of training in (populated) virtual environments. Regardless of the outcome of such studies, the present research makes one thing apparent: the onlookers in a virtual environment may be fake, but their social effects can be felt all the same.

References

1. Baldwin, N., Branyon, J., Sethumadhavan, A., Pak, R.: In search of virtual social facilitation effects. Proc. Hum. Factors Ergon. Soc. **59**(1), 90–94 (2015)
2. Bond, C.F., Titus, L.J.: Social facilitation: a meta-analysis of 241 studies. Psychol. Bull. **94**(2), 265 (1983)
3. De Paepe, A.L., Crombez, G., Legrain, V.: Remapping nociceptive stimuli into a peripersonal reference frame is spatially locked to the stimulated limb. Neuropsychologia **101**(May), 121–131 (2017). https://doi.org/10.1016/j.neuropsychologia.2017.05.015
4. Durnez, W., Van Damme, S.: Trying to fix a painful problem: the impact of pain control attempts on the attentional prioritization of a threatened body location. J. Pain **16**(2), 135–143 (2015)
5. Hall, B., Henningsen, D.D.: Social facilitation and human-computer interaction. Comput. Hum. Behav. **24**(6), 2965–2971 (2008). https://doi.org/10.1016/j.chb.2008.05.003
6. Hayes, A.L., Ulinski, A.C., Hodges, L.F.: That Avatar is looking at me! social inhibition in virtual worlds. In: Allbeck, J., Badler, N., Bickmore, T., Pelachaud, C., Safonova, A. (eds.) IVA 2010. LNCS (LNAI), vol. 6356, pp. 454–467. Springer, Heidelberg (2010). https://doi.org/10.1007/978-3-642-15892-6_49
7. Holm, S.: A simple sequentially rejective multiple test procedure. Scand. J. Stat. **6**(2), 65–70 (1979)
8. Hoyt, C.L., Blascovich, J., Swinth, K.R.: Social inhibition in immersive virtual environments. Presence Teleoper. Virtual Environ. **12**(2), 183–195 (2003). https://doi.org/10.1162/105474603321640932
9. Mori, M., MacDorman, K.F., Kageki, N.: The uncanny valley. IEEE Rob. Autom. Mag. **19**(2), 98–100 (2012). https://doi.org/10.1109/MRA.2012.2192811
10. Park, S., Catrambone, R.: Social facilitation effects of virtual humans. Hum. Factors J. Hum. Factors Ergon. Soc. **49**(6), 1054–1060 (2007). https://doi.org/10.1518/001872007x249910
11. Rickenberg, R., Reeves, B.: The effects of animated characters on anxiety, task performance, and evaluations of user interfaces. In: Proceedings of the SIGCHI conference on Human factors in computing systems - CHI 2000, vol. 2, no. 1, pp. 49–56 (2000). https://doi.org/10.1145/332040.332406
12. Sanders, G.S.: Driven by distraction : an integrative review of social facilitation theory and research. J. Exp. Soc. Psychol. **17**(3), 227–251 (1981)

13. Strauss, B.: Social facilitation in motor tasks: a review of research and theory. Psychol. Sport Exerc. **3**(3), 237–256 (2002). https://doi.org/10.1016/s1469-0292(01)00019-x
14. Verbruggen, F., Aron, A.R.: Theta burst stimulation dissociates attention and action updating in human inferior frontal cortex. Proc. Natl. Acad. Sci. **107**(31), 13966–13971 (2010). https://doi.org/10.1073/pnas.1001957107/-/DCSupplemental.www.pnas.org/cgi/doi/10.1073/pnas.1001957107, http://www.pnas.org/content/107/31/13966.short
15. Zajonc, R.B.: Social facilitation. Science **149**(3681), 269–274 (1965). https://doi.org/10.1017/cbo9780511628214
16. Zajonc, R.B.: Feeling and thinking: preferences need no inferences. Am. Psychol. (1980). https://doi.org/10.1037/0003-066x.35.2.151
17. Zanbaka, C.A., Ulinski, A.C., Goolkasian, P., Hodges, L.F.: Effects of virtual human presence on task performance. In: Proceedings Artificial Reality and Telexistence, pp. 174–181 (2004)

Investigating the Influence of Optical Stimuli on Human Decision Making in Dynamic VR-Environments

Stefanie Fröh[1(✉)], Manuel Heinzig[1], Robert Manthey[1], Christian Roschke[2], Rico Thomanek[2], and Marc Ritter[1]

[1] Faculty Applied Computer Sciences and Biosciences,
University of Applied Sciences, Technikumplatz 17, 09648 Mittweida, Germany
{stefanie.froeh,manuel.heinzig,robert.manthey,marc.ritter}@hs-mittweida.de
[2] Faculty Media Sciences, University of Applied Sciences,
Technikumplatz 17, 09648 Mittweida, Germany
{christian.roschke,rico.thomanek}@hs-mittweida.de

Abstract. In this paper, we investigate the human decision making process in a virtual environment. The main goal is to find influencing optical and behavioral economical factors for intuitive decisions in Virtual Reality. We therefore place test persons in a virtual corridor with six visually and technically varying doors. The experimental task is to open one of the doors without overthinking or hesitating too long. This is repeated several times while randomizing and recombining optical features in every iteration. Our data shows that most of the introduced determinants actually do have an impact in the user's decision. We can also observe different intensities of impact depending on the factor. It appears that color is by far the most influential component, followed by the complexity of the doors opening process. In contrast, position, spotlights and color brightness show only marginal correlation with choices made by the user.

Keywords: HCI · Virtual Reality · Rapid decision making · Visual factors · Opening doors · Color influence · Virtual gesture interaction

1 Introduction

Development in computer visualization technologies and in particular in Virtual Reality has undergone a rapid growth in recent years [13]. Based on the likewise increasing amount of interaction possibilities that are available to the user in computer games or real world simulations, information about the selection of actions said user makes holds a great deal of importance to scientists and business companies alike. The usage of manipulation techniques can subconsciously guide the user into a desired behavior. Such manipulating actions could be achieved with elements of interactive guidance like visual clues or storytelling.

© Springer Nature Switzerland AG 2020
J. Y. C. Chen and G. Fragomeni (Eds.): HCII 2020, LNCS 12190, pp. 453–467, 2020.
https://doi.org/10.1007/978-3-030-49695-1_30

Consequently, the optical and functional design of virtual environments offers a high potential to manipulate the users decision making process.

Our study focuses on the design and implementation of a virtual environment that offers various optical stimuli in order to influence decisions of a users movement process in VR. Therefore, we created a virtual corridor with a number of closed doors, which the user can open. Those can be distinguished by optical appearance and complexity of their opening technique. Users have to actively move through one of the doors without interrupting their movement process for an unnatural amount of time. Like this, rapid judgment skills become obligatory and the whole process leads to meaningful claims [7].

Using this method, we want to extract and rank the factors according to their influence on the decision making process. As test subjects, we use people from a broad range of ages that are used to gaming in VR. This is necessary to minimize or eliminate basic operational issues, such as motion sickness, that might interfere with our testing methods and allows us to concentrate on meaningful events. People are sent through a dynamic, seed based varying corridor and told to quickly decide on a door to pass through. Characteristics of several runs are accumulated numerically and test subjects undergo a short interview to explain the reasoning behind their actions.

To elucidate our experiments, firstly we break down the touched scientific field (Sect. 2: Related Work) and draw primary conclusions for emerging actions. We then disclose details of our used measurement methods and study setup (Sect. 3: Implementation), explicate the underlying software structure (Sect. 4: Implementation) and discuss the obtained results by drawing conclusions, emerging from the surrounding scientific context (Sect. 5: Results).

2   Related Work

Every human has to face an enormous series of decisions in their everyday life. When to get up in the morning? What to wear? What to eat? Summarized, an average person ends up with approximate 35000 conscious decisions throughout the day [9]. A decision is thereby defined by the process of choosing a preferred option out of two or more [17].

The human normally chooses a method that leads to the best results [11]. It is very unlikely that a person will pick an option that is not beneficial to his needs. An option can thereby be the choice of an object or the choice of an action in a situation. Both object and action will benefit the human in its current process. A decision, however, is not only defined by consciousness. It can also emerge from the unconscious domain [16]. In many cases it's not quite sure which domain is responsible for the actions of test subjects. There are many fields of study the treat the decision making process as well as the visual indications of a human that fuels those processes [1, 12, 20].

Fig. 1. Variation and shared features within the basic object class "door".

2.1 Visual Basics

Human object recognition in general is based on varying semantic perception levels that get combined into one big concept of a *thing*. Therefore, eye and brain perceive and process an objects raw appearance and sort it into a general category, e.g. "car". With increasing time, details such as edges or interesting points become more important and the object is integrated into more specific concepts, e.g. "Volkswagen". This process is correlated with optical clues. Firstly, the overwhelming outline of the object is recognized. Then, details are perceived to achieve a more detailed classification. With this, the human brain builds a hierarchy of basic, major and minor categories [5], each of them based on selection of examples that are learned through experience. Such basic categories are especially interesting for fast object recognition. Items are classified based on relations between their different attributes in corresponding classes. Figure 1 depicts examples of this concept. Each door is classified as such by incorporating a door leaf, frame and an element to operate their opening functionality. Slight variations of the outer shape or ornaments on individual doors serve as characteristic traits to distinguish different doors, but none of those small augments turns them into a telephone.

The effect of colors on a human depends on a plethora of factors. Context is crucial, because the fundamental meaning of some colors and shades vary heavily when viewed in different environments. In addition to the well known psychological effect (blue = calming, red = arousing) more levels of impact exist. There are also attributions based on cultural facts (is *white* considered a *happy, celebrational* or a *sad, grievous* color?), politics (green, red, blue pol. partys) or tradition (in chines history, red = fire, yellow = earth etc.). Some other colors are said to stimulate creativity or even trigger special effects in the receptive system (e.g. optical illusions). Most of those effects only spur to action in very specific situations which are directly designed to trigger the wanted effects and can therefore be neglected. When working with many different colors, there are also certain consequences, that have to be kept in mind while designing a color-related experiment. Most of them only appear while combining or cross-fading colors, so the usage of color-static scenarios would minimize the probability of optical side effects and simplify the experimental concept [14].

3   Method

The main objective of this paper is the analysis, whether varying optical stimuli in virtual environments can manipulate the user at all and if they do, how do the different kinds of stimuli affect the decision process. We therefor build an experimental setup in which we examine the following stimuli: color, position in relation to the user, texture/complexity and highlighting through illumination. All of those will be combined with each other to create various setups and to minimize the distortion of results through learning effects or personal predisposition [6]. Based on the exact combination of selected factors, it is also possible to analyze, which factors are most likely to manipulate the user. With the results, a conceptual virtual environment can be developed to influence user decisions in simulations, games or other VR experiences. The methods used for this are partially based on classical game design theory [2], which is also applicable to modern VR use cases [19].

3.1   Study Setup

In order to ensure a successful execution, a carefully constructed study is required. We want to observe the users behavior in an elaborated environment, which we design and implement using the Unity Game Engine to efficiently build our corridor and arrange the doors in Virtual Reality. The fundamental layout for our virtual environment is a walk-in corridor that contains six doors as stimulating object targets. These doors have a certain 3D model that defines their structural appearance and therefor serves as the first optical stimulus (also called visual factor). A variation of this stimulus takes place by varying the underlying 3D model for every door. The second varied optical factor is the base color of the door's surface. In addition to the realistic color corresponding to the material, we used a palette of some other pure colors that the user can distinguish easily. Factor three is the spawning position of a door relative to the user, who always spawns at the same spot and looks into the same direction. For the fourth and last optical factor we introduce a spotlight that shines from above selected doors, consequently highlighting them on purpose. In this setup, the user can navigate through the corridor for a fixed number of rounds, with each new round leading to a recombination of the factors.

3.2   Colored Design Choices

While planning the colorization of the three dimensional scene, we firstly focused on creating an ordinary, easily comprehensible optical framework to host our manipulative visuals. To prevent overly intense visuals to influence results due to their unrealistic and unfamiliar appearance, we create realism-oriented doors too. This leads to an unpretentious color palette with slight accentuations. With this in mind, used colors are chosen with a preference of achieving high contrast, to enable test subjects to easily distinguish between colors nevertheless. Consequently, we only use "basic colors" *green, blue, yellow and red* to build experimental environments. To further ease a fast perception of the appearance of a door, we choose to only have a single color on their surface. As a welcome side effect, this simplifies the conception of test cases as well as the subsequent evaluation process.

- **Red** has many contrary color effects, which all fall under the hypernym *passion* in some way. More popular implications relate to emotions like fury or love as well as symbolism for fire and heat. It also serves as a biological aid for survival because of its very noticable colorization as an attractor and warning sign, leading to spontaneous orientating responses [22].
- **Blue** is a symbolic color for serenity and safety, connected with the illusion of distance and defensiveness. This calming distance originates from the visual phenomenon, that every object seems more blue the farer it is in the distance. In the same manner, the symbolic meaning of darkness and cold underlines the perception negatively perceived remoteness [22].
- The interpretation of **Yellow** has many diverse facets. The most common one is the feeling of happyness and merryment, paired with the positive reception of a cozy warmth. This is based on the association of yellow with the sun and corresponding biological reactions of the human body when exposed to their light [3]. The more hours of sun in a day, the better most people feel. The decrease in sunny hours during the winter months leads to a growth in depression rates and general negative feelings [3]. Negative connotations of yellow come in the form envy, disturbances and increased alertness for unsuspected courses of events [22].
- Especially when it comes to video games and movies, **Green** often has negative associations. Poisonous liquids, spoiled food and blighted areas in the fictional world often do nothing good for the protagonist. Opposed to this, green is seen as a positive hue in real world objects. Originating from healthy plants and the romantic imagination of "fields of green" which depict the fundamental entities of life, we correlate the color with youth, healthiness and the positive feeling of a growing something new [22].

Additionally, we use a bright spotlight to highlight one of the doors. As the corridor is not completely dark at the beginning, this only serves as a small indication that might nudge testers towards a specific door. All design choices that are relevant to the experiments are summarized in Table 1 with a short outline of their potential significant effect on the perceived virtual world.

Those factors are varied and combined with each other at random. Furthermore, we conduct experiments where only a few factors are modified and others are fixed (e.g. fixed position and lighting, but random colors and corpora). Only with this broad range of tests it is possible to obtain reasonably

Table 1. List and explanation of all varied factors.

Visual factor	Explanation
Corporality	The basic visual appearance of a door, including texture, structural properties, small decorations and material
Color	The primary color of a door. Only pure red, green, yellow and blue are used. They do not manipulate basic appearance, e.g. a wooden door will remain wooden, but painted red
Positioning	The corridor has six positions for doors to spawn. All doors are fully interchangeable within the given spawning positions by random choice. As we have six unique door designs, all of them will be visible
Spotlight	In addition to varying features of the doors itself, we want to examine if lighting clues have any effects on decision making. Two spotlights are therefore placed in our scene at random, slightly lighting two doors

reliable conclusions that enable findings or exclusions of inter-factor correlations and dependencies, from which valuable learnings and inferences might emerge.

3.3   Test Subjects

In order to draw conclusions, it is necessary to collect, summarize and compare data. A user study was conducted to investigate the resulting application that was implemented with our research question in mind. The Subject group has to make a conscious decision during the testing phase and must not fall into a monotonous, absent minded selection process – a phenomenon that is very likely to crop up when a human as to undergo a highly repetitive process such as rapid, intuitive decision-making. As we set a fixed number of repetitions required for each subject to achieve comparability, we have a reasonable degree of control on that matter.

The main selection criteria for our participants was their general interest in using virtual reality and their present experience in VR. We ended up with a fairly low average of 22.4 years of age. The majority of subjects is between 18 and 27 years old. The experiments in VR were conducted over an extended period of time (approximately one month) in order to ensure a sufficient number of test subjects. The test, however, did never change and remained exactly the same for all participants. Neither did social environment or used hardware. We made sure that all tests were taken during the early afternoon to ensure a fairly equal state of body and mind with no subject having to take the test when close to their individual sleep cycle. To increase the validity of our test setup, we added a small group of persons that aged significantly above the expectable scope. In the final arrangement, those 46–52 year old people accounted for 18% of total subjects.

3.4   Testing Setup

All testers, regardless of knowledge, age or interest in technology had to take the same test. When finished with the practical part of our user study, subjects had to take a questionnaire that reviews their movement decisions in detailed self assessment and contributes to the evaluation by providing us with subjective but structured information about the real experience that test persons had and we get a glimpse behind the reasoning in their movement decisions. Due to the psychological background of stimuli and human decision-making, the questions cover several scientific topics which is referred to in Table 2. Literature shows, that there exists a connection between optical stimuli and attention as well as perception [15]. Furthermore, even the most basic concepts of color perception strongly impact human behavior, which has to be taken into account [4].

Table 2. Exemplary questions that users had to take for self-assessment, after they completed the test. The top half shows examples of questions relating to general color perception, the bottom half covers character traits of a user.

Question	Possible answers
Name & age	Words and numbers
Do you considers yourself a European?	Yes or no
Favorite color?	Free answer
What do you think influenced your decision process?	Design, light, colors...
How many consecutive choices could you memorize?	Free number
Was the succession of door perception a relevant factor?	Yes/No
You don't feel well in a situation. Do you still face it?	Yes/No/known consequence

Consequently, the first section of our questionaire is dedicated to general information about the respective testing user and asks questions about the self-implied impact of colors. In addition to questions about age and name of the participant, questions about cultural group and their favorite color are intended to focus on the subjective cultural effect and personal preferences. Questions of the second section deal with attention and perception. An important aspect of attention is selective attention, ergo the subset of information that is captured. In order to analyze this subset, the questions investigate selection criteria that the participant paid attention to. In addition to questions about the decisions themselves, the subsequent questions focus once more on selection criteria and the perception of objects in the 3D Scene. The slight preponderance of this type of questions is intended, since those represent the main focus of our study. Finally, the questions of the last section determine the respondent's generalized character traits. These should allow conclusions about potential influencing and biasing mental backgrounds.

4   Implementation

For the practical implementation, we used the game engine Unity [21] which uses C# as it's primary programming language. This is necessary to create three-dimensional environments with user interaction and Virtual Reality support in an easy way. A game engine is specifically designed for this purpose and decreased the overhead of implementing basic functionality in said domains by providing the needed elements and concepts. This enabled us to focus on building fundamental utilities, environments and sophisticated parts of the code that are directly relevant to our experiments.

4.1   Basic Scene Setup

In Unity, we built a so called `Scene` which serves as container for the three dimensional virtual space in which we can place our objects. Even with the goal of building a dynamically changing corridor, there are some basic elements that remain static for the whole time. This applies to the floor on which the user will stand, as well as for the majority of our wall area, which stays in the same optically neutral state for all of the experiments. We leave intended holes at all positions where dynamically changing environmental elements should appear. Those are inserted via code later.

4.2   Composing Pseudo-Random Scene Setups

An important prerequisite for the dynamic assembling of a scene has to be taken care of before a single line of code is written. To display doors with different shapes, materials and lighting, all used 3D models must be created modular. This ensures that all parts that will have to be varied later, are supporting said behavior. As there are many different possible topologies and conventions for building the internal structure of virtual 3D Objects, such features can't be assumed per se. This modularity has to be in effect all through our scenes optical framework. There are walls and a floor as basic, non varying elements of our setup. All of those have visually empty spaces, where invisible objects are placed for a start. We call them *empties*. At runtime, all empties are replaced by a random selection of real, visible and interactible doors that vary in their respective conceptualized attributes (overall appearance, color, lighting etc.). As we just need some random arrangements, we do not go the extra mile and implement a sophisticated randomization method [10], but rather use Unity's built-in `Random()`-function to create a pseudo-random sequence of index values. The obtained numbers are mapped to appearance elements which then get picked from the fundus and arranged to their determined positions in the three dimensional grid, featuring specified attribute values. Beforehand, the Random Number Generator is initialized with a specified *seed value* to ensure the same sequence of door-variations for all test subjects over all experiments [10].

Table 3. Brief overview of all implemented door variants and their corresponding opening mechanics.

Door	Opens...	Door	Opens...
	...by moving through the door area. (Big Door)		...by grabbing the metal ring and pulling it towards the user. (Medieval Door)
	...by pressing against the metal bar. (Simple Door)		...by grabbing the pivot point and pulling and pushing the complexly moving door. (Evolving Door)
	...by pulling the latch upwards and sliding it to the right in a single, smooth movement. (Creepy Door)		...by grabbing two door knobs and sliding both wings to their corresponding sides. (Sliding Door)

4.3 Interaction

Players have to be able to walk through doors, so implementing an opening mechanic is crucial to represent our experimental design. How to open a door is derivable from their visual identity, but consequently corresponding to changing appearances. As we want to keep the setup close to reality, this is necessary to not confuse test subjects. Complete randomness would allow for doors having a prominent door-handle, yet wanting to be opened with a sliding motion, or other arguably funny but not closely expedient scenarios.

An overview of doors and their opening procedure can be seen in Table 3. Some of the doors opening interactions just consist of the binary option of colliders touching each other and triggering an effect. This is especially true for *Big Door*, where a user just has to walk through (head "colliding" with door

Fig. 2. Comparison of doors with simple and more complex optical features.

area) to activate the `Door is open`-Signal. A little more complex are *Simple Door* and *Medieval Door*, where the tester actually has to execute the typical three dimensional opening motion. They may grab certain meaningfully placed interaction points with their virtual hands, represented by the controllers. Furthermore, those two doors have to have pivot points on which the door itself can rotate around. A certain angle has to be reached before we consider the door as opened.

Sliding Door has a similar technical structure. Interaction points at the handles and to wings to be slid to the sides. We calculate a value depending on the distance the two wings are apart from each other and counts is as *open* when a threshold is reached or one wing reaches its end position, indicating that the gap is big enough to pass through.

The *Evolving Door* once again features a door knob for the user to grab and a rather complex visual animation for opening in the style of spacecraft doors in sci-fi movies. The important movement to be made by the user is a swipe from right to left in an arc-shape that faces towards the person. Like this, it combines rather big pulling and pushing movements. The real challenge for development is the physically correct behavior of all four separate parts of the door, since it involves twisting and turning them in relation to the used force, grabbing position and current opening progress.

The most complex opening is featured in *Creepy Door* where one has to undergo a series of micro movements to finally open the door. Program-wise, this is representation in a succession of conditions that depend on each other and integrates techniques from all other doors. Twisting an object till the correct angular rotation has been achieved, subsequently moving it to the side for a certain distance and tracing a quadrant-shaped path to finish the motion finally triggers the wanted signal. All actions have to be completed in correct chronology. Since the used VR-system was technologically not able emulate realistic haptic

Fig. 3. Example of the implemented 3D corridor with varying doors.

feedback, the correct satisfaction of all conditions had to be ensured via reliably working code and usage errors must be indicated by small, non-disturbing overlays.

All interactions, collisions, errors as well as movements of head and hands are tracked by a supervisor script to easily access all wanted data for analysis after the experiments have been conducted.

5   Results and Discussion

It took the practitioners on average about 20 min to finish a test run. First findings were already made during the experiments. A majority of testers showed surprise when asked about the spotlights in the survey, as they had not noticed them during the run. The data and answers confirmed the assumption, as about 85% of the selected doors did not have activated spotlights. It should be noted that every selection run had two activated spotlights. However, this does not justify the high percentages.

5.1   Influence of Colors

In the given scenario, the color factor qualified as the strongest influencing factor. Colors should be chosen as realistic as possible, as people tend to dislike colors which they don't find fitting for the purpose. Hence, colors should be chosen as familiar – with regards to the present environment – as possible, since the user has a tendency of leaning towards the familiar rather than conspicuous and unusual objects and combinations (known as ambiguity effect) [8]. This was also evident in the survey, as the majority stated that they would only act in unpleasant situations if they could see what was coming their way.

People self-assessed that they did chose doors mainly based on their personal favorite color. However, an alignment with the summarized test data shows that the colored doors were chosen significantly less often than those that had a basic, realistically colored texture (Fig. 4). Around 52% of the selected doors just had their realistic, base colored texture. Selection data of colored textures show that the other colors have a roughly equal distribution and thus no generally more attractive color can be identified. Analysis shows that a manipulation with colorful textures is possible, but difficult to execute, because it correlates with the user's favorite color.

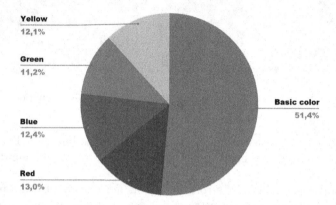

Fig. 4. Percentage of chosen doors by color. It is obvious that, despite being in a virtual environment, test users prefer a familiar, realistic appearance. (Color figure online)

5.2   Influence of Mechanics

The opening mechanics of the doors turned out be a important factor as well. Although during the first iterations, doors described as "pretty" or "beautiful" were given preference, many users turned to doors that open in a satisfying way over time. In general, the functionality of the doors was judged to be decisive by the users.

Looking at the data (Fig. 5), Sliding Door turns out to be the favorite with 28.5% of choices, followed by Creepy Door and Big Door with 18.2% and 17.8%. Simple Door and the Special Door qualified equally as the least selected doors as both recorded approximately the same number of selections. The questionnaire shows, that the users where intrigued by the easy, yet satisfying experience of performing an interaction that requires both controllers and most of the times leads to an immediate but rewarding success.

5.3   Influence of Positions

From the questionnaire, it appeared that the positioning of the doors was not extensively relevant to the users, as only three indicated that they had viewed

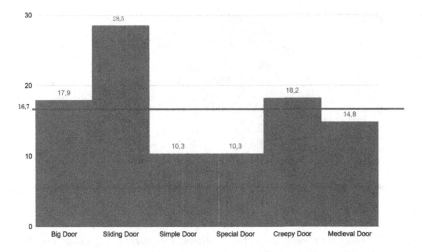

Fig. 5. Percentile distribution of selected doors dependent on their opening mechanics. Test users prefer doors where they can quickly interact in a satisfying, realistic way.

all the doors before deciding on one. Nine users partially indicated that the positioning was considered. As it is often the case [18], real data tells another story. Positioning of the doors seems to at least have some impact on the decision, since doors that appeared within a certain range of the user's field of view were chosen somewhat more frequently (Fig. 6).

The findings of positioning and headlights can be traced back to human consciousness, attention and perception. Thus, brightness information and the associated color changes appear to be less important in our context and attract less attention than the rest of the appearance. An increase in color intensity has only been noticed by a few and thus only serves as a minor eye-catcher. On the other hand, the positioning seems to heavily influence decisions in correlation with visual habits regarding the field of view. It should be noted that the resulting findings are sums and averages for iteratively changing, repetitive selections and can therefore only provide indications and trends for isolated decisions.

In the reflective survey, some users showed slightly negative cognitive capabilities, resulting in faulty memorization of their made selections. In addition, an occurrence of the *Bizarreness Effect* [6] can be suspected, as users commented on conspicuous objects such as the telephone cabinet as opposed to the carpet and used unusual elements of the door as a description of it rather than more common ones such as the unique functionality of each door. In the verbal description of the doors itself, the object recognition of visual perception becomes apparent, as subordinate categories of the basic category door were used to make comparisons.

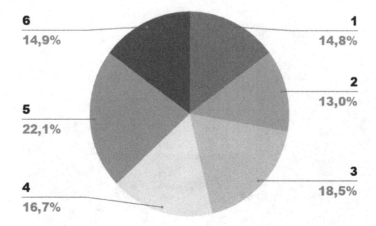

Fig. 6. Distribution of chosen doors by positions. The slightly dominant Pos. 5 is the center-right location in the visual field of view.

6   Conclusion and Future Work

The designed and fully implemented Virtual Environment enabled us to test a wide variety of optical stimuli and their influence on fast human decisions. Starting from scratch with custom made 3D door models to a simple, yet powerful analyzing module, the implemented functionality helped us to achieve our desired goals. The modular structures of our three dimensional models solve as the needed basis for automatically composing random scenery in our experiments and enables expandability for future variations of the test. Same is true for all used scripts and parametrizable functions, whose options can easily be reconfigured to adapt to new scopes.

Regarding our scientific results, we identify the factor *color* to be the most influential one, even though a realistic color scheme with quiet shading was used. Data furthermore allows implications that directly correlate our results to findings of cognitive psychology. To further align our outcome with interdisciplinary state of the art methods, more tests and corresponding adjustments to the overall procedure are needed. To transcend the classical disciplines of natural and cognitive science.

References

1. Abernethy, B.: Visual search strategies and decision-making in sport. Int. J. Sport Psychol. **22**(3–4), 189–210 (1991)
2. Adam, E.: Fundamentals of Game Design - Fundamentals of Game Design 2, 2nd edn. New Riders, London (2010)
3. Denissen, J.J.A., Butalid, L., Penke, L., van Aken, M.A.G.: The effects of weather on daily mood: a multilevel approach (2008). https://www.researchgate.net/publication/23302100_The_Effects_of_Weather_on_Daily_Mood_A_Multilevel_Approach

4. Gaines, K., Curry, Z.: The inclusive classroom: the effects of color on learning and behavior. J. Family Consumer Sci. Educ. **29**(1), 46–57 (2011)
5. Gauthier, I., Anderson, A.W., Tarr, M.J., Skudlarski, P., Gore, J.C.: Levels of categorization in visual recognition studied using functional magnetic resonance imaging. Curr. Biol. **7**(9), 645–651 (1997)
6. Geraci, L., Mcdaniel, M., Miller, T., Hughes, M.: The bizarreness effect: evidence for the critical influence of retrieval processes. Memory Cogn. **41**, 1228–1237 (2013)
7. Gigerenzer, G., Goldstein, D.G.: Simple Heuristics that Makes Us Smart. Oxford University Press, New York (1999)
8. Heath, C., Tversky, A.: Preference and belief: ambiguity and competence in choice under uncertainty. J. Risk Uncertainty **4**(1), 5–28 (1991)
9. Hoomans, D.J.: 35,000 Decisions: The Great Choices of Strategic Leaders, March 2015
10. Knuth, D.E.: The Art of Computer Programming - Volume 2: Seminumerical Algorithms, 3rd edn. Addison-Wesley Professional, Boston (1997)
11. Krantz, D., Kunreuther, H.: Goals and plans in decision making. Judgment Decis. Making **2**, 137–168 (2007)
12. Kundel, H., Nodine, C., Carmody, D.: Visual scanning, pattern recognition and decision-making in pulmonary nodule detection. Invest. Radiol. **13**(3), 175–181 (1978)
13. Lessick, S., Kraft, M.: Facing reality: the growth of virtual reality and health sciences libraries(). J. Med. Libr. Assoc.: JMLA **105**(4), 407–417 (2017)
14. Maloney, L.T., Boyaci, H., Doerschner, K.: Surface color perception as an inverse problem in biological vision. In: Bouman, C.A., Miller, E.L. (eds.) Computational Imaging III, vol. 5674, pp. 15–26. International Society for Optics and Photonics, SPIE (2005)
15. Morgan, S.T., Hansen, J.C., Hillyard, S.A.: Selective attention to stimulus location modulates the steady-state visual evoked potential. Proc. Natl. Acad. Sci. **93**(10), 4770–4774 (1996)
16. Newell, B.R., Shanks, D.R.: Unconscious influences on decision making: a critical review. Behav. Brain Sci. **37**(1), 1–19 (2014)
17. Phillips, S.D.: Toward an expanded definition of adaptive decision making. Career Dev. Q. **45**(3), 275–287 (1997)
18. Pohl, R.F.: Cognitive Illusions - A Handbook on Fallacies and Biases in Thinking. Judgement and Memory. Psychology Press, London (2004)
19. Schell, J.: The Art of Game Design: A Book of Lenses, 1st edn. Elsevier/Morgan Kaufmann, Amsterdam (2008)
20. Tanner, W.P., Swets, J.A.: A decision-making theory of visual detection. Psychol. Rev. **61**(6), 401–9 (1954)
21. Unit Technologies: The world's leading real-time creation platform (2019). https://unity3d.com/. Accessed 31 Jan 2020
22. Welsch, N., Liebmann, C.C.: Farben - Natur, Technik, Kunst, 3rd edn. Springer, Heidelberg (2012). https://doi.org/10.1007/978-3-662-56625-1

A HMD-Based Virtual Display Environment with Adjustable Viewing Distance for Improving Task Performance

Makio Ishihara[1]([⊠]) and Yukio Ishihara[2]

[1] Fukuoka Institute of Technology, Fukuoka 811-0295, Japan
m-ishihara@fit.ac.jp
[2] Shimane University, Matsue, Shimane 690-8504, Japan
iyukio@ipc.shimane-u.ac.jp
https://www.fit.ac.jp/~m-ishihara/Lab/

Abstract. This manuscript builds a HMD-based virtual display environment and conducts an experiment on a relation between viewing distances to the display and task performance. The result implies that longer viewing distances could improve speed, accuracy and precision of mouse manipulation.

Keywords: Task performance · Mouse manipulation · Viewing distance · Virtual display

1 Introduction

The VDT syndrome is a symptom that is caused by extensive use of eyes for long hours and pains in the neck or shoulders due to sitting at desks for long periods of time, and physiological stress that stems from monotonous and continuous work requiring no errors etc.

To deal with the VDT syndrome, A. Uetake et al. [4] discussed an evaluation method of eye fatigue during VDT tasks. They found that eye fatigue is expressed as a function of pupil diameter and focusing strength. T. Katayama et al. [2] investigated the impact of color patterns displayed on a screen on work performance and fatigue. They found that an appropriate contrast between characters and background tends to alleviate much more fatigue. Y. Kato et al. [3] built a posture feedback neck band to alleviate pain in the neck and shoulders. The users wear the band on their neck and the band rings an alarm when their posture becomes misaligned during VDT tasks.

In regard to human ergonomics, international standards of ISO9241-303 specify requirements for output devices, especially for electronic visual displays. It says for example that the viewing distance, which refers to the physical distance between the surface of the computer screen and the user's eyes, should be 30 to 40 cm for children and young people, and more than 40 cm for adults and older people. Though a lot of approaches and efforts from various points of view have

© Springer Nature Switzerland AG 2020
J. Y. C. Chen and G. Fragomeni (Eds.): HCII 2020, LNCS 12190, pp. 468–477, 2020.
https://doi.org/10.1007/978-3-030-49695-1_31

been made to address VDT syndrome over the years, it still remains a problem for many office workers.

As mentioned, optimal viewing distances have been discussed often from the side of human ergonomics but not task performance. Previously, the authors [1] showed that long viewing distances enable users to manipulate the mouse more slowly, more correctly and more precisely than shorter ones. In their study, a series of experiments were conducted for two viewing distances of 0.5 m and 3.5 m from a computer/projection screen with a constant horizontal field of view or FOV. In this study, the aim is to cover discussion with longer viewing distances like 5 m and 10 m, and investigate its impact on task performance.

2   A HMD-Based Virtual Display Environment

To realize longer viewing distances to the computer screen, this study employs a head-mounted display or HMD and builds a virtual computer screen environment in a virtual space. Figure 1 shows a screenshot of the HMD view which the user sees in. There is a virtual computer screen in that view and the user manipulates the contents on it. The contents on the virtual computer screen come from the host computer and all the input made on the virtual computer screen like mouse clicks and drags, goes back to the host computer to update the contents.

Figure 2 shows a look of our prototype system. The system consists of a HMD device of HTC Vive Pro, a high-end host computer of Dell Alienware, and two displays (a dual display). The HMD and two displays are connected to the host computer. The host computer runs Unity (2019.1.14f1) to compose a virtual space where a virtual computer screen is placed and makes a copy of the screen image of the left display then sends it to the virtual computer screen in the virtual space. The user can adjust its viewing distance in real time with a Vive trackpad. The viewing distance can be adjusted between 0.5 m and 128 m.

3   Pilot Experiment

The aim of this experiment is to see how the user accepts a virtual computer screen with adjustable viewing distance functionality in a HMD environment.

Figure 3 shows the design of the experiment. The left diagram shows the top view and the user sees a virtual computer screen just in front of him/her. The virtual computer screen is enlarged with a constant horizontal FOV of 60° as the viewing distance becomes long. The user perceives a small screen at the short viewing distance and does a large screen at the long distance. The right diagram shows the side view and the virtual computer screen is placed along a line at the angular position of 22° below the eye level according to ergonomics of human system interaction in ISO9241.

3.1   Tasks and Subjects

Each subject is asked to view a PDF document on the virtual computer screen for 3 min allowing him/her to adjust the viewing distance as he/she prefers.

Fig. 1. Screenshot of the HMD view.   **Fig. 2.** Hardware setups.

All the change of the viewing distance made by him/her is recoded with times-tamps. The PDF document is chosen from handouts that the authors use in their class of Java Programming in the university. The PDF document is written in Japanese with the font size of 10.5 pt and the font style of HG Maru Gothic M-PRO.

There are 8 subjects aged from 21 to 24. They are students from a course of computer science and engineering in the university and they also have experience in using computers on a daily basis. They all have a good eyesight.

3.2   Results

Figure 4 shows the change of the viewing distance made by Subject 1 for 3 min. The horizontal axis is the elapsed time in second and the vertical one is the view-ing distance in meter. From the figure, the subject examined his/her preferred viewing distance in the middle and finally he/she seemed to find it around 30 m to 40 m. Figure 5 shows the often-adjusted viewing distance. The horizontal axis is the viewing distance in meter and the vertical one is the dwell time in second. From the graph, there were two spikes around viewing distances of 2 m and 34 m. For the viewing distance of 2 m, referring to Fig. 4, most of the plots surely came from a certain period of time at the beginning. It was maybe the time for the subject to get used to the system. Figure 6 shows the cumulative distribution function of the often-adjusted viewing distance.

Figure 7 shows the change of the viewing distance made by another subject 2. The horizontal axis and the vertical one are the same with Fig. 4. From the figure, there were some drastic increases in the middle and this was because it is often hard for users to notice any visual change of the virtual computer screen in case of long viewing distances, leading to having the subject keep moving the virtual computer screen. Finally, he/she seemed to find the preferred viewing

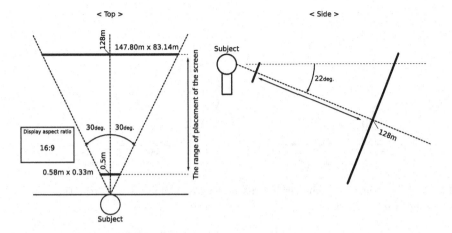

Fig. 3. Experiment design.

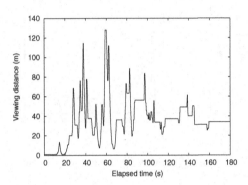

Fig. 4. Change of viewing distance made by Subject 1.

distance less than 5 m. Figure 8 shows the often-adjusted viewing distance and Fig. 9 shows its cumulative distribution function. From the graph, there was a single hill around 2 m and it could be his/her preferred viewing distance.

Figure 10 shows the ratio of preferred viewing distances over the given one x in meter to all. The horizontal axis is the given viewing distance x in meter and the vertical one is the ratio. The preferred viewing distance is here defined as the one where the subject stays for viewing the PDF document for more than 10 seconds and there were 30 pieces of preferred viewing distances extracted from the experiment results. The obtained approximate curve is represented in the figure and it says that the ration of preferred viewing distances over 10 m to all is more than 40%. Furthermore the average of preferred viewing distances is significantly more than 3.5 m that was discussed in the previous work[t(29)=2.94 at $p <.01$].

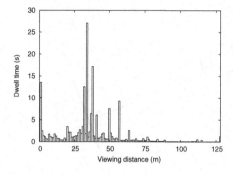 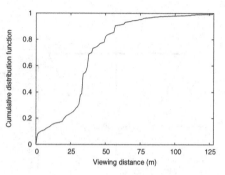

Fig. 5. Dwell time at each viewing distance made by Subject 1.

Fig. 6. Cumulative distribution function from Fig. 5

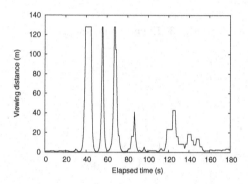

Fig. 7. Change of viewing distance made by Subject 2.

4   Experiment on Task Performance

The aim of this experiment is to evaluate an impact of viewing distances on task performance. The setup of the experiment is the same with the pilot experiment shown in Fig. 3. Only the difference is that three constant viewing distances of 0.5 m, 32.0 m and 128.0 m are given for each subject to perform the given task. The three constant viewing distances are referred to as Near, Middle and Far, respectively.

4.1   Tasks and Subjects

Each subject performs two tasks, Tapping task and Tracing task at each condition: Near, Middle and Far. Tapping task measures accuracy and speed of mouse manipulation of clicking on a target. Figure 11(left) shows a look of Tapping task. Two rectangles are placed on the left and right of the screen separately and the subject is asked to move the mouse cursor to either rectangle and click on it. Next the subject moves the cursor to the other rectangle and clicks on it alternating 100 times in total as quickly and correctly as possible. During the

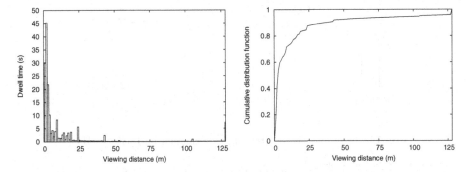

Fig. 8. Dwell time at each viewing distance made by Subject 2.

Fig. 9. Cumulative distribution function from Fig. 8.

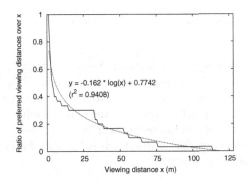

Fig. 10. Rate of preferred viewing distances over the given one.

experiment, the elapsed time to complete the task and the number of misclicks in total are recorded.

Tracing task measures accuracy and speed of mouse manipulation of dragging along a path. Figure 11(right) shows a look of Tracing task. A round path is placed in the center of the screen and the subject is asked to drag the mouse cursor on the path clockwise at 100 revolutions in total as quickly and correctly as possible. During the experiment, the elapsed time to complete the task and the gap between the center line of the round path and the mouse cursor are recorded.

There are 14 subjects aged from 21 to 24. They are students from a course of computer science and engineer in our university and all are right-handed and have experience with manipulating a computer mouse. They also have good eyesight.

4.2 Experiment Procedure

Figure 12 shows a procedure of the experiment. Each subject performs Tapping task first, which is followed by Tracing task. The subject has a practice time

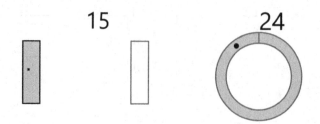

Fig. 11. Tapping task and tracing task defined by ISO9241-411.

1st task:Tapping 2nd task:Tracing

Practice	Sit still 5 min	Experiment 1st	Questionnaire	Sit still 5 min	Experiment 2nd	Questionnaire	Sit still 5 min	Experiment 3rd	Questionnaire

Fig. 12. Procedure of the experiment.

to become familiar with each task before it begins. After that, he/she sits still for 5 min then starts the task at one of the conditions of Near, Middle and Far, and fills out a questionnaire about his/her physical fatigue. He/she sits still for another 5 min then starts the task again at the other condition and fills out the questionnaire. The order of conditions between Near, Middle and Far is balanced among subjects to remove order effects. Each subject performs one trial at each condition for each task, resulting in

$$14 \text{ subjects} \times 2 \text{ tasks} \times 3 \text{ conditions} \times 1 \text{ trial}$$
$$= 84 \text{ trials in total.} \tag{1}$$

4.3   Results

Figure 13 shows speed of mouse manipulation of clicking on a target for Tapping task. The horizontal axis shows three conditions of Near, Middle and Far, and the vertical one does the elapsed time to complete the task in second. Each line represents a difference subject. From the figure, there seems not to be a vivid relation between those conditions and the elapsed time. Some subjects completed the task more quickly for longer viewing distances and the others did not. Figure 14 shows the average of speed across all the subjects (the solid line) and its standard deviation (the dashed line). From the figure, there seems to be a little decrease at Far condition.

Figure 15 shows accuracy of mouse manipulation of clicking on a target for Tapping task. The horizontal axis is the same with Fig. 13 and the vertical one shows the rate of misclicks made by each subject over the task. Each line represents a different subject. From the figure, there seems to be more misclicks

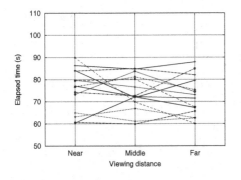

Fig. 13. Elapsed time to complete Tapping task at individuals.

Fig. 14. Elapsed time to complete Tapping task on average across individuals.

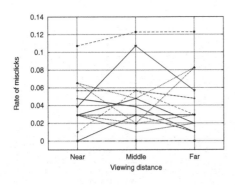

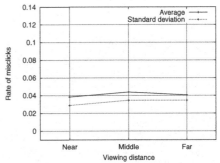

Fig. 15. Rate of misclicks made during Tapping task at individuals.

Fig. 16. Rate of misclicks made during Tapping task on average across individuals.

at Middle condition than the other two. Figure 16 shows the average of accuracy across all the subjects (the solid line) and its standard deviation (the dashed line). From the figure, there is somewhat a tendency for an increase at longer viewing distances.

Figure 17 shows speed of mouse manipulation of dragging along a round path for Tracing task. The horizontal axis shows three conditions of Near, Middle and Far, and the vertical one does the elapsed time to complete the task in second. Each line represents a difference subject. From the figure, there seems to be a certain relation between those conditions and the elapsed time. Most of the subjects completed the task more quickly for longer viewing distances. Figure 18 shows the average of speed across all the subjects (the solid line) and its standard deviation (the dashed line). From the figure, there seems to be more decrease for longer viewing distances.

Figure 19 shows accuracy of mouse manipulation of dragging along a round path for Tracing task. The horizontal axis is the same with Fig. 17 and the vertical one shows the gap between the center line of the round path and the

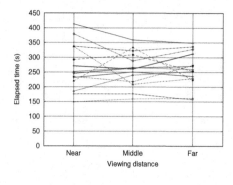

Fig. 17. Elapsed time to complete Tracing task at individuals.

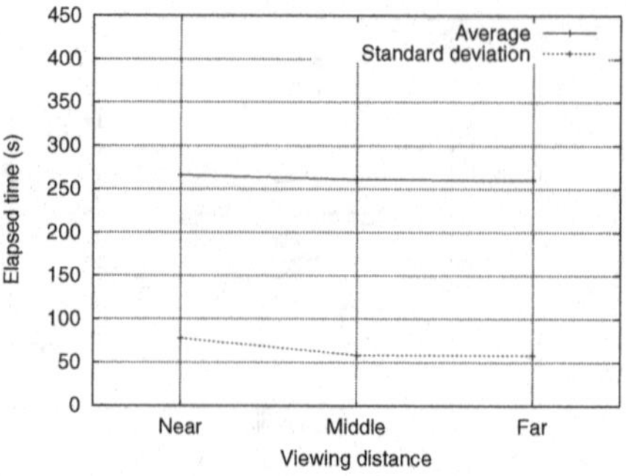

Fig. 18. Elapsed time to complete Tracing task on average across individuals.

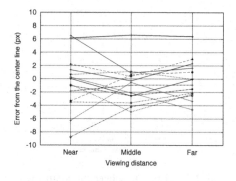

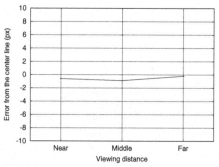

Fig. 19. Tracing errors made during Tracing task at individuals.

Fig. 20. Tracing errors made during Tracing task on average across individuals.

position of the mouse cursor. Each line represents a different subject. From the figure, nearly half the subjects dragged the mouse cursor along the center path more closely at Far condition than Middle one. Figure 20 shows the average of accuracy across all the subjects. From the figure, there seems to be more precise and accurate at Far condition than the other two.

To see the absolute error, Fig. 21 shows the absolute gap between the center line of the round path and the position of the mouse cursor at each subject for each condition. From the figure, nearly half the subjects completed the task with less absolute error at Far condition than Near condition. Figure 22 shows the average across all the subjects. From the figure, there seems to be more precise and accurate for longer viewing distances.

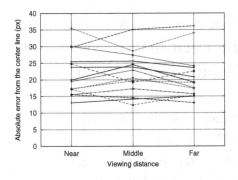

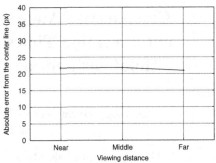

Fig. 21. Absolute tracing errors made during Tracing task at individuals.

Fig. 22. Absolute tracing errors made during Tracing task on average across individuals.

5   Conclusions

This manuscript built a HMD-based virtual display environment and conducted an experiment on a relation between viewing distances to the display and task performance. The result implied that longer viewing distances could improve speed, accuracy and precision of mouse manipulation.

In the future, the authors are going to conduct a further experiment with more subjects and practical tasks.

References

1. Ishihara, M., Ishihara, Y.: Impact of viewing distance on task performance and its properties. IEICE Trans. Inf. Syst. **E101.D**(10), 2530–2533 (2018). https://doi.org/10.1587/transinf.2018EDL8117
2. Katayama, T., Shoyama, S., Tochihara, Y.: Effects of blue background in the negative display mode on VDT work efficiency and fatigue. J. Hum. Living Environ. **22**(1), 29–38 (2015). http://ci.nii.ac.jp/naid/110009973299/en/
3. Kato, Y., Fukuda, S., Suzuki, Y., Ota, S.: Effect of posture feedback band on posture alignment and pain during a visual display terminal task. J. Japan. Soc. Exp. Mech. **16**(4), 315–319 (2017). https://doi.org/10.11395/jjsem.16.315, http://ci.nii.ac.jp/naid/130005300060/en/
4. Uetake, A., Otsuka, M., Takasawa, Y., Murata, A.: On evaluation index for visual fatigue induced during a VDT task. Trans. Inst. Electron. Inf. Commun. Eng. A **83**(12), 1521–1529 (2000). http://ci.nii.ac.jp/naid/110003313913/en/

Comparative Analysis of Mission Planning and Execution Times Between the Microsoft HoloLens and the Surface Touch Table

Sue Kase, Vincent Perry$^{(\boxtimes)}$, Heather Roy, Katherine Cox, and Simon Su

US Army Research Lab, Aberdeen Proving Ground, MD 21005, USA
{sue.e.kase.civ, vincent.p.perry7.civ,
heather.e.roy2.civ, katherine.r.cox11.civ,
simon.m.su.civ}@mail.mil

Abstract. In this paper, we present results of an investigation comparing two visualization technologies: the Microsoft HoloLens and the Microsoft Surface Touch Table. Two-person teams (dyads) played the role of commander's staff tasked with planning the most efficient and safest mission route for a squad of soldiers to extract a repository of intelligence documents from the ruins of a building located in enemy territory. Quantitative and qualitative measures of performance were collected. We focused on two performance measures: total mission planning time and mission execution time (the planned route run in a simulated execution mode). Surprisingly, there was a significant decrease in planning time when using the Surface Touch Table. The dyads needed on average 86% more time to plan the mission using the HoloLens. Additionally, this increase in mission planning time associated with the HoloLens did not produce a more optimal mission solution. In a search for understanding the unexpected results, a content analysis of a preferred visualization questionnaire is described. Analysis results suggested: a more realistic scene invited unnecessary exploration instead of focused time on task; becoming familiar with the HoloLens spilled over into task time; collaborative and communication difficulties stemmed from the HoloLens being designed as a single-user device.

Keywords: Augmented reality · Comparative analysis · Mission planning

1 Introduction

With the standing up of Army Futures Command and the establishment of modernization priorities, the Army is focused on preparing for the future. In the Army's Future Force vision, the HoloLens and other immersive technologies can assist commanders and their staff in conducting mission planning for complex environments such as dense urban terrains and multi-domain battlespaces. One of the six principles of mission command outlined in Army Doctrine Publication (ADP) 6-0 [1] is "create shared understanding." This doctrine states that "a defining challenge for commanders and staffs is creating shared understanding of their operational environment, its problems, and approaches to solving them." The U.S. Army Functional Concept for Mission

This is a U.S. government work and not under copyright protection in the U.S.;
foreign copyright protection may apply 2020
J. Y. C. Chen and G. Fragomeni (Eds.): HCII 2020, LNCS 12190, pp. 478–492, 2020.
https://doi.org/10.1007/978-3-030-49695-1_32

Command (AFC-MC) [2] describes visualization and collaboration devices as allowing the command and staff to view the common operational picture and communicate internally and externally thereby enabling continued, sustained operations.

Supporting the realization of these important doctrinal requirements, the Army is investing $480 million dollars ruggedizing an augmented reality (AR) device, the Microsoft HoloLens 2, as part of the Integrated Visual Augmentation System (IVAS) project [3]. There appears to be a rush to assemble immersive platforms composed of mixed reality devices despite little scientific evidence that using immersive technologies produces decision making performance benefits [4, 5]. In general, little is known about individual and team behavior associated with immersive environments. Empirical investigations of immersive technologies supporting collocated, remote, and distributed teams are sparse. We are working towards closing this knowledge gap by conducting a series of analytic comparisons between 3D and 2D visualization technologies in a mission planning context [6–8]. This study focused on determining if a 3D representation of the mission terrain produced by the Microsoft HoloLens produced better performance, defined by mission planning and execution times, than a more traditional 2D flat-screen display of the mission terrain.

In the next section of the paper, we overview the experimental investigation including information pertaining to participants, design, and metrics. Section 3 details a comparative analysis of mission planning and execution times as well as a context analysis of the participants' preferred visualization technology for performing the mission planning task. Section 4 offers several observations as to why the data analysis results were somewhat surprising. Finally, Sect. 5 concludes the paper.

2 Experiment

We conducted an experimental investigation to understand if an advanced 3D visualization technology improves mission planning performance when compared to a more traditional 2D visualization technology.

2.1 Participants

24 science and technology researchers, 16 male, 8 female, spanning the ages 24–51 (M = 35.00, SD = 8.14) participated in the mission planning experiment. All of the participants were employees at the Army Research Laboratory and volunteered for the experiment. The participants were paired in two-person teams (called dyads). The participants shared an interest in using an augmented reality device for experimentation. Basic information on playing video games and previous experience with AR was provided by the participants. None of the participants had extensive experience using AR devices.

2.2 Experimental Design

The narrative underlying the experiment requested dyad members to play the role of command staff tasked with planning the best mission route (i.e., shortest, safest) for a squad of soldiers to retrieve a repository of intelligence documents believed to be located within the ruins of a large building in enemy-held territory. The end point locations of the mission route, helicopter entry and ship extraction, were constants that could not be changed by the dyad. Mission variables the dyad needed to consider when planning the route included: coverage offered by the waterfront tree line; estimated number and patrol routes of enemy forces, occupant affiliation of a nearby small village; navigating the remnants of a large multi-room building, and estimated location of the document repository.

The experiment conditions focused on the dyads performing the mission planning task using two different visualization technologies separately. One of the devices, the Microsoft HoloLens 1, is a commercial off-the-shelf AR device with the capability to superimpose data collected and generated from modeling and simulation onto the actual physical environment of the HoloLens user in the form of a 3D holographic image. The other device, a Surface Touch Table, is similar in capabilities to Microsoft Surface tablets and laptops. The Surface Touch Table is a Samsung SUR40 40" interactive multi-touch display positioned horizontally. The Surface Touch Table displays images in 2D and uses Microsoft PixelSense for touch recognition. Figure 1 shows both visualization technologies; the Microsoft HoloLens and clicker on the left, and the Surface Touch Table on the right.

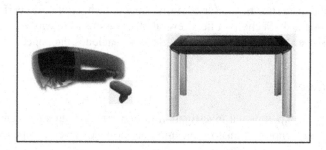

Fig. 1. Visualization devices used in the experiment. Microsoft HoloLens and clicker (left side) and Surface Touch Table (right side).

While using the HoloLens the dyad could walk around the holographic image of the mission terrain, thereby changing their viewing perspective in reference to the image. Each dyad member's HoloLens and clicker enabled marking of symbols and routes on the terrain. The AR visualization environment allowed the dyad to use hand gestures and communicate with each other during mission planning. The dyads could optimize their mission plan using an iterative 'run and re-plan' workflow similar to a wargaming simulation. Figure 2 shows the 3D holographic image of the mission terrain as viewed through a dyad member's HoloLens. In Fig. 2, the vertical blue arrow in the center of the building ruins estimates the location of the targeted document repository. The blue lines are example routes constructed by the dyad to retrieve the documents and reach an extraction point on the waterfront. The black squares to the left of the building are a menu of route planning tools.

Fig. 2. 3D holographic image of the mission terrain viewed from a HoloLens device.

Fig. 3. 2D image of the mission terrain displayed on the Surface Touch Table.

While using the Surface Touch Table the dyad could walk around the 2D image of the mission terrain. The rotate, pan, and zoom capabilities of the Surface Touch Table were disabled making the interaction experience similar to utilizing a more traditional 2D representation of terrain in the form of a paper map or a sand table. Similar to several individuals gathered around a large monitor display, the dyad members were able to use hand gestures and communicate with each other during mission planning. The tools menu and simulation capabilities functioned in the same manner as the HoloLens environment. Figure 3 shows the 2D representation of the mission terrain on the Surface Touch Table.

We followed a within-subjects design method where each dyad had the opportunity to plan the mission using both of the visualization technologies (HoloLens and Surface Touch Table). Dyads were randomly assigned one of the technologies to use first. All participants performed the same mission planning task in the same laboratory under the same conditions. Participants received an interactive training session on each device before beginning the mission planning task. The estimated time to complete the study was one and a half hours.

2.3   Measures

All participants were recorded on video using an external camera while performing the mission planning task using both visualization technologies. In addition, during the HoloLens condition, the field of vision through each dyad member's HoloLens device was recorded capturing their interaction with the hologram of the mission terrain. For example, Fig. 4 shows the HoloLens views from each dyad member and their corresponding physical position while viewing the 3D-generated mission terrain captured by the external camera.

Fig. 4. HoloLens views of each dyad member with the turquoise Gaze disc indicating their current focus (left side). Corresponding video capture from the external camera showing the physical position of each dyad member while viewing the 3D-generated mission terrain (right side).

Qualitative data were collected by 11 questionnaires which recorded each participant's impressions during the mission planning task. The broad range of subjective measures addressed in the questionnaires included: system usability, user engagement, team efficacy and performance, shared situational awareness, and task load assessment. More specific subjective measures focused on visualization topics such as simulator sickness, shared AR experience, and preferred visualization mechanism.

Quantitative data measuring dyad performance on the task were collected based on each dyad's interaction with the mission terrain. Performance metrics pertaining to the mission route included: number of path segments making up the route, number of deleted path segments, total route distance, time to plan the mission, simulated mission execution time, and total time it took for the dyad to complete the task. Additional objective measures involving other environmental variables in the terrain included: number of physical obstacles the squad ran into due to poor planning (e.g., mistaking window access for a wall), number of times the squad was detected by enemy patrols, length of time the squad waited at the extraction point for the ship (i.e., thereby open to enemy detection), and success or failure in obtaining the intelligence documents.

For this paper our comparative analysis focuses on two of the time-based performance metrics (1) the length of time the dyad needed to plan the mission route using each of the visualization technologies, and (2) the execution time of the simulated mission route.

3   Results

3.1   Mission Planning and Execution Times

All dyads participating in the experiment successfully completed the mission planning task on both the HoloLens and the Surface Touch Table. The time it took the dyads to plan the mission route was recorded for each of the visualization technologies. A data recording error occurred during one of the dyad runs (Dyad 9); therefore, that dyad's data is not included in the analysis results. During planning the mission as well as after the mission plan was completed, the dyads had the opportunity to execute a simulation of the current mission route showing the actions of the squad from helicopter entry to ship extraction. The length of time of the simulation run was recorded and called execution time. Table 1 compares the time recorded for each dyad to plan the mission and the time to execute the mission on each technology. The average mission planning time for each technology was 307.26 (SD = 180.09) seconds for the HoloLens, and 165.43 (SD = 81.93) seconds for the Surface Touch Table. The dyads needed on average 86% more time to plan the mission with the HoloLens than with the Surface Touch Table. A paired-samples t-test was conducted to compare mission planning time when using the Surface Touch Table and the HoloLens. There was a statistically significant decrease in the planning time; $t(10) = -2.47$, $p = 0.03$ when using the Surface Touch Table. The significant difference in planning time was also confirmed by conducting a Wilcoxon Signed Rank test.

The average mission execution time for each technology was 36.87 (SD = 3.76) seconds for the HoloLens, and 36.41 (SD = 4.09) seconds for the Surface Touch Table. There was little difference in execution time across the technologies. On average the execution time of the dyads' missions ran 5% longer on the HoloLens than on the

Surface Touch Table. A paired-samples t-test comparing execution time using both technologies showed non-significance.

Table 1. Time to complete the mission planning task and execution time of the mission plan for each dyad (D) using the two different visualization technologies. Time in seconds.

Dyad	Planning time			Execution time		
	HoloLens	Table	Difference	HoloLens	Table	Difference
D1	126.84	153.25	−26.41	35.34	33.63	1.71
D2	232.29	128.67	103.62	33.20	32.52	0.68
D3	295.16	146.77	148.39	35.78	36.38	−0.60
D4	352.42	185.40	167.02	44.73	46.45	−1.72
D5	118.79	135.78	−16.99	34.57	35.32	−0.75
D6	410.86	312.53	98.33	35.61	34.20	1.41
D7	410.32	159.79	250.53	38.85	39.63	−0.78
D8	121.05	72.09	48.96	35.10	34.74	0.36
D10	225.53	132.34	93.19	33.23	32.64	0.59
D11	350.58	320.25	30.33	42.81	39.51	3.30
D12	736.03	72.91	663.12	36.38	35.51	0.87
Mean	**307.26**	**165.43**	**141.83**	**36.87**	**36.41**	**1.71**
SD	**180.09**	**81.93**	**190.93**	**3.76**	**4.09**	**1.40**

Dependent on random selection, the dyads were assigned to perform the mission planning task on the HoloLens and then on the Surface Touch Table or vice versa. We calculated the time difference to perform mission planning on the HoloLens first in comparison to the Surface Touch Table second. Table 2 (left side) shows the percentage of time the dyads that used the HoloLens first needed to perform the mission planning task. We can see that in general, a dyad will need around 235% more time to perform mission planning on the HoloLens than on the Surface Touch Table when the HoloLens is used first.

The remaining dyads performed mission planning first using the Surface Touch Table and then second on the HoloLens. Again, we calculated the time difference to perform the task on the HoloLens in comparison to the Surface Touch Table. Table 2 (right side) shows the percentage of time the dyads that used the Surface Touch Table first needed to perform the mission planning task. Generally, a dyad will need around 16% more time to perform mission planning on the HoloLens than on the Surface Touch Table when the Surface Touch Table is used first.

Table 2 indicates the visualization technology that was used first to perform mission planning can greatly influence the dyads' time to complete the task. The effect of learning the mission planning task first on the Surface Touch Table suggests the dyads were then much more effective in executing the task using the HoloLens. For example, in Table 2 (left side), all times to perform the task on the HoloLens were much greater than the times to perform the task on the Surface Touch Table. Whereas in Table 2 (right side), Dyads 1 and 5 performed the task in less time using the HoloLens compared to the Surface Touch Table. Comparing the mean time differences in Table 2, 237.6 s (HoloLens first) and 26.8 s (Surface Touch Table first) strongly indicates mission planning time with the HoloLens (a 3D visualization device) can be greatly reduced by first planning the mission using a more traditional 2D visualization device.

Table 2. Increase in time to perform the mission planning task on the HoloLens vs. the Surface Touch Table (in %). Left side: Dyads performed the task first on the HoloLens and then on the Surface Touch Table. Right side: Dyads performed the task first on the Surface Touch Table and then on the HoloLens.

HoloLens First Planning Time		Surface Table First Planning Time	
Dyad	% Increase	Dyad	% Increase
D2	80.53	D1	-17.23
D3	101.10	D5	-12.51
D4	90.09	D6	31.46
D7	156.79	D8	67.91
D10	70.42	D11	9.47
D12	909.50	Mean	15.82
Mean	234.74	SD	34.98
SD	331.95		

Figures 5 and 6 visually summarize the differences in mission planning time (Fig. 5) and execution time (Fig. 6) and the learning effect across both technologies. Numbered dyads appear on the x-axis with time in seconds on the y-axis. Light gray bars indicate dyads which used the Surface Touch Table first and then the HoloLens second to plan the mission; dark gray bars indicate vice versa. Our analysis results show mission planning times when using the HoloLens tended to be greater than mission planning times when using the Surface Touch Table (Fig. 5). There was little overall difference in mission execution times across the technologies (Fig. 6). This suggests the visualization technology has an effect on mission planning time but not on mission execution time. There was a strong learning effect based on which technology was used first for the mission planning task. This suggests mission planning task times when using a 3D visualization device such as the HoloLens can be reduced by first performing the task using a more traditional 2D device such as the Surface Touch Table.

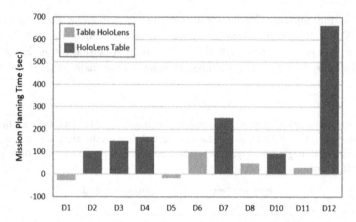

Fig. 5. Difference in mission planning time when using the HoloLens compared to the Surface Touch Table. Numbered dyads on the x-axis; mission planning time in seconds on the y-axis. Light gray bars indicate the dyad used the Surface Touch Table first and the HoloLens second; dark gray bars indicate vice versa.

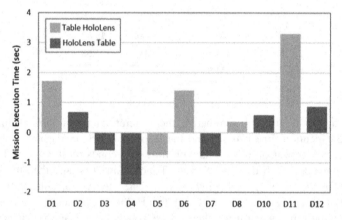

Fig. 6. Difference in execution time when the mission route is simulated using the HoloLens compared to the Surface Touch Table. Numbered dyads on the x-axis; mission execution time in seconds on the y-axis. Light gray bars indicate the dyad used the Surface Touch Table first and the HoloLens second; dark gray bars indicate vice versa.

3.2 Preferred Visualization

In our comparison between the HoloLens and the Surface Touch Table, preliminary analysis results of two performance metrics, mission planning time and simulated mission execution time, showed a significant difference in planning time and no difference in execution time between the two visualization technologies. Surprisingly, dyads required on average 86% more time to plan the mission with the HoloLens than with the Surface Touch Table when not taking into consideration the learning effect of which technology was used first. With greater mission planning time associated with

HoloLens use, we expected dyads to produce more optimal mission planning routes with shorter execution times then those produced using the Surface Touch Table. However, that was not the case, there was only a slight difference in execution time and in the opposite direction—5% longer on the HoloLens than on the Surface Touch Table.

To better understand the mission planning and execution time analysis results, we turned to subjective measures captured in a questionnaire focused on individual dyad member's preferred visualization device for performing a mission planning task. The questionnaire consisted of seven open-ended questions listed in Table 3. Open-ended questions prompt for feedback in a conversation style by asking questions starting with an interrogative word such as 'why', 'what', and 'which'. Responses to open-ended questions go beyond a single-word answer such as 'yes' or 'no'. Singer and Couper [9] reviewed the primary methodological uses of open-ended questions. In this case, the preferred visualization questionnaire gave individual dyad members an opportunity to describe their experience using the technologies. The preferred visualization questionnaire was administered at the end of the experiment after dyads had completed the mission planning task using both visualization technologies.

Table 3. Open-ended questions contained in the preferred visualization questionnaire asked individual dyad members about their preferred visualization technology for performing mission planning tasks.

Which technology did you prefer for mission planning? Why?
Which technology was easier to coordinate/communicate mission planning with your partner?
Which technology did you feel you were better able to work together to achieve the fastest outcome?
Which technology did you feel you were better able to work together to achieve the best outcome?
What suggestions do you have to improve the mission planning scenario when using the Surface Touch Table?
What suggestions do you have to improve the mission planning scenario when using the HoloLens?
What are your thoughts on how augmented reality could support mission planning with deployed Soldiers?

Qualitative data collected by questionnaires and surveys can be analyzed using a content analysis approach in order to distill words contained in the question responses into common themes [10–13]. Our goal was to analyze the responses for frequently occurring themes in use of the technologies for the mission planning task. The first step in analyzing responses to open-ended questions is *coding* the response text. Coding is the process of assigning response categories (codes) to open-ended question responses, or other types of text data after which the text can be analyzed similar to numerical data [14]. The codes help capture what the response is about and summarize the results of the entire survey. Coding text responses to open-ended questions can be conducted manually or automatically with the use of text analytics software. In this case, we manually coded the response text because the total number of participants in the experiment was small and the responses relatively brief in length.

A simplified and reduced 3-step content analysis approach was used to code the responses to the open-ended questions based on Hsieh and Shannon [12]. First, we considered several factors of *presence* identified by Witmer and Singer [15] in early virtual environment research. The concept of presence can be traced back to tele-robotics in experiencing a situation as if one were at the robot's location, or were present at the robot's remote site. Witmer and Singer [15] reviewed a large body of literature and formulated four main factor categories of presence: control, sensory, distraction, and realism. We applied these factor categories to an earlier analysis of survey data collected by a Shared Augmented Reality Experience questionnaire during the same user study and mission planning task [6]. In the second step of the content analysis process, the text responses from the open-ended questions of the preferred visualization questionnaire were coded and categorized into major and minor themes corresponding to Witmer and Singer's [15] factors of presence. In the third step, the emerging themes and categories derived from the response text were compared, contrasted with each other, and where appropriate, grouped to reduce the overall complexity.

Figure 7, provides an aggregated overview of the content analysis results from the preferred visualization questionnaire. Major themes from the text responses were classified into eight categories: scene realism, physical comfort, field of view, engagement, ease of collaboration, scene manipulation, interaction, and time on task (Fig. 7, second section). From top-down these categories were informed by Witmer and Singer's [15] factors of presence and accompanying literature relevant to early virtual environment research (Fig. 7, top section). From the bottom-up the categories emerged from HoloLens-specific topics discussed in the text responses (Fig. 7, third section). The frequency of the topics appearing in the text responses is totaled for each category and shown in the bottom section of Fig. 7.

Three of the eight categories had high frequency counts: scene realism (32), ease of collaboration (26), and scene manipulation (26). The topics discussed under the scene realism category suggest the 3D representation of the mission terrain offered a visually rich environment containing a great deal of information for planning the mission. Dyad members could physically move around the scene enabling identification of terrain obstacles and potential building entrance and exit points. The realism and detail assisted dyads in strategically planning what they considered to be the best mission route. In comparison, when using the 2D mission terrain displayed on the Surface Touch Table, dyads reported difficulty in identifying building entrance and exit points and navigating the interior of the building. Minimal scene content, limited resolution, and distracting shadows were also mentioned as hindering performance in the 2D mission planning environment.

The topics discussed in the ease of collaboration category suggest limitations in collaborative behavior in particular the lack of shared situational awareness when using the HoloLens to plan the mission. Not being able to see what your partner was pointing to because of wearing the HoloLens headset, and what your partner was looking at in the 3D scene were frequent topics of complaint. These feelings of disconnectedness from your partner are not surprising as the HoloLens was originally designed as a

Factors of Presence	Control		Sensory		Realism		Distraction	
Preferred Visualization Categories	Scene Manipulation	Time on Task	Interaction	Engagement	Field of View	Scene Realism	Physical Comfort	Ease of Collaboration
Category Topics	Ability to walk around a 3D scene Helpful to see from different angles Able to manipulate the map Could walk around and see into building	Slower because of needing to move around More time needed to get necessary information Less concerned about time	Slightly more difficult to grasp Harder to use Needs better pointing with mouse or stylus Improve the stability of gaze cursor Cumbersome to go find menu Frustrating mouse function	More immersive Novel Fun Meshing of reality and virtual content	Difficult to see the whole picture while route planning Needed wider field of view Improve the size of view window	Better depiction of reality Increased clarity of scene Scene details visible Offered more visual information Better informed routing strategy Could see door and window access to building Improved understanding of obstacles Improved situational awareness of mission terrain Easier to find more efficient path	Increased eyestrain Caused headache afterwards Needed neck brace Much less comfortable Cumbersome	Couldn't see where partner was pointing Needed a shared pointer Pointing with hand was difficult Not able to see where partner is in the scene Needed gaze ID markers for where partner is looking Needs multi-person drawing support Integrate partner's cursor location in my view
Frequency	26	4	10	5	5	32	5	26

Fig. 7. Overview of content analysis of text responses to open-ended questions in the preferred visualization questionnaire.

single-user system. In comparison, individuals grouped around a large 2D flat-screen display is a common collaborative scenario. The Surface Touch Table allowed dyad members to communicate verbally in conjunction with directly pointing and touching portions of the mission terrain while in close proximity to each other.

Topics discussed in the scene manipulation category portray an interactive and engaging experience with the 3D terrain as a benefit in effectively planning the mission route. Related to the scene realism topics, dyad members reported utilizing physical movement to manipulate the terrain. Although the HoloLens terrain could be manipulated using finger control, dyad members appeared to prefer using their physical location and posture in relation to the terrain as the primary scene manipulation approach. In contrast, the Surface Touch Table representation of the terrain simulated a traditional static map-like modality with disabled rotate, pan, and zoom capabilities. Lack of control over the terrain and unresponsiveness were frequently mentioned in the text responses. The next section discusses how the results from the preferred visualization questionnaire can assist in interpretation of the significant increase in mission planning time required when using the HoloLens without resulting in an execution time benefit.

4 Discussion

Research on the performance benefits associated with state-of-the-art visualization technologies such as the HoloLens has been comparatively vague and imprecise when contrasted with the abundance of usability studies involving 2D flat-screen displays in fields such as human computer interaction, human system integration, and computer-supported collaborative work. Thus, this study investigated performance differences in a simulated mission planning task when using 3D versus 2D visualization technologies.

Dyads (two-person teams) performed the same task comparing two visualization technologies: the Microsoft HoloLens, and a Surface Touch Table. The HoloLens provided dyads with an interactive 3D holographic image of the mission terrain overlaid on their physical environment. The Surface Touch Table provided dyads a flat-screen display with multi-touch recognition. A combined quantitative and qualitative data collection approach was utilized in the experimental design which included: capturing performance metrics generated by the dyads' interaction with the 3D and 2D environments; and recording dyads' impressions of using the technologies through a variety of questionnaires and surveys.

The quantitative data results outlined in the previous section focused on two time-based performances metrics (mission planning time and mission execution time). There was a significant difference in mission planning time between the devices with dyads requiring on average 86% more time to plan the mission using the HoloLens than with the Surface Touch Table. Mission execution time was not significantly different across devices. Dyads were randomly assigned one of the devices to use first (HoloLens then Surface Touch Table, or vice versa). There appeared to be a learning effect: an average of 235% more time to complete the task on the HoloLens than on the Surface Touch Table when the HoloLens was used first; and an average of 16% more time to complete the task on the HoloLens when the Surface Touch Table was used first.

The qualitative data results from a content analysis of open-ended question responses from a preferred visualization questionnaire highlighted three categories with greater frequencies of topic mentions than the other five categories. Two of the three categories with high frequency counts focused on characteristics of the visual environment (scene realism, scene manipulation). The 3D holographic image of the mission terrain offered a visually rich environment where dyad members actively searched for the best route by physically walking around the scene and oftentimes changing their posture to alter their viewing perspective (i.e., stooping to look through a window on the side of the building; standing upright over the building for a bird's eye view). Through the HoloLens, interaction with the 3D terrain was perceived as natural with active control that consistently responded in a real-world manner without delay.

Active search and control in a visually rich environment invited exploration which provided valuable information and understanding of the physics of the mission space but also potentially encouraged time not spent focused on the task at hand. Additionally, the sizable learning effect detected in the previous section may indicate time spent familiarizing oneself with the device instead of time spent on the task. Before performing the mission planning task, the dyads completed a training scenario to learn how to use the HoloLens. We all have expertise using a 2D touch screen device such as a cell phone; however, few of us have a similar level of expertise using a 3D AR or VR device. Possibly, the time the dyad spent on HoloLens training was not enough and therefore time spent learning how to use the HoloLens spilled over into time spent planning the mission. Overall, the HoloLens offered a more realistic, exploratory, novel, and thereby engaging mission planning environment at the cost of longer task completion times. In contrast, the Surface Touch Table offered a 2D representation of the mission planning environment with an adequate amount of information and detail to keep the dyad focused on task which resulted in shorter task completion times.

The third category with a high frequency of topic mentions focused on collaboration and communication between the dyad members (ease of collaboration). Even though a synchronized scene was displayed across dyad members through their HoloLens [8], the disconnectedness in collaborative behavior in the 3D environment such as not knowing where your partner was pointing to or what your partner was looking at in the scene could contribute to an increase in task completion time. Oftentimes, dyad members were physically positioned at opposite sides of the terrain requiring a verbal exchange of communication in order to decide the next location of a path marker. In comparison, using the Surface Touch Table, dyad members could make a timely path marker decision by pointing at a location on the touch screen and nodding, with no or very little verbal exchange required. The limitations in collaborative behavior associated with HoloLens use would certainly decrease the level of shared situational awareness across dyad members resulting in more time needed to plan the mission.

Our above observations shed some understanding on the substantial difference found in mission planning time between the Microsoft HoloLens and the Surface Touch Table. Why a more efficient mission route with a shorter execution time was not consistently produced using the HoloLens is less understood. The HoloLens offered a more realistic 3D environment for performing the task which could be actively searched and controlled by the dyad. Experimentation on a larger scale with a more complex scene and challenging task, and a larger participant pool, as well as, revisiting the training requirement for using a 3D device is necessary to further our investigation of mission planning performance.

5 Conclusion

The U.S. Army is increasingly supporting the use of immersive environments for mission command in complex environments such as dense urban terrains and multi-domain battlespaces. However, technological advancements in immersive devices are accelerating with limited information and empirical evidence on the actual decision-making performance benefits. This study is the most recent in a series of analytic comparisons between 3D and 2D visualization technologies in a mission planning context. Here, we focused on determining if a 3D representation of the mission terrain produced by the Microsoft HoloLens improved mission planning and execution times compared to a 2D representation of the mission terrain on a Surface Touch Table. Results indicated a significant difference in mission planning time between the visualization devices with on average 86% more time required to plan the mission using the HoloLens. Surprisingly, mission execution time did not benefit from the increased time in planning the mission. There appeared to be a large learning effect depending on which device was used first. A content analysis of open-ended responses to a preferred visualization questionnaire was helpful in understanding the performance results.

Acknowledgments. This work was supported in part by the DOD High Performance Computing Modernization Program at The Army Research Laboratory (ARL), Department of Defense Supercomputing Resource Center (DSRC).

References

1. ADP 6-0 (FM 6-0): Mission Command. Headquarters, Department of Army, Washington DC (2012)
2. U.S. Army Training and Doctrine Command (TRADOC) Pamphlet (TP) 525-3-3. U.S. Army Functional Concept for Mission Command (AFC-MC). United States, Army Training and Doctrine Command (2017)
3. Haselton, T.: How the army plans to use Microsoft's high-tech HoloLens goggles on the battlefield (2019). https://www.cnbc.com/2019/04/06/microsoft-hololens-2-army-plans-to-customize-as-ivas.html
4. Raglin, A., et al.: MxR framework for uncertainty based explanation for uncovering adversarial behavior. In: Chen, J.Y.C., Fragomeni, G. (eds.) VAMR 2018. LNCS, vol. 10910, pp. 354–368. Springer, Cham (2018). https://doi.org/10.1007/978-3-319-91584-5_28
5. Trout, T., et al.: Networked mixed reality (MxR) infrastructure for collaborative decision-making. In: Proceedings on International Society for Optics and Photonics (2018)
6. Kase, S., Su, S., Perry, V., Roy, H., Gamble, K.: An augmented reality shared mission planning scenario: observations on shared experience. In: Chen, J.Y.C., Fragomeni, G. (eds.) HCII 2019. LNCS, vol. 11575, pp. 490–503. Springer, Cham (2019). https://doi.org/10.1007/978-3-030-21565-1_33
7. Su, S., Perry, V., Bravo, L., Kase, S., Roy, H., Cox, K.: Virtual and augmented reality applications to support data analysis and assessment of science and engineering. J. Comput. Sci. Eng. (forthcoming)
8. Su, S., Perry, V., Roy, H., Gamble, K., Kase, S.: 3D user interface for a multi-user augmented reality mission planning application. In: Cassenti, D.N. (ed.) AHFE 2019. AISC, vol. 958, pp. 120–131. Springer, Cham (2020). https://doi.org/10.1007/978-3-030-20148-7_12
9. Singer, E., Couper, M.P.: Some methodological uses of responses to open questions and other verbatim comments in quantitative surveys. Methods Data Anal. **11**(2), 115–134 (2017)
10. Patton, M.Q.: Qualitative Research and Evaluation Methods: Integrating Theory and Practice, 4th edn. Sage Publications, Thousand Oaks (2015)
11. Popping, R.: Analyzing open-ended questions by means of text analysis procedures. Bull. de Méthodologie Sociologique **128**(1), 23–39 (2015)
12. Hsieh, H., Shannon, S.: Three approaches to qualitative content analysis, **15**(9), 1277–1288 (2005)
13. Weber, R.P.: Basic Content Analysis. Sage Publications, Newbury Park (1990)
14. Kammeyer, K., Roth, J.A.: Coding responses to open-ended questions. Sociol. Methodol. **3**, 60–78 (1971)
15. Witmer, B.G., Singer, M.J.: Measuring presence in virtual environments. ARI Technical Report 1014. U.S. Army Research Institute, Alexandria, VA (1994)

Effect of Motion Cues on Simulator Sickness in a Flight Simulator

Jiwon Kim[1], Jihong Hwang[2], and Taezoon Park[1(✉)]

[1] Department of Industrial and Information Systems Engineering,
Soongsil University, Seoul, South Korea
tzpark@ssu.ac.kr
[2] Department of Mechanical System Design Engineering,
Seoul National University of Science and Technology, Seoul, Korea

Abstract. The objective of this study is to investigate the effect of sensory conflict on the occurrence and severity of simulator sickness in a flight simulator. According to the sensory conflict theory, it is expected that providing motion cues that match the visual cues will reduce the discrepancy between the sensory inputs and thus reduce simulator sickness. We tested the effect of motion cues thorough a human subject experiment with a spherical type motion platform. After completing pre-experiment questionnaire including Motion Sickness Susceptibility Questionnaire (MSSQ) and Immersive Tendency Questionnaire (ITQ), two groups of participants conducted a flight simulation session with or without motion cues for 40 min. In the simulation session, participants were asked to fly through the gates sequentially arranged along the figure-eight shaped route. The Simulator Sickness Questionnaire (SSQ) was filled out after the exposure to compare groups between with and without motion cues. Physiological data, including electrodermal activity, heart rate, blood volume pressure, and wrist temperature were also collected to find the relationship with perceived simulator sickness. The results showed that simulator sickness and disorientation significantly lowered in motion-based group. Also, nausea and oculomotor were marginally lower when motion cue was given. This study supports sensory conflict theory. Providing proper motion cue corresponding to the visual flow could be considered to prevent simulator sickness.

Keywords: Flight simulator · Simulator sickness · Sensory conflict theory · Virtual reality

1 Introduction

Training through simulators keeps gaining more attention since it saves enormous costs and enables a positive transfer to the real task. Despite these advantages, the use of simulators has limitations due to the occurrence of simulator sickness. Simulator sickness is, as the name suggests, a special form of motion sickness. Whereas general motion sickness occurs through vestibular stimulation, simulator sickness can occur with only visual cue. There are a couple of theories to explain the cause of simulator sickness. According to sensory conflict theory, when only a visual stimulus is given, a collision with the sense from vestibular and visual cue may occur, causing motion

© Springer Nature Switzerland AG 2020
J. Y. C. Chen and G. Fragomeni (Eds.): HCII 2020, LNCS 12190, pp. 493–506, 2020.
https://doi.org/10.1007/978-3-030-49695-1_33

sickness [1]. Meanwhile, the development of the motion platform, which started with the Stewart platform, enables the simulator to provide not only visual stimuli but also vestibular proprioceptive stimuli. However, it is not yet clear whether a simulator with a motion platform can reduce simulator sickness because if sensory conflict theory is the cause of motion sickness, it's hard to explain how to adapt to motion sickness when conflict continues [2]. Another model is called as postural instability theory [3]. Postural stability theory suggests that motion sickness occurs as the body slips the ability to control the stability of the posture during swaying in real or virtual reality.

Most people do not feel motion sickness when they are in a common situation where motion and visual cues coincide. But, they could feel sick in certain situations, such as when riding a vehicle, playing games, or experiencing virtual reality through a head-mounted display. On the other hand, we do not have symptoms called motion sickness when we study or work in our daily lives. In this sense, sensory conflict theory suggests that visual-vestibular sensory coherence can decrease sickness in simulators. According to Kennedy et al. (1993), the following three factors cause illness: simulator factors, individual factors, and simulated task factors [4]. One reason why analyzing the sensory conflict theory is important is that it could be determined if we can control motion sickness factors at the simulator factors level. If the cause of motion sickness is sensory conflict, the engineer has to design the cues so that they do not collide. Investigation about the theory can give directions to design guidelines from an engineering perspective. Individual factors are dealt with by postural stability theory and adaptation [5]. However, these are difficult to manipulate into design elements in applications. Simulated task factors are related to flight scenarios or vehicles [5].

In this paper, experiments were conducted to determine the effect of motion cues on simulator sickness. This experiment assumes that each sensor can independently indicate the orientation or motion of the body. It can explain why the sickness is caused by inconsistencies in cues from each organ. It has been hypothesized that the visual and vestibular system will receive cues that are as similar as possible by spherical motion simulator, resulting in lower sensory conflict and reduced simulator sickness.

This study aims to investigate the effect of sensory conflict on the occurrence and severity of simulator sickness in a flight simulator. The spherical motion-based simulator and fixed-based simulator were set to provide sensory cues. Also, the relationship between simulator sickness and other indicators measured by the questionnaire, such as motion sickness susceptibility and individual immersion tendency, is analyzed.

2   Background

2.1   Theoretical Models of Simulator Sickness

Simulator sickness is a well-known unintended adverse reaction when trained in a simulated environment, such as a flight simulator. Reason and Brand (1975) have suggested sensory conflict theory, which claims that simulator sickness is caused by mismatches among different sensory inputs [1]. The theory has been reviewed in various aspects and is generally accepted [6–9]. According to the theory, it is expected that providing motion cues that match the visual cues will reduce the discrepancy between the sensory inputs and thus reduce simulator sickness.

Another reason which causes the sickness is vection. Vection does not contradict against sensory conflict theory. According to Hettinger et al. (1990), the interpretation of the sensory conflict theory of motion sickness suggested that in fixed simulators, vection could be a necessary prerequisite for simulator sickness [10]. Illusory self-motion, called vection, commonly induces in the fixed simulator because the motion of the pilot is fixed and the visual cue is flowing. The pilot's perception of himself and real feeling isn't consistent. Previous studies have shown that participants who experienced visually induced motion sickness reported vection, and that vection could precede visually induced motion sickness [11, 12]. In other words, users who experienced illusory self-motion are more likely to have symptoms of simulator sickness [12]. The motion simulator that can generate inertial cues reduces the occurrence of vection because the visual flow and real motion match over a certain level. However, it is not experimentally supported yet due to the Stewart platform simulator with a limited rotation angle. The conventional motion platform has difficulties in providing appropriate motion cues that match the visual flow.

2.2 Effect of the Motion Cues on Simulator Sickness

McCauley and Sharkey (1992) noted that a teleoperating system with virtual reality can cause inconsistency due to the lack of vestibular stimulus corresponding to the visual cue [13]. Kennedy et al. (1987) explained that the head movements of the pilot during simulation is the reason for reducing simulator sickness in motion-based simulators than fixed ones [14]. They explained based on Sinacori's (1970) observation that head movements in motion-based simulators are similar to head movements in real helicopter maneuvers, whereas head movements in static simulators were dissimilar [15]. Aykent et al. (2013) conducted an experimental study using a driving simulator, which showed nausea, dizziness, eyestrain, and tiredness were significantly decreased in the dynamic simulator than the static one [16]. However, most of the studies in flight simulators did not reduce simulator sickness even when motion cues were provided [13, 17, 18]. Sharkey and McCauley (1992) noted that the motion-based cab's movement can be reduced before visually described acceleration stops, resulting in false cues [17]. In other words, it can be accelerated in the opposite direction to the aircraft in the simulation. False cues could induce the inconsistency between visual and motion cue. Providing appropriate motion cues with the motion-based simulator is important to prove sensory conflict theory empirically.

2.3 Impact of Individual Immersive Tendency on Simulator Sickness

Previous studies have shown that the relation of sense of presence and simulator sickness [19, 20]. Witmer and Singer (1993) reported that there is a positive correlation between Simulator Sickness Questionnaire (SSQ) scores and Presence Questionnaire (PQ) scores ($r = 0.426$, $p = .001$) [19]. They noted that participants reporting more simulator sickness symptoms in virtual reality responded to less sense of presence than those who report fewer illnesses [19]. However, the relationship between immersive tendency and simulator sickness was not reported on their paper.

Witmer and Singer (1993) developed an immersive tendency questionnaire (ITQ) consisting of three subscales through cluster analysis [19]. The three subscales are Involvement (7 items), Focus (7 items) and Games (2 items). ITQ consists of a total of 18 items, including 2 items not included in three subscales. Afterward, Jerome and Witmer (2002) revealed that the effect of immersive tendency on simulator sickness was found to be positive through structural equation modeling using questionnaires (.15, p < .05) [20]. However, it is not yet known that each subscale of the immersive tendency is associated with which symptoms of simulator sickness.

2.4   Hypothesis

What is not revealed in previous studies is whether simulator sickness occurs less by providing the appropriate motion cues that matches the visual cues. Also, it is not yet clear which subscales of immersive tendency (Involvement, Focus, Games) are associated with symptoms of simulator sickness. Therefore, the hypothesis of the study is compared to fixed-based simulator (without motion), motion-based simulator (with motion) will reduce simulator sickness due to the sensory conflict theory. In this study, the experiment was carried out using a spherical motion platform to minimize false cues. An empirical experiment was conducted to reveal the effect of proper motion cues in flight simulator. On the other hand, the correlations between the individual's immersive tendency and their subscales (Involvement, Focus, and Games) and simulator sickness symptoms (nausea, oculomotor, disorientation, and total severity) were analyzed to investigate the relation between them.

3   Method

3.1   Participants

Fifteen (10 men, 5 women) university students participated in the study with a mean age of 26.1 years (SD; Standard Deviation = 2.19). They were divided into two groups and assigned to different types of simulators. One group (7 men) named 'Motion-based' experienced the motion-based simulator with the mean age of 27.6 years (SD = 2.15). The other group (3 men, 5 women) named 'Fixed-based' experienced a fixed-based simulator with the mean age of 24.88 years (SD = 1.36). Before the experiment, participants were informed that the simulation with the head-mounted display could occur nausea or simulator sickness and they could stop the experiment anytime they want.

3.2   Apparatus

Flight simulator software used in the study was Lockheed Martin's Prepar3D. It could simulate various flight environments with different conditions. The virtual environment implemented for this experiment used a head-mounted display VIVE Pro Eye form

HTC, which provides a resolution of 1440 × 1600 pixels per eye (2880 × 1600 pixels combined) and 110° of field of view. Biosignals were recorded by an Empatica E4 Wristband. It can collect electrodermal activity (galvanic skin response), heart rate, blood volume pressure and the temperature of the wrist. Heart rate was measured once per second. Blood volume pressure was measured at 64 Hz. Electrodermal activity and temperature were measured at 4 Hz. The experiment was conducted in an immersive virtual reality environment equipped with a spherical type motion simulator using the multi-degree of freedom platform at UNIST (Ulsan National Institute of Science and Technology, Korea). The motion simulator independently controls rotation and translation motion, and provide unlimited yawing rotations [21]. For the safety of the participants, the angle of roll and pitch was limited up to 20°. The spherical type motion simulator generates closely matching body motions with the actual flight motion. In the fixed condition, motion cues were not provided to the participants.

3.3 Manipulation and Measurements

Independent Variable. An independent variable in this study was whether there is the motion cues. With motion and without motion were the levels of the independent variable. A fixed-based simulator used to give only visual cue, whereas a motion-based simulator could give both visual and motion cue.

Dependent Variable and Measurement. Simulator sickness was the main interest of the study. It was measured by the Simulator Sickness Questionnaire (SSQ). By SSQ, nausea, oculomotor, disorientation, and total severity were collected. Also, the biosignal was determined as a quantitative and objective data that can determine whether the simulator sickness occurred. Biosignal records were measured by Empatica E4 wristband. The SSQ was used as a subjective indicator of simulator sickness, and biosignals were used as an objective one.

Questionnaires. Participants were asked to complete two surveys before the simulation which include motion sickness susceptibility questionnaire (MSSQ) and immersive tendency questionnaire [22]. A short form of motion sickness susceptibility questionnaire asks about their experience of motion sickness when riding various vehicles or park attractions in the past. The questionnaire divide into two sections. First section A is about the experience before age 12, whereas section B is about the past 10 years. The MSSQ percentile scores in this experiment ranged from 0 to 92.37. The average percentile score of the 'Motion-based' group was 42.11 (SD = 30.29) and the 'Fixed-based' group was 43.65 (SD = 33.12).

In the related paper, 18 items with verified scale reliability were used as ITQ [19]. In ITQ, 3 subscales were labeled as involvement, focus, and games. The questionnaire consists of questions asked about immersive tendencies based on the participant's experience. The average total ITQ score of the 'Motion-based' group was 72.29 (SD = 5.09) and the 'Fixed-based' group was 72.50 (SD = 13.38).

After exposure to the virtual reality simulation, each participant was completed SSQ [4]. The questionnaire contains 16 specific symptoms. Participants were asked to rate symptoms from 0 to 3 (None = 0; Slight = 1; Moderate = 2; Severe = 3). 16 specific symptoms are classified on 3 subscales: Nausea, Oculomotor, and Disorientation. The total severity representing the overall simulator sickness can be calculated by multiplying the sum of these three subscales with the weight 3.74. The results for this SSQ score are discussed in Sect. 4.

3.4   Procedures

Participants were fully informed about the experiment that the simulation could cause simulator sickness and they have a right to stop anytime. They were given brief information about the biosignal recording device and the experimental procedures. All participants filled the pre-exposure questionnaires which include MSSQ and ITQ. After wearing the biosignal recording device, Empatica E4 wristband, each participant had a 10 min electrode stabilization period and a 5 min baseline measuring period. Participants received a training period of about 5 min to practice controlling aircraft, and they conducted the main experiment for about 40 min. Experiment scenario designed in Prepar3D guided the participant to fly through a figure-eight route in the sky where the gates are arranged to pass through sequentially. Through the experiment, participants were asked about their current simulator sickness symptoms in 4-point scale (0 to 3; None = 0; Slight = 1; Moderate = 2; Severe = 3) every two minutes. Before the experiment, participants were informed about the symptoms of simulator sickness such as nausea, oculomotor and disorientation. After performing the simulation, participants completed simulator sickness questionnaire.

4   Results

4.1   Subjective Indicator: Simulator Sickness Questionnaire

In this experiment, two different groups of virtual reality flight simulations were compared using 'Motion-based' and 'Fixed-based'. A total of 15 data were collected from each group. By the Kolmogorov-Smirnov test and Shapiro-Wilk test, it was confirmed that the normality assumptions were met. Levene's test was also performed to confirm that the two groups were following the equality of variances. Levene's test indicated equal variances of Nausea (F = 0.274, p = .609), Oculomotor (F = 0.242, p = .631), Disorientation (F = .041, p = .842), Total Severity (F = 0.031, p = .864).

The results showed that total severity, which means simulator sickness (F(1, 13) = 4.8, p = .047), and disorientation (F(1, 13) = 6.665, p = .023) were significantly lower for the motion-based group than for the fixed-based group. The nausea (F(1, 13) = 2.614, p = .130) and oculomotor (F(1, 13) = 3.431, p = .087) which is the symptoms of simulator sickness were marginally lower for the motion-based group than another (Table 1) and (Fig. 1).

Table 1. Descriptive statistics for SSQ symptoms

Symptom	Condition	N	Mean	SD	SEM
Nausea	Motion based	7	35.4	30.02	11.35
	Fixed based	8	63.2	35.67	12.61
Oculomotor	Motion based	7	45.5	25.52	9.64
	Fixed based	8	73.0	31.11	11.00
Disorientation	Motion based	7	39.8	44.33	16.76
	Fixed based	8	94.0	37.02	13.09
Total severity	Motion based	7	47.0	32.38	12.24
	Fixed based	8	86.0	36.04	12.74

SD: Standard deviation, SEM: Standard error of the mean

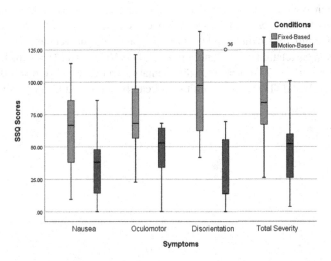

Fig. 1. Box plot of SSQ results for each symptom for two conditions

4.2 Objective Indicators: Biosignal Records

Biosignals were compared to simulator sickness severity on the 0 to 3 scale which was asked every two minutes in the simulation period. For the analysis of the physiological response, the baseline was measured for each signal through a baseline period of 5 min. The baseline was subtracted from the biosignals recorded every two minutes after exposure to the simulator. Analysis of the experimental data proceeded with the difference from baseline.

Blood volume pressure (BVP) data from two groups met equal variances assumption by Levene's test. However, heart rate (HR), electrodermal activity (EDA) and temperature (TEMP) do not satisfy the equality of variance. Therefore, an analysis of variance (ANOVA) was conducted with only BVP records. Other biosignals such as HR, EDA and TEMP were analyzed by Welch's ANOVA. It is because the analysis method can be used even if equality of variances are not assumed [23].

Results of Objective Indicators. The difference in BVP from baseline was significantly higher in the group with motion cues than another group without motion, $F(1, 280) = 19.370, p < .001$. Also, the difference from the baseline of HR was significantly higher in the motion simulation group than the fixed simulation group, $F(1, 233.796) = 60.669$, $p < .001$. The differences from the baseline of EDA ($F(1, 252.684) = 16.098, p < .001$) and TEMP ($F(1, 255.430) = 11.828, p = .001$) were significantly higher in the fixed-based simulator group than motion-based simulator group.

4.3   Expected Correlation Between Simulator Sickness and Others

Relation to Immersive Tendency. In the ITQ questionnaire, labeled as involvement, focus, and games, higher scores indicate that the individuals are more immersive. A correlation analysis between SSQ symptoms and GAMES label revealed that participants' experience with the more frequent (Q21) and deeply involved (Q10) in the game, the less simulator sickness (total severity) occurred ($r(13) = -.755, p = .001$). Also, symptoms of simulator sickness and the GAMES subscale showed negative correlation, and the Pearson correlation coefficients are as follows: Nausea ($r(13) = -.611, p = .016$), Oculomotor ($r(13) = -.747, p = .001$), disorientation ($r(13) = -.731, p = .002$) (Fig. 2). Other labels and total ITQ score weren't significantly correlated to SSQ scores.

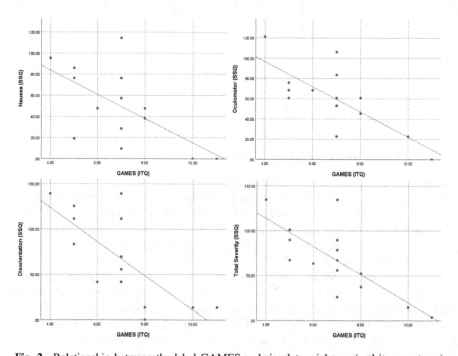

Fig. 2. Relationship between the label GAMES and simulator sickness (and its symptoms)

Relation to Motion Sickness Susceptibility. Motion sickness susceptibility questionnaire is well known as a predictor of the simulator sickness. However, in this experiment, there was no significant correlation between MSSQ and SSQ.

The Relation Between Immersive Tendency and Motion Sickness Susceptibility.
There was a positive Pearson correlation between the MSSQ raw (MSA + MSB) score and total ITQ score (r(13) = .607, p = .016). There was also a positive correlation with the MSSQ raw score and the FOCUS scale of ITQ (r(13) = .684, p = .005). Participants with high susceptibility scores who frequently experienced motion sickness, both when childhood (MSA) and adults (MSB), tended to maintain focus on their activities more than others who scored lower in MSSQ (Table 2).

Table 2. The results of the Pearson correlation analysis between MSSQ and ITQ

	Scores	Involvement	Focus	Games	ITQ Score
Coefficient	MSA	.212	.618*	.217	.528*
Sig.	(childhood)	.447	.014	.437	.043
Coefficient	MSB	.331	.699**	.161	.646**
Sig.	(adults)	.229	.004	.567	.009
Coefficient	MSSQ raw	.277	.684**	.201	.607*
Sig.	(MSA + MSB)	.318	.005	.472	.016
Coefficient	MSSQ %tile	.295	.653**	.274	.603*
Sig.		.286	.008	.323	.017

** Correlation is significant at the 0.01 level, * Correlation is significant at the 0.05 level (two-tailed)

4.4 Temporal Aspects of the Simulator Sickness

As the simulation time passed, the severity of simulator sickness (0 to 3) gradually increased. A linear regression was calculated to predict simulator sickness severity based on exposure time. A significant regression equation was found ($F(1, 280) = 37.615$, $p < .001$), with an R^2 of .118. Participants' predicted simulator sickness severity is equal to .277 + .026 * (Simulation time) when the simulation time is measured in minutes. Simulator sickness increased .026 for each minute of simulation time. Results of the Pearson correlation also indicated that there was a significant positive association between simulation time and simulator sickness severity, r(280) = .344, p < .001 (Fig. 3).

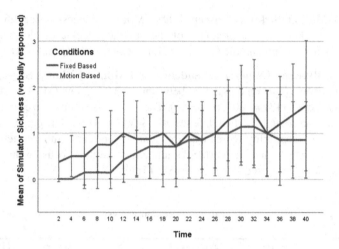

Fig. 3. Severity of simulator sickness over time (with 95% confidence interval bars)

5 Discussion

The experimental result showed significant differences in simulator sickness and disorientation depending upon the existence of motion cues. Also, there are marginally significant differences in nausea and oculomotor between the motion-based group and the fixed-based group. The results of the subjective index (SSQ) support the evidence for the sensory conflict theory. The spherical motion-based simulator provided proper motion cues, which reduced the mismatch between visual and vestibule-proprioceptive signal. In terms of flight posture, it can be explained based on a discussion by Kennedy et al. (1987), which states that the pilot's head movements are more similar to the head movements of a real helicopter in a motion-based simulator [14]. This study was conducted using fixed-wing aircraft, not helicopters, but a spherical motion platform was used to provide a motion similar to the angle at which the actual plane would tilt. Providing proper motion cues that correspond to visual cues can reduce simulator sickness by reducing the magnitude of sensory conflict and providing realistic head movements in flight.

5.1 Discussions on the Physiological Response

The change in biosignal was analyzed by the difference between the signal measured at the interval of 2 min and the signal measured at the baseline (5 min). The results showed that BVP and HR were higher in the motion-based group and EDA and TEMP were higher in the fixed-based group. BVP and EDA support the results of the subjective questionnaire SSQ, but HR and TEMP are not. The BVP and EDA results indicate that simulator sickness is less severe with motion cues, which supports the SSQ results. However, HR and TEMP results suggest that simulator sickness is more severe when there are motion cues, contrary to the subjective questionnaire results.

Blood Volume Pulse. According to reviewed by Dahlman (2009), BVP falls as a result of sympathetic domination as motion sickness progresses [24, 25]. Besides, the BVP response was highly variable between individuals and varied depending on the context [24, 26]. In the study of Cowings et al. (1986), the volume pulse decreased sharply at the onset of motion sickness stimulation and then gradually increased as motion stimulation continued [26]. The 0 to 3 verbally asked simulator sickness scale and the BVP response difference from baseline responded every two minutes were negatively correlated with $r(280) = -.197$ and $p = .001$. The correlation results support previous studies that BVP decreased with motion sickness progresses.

Heart Rate. R. Liu et al. (2017) discussed that HR declined at the beginning of exposure and then increased in the last few minutes [27]. Similar patterns were founded in this experiment. After the onset of the simulation, HR gradually decreased for about 28 min in both groups, then slowly increased at the end. The 0 to 3 verbally asked simulator sickness scale and the HR response difference from baseline responded every two minutes were negatively correlated with $r(280) = -.290$ and $p < .001$. In this experiment, the motion-based simulator participants who responded that they felt relatively less simulator sickness increased HR than baseline when exposed. On the other hand, there are contrast results in other studies [28, 29]. In their studies, HR was decreased when sickness induced. Further research on the relationship between HR and motion sickness is needed.

Electrodermal Activity. EDA and TEMP rose with inducing simulator sickness compared to other signals. EDA is generally known as a physiological response that increases with motion sickness [30, 31] or nausea [32]. The 0 to 3 verbally asked simulator sickness scale and the EDA response difference from baseline responded every two minutes were positively correlated with $r(280) = .227$ and $p < .001$. The correlation between simulator sickness and EDA matched with the results of previous studies.

Temperature. TEMP is known to decrease as motion sickness occurs [30]. The 0 to 3 verbally asked simulator sickness scale and the TEMP response difference from baseline responded every two minutes were negatively correlated with $r(280) = -.176$ and $p = .003$. The correlation between simulator sickness and TEMP was found to support the results of the previous study. However, SSQ results are not supported by TEMP. In this experiment, TEMP was higher in the fixed-base group with more simulator sickness than motion-base group. Motion simulator experiments were conducted in a relatively well ventilated large laboratory, while fixed simulator experiments were conducted in a closed, narrow laboratory. The laboratory environment may have affected the subject's temperature.

5.2   Positive Correlation Between Immersive Tendency in Game and Simulator Sickness

These were two questions that correspond to the GAMES subscale in ITQ [19].

1) Do you ever become so involved in a video game that it is as if you are inside the game rather than moving a joystick and watching the screen?

2) How often do you play arcade or video games? (OFTEN should be taken to mean every day or every two days, on average.)

It was a question of how often and how involved to play the game. Subjects who were more involved and more likely to play games felt less symptoms of simulator sickness. This can be interpreted as a game experience that help people feel less sick. For non-pilots, the flight simulator may feel like a game. When experiencing a simulator that feels like a game, people who have been more involved and frequently played games in the past may have become resistant to game sickness.

5.3   Simulator Sickness over Simulation Time

In this experiment, simulator sickness gradually increased in both groups as simulation time elapsed. The results of regression analysis using only fixed simulator results, a regression equation was found ($F(1, 140) = 16.653$, $p < .001$), with an R^2 of .106. Fixed-based simulator participants' predicted severity is equal to $.448 + .025 * (Simulation Time)$ score when the simulation time is measured in minutes. Fixed-based participants' severity of simulator sickness increased .025 for each minute of simulation time. In comparison, the results of regression using only motion simulator results, an equation was found ($F(1, 138) = 26.061$, $p < .001$), with an R^2 of .399. Motion-based simulator participants' predicted severity is equal to $.064 + .028 * (Simulation Time)$ score. Motion-based participants' severity of simulator sickness increased .028 for each minute of simulation time. The coefficient of the equation is similar in both conditions, whereas the y-intercept is higher in the fixed simulator, so the onset of symptoms is faster when there was no motion cues.

6   Conclusions

This study investigates how simulator sickness changes with the presence of motion cue. Participants in the group with motion cues felt significantly less simulator sickness and disorientation, and marginally less nausea and oculomotor. This supports the study of sensory conflict theory and subjective vertical conflict called vection which often leads to motion sickness. This result suggests that it may be helpful to provide a suitable motion cue that matches the visual flow to reduce simulator sickness. In the case of biosignals, BVP, HR, EDA, and TEMP were measured. Simulator sickness severity scale which were participants reported positively correlated with EDA, whereas negatively correlated with BVP, HR, and TEMP.

There are a couple of limitations to generalize the findings of this study. Since this experiment was conducted with adult college students, not actual pilots, it is prudent to apply experimental results directly to pilots who have experienced real motion. Also, the number of subjects was small as 15 in total, and the experiment was conducted with the between-subject design. Although we can avoid carry-over or order effects there are potential worries that the two groups may have different inclinations or individual differences. The motion-based group consisted of 7 men only, and the fixed-based group consisted of 3 men and 5 women. Motion sickness susceptibility due to these gender differences may vary. In this experiment, the average MSSQ percentile of the motion-based group was 42.11 (SD = 30.29) and the average of the fixed-based group was 43.65 (SD = 33.12). Motion sickness susceptibility acquired from MSSQ between the two groups was quite similar, but the effects of gender differences may have been confounded in the results.

Acknowledgment. This work is financially supported by the Institute of Civil-Military Technology Cooperation funded by the Defense Acquisition Program Administration and Ministry of Trade, Industry, and Energy of Korea government under grant No. 17-CM-RB-27.

References

1. Reason, J.T., Brand, J.J.: Motion Sickness. Academic Press, London (1975)
2. Stoffregen, T.A., Riccio, G.E.: An ecological critique of the sensory conflict theory of motion sickness. Ecol. Psychol. **3**(3), 159–194 (1991)
3. Riccio, G.E., Stoffregen, T.A.: An ecological theory of motion sickness and postural instability. Ecol. Psychol. **3**(3), 195–240 (1991)
4. Kennedy, R.S., Lane, N.E., Berbaum, K.S., Lilienthal, M.G.: Simulator sickness questionnaire: an enhanced method for quantifying simulator sickness. Int. J. Aviat. Psychol. **3**(3), 203–220 (1993)
5. Aykent, B., Merienne, F., Guillet, C., Paillot, D., Kemeny, A.: Motion sickness evaluation and comparison for a static driving simulator and a dynamic driving simulator. Proc. Inst. Mech. Eng. Part D: J. Automob. Eng. **228**(7), 818–829 (2014)
6. Kennedy, R.S., Hettinger, L.J., Lilienthal, M.G.: Simulator sickness. In: Motion and Space Sickness, pp. 317–341 (1988)
7. Kolasinski, E.M.: Simulator sickness in virtual environments, vol. 1027. US Army Research Institute for the Behavioral and Social Sciences (1995)
8. Schmäl, F.: Neuronal mechanisms and the treatment of motion sickness. Pharmacology **91** (3–4), 229–241 (2013)
9. Shupak, A., Gordon, C.R.: Motion sickness: advances in pathogenesis, prediction, prevention, and treatment. Aviat. Space Environ. Med. **77**(12), 1213–1223 (2006)
10. Hettinger, L.J., Berbaum, K.S., Kennedy, R.S., Dunlap, W.P., Nolan, M.D.: Vection and simulator sickness. Mil. Psychol. **2**(3), 171–181 (1990)
11. Ji, J.T., So, R.H., Cheung, R.T.: Isolating the effects of vection and optokinetic nystagmus on optokinetic rotation-induced motion sickness. Hum. Factors **51**(5), 739–751 (2009)
12. Koohestani, A., et al.: A knowledge discovery in motion sickness: a comprehensive literature review. IEEE access **7**, 85755–85770 (2019)
13. McCauley, M.E., Sharkey, T.J.: Cybersickness: perception of self-motion in virtual environments. Presence: Teleoper. Virtual Environ. **1**(3), 311–318 (1992)
14. Kennedy, R.S., Berbaum, K.S., Lilienthal, M.G., Dunlap, W.P., Mulligan, B.E.: Guidelines for alleviation of simulator sickness symptomatology (No. NAVTRASYSCEN-TR-87-007). Naval Training Systems Center Orlando FL (1987)
15. Sinacori, J.B.: Validation of ground based simulation. J. Am. Helicopter Soc. **15**(3), 10–21 (1970)
16. Aykent, B., Merienne, F., Paillot, D., Kemeny, A.: Influence of inertial stimulus on visuo-vestibular cues conflict for lateral dynamics at driving simulators (2013)
17. Sharkey, T., McCauley, M.: Does a motion base prevent simulator sickness? In: Flight Simulation Technologies Conference, p. 4133, January 1992

18. Kaufeld, M., Alexander, T.: The impact of motion on individual simulator sickness in a moving Base VR simulator with head-mounted display (HMD). In: Chen, J., Fragomeni, G. (eds.) HCII 2019. LNCS, vol. 11574, pp. 461–472. Springer, Cham (2019). https://doi.org/10.1007/978-3-030-21607-8_36

19. Witmer, B.G., Singer, M.J.: Measuring presence in virtual environments: a presence questionnaire. Presence 7(3), 225–240 (1998)

20. Jerome, C.J., Witmer, B.: Immersive tendency, feeling of presence, and simulator sickness: formulation of a causal model. In: Proceedings of the Human Factors and Ergonomics Society Annual Meeting, vol. 46, no. 26, pp. 2197–2201. SAGE Publications, Los Angeles, September 2002

21. Lee, S., Park, S., Son, H.: Multi-DOFs motion platform based on spherical wheels for unmanned systems. In: 2016 13th International Conference on Ubiquitous Robots and Ambient Intelligence (URAI), pp. 35–37. IEEE, August 2016

22. Golding, J.F.: Predicting individual differences in motion sickness susceptibility by questionnaire. Pers. Individ. Differ. 41(2), 237–248 (2006)

23. Moder, K.: Alternatives to F-test in one way ANOVA in case of heterogeneity of variances (a simulation study). Psychol. Test Assess. Model. 52(4), 343–353 (2010)

24. Dahlman, J.: Psychophysiological and performance aspects on motion sickness. Doctoral dissertation, Linköping University Electronic Press (2009)

25. Brodal, P.: The Central Nervous System: Structure and Function. Oxford university Press, Oxford (2004)

26. Cowings, P.S., Suter, S., Toscano, W.B., Kamiya, J., Naifeh, K.: General autonomic components of motion sickness. Psychophysiology 23(5), 542–551 (1986)

27. Liu, R., Peli, E., Hwang, A.D.: Measuring visually induced motion sickness using wearable devices. Electron. Imaging 2017(14), 218–223 (2017)

28. Holmes, S.R., Griffin, M.J.: Correlation between heart rate and the severity of motion sickness caused by optokinetic stimulation. J. Psychophysiol. 15(1), 35 (2001)

29. Sugita, N., et al.: Quantitative evaluation of effects of visually-induced motion sickness based on causal coherence functions between blood pressure and heart rate. Displays 29(2), 167–175 (2008)

30. Kim, Y.Y., Kim, H.J., Kim, E.N., Ko, H.D., Kim, H.T.: Characteristic changes in the physiological components of cybersickness. Psychophysiology 42(5), 616–625 (2005)

31. Hu, S., Grant, W.F., Stern, R.M., Koch, K.L.: Motion sickness severity and physiological correlates during repeated exposures to a rotating optokinetic drum. Aviat. Space Environ. Med. 62, 308–314 (1991)

32. Crampton, G.H.: Studies of motion sickness: XVII. Physiological changes accompanying sickness in man. J. Appl. Physiol. 7(5), 501–507 (1955)

Crew Workload Considerations in Using HUD Localizer Takeoff Guidance in Lieu of Currently Required Infrastructure

Daniela Kratchounova[1]([⊠]), Mark Humphreys[2], Larry Miller[3],
Theodore Mofle[4], Inchul Choi[4], and Blake L. Nesmith[4]

[1] Federal Aviation Administration Civil Aerospace Medical Institute,
Oklahoma City, OK, USA
Daniela.Kratchounova@faa.gov
[2] Precision Approaches, Irvine, CA, USA
Mark.Humphreys3@gmail.com
[3] Federal Aviation Administration Flight Technologies and Procedures Division,
Oklahoma City, OK, USA
Larry.C.Miller@faa.gov
[4] Cherokee Nation 3S, Catoosa, OK, USA
{Theodore.C-CTR.Mofle, Inchul.CTR.Choi,
Blake.L-CTR.Nesmith}@faa.gov

Abstract. The purpose of this research was to examine the crew workload considerations for using HUD with localizer guidance symbology in lieu of currently required infrastructure for lower than standard takeoff minima and within the larger conceptual framework of external (runway) and internal (flight deck) visual cues, HUD guidance symbology, and RVR visibility. To identify the differential contributions of these factors, three baseline conditions without HUD localizer guidance symbology and two conditions with HUD localizer takeoff guidance symbology were used. Currently, only about 30% of the CAT I runways in the NAS are equipped with CLL. Therefore, the human factors considerations in using HUD localizer guidance in lieu of CLL in low visibility conditions were of principal interest. The results of this study have the potential to inform operational credit changes that would allow more reduced visibility takeoffs and increase the number of viable airports available for takeoff under low visibility conditions. The research was conducted on a Boeing 737-800NG Level D simulator at the FAA Flight Technologies & Procedures Division facility in Oklahoma City, Oklahoma.

Keywords: Head-up display (HUD) · Aviation human factors · Crew workload

1 Introduction

Today, head-up displays (HUDs) are standard equipment for many business and commercial aircraft. Their use is encouraged in all phases of flight and mandated by many airlines during critical phases of flight. Research in the past four plus decades suggests that there are a number of advantages in using HUDs. These include:

J. Y. C. Chen and G. Fragomeni (Eds.): HCII 2020, LNCS 12190, pp. 507–521, 2020.
https://doi.org/10.1007/978-3-030-49695-1_34

- Reduced head-down time;
- Reduced time to refocus between flight deck instruments and the external scene;
- Reduced scanning;
- Improved awareness of the outside environment;
- Improved flight performance over traditional head-down displays (HDDs);
- Increased accuracy in flight path tracking;
- Ability to safely perform lower than standard visibility operations;
- Ability to display enhanced, synthetic and combined vision imagery overlaid with conformal symbology, augmenting the external scene in reduced visibility conditions.

Nevertheless, reports of perceptual and cognitive issues with the use of HUD have persisted over the course of last several decades. Previous reviews [1–3] have provided ample coverage of the longstanding argument about the effects of the perceptual (e.g., misaccommodation) and cognitive (e.g., attention tunneling) issues associated with the use of HUDs reported in the literature. Herein, only a brief background is provided.

The purpose of this research was to examine the crew workload considerations for using HUD with localizer guidance in lieu of currently required infrastructure for lower than currently authorized visibility minima. In addition, feedback on the equivalent level of safety between using HUD with localizer guidance and using HUD with runway centerline lighting (CLL) was solicited from the pilot participants. The results have the potential to inform operational credit changes that would allow more reduced visibility takeoffs and increase the number of viable airports (with reduced infrastructure characteristics) available for takeoff under low visibility conditions. The research was conducted on the Boeing 737-800NG Level D simulator at the Federal Aviation Administration (FAA) Flight Technologies & Procedures Division facility in Oklahoma City, Oklahoma.

1.1 Background

HUDs evolved as the original aviation augmented reality (AR) device long before AR was contemplated as a worthy notion in the aesthetic of cool. Looking back, HUDs were developed with collimated optics to allow the pilot to monitor primary flight information while maintaining visual contact with the outside environment, with the central assumption that the eyes can focus at optical infinity when viewing collimated imagery. Specifically, collimation was intended to position the HUD symbology at the same optical depth as the outside world. In theory, this would assist with eye accommodation and reduce the time necessary to refocus. However, in the 1980s, a repeated experimental observation was reported: when viewing collimated images, instead of automatically focusing at optical infinity, the eyes lapse inward toward their dark focus, or resting accommodation distance [4–6]. Such positive misaccommodation was considered an issue because it could impair pilots' ability to detect targets and judge their distance and size. The supposed perceptual consequence of positive misaccommodation was that the visual scene outside appeared reduced in apparent size. This caused distant objects to appear farther away than they are, and anything below the line of sight (e.g., terrain, runway), to appear higher relative to the horizon [7].

After HUDs entered operational use, research studies continued to report that not only did collimation fail to pull the pilot's focus outward to optical infinity, but possibly it also deepened misaccommodation [4–6]. When using a HUD, about one third of the pilots reported experiencing an increased tendency toward spatial disorientation [8–10]. Fischer, Haines, and Price [11] noted instances when pilots failed to attend simultaneously to both the HUD symbology information and the outside world. Pilots also reported a tendency to focus at the near distance, on the HUD combiner glass, instead of on the external scene [9]. Furthermore, pilots found it necessary to use volitional accommodation when shifting attention between HUD symbology and the outside environment [12]. The HUD myopia seemed to act as a special case of a phenomenon identified as instrument myopia [13].

In the late 1980s and early 1990s, Newman [14] and Weintraub and Ensing [3] contended that there was a substantial amount of evidence supporting the notion of collimated HUDs actually pulling pilot's focus outward, even if it was not always to optical infinity. They argued that earlier research findings were an artifact of the display technology available at that time, and might be attributable to the poor optical quality of HUD and external scenes imagery used in those prior studies. They maintained that if the external visual cues were of poor quality because of reduced visibility, for example, high-quality HUD images would actually pull the pilots' focus outward, and consequently, partially offset the tendency for the point of accommodation to be closer than the objects in the external environment. In addition, as reported by Foyle et al. [15], the misaccommodation argument had fallen short of explaining the failure to process simultaneously the outside world information and HUD-like symbology information when using non-collimated displays. They suggested that these results could be attributed to attentional rather than to visual factors. That is, pilots actually switch attention back and forth between the HUD and the external scene instead trying to perceive both at the same time.

Nonetheless, results from a number of studies suggested that there was a potential issue with switching attention between the internal and external scene when using HUD, as well. More specifically, that HUD symbology could capture pilots' attention and impair their ability to detect events in the external environment. This effect has been referred to as cognitive tunneling or cognitive capture [15, 16]. Problems associated with cognitive tunneling seemed to revolve around pilots' ability to be effective in switching attention between the HUD and other elements in the same visual scene. As opposed to switching attention between the HDDs and the outside world, switching attention between the HUDs and the outside world involved mentally shifting attention between stimuli within the same visual space. Namely, the latter did not involve a change in visual accommodation [17–19]. Rather, cognitive capture occurred when pilots failed to switch attention and instead fixated on one element of HUD symbology at the expense of other information, either on the HUD or in the external scene.

Previous research observed an altitude/path performance trade-off and proposed two models of visual/spatial attention as potentially viable explanations for it: object-based and location-based [20]. The object-based attentional model predicted that the altitude/path performance trade-off should not be affected by a reduction in the distance between altitude and path information as presented on the display. The location-based attentional model suggested that efficient concurrent processing of two separate information sources was only possible when both sources were within the same attentive field. Later, to study the differences between the object-based and location-based attentional models of the altitude/path performance trade-off, Foyle et al. [15] conducted two experiments. The results indicated that synchronized processing of both the HUD and the outside world information occurred only in conditions that required visual/attentional scanning. The authors argued that due to its volitional nature, visual scanning in a pattern following known locations of information might be more efficient in alleviating the altitude/path performance trade-off. Particularly, when gathering specific information was required and participants were prepared to process it, attentional tunneling was eliminated by scanning for information in a particular predefined order.

McCann, Lynch, Foyle, and Johnston [21] and McCann, Foyle, and Johnston [22] examined the potential cost of attention switching. The results showed that differential motion between symbology with fixed position on the HUD and the optical flow of the world outside was a possible source of attentional tunneling. They found that the differential motion led to increased attention-switching times. Shelden, Foyle, and McCann [23] and Levy, Foyle, and McCann [24] proposed that a set of symbology that appears to be a part of the outside world, i.e., to be conformal to it [25], would alleviate the tunneling. Their results supported the notion that scene-linked symbology yielded improved performance and that the performance advantage is attentional. That is, attention can be divided between scene-linked symbology and the outside world [24]. Furthermore, the authors made a distinction between two separate methods that could make the symbology look as if as it was an integral part of the outside world: scene enhancement and scene augmentation. Scene enhancements would add more saliency to features of already existing objects in the outside world, where scene augmentations would involve the addition of virtual objects that are otherwise non-existent in the real world. In both cases, the HUD symbology would be moving in unison with the external scene. The results further indicated that making the HUD symbology conformal to its outside counterpart to form a single perceptual object, along with flight task integration, supported synchronized processing which in turn yielded performance advantages and had the potential to mitigate the problem of attentional tunneling [23].

Wickens and Long [25] examined the impact of positioning conformal and non-conformal symbology in head-up or head-down locations to determine the comparative influences of three factors: space-based cost of clutter, space-based cost of scanning, and object-based benefit of conformality. Their results not only aligned with prior research findings about HUDs' significant contribution to safety, but also reinforced the notion that the negative impact of clutter was very real. The authors strongly cautioned against adding too much non-conformal symbology to HUDs.

We could not find a comprehensive review of the literature on the direct effects of clutter, and more specifically, the effects of the amount of information when presented on HUDs. Nevertheless, a large body of research has addressed the subject of display clutter in general. In summary, preserving the most relevant and unambiguous visual cues pilots use is an art form. It could be successfully accomplished through enhancement, augmentation, task integration, and synchronization of those visual cues in the near and far domain. However, if overdone, the intended benefits might very well be nullified by the resulting clutter [26–29].

So far, the results from applied research literature on the subject of why it might be difficult for pilots to monitor primary flight information while maintaining visual contact with the outside environment are remarkably inconclusive. Interestingly, findings from prior basic research by Neisser and Becklen [30] foreshadowed the results of Foyle et al. [15] mentioned earlier. The authors asserted that selective attention was a direct consequence of skilled perception and did not require any special mechanisms to reject unwanted information. They reported that without any prior practice, it was easy to attend to one dynamically changing scene/episode and ignore another, even when the two were presented in transparent visual overlap. Moreover, they concluded that what outlined one episode and differentiated it from the other was not its location or clarity, but its inherent relevance, structure, and the continuous and coherent sequence of motion. In other words, in order to follow one dynamically changing event rather than another, one must have already made a decision to attend the former rather than the latter. Neisser and Becklen [30] did not address the question of whether selective attention would have improved had the participants been given the opportunity to practice. Later, Spelke, Hirst, and Neisser [31] conducted research on complex unimodal (e.g., visual) dual-task performance and found that better performance could be achieved if participants were allowed to practice the tasks in combination. However, two questions remained unanswered: how to combine tasks successfully and specifically, what aspects of the tasks would make their combination successful in terms of performance. The case of transparent visual overlap of dynamically changing events is a rare and unnatural occurrence for which the human visual system is "unprepared." Training to follow two simultaneous dynamic episodes that are visually overlapped, even if they are related, should therefore encompass strategies that allow them to be combined more easily. Littman and Becklen [32] in effect replicated Neisser and Becklen [30] with one exception: participants were required to fixate on a spot in the center of the visual field during 50% of the trials. The results demonstrated that selective looking could be accomplished without eye movements, and that it was not more difficult to follow either a single event, or one of two superimposed events, when such fixation was required. A similar strategy could help with minimizing the incompatibilities (e.g., movement in the periphery) in complex dual visual tasks. The authors concluded that eye movements do not initiate a perceptual act. Rather, they are dependent upon perceptual expectations.

Research on flight performance has shown that without a direct presentation of the flight path, the pilot was required to visually scan the flight deck instruments and mentally transform the information to determine the path of the aircraft [11]. HUD symbology typically includes active flight path information (e.g., flight path vector). This allows for a more natural, intuitive control. Numerous early studies have shown that using HUD with flight path symbology produced superior flight path maintenance and landing precision relative to traditional flight director instrumentation [33–35]. More recent, high-fidelity HUD research conducted in applied settings, and in the context of multi-crew commercial flight operations, is a research area that could benefit from more study.

Training is often suggested as a solution to human factors issues. Nevertheless, it is almost never the sole remedy for inadequate design. Therefore, it is plausible to expect that to complement the continuous improvements of HUDs design over the years; robust training curricula would help pilots learn how to monitor primary flight information on a HUD while maintaining visual contact with the outside environment, in an efficient and effective fashion. In theory, such training would also improve their awareness of the potential for attention capture and ultimately, help them counter it at its onset. It is unknown however, whether it is possible to train pilots to overcome the effects of cognitive tunneling when using HUD, or how much training would be needed if it were possible to do so.

Personal correspondence containing observations from a pilot subject matter expert indicated that almost all pilots new to HUD focus on the flight path vector only for the first 2–3 h of HUD exposure. In the next 4–6 h, they start to open their scan to the other information displayed on the HUD. From 7 h on, they have the ability to move their gaze back and forth between the HUD symbology and the outside world. It is unknown if this gaze shifting can be taught early in a training program. Nevertheless, it seems to be a function of time and exposure to the HUD, before the brain can "gaze shift" (M. Humphreys, personal communication, January 6, 2020).

1.2   HUD Operations Research Gap

Presently, Instrument Flight Rules (IFR) for lower-than-standard takeoff minimums allow commercial aircraft takeoffs as low as 300 ft Runway Visual Range (RVR) using High-Intensity Runway Lights (HIRL), CLL, and HUD takeoff guidance symbology. This type of commercial operation is only approved for runways with the lowest Category III Instrument Landing System (ILS) minima and the associated runway infrastructure, such as additional RVR sensors, touchdown zone lighting, and lead on/off lights. This limits 300 ft RVR takeoff operations to only a few airports and runways in the National Airspace System (NAS). To expand this capability to additional airports and potentially increase the NAS throughput, the FAA Civil Aerospace Medical Institute (CAMI) Human Factors Division assessed HUD localizer-guided low-visibility takeoffs using a Category I (CAT I) localizer and reduced airport infrastructure.

2   Method

Twenty-four pilot crews participated in this research: 12 airline crews and 12 business jet crews. For normal operations scenarios, five levels of "Type of guidance", three levels of "RVR", and two levels of "Lighting conditions were examined (Table 1).

Table 1. Research matrix

Type of guidance	RVR (ft)					
	300		500		700	
Baseline 1: HUD, No LOC[a] guidance, RCLM[b] only	Day	Night	Day	Night	Day	Night
Baseline 2: HUD, No LOC guidance, CLL[c]	Day	Night	Day	Night	Day	Night
Baseline 3: No HUD, CLL	Day	Night	Day	Night	Day	Night
Condition 1: HUD, LOC guidance, RCLM only	Day	Night	Day	Night	Day	Night
Condition 2: HUD, LOC guidance, No RCLM, No CLL	Day	Night	Day	Night	Day	Night

[a]LOC = localizer
[b]RCLM = Runway Centerline Markings
[c]All CLL conditions assume existing RCLM

For normal operation scenarios, crosswinds speed ranging between 3 knots (calm) and 22 knots[1] and varying direction were randomly assigned to scenarios. For abnormal operations (failure cases) scenarios, crosswinds between 3 knots (calm) and 15 knots were applied. All tailwinds were limited to 10 knots (Boeing 737-800NG Airplane Flight Manual Limitation). Six abnormal operational conditions were included in this research, as well. They encompassed engine malfunctions, failure of the localizer transmitter, slewing of the localizer azimuth, and loss of HUD. All experimental trials were conducted on a CAT I runway at Memphis International Airport.

For the purposes of this study, NASA Task Load Index (TLX) rating scale was used to assess crew workload [36]. Specifically, both the pilot flying (PF) and the pilot monitoring (PM) completed the pen-and-paper version of the NASA TLX questionnaire after each experimental run. In addition, after each run, pilots were encouraged to provide additional verbal feedback regarding the level of workload they experienced, the personal techniques they applied when using the HUD symbology, as well as, how they dynamically allocated their attention to monitor primary flight information while maintaining visual contact with the outside environment.

2.1 Procedures

Each pilot crew was briefed on the purpose of the research, viewed a video introducing the HUD localizer takeoff guidance symbology implemented on the Rockwell Collins Head-up Guidance System (HGS) Model 6700 as installed on the FAA's Boeing 737-800NG Level D simulator, and received a safety briefing. A 3-hour simulator familiarization session followed. The purpose of the session was to make the pilots familiar

---

[1] AC 120-28D - Criteria for Approval of Category III Weather Minima for Takeoff, Landing, and Rollout.

and comfortable with the HUD symbology set, flight deck controls, and simulator handling qualities. For the data collection portion of this research, each crew completed 96 takeoff scenarios including 60 normal and 36 abnormal conditions over the course of two days. Each pilot flew 48 scenarios as a PF and 48 as a PM. During the debriefing session, each crew completed the NASA TLX pairwise comparison, and provided feedback regarding the equivalent level of safety of using HUD localizer guided takeoff symbology in lieu of CLL. Specifically, based on their overall experience, the crews reflected on whether it was equally safe to use HUD localizer guidance symbology in lieu of CLL and to what RVR levels. In addition, they made suggestions relating to other conditions/factors (crosswind limitation, additional training, etc.) to be considered in the decision-making process for future operational approval of using HUD with localizer guidance in lieu of currently required infrastructure for lower than standard takeoff minima.

3   Results

The total NASA TLX scores displayed issues with normality, violating the assumptions needed for parametric statistics. To address these issues and satisfy the assumption of normality, a natural log transformation was applied to the total workload scores. The equal variance assumption was met according to Hartley's F_{max} test (F_{max} (15, 191) = 1.44) against the critical value of 2.0964 [37, 38]. Accordingly, statistical results are reported with the natural log transformed data. However, for ease of interpretation, tables and graphs report untransformed total workload scores.

An Analysis of Covariance (ANCOVA) was conducted to evaluate the main effects of Type of Guidance and RVR on crew workload with Crosswind Component as a covariate. To calculate the Crosswind Component, the wind speed magnitude assigned to each scenario was multiplied by the absolute value of sine of the relative wind angle to the aircraft (Eq. 1). The ANCOVA model included Crew as a random effect to account for variance in the subjective measure of workload. In addition, Lighting Condition (day/night) and Pilot Role (PF and PM) were set as random factors in the model.

$$XWC = |V \times \sin(\theta)| \tag{1}$$

where
XWC = Crosswind Component
V   = wind speed (kt)
Θ = relative angle of wind to aircraft

Analyses of total workload scores revealed no significant interaction effects. Therefore, all factors were evaluated as main effects. Type of Guidance had a significant effect on total workload scores (F (4, 2838) = 24.74, $p < 0.001$, $\eta^2 = 0.034$).

Bonferroni correction for multiple testing was applied. The results further indicated that when using HUD, with no localizer guidance, and RCLM only (Baseline 1), the crews reported experiencing significantly higher workload than when using either HUD, with no LOC guidance, and CLL (Baseline 2) ($p < 0.001$) or HUD, with LOC guidance, and RCLM only (Condition 1) ($p < 0.001$). When using HUD with LOC guidance, no RCLM, and no CLL (Condition 2), the crews experienced significantly higher workload than in any other type of guidance condition (Fig. 1 and Fig. 2).

The results showed no significant differences in crew workload between HUD, no LOC guidance, and CLL (Baseline 2) as compared to HUD, with LOC guidance, and no CLL (Condition 1) indicating equivalent levels of crew workload in the conditions of principal concern in this research. Furthermore, results did not show a significant difference between No HUD, with CLL (Baseline 3) compared to HUD, No Localizer guidance, with CLL (Baseline 2) or compared to HUD, With Localizer guidance, RCLM only (Condition 1).

In addition, RVR level also had a significant effect on total NASA TLX scores (F (2, 2838) = 24.74, $p < 0.001$, $\eta^2 = 0.048$). Bonferroni correction for multiple testing was applied, and the results indicated that in the 300 ft RVR condition, the crew experienced significantly higher workload than in the 500 ft RVR ($p < 0.0001$) and 700 ft RVR ($p < 0.0001$) conditions, respectively. In the 500 ft RVR condition the pilots experienced significantly higher workload than in the 700 ft RVR ($p = 0.013$) condition (Fig. 1 and Fig. 2).

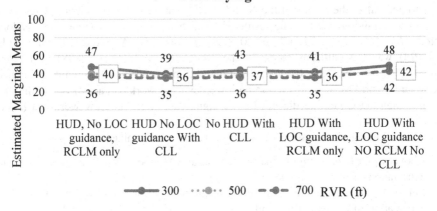

Fig. 1. Estimated marginal means of total NASA TLX scores for PF by Type of Guidance and RVR (The model's covariate value for mean Crosswind Component was assessed at 9.39.)

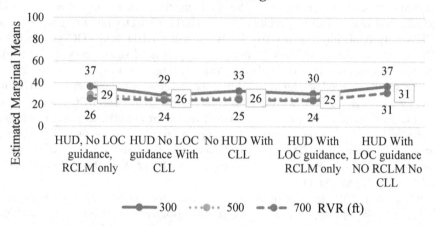

Fig. 2. Estimated marginal means of total NASA TLX scores for PM by Type of Guidance and RVR (The model's covariate value for mean Crosswind Component was assessed at 9.39.)

The covariate, Crosswind Component, was found to have a significant effect on the total NASA TLX scores (F (1, 2838) = 93.933, $p < 0.0001$, $\eta^2 = 0.032$), and the coefficient of Crosswind Component was 0.446. In the current model, individual crews and Pilot Type (airline or business jet pilot) were considered mutually inclusive. Therefore, to refine the model, mitigate the subjectivity of the TLX measure, and be able to generalize the results of the NASA TLX measure to the population; Crew was treated as a random factor. The results showed that Crew had a significant random effect (F (23, 2838) = 71.769, $p < 0.0001$, $\eta^2 = 0.368$). As expected, Pilot Role (PF/PM) was a significant factor in the model, as well (F (1, 2838) = 512.253, $p < 0.0001$, $\eta^2 = 0.153$). Parameter estimation indicated a 10.70-point difference between PF and PM, with PM reporting lower levels of workload across all conditions. Lastly, Lighting Condition did not have a significant effect on crew workload (F (1, 2838) = 0.236, $p = 0.627$).

The following abnormal operations scenarios were examined:

- Above V_1 Continue: engine malfunction at an IAS above V_1 (122 knots), with an expectation of continued take-off
- Below V_1 Abort: engine malfunction at an IAS below V_1 (105 knots), with an expectation of a rejected take-off
- Below V_{mcg} Abort: engine malfunction at an IAS below V_{mcg} (95 knots), with an expectation of a rejected take-off
- LOC Fail: failure of the localizer, removing centerline guidance capability from the HUD at 70 kt
- LOC Bend: slewing of the localizer azimuth at 50 knots, causing a drift of centerline guidance from the HUD
- Loss of HUD at V_R (132 knots)

Similar patterns emerged in the crew workload data during both normal and abnormal (failure conditions) operations. That is, there was an inverse relationship between RVR and crew workload scores. However, during the abnormal operations scenarios the reported crew workload levels were slightly more elevated on the NASA TLX scale. More specifically, Fig. 3 suggests that there is a pattern of higher workload scores during the three engine failure conditions than the other malfunctions.

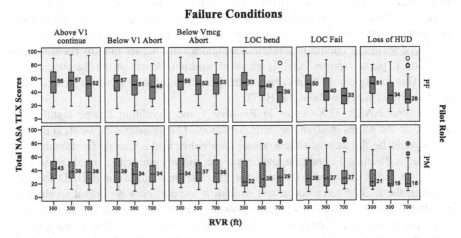

Fig. 3. Total NASA TLX scores per Failure Condition, RVR, and Pilot Role

4   Discussion

The purpose of this research was to examine the crew workload considerations for using HUD with localizer guidance symbology in lieu of currently required infrastructure (i.e., CLL) for lower than standard takeoff minima and within the larger conceptual framework of near domain (flight deck) and far domain (runway environment) visual cues, HUD guidance symbology, HUD utility, and RVR visibility. To identify the differential contributions of these factors, three baseline conditions without HUD localizer guidance symbology and two conditions with HUD localizer takeoff guidance symbology were used (Table 1). The baseline conditions included currently existing runway infrastructure and markings (e.g., CLL, RCLM) where Baseline 1 and 2 were flown with the HUD and Baseline 3 without the HUD. The two experimental conditions included HUD localizer guidance symbology. Specifically, Condition 1 included RCLM and excluded CLL. Condition 2 excluded both CLL and RCLM.

For this research, RVR conditions within the continuum between 300 ft and 1000 ft were selected. We selected this continuum based on FAA Policy Order 8400.13F [39] regarding takeoffs with (a) HUD localizer guidance, CLL, and HIRLs at 300 ft RVR; and (b) RCLM, HIRLS or CLL at or below 1000 ft RVR. Currently, only about 30% of the CAT I runways in the NAS are equipped with CLL. Therefore, the human factors considerations in using HUD localizer guidance in lieu of CLL, within the RVR continuum defined above were paramount for this research. The experimental conditions of principal interest in that regard were Baseline 2, Baseline 3 and Condition 1 (Table 1).

No significant differences were found in the total NASA TLX scores when comparing Baseline 2 and Baseline 3, Baseline 3 and Condition 1; and Baseline 2 and Condition 1. We attribute these results to the availability of salient runway centerline visual cues in the near and/or far domains. Namely, HUD localizer guidance symbology (near domain) and RCLM (far domain) in Condition 1, and CLL (far domain) in Baseline 2 and Baseline 3. In particular, all three conditions included one of these combinations providing the necessary information about the runway centerline position in reduced visibility conditions. While not significantly higher than in Baseline 2 or Condition 1, pilots reported slightly elevated workload levels in the Baseline 3 condition. This finding could be ascribed to the general discontent pilots expressed when asked to fly scenarios without the HUD.

The total NASA TLX scores in Baseline 1 and Condition 2 were significantly higher than the scores in all of the other conditions. One plausible explanation of these results could be the lack of salient visual cues either in the near or far domains. For example, in Baseline 1 condition, the only direct runway centerline visual cue was the RCLM. In the RVR conditions used for this research and without HUD localizer guidance, the RCLM were not salient enough to support crew workload levels comparable to those conditions where more salient (stand alone or in combination) visual cues were available. In Condition 2, the only direct runway centerline visual cue was the HUD localizer guidance (near domain) and no CLL or RCLM were available. In this condition, crews reported significantly higher workload levels than in any other condition included in this research. However, even in this most challenging experimental condition, the average reported crew workload levels stayed below the midpoint on the NASA TLX scale.

In summary, the overall crew workload levels reported by the crews across the baseline and experimental conditions were low to moderate in the normal operations scenarios included in this research (Fig. 1 and Fig. 2). The median total workload scores during abnormal operations scenarios (failure conditions) did not exceed moderate levels on the NASA TLX scale (Fig. 3). In line with the results from the statistical analyses and considering the remarkably consistent feedback from the pilot crews in favor of the use of HUD localizer guidance for takeoff, we attribute these results also to the high levels of information redundancy and number of safeguards typical for modern flight decks and multi-crew operations.

During the debriefing sessions, and in addition to the empirical data collected during the experimental trials, we requested that pilot participants give their personal recommendation for the lowest RVR they considered as equally safe for using HUD localizer guidance symbology in lieu of CLL. Figure 4 shows the frequency count of their responses. Notably, some pilots expressed difficulty to directly compare the HUD localizer guidance symbology and centerline lighting (e.g., "While I don't believe HUD localizer guided to symbology is 'equivalently safe' to operations with centerline lighting, I believe it is safe within certain RVR limitations [I estimate this to be 500 RVR].").

Pilots Responses: Equivalent Level of Safety (ELOS)

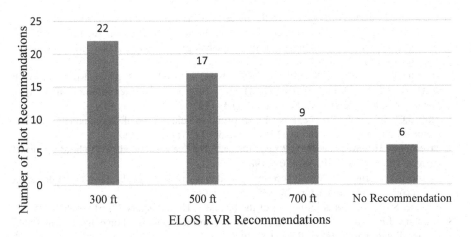

Fig. 4. Frequency count of pilot responses to the question: "Is it equally safe, and down to what RVR, to use HUD LOC guidance symbology in lieu of centerline lights?" (If pilots included two RVR recommendations (e.g., 300 ft RVR day and 500 ft RVR night), the more conservative RVR recommendation was included in the count.)

Inspired by the many years' worth of previous HUD research into the way pilots monitor primary flight information while maintaining visual contact with the outside environment, we sought to obtain more insight into it, and specifically in the context of this study. To accomplish that, we encouraged pilots to share feedback about the techniques they used in this regard for each of the experimental conditions. Pilots reported that they dynamically switch attention between the HUD symbology (near domain) and the outside environment (far domain). The amount of time they reported looking at the symbology versus looking outside changed with the amount of available outside visual cues. When their attention was focused on the HUD symbology, they reported remaining aware of the outside visual cues and used them as a secondary means for confirming they were continuing on centerline. In conditions with enough external cues visible, the pilots reported using the task-relevant HUD symbology (e.g., flight path vector and flight guidance cue) in combination and aligning it with the available outside visual cues (e.g., centerline markings, lighting structures) also while remaining aware of the optical flow in their peripheral vision. This feedback was consistent with findings from previous research [15, 17–19]. More specifically, the pilots' verbal feedback supported the notion that due to its volitional nature, visual scanning in a known pattern may mitigate attentional tunneling. On multiple occasions, pilots did report "tunneling" on the flight path vector and the flight director. However, they reiterated the volitional nature of the "tunneling" as a conscious attempt to exclusively focus on that part of the HUD symbology while remaining fully aware of the rest of the inside and outside visual cues.

Additional research is needed to investigate the relationship between HUD training, level of proficiency, performance, and workload in both normal and abnormal operations.

References

1. Crawford, J., Neal, A.: A review of the perceptual and cognitive issues associated with the use of head-up displays in commercial aviation. Int. J. Aviat. Psychol. **16**, 1–19 (2006)
2. Newman, R.L.: Helmet-mounted display symbology and stabilization concepts. Crew Systems Consultants, San Marcos, TX (1995)
3. Weintraub, D.J., Ensing, M.: Human Factors Issues in Head-Up Display Design: The Book of HUD (CSERIAC State of Art Report). Crew System Ergonomics Information Analysis Center, Wright-Patterson Air Force Base, OH (1992)
4. Hull, J.C., Gill, R.T., Roscoe, S.N.: Locus of the stimulus to visual accommodation: where in the world, or where in the eye? Hum. Factors **24**, 311–319 (1982)
5. Iavecchia, J.H., Iavecchia, H.P., Roscoe Illiana, S.N.: Eye accommodation to head-up virtual images. Hum. Factors **30**, 689–702 (1988)
6. Norman, J., Ehrlich, S.: Visual accommodation and virtual image displays: target detection and recognition. Hum. Factors **28**, 135–151 (1986)
7. Roscoe, S.N.: Bigness is in the eye of the beholder. Hum. Factors **27**, 615–636 (1985)
8. Barnette, J.F.: Role of head-up display in instrument flight. Air Force Instrument Flight Center, Randolph Air Force Base, TX (1976)
9. Jarvi, D.W.: Investigation of spatial disorientation of F-15 Eagle pilots. Aeronautical Systems Division, Wright-Patterson Air Force Base, OH (1981)
10. Newman, R.L.: Operational problems associated with head-up displays during instrument flight. Crew Systems Consultants, Yellow Springs, OH (1980)
11. Fischer, E., Haines, R.F., Price, T.A.: Cognitive issues in head-up displays. NASA Scientific and Technical Information Branch (1980)
12. Morey, J.C., Simon, R.: Attention factors associated with head-up display and helmet-mounted display systems. Dynamics Research Corp., Wilmington (1993)
13. Hennessy, R.T.: Instrument myopia. JOSA. **65**, 1114–1120 (1975)
14. Newman, R.L.: Improvement of head-up display standards. volume 1. Head-up display design guide. Appendix. Air Force Aeromedical Research Laboratory, Wright-Patterson Air Force Base, OH (1987)
15. Foyle, D.C., McCann, R.S., Sanford, B.D., Schwirzke, M.F.J.: Attentional effects with superimposed symbology: implications for head-up displays (HUD). In: Proceedings of the Human Factors and Ergonomics Society Annual Meeting, pp. 1340–1344. SAGE Publications, Los Angeles (1993)
16. Prinzel III, L.J., Risser, M.: Head-up displays and attention capture. NASA Langley Research Center, Hampton (2004)
17. Haines, R.F., Fischer, E., Price, T.A.: Head-up transition behavior of pilots with and without head-up display in simulated low-visibility approaches. NASA Scientific and Technical Information Branch (1980)
18. Weintraub, D.J., Haines, R.F., Randle, R.J.: The utility of head-up displays: eye-focus vs decision times. In: Proceedings of the Human Factors Society Annual Meeting, pp. 529–533. SAGE Publications, Los Angeles (1984)
19. Weintraub, D.J., Haines, R.F., Randle, R.J.: Head-up display (HUD) utility, II: runway to HUD transitions monitoring eye focus and decision times. In: Proceedings of the Human Factors Society Annual Meeting, pp. 615–619. SAGE Publications, Los Angeles (1985)
20. Foyle, D.C., Sanford, B.D., McCann, R.S.: Attentional issues in superimposed flight symbology. In: 6th International Symposium on Aviation Psychology, Columbus, OH, pp. 577–582 (1991)

21. McCann, R.S., Lynch, J., Foyle, D.C., Johnston, J.C.: Modelling attentional effects with head-up displays. In: Proceedings of the Human Factors and Ergonomics Society Annual Meeting, pp. 1345–1349. SAGE Publications, Los Angeles (1993)
22. McCann, R.S., Foyle, D.C., Johnston, J.C.: Attentional limitations with head-up displays. In: Proceedings of the 7th International Symposium on Aviation Psychology, pp. 70–75 (1993)
23. Shelden, S.G., Foyle, D.C., McCann, R.S.: Effects of scene-linked symbology on flight performance. In: Proceedings of the Human Factors and Ergonomics Society Annual Meeting, pp. 294–298. SAGE Publications, Los Angeles (1997)
24. Levy, J.L., Foyle, D.C., McCann, R.S.: Performance benefits with scene-linked HUD symbology: an attentional phenomenon? In: Proceedings of the Human Factors and Ergonomics Society Annual Meeting, pp. 11–15. SAGE Publications, Los Angeles (1998)
25. Wickens, C.D., Long, J.: Conformal symbology, attention shifts, and the head-up display. In: Proceedings of the Human Factors and Ergonomics Society Annual Meeting, pp. 6–10. SAGE Publications, Los Angeles (1994)
26. Ververs, P.M., Wickens, C.D.: Head-up displays: effect of clutter, display intensity, and display location on pilot performance. Int. J. Aviat. Psychol. 8, 377–403 (1998)
27. Kaber, D.B., Alexander, A.L., Stelzer, E.M., Kim, S.-H., Kaufmann, K., Hsiang, S.: Perceived clutter in advanced cockpit displays: measurement and modeling with experienced pilots. Aviat. Space Environ. Med. 79, 1007–1018 (2008)
28. Kaber, D., et al.: Testing and validation of a psychophysically defined metric of display clutter. J. Aerosp. Inf. Syst. 10, 359–368 (2013)
29. Boston, B.N., Braun, C.C.: Clutter and display conformality: changes in cognitive capture. In: Proceedings of the Human Factors and Ergonomics Society Annual Meeting, pp. 57–61. SAGE Publications, Los Angeles (1996)
30. Neisser, U., Becklen, R.: Selective looking: attending to visually specified events. Cogn. Psychol. 7, 480–494 (1975)
31. Spelke, E., Hirst, W., Neisser, U.: Skills of divided attention. Cognition 4, 215–230 (1976)
32. Littman, D., Becklen, R.: Selective looking with minimal eye movements. Percept. Psychophys. 20, 77–79 (1976). https://doi.org/10.3758/BF03198709
33. Boucek, G.P., Pfaff, T.A., Smith, W.D.: The use of holographic head-up display of flight path symbology in varying weather conditions (SAE technical paper series 831445). Society of Automotive Engineers, Warrendale (1983)
34. Bray, R.S.: A head-up display format for application to transport aircraft approach and landing. NASA, Moffett Field, CA (1980)
35. Lauber, J.K., Bray, R.S., Harrison, R.L., et al.: An operational evaluation of head-up displays for civil transport operations-NASA/FAA phase III final report. NASA Scientific and Technical Information Branch (1982)
36. Hart, S.G.: NASA task load index (TLX). Volume 1.0; paper and pencil package. NASA Ames Research Center, Moffett Field, CA (1986)
37. O'Brien, R.G.: A simple test for variance effects in experimental designs. Psychol. Bull. 89, 570 (1981)
38. Kirk, R.E.: Experimental Design: Procedures for the Behavioral Sciences, 3rd edn. Brooks/Cole, Pacific Grove (1995)
39. Federal Aviation Administration: Order 8400.13F. U.S. Department of Transportation, Washington, DC (2019)

Performance, Simulator Sickness, and Immersion of a Ball-Sorting Task in Virtual and Augmented Realities

Crystal Maraj[(✉)], Jonathan Hurter, and Sean Murphy

Institute for Simulation and Training,
University of Central Florida, Orlando, FL 32826, USA
{cmaraj,jhurter,smurphy}@ist.ucf.edu

Abstract. Virtual Reality (VR) and Augmented Reality (AR) can be defined by the amount of virtual elements displayed to a human's senses: VR is completely synthetic and AR is partially synthetic. This paper compares VR and AR systems for variations of three ball-sorting task scenarios, and evaluates both user performance and reaction (i.e., simulator sickness and immersion). The VR system scored higher, with statistical significance, than the AR system in terms of effectiveness per each scenario and completion rate of all scenarios. The VR system also scored significantly lower than the AR system in terms of percentage error and total false positives. The VR group scored significantly lower than the AR group in efficiency performance: the VR group had less time spent in each scenario, less total time duration, and higher overall relative efficiency. Although post-scenario simulator sickness did not differ significantly between VR and AR, the VR condition had an increase in disorientation from pre-to-post scenarios. Significant correlations between performance effectiveness and post-scenario simulator sickness were not found. Finally, the AR system scored significantly higher on the immersion measure item for the level of challenge the scenarios provided. AR interface issues are discussed as a potential factor in performance decrement, and AR interface solutions are given. AR may be preferred over VR if disorientation is a concern. Study limits include causality ambiguity and experimental control. Next steps include testing VR or AR systems exclusively, and testing whether the increased challenge from the AR immersion is beneficial to educational applications.

Keywords: Augmented Reality · Virtual Reality · Performance · Simulator Sickness · Immersion

1 Introduction

This paper investigates different paradigms of emerging and expanding technologies, in terms of user performance and user reaction (i.e., simulator sickness and immersion): forms of Virtual Reality (VR) and Augmented Reality (AR) are compared through the task of sorting virtual balls. The impetus of the research is to understand how a ball-sorting task, which can be linked to other applications, can be completed in two

© Springer Nature Switzerland AG 2020
J. Y. C. Chen and G. Fragomeni (Eds.): HCII 2020, LNCS 12190, pp. 522–534, 2020.
https://doi.org/10.1007/978-3-030-49695-1_35

combinations of Head-Mounted Displays (HMDs), or visual goggles, and controllers. Three ball-sorting scenarios were implemented. The aim is to inform future applications within VR and AR tasks.

1.1   Virtual Reality and Augmented Reality

The amount of virtual elements displayed to a human's senses can define VR and AR. VR provides a completely fabricated, new environment via software; AR alters, or augments, the display of a real environment with additional display input, such as computer-generated graphics (Chavan 2016). VR is completely synthetic and AR is partially synthetic. Recreational VR and AR games continue to be a popular form of technology; however, applications have been increasingly expanding in the education, healthcare, and manufacturing fields through serious games and simulations.

1.2   Games, Serious Games, and Simulations

VR games have been commercially available since the 1990s on the Nintendo Virtual Boy, although these first attempts at making popular VR gaming consoles failed (Kushner 2014). Yet, new VR HMDs have differentiated themselves from their predecessors with enhanced display resolution, low latency, and computing power (Kress et al. 2014). Following the attempts at early VR gaming, one of the first AR systems—ARQuake—was created. Through the extension of the First-Person Shooter (FPS) game Quake, ARQuake utilized two core elements of AR: tracking (of a players' orientation and position) and overlaying computer-generated graphics onto real environments (Piekarski and Thomas 2002). Since then, AR gaming has branched off into two directions: HMD gaming and mobile phone gaming.

Serious games are fundamentally games intended for not solely entertainment purposes (Susi et al. 2007). Serious games can utilize game characteristics as a means for learning goals. Serious games differ from edutainment (a merging of entertainment into education), in that edutainment typically uses drill and practice activities to teach lower-order thinking skills, whereas serious games typically facilitate learning of higher-order thinking skills (Charsky 2010).

The element of simulation is to mirror and represent some aspect of the real world (Aldrich 2009). Training with virtual simulations offers reduced time and cost, and is flexible for modification of a workplace (Grajewski et al. 2015). According to Aldrich (2009), when comparing serious games and educational simulations, serious games tend to be more engaging, with less fidelity and transferability than educational simulations.

2   Current Task Background

The current effort focuses on the simplified task of sorting virtual, colored balls of different sizes, accomplished through either a VR or AR system. This task involves grasping and placing, and thus potentially relates to games, serious games, and simulation aspects. This task is thought to involve spatial ability, such as through depth perception of ball location and how close one needs to be to a ball to grasp it. Since the task involves balls of different sizes, one can see how well different-sized balls can be manipulated. In terms of the ball-sorting task, similar tasks are visible.

Cidota et al. (2016) looked at participants who used their fingers to clasp a virtual object and place it in a box, in both VR and AR conditions: one used their hands as an interface for the task in both VR and AR. Young et al. (2014) also tested a VR glove (and a high-cost VR HMD) for ordering randomly-shuffled, numbered boxes in ascending order; and participants in this condition underperformed in comparison to a condition which differed through manipulation via a handheld controller and visuals via a consumer-grade VR HMD. Krichenbauer et al. (2018) used the same object place-ment task, with the same controller (i.e., a 3D input device), for VR and AR conditions: participants performed better in the AR condition than in the VR condition. Further, a system for virtually sorting red and blue balls into appropriate holes was detailed for reducing phantom limb pain (Zweighaft et al. 2012). Finally, sorting has become a game mechanic: Sort 'Em is a VR game (Steam, n.d.); in contrast, a serious game focused on sorting (and teaching) different types of waste has also been created (Menon et al. 2017). The latter game used gesture-based interaction (via a Microsoft Kinect system).

Various crucial points are taken from the current state of similar tasks. Comparing a VR system using a handheld controller with an AR system using a hand as an interface has yet to be investigated. Despite this, the value of a sorting task is noticeable, noted by applications in clinical therapy and instruction. In any case, the user's performance, simulator sickness, and immersion in these differing systems have implications for further use cases and practical applications, rendering a need for further research. This paper seeks to better understand the relationship between participants and the systems of VR and AR, through the task of sorting different-colored balls. The VR system consisted of the HP Mixed Reality headset and controllers, whereas the AR system consisted of the Meta 2 headset and one's hand(s) as controller(s). Hereinafter, the total VR system will be referred to as the HP Mixed Reality, and the total AR system will be referred to as the Meta 2.

3   Simulator Sickness

A current standard for measuring Simulator Sickness (SS) is the Simulator Sickness Questionnaire (SSQ), a self-report survey developed by Kennedy et al. (1993). Sim-ulator sickness comprises ranked categories of Disorientation, Oculomotor, and Nausea subscales. By looking at the descriptive SSQs of participants exposed to virtual environments, Lampton et al. (1994) concluded that SS might lead to undesirable effects. According to a review paper, there are many potential factors that can influence SS, such as the individual characteristics of age and gender; simulator characteristics, including field of view; and task characteristics, such as session duration and maneuver intensity (Johnson 2005).

Pettijohn et al. (2019) compared the use of two different HMDs, one VR and one AR, for SS differences. The researchers implemented three motion conditions (i.e., no motion, synchronous motion, and asynchronous motion); the task was to destroy a virtual hostile ship with a machine gun. The findings showed no significant differences in SS between the VR and AR headsets.

Muth et al. (2006) tested whether uncoupled motion had any effect on overall performance (measured by task completion time and task accuracy) by having participants complete a motor task consisting of maneuvering a vehicle between cones in a virtual driving game. Participants played the game in two conditions: whilst seated in a moving vehicle and whilst seated in a stationary vehicle. Performance was lessened and SS was higher for the motion condition when compared to the stationary condition. Note, the task of the driving game did not incorporate a VR or AR HMD.

4   Immersion

To further clarify participant reactions to different VR and AR systems, a participant's sense of immersion may be investigated. Jennett et al. (2008) have pinpointed a type of immersion believed to be part of a positive experience, at least for gaming: "Immersion involves a lack of awareness of time, a loss of awareness of the real world, involvement and a sense of being in the task environment. Most importantly, immersion is the result of a good gaming experience." (p. 657). These latter authors developed the immersion questionnaire. The present study incorporated a modified immersion questionnaire, which this paper's authors term the immersion measure.

5   Research Questions

The following questions were developed to assess different HMD systems, for the task of sorting virtual balls.

RQ1: Is there a statistically significant difference between the HP Mixed Reality and Meta 2 for effectiveness for each of the three scenarios, completion rate, percentage error, and total false positives?

RQ2: Is there a statistically significant difference between the HP Mixed Reality and Meta 2 for efficiency (i.e., trial time duration for each of the three scenario, total time duration, and overall relative efficiency)?

RQ3: Is there a statistically significant difference between the HP Mixed Reality and Meta 2 for post-test SS, including SS subscales (i.e., Nausea, Oculomotor, and Disorientation) and Total SS?

RQ4: Is there a statistically significant difference between pre-test and post-test SS, including SS subscales (i.e., Nausea, Oculomotor, and Disorientation) and Total SS, in the HP Mixed Reality condition?

RQ5: Is there a statistically significant difference between pre-test and post-test SS, including SS subscales (i.e., Nausea, Oculomotor, and Disorientation) and Total SS, in the Meta 2 condition?

RQ6: Is there a correlation between post-test SS (including SS subscales [i.e., Nausea, Oculomotor, and Disorientation] and Total SS) and performance (i.e., effectiveness: trial 3; time duration: trial 3, completion rate, total false positives, and percentage errors) for the HP Mixed Reality and Meta 2 conditions?

RQ7: Is there a statistically significant difference between the HP Mixed Reality and Meta 2 for immersion?

6   Method

6.1   Participants

Forty-two individuals from the University of Central Florida (UCF) and its surrounding areas participated in the study. Post analyses indicated 20 males and 22 females volunteered. Ages ranged from 19 to 34 years ($M = 22$, $SD = 3.38$). Participants were vetted during the sign-up process using the Institute for Simulation and Training SONA system (i.e., an online sign-up portal). In order to participate, each individual had to meet inclusion criteria: an age of at least 18 years, United States citizenship, normal or corrected-to-normal vision, no previous history of seizures, and no color blindness. Following the study, the latter lasting up to one hour, participants received $10 compensation for their time and travel.

6.2   Experimental Design

A between-subjects design was employed to assess the difference between the HP Mixed Reality (VR) system and the Meta 2 (AR) system to complete a ball-sorting task. The Independent Variable (IV) was the type of system (i.e., the headset and its related controller[s]). The Dependent Variables (DVs) were the ball-sorting task scenario measurements (i.e., performance outcomes and survey data). Additionally, a within-subjects design was conducted to assess SS, with the IV being the ball-sorting task scenarios, and the DV being the pre-to-post SS scores.

6.3   Testbed

The three scenarios were executed through a single application on one desktop computer (see Table 1 for the desktop specifications). A tutorial and the three scenarios were developed in the Unity game engine; Unity was selected for its user-friendly development interface and capability to support different software development kits.

Table 1. Desktop specifications.

Component	Specification
Operating system	64-bit Windows 10 Enterprise
Processor	Intel Core i7-8700 CPU @ 3.20 GHz
Graphics card	NVIDIA GeForce GTX 1080 Ti (2)
Software	Meta SDK 2.7.0 Mixed Reality Portal Version 10.0.17134.1 Unity 2018.2 16f1 Personal (64-bit)

The tutorial required the participant to practice using the controller scheme respective of the headset (i.e., two handheld Mixed Reality controllers for the HP Mixed Reality headset and physical hand gestures for the Meta 2 headset).

In the tutorial, participants were instructed to pick up colored balls (i.e., red and blue balls) from within a purple box and sort them into respective colored boxes (i.e., red balls were to be sorted into a red box, and blue balls were to be sorted into a blue box; for HP Mixed Reality and Meta 2 examples, see Fig. 1). The AR interface (which did not differ between the tutorial and the scenarios) used a blue status indicator, or highlight, that hovered over each hand when each hand was near a ball. Each indicator was a hollow circle until a fist was made; then the hollow circle would become a filled blue circle. The filled blue circle meant a ball was grabbed; a grabbed ball could be moved by moving one's fist and the ball could be dropped by undoing the fist and opening one's hand. In contrast, the VR interface (which did not differ between the tutorial and the scenarios), used a single button on each controller to grab a ball. A ball could be moved while the button was held down, and the ball could be released when the button was released. The tutorial had a maximum time-limit of 10 min and allowed for the participant to sort 10 red balls and 10 blue balls. Further, the participant was allowed to sort with one hand or with both their hands; instruction regarding hand strategy was not given to the participant. When the participant was ready to move on, the tutorial ended and the first of the three scenarios began.

Fig. 1. Ball-sorting scenario within HP Mixed Reality (left) and Meta 2 (right) conditions. (Color figure online)

Each of the three scenarios required the participant to apply what they practiced in the tutorial: the participant's task was to sort a given number of red and blue balls into their respective color-coded boxes within a 5-min time limit. The first scenario contained 20 red balls and 20 blue balls; all balls had a diameter of 0.15 m. A difficulty curve was introduced in each subsequent scenario: the number of balls would increase (i.e., adding 5 red balls and 5 blue balls), and the size of the balls would decrease (i.e., decreasing the diameter of each ball by 0.025 m). As the participant completed each scenario, the software enacted a process of taking input, processing that input, and outputting the processed results.

The input in the software process was the participant's controller input and ball manipulation. The software processed the input by utilizing virtual colliders on the balls, the boxes, and the rest of the environment: if the balls collided with the correct corresponding box, the software processed the ball manipulation as correctly sorted; if the balls collided with the incorrect box, the software processed the ball manipulation as incorrectly sorted; if the balls collided with any other element of the virtual environment, the software processed the ball manipulation as dropped. The software outputted the processed results into a collective virtual dataset; this dataset was parsed into objective data measurements and logged into a Comma-Separated Values (CSV) file stored onto the desktop.

6.4 Measurements: Surveys

The survey measures used during the data collection procedure included a demographics questionnaire, the SSQ, and the immersion measure.

Demographics Questionnaire. The demographics questionnaire collected biographical data, such as age, gender, educational experience, and computer game usage.

Simulator Sickness Questionnaire (SSQ). The SSQ measured the user's response to the VR and AR systems, in terms of SS symptoms: responses comprised 16 symptoms, rated from none (0) to severe (3). The responses were scored into four subscales (i.e., Nausea, Oculomotor, and Disorientation), as well as a weighted, Total SS score (Kennedy et al. 1993).

Immersion Measure. The immersion measure comprised eight questions related to the level of immersion experienced during the three presented scenarios. The questions were rated from strongly disagree (1) to strongly agree (5; Jennett et al. 2008).

6.5 Measurements: Performance

Objective performance data was tracked and logged into a CSV file. Participant ID and type of system (i.e., HP Mixed Reality and Meta 2) were logged as identifiers for each file; each logged dataset within the file was labeled with unique timestamps. Performance data included effectiveness and efficiency measurements.

Effectiveness was tracked through four metrics: per-scenario trial effectiveness, completion rate, percentage error, and total false positives. Per-scenario trial effectiveness, expressed in percentage, was calculated by dividing the number of balls correctly sorted by the total number of balls in the given scenario. Completion rate, expressed in percentage, was found by dividing the number of successful scenarios by the total amount of scenarios (i.e., 3); a successful scenario was defined as answering yes to the question, "Did the participant sort all balls, whether correctly or incorrectly, within the scenario time limit?" Percentage error, expressed in percentage, was calculated by dividing the sum of balls incorrectly sorted and balls dropped by the total number of balls in the given scenario. Total false positives, expressed in percentage, were found by dividing the number of balls dropped by the total number of balls in the given scenario.

Efficiency was tracked through three metrics: per-scenario trial time duration, total time duration, and overall relative efficiency. Per-scenario trial time duration, expressed in minutes, was measured by the time it took the participant to complete the scenario; completion of the scenario was determined by a) having all balls sorted or dropped within the scenario; or b) the maximum allotted time of 5 min passing. Total time duration, expressed in minutes, was measured by adding all three per-scenario trial time durations. Overall relative efficiency (see Eq. 1), expressed in percentage, incorporated completion rate and per-scenario trial time duration (Mifsud 2015):

$$Overall\ Relative\ Efficiency = \frac{\sum_{j=1}^{R}\sum_{i=1}^{N} n_{ij}t_{ij}}{\sum_{j=1}^{R}\sum_{i=1}^{N} t_{ij}} \times 100\% \tag{1}$$

For the purpose of this study, N represents the three scenarios, R represents the number of participants in the individual dataset (i.e., one participant per dataset), n_{ij} represents the result of scenario completion (i.e., completion rate), and t_{ij} represents time spent completing the scenario (i.e., per-scenario trial time duration).

6.6   Procedure

Prior to the study, a random number generator was used to order the conditions. Upon participant arrival, the experimenter greeted and escorted the individual to the lab space. Next, the experimenter presented the informed consent form and asked the participant to read, date, and sign the form. If the participant agreed to participate in the study, the experimenter administered a color blindness test. Only if the participant passed the color blindness test would the experiment continue: the experimenter would then provide the demographics questionnaire to complete.

Next, the experimenter administered the pre-scenarios SSQ to obtain a baseline from each participant. Thereafter, the participant viewed an instructional PowerPoint about the experiment. The instructional PowerPoint provided information on the purpose of the experiment, the task to complete, tools (i.e., HMD and form of controller), and instructions on the control scheme for a participant's given condition. Additionally, the Meta 2's PowerPoint included a discussion on the Meta 2's environmental mapping process. After the participant was allowed practice using their condition's control scheme (i.e., handheld controllers or physical hand gestures) in the tutorial, the participant began the ball-sorting task scenarios. Following each scenario, the participant received a one-minute break. After the last break, each participant completed the post-scenarios SSQ and immersion measure. Finally, the experimenter provided the participant with a compensation receipt and then dismissed him or her.

7 Results

Preliminary tests were conducted to test for normality, outliers, and homogeneity of variance. Regarding normality, the data violated the test of assumptions on the Kolmogorov-Smirnov Test (with Lilliefors significance correction) and the Shapiro-Wilk Test. Outliers were verified using the 5% trim mean as well as the inspection of the box plots. Three data points were identified as potential outliers; however, the data points were left in the data set after checking the experimental log and finding no inconsistencies. Homogeneity of variance was assessed via non-parametric tests. As a result, the non-parametric tests were used for data analysis.

7.1 Data Analysis

RQ1. There was a statistically significant difference between the HP Mixed Reality and Meta 2 for effectiveness for each of three scenarios, completion rate, percentage error, and total false positives. The Mann-Whitney U Test indicated statistically significant findings (see Table 2).

Table 2. Significant effectiveness differences between the HP Mixed Reality and Meta 2.

Effectiveness	HP Mixed Reality: Md; n	Meta 2: Md; n	U	Z	p	Effect size (Eta squared)
Effectiveness scenario 1	100; 21	97.5; 21	102.5	−3.35	.001	.52
Effectiveness scenario 2	100; 20	96; 21	50	−4.76	.000	.74
Effectiveness scenario 3	100; 20	93.3; 21	50	−4.75	.000	.74
Completion rate	100; 21	0; 21	30	−5.19	.000	.80
Percentage error	0; 20	2.67; 21	34.5	−4.82	.000	.74
Total false positives	0; 20	2.67; 21	21.5	−5.29	.000	.83

RQ2. There was a significant difference between the HP Mixed Reality and Meta 2 for efficiency (i.e., trial time duration for each of the three scenario, total time duration, and overall relative efficiency). The Mann-Whitney U Test indicated statistically significant findings (see Table 3).

Table 3. Significant efficiency differences between the HP Mixed Reality and Meta 2.

Efficiency	HP Mixed Reality: *Md; n*	Meta 2: *Md; n*	*U*	*Z*	*p*	Effect size (Eta squared)
Trial time duration scenario 1	1 min 13 s; 21	3 min 23 s; 21	5.00	−5.42	.000	.84
Trial time duration scenario 2	1 min 20 s; 20	4 min 27 s; 21	2.00	−5.44	.000	.85
Trial time duration scenario 3	1 min 47 s; 20	4 min 52 s; 21	4.00	−5.41	.000	.84
Total time duration	4 min 23 s; 21	12 min 6 s; 21	4.00	−5.49	.000	.85
Overall relative efficiency (%)	100; 20	0; 21	21	−5.36	.000	.84

RQ3. A Mann-Whitney U tested revealed no statistically significant differences between the HP Mixed Reality and Meta 2 for SS, in terms of post-test SS subscales (i.e., Nausea, Oculomotor, and Disorientation) and Total SS.

RQ4. A Wilcoxon Signed-Rank Test revealed a statistically significant increase in Disorientation following the three test scenarios in the HP Mixed Reality condition, $z = -2.14$, $p < .05$, with a medium effect size ($r = .33$). The pre-test median score increased from ($Md = .00$) to post-test median score ($Md = 6.98$).

RQ5. A Wilcoxon Signed-Rank Test revealed no statistically significant difference between pre-test and post-test SS, in terms of SS subscales and Total SS, in the Meta 2 condition.

RQ6. There were no statistically significant Spearman's correlations found between post-test SS (i.e., neither SS subscales nor Total SS) and performance (i.e. effectiveness: trial 3; time duration: trial 3; completion rate, total false positives, and percentage errors) for the HP Mixed Reality and Meta 2 conditions.

RQ7. A Mann-Whitney U Test revealed a statistically significant difference between the HP Mixed Reality and Meta 2 for the immersion measure statement "The scenarios were challenging." See Table 4 for statistical findings.

Table 4. Significant immersion differences between the HP Mixed Reality and Meta 2.

Immersion measure	HP Mixed Reality: *Md; n*	Meta 2: *Md; n*	U	Z	p	Effect size (Eta squared)
Challenging scenarios statement	2; 20	3; 21	65.5	−3.90	.000	.61

8 Discussion

In terms of objective performance for the ball-sorting task, participants were more effective and efficient with the VR system. This suggests a higher level of objective usability for the VR system, as it allows one to complete the task at an easier level. Perhaps the AR system had interface difficulties, such as the ability to grab a ball or how the system could only control objects displayed within the HMD (i.e., if a grabbed ball left the headset's field of view, the ball was no longer registered as grabbed). Note, AR participants were told (in the instructional PowerPoint) that if a ball moved out of their view, it was no longer considered in their possession. Given both systems differed on both HMD and controller, the attribution of usability causality is ambiguous. To improve the AR interface, various solutions are given: additional feedback via a haptic armband may be used to alert when a ball is grasped in AR; and allowing the software to remember if an off-screen ball was continuously grasped might affect performance. Ultimately, maturation appears needed for the AR system's usability.

Further, the higher challenge in the AR system may also be due to immersion, and thus can be interpreted as AR having a positive challenge that captivates participants. Although this challenge may benefit games, more serious applications could be hindered. For example, surgery may benefit from a bare-hand interface to explore medical images (Gallo et al. 2011); perhaps future surgery could involve a bare-hand interface merged with AR visuals, due to the restriction of using handheld controllers during surgery. This is a potential way AR maturation for object selection tasks has practical merit.

Between the VR and AR systems, the relatively stationary task of ball-sorting produced similar SS. Still, participants in the VR system experienced increased disorientation from pre- to post-scenarios. Methods on eradicating disorientation in tasks similar to ball-sorting may debar SS effects in VR. When disorientation is a concern, the application of AR may be a more forgiving option than VR, in terms of SS.

8.1 Limitations

The ball-sorting task contained notable limitations. One limitation relates to defining the source of performance and reaction (i.e., SS and immersion) differences, since the systems differed in both HMD and controllers. Another limitation focuses on the study design: there was little to no control over the participant's method for sorting the balls into the bins (e.g., whether to use one or two hands when sorting); this lack of control could have impacted participant performance. Finally, it is difficult to generalize the research findings outside of the ball-sorting task completed via the VR and AR systems.

9 Conclusion

This paper investigated aspects of both VR and AR systems, in terms of both users' performance and reaction (i.e., SS and immersion), with regards to a virtual ball-sorting task. The task goal and scenarios were similar, but the tools differed between VR and AR. As VR provides enhanced performance in both effectiveness and efficiency, AR may require further maturation of interface conventions. In opposition, AR is more suitable for low-disorientation settings than VR, at least for the systems and task compared.

9.1 Next Steps

The next steps of the study include determining if the increased challenge relating to immersion in AR is beneficial to educational applications or is restrictive and provides undue workload. Another step would be to test the ball-sorting task using exclusively either VR or AR systems. Also, tweaking the AR interface system could impact performance. Finally, another experimental design would be to test different natural, hand-based interfaces (e.g., haptic gloves) to complete identical ball-sorting tasks.

Acknowledgments. This research was sponsored by Gino Fragomeni of the U.S. Army Research Laboratory Human Research Engineering Directorate Advanced Training and Simulation Division (ARL HRED ATSD), under contract W911QX-13-C-0052. However, the views, findings, and conclusions contained in this presentation are solely those of the author and should not be interpreted as representing the official policies, either expressed or implied, of ARL HRED ATSD or the U.S. Government. The U.S. Government is authorized to reproduce and distribute reprints for Government.

References

Aldrich, C.: The Complete Guide to Simulations and Serious Games. Wiley, Somerset (2009)

Charsky, D.: From edutainment to serious games: a change in the use of game characteristics. Games Cult. 5(2), 177–198 (2010)

Chavan, S.: Augmented reality vs. virtual reality: differences and similarities. Int. J. Adv. Res. Comput. Eng. Technol. 5(6), 1947–1952 (2016)

Cidota, M.A., Clifford, R.M., Lukosch, S.G., Billinghurst, M.: Using visual effects to facilitate depth perception for spatial tasks in virtual and augmented reality. In: 2016 IEEE International Symposium on Mixed and Augmented Reality (ISMAR-Adjunct), pp. 172–177. IEEE, September 2016

Gallo, L., Placitelli, A.P., Ciampi, M.: Controller-free exploration of medical image data: experiencing the Kinect. In: 2011 24th International Symposium on Computer-Based Medical Systems (CBMS), pp. 1–6. IEEE, June 2011

Grajewski, D., Górski, F., Hamrol, A., Zawadzki, P.: Immersive and haptic educational simulations of assembly workplace conditions. Proc. Comput. Sci. **75**, 359–368 (2015)

Jennett, C., et al.: Measuring and defining the experience of immersion in games. Int. J. Hum. Comput. Stud. **66**(9), 641–661 (2008)

Johnson, D.M.: Introduction to and review of simulator sickness research. (Research Report No. 1832) (2005). https://apps.dtic.mil/dtic/tr/fulltext/u2/a434495.pdf

Kennedy, R.S., Lane, N.E., Berbaum, K.S., Lilienthal, M.G.: Simulator sickness questionnaire: an enhanced method for quantifying simulator sickness. Int. J. Aviat. Psychol. **3**(3), 203–220 (1993). https://doi.org/10.1207/s15327108ijap0303

Kress, B., Saeedi, E., Brac-de-la-Perriere, V.: The segmentation of the HMD market: optics for smart glasses, smart eyewear, AR and VR headsets. In: Photonics Applications for Aviation, Aerospace, Commercial, and Harsh Environments V, vol. 9202, p. 92020D, September 2014

Krichenbauer, M., Yamamoto, G., Taketom, T., Sandor, C., Kato, H.: Augmented reality versus virtual reality for 3D object manipulation. IEEE Trans. Visual Comput. Graph. **24**(2), 1038–1048 (2018)

Kushner, D.: Virtual reality's moment. IEEE Spectr. **51**(1), 34–37 (2014)

Lampton, D.R., Kolasinski, E.M., Knerr, B.W., Bliss, J.P., Bailey, J.H., Witmer, B.G.: Side effects and aftereffects of immersion in virtual environments. Proc. Hum. Factors Ergon. Soc. Ann. Meet. **38**(18), 1154–1157 (1994). https://doi.org/10.1177/154193129403801802

Menon, B.M., Unnikrishnan, R., Muir, A., Bhavani, R.R.: Serious game on recognizing categories of waste, to support a zero waste recycling program. In: 2017 IEEE 5th International Conference on Serious Games and Applications for Health (SeGAH). IEEE (2017). https://doi.org/10.1109/segah.2017.7939292

Mifsud, J.: Usability metrics – a guide to quantify the usability of any system [Blog post], 22 June 2015. https://usabilitygeek.com/usability-metrics-a-guide-to-quantify-system-usability/

Muth, E.R., Walker, A.D., Fiorello, M.: Effects of uncoupled motion on performance. Hum. Factors: J. Hum. Factors Ergon. Soc. **48**(3), 600–607 (2006). https://doi.org/10.1518/001872006778606750

Pettijohn, K.A., Peltier, C., Lukos, J.R., Norris, J.N., Biggs, A.T.: Comparison of virtual reality and augmented reality: Safety and effectiveness (2019). https://apps.dtic.mil/dtic/tr/fulltext/u2/1068493.pdf

Piekarski, W., Thomas, B.: ARQuake: the outdoor augmented reality gaming system. Commun. ACM **45**(1), 36–38 (2002)

Steam (n.d.): Sort 'em [Game website]. https://store.steampowered.com/app/594360/Sort_Em/

Susi, T., Johannesson, M., Backlund, P.: Serious games - an overview (Technical Report HS-IKI-TR-07-001) (2007). https://www.diva-portal.org/smash/get/diva2:2416/FULLTEXT01.pdf

Young, M.K., Gaylor, G.B., Andrus, S.M., Bodenheimer, B.: A comparison of two cost-differentiated virtual reality systems for perception and action tasks. In: Proceedings of the ACM Symposium on Applied Perception, pp. 83–90. ACM, August 2014

Zweighaft, A.R., et al.: A virtual reality ball grasp and sort task for the enhancement of phantom limb pain proprioception. In: 2012 IEEE Systems and Information Engineering Design Symposium (2012). https://doi.org/10.1109/sieds.2012.621513

Robots in VAMR

The Effects of Asset Degradation on Human Trust in Swarms

August Capiola[1(✉)], Joseph Lyons[1], Izz Aldin Hamdan[2],
Keitaro Nishimura[3], Katia Sycara[3], Michael Lewis[4], Michael Lee[2],
and Morgan Borders[5]

[1] Air Force Research Laboratory, Wright-Patterson AFB, OH 45433, USA
august.capiola.1@us.af.mil
[2] General Dynamics Information Technology, Dayton, OH 45431, USA
[3] Carnegie Mellon University, Pittsburgh, PA 15213, USA
[4] University of Pittsburgh, Pittsburgh, PA 15260, USA
[5] Wright State University, Dayton, OH 45435, USA

Abstract. Human-swarm interaction (HSwI) research investigates interactions between human operators and robotic swarms. Swarms comprise assets, which operate as a unified group to complete goals like target foraging and shape configuration for asset movement optimization. Though the algorithmic specifications of swarm operations make them robust to individual asset loss, it is unknown how viewing asset degradations affects operator trust towards swarms. To investigate this relationship, modifications to an extant simulator of swarm foraging behaviors were implemented to portray functional asset degradation. Participants viewed recordings of swarms foraging, each comprising a randomized percentage of asset degradation. After each recording, participants rated their intentions to rely on the swarms in a target foraging task. Results showed an effect of differential asset loss on participants' intentions to rely on swarms. Post hoc analyses showed that participants had greater intentions to rely on swarms in a future target foraging task when 5% and 15% of assets were degraded compared to 20% and 50%. Limitations and ideas for future research on trust in HSwI during target foraging tasks are discussed in detail.

Keywords: Trust · Swarms · Asset degradation

1 Introduction

Swarms comprise robots operating autonomously via local control laws based on robot location and environmental characteristics [1]. During foraging tasks, swarms navigate through an unknown environment to find targets. This behavior could be advantageous for mission effectiveness during searches in uncertain environments where a human operator lacks sufficient knowledge to plan specific route plans. Examples of such contexts include disaster response and search and rescue missions when the human

Distribution A. Approved for public release; distribution unlimited. 88ABW-2020-0330; Cleared 31 JAN 2020.

J. Y. C. Chen and G. Fragomeni (Eds.): HCII 2020, LNCS 12190, pp. 537–549, 2020.
https://doi.org/10.1007/978-3-030-49695-1_36

operator lacks either sufficient knowledge of the target domain to adequately plan or lacks the time to plan effectively. That is, assets which compose swarms move as a whole to find targets based on nearest-neighbor algorithms as opposed to top-down route plans. However, given the opaque nature of swarm algorithms, swarm performance is not easily perceived or understood by human operators [2]. Further, if assets composing the swarm were to degrade and affect foraging behaviors, it is unclear how this would affect human trust towards swarms.

As humans may be unable to monitor and/or verify swarm performance, proper levels of trust towards swarms is critically important for human-swarm interaction (HSwI), especially when the agents behave unexpectedly [3]. Further, the use of swarms in contested environments will most certainly be met with countermeasures by adversaries which will impact some, or all, of the individual vehicles as well as potentially impacting the overall control algorithms governing the swarm. The ability of the swarm to obtain some objective goal-state may be robust to the loss of some assets [4], yet the observable loss of assets may impact operator beliefs regarding the swarm's overall effectiveness. Thus, studies are needed to identify and understand degradation thresholds which may impact operators' trust towards the swarm. If human operators lose trust of an otherwise viable swarm, they may abort a mission reducing mission effectiveness.

The present research investigated the effects of asset degradations within robotic swarms on human operator trust towards those swarms. Specifically, we investigated whether increasing the number of assets which degrade in a swarm had a practical effect on operator intentions to rely on the swarm in a target foraging task.

1.1 Asset Degradations

Swarms operate via algorithms which allow the population of assets to move throughout an environment [1]. Swarms leverage group emergent behaviors based on local interactions to attain goals, and individual assets are presumed to be relatively incapable of achieving goals on their own. However, as swarms operate via local control laws, degraded assets can affect their nearest neighbors. Put another way: assets which deviate from a swarm's flocking pattern (in the context of a foraging task) can pull other assets away from their ongoing trajectory. This could lead to only minor swarm flocking alterations that can easily be restored (see Fig. 1). However, this could also severely hinder functionality of the swarm and cause assets to go askew without the ability to return to the collective swarm (see Fig. 2). In both cases, degraded assets may drag some functional assets away from the majority of the swarm for a finite period of time. In extreme cases, assets may become totally ostracized from the swarm and remain disconnected from the larger swarm.

Each of these examples demonstrates that asset degradation can be nearly nominal or detrimental to the swarm. However, what is not clear is how this affects operator trust in these swarms, as the features of the swarm may manifest in observable characteristics that could sway operator trust. Said another way: though swarm performance (i.e., foraging efficiency) may or may not be hindered, there is a dearth of research on how operators perceive swarms foraging, let alone how degradations affect trust towards swarms. As trustworthiness perceptions and trust towards automation are antecedents towards reliance behaviors [5], it becomes critically important to understand what perceptions and intentions precede behavioral engagement for operators monitoring swarm foraging behaviors.

1.2 Trust and HSwI

Humans do not easily understand swarm performance [2]. Humans tend to judge swarm behaviors not by parameters most relevant for performance (e.g., underlying algorithm functionality) but instead by features such as their overall shape outline or convex haul [6], suggesting the importance of visual swarm features as an influence on operator attitudes. Seeing one or more rouge "degraded" assets may or may not disrupt the swarm's overall performance, but it is not clear whether these deviations affect human trust in swarms. In fact, the local control laws governing swarm behavior may create an ideal situation for the application of human trust evaluations consistent with System-Wide Trust Theory. System-Wide Trust theory suggests that humans will treat all components of a system as a whole system, such that degradations to one facet of the system will pervade into beliefs of the other system components [7, 8]. For instance, Geels and colleagues [7] investigated how one fallible gauge affects the perceived reliability of three other infallible gauges. Participants monitored a system comprising four gauges, one with fallible reliability (70% reliable) and three with infallible reliability (100% reliable). The results demonstrated that participants' perceived those infallible gauges as less than optimal due to the former system "pulling down" the perceived reliability of the latter three. Put simply: the 70% gauge led people to perceive the 100% systems as less reliable, showing evidence that people judge systems as a whole rather than by their components. In the current research on HSwI, asset degradation within a swarm may negatively impact one's beliefs of the overall swarm as a whole, regardless of the actual swarm performance.

Some research shows that operators may be able to time their input affecting swarm behavior leading to better performance in a shape configuration task [9]. That is, operators were able to approximate when they could offer input for a swarm to converge into a specific shape, thus demonstrating an observation termed neglect benevolence, colloquially waiting "not too little, not too long" to offer an input [4, 9]. Though past research has shown operators may learn to understand the subtleties of swarm behavior leading to optimum performance in a shape configuration task, it is not clear if this is the case in foraging tasks. Moreover, it is unknown how asset degradation—which may or may not affect swarm performance—impacts human trust in HSwI. Trust has implications for HSwI because improper human input during foraging [4] and shape configuration [9] tasks can actually impede objective swarm performance. That is, people may improperly calibrate their trust towards swarms and thus interfere with inputs to swarms when it is not optimal to do so. To circumvent this tendency and instead leverage optimal operator delay in inputs—or neglect benevolence [4]—researchers have investigated how humans might learn to recognize when to interfere with swarm behavior [9]. However, pending an operator may be unable to evaluate precisely how a swarm is performing, trust towards swarms will become critically important, particularly when anomalies such as asset degradations occur.

1.3   The Present Research

The present research investigated whether human trust in swarms is affected by asset degradation in a simulated swarm foraging task. Implications for this research concern display considerations and design strategies to leverage appropriate trust in human-swarm interactions. Based on the findings from System-Wide Trust Theory [7], as well as general assumptions from the trust in automation literature [5, 10], we hypothesize that:

> H_1: There is a negative relationship between percentage of asset degradations and operators' trust towards the swarms those assets compose.

To glean a better understanding of participants' trust towards swarms in the foraging task comprising a novel manipulation, we conducted a post hoc data inspection of the qualitative data comprising participants' free responses about why they would or would not trust the swarm.

2   Method

2.1   Design

The study was a within-subjects design. Participants viewed pre-recorded swarm foraging behavior in a simulator across six trials. For each trial, the swarms' foraging behaviors were visualized with a variety of asset degradations beginning 1-min into a 3-min foraging task. The swarms demonstrated 5, 10, 15, 20, 25, and 50% of assets composing the swarm were degraded per trial. Thus, each participant viewed six randomized trials in total, each containing unique levels of asset degradations. After each trial, participants answered self-reported measures of their intentions to rely on the swarm in a target foraging task and explained their assessments.

The present research is a first-step in exploring the effects of swarm asset degradation on human trust in HSwI. No operator (human) inputs were recorded, as humans were not given the option to augment the swarm's behaviors during foraging. Participants were only to view swarm behaviors across several trials of unique degradations and rate their intentions to rely on that swarm.

2.2   Simulator

The simulator [4] was created in Microsoft Visual Studio 2017. Parameters for swarm manipulations (i.e., percent of degradations, number of targets, no-fly zone locations) were specified in a text file. For all conditions, the swarm comprised 256 assets, with a simulated terrain landscape sized at 500 meters. Swarm assets are initially displayed in white. The swarm began foraging in the center of the digital landscape, with an obfuscated display. As the swarm searched for targets, the obfuscated area is reduced, revealing no-fly zones and targets. No-fly zones are depicted in red on the landscape (see Figs. 1 and 2). Non-degraded assets are incapable of penetrating these regions; however, degraded assets can pass through those regions—signaling a state consistent with a lost connection to the swarm's control laws. When a target is in the vicinity of the swarm, it is partially identified (visible to the swarm) and displayed as a purple square object. Once the target is acquired by the swarm, it is displayed in green. At 1-min into each recording, a set proportion of assets turned red. Those red assets then continued on their specified orientation and trajectory until they would "fly" off of the landscape. Each simulation was recorded using Xbox Game Bar, which is built into Windows 10.

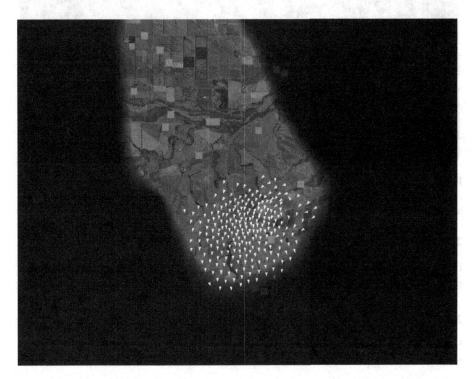

Fig. 1. Example of minimal asset degradation in a swarm. Red assets are degraded, while white are functional. Green blocks are acquired targets, while purple are not yet acquired. Red sections are no-fly zones. Visually occluded areas are undiscovered. (Color figure online)

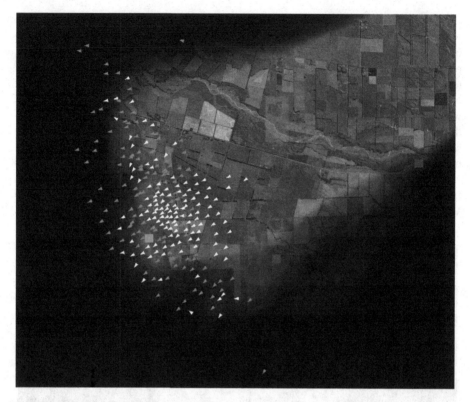

Fig. 2. Example of major asset degradation in a swarm. Red assets are degraded, while white are functional. Green blocks are acquired targets, while purple are not yet acquired. Red sections are no-fly zones. Visually occluded areas are undiscovered. (Color figure online)

2.3 Participants

Forty-seven participants (23 female), aged 18–41 years ($M = 23$) participated in the present study for $10/30 min.

2.4 Independent and Dependent Variables

Several self-report measures at baseline and between trials were assessed in this study. However, for the present research, we focus only on those variables reported below.

Manipulations. The key manipulation in the present research was percentage of assets degraded per trial. Specifically, in six trials, swarm comprised assets degraded by 5, 10, 15, 20, 25, and 50% 1-min into each three-minute trial. Importantly, only one degradation manipulation occurred per trial. The order of degradations was randomized per participant, such that a true within-subjects repeated-measures design could be maintained.

Reliance Intentions. Trust was assessed with a subset of items from the 10-item Reliance Intentions Scale [11]. Participants were asked four questions regarding their intentions to rely on the swarm in a future target foraging task (i.e., "I would rely on the swarm in a future target foraging task without hesitation," "I think using the swarm will lead to positive outcomes," "I would feel comfortable relying on the swarm in a target foraging task in the future," and "If I were facing a very hard target foraging task in the future, I would want to have this swarm with me") and to rate their responses on a 5-point scale (1 = Strongly Disagree to 5 = Strongly Agree). Reliability for the Reliance Intentions scale at each time point can be found in Table 1. In addition to assessing reliance intentions, participants were asked to explain why they would be willing to trust the swarm in a future target foraging task, even if they could not monitor that swarm's actions. The open ended response was used for post-hoc qualitative data assessment.

Table 1. Mean (*SD*) reliance intentions (RI) and scale reliability at each degradation trial (*N* = 47).

	5% degraded assets	10% degraded assets	15% degraded assets	20% degraded assets	25% degraded assets	50% degraded assets
Mean (*SD*)	3.57 (0.96)	3.34 (0.88)	3.55 (0.70)	3.1 (0.93)	3.26 (0.67)	3.11 (0.81)
RI α	.94	.86	.84	.90	.80	.79

2.5 Design Control

In each trial, the cause for asset degradation was explained as the possibility that swarms will "encounter unexpected countermeasures, and it is unknown how many assets will be affected by such occurrences." There were 50 targets in each condition (2 with set locations; 48 were randomly placed per trial); no-fly zones were identical per trial in terms of size and location to avoid confounding environment difficulty. The swarm originated in the center of the landscape in each trial.

2.6 Procedure

Participants were greeted and ushered into the laboratory. There, they reviewed an informed consent document. Upon consenting to participate, participants completed a demographic questionnaire. Participants then read through a training slideshow to give them information on what robotic swarms are and their purpose for target foraging tasks, followed by a three-minute sample video of swarms foraging for targets. This sample video did not contain an obfuscated display or no-fly zones, nor did any proportion of the swarm degrade. After the training was complete, participants viewed six videos of swarms foraging for targets, each with a different percentage of degradations per trial. Each trial was interpolated with self-report measures. After the sixth and final trial, participants' questions were answered and they received remuneration for their participation.

3 Results

3.1 Test of a Priori Hypotheses

The mean *(SD)* responses and scale reliabilities for reliance intentions at each degradation can be found in Table 1. As all participants received each level of the degradation manipulation in a randomized order, repeated-measures ANOVAs were conducted using the "afex" package [12] in the R programming language [13]. For reliance intentions the data failed to meet the assumptions of sphericity based on Mauchley's W test of sphericity, and thus was corrected with the Greenhouse-Geisser correction (note the *df*s reported). We found evidence that the proportion of asset degradation had an impact on participants' intentions to rely on swarms, $F(3.66, 164.75) = 3.77$, $p < .01$. A trend can be seen such that greater degradations led to a reduced intention to rely on swarms in subsequent foraging tasks (see Fig. 3). A Tukey's honestly significant difference (HSD) post hoc test showed that this difference resided between the 5% ($M = 3.57$, $SE = .16$) degradation and the 20% ($M = 3.1$, $SE = .16$), $t(225) = 3.14$, $p = .023$, and 50% degradations ($M = 3.11$, $SE = .16$), $t(225) = 2.89$, $p = .048$. In addition, there was a significant difference between the 15% degradation ($M = 3.55$, $SE = .16$) and the 20%, $t(225) = 3.14$, $p = .023$, and 50% degradations $t(225) = 2.89$, $p = .048$. Post hoc assessments of the open-ended qualitative reports were interpreted and will be reported next. Thus, we have found some evidence that trust evaluations in this HSwI context were affected by

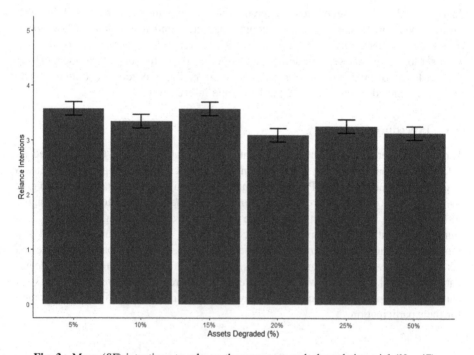

Fig. 3. Mean *(SE)* intentions to rely on the swarm at each degradation trial ($N = 47$).

asset degradations, and the pattern of results surrounding the reliance intentions were consistent with System-Wide Trust Theory [7]. That is, participants reported they would rely less on swarms which had 20% or 50% of their assets degraded compared to 5% and 15%.

3.2 Post-hoc Qualitative Data Inspection

Qualitative data from participants showed that although participants did recognize that different proportions of assets were indeed degrading across trials, participants may have deferred to the number of targets the swarms detected to inform their trust in the swarm. For example, in the 50% degradation condition, one participant wrote "Even though [the] majority of them turned red and the swarm got split up a little, they were still able to come back together and find targets." Though this condition comprised the greatest number of degradations, the participant still considered the swarm collecting targets successfully in their rating of trust. In comparison, in the 5% degradation condition, a participant wrote "Even though they lost only a few red ones, the white ones couldn't seem to figure out how to switch directions. They only found one target." Another participant commented in the 5% degradation condition "…still…unclear about its talent to target foraging as there are not many targets shown to the swarm."

Harkening to research on non-performance aspects such as shape and convex haul influencing trust in HSwI [6], one participant wrote "Unlike the previous swarms, this one as a whole moved in a way that allowed each unit to stay together. In the beginning when presented with multiple no fly zones, the swarm accounted for each and made adjustments to its heading and velocity to allow the units who would be stuck to join back up. When units went red it also accounted for their velocity and heading and continued to fly as if they were still part of the swarm even if they were not." This comment was made in the 20% degradation condition and shows that participants are at least considering some of the non-performance aspects relevant to trust in HSwI found in past research [6].

Other participants mentioned that because the swarm is not completely accurate, they would always require monitoring. For example, one participant wrote in several trials "Not 100% accurate and so will require monitoring." A participant wrote "Monitoring the swarm is essential to make sure nothing goes wrong" in the 50% degradation condition, while another participant wrote "…can't trust completely if assets degrade" in the 20% condition. These comments may have implications for considering participants automation schemas—particularly their "all or none" thinking —in HSwI [14]. Still, other participants noted that there is a balance between targets acquired versus degradations withstood. One statement from a participant in the 50% degradation trial wrote "Many assets…became degraded but many [targets] were identified." Finally, other participants wanted more information on the swarm. Participants in the 25% degradation condition wrote "I don't understand the cause of the degradation" and "If I know more information about the red/degraded swarm members and potential consequences my answer may change" referring to their trust assessments.

These qualitative remarks suggest that participants did consider how many targets the swarms collected as well as the number of degradations the swarm encountered. This suggests that participants weigh meaningful performance information (i.e., how many targets are found in a foraging task) as well as surface-level characteristics like overall shape outline, which could challenge past research [6]. The contextual constraints of this task differ from extant research, such that assets were degraded randomly across trials in the present research. Future research is needed to test these post-hoc suggestions with *a priori* hypotheses and experimental manipulations.

4 Discussion

The present research investigated the effects of swarm asset degradation on operator trust towards the swarms. Specifically, the proportion of assets in a swarm were degraded across randomly assigned trials, which participants viewed and then rated on a theoretically relevant self-report scale. The overarching findings show that as swarms lost different proportions of assets, reliance intentions did vary based on those differing degradations. With respect to the extant theories concerning trust towards systems, we did find some evidence that human trust evaluations were consistent with System-Wide Trust Theory. As System-Wide Trust Theory suggests that humans treat all components of a system as a whole system such that degradations to one facet of the system will pervade into beliefs of the other system components [7, 8], we expected reliance intentions to degrade when the swarm lost more assets. We did find this to be the case, such that participants had greater intentions to rely on the swarms in future target foraging tasks when they were degraded by 5% or 15% compared to 20% or 50%.

In HSwI, participants are often unable to understand exactly how and why the swarm operates as it does [2]. However, based on our qualitative data assessment, participants did seem to prioritize the target acquisition as an important aspect for whether or not they would trust the swarm. However, future research must validate our post hoc suggestions based on the qualitative data. To our knowledge, this pilot experiment was the first of its kind to manipulate the proportion of asset degradations to explore the effect on operator perceptions and intentions. However, future work should implement several changes to the extant protocol to investigate the role of trust in HSwI further, and we outline those suggestions below.

Finally, there is an assumption that as swarms leverage group emergent behaviors based on local interactions, individual assets are relatively incapable of achieving goals on their own [1]. However, in this experiment, we found that this may not always be the case. Indeed, when degradation percentage increased, swarms did in fact find more targets in the 3-min window. Though this simulation and performance outcome may be rather specific in terms of context and goal-state, respectively, compared to operational scenarios swarms are envisioned to operate, future research on simulations and virtual environments should consider instances where manipulations to psychological constructs—in this case trust—can simultaneously affect another performance outcome in the stimuli—in this case the swarm foraging success. Likewise, we found evidence that in many cases participants did appear to understand swarm performance (i.e., find targets and maintain a cohesive convex hull). Extant research has shown that humans do not easily understand swarm performance [2], but some HSwI do afford people to learn how swarms behave [4, 9]. The present scenario was simplified, such that participants were trained on how performance is measured (e.g., targets found) prior to beginning the experimental session. Though less complex than Nagavalli et al.'s work on emergent neglect benevolence, our instructions may have increased the transparency of swarm performance. As such, future work on trust in HSwI may simply ensure participants do understand what they should be looking for in HSwI simulations to get a better understanding of the effects of experimental manipulations on outcomes of interest.

Trust has implications for HSwI. Improper human input during extant collaborative foraging [4] and shape configuration [9] tasks impede swarm performance. Researchers have investigated how humans might learn to recognize when to interfere with swarm behavior [9] to circumvent mistimed human inputs. The present work showed evidence that anomalies such as asset degradations do impact trust towards swarms, which extends the findings from System-Wide Trust Theory [7, 8] to a new context and has implications for future work on investigating trust in HSwI, particularly in efforts to uncover what emergent swarm features have an effect on neglect benevolence [9].

4.1 Limitations and Future Research

The present study is not without limitations. As mentioned above, participants were unable to offer inputs to redirect the swarm's trajectory. Past research has implemented the ability for operators to shift the trajectory of swarms in a shape orientation task [9]. Preliminary findings show that human operators may learn to strategize when offering an input to redirect the swarm is best for task-dependent performance (i.e., shifting from starting orientation to a different goal orientation). Future research is needed to investigate the association of operator input and trust towards the swarm. It is often surmised that offering input to an automated system which overrides its assumed trajectory is indicative of lowered trust [15]. Investigating the role of operator input on trust in swarms during a target foraging task is a promising step for HSwI researchers to uncover the role of trust and reliance in these interactions. As swarm technologies develop, humans and swarms may begin to transition from a user-automation context to a user-partner context (e.g., the distinction between an *automated* versus *autonomous* partner; [3]). As such, investigating psychological trust from users to swarms—and the effects of said trust onto task-based performance outcomes—will be a crucial area of interest in HSwI foraging tasks.

In addition, participants did not know the number of targets that the swarm could have collected per trial, only the number that they did collect. Knowing the possible targets the swarms could acquire may have made the swarm performance more salient for participants to perceive, leading to more informed perceptions. Transparency of data presentation has been shown to facilitate calibrated trust in human factors research [16]. Future research may investigate whether this increase in performance transparency has a similar effect on perceptions of swarm trustworthiness. Additionally, though it is shown in past research [2] that operators have difficulty interpreting swarm behavior, it would be interesting to have experts in engineering and/or robotics team with a swarm in a foraging task. Their expertise may influence their perceptions because they are more likely to be aware of what they can and cannot glean when making a trust assessment when viewing a swarm's behavior.

Finally, in each of the trials, swarms did perform differently. That is, swarms collected anywhere between 1 and 8 targets per trial. As the no-fly zones were not randomized per trial, swarms could have navigated to an area where they were disrupted more or less once the degradation took place, which would have a different impact on overall swarm asset loss and potentially target acquisition in the remainder of the trial. Future iterations may wish to systematically control for how many targets a swarm collected in order to investigate the effects of objective performance on operator trust. Participants commented in their self-report explanation that although the swarm did in fact display few degradations in the 5% trial, they still did not collect enough targets to be truly unmonitored. In fact, several said they preferred to monitor the swarm's actions regardless of the number of assets the swarm collected, even in the 5% trial. Also in the 5% trial, swarms only found one target, thus potentially confounding the degradation manipulation with poor performance (i.e., finding targets). It is possible that participants may have prioritized the target acquisition to inform their trust, but we cannot assume this to be the case. Moreover, the condition which comprises the greatest number of target acquisitions was in fact the 50% degradation trial, which only further strengthens the point that we ought to control this in subsequent iterations using these asset degradation manipulations. Future research will need to systematically control for these limitations and explore their effects on trust.

The trust process assumes that for trust to emerge, there must be some kind of perceptible vulnerability and risk inherent in the context [17]. Put simply: for trust to be relevant, something must be at stake. In the present experiment, the participants were told to view swarm behavior in six trials, and based on those recordings to rate their perceptions and intentions to rely on the swarms. However, in this task, the participants were not under any salient risk. That is, if the swarm lost more or less assets, it did not affect the participant. Moreover, participant remuneration was not affected by swarm performance, which may be critical for instilling task-based vulnerability. Using the novel manipulations from the present experiment, one way to determine whether participants vary in their perceptions of swarms degrading at different rates is to have the swarm performance affect the participant in some task-related way and allow participants to have some input onto the swarm's performance. A similar interpretation comes from the trust in automation literature, where choosing between varying levels of manual and autonomous control can be used to infer trust towards automation [18]. In this way, task risk becomes more salient and the actual ability to influence swarm behaviors keeps the participant engaged, such that the HSwI is more of a collaboration rather than a monitoring task.

4.2   Conclusion

The present research investigated the effects of percentage of swarm asset degradation on operator trust in HSwI. Findings from this study show a relationship between the proportion of assets degraded and operator trust towards the swarms and align with our hypotheses which leverage the System-Wide Theory of Trust [7, 8]. This research is a first step for exploring the effects of individual asset degradations on trust in HSwI, providing fodder for future research on trust in HSwI when humans have the ability to offer inputs to the swarms foraging behaviors, thus acting more so as a human-swarm team.

References

1. Kolling, A., Walker, P., Chakraborty, N., Sycara, K., Lewis, M.: Human interaction with robot swarms: a survey. IEEE Trans. Hum.-Mach. Syst. **46**(1), 9–26 (2015)
2. Nam, C., Walker, P., Lewis, M., Sycara, K.: Predicting trust in human control of swarms via inverse reinforcement learning. In: 2017 26th IEEE International Symposium on Robot and Human Interactive Communication (RO-MAN), pp. 528–533. IEEE, Torino (2017)
3. de Visser, E.J., Pak, R., Shaw, T.H.: From 'automation' to 'autonomy': the importance of trust repair in human–machine interaction. Ergonomics **61**(10), 1409–1427 (2018)
4. Walker, P., Nunnally, S., Lewis, M., Kolling, A., Chakraborty, N., Sycara, K.: Neglect benevolence in human control of swarms in the presence of latency. In: 2012 IEEE International Conference on Systems, Man, and Cybernetics (SMC), pp. 3009–3014. IEEE, Torino (2012)
5. Lee, J.D., See, K.A.: Trust in automation: designing for appropriate reliance. Hum. Factors **46**(1), 50–80 (2004)
6. Nam, C., Li, H., Li, S., Lewis, M., Sycara, K.: Trust of humans in supervisory control of swarm robots with varied levels of autonomy. In: 2018 IEEE International Conference on Systems, Man, and Cybernetics (SMC), pp. 825–830. IEEE, Torino (2018)
7. Geels, K., Rice, S., Schwark, J., Hunt, H., Sandry, J.: Applying the reliance-compliance model to system-wide trust theory in an aviation task. In 16th International Symposium on Aviation Psychology, pp. 215–220. Curran, New York (2011)
8. Keller, D., Rice, S.: System-wide versus component-specific trust using multiple aids. J. Gen. Psychol. **137**(1), 114–128 (2010)
9. Nagavalli, S., Chien, S.Y., Lewis, M., Chakraborty, N., Sycara, K.: Bounds of neglect benevolence in input timing for human interaction with robotic swarms. In: Proceedings of the Tenth Annual ACM/IEEE International Conference on Human-Robot Interaction, pp. 197–204. ACM, New York (2015)
10. Hoff, K.A., Bashir, M.: Trust in automation: integrating empirical evidence on factors that influence trust. Hum. Factors **57**(3), 407–434 (2015)
11. Lyons, J.B., Guznov, S.Y.: Individual differences in human–machine trust: a multi-study look at the perfect automation schema. Theor. Issues Ergon. Sci. **20**(4), 440–458 (2019)
12. Singmann, H., Bolker, B., Westfall, J., Aust, F.: afex: analysis of factorial experiments. R package version 0.13–145 (2015)
13. R Core Team R: A language and environment for statistical computing. R Foundation for Statistical Computing (2018). https://www.R-project.org/
14. Merritt, S.M., Unnerstall, J.L., Lee, D., Huber, K.: Measuring individual differences in the perfect automation schema. Hum. Factors **57**(5), 740–753 (2015)
15. Parasuraman, R., Riley, V.: Humans and automation: use, misuse, disuse, abuse. Hum. Factors **39**(2), 230–253 (1997)
16. Lyons, J.B., et al.: Shaping trust through transparent design: theoretical and experimental guidelines. In: Savage-Knepshield, P., Chen, J. (eds.) Advances in Human Factors in Robots and Unmanned Systems. AISC, vol. 499, pp. 127–136. Springer, Cham (2017). https://doi.org/10.1007/978-3-319-41959-6_11
17. Mayer, R.C., Davis, J.H., Schoorman, F.D.: An integrative model of organizational trust. Acad. Manag. Rev. **20**(3), 709–734 (1995)
18. Lee, J., Moray, N.: Trust, control strategies and allocation of function in human-machine systems. Ergonomics **35**(10), 1243–1270 (1992)

Visual Reference of Ambiguous Objects for Augmented Reality-Powered Human-Robot Communication in a Shared Workspace

Peng Gao, Brian Reily, Savannah Paul, and Hao Zhang[(⊠)]

Human-Centered Robotics Lab, Colorado School of Mines,
1500 Illinois Street, Golden, CO 80401, USA
{gaopeng,breily,savannahpaul,hzhang}@mines.edu

Abstract. In shared workspaces, teammates working with a common set of objects must be able to unambiguously reference individual objects in order to effectively collaborate. When teammates are autonomous robots, human teammates must be able to communicate their intended reference object without overtly interfering with their workflow. In human-robot interaction, the problem of visual reference is defined as identifying the specific object referred to by a human (e.g., through a pointing gesture recognized by an augmented reality device), and relating this object to the associated object in the robotic teammate's field of view, thereby identifying the intended object from a set of ambiguous objects. As human and robot teammates typically observe their shared workspace from differing perspectives, achieving visual reference of objects is a challenging yet crucial problem. In this paper, we present a novel approach to visual reference of ambiguous objects that introduces a graph matching-based approach which fuses visual and spatial information of the objects in a shared workspace through augmented reality-powered human-robot communication. Our approach represents the objects in a scene with a graph where edges encoding the spatial relationships among objects and attribute vectors describing each object's appearance associated with each node. Then, we formulate visual object reference for human-robot communication in a shared workspace as an optimization-based graph matching problem, which identifies the correspondence of nodes in graphs built from the human and robot teammates' observations. We conduct extensive experimental evaluation on two introduced datasets, showing that our approach is able to obtain accurate visual references of ambiguous objects and outperforms existing visual reference methods.

Keywords: Visual reference · Human-robot communication · Collaborative perception · Augmented reality · Graph matching

© Springer Nature Switzerland AG 2020
J. Y. C. Chen and G. Fragomeni (Eds.): HCII 2020, LNCS 12190, pp. 550–561, 2020.
https://doi.org/10.1007/978-3-030-49695-1_37

1   Introduction

Human-robot teaming and interaction in shared space has been recently attracting significant attention. In such scenarios, autonomous robots work alongside humans in shared workspaces and cooperate with them to complete collaborative tasks together. A critical capability required for human-robot teaming in shared workspaces is effective communication between robots and humans [1]. Recently, augmented reality (AR) has been proposed as a promising solution to improving human-robot communication, offering the revolutionary capability to visualize virtual information with the real world scene through the use of head-mounted displays or hand-held devices [2,3], in order to more intuitively deliver information to a human.

Visual reference of objects in a shared space is essential to enabling AR-powered human-robot communication. Visual reference in human-robot communication is defined as the problem of a robot correctly visually identifying a specific object within the robot's field of view that has been referred to by a human within their own field of view. Figure 1 illustrates a motivating example of visual reference for AR-powered human-robot communication in a shared workspace. A human teammate wears an AR headset and uses a pointing gesture recognized by the AR device to refer to one of the objects in the shared workspace that she wants the robot to pick up. Then, the robot must identify the specific object referred to by the human teammate within its own field of view, before taking an action to manipulate the object. Scenarios that require visual object references are common in many real-world applications, such as

Fig. 1. A motivating example of visual reference of ambiguous objects for AR-powered human-robot communication in a shared workspace. When the human teammate selects an object through a pointing gesture recognized by the AR headset, the robot teammate needs to identify the object referred to by the human within its own field of view, without being confused by other similar objects in the shared space.

assembling, manufacturing, and multi-robot multi-human teaming in field environments, in which many relevant objects exist in shared space.

Due to the importance of visual reference, many methods have been developed to address this problem of identifying a referenced object in multiple views. The first category consists of methods based on visual appearance similarity between objects, e.g., using matched key-points to track the same object in a video [4], utilizing the similarity between region-based global features to identify if two instances of objects are the same [5] or leveraging feature attributes for object re-identification [6]. The second category of existing methods employ a synchronization algorithm to identify the same objects in multiple views by enforcing a circle consistent constraint, e.g., formulating visual reference as a semi-definite problem [7], solving a relaxed convex problem to associate the same object over multiple views [8,9], or formulating this disambiguation as a top-rank eigenvector-decomposition problem [10,11]. The third category of methods to refer to the same object among multiple views consists of approaches based on spatial information among objects, e.g., formulating the visual reference problem as a linear assignment problem which can be solved by the Hungarian [12] or Sinkhorn algorithms [13], identifying a matching node between two graphs by solving the quadratic assignment problem (also known as pairwise graph matching) [14,15], and referring to the same point in multiple point clouds by employing iterative closest point techniques [16].

While these existing methods have obtained promising performance in subareas of visual reference, addressing the problem of disambiguation of object references in a real-world environment in a unified fashion (i.e., incorporating visual and spatial information) is still hard to solve due to two major challenges. The first major challenge for visual object reference is the ambiguity among the multiple objects in shared workspace. Humans and robots typically observe a shared workspace from different points of view. From one teammate's perspective, multiple objects can have a similar appearance (i.e., perceptual aliasing), which will cause the visual appearance and synchronization-based methods to fail, as they require the objects in multiple views to be unique. From different perspectives (e.g., both the robot's and human's), the same object can often exhibit a different visual appearance, such as objects that are different colors on various sides. Thus, using only visual appearance to identify correspondences among objects is insufficient to solve the visual reference problem. The second major challenge for visual object reference is the deformation in the spatial relationships among objects. The position of multiple objects can be obtained from a depth sensor (e.g., using an RGB-D camera). Due to the noise and resolution limit in depth measurement, the position of objects recovered from 2D image coordinates and depth values contain inaccuracies which will lead to deformation in the constructed spatial relationship of objects. Thus, relying solely on spatial relationships among objects is also insufficient to enable effective visual referencing.

In this paper, we propose a graph matching method for visual reference that integrates visual and spatial information describing the objects to identify the correspondence of objects between the robot's view and the human teammate's view. From the robot teammate's perspective, we represent multiple detected objects as a graph, where each node corresponds to a detected object, where edges between nodes describe the spatial distance between objects and an attribute vector associated with each node describes the object's visual appearance. We represent the human teammate's perspective with a similar graph. Thus, our graph representation integrates both visual and spatial information about the detected objects in both observations. Given these two graph representations generated from the robot's and human teammate's observation, we formulate visual reference as a graph matching problem, which uses constrained optimization to identify corresponding objects between two views based on the similarity of the visual and spatial information of the objects encoded in each graph.

The contributions of this research are twofold:

- We formulate visual reference as a graph matching problem, which integrates visual and spatial information of objects into a unified graph representation for correspondence identification between two views to improve representation expressiveness and reduce or remove the ambiguity inherent in visual reference.
- We develop a heuristic optimization algorithm to solve the proposed non-convex graph matching problem, which has no closed-form solution.

The remainder of the paper is organized as follows. In Sect. 2, we introduce the proposed graph matching approach to visual reference of ambiguous objects, including our problem formulation and optimization algorithm. In Sect. 3, we present our experimental results on multiple datasets. Finally, we conclude this work in Sect. 4.

2   The Proposed Approach

Notation. The matrices are denoted as boldface capital letters, e.g., $\mathbf{M} = \{\mathbf{M}_{i,j}\} \in \mathbb{R}^{n \times m}$ with $\mathbf{M}_{i,j}$ denoting the element in the i-th row and j-th coloumn of $\mathbf{M}$. Vectors are represented as boldface lowercase letters $\mathbf{v} \in \mathbb{R}^n$. In addition, $\mathbf{m} \in \mathbb{R}^{nm}$ is the vectorized form of a matrix $\mathbf{M} \in \mathbb{R}^{n \times m}$, which is a concatenation of each column in $\mathbf{M}$ into a vector.

2.1   Problem Formulation

The problem of visual reference is to identify the same objects in a shared workspace observed by a robot and a human teammate from their respective fields of view. In this work, we design a graph matching-based method to address visual reference.

Given an observation from by a robot or a human teammate, we represent it as a graph $\mathcal{G} = \{\mathcal{V}, \mathcal{F}, \mathcal{S}\}$. In graph $\mathcal{G}$, $\mathcal{V} = \{\mathbf{v}_1, \mathbf{v}_2, \ldots, \mathbf{v}_n\}$ denotes the node set, which represents the 3D central positions of the objects in the observation, where $\mathbf{v}_i = \{x, y, z\}$ denotes the 3D central position of the i-th object and n is the number of objects. The appearance set $\mathcal{F} = \{\mathbf{f}_1, \mathbf{f}_2, \ldots, \mathbf{f}_n\}$ denotes the set of visual appearance features of the objects, where $\mathbf{f}_i$ is a feature vector describing the appearance of the i-th object located at $\mathbf{v}_i$. $\mathcal{S} = \{s_{i,j}, i, j = 1, 2, \ldots, n, i \neq j\}$ denotes the set of spatial relationships among the objects, where $s_{i,j}$ denotes the distance between the i-th object located at $\mathbf{v}_i$ and the j-th object located at $\mathbf{v}_j$.

In visual reference, the objects observed by a robot and a human teammate in their own fields of view can be respectively represented as two graphs $\mathcal{G} = \{\mathcal{V}, \mathcal{F}, \mathcal{S}\}$ and $\mathcal{G}' = \{\mathcal{V}', \mathcal{F}', \mathcal{S}'\}$. Given the graph representations, one way to identify the correspondences of objects in two views is based on visual similarities of objects, which is denoted as $\mathbf{a} = \{\mathbf{a}_{i,i'}\} \in \mathbb{R}^{nn'}$, where $\mathbf{a}_{i,i'}$ represents the similarity between the feature vectors $\mathbf{f}_i \in \mathcal{F}$ of the i the object in graph $\mathcal{G}$ and $\mathbf{f}'_i \in \mathcal{F}'$ of the i' object in graph $\mathcal{G}'$, which can be computed using a dot product of two feature vectors:

$$\mathbf{a}_{i,i'} = \frac{\mathbf{f}_i \cdot \mathbf{f}'_i}{\|\mathbf{f}_i\|\|\mathbf{f}'_i\|} \tag{1}$$

In order to obtain the correspondence of objects in two different graphs $\mathcal{G}$ and $\mathcal{G}'$ given this appearance similarity, a common way is to solve the following linear assignment problem,

$$\max_{\mathbf{X}} \mathbf{a}^\top \mathbf{x}$$
$$\text{s.t.} \quad \mathbf{X}\mathbf{1}_{n' \times 1} \leq \mathbf{1}_{n \times 1}, \mathbf{X}^\top \mathbf{1}_{n \times 1} \leq \mathbf{1}_{n' \times 1} \tag{2}$$

where $\mathbf{x} = \{\mathbf{x}_{ii'}\} \in \{0, 1\}^{nn'}$ denotes the vectorized correspondence matrix $\mathbf{X} \in \{0, 1\}^{n \times n'}$, with $\mathbf{X}_{ii'} = 1$ denoting that the i-th node in $\mathcal{V}$ and the i'-th node in $\mathcal{V}'$ are matched, and $\mathbf{1}$ is a vector with all elements equal to 1. In general, the problem in Eq. (2) can be solved by the Hungarian [12] or Sinkhorn algorithms [13]. The constraints in Eq. (2) are designed to enforce the one-to-one correspondence: each row or column in $\mathbf{X}$ can at most have one element equal to 1, and all others are equal to 0.

However, this visual-based matching can not address the ambiguity in object appearance, e.g., two different objects may look similar or the same object observed from different perspectives may look different. Another way to refer the same object in different views is based upon spatial relationships among objects. The distance-based spatial similarity can be denoted as $\mathbf{S} = \{\mathbf{S}_{ii',jj'}\} \in \mathbb{R}^{nn' \times nn'}$, where $\mathbf{S}_{ii',jj'}$ represents the similarity of the distance $s_{i,j} \in \mathcal{S}$ and the distance $s'_{i',j'} \in \mathcal{S}'$, which can be computed by:

$$\mathbf{S}_{ii',jj'} = \exp\left(-\frac{1}{\beta}(s_{i,j} - s'_{i',j'})^2\right) \tag{3}$$

This similarity is computed using the nonlinear exponential function, with β as a hyperparameter, to transfer any non-negative input to an output value between 0 and 1. Then, visual reference can be formulated as the quadratic assignment problem as follows,

---

Algorithm 1: The proposed algorithm to solve the formulated non-convex optimization problem in Eq. (5).

Input : $\mathbf{S} \in \mathbb{R}^{nn' \times nn'}$ and $\mathbf{a} \in \mathbb{R}^{nn'}$
Output: $\mathbf{X} = \in \{0,1\}^{n \times n'}$

1: Initialize the correspondence matrix $\mathbf{X}$
2: Compute $\mathbf{P}$ and $\mathbf{q}$ according to Eq. (6)
3: **while** *not converge* **do**
4:     Compute the jump vector $\mathbf{z}$ by Eq. (8)
5:     Normalize $\mathbf{z}$ using bistochastic normalization
6:     Update $\mathbf{X}$ with the reweighted jump vector by Eq. (9)
7: **end**
8: Discretize $\mathbf{X}$ using the Hungarian algorithm
9: **return** $\mathbf{X}$

$$\max_{\mathbf{X}} \mathbf{x}^\top \mathbf{S} \mathbf{x}$$
$$\text{s.t.} \quad \mathbf{X} \mathbf{1}_{n' \times 1} \leq \mathbf{1}_{n \times 1}, \mathbf{X}^\top \mathbf{1}_{n \times 1} \leq \mathbf{1}_{n' \times 1} \tag{4}$$

Generally, Eq. (4) is NP-hard and can be solved by existing heuristic algorithms [14]. Due to noise in measurement or variations in the sensing environment, the position of objects obtained by sensors is inaccurate, which will lead to deformation in spatial relationships (e.g., distance) among objects. Thus, only using spatial information for visual reference is insufficient.

In this paper, in order to accurately reference the same object in two different views despite the ambiguity in the appearance of objects and the deformation in the position of objects, we formulate visual reference as a graph matching problem defined in an optimization framework, which integrates both the visual and spatial information of objects for visual reference. The final correspondences of the same objects in different views can be obtained by solving the following optimization problem:

$$\max_{\mathbf{X}} \lambda_1 \mathbf{a}^\top \mathbf{x} + \lambda_2 \mathbf{x}^\top \mathbf{S} \mathbf{x}$$
$$\text{s.t.} \quad \mathbf{X} \mathbf{1}_{n' \times 1} \leq \mathbf{1}_{n \times 1}, \mathbf{X}^\top \mathbf{1}_{n \times 1} \leq \mathbf{1}_{n' \times 1} \tag{5}$$

The first term in Eq. (5) represents the accumulated similarity between visual appearances of the objects in the two graphs, which sums all visual appearance similarities $\mathbf{a}_{i,i'}$ of the feature vectors $\mathbf{f}_i \in \mathcal{F}$ and $\mathbf{f}'_i \in \mathcal{F}'$. The second term denotes the accumulated spatial similarities of the objects in two graphs, which sums all distance similarities $\mathbf{S}_{ii',jj'}$ of two edges $s_{i,j} \in \mathcal{S}$ and $s'_{i',j'} \in \mathcal{S}'$. $\lambda_1 \geq 0$ and $\lambda_2 \geq 0$ are hyperparameters to control the importance of the visual and spatial similarities, which satisfy $\lambda_1 + \lambda_2 = 1$.

2.2 Optimization Algorithm

Since our proposed graph matching formulation is a non-convex optimization problem, which has no closed-form solution, we design an optimization algorithm based on random walks with the reweighted jump technique [14] to solve the proposed optimization problem in Eq. (5). The proposed optimization algorithm is presented in Algorithm 1.

In Step 2, we first convert the similarity matrix in Eq. (5) to a stochastic form $\mathbf{P} \in \mathbb{R}^{nn' \times nn'}$ and $\mathbf{q} \in \mathbb{R}^{nn'}$ as follows:

$$\mathbf{P} = \mathbf{S}/ \max_{i} \sum_{j} \mathbf{S}_{i,j}$$

$$\mathbf{q} = \mathbf{a}/ \max_{i} \mathbf{a}_i \tag{6}$$

By dividing by the maximum elements, Eq. (6) can normalize the original matrix without losing relative similarity. Then the original formulation in Eq. (5) is converted to the following form:

$$\max_{\mathbf{X}} \lambda_1 \mathbf{q}^\top \mathbf{x} + \lambda_2 \mathbf{x}^\top \mathbf{P} \mathbf{x}$$

$$\text{s.t.} \quad \mathbf{X} \mathbf{1}_{n' \times 1} \leq \mathbf{1}_{n \times 1}, \mathbf{X}^\top \mathbf{1}_{n \times 1} \leq \mathbf{1}_{n' \times 1} \tag{7}$$

Then in Step 4, we define the reweighting jump vector as $\mathbf{z} \in \mathbb{R}^{nn'}$ to jump out of local optima, which is inspired by the PageRank algorithm [14].

$$\mathbf{z}^r = \exp\left(\mathbf{x}^r \circ \mathbf{a}/ \max\left(\mathbf{x}^r \circ \mathbf{a}\right)\right) \tag{8}$$

where $\circ$ denotes the entry-wise product and r denotes the r–th iteration. The node appearance similarity $\mathbf{a}$ is introduced to guide the jump toward a direction such that similar objects can be better matched.

In Step 5, we employ bistochastic normalization to normalize each row and column in $\mathbf{z}$ to enforce the one-to-one correspondence.

In Step 6, to facilitate $\mathbf{X}$ to jump out of local optima, $\mathbf{X}$ is updated by:

$$\mathbf{x}^{r+1} = \alpha\left(\mathbf{q} + \mathbf{x}^{r\top} \mathbf{P}\right) + (1 - \alpha)\mathbf{z}^r \tag{9}$$

where α is a hyper-parameter that controls the update rate, and $\alpha = 0.3$ in the following experiments.

In Step 8 after convergence, we discretize the matrix $\mathbf{X} \in \mathbb{R}^{n \times n'}$ into binary form by using the Hungarian algorithm. The complexity of the proposed Algorithm 1 is dominated by matrix $\mathbf{S}$, which is $O((nn')^2)$.

3   Experiment

3.1   Experimental Setup

In order to evaluate our proposed visual reference method in AR-powered human-robot communication, we collected two datasets: (1) the multi-view object identification dataset (MOI); and (2) the multi-robot coordination dataset (MRC), seen illustrated in Fig. 2. In each dataset, 30 data instances are used to

(a) MOI   (b) MRC

Fig. 2. Illustrations of MOI and MRC datasets.

evaluate our approach. Each data instance contains a pair of RGB-D observations observed by 3D structured-light cameras from two different perspectives. Both of the datasets include the color and HOG features of objects to describe the appearance of objects, 3D position of objects recovered from RGB-D observations and the ground truth of the correspondences of the objects in two perspectives, which are labeled manually in MOI or detected from the QR code in MRC.

We evaluated our method on the MOI and MRC datasets by comparing with three existing methods: (1) **SM** [15], a spatial-based matching method; (2) **RRWM** [14], which uses the distance relationships of objects to identify the correspondence of objects; and (3) **ATT** [6], which uses attribute features to describe object for re-identification. We use each author's original MATLAB code in our comparison. Our visual-spatial graph matching method is also implemented in MATLAB and sets $\lambda_1 = 0.5$ and $\lambda_2 = 0.5$ for evaluation.

We adopt *accuracy, precision* and *recall* as metrics to evaluate the performance of visual reference. From the perspective of graph matching [14], given the visual correspondences of the objects, *accuracy* is defined as the number of correct correspondences over the total number of the ground truth of object correspondence. From the perspective of object retrieval [17], *precision* is defined as the fraction of correctly retrieved object correspondences over all retrieved objects, and *recall* is defined as the ratio of retrieved correct correspondences over all of the ground truth of correspondences.

Table 1. Quantitative experimental results on the MOI and MRC datasets.

Method	MOI			MRC		
	Accuracy	Precision	Recall	Accuracy	Precision	Recall
SM [15]	0.2646	0.2792	0.1874	0.2861	0.2142	0.1926
RRWM [14]	0.2917	0.3440	0.2207	0.3053	0.3262	0.1378
ATT [6]	0.5669	0.6455	0.5579	0.6289	0.6476	0.5211
Ours	**0.8496**	**0.8579**	**0.8056**	**0.8590**	**0.7926**	**0.8434**

3.2   Results on the MOI Dataset

We first evaluate our proposed method on the multi-view object identification dataset. In MOI, the objects are observed from the overhead perspective, in which most classes of the objects have a similar appearance (e.g., multiple apples look similar visually) and the positions of object are inaccurate due to sensing error from the camera angle. Since all the objects are close to each other, the inaccurate positions of object will lead to large deformations in the distance relationships between objects.

The qualitative results are presented in Fig. 3. We can observe that ATT, using only visual information about the objects for visual reference, can only distinguish the objects in different classes that have unique appearances. Due to the existence of ambiguity in objects' appearance, apples in two perspectives are identified incorrectly. The results obtained from the spatial-based method RRWM indicate that using spatial information is robust to the ambiguity in objects' appearance. However, since there exists deformation in the spatial relationships of objects, only using spatial information is still insufficient. Our proposed method integrating both visual and spatial information of objects for visual reference can correctly identify the correspondences of objects in two perspectives and obtain the best performance.

The qualitative results for visual reference in MOI are reported in Table 1. The results indicate that only using spatial-based features (SM and RRWM) causes poor performance for visual reference due to the deformation in the distances between pairs of objects. The visual-based method (ATT) obtains an improved performance but is still worse than our approach due to ambiguity in visual appearance of objects. Our approach achieved the best performance,

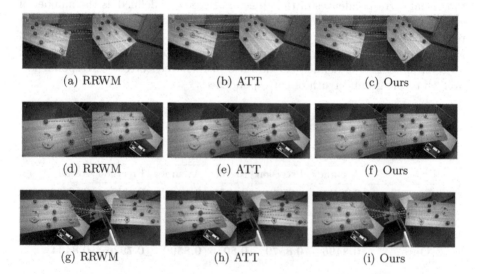

Fig. 3. Qualitative experimental results on the MOI dataset with comparison of our proposed method with RRWM and ATT. Green lines denote correct correspondences and red lines denote incorrect correspondences. [Best viewed in color.]

which can address the challenges caused by the ambiguity in visual appearance and deformation in spatial relationships of objects.

3.3   Results on the MRC Dataset

We also evaluate our approach on the multi-robot coordination dataset, which is more challenging compared to the MOI dataset. Most object instances in MRC have an identical appearance, which indicates larger ambiguity in objects' appearance. In addition, the object instances are observed far away from the sensing camera, which leads to larger deformations in objects' spatial relationships. Thus, MRC is a very challenging dataset for the evaluation of visual reference.

To visualize object correspondences, the qualitative experimental results of visual reference for MRC are presented in Fig. 4. Results obtained by the other two best performing methods (RRWM and ATT) are also compared in the figure. We can see that RRWM cannot well identify correspondence of the objects. ATT obtains improved performance, in which unique objects can be correctly identified, but ATT again failed for the objects with identical appearance. As with the MOI dataset, our graph matching approach obtains the best results on object correspondence identification for visual reference.

The quantitative results on MRC dataset are also presented in Table 1. We observe that graph matching methods (SM and RRWM) perform badly, due to the large deformation existed in the spatial relationships of objects. ATT achieves better performance due to the existence of the objects with unique appearance.

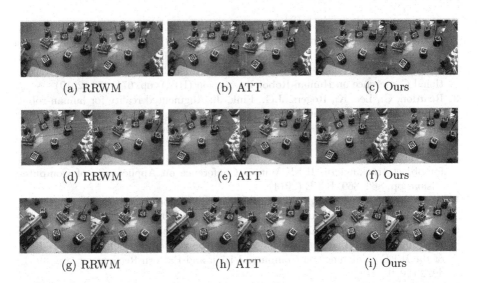

(a) RRWM   (b) ATT   (c) Ours

(d) RRWM   (e) ATT   (f) Ours

(g) RRWM   (h) ATT   (i) Ours

Fig. 4. Qualitative experimental results on the MRC dataset with comparison of our proposed method with RRWM and ATT. Green lines denote correct correspondences and red lines denote incorrect correspondences. [Best viewed in color.]

Our approach obtains the best performance on MRC, and outperforms ATT, due to our approach's ability to integrate visual and spatial information about objects.

4   Conclusion

In this paper, we present an approach to enable visual reference of ambiguous objects in a workspace shared between human and robot teammates utilizing augmented reality-powered human-robot communication. We introduce a novel graph matching-based approach that is able to fuse visual and spatial information describing the objects as seen from each teammate's perspective, where these objects as represented with graph edges describing spatial structure and attribute vectors describing visual appearances. We formulate our approach as a constrained optimization problem that identifies the correspondences of nodes in graphs built from both the human and robot's observations. Through extensive evaluation on two datasets, we show that our approach provides accurate visual reference of ambiguous objects from human and robot perspectives, and is able to outperform existing state-of-the-art visual reference methods.

Acknowledgments. This work was partially supported by ARL W911NF-17-2-0181, ARO W911NF-17-1-0447, USAFA FA7000-18-2-0016, DOE DE-FE0031650, IIS-1849348, and NSF CNS-1823245.

References

1. Reardon, C., Zhang, H., Fink, J.: Shaping of shared autonomous solutions with minimal interaction. Front. Neurorobot. **12**, 54 (2018)
2. Williams, T., Szafir, D., Chakraborti, T., Phillips, E.: Virtual, augmented, and mixed reality for human-robot interaction (VAM-HRI). In: ACM/IEEE International Conference on Human-Robot Interaction (HRI), pp. 671–672 (2019)
3. Reardon, C., Lee, K., Rogers, J.G., Fink, J.: Augmented reality for human-robot teaming in field environments. In: Chen, J.Y.C., Fragomeni, G. (eds.) HCII 2019. LNCS, vol. 11575, pp. 79–92. Springer, Cham (2019). https://doi.org/10.1007/978-3-030-21565-1_6
4. Nebehay, G., Pflugfelder, R.: Consensus-based matching and tracking of keypoints for object tracking. In: IEEE Winter Conference on Applications of Computer Vision, pp. 862–869. IEEE (2014)
5. Zhao, R., Oyang, W., Wang, X.: Person re-identification by saliency learning. IEEE Trans. Pattern Anal. Mach. Intell. **39**(2), 356–370 (2016)
6. Zhao, Y., Shen, X., Jin, Z., Lu, H., Hua, X.-S.: Attribute-driven feature disentangling and temporal aggregation for video person re-identification. In: Proceedings of the IEEE Conference on Computer Vision and Pattern Recognition, pp. 4913–4922 (2019)
7. Leonardos, S., Zhou, X., Daniilidis, K.: Distributed consistent data association via permutation synchronization. In: IEEE International Conference on Robotics and Automation (2017)

8. Hu, N., Huang, Q., Thibert, B., Guibas, L.J.: Distributable consistent multi-object matching. In: IEEE Conference on Computer Vision and Pattern Recognition (2018)
9. Zhou, X., Zhu, M., Daniilidis, K.: Multi-image matching via fast alternating minimization. In: IEEE International Conference on Computer Vision (2015)
10. Maset, E., Arrigoni, F., Fusiello, A.: Practical and efficient multi-view matching. In: IEEE International Conference on Computer Vision (2017)
11. Pachauri, D., Kondor, R., Singh, V.: Solving the multi-way matching problem by permutation synchronization. In: Advances in Neural Information Processing Systems (2013)
12. Almohamad, H., Duffuaa, S.O.: A linear programming approach for the weighted graph matching problem. IEEE Trans. Pattern Anal. Mach. Intell. **15**(5), 522–525 (1993)
13. Wang, R., Yan, J., Yang, X.: Learning combinatorial embedding networks for deep graph matching. In: IEEE International Conference on Computer Vision (2019)
14. Cho, M., Lee, J., Lee, K.M.: Reweighted random walks for graph matching. In: Daniilidis, K., Maragos, P., Paragios, N. (eds.) ECCV 2010. LNCS, vol. 6315, pp. 492–505. Springer, Heidelberg (2010). https://doi.org/10.1007/978-3-642-15555-0_36
15. Leordeanu, M., Hebert, M.: A spectral technique for correspondence problems using pairwise constraints. In: Tenth IEEE International Conference on Computer Vision, ICCV 2005, vol. 2, pp. 1482–1489. IEEE (2005)
16. Sobreira, H., et al.: Map-matching algorithms for robot self-localization: a comparison between perfect match, iterative closest point and normal distributions transform. J. Intell. Robot. Syst. **93**(3–4), 533–546 (2019)
17. Suh, Y., Adamczewski, K., Mu Lee, K.: Subgraph matching using compactness prior for robust feature correspondence. In: Proceedings of the IEEE Conference on Computer Vision and Pattern Recognition, pp. 5070–5078 (2015)

Safety in a Human Robot Interactive: Application to Haptic Perception

Vamsi Krishna Guda, Damien Chablat$^{(\boxtimes)}$, and Christine Chevallereau

Laboratoire des Sciences du Numérique de Nantes (LS2N), UMR CNRS 6004,
44300 Nantes, France
{Vamsikrishna.Guda,Christine.Chevallereau}@ls2n.fr,
Damien.Chablat@cnrs.fr

Abstract. Usually, traditional haptic interfaces, such as Virtuose 6DOF [1], are used in the design phases by engineers [2]. Such interfaces are safe. However, the user can apply a force/torque but cannot really feel textures and appreciate material quality. These interfaces have a limited workspace, low stiffness and are very expensive. New haptic interfaces using an industrial robots or a cobot (robots specially designed to work in Human-Robot environments) can be used as a haptic interface with intermittent contacts [3,4]. For application considered in this paper, the cobot carries several specimens of texture on its end-effector, to allow contact between a finger of the user and the robot.

Safety is an important aspect in Human Robot Interactions (HRI) [5], even with the use of cobots, because contacts are expected. The purpose of this paper is to introduce a new methodology to define the basic placement of the robot in relation to the human body and for the planning and control of movements during HRIs to ensure safety.

Keywords: Human safety · Motion capture · Haptic interface · Workspace · Robot base location

1 Introduction

Safety is important in interactions between human and robots (HRI). Robots can perform powerful and fast movements that can be dangerous to the humans around them. Involuntary contact between these robots and humans is a threat. This is particularly important in a virtual reality context where humans equipped with a headset will not be able to anticipate the robot's movements. Today more than ever, men work closely with robots. In the case of intermittent contact interface ICI, contact is inevitable between humans and robots. Cobots are best suited to such a scenario, but in terms of human safety, accident prevention can always be improved [6]. These robots are designed to work at limited speeds during potential contacts. Moreover, it must be ensured that the desired contacts with the robot during interaction will not result into an necessary restart of the robot after a safety stop [7].

© Springer Nature Switzerland AG 2020
J. Y. C. Chen and G. Fragomeni (Eds.): HCII 2020, LNCS 12190, pp. 562–574, 2020.
https://doi.org/10.1007/978-3-030-49695-1_38

The model of haptic perception is the human sense of touch. The deep sensibility is an integral part of this human sense. It includes the senses of force, position and movement of the different parts of the human body. In our case the objective is development of a new generation of haptic devices called intermittent contact interfaces (ICI) [8]. ICI are based on the principle of controlling a robot to follow the user's movements remotely, and only come into contact when a haptic interaction must be created, for example to simulate a contact between his hand and the virtual environment. The combination of visual virtual reality and haptic device can provide users with the sensation of touching virtual objects of varying shapes, using pseudo-haptic effects [9, 10].

2   Context of the Study

The context of the study is the evaluation of the perceived quality of a virtual car interior during the first design phases. In a given scenario, the user sits in the real world for a visual virtual reality experience inside the car. The user wears a helmet and cannot see the robot, which explains the safety problem (Fig. 1). While the user is trying to interact with the virtual object in the environment, the robot must come and position a sample of the material associated with the local surface, in order to provide a tactical sense of touching the object [11,12]. A motion capture system based on HTC vive trackers is used to know the position of the body and especially the hand used for interaction as well as the position of the chair and the robot [13] (Fig. 2). Currently, the prop can carry six different materials (Fig. 3). The robot is fixed on a 75 cm high table and the user sits on a seat 60 cm above the floor.

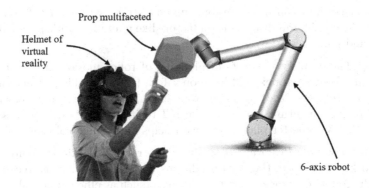

Fig. 1. Conceptual scheme of the experimental platform

So in this scenario, ideally we want the robot workspace to cover all the virtual environment (in this case the passenger compartment of the car) the user could interact. Figure 4 depicts the interior of a Dacia Duster and three areas to touch.

Fig. 2. The complete system setup for human robot interaction

In this process the robot should avoid unwanted collisions with the user. In this context we have two types of contacts: (i) task contacts and (ii) unwanted contacts.

Task contacts are contacts that are related with the actual task of the robot and therefore they are expected and mainly initiated by the robot. They are located on the frontiers of the virtual environment and occurs between the end-effector and the human's hand.

Unwanted contacts are collisions that happen when the robot end-effector or robot body comes in contact with the user while it is not expected in the task description.

To manage these collisions, we come up on a strategy for safety of user in ICI scenario. We consider multiple control factors like planning, workspace /working posture and placement.

Planning: There are two aspects of planning of robot motion in this scenario: (i) reaching the desired next ICI location safely, (ii) being able to track the user hand at the frontier of the virtual environment without having collision with the user, to prepare a future motion of the ICI to its desired location as soon as possible. Having a better planning control helps in avoiding collisions.

Workspace/Working Posture: Constraining the robot's working posture for the entire workspace reduces the risk of collisions. In practice this avoid reconfiguration of the robot to change of working posture (such as elbow up or elbow down configuration) and such large amplitude motion can lead to collision.

Placement: The placement of the robot with respect to the user and the environment has to be defined in order that the robot is able to carry the prop to the limit of the virtual environment that the user wants to explore while avoiding collision with the human. It is better if all the part of the robot is keep outside of the interior of the virtual car. This requirement is especialy difficult to reach for the region defined by S_3 (see Fig. 4).

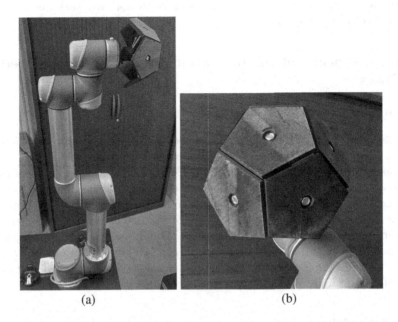

(a)   (b)

Fig. 3. (a) The UR5 robot with a prop attached to the end-effector and (b) The prop used to carry six sample textures. The lateral surface of the prop are denoted 1 to 5 and can be changed by a rotation of the last axis of the robot. The frontal surface of the prop is denoted 6. A displacement of the robot is required to present a lateral surface and then the frontal surface at the same cartesian location

Fig. 4. Example of virtual environment and a set of regions to be reached

Find a convenient location for the robot is an not easy task and it is the main subject of the paper.

3   Base Placement of the Robot for Reach the Desired Poses

3.1   Requirement

The base placement of the robot, is defined in order to be able to place the prop at the point that the human want to explore. Since the robot arm studied has dimension which are close to the dimension of human arm, the ideal robot location would be in the location where the user is seated. However to avoid collisions, we cannot place the robot there. In fact, we would like the robot to be located outside the passenger compartment of the virtual car. It is expected that the user body (specially the chest and neck) should be outside the workspace of the robot, such that there will be no possibility of contact between body parts of the user and the robot's arm. The robot placement should be such that it can reach all the desired contact regions in the required orientation.

3.2   Methodology

The Robot. The cobot used in this paper is UR5 from Universal Robots [14]. It is a 6 DOF robot able to interact with humans in a shared space or to work safely in close proximity. We constrain the posture of the robot to stay in a single aspect, i.e. a particular configuration [15]. In this case, it is elbow up. This helps us in avoiding crossing singularities, during motions. The selection of the specific posture is done by studying the various reachability ranges of different postures and selecting the posture with maximum reachability range without collision between the arm and its support.

Now, for the posture of the robot defined as elbow up, the workspace of the robot is defined as the position location of the effector with respect to the base of the robot, defining a range of orientations for the end-effector.

The workspace is calculated using the ROS package Reuleaux, via a discrete set of spheres of 5 cm diameter. For each center of the sphere and desired orientation of the end-effector, the inverse geometric model is used (with imposed posture) and if a solution exist, the sphere is conserved. At this point, we have all the information about each point in the workspace that can be reached with the preset posture of the robot. If several orientation of the end effector is desired, the intersection of the workspace for each orientation is defined. The workspace of the robot for two orientations and the intersections of both orientations are illustrated on Fig. 6.

These orientations under test are obtained as a factor of the surfaces of the prop that will be used for this tests. The prop that we consider has 6 surfaces. Figure 5 shows the major frames of interest in this test scenario. the TCP frame is the frame at the end of robot without any attachment. We will need to consider two transforms from the TCP to the surface of the prop in contact. For the S_2 Region as shown in Fig. 7. We will considering that all the six surfaces of the prop can be touched. In this region we can have maximum surface interaction with robot prop to compare the feeling with several texture.

When building the workspace, the table linked to the robot is taken into account as an obstacle, but since the pose of the robot in the environment is not known, the other obstacles are not considered.

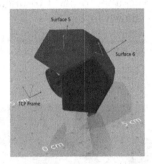

Fig. 5. The prop used in this experiment

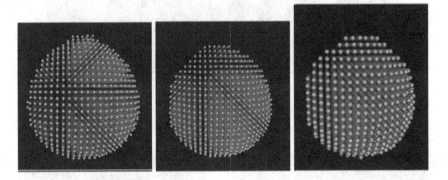

Fig. 6. The workspace of the robot are build for orientation 1 (denoted W_1), orientation 2 (denoted W_2) and for both orientation by intersection of W_1 and W_2 to obtain W_3.

The Task. For interaction between the virtual environment and robot tool, lets consider three major regions in the passenger compartment of the car. These regions are defined as S_1, S_2 and S_3 located at the extremes of the car for the driver: the door, the dash board and the seat next to the user/driver. In the three regions S_1, S_2 and S_3, we define four points $P_1, \ldots, P_4$ that we want the robot to reach.

For S_1 region as shown in Fig. 8, which is the door close to the user, we want for the robot being able to reach this surface with the prop surface 6. This correspond to the orientation 1. The points must belong to the workspace W_1 shown in Fig. 6

For the S_2 region, shown in Fig. 7, we can have a maximum surface interaction with robot prop, we imposed that the surface 6 or surface 1 to 5 of the prop can be presented in order to test several material. A rotation of the last axis of the robot allows to change the surface of the prop from surface 1 to 5. To achieve this, the points has to be reachable by the two orientations. The points must belong to the workspace W_3 shown in Fig. 6.

Finally, the S_3 region is defined in the middle of the seat close to driver, as shown in Fig. 9. For this task, the points must belong to workspace W_2 shown in Fig. 6.

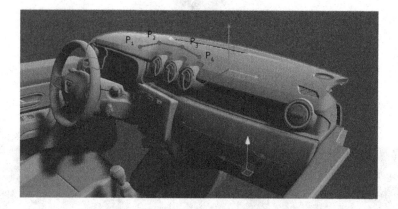

Fig. 7. S_2 - region

Fig. 8. S_1 - region   **Fig. 9.** S_3 - region

The Robot Placement. Now to find the best base placement of the robot, we discretize the possible position of the robot. The set of possible location are expressed as a set of sphere of 8 cm of diameter that represent the paving of the space.

If the robot is fixed on the floor, the paving can include only sphere at the level of the floor. In more general case, as the one studied here, a 3D paving can be considered. The vertical coordinate of the best pose of the robot will defined the good height for the table supporting the robot.

The task is defined as previously by the set of points that we want to reach with a given orientation. The workspace generated for each orientation of region is also used (This is called as reachability map [16]). A point can be reach if it belongs to the workspace associated to the desired orientation (for example W_1).

The algorithm developed is based on the Reuleaux package [17] available via ROS [18] and using libraries [19,20].

The methodology can include any number of point tasks. For each point associated with one orientation i.e. one workspace W_i, all the sphere inside of the workspace is covered and placed at the point studied, and the corresponding pose of the robot is registered. The location of the based is associated to the sphere paving the possible placement of the robot. The number of point reachable from this base location is increased.

After considering all the point of interest (12 point in our study), the possible placement of the robot to achieve the task is defined as the sphere where the number of reachable is maximum.

From this set of base locations, we remove the base locations that coincide with the location of the user. Depending on the number of desired points that can be reached, the points are categorized. This gives the possible robot base location more suited for this scenario.

Algorithm 1: Base Placement of the Robot

Result: Set of robot base locations
input (Reachability Map, Task Points);
procedure 1 create basemap;
for each task point P_i **do**;
INVtransform from P_i and obtain b the base location of the robot;
cluster b and assign the spheres S_k;
increment the index associated to sphere S_k;
save S_k;
end for;
end procedure;
procedure 2 base placement;
access spheres S_k;
find spheres with max base index;
exclude the spheres from inside the car;
end procedure;

3.3   Results

Test were performed to find the robot base placement for given set of point the robot has to reach with a defined orientation. In the tested scenario, the dimension of the table under consideration is 75 cm high and 53 cm long and wide. The base of the robot is located in the middle of the table to ensure its stability. A total of 12 task points have been defined: four task points in S_3 region (Chair), four task points in S_1 region (Door), and four task points in S_2 region (Dash board) with two sets of different orientation.

The possible robot base location are illustrated by blue sphere in Fig. 10. The base location are outside the passenger compartment of car. Multiple robot base locations were found that could reach all the desired positions (Figs. 11, 12 and 13).

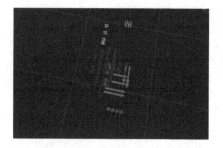

Fig. 10. Base placement for S_1, S_2 and S_3 (Color figure online)

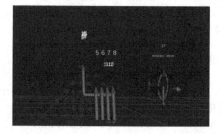

Fig. 11. Side view for S_1, S_2 and S_3

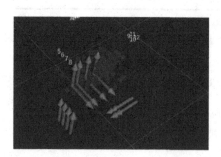

Fig. 12. Front view for S_1, S_2 and S_3

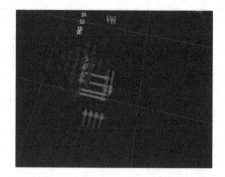

Fig. 13. Top view for S_1, S_2 and S_3

4   Obstacles Avoidance

In the previous study, the obstacle of the environment (the chair and the human) was not taken into account since the location of the robot was not known. Thus the next step is to check for the selected pose location (in Fig. 10) that the points can be reached when the real environment are taken into account.

In this environment, we introduce a model of the chair and the human in rest position. For the user's body, the dimensions considered, for user cover 75% of men and women of age group 25–55 in France. The volume dimensions of the cuboid are 185 cm in height and 60 cm in width and 30 cm in thickness (Fig. 14).

First the location of the robot corresponding to the actual height of the table is considered. For each pose location, the following task is considered: go from home position to each points successively.

From several candidate poses of the robot, the task cannot be achieved. For others, the task can be achieved. Two main problems were encountered:

An illustration of the result is shown for the case illustrated in Fig. 14. The configuration of the robot to reach a point on the passenger chair is shown in Fig. 15, the robot is close to the legs of the human. The configuration of the robot to reach a point on the dashboard is shown in Fig. 16, the robot configuration is convenient, it is far from the human.

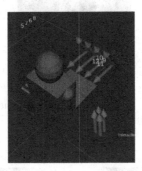

Fig. 14. Base location in blue and tasks points with the desired orientation in pink, 75 cm table height (Color figure online)

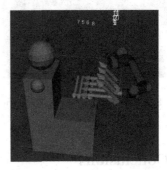

Fig. 15. Interaction at chair, 75 cm height   **Fig. 16.** Interaction at dash, 75 cm height

To improve, the robot base placement, we can change the height of the table used. Several tests are done to determine the effect of changing the height of the table, on the position of robot base and its effect on the inclusion of the robot in the passenger compartment of the car. For performing the tests, the task points shown in Fig. 17 are considered.

When the robot tries to reach the chair task points, we can see from Fig. 15 that the robot goes to the passenger compartment of the car. Conversely, the same problem does not occur in Fig. 19, as the height to the table is reduced by 15 cm. Similar result is shown in Fig. 18 with reduced base table dimensions. It can be concluded that it is better to use a table of 60 cm height that 75 cm height for the given scenario.

Fig. 17. Base location in blue and tasks points with the desired orientation in pink, 60 cm height (Color figure online)

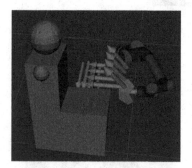

Fig. 18. Interaction at dash, 60 cm height   **Fig. 19.** Interaction at chair, 60 cm height

5   Conclusions

In this article, a collaborative robot is used as a haptic interface with intermittent contact. This interface is used when designing car passenger compartment to choose the textures of the materials used. The work presented allows to choose a robot placement so that the end-effector reaches the areas of interest in the environment while ensuring the absence of collision between the robot and the user. An algorithm has been proposed define convenient placement of the robot base in order to reach several areas of interest. First results are obtained using a given height of the table that support the robot base. The results show an accessibility of the task but also show a robot insertion in the passenger compartment. Changing this height setting prevents this intrusion and therefore improves user safety.

Acknowledgement. This work was funded under the LobbyBot project, ANR-17-CE33 [21]. The authors of the article thank the members of the project for their help in carrying out this work, Lionel Dominjon, Sandrine Wullens, Allexandre Bouchet, Javier Posselt, Maud Marchal, Anatol Lecuyer and Victor Rodrigo Mercado Garcia.

References

1. Perret, J., Vercruysse, P.: Advantages of mechanical backdrivability for medical applications of force control. In: Conference on Computer/Robot Assisted Surgery (CRAS), pp. 84–86 (2014)
2. McNeely, W.A.: Robotic graphics: a new approach to force feedback for virtual reality. In: Proceedings of IEEE Virtual Reality Annual International Symposium, pp. 336–341. IEEE (1993)
3. Araujo, B., Jota, R., Perumal, V., Yao, J.X., Singh, K., Wigdor, D.: Snake charmer: physically enabling virtual objects. In: Proceedings of the TEI 2016: Tenth International Conference on Tangible, Embedded, and Embodied Interaction, pp. 218–226. ACM (2016)
4. Kim, Y., Kim, Y.: Versatile encountered-type haptic display for VR environment using a 7-DOF manipulator. In: Proceedings of the IEEE/RSJ International Conference on Intelligent Robots and Systems (IROS 2016) (2016)
5. Goodrich, M.A., Schultz, A.C., et al.: Human-robot interaction: a survey. Found. Trends® Hum.-Comput. Interact. **1**(3), 203–275 (2008)
6. Cherubini, A., Passama, R., Crosnier, A., Lasnier, A., Fraisse, P.: Collaborative manufacturing with physical human-robot interaction. Robot. Comput.-Integr. Manuf. **40**, 1–13 (2016)
7. Long, P., Chevallereau, C., Chablat, D., Girin, A.: An industrial security system for human-robot coexistence. Ind. Robot Int. J. **45**(2), 220–226 (2018)
8. De La Cruz, O., Gosselin, F., Bachta, W., Morel, G.: Contributions to the design of a 6 DOF contactless sensor intended for intermittent contact haptic interfaces. In: 2018 3rd International Conference on Advanced Robotics and Mechatronics (ICARM), pp. 130–135. IEEE (2018)
9. Ban, Y., Kajinami, T., Narumi, T., Tanikawa, T., Hirose, M.: Modifying an identified curved surface shape using pseudo-haptic effect. In: 2012 IEEE Haptics Symposium (HAPTICS), pp. 211–216. IEEE (2012)
10. Lécuyer, A.: Simulating haptic feedback using vision: a survey of research and applications of pseudo-haptic feedback. Presence Teleoperators Virtual Environ. **18**(1), 39–53 (2009)

11. Mercado, V.R., Marchal, M., Lécuyer, A.: ENTROPiA: towards infinite surface haptic displays in virtual reality using encountered-type rotating props. IEEE Trans. Vis. Comput. Graph. (2019). https://doi.org/10.1109/TVCG.2019.2963190

12. Salazar, S.V., Pacchierotti, C., de Tinguy, X., Maciel, A., Marchal, M.: Altering the stiffness, friction, and shape perception of tangible objects in virtual reality using wearable haptics. IEEE Trans. Haptics (ToH) 13(1), 167–174 (2020)

13. Tomić, M., Chevallereau, C., Jovanović, K., Potkonjak, V., Rodić, A.: Human to humanoid motion conversion for dual-arm manipulation tasks. Robotica 36(8), 1167–1187 (2018)

14. Ostergaard, E.H.: Lightweight robot for everybody [industrial activities]. IEEE Robot. Autom. Mag. 19(4), 17–18 (2012)

15. Wenger, P.: Cuspidal and noncuspidal robot manipulators. Robotica 25(6), 677–689 (2007)

16. Zacharias, F., Borst, C., Hirzinger, G.: Capturing robot workspace structure: representing robot capabilities. In: 2007 IEEE/RSJ International Conference on Intelligent Robots and Systems, pp. 3229–3236. IEEE (2007)

17. Makhal, A., Goins, A.K.: Reuleaux: robot base placement by reachability analysis. ArXiv e-prints, October 2017

18. Quigley, M., et al.: ROS: an open-source robot operating system. In: ICRA Workshop on Open Source Software, Kobe, Japan, vol. 3, no. 3.2, p. 5 (2009)

19. KDL kinematics and dynamics library (KDL), June 2019. http://wiki.ros.org/kdl

20. FCL flexible collision library, June 2019. https://github.com/flexible-collision-library/fcl

21. Lobbybot project. https://www.lobbybot.fr/

Virtual Reality for Immersive Human Machine Teaming with Vehicles

Michael Novitzky[1]([✉]), Rob Semmens[2], Nicholas H. Franck[1],
Christa M. Chewar[1], and Christopher Korpela[1]

[1] United States Military Academy, West Point, NY 10996, USA
{michael.novitzky,christa.chewar,christopher.korpela}@westpoint.edu
[2] Naval Postgraduate School, Monterey, CA 93943, USA
semmens@nps.edu
https://www.westpoint.edu/, https://my.nps.edu/

Abstract. We present developments in constructing a 3D environment and integrating a virtual reality headset in our Project Aquaticus platform. We designed Project Aquaticus to examine the interactions between human-robot teammate trust, cognitive load, and perceived robot intelligence levels while they compete in games of capture the flag on the water. Further, this platform will allows us to study human learning of tactical judgment under a variety of robot capabilities. To enable human-machine teaming (HMT), we created a testbed where humans operate motorized kayaks while the robots are autonomous catamaran-style surface vehicles. MOOS-IvP provides autonomy for the robots. After receiving an order from a human, the autonomous teammates can perform tasks conducive to capturing the flag, such as defending or attacking a flag. In the Project Aquaticus simulation, the humans control their virtual vehicle with a joystick and communicate with their robots via radio. Our current simulation is not engaging or realistic for participants because it presents a top-down, omniscient view of the field. This fully observable representation of the world is well suited for managing operations from the shore and teaching new players game mechanics and strategies; however, it does not accurately reflect the limited and almost chaotic view of the world a participant experiences while in their motorized kayak on the water. We present creating a 3D visualization through Unity that users experience through a virtual reality headset. Such a system allows us to perform experiments without the need for a significant investment in on-water experiment resources while also permitting us to gather data year-round through the cold winter months.

Keywords: Underlying and supporting technologies · VAMR technologies and techniques for human-robot interaction · Virtual reality · Human-robot teaming · Simulation

---

The views and conclusions contained herein are those of the authors and should not be interpreted as necessarily representing the official policies or endorsements, either expressed or implied, of the U.S. Department of Defense or the U.S. Government.

© Springer Nature Switzerland AG 2020
J. Y. C. Chen and G. Fragomeni (Eds.): HCII 2020, LNCS 12190, pp. 575–590, 2020.
https://doi.org/10.1007/978-3-030-49695-1_39

1   Introduction

Modern systems are combining manned vehicles with autonomous vehicles to perform tasks in challenging environments. For example, the U.S. Army has the Manned-Unmanned Teaming (MUM-T) program in which manned aircraft work with unmanned aerial systems (UAS) [40]. The U.S. Air Force's "Loyal Wingman" project is exploring manned-unmanned teaming in which an UAS and a manned aircraft work directly on missions such as air interdiction, attack on integrated air defense systems, and offensive counter air [17]. We have developed a similar manned-unmanned teaming concept in the marine domain called Project Aquaticus [21,23–25,27–29,31–33]. The marine domain is more accessible for deploying autonomous vessels (no approval is required from government agencies and vehicles can be easily stopped on the water) and yet still challenging, given the elements in the environment. As seen in Fig. 1, our manned vessels are motorized kayaks and our autonomous teammates are autonomous surface vehicles (ASVs). Project Aquaticus has been designed to explore the interplay between human cognitive load, robot autonomy, and human-robot teammate trust. The nominal composition of Project Aquaticus is to have two humans and two robots on the same team competing in a game of capture the flag against a similarly situated team. It is our goal to provide lessons learned from our platform in the marine domain to other challenging environments.

The testbed has already demonstrated a level of maturity [26] as it has collected and published real-world data for publicly available data sets at: www.aquaticus.org. Researchers have been able to leverage the datasets to extract successful tactics [36]. However, in order to run these real-world experiments, it requires a substantial amount of resources in terms of hardware and personnel and can only be performed during the ideal summer months. As an alternative to real-world testing, we have begun utilizing our Project Aquaticus simulation in order to gather participants in larger numbers and at anytime of the year. A drawback with our Project Aquaticus simulator is that it offers participants an overhead 2D view of the playing field which is a completely different experience than what participants encounter in our real-world testbed.

Our goal with this work is to have participants immersed in a virtual world playing capture the flag games. We will leverage the Unity 3D gaming environment to do this. A first step for this effort is to create the Project Aquaticus field and import vehicles into the Unity 3D space. A second and vital step is to then connect the Unity 3D vehicles to our MOOS-IvP Project Aquaticus simulation. This way, the Unity 3D environment acts as a 3D visualization and allows us to leverage its built in support for virtual reality headsets. A key component to this will be the need to add a camera view that is anchored to the human operated vehicle relevant to that participant.

Fig. 1. A view from a vessel on the water. In the distance is the blue flag surrounded by blue and red vehicles. (Color figure online)

2   Related Work

Simulation has been a key technology to enable robotics. In particular for field robotics, the use of simulation allows developers and experimenters to focus on development prior to tackling the difficulties of real-world testing and deployment. Additionally, if a simulator can better approximate the environment in terms of sensing it greatly reduces development time. There are a number of 3D simulators that are leveraged for robotics development including 4DV-Sim, Actin, Gazebo, Morse, OpenHRP, OpenRAVE, RoboDK, Unity, V-Rep, and Webots.

2.1   Virtual Reality for Human-Machine Teaming

Virtual Reality headsets are a natural way to study human-robot interaction. Lipton et al. [18] use virtual reality headsets and controllers to teleport the human inside the robot's mind to teleoperate a humanoid robot. Taheri et al. immerse people into virtual 3D car simulations where participants wore virtual reality headsets to study their driving characteristics [37]. Ropelato et al. also used 3D virtual reality headsets but to observe humans driving so that an artificial tutor could improve their driving [34].

2.2   Virtual Reality for Training of Tactical Judgment

Virtual reality has been the military's *training environment of the future* for the past thirty years [20]. There have been many efforts and studies to determine the utility and training benefits of virtual reality for the military [1,5]. In *Experience*

on Demand: What Virtual Reality Is, How It Works, and What It Can Do,
Bailenson discusses all of the benefits of virtual reality for learning. In a perfect
system, virtual reality enables learning by doing, spaced practice and repetition,
practice in decision making, the low-cost opportunity for productive failure, and
arousal and affect [4]. It is no wonder that the military desires to take advantage
of these benefits, even without considering the benefits of cost-savings or safety.

Simulation, in a broad sense, is how those in the military learn professional
judgment. Simulation can be very low fidelity, such as tactical decision games.
For example, the Infantry Journal published *Combat Problems for Small Units,*
in 1943. This book contains 27 tactical situations in which the reader is asked
for what commands they would issue at several points in the scenario. This
intends to put the reader in the situation as much as possible. After making
a decision, the reader then turns the page and sees an exemplar answer. The
reader can then compare their commands to suggested commands. Committing
to an answer before being shown an exemplar answer is one example of active
learning [6] and Ai-Lim Lee and colleagues have shown that virtual reality has a
significant relation with active learning, which in turn, has a significant relation
with learning outcomes [3]. It should be the case that virtual reality offers an
environment for similar decision making without the reliance on the individual's
imagination, which can vary.

However, some learning concerns have impeded the realization of a virtual
reality nirvana. One concern is transfer [38]. Concerning virtual reality, issues
of transfer take two forms. The first is that the fidelity of the simulation is
sufficient to mimic reality, so that when trainees experience similar stimuli in the
real world, the trainees make benefit of the training, and make the appropriate
decision. The second is that virtual reality should avoid negative transfer, where
attentional cues learned or ways of interacting that only work in the virtual
world are misused in the actual world. In educational settings, transfer is often
assumed, but not tested. Virtual reality can add to the complexity of measuring
transfer, as Zaal and Sweet found in examining stall recovery training for pilots
[41].

Outside of learning issues, the military has other practical issues [8]. Identifying what tasks one should practice, to what level of proficiency, and how
frequently is persistent. This issue persists because there is a multivariate solution space that includes the capability and availability of the simulator, and the
cost and danger of performing the same training in reality. For example, interest
in purchasing flying simulators and tank simulators is often cost-driven because
the actual equipment is expensive to operate.

We believe the real value of virtual reality is not in learning procedures; it is in
learning judgment. It is learning what attentional cues hold valuable information,
making a decision based on that information, and then seeing the consequences.
Learning to recognize or recall tactics is easy. Learning the judgment to employ
any given tactic requires experience.

A tactic is simply an action taken to achieve a goal. There are individual
tactics, such as individual movement techniques that allow a soldier to move to a

better position while minimizing the chances of getting shot. The Army teaches three of these: low crawling, high crawling, and 3–5 s rush. These individual tactics support collective tactics, such as fire and maneuver, where some people shoot while others move forward, and then switch.

These particular tactics exist due to a combination of technology and human ability (or inability.) Concerning technology, the current rifle is accurate and allows one person to place well-aimed fire quickly. By contrast, muskets were neither and required a different tactic. Concerning the human, it is much easier to point the rifle accurately when one is on the ground than when running.

This is also true for sports. In most sports, the ball moves faster than the players. Therefore, players arrange themselves to receive the ball where they can do something with it, or allow teammate to receive the ball. The other team tries to prevent that. By contrast, in a game called pushball, the ball moves slower than the players. As a result, the players arrange themselves very differently. Formations are similar to a scrum.

In the current work, virtual reality allows us to change the capability of the robot. We can make it faster, or slower, or more adaptable or less. This is what is required to study the development and judgment of tactics. We will say more about this in future work.

2.3   Previous Project Aquaticus Virtual Reality Efforts

For our previous work [22], we investigated the integration of the Gazebo 3D simulator [15] which is maintained by OSRF. Gazebo was featured as the simulation environment for the Virtual Robotics Challenge (VRC), a component in the DARPA Robotics Challenge in July of 2013 [2]. Gazebo also supports the Oculus Rift VR headsets [19]. In our previous report [22], we described how we were able to import some of our vehicle models into Gazebo. However, this became a time sink for our team. Utilizing all that Gazebo had to offer, required more specialized skill, specifically 3D CAD modeling which at the time we were not yet proficient. Oftentimes, the models would fail to load. If they did load, then the scale would be off or the texture would not load properly. Our initial difficulties with Gazebo models was only part of our frustration. Only the earlier SDK versions of Oculus Rift VR headsets, which have been discontinued, are supported. This means that in order to use this system, we would have to find previously used devices through sites like eBay. Thus, our attempts at incorporating a 3D visualization and virtual reality headset stalled.

As part of our second attempt at virtual reality for Project Aquaticus [25], we came upon meshcat-python which is a WebGL 3D visualizer for Python [13]. MeshCat is a remotely-controllable 3D viewer, built on top of Three.js [7]. It was heavily used by the MIT DRC Team for the DARPA Robotics Challenge as a command and control interface for their humanoid robot [12]. Our initial experience with meshcat-python was phenomenal [25], as we began using meshcat-python as a 3D visualizer for our Project Aquaticus datasets. With minimal trial and error, we were able to import all of our vehicle models and create a simulated Project Aquaticus field. We connected the meshcat-python visualizer to our logged vehicle datasets. Our tool could playback previously recorded games in the 3D environment and has a floating camera for one to observe each game. A compelling part of meshcat-python is that it is based on Three.js which has support for Google Cardboard [9]. Google Cardboard [16] is a virtual reality (VR) platform developed by Google for use with a head mount that contains a smartphone. We were able to enable Google Cardboard support from within meshcat-python and use smartphones on hand for a virtual reality experience.

While meshcat-python was a great start to implementing a 3D version with Virtual Reality support for Project Aquaticus, it lacked certain tools amenable to creating an immersive world for our participants. We now describe our integration of Unity 3D into the Project Aquaticus simulation. Unity 3D allows us to create higher fidelity 3D simulations of our capture the flag playing field.

3   System Design

3.1   Game Mechanics

Initially, our virtual reality experiments will continue the game mechanics that were used during on-water data gathering [26]. In the on-water experimental work on Aquaticus, the nominal composition of Project Aquaticus is to have two humans and two robots on the same team competing in a game of capture the flag against a similarly composed team.

Each Project Aquaticus game took place in the area of the Charles River immediately adjacent to the MIT Sailing Pavilion. The field for the game extends along the entire 160 m dock and 80 m into the river, as seen in Fig. 2. Boundaries of the field are marked with floating buoys. The field is divided in half: one half (to the left of Fig. 2) of the field is the blue team's territory and the other half is the red team's territory. A team's flag, a small buoy in the team's color at a known GPS coordinate, is located approximately in the rear center of each of their territories. Teams start with all players near their respective flag. The flag buoys are not moved during the game - participants and robots instead grab a virtual flag (for safety to avoid collisions) and take it back to their flag zone.

To score a point, the participant must go to their opponent's side of the field, virtually grab the flag and make it back to their home flag without being tagged or going out of bounds. A buoy is located at the end of each side to indicate the original flag position. However, the players manipulate a virtual flag to keep the complexity low (no need for physical interaction) and focus on human-robot interaction with fully autonomous robots while avoiding unnecessary collisions. Virtual flag management is coordinated by the autonomous central game controller on the shoreside computer. Players request flag grabs from the central game controller which is granted to them if they are (a) within the opposing team's flag zone (b) if the virtual flag is located within the flag zone, and (c) the requesting vehicle is untagged. Players can defend their side of the field through the use of tags. To tag an opponent, a request is made to the central game manager that checks if (x) the requesting vehicle is in their home field side, (y) that the opponent vehicle is both on the requesting vehicles side and within 10 m of the requesting vehicle, and (z) the tagger is untagged. A tagged player must untag themselves by returning to their home flag zone. If a player is carrying a virtual flag and is tagged, then the flag is automatically reset to its original location.

3.2 Autonomous Teammates and Interaction

The robots are truly autonomous teammates. As described in [26], the robots leverage the MOOS-IvP marine autonomy open source project. During on-water experiments, humans put the robots into one of several modes that are conducive to playing games of capture the flag such as attack the flag, defend the flag, cover me and follow me. These robot teammates continue to perform this task while avoiding collisions and untagging themselves until told to switch tasks. As seen in Fig. 3, the participants interact with their teammates and simulated vehicle through an audio headset and game controller.

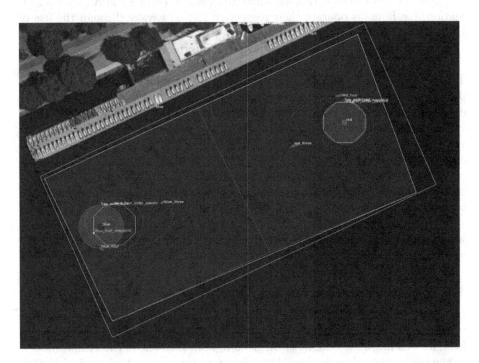

Fig. 2. An image of our pMarineViewer tool. It provides command and control during experiments and the view for each simulation. As can be seen, the top down view is perfect for getting an overall picture of the game state. However, the top down view gives the participants a fully observable view of the game which is great for training but a poor approximation of what a human can perceive while performing on-water experiments.

3.3   Current Simulation

The current simulation topology is seen in Fig. 3. The topology includes a central server to run the Aquaticus game mechanics while we run hardware-in-the-loop for all of the simulated vehicles. The current simulation is supported by several MOOS-IvP applications including *pMarineViewer* and *uSimMarine*. The *pMarineViewer* application, seen in Fig. 2, is a MOOS application written using FLTK and OpenGL for rendering vehicles and associated information and history during operation or simulation. The user is able manipulate a map display to see multiple vehicle tracks and monitor key information about individual vehicles. In the primary interface mode the user is a passive observer, only able to manipulate what the user sees and not able to initiate communications to the vehicles. However there are hooks available to allow the interface to accept field control commands. The *uSimMarine* application is a simple 3D vehicle simulator that updates vehicle state, position and trajectory, based on the present actuator values and prior vehicle state. The typical usage scenario has a single instance of *uSimMarine* associated with each simulated vehicle. During the Aquaticus simulation, the humans operate their respective virtual kayaks through the use of USB game controllers. In order to interact with the game and their teammates, the participants use the human-robot speech interface.

Project Aquaticus is both real-world vessels and a simulation environment. The benefits of using the simulator are that it allows for relatively inexpensive data collection as compared to maintaining experimental vessels in a maritime environment during periods of inclement weather. The current limitation of the Project Aquaticus simulator is that it gives the participant(s) an allocentric or god's eye view of the environment, as seen in Fig. 2. This view provides perfect situational awareness. This simplifies the cognitve load as compared to the egocentric perspective while conducting operations. Maintaining situational awareness is much more challenging egocentrically, especially while coordinating with teammates and directing a robot on the water. To create a first person perspective for each participant that is reflective of the actual on-water experience, we create a plug-in for the Project Aquaticus simulator that connects to a 3D visualization and a virtual reality headset, as seen in Fig. 5.

3.4   Project Aquatiucs Field in Unity 3D

In order to leverage Unity 3D's capability as a visualization engine, models of the vehicles and objects have been imported and organized to reflect the real-world field, as seen in Fig. 4. Care must be given to keep the ratio of the vehicle models to the field size as close as possible to the on-water games. As described further below, each Unity 3D vehicle will connect to the Project Aquaticus simulation for their pose information.

3.5   Bridge Between Project Aquaticus 2D Simulation and Unity 3D

The integration between the Project Aquaticus simulator and Unity 3D is seen in Fig. 5. A new MOOS-IvP application named *pUnity* was created for the purposes

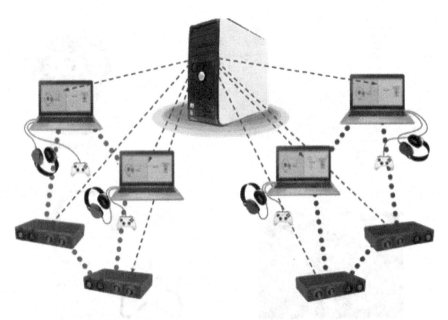

Fig. 3. The simulation network topology for our Project Aquaticus capture the flag competition. Each vehicle communicates with our centralized game server which handles the game mechanics such as tagging, flag management, and safety penalties. Each nominal team is composed of two humans and two autonomous robots. Depicted are human interfaces where each participant uses a laptop that presents a simulated overhead view of the field. The participants use a headset for speech recognition and audio cues and a game controller to control their vehicle. The autonomous robots are run by our payload autonomy boxes (called PABLOs) which include a Raspberry Pi that runs our autonomy software. Our autonomous surface vehicles also utilize their own PABLO box. All simulations are run as hardware-in-the-loop.

Fig. 4. A view of the Project Aquaticus capture the flag field in the Unity 3D world.

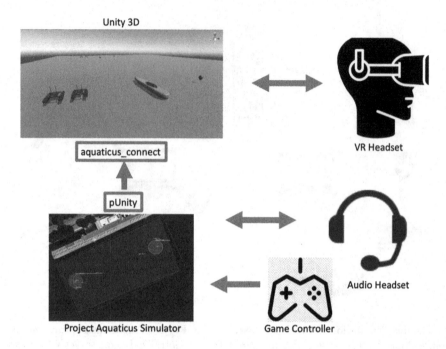

Fig. 5. The main contribution of this work is the integration of the Unity 3D visualization framework with the Project Aquaticus simulation. This is accomplished by the creation of the MOOS-IvP application *pUnity* and the Unity 3D C# script called *aquaticus_connect*. Each vehicle has a respective *pUnity* and *aquaticus_connect* in which the Project Aqauticus simulator produces location information for the Unity 3D visualizer to place the vehicle in the appropriate pose. Virtual reality immersion for Project Aquaticus is created by leveraging Unity 3D's support for virtual reality headsets.

of bridging the Project Aquaticus simulation to the Unity 3D visualization. A *pUnity* application is associated with each MOOS-IvP vehicle community. The *pUnity* application subscribes to the MOOS variable NODE_MESSAGE which contains the vehicle's name, x location, y location, and heading. In order to connect to the Unity 3D visualizer, *pUnity* acts as a TCP server. Once connected, *pUnity* forwards the NODE_MESSAGEs to the corresponding TCP client program attached to each Unity 3D vehicle.

A new C# script called *aquaticus_connect* was created to attach each vehicle object in Unity 3D to their respective MOOS-IvP vehicle community. Each *aquaticus_connect* is a TCP client that connects to a specific *pUnity* MOOS-IvP application based on startup parameters of IP address and port. As *pUnity* passes NODE_MESSAGEs to *aquaticus_connect*, the script in turn changes the location of the 3D vehicle within the Unity 3D engine. This setup allows for a flexible number of vehicles to be visualized.

Virtual Reality Headset. The second step is to integrate a virtual reality headset into our 3D visualization. The most popular virtual reality headsets are the Oculus [14], HTC Vive [10], and Valve Index [11]. Our top choice is the Valve Index as it has the best resolution and highest frame rate possible – which is key to reduce the possibility of motion sickness which leads to a higher number of recruited participants. We can anchor the headset's view to the participant's vehicle location. Thereby creating the 3D simulated world with the headset view anchored to the participant's virtual vehicle yet responsive to the participant's head motions to look around the environment while playing virtual games of capture the flag.

3.6 Single Player Experience

As seen in Fig. 5, the single player experience will continue to use the game controller to move the vehicle around and interact with the game mechanics such as tag opponents and grab the flag while they will use an audio headset to communicate with their teammates and receive game events. Instead of the participant looking at a monitor displaying the Unity 3D visualization from their vehicle's perspective, they will wear a virtual reality headset. Thus, when the participant moves their head around, the virtual reality view will adjust accordingly. As the view moves with the vehicle within the simulation, the participant will experience a view more akin to what they would experience playing games of capture the flag on the water in their motorized kayaks.

3.7 Local Multiplayer

The 2D version of Project Aquaticus is capable of having multiple participants in the same competition. As seen in Fig. 3, the original system is capable of being run on Raspberry Pis. Extending it to multiple player virtual reality means increasing the capability of each participant's machine to a PC with a video card capable of smoothly re-creating the 3D environment.

4 Future Work

4.1 Work to Finish the VR Platform

Visually, the Project Aquaticus capture the flag field within Unity 3D requires a few additions. This includes the "chalk" on the water that marks the boundaries of the play area. Additionally, some scenery will add to the ability of participants to gain a visual estimate of speed, as included with Unity 3D.

We need to include collision physics, as that is related to some of the tactics we wish to study. While in the simulation the robots are running collision avoidance algorithms, just as they would on the water, there is no simulation of collision physics. In our current Project Aquaticus 2D simulation the vehicles can go through each other. To improve the study of these tactics, a basic collision model will need to be implemented.

4.2   Future Potential Experiments

In concurrent work, we analyzed four of the existing Aquaticus games [36]. We used video analysis to identify tactics that players used. We identified five tactics, but there could be more. We also attempted to characterize difference in game play between experienced players and brand new players. The results were inconclusive, in part because one novice performed very well. There is the potential that "the novice" was on the sailing team and that he was able transfer his knowledge of watercraft performance into the game. This is speculation, as we were not systematically collecting data about prior experience.

This experimental platform offers several advantages in studying the development of tactical judgment. First, we can assume that few participants will not have familiarity with playing capture the flag with a robot teammate in a virtual reality kayak. This will help control for prior tactical knowledge. The second is that games are short. This provides the opportunity to conduct a game, have an after action review where we record their learning, have participants conduct a plan, play again, review and plan again, play one more time, and then debrief the experiment, all within an hour. The relatively few number of teammates puts a limit on the complexity of their plan. This helps the research team identify the tactics, even when they enact them concurrently. Finally, VR offers the opportunity to easily change the characteristics of the entities and the environment. For example, we can easily make the humans faster than the robots, or vice versa. We can introduce a strong current, where it is easy for everybody to go in one direction, but hard to go in the other. Either of these should eventually lead to a change in tactics, but how that change is realized remains to be seen.

Another question to explore is when and how often robots should provide status updates to the human? In the game, the humans are under some cognitive load as they maneuver themselves and send maneuver commands to the robot. Semmens, et al. asked people who were driving if it was a good time to receive non-essential information [35]. They found that there were many times when it was ok to receive information, and some times when it was not. It was not a good time when people were trying to do something, such as turning left, or figuring out the GPS. This platform will allow us to explore the same type of question for people in a contested environment. This might inform future communications systems that could hold information until the human is ready.

Finally, this platform may be used to investigate adaptive thinking skills or tactical planning skills, as others have before [30,39]. It is unclear what the benefit of training repetition and low-cost failure are for tactical judgment in specific, and human development in general. There could be benefits to tactical confidence, increases in growth mindset and willingness to learn, and fortification of grit. None of that may prove true, but this platform will allow us to find out.

5   Conclusions

We have introduced the utility and our plan to integrate a 3D virtual reality simulation into our experiments for the Aquaticus Project. Aquaticus captures the richness (and chaos) of real-world human-robot teaming within a structured game of capture-the-flag on the water. As described in Sect. 3.3, our current 2D top-down simulator is a great learning tool and useful for command and control from the shore. Yet, the current simulation view does not capture the chaos that a participant experiences from being in their own vehicle with a view from the water. We presented our previous efforts in trying to bring about a 3D visualizer and VR headset and why it stalled. Lastly, we presented our current progress using the Unity 3D visualization tool with our real-time simulator.

Acknowledgments. We thank Hugh R. R. Dougherty, Caileigh Fitzgerald, Paul Robinette, Michael R. Benjamin, and Henrik Schmidt for their contributions to this initial work with Gazebo and Meshcat-python. We also thank Clearpath Robotics for furnishing us with a model of their Heron M300 autonomous surface vehicle.

References

1. Virtual Reality: State of Military Research and Applications in Member Countries (La realite virutelle: L'etat actuel des travaux de recherche et des applications militaires dans les pays membres de l'Alliance). Technical report, RTO-TR-018, NATO RESEARCH AND TECHNOLOGY ORGANIZATION NEUILLY-SUR-SEINE, FRANCE, February 2003. https://apps.dtic.mil/docs/citations/ADA411978
2. Aguero, C., et al.: Inside the virtual robotics challenge: simulating real-time robotic disaster response. IEEE Trans. Autom. Sci. Eng. **12**(2), 494–506 (2015). https://doi.org/10.1109/TASE.2014.2368997
3. Lee, E.A., Wong, K.W., Fung, C.C.: How does desktop virtual reality enhance learning outcomes? A structural equation modeling approach. Comput. Educ. **55**(4), 1424–1442 (2010). https://doi.org/10.1016/j.compedu.2010.06.006. https://linkinghub.elsevier.com/retrieve/pii/S0360131510001661
4. Bailenson, J.: Experience on demand: what virtual reality is, how it works, and what it can do (2019). oCLC: 1037811122
5. Beal, S.A.: Using games for training dismounted light infantry leaders: emergent questions and lessons learned. Technical report, 1841, US Army Research Institude for the Behavioral and Social Sciences (2005). https://doi.org/10.1037/e423262005-001. http://doi.apa.org/get-pe-doi.cfm?doi=10.1037/e423262005-001, type: dataset
6. Bonwell, C.C., Eison, J.A.: Active Learning: Creating Excitement in the Classroom. 1991 ASHE-ERIC Higher Education Reports. ERIC (1991)
7. Cabello, R.: Three.js, November 2018. https://threejs.org/. Accessed 02 Nov 2018
8. Campbell, C.H., Knerr, B.W., Lampton, D.R.: Virtual environments for infantry soldiers: virtual environments for dismounted soldier simulation, training and mission rehearsal. Technical report, ARI-SP-59, ARMY RESEARCH INST FOR THE BEHAVIORAL AND SOCIAL SCIENCES ALEXANDRIA VA, May 2004. https://apps.dtic.mil/docs/citations/ADA425082

9. Catanzariti, P.: Bringing VR to the web with google cardboard and three.js, November 2018. https://www.sitepoint.com/bringing-vr-to-web-google-cardboard-three-js/. Accessed 02 Dec 2018

10. HTC Corporation: HTC VIVE. https://www.vive.com/. Accessed 14 Aug 2019

11. Valve Corporation: Valve index. https://www.valvesoftware.com/en/index/headset/. Accessed 14 Aug 2019

12. DARPA: MIT DARPA robotics challenge team, November 2018. http://drc.mit.edu/. Accessed 02 Nov 2018

13. Deits, R.: Meshcat-Python, November 2018. https://github.com/rdeits/meshcat-python/. Accessed 02 Nov 2018

14. Facebook Technologies, L.: Oculus rift. https://www.oculus.com/. Accessed 14 Aug 2019

15. Foundation, O.S.R.: Gazebo, February 2018. http://gazebosim.org/. Accessed 02 Feb 2018

16. Google: Google cardboard, November 2018. https://vr.google.com/cardboard/. Accessed 02 Dec 2018

17. Kearns, K.: RFI: Autonomy for Loyal Wingman. Air Force Research Laboratory (AFRL), July 2015

18. Lipton, J.I., Fay, A.J., Rus, D.: Baxter's homunculus: virtual reality spaces for teleoperation in manufacturing. IEEE Robot. Autom. Lett. 3(1), 179–186 (2018)

19. LLC., O.V.: Oculus rift, February 2018. https://www.oculus.com/. Accessed 02 Feb 2018

20. Lynn, V.L., Cherry, P., Brady, E., Droulihet, P., Evers, W.: Army science board 1991 summer study - army simulation strategy. Technical report, Army Science Board, Washington, December 1991. https://apps.dtic.mil/docs/citations/ADA250382

21. Novitzky, M., Benjamin, M.R., Robinette, P., Dougherty, H.R., Fitzgerald, C., Schmidt, H.: Virtual reality for immersive simulated experiments of human-robot interactions in the marine environment. In: Workshop on Virtual, Augmented and Mixed Reality for Human-Robot Interaction at HRI 2018, Chicago, March 2018

22. Novitzky, M., Benjamin, M.R., Robinette, P., Dougherty, H.R., Fitzgerald, C., Schmidt, H.: Virtual reality for immersive simulated experiments of human-robot interactions in the marine environment. In: ACM/IEEE International Conference on Human-Robot Interaction (HRI) 2018 Workshop on Virtual, Augmented, and Mixed Reality (VAM) for Human-Robot Interaction. ACM (2018)

23. Novitzky, M., Dougherty, H.R.R., Benjamin, M.R.: A human-robot speech interface for an autonomous marine teammate. In: Agah, A., Cabibihan, J.-J., Howard, A.M., Salichs, M.A., He, H. (eds.) ICSR 2016. LNCS (LNAI), vol. 9979, pp. 513–520. Springer, Cham (2016). https://doi.org/10.1007/978-3-319-47437-3_50

24. Novitzky, M., Fitzgerald, C., Gleason, D., Robinette, P., Benjamin, M.R., Schmidt, H.: Integrating a multi-modal interface in a marine human-robot teaming testbed. In: IEEE International Conference on Robotics and Automation (ICRA) workshop on Human-Robot Teaming Beyond Human Operational Speeds (RT-DUNE). IEEE, Montreal, May 2019

25. Novitzky, M., Fitzgerald, C., Robinette, P., Benjamin, M.R., Schmidt, H.: Updated: virtual reality for immersive simulated experiments of human-robot interactions in the marine environment. In: Proceedings of the Workshop Virtual, Augmented, and Mixed Reality for Human-Robot Interaction ACM/IEEE International Conference on Human-Robot Interaction. ACM/IEEE, Daegu, March 2019

26. Novitzky, M., Robinette, P., Benjamin, M.R., Fitzgerald, C., Schmidt, H.: Aquaticus: publicly available datasets from a marine human-robot teaming testbed. In: Companion of the 2019 ACM/IEEE International Conference on Human-Robot Interaction. Daegu, March 2019

27. Novitzky, M., Robinette, P., Benjamin, M.R., Gleason, D.K., Fitzgerald, C., Schmidt, H.: Preliminary interactions of human-robot trust, cognitive load, and robot intelligence levels in a competitive game. In: Companion of the 2018 ACM/IEEE International Conference on Human-Robot Interaction, pp. 203–204 (2018)

28. Novitzky, M., Robinette, P., Fitzgerald, C., Dougherty, H.R.R., Benjamin, M., Schmidt, H.: Issues and mitigation strategies for deploying human-robot experiments on the water for competitive games in an academic environment. In: Proceedings of the Workshop Dangerous HRI: Testing Real-World Robots has Real-World Consequences ACM/IEEE International Conference on Human-Robot Interaction. ACM/IEEE, Daegu (2019)

29. Novitzky, M., Robinette, P., Gleason, D.K., Benjamin, M.R.: A platform for studying human-machine teaming on the water with physiological sensors. In: Workshop on Human-Centered Robotics: Interaction, Physiological Integration and Autonomy at RSS 2017, Cambridge, July 2017

30. Pleban, R.J., Vaughn, E.D., Sidman, J., Geyer, A., Semmens, R.: Training platoon leader adaptive thinking skills in a classroom setting. Research Report 1948, U.S. Army Research Institute for the Behavioral & Social Sciences, Arlington (2011). http://www.dtic.mil/dtic/tr/fulltext/u2/a544978.pdf

31. Robinette, P., Novitzky, M., Benjamin, M.R.: Trusting a robot as a user versus as a teammate. In: Workshop on Morality and Social Trust in Autonomous Robots at RSS 2017, Cambridge, July 2017

32. Robinette, P., Novitzky, M., Benjamin, M.R.: Longitudinal interactions between human and robot teammates in a marine environment. In: In Workshop on Longitudinal Human-Robot Teaming at HRI 2018, Chicago, March 2018

33. Robinette, P., Novitzky, M., Benjamin, M.R., Fitzgerald, C., Schmidt, H.: Exploring human-robot trust during teaming in a real-world testbed. In: Companion of the 2019 ACM/IEEE International Conference on Human-Robot Interaction, March 2019

34. Ropelato, S., Zünd, F., Magnenat, S., Menozzi, M., Sumner, R.: Adaptive tutoring on a virtual reality driving simulator. In: 1st Workshop on Artificial Intelligence Meets Virtual and Augmented Worlds (AIVRAR) in Conjunction with SIGGRAPH Asia 2017, ETH Zurich (2017)

35. Semmens, R., Martelaro, N., Kaveti, P., Stent, S., Ju, W.: Is now a good time? An empirical study of vehicle-driver communication timing. In: Proceedings of the 2019 CHI Conference on Human Factors in Computing Systems, CHI 2019, pp. 1–12. Association for Computing Machinery, Glasgow, May 2019. https://doi.org/10.1145/3290605.3300867

36. Semmens, R., Novitzky, M., Robinette, P., Lieberman, G.: Insights into Expertise and Tactics in Human-Robot Teaming

37. Taheri, S.M., Matsushita, K., Sasaki, M.: Development of a driving simulator with analyzing driver' characteristics based on a virtual reality head mounted display. J. Transp. Technol. **7**(03), 351 (2017)

38. Thorndike, E.L., Woodworth, R.S.: The influence of improvement in one mental functionupon the efficiency of other functions: III. Functions involving attention, observation and discrimination. Psychol. Rev. **8**(6), 553–564 (1901). https://doi.org/10.1037/h0071363

39. Tucker, J., Semmens, R., Sidman, J., Geyer, A., Vaughn, E.: Training tactical-level planning skills: an investigation of problem-centered and direct instruction approaches. Technical report, U. S. Army Research Institute for the Behavioral & Social Sciences, Arlington (2011). http://www.dtic.mil/dtic/tr/fulltext/u2/a545362.pdf

40. Whittle, R.: MUM-T is the word for AH-64E: helos fly, use drones. Breaking Defense, January 2015

41. Zaal, P.M.T., Sweet, B.T.: The challenges of measuring transfer of stall recovery training. In: 2014 IEEE International Conference on Systems, Man, and Cybernetics (SMC), pp. 3138–3143, October 2014. https://doi.org/10.1109/SMC.2014.6974410, ISSN 1062-922X

A Robotic Augmented Reality Virtual Window for Law Enforcement Operations

Nate Phillips, Brady Kruse, Farzana Alam Khan, J. Edward Swan II,
and Cindy L. Bethel$^{(\boxtimes)}$

Mississippi State University, Mississippi State, MS 39762, USA
{Nathaniel.C.Phillips,brady.kruse}@ieee.org, fk141@msstate.edu,
swan@acm.org, cbethel@cse.msstate.edu

Abstract. In room-clearing tasks, SWAT team members suffer from a lack of initial environmental information: knowledge about what is in a room and what relevance or threat level it represents for mission parameters. Normally this gap in situation awareness is rectified only upon room entry, forcing SWAT team members to rely on quick responses and near-instinctual reactions. This can lead to dangerously escalating situations or important missed information which, in turn, can increase the likelihood of injury and even mortality. Thus, we present an *x-ray vision* system for the dynamic scanning and display of room content, using a robotic platform to mitigate operator risk. This system maps a room using a robot-equipped stereo depth camera and, using an augmented reality (AR) system, presents the resulting geographic information according to the perspective of each officer. This intervention has the potential to notably lower risk and increase officer situation awareness, all while team members are in the relative safety of cover. With these potential stakes, it is important to test the viability of this system natively and in an operational SWAT team context.

Keywords: Augmented reality · Situation awareness · X-Ray Vision · Robotics

1 Introduction and Motivation

A major concern in our country and around the world is the challenges law enforcement officers face during incident responses and the attention they receive as a result of the actions and decisions made during these responses [3]. The focus of this paper is to describe the design and development process for an augmented reality virtual window to provide *x-ray vision*, through which otherwise occluded objects can be seen in unknown, potentially dangerous, and stressful environments in the context of a common SWAT (special weapons and tactics) team task.

The original version of this chapter was revised: the forgotten acknowledgement was added. The correction to this chapter is available at
https://doi.org/10.1007/978-3-030-49695-1_44

J. Y. C. Chen and G. Fragomeni (Eds.): HCII 2020, LNCS 12190, pp. 591–610, 2020.
https://doi.org/10.1007/978-3-030-49695-1_40

As an example, a SWAT team is standing outside of an apartment during a high-stress, slow, and methodical building search operation as part of serving a drug search warrant. They have a non-weaponized tactical robot, and they send it into the apartment to gain situation awareness and reconnaissance information prior to entry. The SWAT team breacher is able to open any door to provide access for the robot. The team members wear augmented reality (AR) head-mounted displays integrated with their helmets [46]. Visual images are provided to SWAT team members from both a through-the-camera view, seen from the robot's perspective, and an AR virtual window view, seen from the point of view of each team member wearing an AR head-mounted display. Providing video information to SWAT officers by sending a robot into the environment prior to entry improves planning and decision-making by the officers. With more information about the situation, better decisions can be made and more lives can be protected, both officers and public. It is expected that overall team performance, situation awareness, and safety will be enhanced through this *x-ray vision* approach.

2   Background

In order to accomplish this approach, we use *augmented reality* (AR). AR, sometimes also known as *mixed reality*, supplements our natural senses by overlaying additional information on top of what is natively sensed [11]. However, this approach does have some limitations and downsides; human attention is limited, and additional informational inputs can quickly surpass that limit [14,15]. Further, cognitive processing for certain types of information, particularly as it relates to depth, may interact negatively with what can be seen in the real world [35]. These problems lead to two main issues for *X-Ray Vision*: perceptual problems associated with AR and situation awareness concerns inherent to human psychology. Even beyond these factors, human-robot integration also represents a significant challenge for this sort of task.

2.1   Perception and Augmented Reality

Successful AR x-ray vision, which has been a significant area of interest [1,16,27,34,35], is perhaps the most important component of this task. Accurate and accessible augmentation of the environment is a necessity in order to improve outcomes for SWAT teams. As such, this task requires the creation of 3D images that appear to occupy specific locations concurrent with the measured position of those objects in the real world. To do this, we make use of *depth cues*, environmental variables used by the human perceptual system to generate a sense of depth. These include occlusion, stereopsis, accommodation, contrast, motion parallax, familiar size, and many more [10,11]. Significant research has been done to determine the relative effectiveness of each of these cues and how they affect augmented reality depth perception [10,11,24,25,33,40,41,44]; however, a comprehensive approach for accurate depth perception within AR has been an elusive goal [11,24,33].

This is further complicated by the limited nature of most AR displays. While displays have improved dramatically over the last decade, they are still fundamentally limited. Few or no commercially available AR displays allow the adjustment of each depth perception parameter [40]. Thus, parameters like multi-focal accommodation, which are relatively difficult to design into mobile display technology, are often unavailable [29, 32]. Other parameters, such as brightness, can generally be adjusted, but current hardware limits fall short of the brightness of a typical sunny day [47]. Fortunately, this particular application is able to make use of several important depth perception cues, including stereopsis and motion parallax.

Stereopsis, or the combination of stereo images in human eyes to create a depth effect, has been found to have a strong effect on depth perception within arm's reach [10, 23, 25]. Beyond that, however, the effectiveness of this depth cue deteriorates with distance [10, 23]. On its own, stereopsis would likely represent a potentially fallible depth cue for this application [39, 42]. Fortunately, it is also paired with motion parallax, which has been found in several studies to notably increase depth estimation accuracy [7, 8, 42]. Even in real-world studies, motion parallax is an important depth cue; its availability improves depth estimation and undermines several types of optical depth illusions [7, 8]. Other depth cues, such as familiar size, contrast, or texture, may have an impact on depth perception [37, 38], but those effects, with one exception, are notably less significant than the effects of stereopsis and motion parallax.

In a vacuum, we would expect stereopsis and motion parallax to be generally sufficient for locating objects in depth [39, 42]. However, there is a complication: *occlusion*, in which an object in front blocks the view of an object behind, is one of the most salient visual cues for human vision [10, 26]. In this task, where occlusion is necessarily ignored, there is a significant perceptual conflict between seeing an opaque wall and perceiving virtual 3D data beyond it. In some cases, this can cause the depth of the virtual data to be perturbed [5, 35]. In order to deprecate this perceptual conflict, we make use of the *window metaphor*. The window metaphor is a way of contextualizing the display of data past an apparently solid object [5]. Generally, humans have no experience with or grasp of seeing a collection of images through an opaque object. However, we do understand the context of a window, a bounded box that lets us see beyond some barrier. Where a boundary-less mass of floating stimuli beyond a wall might be confusing and bewildering, a neat, bounded window through a wall could be expected to be more perceptually understandable and approachable. Indeed, research on this window metaphor or similar concepts has generally found improvement in depth perception estimations, though further research should be done to confirm this phenomenon [5, 35]. Thus, we expect that the window metaphor will increase user understanding of depth and help prevent information overload.

2.2   SWAT Team Integration and Deployment

Even with the carefully engineered approach described above, this system would be ineffective if it could not be integrated with the target audience, a SWAT team. The complex integration of robotics and augmented reality has the potential to be either a successful extension of SWAT team awareness or a dangerous distraction that yields little operational value. While we do not yet have data on this use case, extrapolation from previous research can help us determine which characteristics are likely to lead to positive outcomes and which are not.

First, it is important to note that tactical robot integration is a challenging task and is difficult to do well [49]. It is easy to create system features that almost inherently detract from team goals: embedded operator requirements, robots that interfere with team performance, or distracting control schemes [2,31]. However, positive responses have been garnered from some system features [2,31]. Broadly speaking, these seem to point toward a desire for greater robot autonomy, robot features that draw fire away from (and not toward) team members, and robot features that allow potential offloading of team tasks onto the robot [2]. While these characteristics don't necessarily map 1-to-1 with this proposed system, there are still many general lessons to learn from these results.

The clear first lesson is that the proposed system needs to be easy-to-use. Team members are unlikely to want to spend valuable time trying to troubleshoot or set up a system that is buggy or difficult to use. Such a distraction would detract from their core task and increase the likelihood of negative outcomes. SWAT team members are also unlikely to want to dedicate a full-time operator to managing the robot [2]. Further, a robot with greater independence would also be better able to draw fire away from team members and help the team more efficiently clear rooms. As such, while it is beyond the purview of this project, developing limited or supervised autonomy that allows a robot to move between rooms, following police search protocols, would likely be a useful addition to this set of tools.

Finally, there are a few attributes of this system that have not been previously investigated and which may be difficult to integrate into tactical teams. A primary concern would be how officers will react to wearing mobile AR displays. Clearly, in the long term and for live use cases, wearing anything that interferes with body armor or head protection would be met with an almost-immediate rejection. However, if the technology otherwise proves worthwhile and usable, it is possible that hardened versions of AR displays could be produced and integrated into body armor. Another potential factor would be the degree to which the AR display becomes a distraction when officers are in the process of clearing a room. This, however, seems like it could be easily counter-acted with a minimal display footprint and/or with a manual AR-on/AR-off switch. It is expected that our evaluation of this system will determine how to best support tactical team performance and usability.

2.3   Situation Awareness

The crux of the issue, however, is *situation awareness*: the general understanding and grasp of a given task environment. This is the very quality that is expected to improve with this system [13,14,43]. As previous research has discovered,

Situational Awareness.jpg

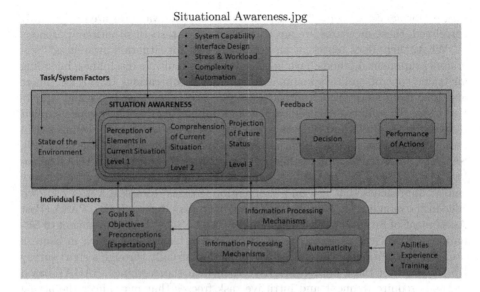

Fig. 1. Situation awareness model for dynamic decision making [14].

it is entirely possible to reduce situation awareness with some types of seemingly positive interventions. In particular, it is surprisingly easy to overwhelm or distort human cognition with too much information, particularly extraneous or difficult-to-incorporate information [13,14]. Thus, in the design and testing of our system, we should consider whether it truly improves situation awareness or whether it, in fact, reduces it.

First, it is important to more fully examine the underlying concept of situation awareness (See Fig. 1). Situation awareness informs human decision-making by encompassing underlying perceived data; in a very real sense, situation awareness can be interpreted as our own internal model of our environment. For 'good' situation awareness, the internal model of the environment would be both accurate and focused on the features that actually matter; for 'poor' situation awareness, the internal model might be inaccurate or not useful for the situation. As such, situation awareness is composed of three main components: perception, comprehension, and prediction [14,17]. In order to build an accurate model, information must be perceived and its implications understood. For complex scenarios, better understanding of the underlying information leads to improved predictions about the state of the environment.

However, it is worth noting that better situation awareness does not inherently result in better task performance [14,15]. It is entirely possible for an operator to have excellent situation awareness and make a mistake or for an operator to have poor situation awareness and blunder into a better performance. It is even possible for an operator to be very confident in his or her situation awareness, but actually have a poor understanding of the situation [14,15]. As such, while task performance or user self-judgment and situation awareness are likely highly correlated, these measures are not themselves ideal tests of situation awareness.

What, then, does represent an exemplary test for situation awareness? Several measurement methods have been drawn from multiple disciplines, including air traffic control, military command, and robotic operations [15,17,49]. There are three main methodical approaches: *explicit* tests, *implicit* tests, and subjective tests. We mainly focus on explicit and implicit methodology, since explicit tests are both direct and objective and implicit tests are directly connected to task performance, and, as such, are generally considered sound methods [17]. SAGAT (Situation Awareness Global Assessment Technique), ASAGAT (Analog SAGAT), and QASAGAT (Quantitative Analog SAGAT) are three very similar approaches that use mid-intervention 'freezes' to assess a user's knowledge in the moment [15,17]. CARS (Crew Awareness Rating Scale), PASA (Post Assessment of Situation Awareness), and SPASA (Short Post Assessment of Situation Awareness) are examples of retrospective techniques, which measure a user's understanding of the task after completion, usually through a short survey [15,17]. Both of these approaches have their own shortcomings. SAGAT-based methods require frequent and intrusive task freezes that may affect the actual cognitive task approach or may bias the operator toward focusing specifically on what is being tested [15,17]. The retrospective techniques, in contrast, occur post-task and so do not interfere with task cognition; however, they produce results that may not be indicative of an operator's effective situation awareness within the task [15,17]. All of these approaches focus on the functional application of the task and individual parameters relating to task performance. However, the primary aspect of situation awareness that this system improves is perception. As such, one of the key questions we must ask in our research is: *How can we measure the effect of this system on an operator's spatial perception?*

3   Approach

The design approach for this project can be viewed as occurring in three distinct steps: (1) determining ideal system parameters from research and task stakeholders, (2) implementing the x-ray vision system, and (3) gauging the system's effectiveness. The following section contains explanations and information pertinent to the current methods used by SWAT teams, the technical execution of our project thus far, and potential future experiments meant to measure memory retention, general performance, and perceptual accuracy.

3.1   Tactical Room-Clearing

SWAT police teams are called in to safely and effectively resolve certain situations where the threat of violence is considered high: counter-terrorism operations, drug raids, high-risk search warrants, hostage situations, or apprehension and arrest of armed suspects. These situations are extremely stressful and can easily lead to unnecessary loss of life, as in the several recorded instances of

Fig. 2. A team member performing mirror reconnaissance. Note that the view the team member sees here is rotated and displaced from his current perspective.

swatting deaths. In particular, room clearing operations require team members to enter a novel environment/situation and evaluate it for potential threats. There are currently two methods for entering a room – blind entry and mirror entry. In blind entry, team members typically go into a room with no visual knowledge of what is on the other side. In mirror entry (See Fig. 2), a team member uses a mirror on a pole to examine the contents of the room from cover before entering. Both of these approaches have notable problems; both leave team members with an imperfect awareness of the environment. In mirror entry, even though some environment information is imparted, this information is distinctly limited. The field of view is small, the mirror itself is awkward and difficult to use, and only one member of the team is be able to scan the room at a time. The information from the mirror is also displaced with respect to the team and requires mental rotation and translation to transform it into the team member's own point of view. This displacement, in particular, has been shown to reduce task performance and increase cognitive load [12,28,45], which likely is related to significantly reduced situation awareness.

In contrast to these methods, our system offers a less cognitively demanding and potentially less dangerous approach. Officers will be able to send a robot, equipped with a stereo camera, in ahead of the team. The robot will stream the depth image of the room to team members wearing mobile head-mounted AR displays. This information will be presented to the team members from their own perspective through an adjustable window. As such, the final result will be an egocentric view of the room, from each operator's perspective – no risk to officers and no awkward mental re-orientation required! Clearly, such an outcome (if it can be successfully incorporated into SWAT practice) could potentially, and dramatically, reduce the risk associated with standard room-clearing operations.

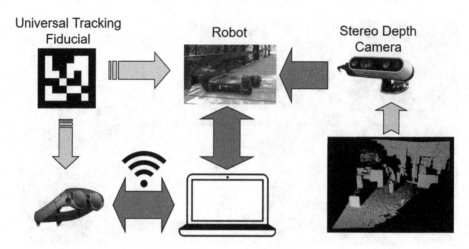

Fig. 3. Connection flow chart for the X-Ray Vision System. Depth images are taken by the stereo depth camera, processed, and delivered to a subscriber AR system through a secure network. Note that the robot and AR system positions are synchronized through the use of a universal tracking fiducial.

3.2   Apparatus

The Depth Camera. The Intel RealSense D435 stereo depth camera is designed specifically for low-light environments and supports a wide field of view out to ten meters, which is ideal for this use case [22]. The depth camera is used in tandem with the robot controlled by the SWAT team; this is comparable to approaches used in previous work [6]. In this system, the depth camera will generate RGB point cloud data (PCD) in real-time, which is immediately transferred to the operators' head-mounted displays.

The depth camera is rigged with a combination of Robot Operating System (ROS) and SLAM software and is equipped with gyroscopic hardware [4,20]. Using these features, depth data can be either taken in independent 'snapshots' or can be used to continuously build a single environmental map. Interestingly, this data can also be stored for later retrieval and analysis, which may be useful for certain law enforcement applications.

The Magic Leap AR System. The Magic Leap headset is a self-contained mobile AR display device. It supports automatic SLAM (simultaneous localization and mapping) environment and position mapping; speech, gesture, and peripheral-based control schemes; standard network protocols; approximately three hours worth of battery life; a 40° horizontal field of view; and a target refresh rate of 60 frames per second. Once the system program has been uploaded to each Magic Leap, they will operate completely independently (aside from syncing and depth data delivered over the network). This is particularly key in that the device will not limit team mobility while in use, nor will charging issues represent a significant constraint for most scenarios (Fig. 4).

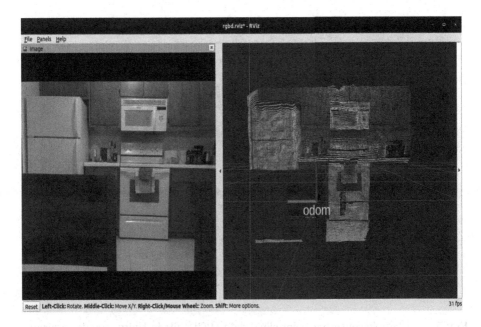

Fig. 4. A screenshot of a scanned room in Rviz

In interacting with the stereo depth camera, Unity, aided by certain tools and libraries, converts the output into a format which can be directly uploaded to the Magic Leap [19,21]. The output is then displayed to operators as a mesh (see Figs. 5, 6 and 7).

As previously stated, by generating and displaying these environments, we are supplying SWAT teams with a safer and more efficient room surveying approach. The additional information these methods provide, combined with the intuitive perceptual understanding that AR supports, represents a potential advancement over the state of the art-provided that the positive aspects of this system outweigh any hidden costs.

3.3 Implementation

In order to implement this system (See Fig. 3), we use several connected components. First, we make use of a Jaguar V4 robot chassis, equipped with an Intel RealSense D435 camera. This robot will contain a computing system (supported by a secure wireless network) that allows the transfer of the point cloud room layout to team members. Each team member will be equipped with a Magic Leap AR system that provides stable augmentation and virtual images. Finally, the relative positions of both the robot and the Magic Leap systems will be synchronized and tracked using a printed fiducial. As an example of the system in action, see Figs. 8 and 9.

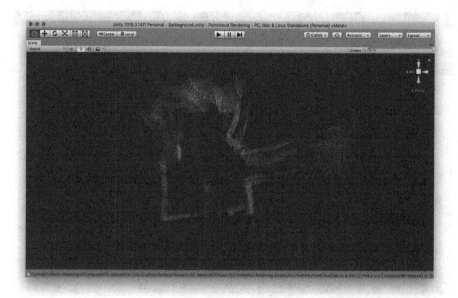

Fig. 5. An example converted point cloud data (PCD) file in Unity (top-down view).

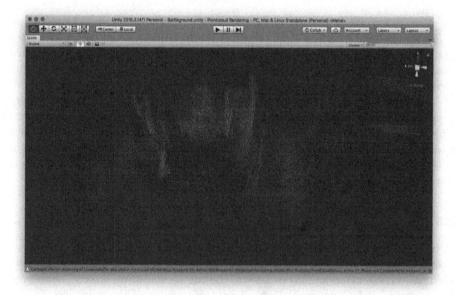

Fig. 6. An example converted point cloud data (PCD) file in Unity (camera view).

The current system development is focused on the structure and design of the robotic platform. Interface improvements might also help improve the system's

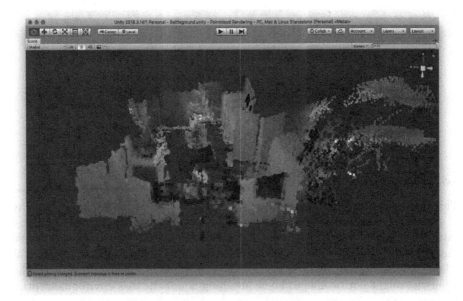

Fig. 7. The same data as Fig. 6, but with point size increased, giving the mesh a blocky appearance.

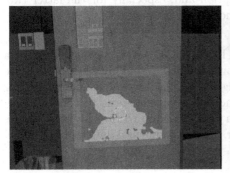

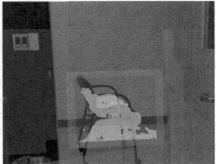

(a) The scanned depth data, as viewed through a closed door.

(b) The scanned depth data, with the scanned room visible.

Fig. 8. The X-Ray Reconnaissance System, displaying a standard office chair.

effectiveness and usability, while adding color and meshing to the displayed point cloud output may improve scene recognition. Certain practical issues, such as the frequency of displayed mesh updates, are also being investigated. These issues should be relatively easy to mitigate or solve with additional analysis. Finally, the important issue of testing and verification is being addressed.

Fig. 9. The X-Ray Reconnaissance System, from several perspectives.

3.4   System Effectiveness

This brings us to evaluating our system's effectiveness – what traits are worthy of analysis? Considering the nature of this intervention and the lack of predictive features, it seems best to evaluate the perceptual validity of this system. Even though perception alone is not comprehensive situation awareness [14,17], it is a key component and represents a notable step forward for team members who otherwise might not be able to know anything about the task environment prior to entry.

As such, there are at least three possible aspects of perception to consider: *memory*, *task performance*, and *depth perception*. Each of these represents, or is affected by, a part of our overall perception and, especially for the latter two, may be relevant to task performance and situation awareness.

Testing. For each of the approaches listed below, testing would occur in a broadly similar manner. Each experimental approach would have three separate conditions: a real world condition using an actual, physical window; a mirror entry condition; and a x-ray vision condition. This allows us to consider each condition both on its own merits and in comparison to real-world performance, to determine which approach is superior. This experimental data will be supplemented by a post-experiment survey.

Memory Testing. In order to test operators' memory, we propose a simple environmental reconstruction experiment. In this task, an operator would observe and be encouraged to explore an adjacent room by looking in through a fixed window. After a short period of free-moving exploration, the operator will be taken to a new area and tasked with reconstructing the explored scene. This reconstruction can be approached from a variety of angles; the operator could draw the scene from memory on a sketchpad or position physical objects identical to the objects in the observed environment. Further investigation is warranted to determine which of these approaches is best for this application. On the one hand, free-style drawing and spatial reasoning is definitively a practiced skill, with some operators being more proficient and some being dramatically less proficient. On the other hand, allowing the physical adjustment of room objects may provide additional feedback to the operator that they would not otherwise receive.

This experimental approach would allow the investigation of memory decay and accuracy. In particular, it will be interesting to observe how working memory functions when using the x-ray vision system, as opposed to strictly real-world stimuli. These results will help determine how effectively the system replicates real-world memory effects.

Task Performance Testing. Task performance does not necessarily correlate directly with situation awareness [14,15]. However, it may be possible to create a task that specifically is novel enough that training and performance differences don't apply and simple enough that completion is readily achievable.

In particular, team members during room-clearing operations desire to have an accurate and complete model of the room prior to entry so that it can be navigated more easily and potential hiding spots identified and cleared. While effectively simulating a room-clearing task with professional SWAT teams may be difficult, room navigation itself is much simpler – though the task becomes trivially easy upon entry into the room. However, if we require operators to rely solely on information acquired from the intervention, the outcome can be expected to rely heavily upon how well the system supports perception and memory. Thus, it may be useful to employ a monitored blind walking navigation task, where users observe the simulated room and are then instructed to enter it without sight. At that time, they would be given a simple navigation task in order to test their perceptual memory of the room layout. This approach has the advantage of testing task performance in a way that is both relevant to the room-clearing operation and that is, at least at the beginning of the experiment, somewhat unpredictable to operators. As such, this approach may be a better measure of how a SWAT team member interacts with the system than an intervention where they know beforehand how they will be tested. To maintain safety during this experiment, a dedicated observer would be present to ensure that the participant does not run into any physical objects.

The results of this approach would clearly represent the expected effect of situation awareness prior to the room-clearing task. Data could easily be gathered from positional reports by the Magic Leap and could consist of a variety of variables including: elapsed task time; task accuracy; and task errors, for any time a user attempts to walk through a location containing a displayed virtual object.

Depth Perception Testing. Depth perception, in this case, is an important aspect of situation awareness, though a high degree of accuracy isn't necessarily required for a room-clearing task. One way that this might be measured is through a version of triangulated walking [36]. In classical depth perception experiments, triangulated walking tasks involve observing a virtual object that is observed briefly and then disappears. After it disappears, the subject is instructed to walk obliquely toward it while continuously pointing to its perceived location. This task has been observed to be an accurate experimental depth perception measurement and has regularly been used in scientific research [36].

This task could easily be modified for use in a hall; indeed, by having the subject move to several different locations in a hallway, both the perceived distance to the object and the associated memory footprint could be evaluated. This task might also indicate whether being subjected to movement/optical flow in the real world could distort the location of the remembered virtual object(s).

4   Discussion

As this project is still untested, this section primarily focuses on our expected results and any potential confounds. We discuss the expected general results of this system for improving situation awareness, the anticipated use and benefit of AR and the window metaphor, and the possible challenges for the integration of the system into SWAT operations.

4.1   Hypotheses and Predictions

Some of the proposed tests have not been previously tried in this sort of venue before (e.g., memory reconstruction). Other tests either have not been applied in exactly this way before (e.g., blind walking), or dramatically differing technologies and levels of virtuality/depth cuing have been used in previous experiments (e.g., triangulated walking) [30,50]. As such, expected results are hard to predict. We would expect results generated from the system to be approximately equivalent to results generated under real-world conditions – which, for blind and triangulated walking, would indicate generally veridical depth judgments. On the other hand, we would expect results from the mirror test to be significantly worse than the real world for depth tasks and likely also worse for memory reconstruction. The relationship between memory reconstruction and the system may also be more complicated than anticipated; some previous research has theorized that presenting items in augmented reality may have novelty or arousal-inducing effects, which could potentially modify or strengthen the operator's memory of item locations [18]. This effect might be caused by the novelty inherent for most users in AR displays; it might also represent a more general tendency for operators to fixate on virtual content over real-world content. Even so, we would expect that this effect would be relatively minor and that memory reconstruction would be approximately equivalent in both the system and the real world.

4.2   The Window Metaphor—Effectiveness and Usability

Previous research has noted a discrepancy between perception in egocentric and allocentric reference frames, causing cognitive displacement and confusion when participants attempt to rectify their location in the physical and virtual worlds [9, 48]. This phenomenon has been known to cause simulator sickness (or a general feeling of nausea induced by exposure to VR or AR) and other negative effects. In addition, views from non-egocentric frames of reference, referred to as displaced perspective, often exhibit increased cognitive demands for users [12, 28, 45]. This increased attentional overhead may have a negative effect on situation awareness and, thus, likely negative effects on performance in a standard room-clearing task. Thus, this system focuses on egocentric perception from the ground up, sidestepping all of the significant costs of non-user-centered projections.

Another area that is important to consider is the effectiveness of the window metaphor. While we have not yet collected concrete data on this issue, subjective experience seems clear; the window metaphor appears to be an effective way to help operators mentally categorize the perceptual data. Without the window, the displayed data can appear chaotic and difficult to place, but, with the window, analysis and examination seem more intuitive. This may also be reinforced by the need to move. In the absence of a window, all the data can be viewed from a single point, while, with the window, movement or re-positioning of the operator or window is necessary to view more than a small portion of data. Thus, in the presence of the window, operators are incentivized to move about, thus introducing motion parallax depth cues, which help more concretely establish and reinforce distance judgments to the displayed data. It might be interesting to more fully investigate this idea in future experimentation, but, for now, it seems subjectively clear that the window metaphor results in improved situation awareness and depth judgments.

4.3   SWAT Team Contextualization

In contrast, the reception of this system among SWAT team members is likely to be a more complicated variable. On the one hand, pre-task intelligence is expected to be highly valuable to SWAT team members, in terms of both its extrinsic value and its regard among the team members. However, this system will also be associated with several cognitive costs, some of which team members may be aware and some of which they may not be. In particular, the deployment and set-up of this system is expected to take a few minutes of up-front time. In most contexts, this will be trivial, but in an incident where speed is extremely important, deployment of this technology could be stressful or result in increased cognitive demands. Therefore, system deployment procedures, and deployment training, are an important consideration. In addition, this task requires integrating a robotic system into SWAT team procedures. While several such integrations have proven successful and popular, it does still remain that current robotics platforms can be noisy, slow, and cumbersome, as compared to team members [2]. Therefore, while it seems likely that the addition of valuable intelligence and the lower risk of fatalities will offset these characteristics in the mind of SWAT team members, it remains to be seen how exactly they will interact with, and react to, this new technology.

5   Future Work

The clear next step for this project is to polish and finalize the various details of the x-ray vision system and begin testing its effectiveness, first with untrained users and then with SWAT team members. These details, while relatively minor, may have a significant impact on performance and operator reception. Once these are finalized, proper testing and experimentation can begin (see Sect. 4).

5.1   Environment Generation and Integration

One of the primary forthcoming issues to consider is how to display the point cloud room data in the Magic Leap. The underlying problem of getting the data to each Leap is largely solved, but determining the best parameters for displaying it is more open-ended. How often should the displayed scene be refreshed from the camera? Updating too often risks bogging down the Magic Leap's processing power and cause rubber banding; updating too rarely, on the other hand, might cause unexpected perceptual effects or somewhat delay the receipt of critical mission data. Similar questions can be asked about ideal point count to be displayed, the usefulness of meshing or color for operators, and whether previously viewed areas should continue to be displayed or only the area currently visible to the depth camera.

5.2   Robot Design and Performance

Functionally, it is also important to finalize the production design of the robotic platform. The physical location of components and wiring all have to be analyzed for faults or weaknesses before the robot can be used in practical applications. In addition, as mentioned previously, expanding robot autonomy would be an interesting next step for this project. It is well beyond the current scope, but expanding the system to potentially encompass multiple semi-autonomous, independent robots promises to be an exceptional step forward in large-scale room clearing tasks. If such a robotic fleet could effectively communicate with each other and the tactical team, it would be possible to dramatically reduce the time required to clear large buildings or even urban environments.

5.3   Testing and Experimentation

Finally, the most important future work is, arguably, testing and experimentation. As mentioned in Sect. 4, there are a number of experiments that can be used to determine if the x-ray vision system is an effective way to improve perception. However, situation awareness goes beyond more than just perception-an important next step would be scenario-based testing, where team members might have to comprehend or predict based on what they see. These scenarios would be fairly challenging to implement and would have to be presented in a surprising manner so as to better test the team's unprepared reactions and awareness.

Other tests might include data-based analysis of various smaller components of the x-ray vision system: the effect of motion parallax on depth judgments, the effectiveness of the window metaphor vs. an unbounded display, or potentially several other system components.

6   Conclusion

We expect that this x-ray vision system will be an effective aid to tactical SWAT teams in room-clearing tasks. It seems likely that presenting previously unknown room information from an egocentric frame of reference will allow team members to easily and intuitively understand, plan, and react to it. These benefits, too, seem to be free of major downsides that could bog down or hinder team efficiency. As such, it is expected that the x-ray vision system will significantly aid in team situation awareness, though further testing is required.

Acknowledgements. This material is based upon work supported by the National Science Foundation, under awards IIS-1937565, to J.E. Swan II and C.L. Bethel, and IIS-1320909, to J.E. Swan II. We acknowledge a productive collaboration with Mark Ballard, Chief of Police, Police Department, City of Starkville, MS, USA. We also acknowledge the contributions of Mohammed Safayet Arefin.

References

1. Bane, R., Hollerer, T.: Interactive tools for virtual x-ray vision in mobile augmented reality. In: Third IEEE and ACM International Symposium on Mixed and Augmented Reality, pp. 231–239. IEEE (2004)
2. Bethel, C.L., Carruth, D., Garrison, T.: Discoveries from integrating robots into swat team training exercises. In: 2012 IEEE International Symposium on Safety, Security, and Rescue Robotics (SSRR), pp. 1–8. IEEE (2012)
3. Bethel, C.L., May, D.C., Louine, J.: Use of technology by law enforcement. In: 2016 International Police Executive Symposium (IPES). IPES (2016)
4. Bi, Y., et al.: An MAV localization and mapping system based on dual realsense cameras. In: International Micro Air Vehicle Competition and Conference, University of Singapore, Singapore, Technical report (2016)
5. Bichlmeier, C., Sielhorst, T., Heining, S.M., Navab, N.: Improving depth perception in medical ar. In: Horsch, A., Deserno, T.M., Handels, H., Meinzer, H.P., Tolxdorff, T. (eds.) Bildverarbeitung für die Medizin 2007, pp. 217–221. Springer, Heidelberg (2007). https://doi.org/10.1007/978-3-540-71091-2_44
6. Biswas, J., Veloso, M.: Depth camera based indoor mobile robot localization and navigation. In: 2012 IEEE International Conference on Robotics and Automation, pp. 1697–1702, May 2012. https://doi.org/10.1109/ICRA.2012.6224766
7. Bradshaw, M.F., Parton, A.D., Eagle, R.A.: The interaction of binocular disparity and motion parallax in determining perceived depth and perceived size. Perception **27**(11), 1317–1331 (1998)
8. Bradshaw, M.F., Parton, A.D., Glennerster, A.: The task-dependent use of binocular disparity and motion parallax information. Vis. Res. **40**(27), 3725–3734 (2000)

9. Byagowi, A., Moussavi, Z.: Design of a virtual reality navigational (VRN) experiment for assessment of egocentric spatial cognition. In: 2012 Annual International Conference of the IEEE Engineering in Medicine and Biology Society, pp. 4812–4815. IEEE (2012)

10. Cutting, J., Vishton, P.: Perception of space and motion. In: Handbook of Perception and Cognition, 1st edn. Academic Press Inc, San Diego (1995)

11. Drascic, D., Milgram, P.: Perceptual issues in augmented reality. In: Proceedings-SPIE the International Society for Optical Engineering, vol. 2653, pp. 123–134. SPIE International Society for Optical Engineering (1996)

12. Ellis, S.R., Adelstein, B.D., Yeom, K.: Human control in rotated frames: anisotropies in the misalignment disturbance function of pitch, roll, and yaw. In: Proceedings of the Human Factors and Ergonomics Society Annual Meeting, vol. 56, pp. 1336–1340. SAGE Publications, Los Angeles (2012)

13. Endsley, M.R.: Measurement of situation awareness in dynamic systems. Hum. Factors **37**, 65–84 (1995)

14. Endsley, M.R., Garland, D.J., et al.: Theoretical underpinnings of situation awareness: a critical review. Situation Awareness Anal. Measur. **1**, 24 (2000)

15. Endsley, M.R., Selcon, S.J., Hardiman, T.D., Croft, D.G.: A comparative analysis of SAGAT and SART for evaluations of situation awareness. In: Proceedings of the Human Factors and Ergonomics Society Annual Meeting, vol. 42, pp. 82–86. SAGE Publications, Los Angeles (1998)

16. Furness, L.: The Application of Head-Mounted Displays to Airborne Reconnaissance and Weapon Delivery. Wright-Patterson Air Force Base, Ohio, USA (1969)

17. Gatsoulis, Y., Virk, G.S., Dehghani-Sanij, A.A.: On the measurement of situation awareness for effective human-robot interaction in teleoperated systems. J. Cogn. Eng. Decis. Making **4**(1), 69–98 (2010)

18. Hopp, T., Gangadharbatla, H.: Novelty effects in augmented reality advertising environments: the influence of exposure time and self-efficacy. J. Curr. Issues Res. Adv. **37**(2), 113–130 (2016)

19. Pcllibrary (2020). Accessed 06 Feb 2020

20. Slam with d435i (2019). Accessed 06 Feb 2020

21. Pcx (2020). Accessed 06 Feb 2020

22. Intel realsense d435 (2019). Accessed 06 Feb 2020

23. Johnston, E.B., Cumming, B.G., Landy, M.S.: Integration of stereopsis and motion shape cues. Vis. Res. **34**(17), 2259–2275 (1994)

24. Jones, J.A., Swan II, J.E., Singh, G., Kolstad, E., Ellis, S.R.: The effects of virtual reality, augmented reality, and motion parallax on egocentric depth perception. In: Proceedings of the 5th Symposium on Applied Perception in Graphics and Visualization, pp. 9–14. ACM (2008)

25. Julesz, B.: Binocular depth perception without familiarity cues: random-dot stereo images with controlled spatial and temporal properties clarify problems in stereopsis. Science **145**(3630), 356–362 (1964)

26. Jurgens, V., Cockburn, A., Billinghurst, M.: Depth cues for augmented reality stakeout. In: Proceedings of the 7th ACM SIGCHI New Zealand Chapter's International Conference on Computer-Human Interaction: Design Centered HCI, pp. 117–124 (2006)

27. Kersten-Oertel, M., Jannin, P., Collins, D.L.: The state of the art of visualization in mixed reality image guided surgery. Comput. Med. Imaging Graph. **37**(2), 98–112 (2013)

28. Klatzky, R.L., Wu, B., Stetten, G.: The disembodied eye: consequences of displacing perception from action. Vis. Res. **50**(24), 2618–2626 (2010)

29. Konrad, R., Padmanaban, N., Cooper, E., Wetzstein, G.: Computational focus-tunable near-eye displays. In: ACM SIGGRAPH 2016 Emerging Technologies, p. 3. ACM (2016)
30. Kunz, B.R., Wouters, L., Smith, D., Thompson, W.B., Creem-Regehr, S.H.: Revisiting the effect of quality of graphics on distance judgments in virtual environments: a comparison of verbal reports and blind walking. Attention Percept. Psychophys. **71**(6), 1284–1293 (2009)
31. Lalejini, A., Duckworth, D., Sween, R., Bethel, C.L., Carruth, D.: Evaluation of supervisory control interfaces for mobile robot integration with tactical teams. In: 2014 IEEE International Workshop on Advanced Robotics and its Social Impacts, pp. 1–6. IEEE (2014)
32. Liu, S., et al.: A multi-plane optical see-through head mounted display design for augmented reality applications. J. Soc. Inf. Display **24**(4), 246–251 (2016)
33. Livingston, M.A., Ai, Z., Swan, J.E., Smallman, H.S.: Indoor vs. outdoor depth perception for mobile augmented reality. In: 2009 IEEE Virtual Reality Conference, pp. 55–62. IEEE (2009)
34. Livingston, M.A., Dey, A., Sandor, C., Thomas, B.H.: Pursuit of "x-ray vision" for augmented reality. In: Huang, W., Alem, L., Livingston, M. (eds.) Human Factors in Augmented Reality Environments, pp. 67–107. Springer, Heidelberg (2013). https://doi.org/10.1007/978-1-4614-4205-9_4
35. Livingston, M.A., et al.: Resolving multiple occluded layers in augmented reality. In: Proceedings of the Second IEEE and ACM International Symposium on Mixed and Augmented Reality, pp. 56–65. IEEE (2003)
36. Loomis, J.M., Knapp, J.M., et al.: Visual perception of egocentric distance in real and virtual environments. Virtual Adapt. Environ. **11**, 21–46 (2003)
37. McIntosh, R.D., Lashley, G.: Matching boxes: familiar size influences action programming. Neuropsychologia **46**(9), 2441–2444 (2008)
38. O'Shea, R.P., Blackburn, S.G., Ono, H.: Contrast as a depth cue. Vis. Res. **34**(12), 1595–1604 (1994)
39. Palmisano, S.: Perceiving self-motion in depth: the role of stereoscopic motion and changing-size cues. Percept. Psychophys. **58**(8), 1168–1176 (1996)
40. Phillips, N., Massey, K., Arefin, M.S., Swan, J.E.: Design, assembly, calibration, and measurement of an augmented reality haploscope. In: 2019 IEEE Conference on Virtual Reality and 3D User Interfaces (VR), pp. 1770–1774. IEEE (2019)
41. Rieser, J.J., Pick, H.L., Ashmead, D.H., Garing, A.E.: Calibration of human locomotion and models of perceptual-motor organization. J. Exp. Psychol.: Hum. Percept. Perform. **21**(3), 480 (1995)
42. Rogers, B., Graham, M.: Motion parallax as an independent cue for depth perception. Perception **8**(2), 125–134 (1979)
43. Sarter, N.B., Woods, D.D.: Situation awareness: a critical but ill-defined phenomenon. Int. J. Aviat. Psychol. **1**(1), 45–57 (1991)
44. Singh, G., Ellis, S.R., Swan II, J.E.: The effect of focal distance, age, and brightness on near-field augmented reality depth matching. IEEE Trans. Vis. Comput. Graph. (2018)
45. Smith, K.U., Smith, W.M.: Perception and Motion. American Psychological Association (1962)
46. Stevens, J., Eifert, L.: Augmented reality technology in U.S. army training (wIP). In: Proceedings of the 2014 Summer Simulation Multiconference, pp. 1–6. Society for Computer Simulation International, 2685679 (2014)
47. Taylor, A.G.: Develop Microsoft Hololens Apps Now. Springer, Heidelberg (2016). https://doi.org/10.1007/978-1-4842-2202-7

48. Vidal, M., Amorim, M.A., Berthoz, A.: Navigating in a virtual three-dimensional maze: how do egocentric and allocentric reference frames interact? Cogn. Brain Res. **19**(3), 244–258 (2004)
49. Voshell, M., Woods, D.D., Phillips, F.: Overcoming the keyhole in human-robot coordination: simulation and evaluation. In: Proceedings of the Human Factors and Ergonomics Society Annual Meeting, vol. 49, pp. 442–446. Sage Publications, Los Angeles (2005)
50. Willemsen, P., Colton, M.B., Creem-Regehr, S.H., Thompson, W.B.: The effects of head-mounted display mechanics on distance judgments in virtual environments. In: Proceedings of the 1st Symposium on Applied Perception in Graphics and Visualization, pp. 35–38. ACM (2004)

Enabling Situational Awareness via Augmented Reality of Autonomous Robot-Based Environmental Change Detection

Christopher Reardon[1(✉)], Jason Gregory[1], Carlos Nieto-Granda[2], and John G. Rogers[1]

[1] U.S. Army Research Laboratory, Adelphi, MD 20783, USA
{christopher.m.reardon3.civ,jason.m.gregory1.civ,
john.g.rogers59.civ}@mail.mil
[2] University of California, San Diego, San Deigo, CA 92093, USA
cnietogr@ucsd.edu

Abstract. Accurately detecting changes in one's environment is an important ability for many application domains, but can be challenging for humans. Autonomous robots can easily be made to autonomously detect metric changes in the environment, but unlike humans, understanding context can be challenging for robots. We present a novel system that uses an autonomous robot performing point cloud-based change detection to facilitate information-gathering tasks and provides enhanced situational awareness. The robotic system communicates detected changes via augmented reality to a human teammate for evaluation. We present results from a fielded system using two differently-equipped robots to examine implementation questions of point cloud density and its effect on visualization of changes. Our results show that there are trade-offs between implementations that we believe will be constructive towards similar systems in the future.

Keywords: Human-robot teaming · Augmented reality · Simultaneous Localization and Mapping (SLAM) · Change detection · Field robotics

1 Introduction

The real world is an endlessly dynamic and varying place. The ability to detect changes in an environment is important both for intelligent robots to operate in the real world and for robots to operate alongside humans as teammates.

Robots with minimal capabilities may be able to operate using simple reactive or closed-loop control to perform a basic task. This is particularly true where efforts can be made to engineer and instrument the environment to simplify the task space. However, the increased task and environmental complexity present in real-world scenarios will require more sophisticated capabilities, including

This is a U.S. government work and not under copyright protection in the U.S.;
foreign copyright protection may apply 2020
J. Y. C. Chen and G. Fragomeni (Eds.): HCII 2020, LNCS 12190, pp. 611–628, 2020.
https://doi.org/10.1007/978-3-030-49695-1_41

scene understanding so that a robot can reason about essential information such as the state of a task or the feasibility of goal completion [14]. Importantly, this mission-critical information can be deduced from detecting changes in the robot's environment and contributes greatly to whether an autonomous robot can complete a given mission. Take, for example, a search and rescue application where a change may make the goal state unachievable, such as a planned route becoming blocked by rubble. In this case, not only will the autonomous robot not be able to navigate to its intended destination, but the safe execution of the entire mission may be in jeopardy if the change's context indicates a high likelihood of additional adverse events, e.g., falling debris or adversarial activity.

(a)   (b)

Fig. 1. Changes detected in the point cloud model (a) indicate potential locations of devices placed by an adversary (b).

In order for robots to operate alongside humans as teammates, the ability to communicate these detected changes and corresponding reasoning is also important for a variety of cooperative tasks. For example, in autonomous inspection of infrastructure, the ability to detect, identify, and communicate changes that represent structural deterioration to a human is essential for affecting timely repairs. An example in security robotics is the ability for a surveillance robot to detect changes along its regular patrol route that might indicate actions by adversarial agents, e.g., a break-in or the placement of a dangerous device, such as shown in Fig. 1, which a human teammate would want to be informed of immediately. In the context of cooperative tasks involving humans and autonomous robots, the relevant information must be exchanged between the teammates in a timely fashion for optimal and responsive decision making.

Detecting even large changes in complex environments can be challenging for humans [3,13]. Mobile robots can autonomously perform metric-based comparisons of sensor readings to detect potential changes, but lack contextual understanding to determine their significance. In addition to the potential for innocuous change in any real world environment, algorithmic methods for robots to

Fig. 2. Augmented reality situational awareness in human-robot teaming.

detect changes can be noisy and yield numerous false positives. Combined, these issues provide significant obstacles for autonomous robots to interpret and act upon detected changes. We believe that a human-robot team working cooperatively to detect, interpret, and act upon changes offers a powerful means to overcome their mutual shortcomings. Together, the human and robot possess the capabilities to detect and identify changes of importance in any specific scenario context; however, the critical challenge becomes creating an efficient method of communicating, interpreting, and prioritizing changes.

We present a novel approach to address this challenge that uses Augmented Reality (AR) to create a human-robot team where the robot identifies changes, communicates them via AR to the human teammate, who can then interpret their context for further action. Our system is intended to address the general case of detecting changes in an arbitrary environment without external instrumentation and presenting them to a human teammate using AR, building upon previous work in [10]. The AR system we employ is a head-mounted device (HMD) worn by the human teammate, who is co-located in the environment with the robot (Fig. 2). This allows the robot to present augmented visualizations via the HMD to provide situational awareness to the human teammate, which enables improved decision making and collaboration. We believe this is the first example of the use of AR for communicating and interpreting environmental changes detected by an autonomous robot to a human teammate.

Detection of environmental changes takes place on-board the mobile robot in real time (Fig. 1). A prior model is collected of the environment in a "clean", initial state. This model consists of a point cloud together with an anchoring position and orientation, referred to as a pose, which is registered into a global reference frame. To compare the current state of the environment with this model, a fine alignment is computed using generalized-ICP [12] with the robot's pose from a Simultaneous Localization and Mapping (SLAM) solution as an initial guess. Points in the current scan which are further than the intrinsic sensor noise threshold from the model are clustered into candidate change regions. The candidate change regions of sufficient size are highlighted in the user's AR interface for the human to evaluate for further action.

One important question when implementing a point cloud-based change detection system is: What is the appropriate sampling density with regards to system performance and user experience? To validate our approach and examine this question, we implement and test our system using two otherwise identical robots equipped with different commercial-off-the-shelf LiDAR devices that generate relatively sparse and dense point clouds. Our robots autonomously perform change detection and present changes online to the human teammate via the HMD interface.

We hypothesize (*H1*) that the higher-density LiDAR would provide more accurate detection in all environments than the lower-density LiDAR. Given that expectation, we further hypothesize that (*H2*) when the user is teamed with the higher-density LiDAR robot, the visual presentation to the user would be more discriminative, i.e., correct change detections would be more obvious.

To evaluate these hypotheses, we compare performance between the two robotic systems in two different field environments: in an alleyway street scene and an outdoor driveway with a parking space. Our results show that while the higher-resolution LiDAR does produce a denser point cloud and therefore more true positive detections, when evaluated in field environments there are a number of distinct trade-offs that mean the higher density is not always more accurate, nor does it always provide a better user experience. Full results are discussed in Sect. 5.

2   Background and Related Work

Novelty detection is a broad and robust area of research that generally means the recognition of elements in *test* data that differ from *training* data or a *model* learned from that data [7]. Environmental change detection can be seen as the application of novelty detection to tasks where physical changes in a specific environment, e.g., object addition or removal, are identified on an ongoing basis by comparing continuously reacquired *test* data against a known *model*.

Robots operating in real-world environments have a strong need for accurate change detection, particularly for tasks where one robot or teams of robots repeatedly encounter the same environment. This area of research has broad applications including inspection [5], surveillance [6,18], safety and security [15], and general robust outdoor navigation [14].

Augmented and mixed reality technologies are currently experiencing a period of growth for use in human-robot interaction (HRI) as they present a mechanism for overcoming issues of communication in HRI [16]. Similarly, this work uses AR to overcome issues of communication and contextual understanding in HRI by creating more robust human-robot teams for operation in field environments. Previous work by the authors presented an overview of examined applications in this domain [10].

3 Approach

3.1 SLAM

In our system, both the AR-HMD and the mobile robot construct independent 3D representations of the environment utilizing a Simultaneous Localization and Mapping (SLAM) algorithm. For the AR-HMD, this approach is based upon visual feature tracking and is provided as a black-box solution delivered with the interface (Microsoft HoloLens). The SLAM implementation utilized onboard the robot is based upon *OmniMapper* as described in [17] with further refinements described in [4]. Briefly, the approach is to build a *pose graph* over measurements between adjacent point clouds and loop closures when locations are revisited. These measurements are used to compute a solution to the robot's trajectory in a least squares sense via the nonlinear optimization framework *GTSAM* [1] based upon square root smoothing and mapping [2]. Each point cloud taken along this optimized trajectory solution is then projected into a common frame of reference and accumulated into a point cloud representing the environment.

Of course, using shared environmental information like change detections for teaming between the human and the robot is impossible without a common frame of reference. Alignment of the human and robot teammates' coordinate frames is therefore critical for understanding teammate position. We use the approach presented in previous work [9] to enable this capability. Since both the robot and the AR-HMD can generate a geometric representation of the environment in point cloud format, we can then compute the homogeneous transformation matrix between the robot and human point clouds using the Iterative Closest Point (ICP) algorithm [12]. The initial computation is performed on a coarse estimate provided by the human, and is then recomputed online as the human and robot maneuver through the environment.

3.2 Change Detection

To perform change detection, first a *model* cloud representing the "clean" state of the world is built via the SLAM process described in Sect. 3.1. At any time in the future, the robot can then collect a *test* cloud using the same procedure. This cloud can either be collected completely and then processed, or processed incrementally during collection.

Once a *test* cloud is created, either at the end of a patrol or incrementally online, it is analyzed for changes from the *model* cloud. These clouds are in approximately the same reference frame either through coarse GPS alignment or by originating the maps near the same place, as was done in this paper. Note, however, either of these approximate alignment methods is insufficient to support change detection due to the large errors that inherently result from small rotational alignment errors. Therefore, the alignment of these clouds is first refined with a generalized ICP [12] procedure.

Once the *model* and *test* clouds are accurately aligned, change detection is implemented in PCL [11] via a set of difference segmentation functions and outlier filters. The difference segmentation routine builds a KD-tree of the model to reduce quadratic search complexity to $n \log n$. Each point in the test cloud is then compared with the model via the KD-tree to find the nearest point and its distance. If this distance is greater than a threshold, which in our experimentation is 10 cm, it is accumulated in a new point cloud denoted *change*.

The *change* cloud is then filtered to remove noisy detections by looking for support of at least 10 detection points within a radius of 30 cm. This will remove small isolated groups of detection points which might be due to range error in the sensor or quantization error in the representation used by the mapper. Other errors are possible due to occluded regions in the *model* cloud which happen to be visible due to slight viewpoint variance in the *test* cloud; these regions will be present in the *change* cloud and will lower the precision of the analyzed results in Sect. 4. The segmented changes can be seen in Fig. 1 for an example scenario where a device has been hidden under a bicycle and is detected by the robot system.

3.3 Augmented Reality Interface

Change detections described in Sect. 3.2 are continuously collected as the robot navigates through the environment. Filtered candidate changes are presented to the user via the AR-HMD as translucent red spheres with a radius of 4 cm. An example of changes detected and visualized in the AR-HMD is shown in Fig. 3, where the user can see the detected change locations superimposed over the physical changes in the environment. For the user's reference, the 2D occupancy grid generated by the robot's SLAM implementation (Sect. 3.1) is also visualized as a 2D projection onto the ground plane, with white representing unoccupied and black representing occupied space in the robot's map. Using this information, the user is able to evaluate and identify actual changes for future investigation. For example, the user could prioritize examining a suspicious package or removing debris blocking a road. The locations where visualizations coincide with movable objects are the most likely candidates for such changes.

Future work will be directed at refining the interface through testing different data aggregation, visualization, and interaction types through the HMD with an aim towards improving the interpretability and accuracy of the information displayed, as well as directing the robot to autonomously address changes that the human deems of interest.

4   Experiments

We tested our hypotheses from Sect. 1 through an evaluation of our approach using the complete system online in experiments in two different environments.

By examining the performance of the change detection and AR visualization by teaming a human wearing an AR-HMD with two otherwise identical robots equipped with different resolution LiDAR systems, we are able to reach several valuable conclusions regarding the development, applicability, and configuration of such systems.

(a)

(b)

Fig. 3. Augmented reality visualizations of changes (red spheres) in the two experimental environments: (a) alley and (b) driveway. Also shown are the robot's 2D occupancy grid map as white (unoccupied) and black (occupied) cells projected onto the ground plane, and the current location of the robot (blue box). (Color figure online)

4.1   Hardware

The hardware employed for these experiments included two Clearpath Robotics Jackal robots. This wheeled platform measures $0.508 \times 0.430 \times 0.250$ m and can move at a maximum velocity of 2.0 m/s. Each have an Intel Core i5-4570TE CPU and runs Ubuntu 16.04 and the Robot Operating System (ROS) [8] on board. Each was equipped with a MicroStrain 3DM-GX4-25 inertial measurement unit (IMU) for improved mapping and state estimation performance, and a Ubiquiti Bullet M5 HP 5 GHz WiFi radio for communications.

Because both the change detection (Sect. 3.2) and corresponding visualization of those changes in AR (Sect. 3.3) are highly dependent upon the density of the point clouds collected by the system, we equipped each robot with a different Light Detection and Ranging (LiDAR) device. The first robot was equipped with a lower density Velodyne VLP-16 LiDAR sensor, which has 16 laser rangers oriented with a 1.9° elevation angle separation, a range of 100 m, and collects approximately 300,000 points per second in a 360° azimuthal field of view and a 30° elevational field of view. The second robot was equipped with a higher density Ouster OS1 with 64 laser rangers oriented with a 0.7° elevation angle separation and a range of 120 m that collects over 1.3 million points per second with 360° azimuthal and 45° elevational fields of view. Both robots are shown in Fig. 4.

Fig. 4. The two robots used in our experiments, which are equipped identically with the exception of Velodyne VLP-16 LiDAR (left) and Ouster OS1 LiDAR (right).

The human is equipped with the Microsoft HoloLens AR-HMD[1]. Custom visualization messages are communicated between the robots and the HoloLens using a combination of ROSBridge[2] (on the robots) and ROS#[3] (on the HoloLens).

---

[1] https://www.microsoft.com/en-us/hololens.

[2] http://wiki.ros.org/rosbridge_suite.

[3] https://github.com/siemens/ros-sharp.

4.2   Environments

Two environments were used for these experiments. The first was an alleyway street scene constructed for the purpose of robotics experimentation that features a narrow alley space between two multi-story buildings seen in Fig. 5a. The second was an outdoor driveway with a parking space that is adjacent to trees and a building, as seen in Fig. 5c. Both presented unique features that excited the change detection system in different ways.

(a)   (b)

(c)   (d)

Fig. 5. Environments used in the experiments. (a) and (c) show the alley and driveway environments. (b) and (d) show environments with changes added. In (b), a ball, yellow case, and steel drum were added to the alley scene. In (d), a small All-Terrain Vehicle (ATV) was placed in a parking space. (Color figure online)

The *model* point clouds generated by each robot for each environment are shown in Fig. 6a–6c. The differing density of the clouds due to the different LiDAR resolutions can be clearly seen in the quantity of points and resulting appearance of fidelity.

4.3   Procedure

The procedure for each experiment was as follows. In each environment, following the approach in Sect. 3, a *model* point cloud was collected and stored.

Then, changes in the form of novel objects were placed in the environment that were not present in the model, as depicted in Figs. 5b and 5d. For the next phase, a robot re-explored the environment while collecting *test* clouds and evaluating them online against the *model* cloud. As changes were detected, visualizations were immediately displayed via the AR-HMD interface to a human who was co-present in the environment. *Model, test,* and the robots' change detection performance, as well as video from the AR-HMD user's experience were all recorded for analysis.

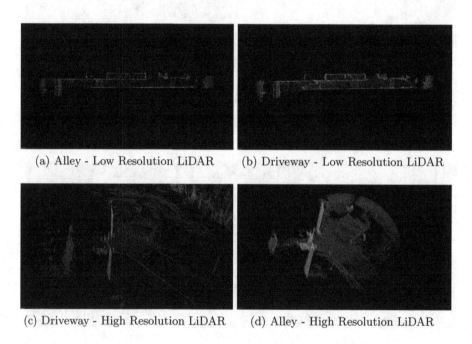

(a) Alley - Low Resolution LiDAR   (b) Driveway - Low Resolution LiDAR

(c) Driveway - High Resolution LiDAR   (d) Alley - High Resolution LiDAR

Fig. 6. *Model* point clouds of each environment for each LiDAR sensor type.

5   Results and Discussion

Recall that our initial hypotheses were:

H1: The robot equipped with the higher resolution LiDAR would provide more accurate detection than the robot with the low-density LiDAR.
H2: Visual presentation to the user will be more discriminative (correct change detections would be more obvious) with the higher resolution LiDAR.

Interestingly, the first hypothesis *H1* did not hold entirely for either environment, given our assumptions, and for different reasons. First, it is worth noting that our change detection algorithm is far from perfect; it can at times produce a large number of false positives. These can be due to small errors and misalignments in the collection, noise in the data, or noise in the environment itself such as random motion effects like wind. In light of this, the density of the point cloud was actually detrimental to the statistical performance of the higher-resolution LiDAR. Where the low-resolution LiDAR would detect a few spurious point changes, the high-resolution would detect a large number. This effect can be seen clearly in the alley environment between Figs. 7a and 7b. Figures 9 and 10 show the actual point cloud detections over time; one can observe the relative number of false positives in particular. Further, even though the alley has many of the visual aspects of a real street scene, because it is part of a larger "mock" staged environment contained in large building it is not subject to environmental changes such as wind. The effect of wind noise on the system was highly

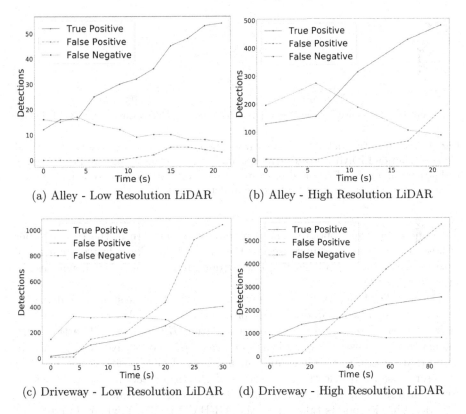

(a) Alley - Low Resolution LiDAR   (b) Alley - High Resolution LiDAR

(c) Driveway - Low Resolution LiDAR   (d) Driveway - High Resolution LiDAR

Fig. 7. True positive, false positive, and false negative detection results from the two robot configurations (lower and higher resolution LiDAR) in two environments (alley street scene and outdoor driveway with a parking space). Note the difference in detections scale.

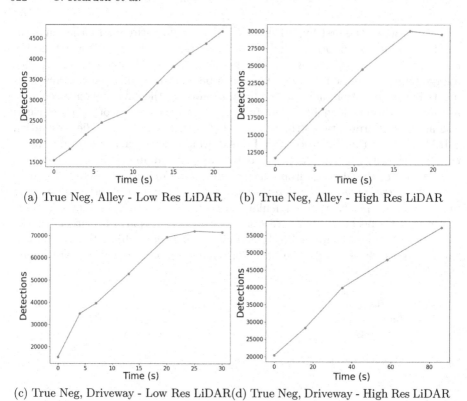

(a) True Neg, Alley - Low Res LiDAR   (b) True Neg, Alley - High Res LiDAR

(c) True Neg, Driveway - Low Res LiDAR(d) True Neg, Driveway - High Res LiDAR

Fig. 8. True negative detection results from the two robot configurations (lower and higher resolution LiDAR) in two environments (alley street scene and outdoor driveway with a parking space). Presented separately from Fig. 7 due to relative magnitude vs. other detection types. Note the difference in detections scale.

pronounced for *both* robots in the driveway scene, as seen in the high number of false positives as time increased in Figs. 7c and 7d. The relative quantity of false positives from wind blowing on surrounding vegetation is shown best in Figs. 11d and 12d.

Despite the difficulty of noisy environments and the system's tendency to be sensitive to these small errors and produce a large number of false positives, we were pleased to find support for invalidating *H2* as well. While this work did not include a user study and therefore cannot be conclusive, anecdotally we found that despite relatively significant numbers of false positives visualized to the user, because of the tight clustering of change detection visualizations on true changes, the noisy data was easily filtered out by a human user. This is illustrated in viewpoints taken from the AR-HMD in Fig. 3, where despite false change detections to the left in Fig. 3a one can clearly see the changes clustered on the objects, and likewise despite false changes in the grass and trees in Fig. 3b, one's attention is immediately drawn to the changes indicated on the ATV.

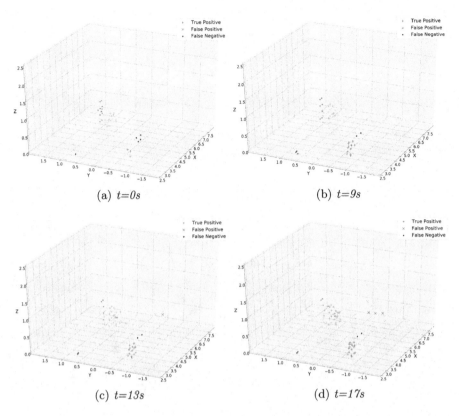

(a) $t=0s$ (b) $t=9s$

(c) $t=13s$ (d) $t=17s$

Fig. 9. Example results from the lower resolution LiDAR-equipped robot in the alley scene (Fig. 5b). Plots (a)–(d) spatial representations of true positive, false positive, and false negative detections at progressing time lapses. The robot begins at position $(2, 0, 0)$ and proceeds along the X axis. True positives on the right, centered around $(3.5, -0.5, 0.25)$, are change detections intersecting the yellow case in Fig. 5b. True positives on the left near $(6.5, 1, 0.5)$ are change detections intersecting the black drum. The ball in Fig. 5b was not detected.

With these results in mind, we can define a set of trade-offs and design decisions that we believe may be constructive towards further refinements of similar systems in the future. The LiDAR resolution had significant and somewhat unexpected trade-offs. As noted above, there was a significant magnifying effect on the false positive detections for the high-resolution LiDAR. Extensive outdoor environments where no barriers exist to LiDAR scans present a computational challenge to both robots. In the driveway environment, the processing time for the lower-resolution LiDAR robot was demonstrably longer than in the alley, resulting in about half as many *test* clouds being processed per unit time. This effect was much worse for the other robot, as the size of the point cloud on a high-resolution LiDAR like the Ouster OS1 makes the change detection algorithm, while not completely intractable, too slow to run on our robot's hardware in

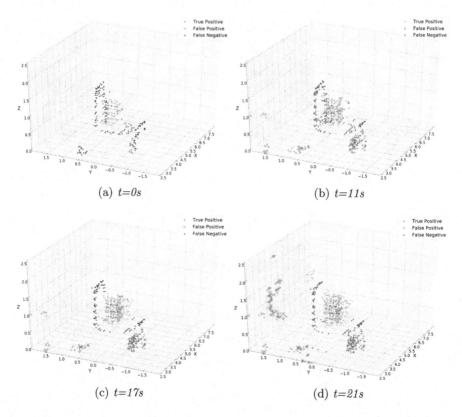

Fig. 10. Example results from the higher resolution LiDAR-equipped robot in the alley scene (Fig. 5b). Plots (a)–(d) show spatial representations of true positive, false positive, and false negative detections at progressing time lapses. The robot begins at position $(2, 0, 0)$ and proceeds along the X axis. True positives on the right, centered around $(3.5, -0.5, 0.25)$, are change detections intersecting the yellow case in Fig. 5b. True positives on the left near $(6.5, 1, 0.5)$ are change detections intersecting the black drum. True positives on the left near $(3, 0.75, 0.1)$ are detections intersecting the ball.

any reasonable timeframe. For this reason we applied a threshold to the LiDAR, limiting any laser return to 50 m in an effort to reduce the point cloud size. For a more fair comparison we made a corresponding change in the post-processing of the results from the low-resolution LiDAR robot, discarding detections over 50 m.

In terms of object detection, the higher-resolution LiDAR robot was the only robot to successfully detect the ball in the alley scene (Fig. 5b). For a visualization of that detection compare Fig. 9 with Fig. 10. Note the ball location at $(3, 0.75, 0.1)$. It is possible that with better tuning of the change detection the ball could be detected by the lower-resolution LiDAR; however, it is entirely possible that the low number of points returned from such a small object will always be filtered.

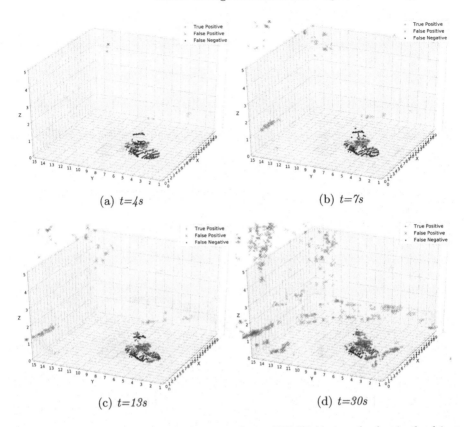

(a) *t=4s*

(b) *t=7s*

(c) *t=13s*

(d) *t=30s*

Fig. 11. Example results from the lower resolution LiDAR-equipped robot in the drive-way scene (Fig. 5(d)). Plots (a)–(d) show spatial representations of true positive, false positive, and false negative detections at progressing time lapses. The robot begins at position $(0,0,0)$ and proceeds along the X axis. True positives on the left near $(7,5,0.5)$ are change detections intersecting the small ATV in Fig. 5d. The numerous false positives in the space over 10 m from the origin coincide with vegetation in the scene blowing in the wind.

Finally, the purpose of this system is ultimately to present changes to the human for evaluation of further action. Given the concerns of tractability of computation, accuracy of detection, and sufficiency of information, and given our change detection approach, unless there is a need to detect small changes in the environment, we believe that a robot equipped lower resolution LiDAR may be capable of detecting and presenting changes to the human user via the AR-HMD just as well, if not better, than a robot equipped with a higher-resolution LiDAR. We caveat this with the expectation that given sufficient optimization for computation, detection accuracy, and information downsampling (e.g., through filtering and clustering) in the user interface, the system with a higher-resolution LiDAR should be able to be made to outperform the lower-resolution.

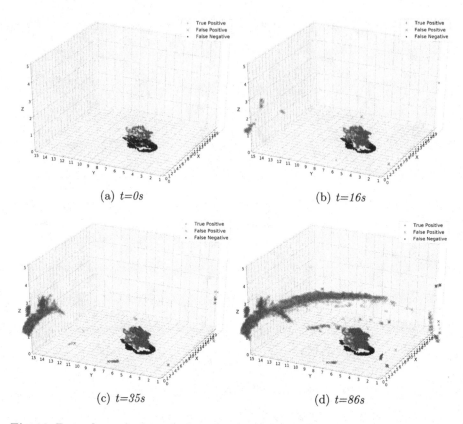

(a) $t=0s$ (b) $t=16s$

(c) $t=35s$ (d) $t=86s$

Fig. 12. Example results from the lower resolution LiDAR-equipped robot in the driveway scene (Fig. 5d). Plots (a)–(d) show spatial representations of true positive, false positive, and false negative detections at progressing time lapses. The robot begins at position $(0,0,0)$ and proceeds along the X axis. True positives on the left near $(7,5,0.5)$ are change detections intersecting the small ATV in Fig. 5d. The numerous false positives in the space over $10\,m$ from the origin coincide with vegetation in the scene blowing in the wind.

6   Conclusion

In this paper we present an approach to provide situational awareness of change detections found by an autonomous robot to its human teammate. This approach is motivated by the complimentary observations that 1) change detection can be challenging for humans yet entirely tractable for properly equipped and programmed autonomous robots, and 2) understanding change context is easy for humans and challenging to implement on an autonomous robot. The approach presented compares observed *test* point clouds against an *a priori* collected *model* cloud to generate change detections. Our system enables the robot to communicate detected changes via AR visualizations to the human teammate for evaluation. To field such a system, an important consideration is the sampling density of the point cloud. We implement our system on two otherwise identical robots with different resolution LiDAR sensors and examine two hypotheses about the system's change detection performance and visualization interpretability. Our results lead us to conclude that higher resolution is not simply better, and we identify several trade-offs between implementations. We observe that regardless of the implementation and although a full human study is out ot scope of this paper, there is evidence that our approach is sufficient to provide situational awareness of changes in the environment to human teammates.

References

1. Dellaert, F.: Factor graphs and GTSAM: a hands-on introduction. Technical report, Georgia Institute of Technology (2012)
2. Dellaert, F., Kaess, M.: Square Root SAM: simultaneous localization and mapping via square root information smoothing. Int. J. Robot. Res. **25**(12), 1181–1203 (2006)
3. Durlach, P.J.: Change blindness and its implications for complex monitoring and control systems design and operator training. Hum.-Comput. Interact. **19**(4), 423–451 (2004)
4. Gregory, J., et al.: Application of multi-robot systems to disaster-relief scenarios with limited communication. In: Wettergreen, D.S., Barfoot, T.D. (eds.) Field and Service Robotics. STAR, vol. 113, pp. 639–653. Springer, Cham (2016). https://doi.org/10.1007/978-3-319-27702-8_42
5. Marsland, S., Nehmzow, U., Shapiro, J.: On-line novelty detection for autonomous mobile robots. Robot. Auton. Syst. **51**(2–3), 191–206 (2005)
6. Núñez, P., Drews, P., Rocha, R., Campos, M., Dias, J.: Novelty detection and 3D shape retrieval based on Gaussian mixture models for autonomous surveillance robotics. In: 2009 IEEE/RSJ International Conference on Intelligent Robots and Systems, pp. 4724–4730. IEEE (2009)
7. Pimentel, M.A., Clifton, D.A., Clifton, L., Tarassenko, L.: A review of novelty detection. Sig. Process. **99**, 215–249 (2014)
8. Quigley, M., Faust, J., Foote, T., Leibs, J.: ROS: an open-source Robot Operating System. In: ICRA Workshop on Open Source Software (2009)
9. Reardon, C., Lee, K., Fink, J.: Come see this! Augmented reality to enable human-robot cooperative search. In: Proceedings of the 2018 IEEE Symposium on Safety, Security, and Rescue Robotics (2018)
10. Reardon, C., Lee, K., Rogers, J.G., Fink, J.: Augmented reality for human-robot teaming in field environments. In: Chen, J.Y.C., Fragomeni, G. (eds.) HCII 2019. LNCS, vol. 11575, pp. 79–92. Springer, Cham (2019). https://doi.org/10.1007/978-3-030-21565-1_6
11. Rusu, R.B., Cousins, S.: 3D is here: point cloud library PCL. In: 2011 IEEE International Conference on Robotics and Automation, pp. 1–4. IEEE (2011)
12. Segal, A., Haehnel, D., Thrun, S.: Generalized-ICP. In: Robotics: Science and Systems, vol. 2, p. 435 (2009)
13. Simons, D.J., Chabris, C.F.: Gorillas in our midst: sustained inattentional blindness for dynamic events. Perception **28**(9), 1059–1074 (1999)
14. Sofman, B., Neuman, B., Stentz, A., Bagnell, J.A.: Anytime online novelty and change detection for mobile robots. J. Field Robot. **28**(4), 589–618 (2011)

15. Sturari, M., Paolanti, M., Frontoni, E., Mancini, A., Zingaretti, P.: Robotic platform for deep change detection for rail safety and security. In: 2017 European Conference on Mobile Robots (ECMR), pp. 1–6. IEEE (2017)
16. Szafir, D.: Mediating human-robot interactions with virtual, augmented, and mixed reality. In: Chen, J.Y.C., Fragomeni, G. (eds.) HCII 2019. LNCS, vol. 11575, pp. 124–149. Springer, Cham (2019). https://doi.org/10.1007/978-3-030-21565-1_9
17. Trevor, A.J.B., Rogers, J.G., Christensen, H.I.: OmniMapper: a modular multimodal mapping framework. In: 2014 IEEE International Conference on Robotics and Automation (ICRA), pp. 1983–1990, May 2014. https://doi.org/10.1109/ICRA.2014.6907122
18. Vieira, A.W., Drews, P.L., Campos, M.F.: Spatial density patterns for efficient change detection in 3D environment for autonomous surveillance robots. IEEE Trans. Autom. Sci. Eng. **11**(3), 766–774 (2014)

Construction of Human-Robot Cooperation Assembly Simulation System Based on Augmented Reality

Qiang Wang[1], Xiumin Fan[1,2(✉)], Mingyu Luo[1], Xuyue Yin[1],
and Wenmin Zhu[1]

[1] Institute of Intelligent Manufacturing and Information Engineering,
School of Mechanical Engineering, Shanghai Jiao Tong University,
Shanghai 200240, China
xmfan@sjtu.edu.cn
[2] Shanghai Key Lab of Advanced Manufacturing Environment,
Shanghai 200030, China

Abstract. Human-Robot cooperation (HRC) is the developing trend in the field of industrial assembly. Design and evaluation of the HRC assembly workstation considering the human factor is very important. In order to evaluate the transformational construction scenario of a manual assembly workstation to a HRC workstation fast and safely, a HRC assembly simulation system is constructed which is based on Augmented Reality (AR) with human-in-loop interaction. It enables a real operator to interact with virtual robot in a real scene, and the assembly steps of real workers can be restored and mapped to a virtual human model for further ergonomic analysis. Kinect and LeapMotion are used as the sensors for human-robot interaction decision and feedback. An automobile gearbox assembly is taken as an example for different assembly task verification, operators' data are collected and analyzed by RULA scores and NASA-TLX questionnaires. The result shows that the simulation system can be used for the human factor evaluation of different HRC task configuration schemes.

Keywords: Augmented Reality · Human-Robot Cooperation · Human factors

1 Introduction

Human-Robot Cooperation assembly is the developing trend of industrial assembly field in the future. How to design and evaluate HRC assembly station is a current research hotspot, but there hasn't been much research of human factors evaluation for HRC assembly work station planning. With the development of Virtual Reality (VR) and Augmented Reality, more and more researchers apply VR/AR technologies to industrial simulation and training. It can not only be used to train and guide operators, but also to collect operators' motion data for later analysis.

The HRC simulation system based on AR and VR can measure human factor data more realistically and securely. Matsas et al. [1] proposed a VR training system to solve human-robot contact and collision problems through visual and sound interaction. Qiyue Wang et al. [2] proved the safety and effectiveness of the VR welding system

© Springer Nature Switzerland AG 2020
J. Y. C. Chen and G. Fragomeni (Eds.): HCII 2020, LNCS 12190, pp. 629–642, 2020.
https://doi.org/10.1007/978-3-030-49695-1_42

with HRC through the VR simulation experiment. Besides, Neuhoefer et al. [3] compared the simulation experiments of HRC based on VR and AR respectively, and proved that AR could bring more real simulation environment to participants than VR. D. Ni [4] designed an AR human-robot cooperation system based on tactile feedback. By collecting the depth image to reconstruct the model, and combining with the tactile sensor to define the welding path, the accuracy of welding operation was improved. Michalos et al. [5] developed an AR-based human-robot interaction system with a tablet PC, which improves the safety of operators and productivity by safety area division, production data visualization and voice alarm. However, it also points out that in the industrial scene, it is necessary to work with both hands, so wearing AR glasses will be a better choice, and the human factors are not considered enough in the system design process.

Based on the research above, this paper proposes to use AR to build a HRC assembly simulation system for real operators. The idea of human-in-the-loop is adopted for the human-robot interaction so as to build the system framework and lay the foundation for the subsequent exploration of human factors.

2 Simulation System Architecture

This paper builds the system architecture based on the communication of heterogeneous software platforms, respectively Unity in Window and ROS (Robot Operating System) in Ubuntu. The merit is that it can make full use of the advantages of each platform. It can not only use the development ability of ROS environment for quick, flexible and efficient debugging and compilation, but also use the excellent 3D engine rendering ability of Unity environment to present the virtual reality fusion scene. Moreover, the multi-platform architecture improves the adaptability and transportability of system. The modules between the two platforms are independent of each other, so that the verification experiment and workstation construction can be carried out with little changes in robot simulation.

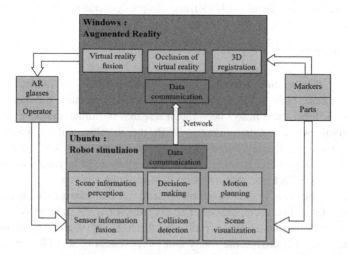

Fig. 1. Architecture of HRC simulation system

The architecture is shown in Fig. 1. The orange blocks on both sides of the diagram denote the real scene. The light red block in the diagram below shows the simulation system related to the virtual robot, reflecting the perception, decision-making and feedback of the robot in HRC. The blue block in the diagram above shows the augmented reality display system related to the real operator, reflecting the observation method of the virtual reality fusion scene when the human is in the simulation loop. The green block shows the communication between the two heterogeneous software platform.

In the construction of the robot simulation system based on AR, the robot simulation module judges the status of the robot and plan the motion path according to the interaction content, environment changes and predefined tasks in real time. The augmented reality display module is used to display the virtual robot and its motion in front of an operator through AR glasses.

In this paper, Rosbridge communication protocol [6] is used to realize the network communication between heterogeneous platforms. Its core idea is to use websocket protocol as a bridge to transmit data between ROS and non ROS environments. From the perspective of ROS, data is a message node in ROS. From the perspective of non ROS, data is in JSON data format. The Rosbridge protocol is equivalent to the translation between ROS and non ROS environments, and realizes full duplex communication.

Figure 2 shows the Rosbridge communication protocol integration under the ROS message publishing mode. The ROS side sets the \rosbridge_server as the message node, subscribes to the \joint_states message data, converts data to JSON format, and sends the subscribed \joint_states message to the network. On the Unity side, the Rosbridge Client receives data and drives the virtual robot to move in real time.

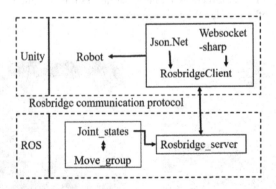

Fig. 2. Data communication based on Rosbridge

After the HRC simulation system is built, the robot driving display is shown in Fig. 3. The robot assembly simulation module based on ROS completes the motion planning and uses the heterogeneous platform communication mechanism to send the motion data. On the other hand, the augmented reality display module based on Unity receives the motion data and drives the AR robot to move in real time.

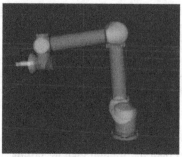

a) Robot motion planning in ROS   b) Display of virtual robot in AR

Fig. 3. Robot motion simulation with data driven from operator

3   Selection of AR Display Scheme

The display device determines the final virtual-real scene fusion effect. Generally, according to different display equipment, it can be divided into head mounted displays which are also called AR glasses, mobile displays such as mobile phones, flat or fixed displays such as computer screens or projectors. In the assembly operation, operators need both hands to work while constantly changing the viewing angle. Using AR glasses as display devices can make virtual-real scene fusion on the premise of freeing hands.

The display scheme with AR glasses can be divided into video see through (VST) mode and optical see through (OST) mode according to the display principle [7]. The biggest difference between the two schemes is the way to obtain the real scene image, in which VST is obtained by camera, while OST is obtained by eyes. Figure 4 shows the display effect under the two schemes.

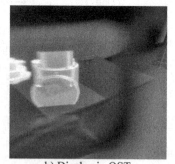

a) Display in VST   b) Display in OST

Fig. 4. Effect comparison of different AR scheme

In OST mode, the real scene is observed by eyes. However, the 3D registration position obtained by a camera is the position of the camera relative to the real scene matrix P_{co} rather than the position of eyes relative to the real scene matrix P_{eo}. Therefore, in the OST mode, the camera needs to calibrate the pose of eyes and itself one more time than the VST mode, so as to obtain the relative matrix P_{ec}. The relationship among the three matrix is as follow:

$$P_{ec} = P_{eo} * P_{co} \tag{1}$$

From the perspective of principle and display effect, compared with the VST mode, the OST mode has the following problems:

1) Limitation of the accuracy and universality of camera-eye calibration. The calibration method of P_{ec} is monocular, which can't completely calibrate the binocular coordinates, and the subjective cognition will affect the accuracy of the calibration matrixes. In addition, due to the different physiological structure, observation ability and cognition of each person, the calibration need to be conducted for different users.

2) Registration delay error between the virtual scene and the real world. The 3D registration needs additional calculation time, while the real scene directly enters eyes through light reflection almost without time delay. It leads to the inconsistency between the superposition of the virtual scene and the real world, resulting in a sense of violation.

3) Field of view (FOV) limitation of AR glasses at present time. Due to the FOV limitation of display screen, virtual objects can't be fully presented within the scope of eyes, resulting in the cognitive discordance.

As a result, the VST mode is superior to the OST mode in terms of registration accuracy, display effect and real-time performance. By measuring the data of 16 users wearing AR glasses and manually adjusting the coincidence degree of virtual object and real scene, Plopski [8] also proved that through VST, the operator could better judge the location of virtual model in real world. Therefore, this paper chooses the VST scheme to implement the AR module.

4 Design the Human-Robot Interaction Scheme

The interaction scheme with safe and natural way is the premise and advantage of human-robot collaboration [9]. This paper presents a human-robot interaction model based on sensors and AR technology, as shown in Fig. 5.

In the process of interaction, the operator has autonomy without additional design, while the robot needs to perceive the environmental information and the operator's intention to judge and make decisions according to the information processing, so as to realize the real-time interaction with the operator. In this section, Kinect and Leap-Motion are used as sensors to acquire the environmental information and hands interaction information of an operator, then establish a decision mechanism to integrate multiple interaction information, so that the robot can make decision independently.

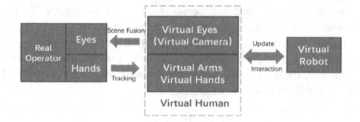

Fig. 5. Human robot interaction model

4.1 Interaction Information Tracking Based on Kinect

Microsoft Kinect is used to track the motion of operators' limbs and real environment. A Kinect structure is shown in Fig. 6. The camera can obtain color image with a resolution of 1920 × 1080, and the depth image can be obtained by time of flight technology to generate point cloud information with a resolution of 512 × 424. Therefore, Kinect can be used to collect the 3D information of real environment and map this information to the simulation space of the virtual robot, so as to realize the robot's perception of the external world.

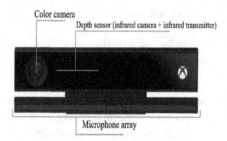

Fig. 6. Kinect structure

However, the size of point cloud information obtained by Kinect is too big, and a frame of image has more than 200000 point cloud. Figure 7 shows the comparison between original image and point cloud image, which can't be imported into the simulation environment for real-time calculation. So Octomap [10] method is used to reconstruct point cloud information, and the octree structure is used to store the depth image. By sacrificing the accuracy, the calculation efficiency is greatly improved. Figure 8 shows the point cloud transforming into octomap model.

For the octomap models, the higher the resolution is, the more real and rich the 3D information is, and the slower the calculation speed is, and vice versa. In addition, the size of data can be controlled by setting the range of the octomap model, then the calculation speed can be changed at the same time. Considering that the HRC assembly is a close operation between human and robot, the activity range of the robot is within 1 m, so the final parameters in octomap model are determined as the resolution of 0.05 m and the sensing distance of 1 m.

a) Color image   b) Point cloud

Fig. 7. Comparison between image and point   **Fig. 8.** Octomap model

4.2   Gesture Recognition for Interaction Based on LeapMotion

Interaction by hand gesture is one of the basic ways of communication between human beings and the outside world, and it is an intuitive and natural non-contact interaction method [11]. Through image recognition, specific gestures can be designed and used as means of human-robot interaction to realize the robot's judgment on human action. LeapMotion sensor is used for hand gesture recognition. As shown in Fig. 9, Leap-Motion can capture 215 frames image per second, and calculate the position of hands in cartesian coordinates of right hand. What's more, it can detect more than 20 joints of hand with an accuracy of 0.01 mm. Figure 10 shows the results of hand detection using LeapMotion.

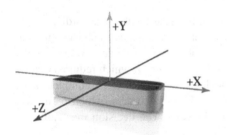
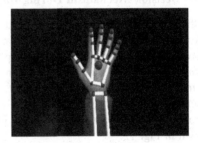

Fig. 9. LeapMotion   **Fig. 10.** Hand detection with LeapMotion

Gesture pictures			
Gesture name	OK	PREV	NEXT
Gesture semantics	The operator is ready, robot starts to work	Command robot to continue Previous action	Command the robot to continue next action

Fig. 11. Hand gesture definition

For the easiness of human-robot interaction, the naturalness (whether it is too difficult to make gestures), discrimination (whether it has obvious feature differentiation), intuitiveness (whether gestures conform to human behavior logic and associative content) of gestures are considered. Three gestures are selected and the semantics of each one are defined, as shown in Fig. 11. They are OK (ready to begin), PREV (the previous step) and NEXT (the next step) respectively. They are consistent with the corresponding semantics of the human behavior logic, and are commonly used in interpersonal communication. They don't affect the human behavior logic, so as to ensure the natural and intuitive of human behavior.

Experiments on above three gestures are carried out, as shown in Table 1. The average recognition rate is 99.46%, close to 100%, which means these hand gestures can be recognized effectively and accurately.

Table 1. Experimental data of gestures recognition

Hand gesture	Total test number	Correct recognized number	Recognition rate
OK	1445	1434	99.24%
PREV	1065	1062	99.72%
NEXT	850	845	99.41%
Average	1120	1114	99.46%

4.3 Decision Mechanism During Interaction

In the process of assembly, robots need to constantly make feedback according to the information input from sensors. Therefore, a decision mechanism is established to help robots make decisions. The first principle that a robot needs to abide is safety, which ensures the safety of humans. The second principle is efficiency, which requires a robot to make decisions quickly in a short time and ensure the efficient completion of assembly tasks. The third principle is response to humans' orders, which requires a robot to accurately execute the orders given by humans. The decision mechanism is shown in Fig. 12.

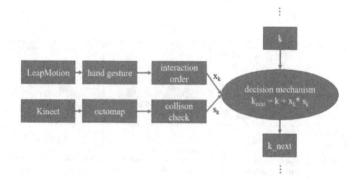

Fig. 12. Decision mechanism

The gesture recognition is obtained from LeapMotion and converted into interaction commands. In Fig. 12, the x_k represents the k steps of assembly operations when the interaction command from the outside is obtained. When operators give the NEXT operation command, then $x_k = 1$. When operators give the PREV operation command, then $x_k = -1$.

The octomap model is obtained from Kinect and used for collision detection with the virtual robot. The s_k represents the collision detection and motion planning results in the current scene. When the robot occurs collision interference or fails to complete the motion planning, then $s_k = 0$. When the robot is not interfered with the octomap model, then $s_k = 1$.

If the robot is currently in the kth step of assembly operations, and after integrating the interaction command and octomap model information, the robot can make the decision for the next assembly operation k_{next}:

$$k_{next} = k + x_k * s_k \qquad (2)$$

By this means, the robot decision-making process can comprehensively consider the external scene information and the operator's instructions to carry out an automatic obstacle avoidance planning, which ensures a natural, safety and real-time interaction.

5 Experiments and Analysis

5.1 Prototype System and Experiments Design

A HRC assembly simulation prototype system is constructed which includes hardware and software. The hardware configuration is shown in Fig. 13, two computers are needed. The one is installed with Ubuntu system for robot motion planning, and the other is installed with Windows system for augmented reality display. Kinect and LeapMotion are connected to computer in Ubuntu system as robot sensors, and also used for driving digital human model for human factor analysis. RealSense and NDI AR glasses are connected to computer in windows system as AR camera and display screen. Router is used to build network to complete communication between two computers.

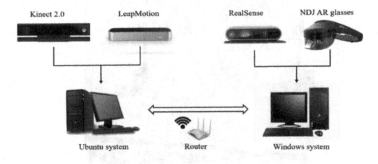

Fig. 13. Hardware device configuration

The software architecture makes full use of advantages of the module independence of ROS platform. Each module directly uses ROS to build message nodes for data distribution and transmission. The advantage is that it improves the independence and integrity of each module, and can easily and quickly add new functions to each module, as shown in Fig. 14.

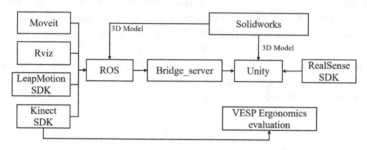

Fig. 14. Modules structure of software system

An automobile gearbox is taken as an assembly object for testing. In this HRC assembly experiment, the layout configuration of the assembly workstation is as shown in Fig. 15. Some parts for assembly process steps are selected, and these assembly parts are assembled to the lower gearbox house which is placed in the center of the workbench and fixed. A real operator and a virtual robot complete the assembly task together. According to the characteristics of strong load capacity and low flexibility of robots, and weak load capacity and high flexibility of human, heavier parts are assigned to the robot, while parts with higher assembly flexibility requirements are assigned to the operator. The assembly task assignment schemes are shown in Fig. 16.

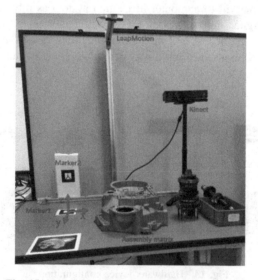

Fig. 15. Assembly workstation for HRC experiment

Assembly steps	① Differential installation	② Output shaft installation	③ Input shaft installation	④ Reverse gear installation	⑤ Reverse gear shaft installation
Assembly scheme 1	Robot	Human	Robot	Human	Human
Assembly scheme 2	Robot	Robot	Human	Human	Human

Human assembly   Robot assembly

Fig. 16. Assembly task assignment scheme

Six testers are invited to repeatedly assemble and disassemble task for 10 times under each experimental scheme, so as to ensure the stability of experimental results. The starting of the robot's movement is controlled by hand gesture. When each tester completes assembly operation, he use the "next" gesture to send command to the robot. It should be noted that only when the robot needs to be stopped and restarted, the interaction gesture would be used. Otherwise, the robot will continue to finish its operation steps. For example, in assembly scheme 1, the robot will maintain a waiting state after completing the first step. When each tester finishes the second step, the third step needs to be started with a hand gesture. On the contrary, in assembly scheme 2, the robot continuously carries out the first and second assembly step without waiting for gesture commands.

Figure 17 shows the process of assembly experiment. The picture a) is the third-person perspective of HRC assembly experiment, and the picture b) is the first-person perspective of the operator in HRC assembly experiment. During the experiment, Kinect is used to obtain the testers' motion data, and Rapid Upper Limb Assessment (RULA) is used to analyze the testers' physiological fatigue. After experiment, all testers are invited to fill in the National Aeronautics and Space Administration-Task Loads Index (NASA-TLX) [12] questionnaires, and the data are used to analyze the testers' psychological fatigue.

a)Third-person perspective of experiment   b)First-person perspective of experiment

Fig. 17. HRC assembly experiment

5.2   Results Analysis

Virtual Engineering Simulation Platform (VESP) [13] is a virtual simulation system developed on the basis of OpenSceneGraph. In this paper, Kinect is used to collect the real testers' data, and these data are used to drive the virtual human movement. The posture of the virtual human is evaluated by RULA through the human factor evaluation module in VESP. As shown in Fig. 18, the picture a) shows a virtual human with corresponding posture after collecting a real tester's data and mapping to this virtual human, and the picture b) shows the RULA results obtained from VESP.

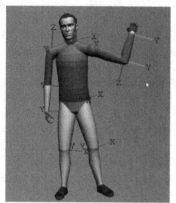
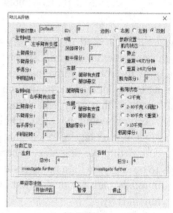

a) Virtual human   b) RULA results

Fig. 18. Analysis of psychological fatigue in VESP

Figure 19 shows the distribution quantity of the two assembly schemes in each scoring interval of RULA. It can be seen that scheme 1 has a larger number of scores in the high score interval, which indicates that the HRC assembly scheme 1 is not reasonable enough and needs to be changed. In contrast, scheme 2 is more reasonable. The average RULA score of scheme 1 is 2.7, close to 3, which belongs to evaluation level II. It means further investigation and research are needed and possible modification may need. The average RULA score of scheme 2 is 2.08, close to 2, which belongs to evaluation level I and is in the acceptable range.

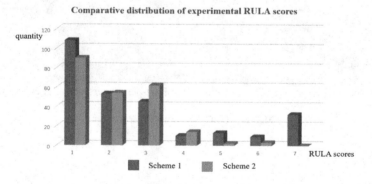

Fig. 19. RULA score comparison

Figure 20 shows the scores of each dimension in NASA-TLX of the two schemes. It can be seen that the score of scheme 2 is lower than that of scheme 1 in all dimensions, which indicates that the task allocation of scheme 2 enables testers to complete tasks more comfortably, reduces the psychological load level in all dimensions. The result of NASA-TLX is consistent with the result of RULA score.

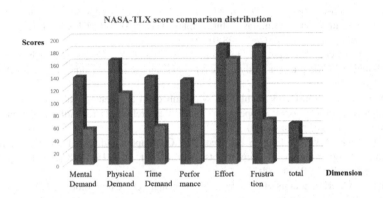

Fig. 20. NASA-TLX score comparison

Compared with the difference between two schemes, scheme 2 isolates the tasks of human and robot. There are no frequent tasks switching between human and robot, which reduces the memory demand of human and frequent contacts with robot, so it can get a better evaluation score. Therefore, it is necessary to avoid frequent switching between human and robot assembly tasks, otherwise it will cause unnecessary psychological burden to the operator.

6   Conclusions

Aiming at the lack of simulation links in the design and transformation of HRC workstation, a method of building a simulation system for HRC workstation based on AR is proposed. A hand-eye interaction model of virtual human is presented, which is realized through AR glasses, LeapMotion and Kinect sensors. These sensors are used for environmental information perception and gesture recognition to complete the natural interaction between human and robot.

Take the assembly workstation transformation of an automobile gearbox as an example, an HRC assembly simulation prototype system including software and hardware is built. RULA by digital human model and NASA-TLX questionnaire are used for testers' data analysis. With human factors analysis, the advantages and disadvantages of each HRC assembly schemes are easily obtained. The results show that the simulation system can used for the evaluation human factor of different HRC tasks configuration planning.

Acknowledgement. The work is partially supported by the NSFC project (51475291) and MIIT project (19GC04252), China. The authors are grateful to the editors and anonymous reviewers for their valuable comments.

References

1. Matsas, E., Vosniakos, G.C.: Design of a virtual reality training system for human–robot collaboration in manufacturing tasks. Int. J. Interact. Des. Manuf. (IJIDeM) 11(2), 139–153 (2017). https://doi.org/10.1007/s12008-015-0259-2
2. Wang, Q., Cheng, Y., Jiao, W., Johnson, M.T., Zhang, Y.: Virtual reality human-robot collaborative welding: a case study of weaving gas tungsten arc welding. J. Manuf. Process. 48, 210–217 (2019)
3. Neuhoefer, J.A., Kausch, B., Schlick, C.M.: Embedded augmented reality training system for dynamic human-robot cooperation. Nato Research and Technology Organization Neuilly-Sur-Seine, France (2009)
4. Ni, D., Yew, A.W.W., Ong, S.K., Nee, A.Y.C.: Haptic and visual augmented reality interface for programming welding robots. Adv. Manuf. 5(3), 191–198 (2017). https://doi.org/10.1007/s40436-017-0184-7
5. Michalos, G., Karagiannis, P., Makris, S., Tokçalar, Ö., Chryssolouris, G.: Augmented reality (AR) applications for supporting human-robot interactive cooperation. Procedia CIRP 41, 370–375 (2016)
6. Crick, C., Jay, G., Osentoski, S., Pitzer, B., Jenkins, O.C.: Rosbridge: ROS for Non-ROS users. In: Christensen, H.I., Khatib, O. (eds.) Robotics Research. STAR, vol. 100, pp. 493–504. Springer, Cham (2017). https://doi.org/10.1007/978-3-319-29363-9_28
7. Azuma, R.T.: A survey of augmented reality. Presence: Teleoper. Virtual Environ. 6(4), 355–385 (1997)
8. Plopski, A., Moser, K.R., Kiyokawa, K., Swan, J.E., Takemura, H.: Spatial consistency perception in optical and video see-through head-mounted augmentations. In: 2016 IEEE Virtual Reality (VR), pp. 265–266. IEEE (2016)
9. Zhu, W., Fan, X., Zhang, Y.: Applications and research trends of digital human models in the manufacturing industry. Virtual Real. Intell. Hardw. 1(6), 558–579 (2019)
10. Hornung, A., Wurm, K.M., Bennewitz, M., Stachniss, C., Burgard, W.: OctoMap: an efficient probabilistic 3D mapping framework based on octrees. Auton. Robots 34(3), 189–206 (2013). https://doi.org/10.1007/s10514-012-9321-0
11. Nguyen, V.T.: Enhancing touchless interaction with the leap motion using a haptic glove. University of Eastern Finland, Joensuu (2014)
12. Hart, S.G., Staveland, L.E.: Development of NASA-TLX (Task Load Index): results of empirical and theoretical research. In: Advances in Psychology, North-Holland, vol. 52, pp. 139–183 (1988)
13. Qiu, S., Fan, X., Wu, D., He, Q., Zhou, D.: Virtual human modeling for interactive assembly and disassembly operation in virtual reality environment. Int. J. Adv. Manuf. Technol. 69(9–12), 2355–2372 (2013). https://doi.org/10.1007/s00170-013-5207-3

Using Augmented Reality to Better Study Human-Robot Interaction

Tom Williams[1][(✉)], Leanne Hirshfield[2], Nhan Tran[1], Trevor Grant[2],
and Nicholas Woodward[1]

[1] MIRRORLab, Colorado School of Mines, Golden, CO, USA
`twilliams@mines.edu`
[2] SHINE Lab, University of Colorado, Boulder, CO, USA
`https://mirrorlab.mines.edu/`
`https://shinelaboratory.com/`

Abstract. In the field of Human-Robot Interaction, researchers often techniques such as the Wizard-of-Oz paradigms in order to better study narrow scientific questions while carefully controlling robots' capabilities unrelated to those questions, especially when those other capabilities are not yet easy to automate. However, those techniques often impose limitations on the type of collaborative tasks that can be used, and the perceived realism of those tasks and the task context. In this paper, we discuss how Augmented Reality can be used to address these concerns while increasing researchers' level of experimental control, and discuss both advantages and disadvantages of this approach.

Keywords: Human-Robot Interaction · Augmented Reality · Research Methods

1 Introduction

One of the greatest challenges in the development of interactive robots is the enabling of autonomous natural language capabilities [1]. Natural language understanding and generation are in general difficult problems to study due to the flexibility, ambiguity, and compositionality of natural language – the very reasons that make natural language such a powerful communication modality in the first place. But natural language interaction is *particularly* difficult to study within the context of human-robot interaction. While traditional natural language processing methods may be evaluated on text corpora, natural language communication in human-robot interaction is necessarily situated [2], with incredible sensitivity to that situated context [3,4], and is almost entirely formulated as task-based dialogues [5], creating a need for situated, task-based study and evaluation of proposed and developed natural language architectures [6,7].

Unfortunately, task-based evaluations themselves come with a host of challenges. In order for a task-based evaluation to be meaningful, it must allow for *joint action* [8] – communication and coordination of actions that change the

© Springer Nature Switzerland AG 2020
J. Y. C. Chen and G. Fragomeni (Eds.): HCII 2020, LNCS 12190, pp. 643–654, 2020.
https://doi.org/10.1007/978-3-030-49695-1_43

state of human and robot teammates' shared context [9]. This in turn necessarily requires both parties to be able to *perceive* their shared environment, and for both parties to be able to take actions that *manipulate* their shared environment. Due to the difficulty of robot perception and action, human-robot experiments are often conducted through a *Wizard-of-Oz paradigm* [10–12] in which some or all of the robot's perception, cognition, or action is remotely dictated by an unseen human confederate, in theory allowing for study of interaction patterns before all technical challenges needed to truly enable such interactions are fully addressed.

Unfortunately, even Wizard-of-Ozing robot perception and action can be extremely challenging. Because there is no straightforward way of "telling" a robot what it sees and where it sees it, simplifying approaches to robot perception are typically needed, in one of two forms. First, the positions and properties of objects in the environment may be hard-coded a priori [13]. This allows a realistic interaction context to be presented to human participants that would look no different if the robot's perception were truly autonomous. However, it may preclude the possibility for collaborative interaction tasks involving joint action, as the objects in the environment cannot be manipulated without changing their (not truly observable) pose. On the other hand, objects in the scene may be augmented on all sides with fiducial markers [14,15]; an approach that allows for fully manipulable and perceivable task contexts, but which necessarily changes the *human's* perception of their environment, such that it no longer truly looks as it would if the robot had full perceptual capabilities, and moreover such that human perception of task-relevant objects may in fact be impaired.

Similarly, Wizard-of-Ozing of robot motion also presents a significant challenge. Wizard-of-Ozing of actions in human-robot interaction typically involves human teleoperators manually selecting dialogue actions [16,17], hard-coded physical actions like gestures [18,19], or full-body motions like traveling or turning [20,21]. As with wizarding approaches to robot perception, these approaches present interaction contexts to human participants that would look no different if the robot's actions were truly autonomous, but which may preclude the possibility for collaborative interaction task involving joint action, due to the difficulty of Wizarding within this framework the dextrous manipulation actions like grasping, picking, and placing that are necessary for truly collaborative tasks.

To address these problems, some researchers have begun to move the human-robot interaction *context* into a virtual domain, such as Lemaignan et al.'s *Free-play Sandbox* [22], Paiva et al.'s work within the EMOTE project [23,24] and in the context of the game *Sueca* [25], Kory and Breazel's storytelling work with Dragonbot [26], and Ramachandran and Scassellati's work on intelligent robot tutors [27]. In these approaches, humans and robots collaborate with respect to some task on a tablet computer. By moving the task into a virtual domain, this technique allows a robot to be fully autonomous without any perceptual or dexterous manipulation capabilities; a robot may instead directly access and manipulate the state of the collaborative task context by interfacing with the tablet responsible for displaying that context. However, this approach may also limit the perceived capability or agency of the robot teammate, due to such robots' real lack of capability and agency outside of the virtual domain. Moreover, working within this approach may limit the extensibility of researchers' work, in that advances in manipulation and perception will not clearly provide an opportunity to move the robot's operation from its virtual task context out to a more realistic, physically situated domain.

We argue that many of these challenges may be addressed using Augmented Reality technologies, by moving task-relevant objects from the physical world into the virtual world. Consider, for example, the game of *Sueca*, used as a task context by Correia et al. [25]. In order to study human-robot collaboration, the card game is played on an electronic tabletop, using a mixture of physical cards (played by humans) and virtual cards (played by the robot), with the physical cards instrumented with fiducial markers. There are at least three limitations of this approach. First, the authors report that this instrumentation was found to be jarring by participants. Second, this arrangement subtly treats human and robots players differently. Finally, this instrumentation may only really be feasible for certain types of games. In contrast, if players were instrumented with augmented reality headsets, each player *and robot* could manage a hand of virtual cards, addressing all of the concerns and challenges listed above while only minimally changing the appearance and interaction style from that of a normal game.

2   Case Study: Using Augmented Reality to Study the Use of Augmented Reality in Human-Robot Interaction

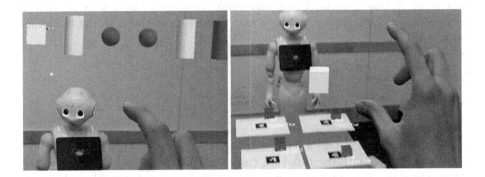

Fig. 1. Experiment in progress.

In this section, we present a case study of how AR might be used to improve the study of human-robot interaction. In fact, this case study will examine how we are using augmented reality objects to more easily study the general use of augmented reality in human-robot communication. In recent theoretical and experimental work, we have been exploring the space of possible robot gestures in human-robot interaction, including both physical gestures, and AR visualizations that may serve the same role as those gestures for armless robots or in privacy-sensitive applications [28]. Recently, for example, we have investigated the benefits of one particular type of augmented reality gesture, *allocentric gesture*, through online experiments in which participants watched videos in which simulated views of such gestures were displayed [29,30]. In our present work, we are now beginning to explore the effectiveness of this form of gesture in the real world using the Microsoft Hololens, in order to further interrogate our previously suggested hypotheses [31] regarding how these gestures may be differentially effective in the context of human-robot interactions under different mental workload conditions. Our main research question in this work is whether different types of human-robot communication (allocentric augmented reality gesture in the form of 3D arrows pointing to targets, and/or rich natural language) are more effective under different types of mental workload (working memory load, visual perceptual load, and auditory perceptual load). While this is experiment directly revolves around Augmented Reality, we are actually using Augmented Reality in supplemental ways not related to our core research questions in order to facilitate the research itself. Specifically, within this experiment, there are two different types of objects that are relevant to the task: **blocks** that the user must **pick**, and **bins** into which the user must **place** those blocks. This is a simple task in which the robot's job is purely communicative; it must periodically refer to different blocks, through either language or gesture. Accordingly, at least as described thus far, this is a task that could be easily implemented using physical bins and physical blocks, potentially with fiducial markers attached to the blocks so that the robot could easily determine where to visualize AR gestures with respect to those blocks. In our case, however, we decided to use an entirely virtual set of task objects (boxes and bins), because it allowed us to reap a number of benefits, alluded to above and thoroughly detailed in the following sections (Fig. 1).

2.1   Advantages

No Need for Object Recognition

By using virtual objects, we obviate the need for object recognition in our experiments; because the robot used in our experiment (the Softbank Pepper) is directly interfaced with the Hololens, these task-relevant objects effectively live within the robot's world rather than the human's. Accordingly, the robot has oracle knowledge of the position of all bins without any sort of object recognition *and* without hardcoding the positions of those task-relevant objects. This drastically improves the consistency of interaction within the experiment; traditional object recognition is prone to errors in detection that could potentially introduce latency when, for example, a participant attempts to place an object in a bin that has not been detected by the robot, or when a participant manipulates a target object outside of the field of view of the robot. Essentially, virtual objects remove the barrier between the view of the participant and the robot's under-standing, as both human and robot can instead share the same knowledge of the environment. Eliminating the need for object recognition also increases the computational efficiency of the experiment, as more computational resources can be dedicated to simulating the interaction with and movement of virtual objects through 3D space, as well as the multitude of tasks assigned to the player, instead of being dedicated to task-irrelevant processes such as object recognition.

No Need for Motion Capture

Similarly, our use of virtual objects allows us to precisely track the exact positions of all task-relevant objects at each point in time throughout the experiment, as well as the exact moments in time when actions were taken on those objects (e.g., pick-and-place actions), as those actions can be automatically logged through the technology that enables them in the first place (i.e., the Hololens). This obvi-ates the need for expensive Motion Capture systems and/or interaction garments that are otherwise often needed to precisely track participants' and robots' move-ments during human-robot interaction experiments (cp. [32]) (or costly manual annotation of such events from manual camera data analysis). The use of virtual objects, especially for the objects that participants interact with to place in vir-tual bins, also allows for their manipulation without the use of tabletop fiducials or a world-coordinate system (cp. [33]). Allowing the interactive virtual objects to be freely placed in space without the utilization of physical markers prevents unnecessary complications in the basic interaction design of the experiment, which could otherwise negatively impact the participant's ability to focus on the tasks they are given. Eliminating motion capture also eliminates the overhead of computationally-expensive algorithms for processing the resulting data. This is particularly important, because it is the standalone AR technology (i.e, the Hololens) that must render every virtual object within the experiment, rather than a desktop computer or other device with more computational power. As such, motion capture could potentially introduce processing delays that would have a negative impact on the ability for participants to seamlessly interact with virtual objects. Avoiding the use of motion capture simplifies the fundamental interaction systems within the experiment without detracting from the interac-tive experience of moving objects around.

Dynamic Environmental Changes Within Tasks

Our use of virtual objects allowed us to dynamically change the task environ-ment during the course of a task, in ways that would not have been otherwise feasible. In the preliminary work discussed in this section, we aimed to study how different types of mental workload modulated the relative effectiveness of different communication modalities. One form of workload we were particularly interested in studying was visual perceptual workload, measured as the distinc-tiveness of target objects within a task with respect to distractor objects. By using virtual objects within our pick-and-place task, as soon as an object was picked-and-placed, it could be automatically replaced by a new virtual object, without experimenter intervention, according to a schedule that maintained a consistent level of visual similarity/dissimilarity within a task block.

Besides the virtual elements, the physical environment can also be dynamically manipulated using AR techniques beyond standalone AR headset. Lindlbauer et al. [34] designed a new form of mixed reality technique, Remixed Reality, that uses multiple RBG-D cameras to reconstruct live representation of an environment. Just as rendered geometry can be easily modified in real time in virtual reality, Remixed Reality allows easy changes in the physical environment, including spatial changes (e.g. erasing objects), changes in appearance (e.g. altering textures of objects), temporal changes (e.g., pausing time), and viewpoint changes (e.g. see a different viewpoint without moving to a new location). Future HRI experiments may leverage such system to manipulate a variety of important environmental features, such as the visual similarity/dissimilarity between physical and virtual objects. The knowledge of the physical environment enabled by this approach also allows virtual objects to be placed properly in the real world and facilitates even more natural interaction.

Within our own experiment, the ability to immediately repopulate objects within the experimental space provided many benefits not only in the pragmatics of running participants through the experimental paradigm (i.e. by allowing the experimenter to monitor interactions between the human participant and the robot, rather than making themselves an extraneous factor within the interaction), but also to the internal validity of the task bed itself. Maintaining steady manipulations of various cognitive resources requires a level of consistency within the stimulus presentation that would not be possible if a human experimenter were to manually set trials for individual participants. The use of the AR system also allows for better tracking of various measures that are relevant to determining the amount of workload a human participant is under during a given time period. Factors such as when a stimulus was presented as well as when a participant responded to that presentation can provide more nuanced information about the level of load an individual is under at that particular time than relying on participant performance metrics alone. The ability for experimenters to dynamically change the AR task environment therefore provides not only a pragmatic function, but also a level of rigorous measurement that would be unavailable, or difficult to implement, within in a purely naturalistic setting.

Dynamic Environmental Changes Between Tasks

Our experiment was executed as a within-subjects experiment in which participants were presented with a series of task contexts whose sets of constituent task objects varied with respect to visual similarity/dissimilarity. Our use of virtual objects allowed us to instantaneously provide new task contexts with carefully controlled placement of objects, without experimenter intervention, and without any opportunity for experimenter error in selection and placement of task-relevant objects. In fact, this allowed us to run a complex within-subjects experiment situated within a series of realistic pick-and-place task scenarios, without any need for experimenter involvement whatsoever during the experimental task.

Functionally, this allows the researcher to spend more time running tasks and collecting data than would have been possible in a situation in which an experimenter had to continually reset the scene for each individual task manipulation. Other experimental benefits are that the transitions between these different tasks allow for more tight control of what is presented to the user. The AR environment allows for more controlled periods of rest between task blocks. Though not directly used in our experimental paradigm, the ability to dynamically shift between different task configurations allows for algorithmic difficulty adjustments within an experimental paradigm that might be difficult to implement in a more traditional HRI experimental setup.

Reducing Extraneous Variables in Experimental Designs

In addition to adding the more robust environmental changes detailed above, the AR environment also reduced the need for the experimenter to change and manipulate physical objects throughout the experiment. Despite researchers best efforts to be consistent during wizard-of-oz studies, constant moving and manipulating of physical objects in our study by an actual human could have introduced any number of intentional extraneous variables into the experiments. For example, moving new blocks to and from the participant's table could be done unintentionally with slightly different timings, which would introduce variable amounts of time for the participant to perceive a new block, and their possible response time to search/sort could ultimately be effected. The effects of extraneous variables become magnified as the dependent measures in a study become more granular. For example, in the author's prior study [35] using non-invasive brain measurement (via functional near-infrared spectroscopy) to measure working memory load, the effects of extraneous variables were difficult to mitigate due to the sensitive nature of the brain measurement equipment. In that study, a virtual block (on the computer) was rotated while participants tallied the number of specific colors that they saw on the rotating block. There was an additional condition that mimicked the virtual block condition, where tangible blocks were actually placed in front of participants and spun in a circle manually by the researchers. Besides being difficult to spin in a circle consistently in all of the tangible block trials, there was also concern that motion artifacts were introduced into the brain data during the tangible block condition, because participants craned their neck to follow the spinning block on the table in a way that differed slightly from their movements while simply viewing the spinning block on a monitor. We include this anecdotal story to show how extraneous variables can be introduced that are caused by researcher error while manipulating physical objects in experiments, or via participant movement that are related to moving physical objects around in their environment. Clearly this 'physical movement' on the part of participants may not be as much of a concern if researchers are not including highly sensitive cognitive and physiological measurements in their study, but it is worth considering that even the NASA-TLX self-assessment of workload [36] contains a sub-scale item for 'physical load', and if there are any extraneous physical variables introduced in the study, that effect could find its way into the overall NASA-TLX score of workload.

2.2   Limitations

While augmented reality offers advantages in terms of enhancing the study of human-robot interaction, it also comes with several challenges:

Visual Quality

Most headsets do not render virtual elements across the wearer's full scope of vision. The inability to cover peripheral vision obviates the user from achieving full immersion. In our HRI experiment where user was asked to interact with virtual objects, the illusion of a natural interaction disappeared when these objects got artificially cropped beyond the edge of the glasses' narrow field of view. Additionally, the visual fidelity of AR Head-Mounted Displays needs improvement to make the user more immersed in the experiment to the point that they forget they are wearing a headset. Enhancing the visual fidelity of the experience and increasing the field of view of the headset also bring with them another set of challenges relating to processing power and battery life. Our study utilized two Microsoft HoloLens 1, and they were switched every two hours to ensure that they both had enough battery to run for an entire day.

User Fatigue

The current generation of mixed reality headset may not be a good fit for tasks that require content to be within two meters and visualized at a high level of precision. Recent studies reports two optical problems that prevent participants from achieving task performance as well as the naked eyes [37]. A phenomenon called focal rivalry prevents human eyes from simultaneously focusing on both virtual and real objects. Another optical issue known as vergence-accommodation conflict stymies the natural ability of our eyes to focus at the correct distance. Our eyes naturally turn inwards to triangulate on an object as it approaches, but the lenses in headsets have fixed focal length. Attempting to manipulate virtual objects using software can't fool the eyes either. What is more, these two issues cause eye fatigue when the user is wearing the headset for some time.

In our experiment, we followed Microsoft's recommendation to design virtual contents to be 1–2 m farther away from the user. We also gave participants breaks between each in-subject round so that eye fatigue would not affect the mental workload of the user, which was one of the factors we manipulated and measured. Though, future natural interaction experiments such as AR-assisted surgery and precise engineering repair may find the AR experience to be artificial when tasks require users to interact with content within arm's reach and to engage with content at any focal points.

3 Previous Work in Augmented Reality for Human-Robot Interaction

Finally, it is worth briefly summarizing how augmented reality is being used by other researchers in the context of human-robot interaction. Work on AR-for-HRI has slowly but steadily been progressing for at least twenty-five years [38–42], with the majority of work focusing either on increasing the flexibility of users' control over robots or increasing the expressivity of users' view into the internal models of those robots [43]. In the past few years, however, there has been a dramatic increase in work in the area [44,45], with approaches being presented that use AR for robot design [46], calibration [47], and training [48], and for communicating robots' perspectives [49], understanding [50] intentions [51,52] and trajectories [53–56]. Most relevant to this paper is work from Amor et al., who, while using projection-based rather than heads-up-display-based AR visualizations, explicitly use AR in order to *align perspectives* between humans and robots [57]. But to the best of our knowledge, there has been no previous work that has specifically reflected on the ability of AR technologies to increase the simplicity and control for experimental research in human-robot interaction. To demonstrate this effectiveness, we present a case study of the benefits gained by using AR in the context of a recent HRI experiment performed in our lab.

4 Conclusion

Augmented Reality and other spatial computing .paradigms stand to change the face of human-robot interaction, robotics in general, and in fact all of computing, in both academic research and its application in industry. In this paper we have discussed a number of advantages and disadvantages of also using Augmented Reality to facilitate the performance of such research itself. In future work it will be valuable to expand upon the insights provided in this paper to explore how other types of spatial computing paradigms may provide similar benefits to HRI researchers.

Acknowledgments. This work was funded in part by grant IIS-1909864 from the National Science Foundation.

References

1. Mavridis, N.: A review of verbal and non-verbal human-robot interactive communication. Robot. Auton. Syst. **63**, 22–35 (2015)
2. Wainer, J., Feil-Seifer, D.J., Shell, D.A., Mataric, M.J.: The role of physical embodiment in human-robot interaction. In: ROMAN 2006-The 15th IEEE International Symposium on Robot and Human Interactive Communication, pp. 117–122. IEEE (2006)
3. Lemaignan, S., Ros, R., Sisbot, E.A., Alami, R., Beetz, M.: Grounding the interaction: anchoring situated discourse in everyday human-robot interaction. Int. J. Soc. Robot. 4(2), 181–199 (2012). https://doi.org/10.1007/s12369-011-0123-x

4. Kruijff, G.J.M., et al.: Situated dialogue processing for human-robot interaction. In: Christensen, H.I., Kruijff, G.J.M., Wyatt, J.L. (eds.) Cognitive Systems. COSMOS, vol. 8, pp. 311–364. Springer, Heidelberg (2010). https://doi.org/10.1007/978-3-642-11694-0_8

5. Scheutz, M., Cantrell, R., Schermerhorn, P.: Toward humanlike task-based dialogue processing for human robot interaction. AI Mag. **32**(4), 77–84 (2011)

6. Scholtz, J.: Theory and evaluation of human robot interactions. In: 2003 Proceedings of the 36th Annual Hawaii International Conference on System Sciences, pp. 10–pp. IEEE (2003)

7. Foster, M.E., Giuliani, M., Isard, A.: Task-based evaluation of context-sensitive referring expressions in human-robot dialogue. Lang. Cogn. Neurosci. **29**(8), 1018–1034 (2014)

8. Sebanz, N., Bekkering, H., Knoblich, G.: Joint action: bodies and minds moving together. Trends Cogn. Sci. **10**(2), 70–76 (2006)

9. Mutlu, B., Terrell, A., Huang, C.M.: Coordination mechanisms in human-robot collaboration. In: Proceedings of the Workshop on Collaborative Manipulation, 8th ACM/IEEE International Conference on Human-Robot Interaction, pp. 1–6. Citeseer (2013)

10. Kelley, J.F.: An empirical methodology for writing user-friendly natural language computer applications. In: Proceedings of the SIGCHI Conference on Human Factors in Computing Systems, pp. 193–196. ACM (1983)

11. Riek, L.D.: Wizard of Oz studies in HRI: a systematic review and new reporting guidelines. J. Hum.-Robot Interact. **1**(1), 119–136 (2012)

12. Steinfeld, A., Jenkins, O.C., Scassellati, B.: The Oz of wizard: simulating the human for interaction research. In: Proceedings of the 4th ACM/IEEE International Conference on Human Robot Interaction, pp. 101–108. ACM (2009)

13. Williams, T., Scheutz, M.: Resolution of referential ambiguity in human-robot dialogue using dempster-shafer theoretic pragmatics. In: Robotics: Science and Systems (2017)

14. Fiala, M.: ARTag, a fiducial marker system using digital techniques. In: 2005 IEEE Computer Society Conference on Computer Vision and Pattern Recognition (CVPR 2005), vol. 2, pp. 590–596. IEEE (2005)

15. Dudek, G., Sattar, J., Xu, A.: A visual language for robot control and programming: a human-interface study. In: Proceedings of the 2007 IEEE International Conference on Robotics and Automation, pp. 2507–2513. IEEE (2007)

16. Marge, M., et al.: Applying the Wizard-of-Oz technique to multimodal human-robot dialogue. arXiv preprint arXiv:1703.03714 (2017)

17. Villano, M., et al.: DOMER: a Wizard of Oz interface for using interactive robots to scaffold social skills for children with autism spectrum disorders. In: Proceedings of the 6th International Conference on Human-Robot Interaction, pp. 279–280. ACM (2011)

18. Salem, M., Eyssel, F., Rohlfing, K., Kopp, S., Joublin, F.: To Err is human(-like): effects of robot gesture on perceived anthropomorphism and likability. Int. J. Soc. Robot. **5**(3), 313–323 (2013)

19. Mok, B.K.J., Yang, S., Sirkin, D., Ju, W.: A place for every tool and every tool in its place: performing collaborative tasks with interactive robotic drawers. In: 2015 24th IEEE International Symposium on Robot and Human Interactive Communication (RO-MAN), pp. 700–706. IEEE (2015)

20. Rothenbücher, D., Li, J., Sirkin, D., Mok, B., Ju, W.: Ghost driver: a platform for investigating interactions between pedestrians and driverless vehicles. In: Adjunct Proceedings of the 7th International Conference on Automotive User Interfaces and Interactive Vehicular Applications, pp. 44–49. ACM (2015)

21. Sirkin, D., Mok, B., Yang, S., Ju, W.: Mechanical ottoman: how robotic furniture offers and withdraws support. In: Proceedings of the Tenth Annual ACM/IEEE International Conference on Human-Robot Interaction, pp. 11–18. ACM (2015)

22. Lemaignan, S., Edmunds, C., Senft, E., Belpaeme, T.: The free-play sandbox: a methodology for the evaluation of social robotics and a dataset of social interactions. arXiv preprint arXiv:1712.02421 (2017)

23. Sequeira, P., et al.: Discovering social interaction strategies for robots from restricted-perception Wizard-of-Oz studies. In: The Eleventh ACM/IEEE International Conference on Human Robot Interaction, pp. 197–204. IEEE Press (2016)

24. Castellano, G., et al.: Towards empathic virtual and robotic tutors. In: Lane, H.C., Yacef, K., Mostow, J., Pavlik, P. (eds.) AIED 2013. LNCS (LNAI), vol. 7926, pp. 733–736. Springer, Heidelberg (2013). https://doi.org/10.1007/978-3-642-39112-5_100

25. Correia, F., et al.: Just follow the suit! Trust in human-robot interactions during card game playing. In: 2016 25th IEEE International Symposium on Robot and Human Interactive Communication (RO-MAN), pp. 507–512. IEEE (2016)

26. Kory, J., Breazeal, C.: Storytelling with robots: learning companions for preschool children's language development. In: The 23rd IEEE International Symposium on Robot and Human Interactive Communication, pp. 643–648. IEEE (2014)

27. Ramachandran, A., Litoiu, A., Scassellati, B.: Shaping productive help-seeking behavior during robot-child tutoring interactions. In: The Eleventh ACM/IEEE International Conference on Human Robot Interaction, pp. 247–254. IEEE Press (2016)

28. Williams, T., Tran, N., Rands, J., Dantam, N.T.: Augmented, mixed, and virtual reality enabling of robot deixis. In: Chen, J.Y.C., Fragomeni, G. (eds.) VAMR 2018. LNCS, vol. 10909, pp. 257–275. Springer, Cham (2018). https://doi.org/10.1007/978-3-319-91581-4_19

29. Williams, T., Bussing, M., Cabrol, S., Boyle, E., Tran, N.: Mixed reality deictic gesture for multi-modal robot communication. In: HRI (2019)

30. Williams, T., Bussing, M., Cabrol, S., Lau, I., Boyle, E., Tran, N.: Investigating the potential effectiveness of allocentric mixed reality deictic gesture. In: Chen, J.Y.C., Fragomeni, G. (eds.) HCII 2019. LNCS, vol. 11575, pp. 178–198. Springer, Cham (2019). https://doi.org/10.1007/978-3-030-21565-1_12

31. Hirshfield, L., Williams, T., Sommer, N., Grant, T., Gursoy, S.V.: Workload-driven modulation of mixed-reality robot-human communication. In: ICMI Workshop on Modeling Cognitive Processes from Multimodal Data (2018)

32. Lenz, A., Skachek, S., Hamann, K., Steinwender, J., Pipe, A.G., Melhuish, C.: The BERT2 infrastructure: an integrated system for the study of human-robot interaction. In: 2010 10th IEEE-RAS International Conference on Humanoid Robots, pp. 346–351. IEEE (2010)

33. Kato, H., Billinghurst, M., Poupyrev, I., Tachibana, K.: Virtual object manipulation on a table-top AR environment. In: Proceedings of the IEEE and ACM International Symposium on Augmented Reality (ISAR 2000), pp. 111–119 (2000)

34. Lindlbauer, D., Wilson, A.D.: Remixed reality: manipulating space and time in augmented reality. In: Proceedings of the 2018 CHI Conference on Human Factors in Computing Systems, pp. 1–13 (2018)

35. Hirshfield, L., et al.: Human-computer interaction and brain measurement using functional near-infrared spectroscopy. In: Symposium on User Interface Software and Technology: Poster Paper. ACM Press (2018)

36. Hart, S., Staveland, L.: Development of NASA-TLX (task load index): results of empirical and theorical research, Amsterdam, pp. 139–183 (1988)
37. Condino, S., Carbone, M., Piazza, R., Ferrari, M., Ferrari, V.: Perceptual limits of optical see-through visors for augmented reality guidance of manual tasks. IEEE Trans. Biomed. Eng. **67**(2), 411–419 (2020)
38. Milgram, P., Zhai, S., Drascic, D., Grodski, J.: Applications of augmented reality for human-robot communication. In: Proceedings of IROS (1993)
39. Green, S., Billinghurst, M., Chen, X., et al.: Human-robot collaboration: a literature review and augmented reality approach in design. IJ Adv. Robot. Syst. **5**(1), 1–18 (2008)
40. Zhou, F., Duh, H.B.L., Billinghurst, M.: Trends in augmented reality tracking, interaction and display: a review of ten years of ISMAR. In: ISMAR (2008)
41. Van Krevelen, D., Poelman, R.: A survey of augmented reality technologies, applications and limitations. Int. J. Virtual Reality **9**(2), 1–20 (2010)
42. Billinghurst, M., Clark, A., Lee, G.: A survey of augmented reality. Found. Trends Hum.-Comput. Interact. **8**(2–3), 73–272 (2015)
43. Williams, T., Szafir, D., Chakraborti, T.: The reality-virtuality interaction cube. In: VAM-HRI (2019)
44. Williams, T., Szafir, D., Chakraborti, T., Ben Amor, H.: Virtual, augmented, and mixed reality for human-robot interaction. In: Companion of HRI (2018)
45. Williams, T., Szafir, D., Chakraborti, T., Amor, H.B.: Report on the 1st international workshop on virtual, augmented, and mixed reality for human-robot interaction (VAM-HRI). AI Mag. **39**(6), 64 (2018)
46. Peters, C., Yang, F., Saikia, H., Li, C., Skantze, G.: Towards the use of mixed reality for HRI design via virtual robots. In: VAM-HRI (2018)
47. Schönheits, M., Krebs, F.: Embedding AR in industrial HRI applications. In: VAM-HRI (2018)
48. Sportillo, D., Paljic, A., Ojeda, L., Partipilo, G., Fuchs, P., Roussarie, V.: Training semi-autonomous vehicle drivers with extended reality. In: VAM-HRI (2018)
49. Hedayati, H., Walker, M., Szafir, D.: Improving collocated robot teleoperation with augmented reality. In: International Conference on HRI, pp. 78–86. ACM (2018)
50. Sibirtseva, E., et al.: A comparison of visualisation methods for disambiguating verbal requests in human-robot interaction. In: Proceedings of the RO-MAN (2018)
51. Ganesan, R.K., Rathore, Y.K., Ross, H.M., Amor, H.B.: Better teaming through visual cues. IEEE Robot. Autom. Mag. **25**(2), 51–71 (2018)
52. Chakraborti, T., Sreedharan, S., Kulkarni, A., Kambhampati, S.: Alternative modes of interaction in proximal human-in-the-loop operation of robots. arXiv preprint arXiv:1703.08930 (2017)
53. zu Borgsen, S., Renner, P., Lier, F., et al.: Improving human-robot handover research by mixed reality techniques. In: VAM-HRI (2018)
54. Walker, M., Hedayati, H., Lee, J., Szafir, D.: Communicating robot motion intent with augmented reality. In: Proceedings of the HRI, pp. 316–324. ACM (2018)
55. Rosen, E., et al.: Communicating robot arm motion intent through mixed reality head-mounted displays. arXiv preprint arXiv:1708.03655 (2017)
56. Reardon, C., Lee, K., Fink, J.: Come see this! Augmented reality to enable human-robot cooperative search. In: International Symposium on Safety, Security, and Rescue Robotics (2018)
57. Amor, H.B., Ganesan, R.K., Rathore, Y., Ross, H.: Intention projection for human-robot collaboration with mixed reality cues. In: VAM-HRI (2018)

Correction to: A Robotic Augmented Reality Virtual Window for Law Enforcement Operations

Nate Phillips, Brady Kruse, Farzana Alam Khan, J. Edward Swan II,
and Cindy L. Bethel

Correction to:
Chapter "A Robotic Augmented Reality Virtual Window
for Law Enforcement Operations"
in: J. Y. C. Chen and G. Fragomeni (Eds.): *Virtual, Augmented*
***and Mixed Reality*, LNCS 12190,**
https://doi.org/10.1007/978-3-030-49695-1_40

The original version of this chapter was revised. The acknowledgement was inadvertently forgotten. It has been added.

The updated version of this chapter can be found at
https://doi.org/10.1007/978-3-030-49695-1_40

Author Index